ENCYCLOPEDIA OF PUBLIC ADMINISTRATION AND PUBLIC POLICY

ENCYCLOPEDIA OF PUBLIC ADMINISTRATION AND PUBLIC POLICY

DAVID SCHULTZ

☑® Facts On File, Inc.

In memoriam: Tina and Megan, forever.

❈

Encyclopedia of Public Administration and Public Policy

Facts On File, Inc.
132 West 31st Street
New York NY 10001

Library of Congress Cataloging-in-Publication Data

Encyclopedia of public administration and public policy / [edited by] David Schultz
    p. cm.
  Includes bibliographical references and index.
  ISBN 0-8160-4799-5
  1. Administrative agencies—United States—Encyclopedias. 2. Executive departments—United States—Encyclopedias. 3. United States—Politics and government—Encyclopedias. 4. Political planning—United States—Encyclopedias. 5. Public policy (Law)—United States—Encyclopedias. I. Schultz, David A. (David Andrew), 1958– .

JK9.E526 2003
320.973′03—dc21

2003040803

Facts On File books are available at special discounts when purchased in bulk quantities for businesses, associations, institutions, or sales promotions. Please call our Special Sales Department in New York at (212) 967-8800 or (800) 322-8755.

You can find Facts On File on the World Wide Web at http://www.factsonfile.com

Text and cover design by Cathy Rincon
Line art by Patricia Meschino

Printed in the United States of America

VB Hermitage 10 9 8 7 6 5 4 3 2 1

This book is printed on acid-free paper.

CONTENTS

LIST OF ENTRIES

PREFACE

Government can make life more tolerable. Be it defending national borders, putting out fires, educating children, enforcing antidiscrimination laws, or tending to the aged, ill, or handicapped, public administrators, civil servants, and government bureaucracies perform many thankless services that social and economic institutions alone neither can nor want to undertake. Yet it is these tasks that enrich people's lives, making it possible not simply to live, but to live well.

Despite the important role that government plays in our lives, many of its organizations and functions remain a mystery to the average citizen. The *Encyclopedia of Public Administration and Public Policy* is written to help dispel this mystery and clarify what government agencies and their public administrators do and why.

Encyclopedia of Public Administration and Public Policy is designed to provide students, the general public, and perhaps even experts in the field a reference tool that will allow them to understand government and its policy processes more fully. The emphasis is not just on one level of government, but all levels and around the world. Moreover, this volume seeks to include traditional terms while also discussing emerging trends affecting the performance of public administrators and agencies. These trends encompass changes in technology and new orga-

nizational models to deliver public services, including the use of private, nonprofit, and international entities to undertake functions traditionally thought reserved for only the public sector.

Encyclopedia of Public Administration and Public Policy not only examines the organizations of government but also the process of how policies are made and evaluated. It discusses several specific areas of public policy, seeking to inform readers of the actual impact of the government on their lives.

Encyclopedia of Public Administration and Public Policy is the product of many different people, ranging from academics and lawyers to government officials. It includes writers from throughout the United States and the world, giving the volume a flavor for how government and the policy process are viewed from numerous perspectives. While not claiming to be the final word on the topic, *Encyclopedia of Public Administration and Public Policy* covers a lot of ground, providing readers with a quick yet substantial reference.

David Schultz
Hamline University
Saint Paul, Minnesota
dschultz@hamline.edu

ACKNOWLEDGMENTS

Encyclopedia of Public Administration and Public Policy is the product of the work of more than 124 individuals, without whose expertise this volume would never have been possible. They deserve more credit and thanks than I could ever offer them. Their willingness to draft and redraft essays and to volunteer at the last minute to make changes or prepare new topics was critical to the success of this volume.

Moreover, while oftentimes I would like to claim that I have an encyclopedic mind, I realized how little I truly knew when I began this project. Contributors suggested many of the terms and essays, adding to the richness and diversity of *Encyclopedia of Public Administration and Public Policy*. The task of editing, while often onerous, was more than compensated by what I learned and the new friends I made in doing this project.

No doubt, I may have neglected to acknowledge all of those who contributed to this project, but these oversights are not intentional, and I apologize in advance for them.

CONTRIBUTORS

MEGAN ALESSANDRINI, University of Tasmania, Australia

ARI-VEIKKO ANTTIROIKO, University of Tampere, Finland

GAYLE R. AVANT, Baylor University

WILLIAM D. BAKER, Arkansas School for Mathematics and Science

BRANDON BARTELS, The Ohio State University

BRUCE L. BIKLE, California State University at Sacramento

J. MICHAEL BITZER, University of Georgia

KATE BOROWSKE, Hamline University

MICHAEL W. BOWERS, University of Nevada, Las Vegas

EERO CARROLL, Swedish Institute for Social Research, Stockholm University, Sweden

EUGENE CLARK, University of Canberra, Australia

DOUG CLOUATRE, Kennesaw State University

MICHAEL COMISKEY, Pennsylvania State University

ELIZABETH CORLEY, Columbia University

DOUGLAS CRAWFORD-BROWN, University of North Carolina, Chapel Hill

RICHARD P. DAVIS, Jacksonville State University

YASMIN A. DAWOOD, University of Chicago

BRIAN DERDOWSKI, JR., New Jersey

DAVID I. DEWAR, McMaster University, Canada

LISA DICKE, Texas Tech University

CRAIG DONOVAN, Kean University

DAVID EDWARDS, University of Tennessee, Chattanooga

GEOFF EDWARDS, Griffith University, Australia

JOLLY ANN EMREY, California State University, Los Angeles

FRAN EQUIZA, Instituto Internacional de Gobernabilidad, Barcelona, Spain

JAMES C. FOSTER, Oregon State University

SHARON FRIEDRICHSEN, City of San Francisco

MARK FUNKHOUSER, City of Kansas City, Missouri

MILA GASCÓ, Instituto Internacional de Gobernabilidad, Barcelona, Spain

ERNEST ALEXANDER GOMEZ, MPA

KATHLEEN GRAMMATICO, University of Virginia

JAMIE F. GREEN, National Institutes of Health/National Cancer Institute

JONATHAN GREENBLATT, United States Department of Education

JAMES GUTHRIE, Macquarie Graduate School of Management, Sydney, Australia

DONALD P. HAIDER-MARKEL, University of Kansas

CHERYLYN A. HARLEY, The Center for New Black Leadership

BRADLEY D. HAYS, University of Maryland

MICHAEL HENRY, Grant MacEwan College

JESSICA L. HILLS, University of California, San Diego

STEVE H. HOLDEN, University of Maryland, Baltimore County

STEVEN G. JONES, University of Charleston

JAMES H. JOYNER, JR., Troy State University

ROGER L. KEMP, Meriden, Connecticut

STEPHEN KENDAL, University of Canberra, Australia

LA LORIA KONATA, Georgia State University

STEVEN G. KOVEN, University of Louisville

DANIEL C. KRAMER, College of Staten Island, CUNY

ROBERT S. KRAVCHUK, Indiana University

MARTHA M. LAFFERTY, Tennessee Fair Housing Council

DANIEL LEVIN, University of Utah

DAHLIA BRADSHAW LYNN, University of Southern Maine

ANGELA MAGARRY, Tasmania, Australia

GRAHAM MAGARRY, Tasmania, Australia

PATRICK N. MALCOLMSON, St. Thomas University, Canada

ROBERT W. MALMSHEIMER, SUNY College of Environmental Science and Forestry

MATHEW MANWELLER, University of Oregon

JOHN LYMAN MASON, Rhodes College

TRACY MCKAY MASON, University of Nebraska–Lincoln

DAVID A. MAY, Eastern Washington University

LAWRENCE MAYER, Texas Tech University

GREGORY MCCARTHY, Adelaide University, Australia

OLIVIA M. MCDONALD, Regent University

SUSAN MCWILLIAMS, Princeton University

SUSAN GLUCK MEZEY, Loyola University Chicago

CHRISTOPHER Z. MOONEY, University of Illinois at Springfield

VERNON MOGENSEN, Kingsborough Community College, CUNY

RAISSA MUHUTDINOVA-FOROUGHI, University of Utah

RICHARD MUNCEY, Government of South Australia

TINA NABATCHI, Indiana University

STEVE NOBLE, Kentucky Assistive Technology Service Network

DOUGLAS D. OFIARA, Muskie School of Public Service, University of Maine

TIMOTHY J. O'NEILL, Southwestern University

JASON PALMER, United States General Accounting Office

DEMETRA M. PAPPAS, Bryant College

MELISSA PAVONE, City University of New York

SCOTT PETERS, Illinois Institute of Technology

ANTHONY PETROSINO, American Academy of Arts & Sciences

PAUL L. POSNER, United States General Accounting Office

JOAN ORIOL PRATS, Instituto Internacional de Gobernabilidad, Barcelona, Spain

STEVEN PURO, St. Louis University

MARK RAGAN, Rockefeller Institute of Government

CAROLE RICHARDSON, American University

LESELE H. ROSE, University of Utah

RICK SARRE, University of South Australia

GREGORY D. SAXTON, SUNY Brockport

STEFFEN W. SCHMIDT, Iowa State University, Nova Southeastern University Oceanographic Center

ROBERT A. SCHUHMANN, University of Wyoming

DAVID SCHULTZ, Hamline University

PATRICK G. SCOTT, Southwest Missouri State University

OLGA SEKULIC, Court Attorney for the New York State Unified Court System in Manhattan

HOLLY TAYLOR SELLERS, University of Connecticut

CELIA A. SGROI, Oswego State University, SUNY

LINDA K. SHAFER, Allegheny College

ELSA M. SHARTSIS, M.S., Urban Planning

STEPHEN K. SHAW, Northwest Nazarene University

BOB SHEAD, BDO Kendalls

BRIEN SHELLEY, Princeton University

MAURICE C. SHEPPARD, Alma College

MICHAEL SHIRES, Pepperdine University

GILBERT B. SIEGEL, University of Southern California

KATHLEEN M. SIMON, Appalachian State University

BRENT C. SMITH, Western Michigan University

CHRISTOPHER E. SMITH, Michigan State University

T. JASON SODERSTRUM, Iowa State University

JERRY E. STEPHENS, United States Court of Appeals, Oklahoma City, Oklahoma

JOHN B. STEPHENS, University of North Carolina, Chapel Hill

TODD STEPHENSON, Development Associates, Inc.

RUTH ANN STRICKLAND, Appalachian State University

BETH SIMON SWARTZ, Cornell University

STEVEN L. TAYLOR, Troy State University

CAROL TEBBEN, University of Wisconsin, Parkside

SHARON TIMBERLAKE, Muskie School of Public Service, University of Maine

SHANN TURNBULL, Macquarie University, Australia

KELLY TZOUMIS, Roosevelt University

PEKKA VALKAMA, University of Tampere, Finland

RICHARD J. VAN ORDEN, Portland State University

JOHN R. VILE, Middle Tennessee State University

A. J. L. WASKEY, Dalton State College

LYNNE A. WEIKART, Baruch College of Public Affairs

GEOFF WITHERS, Colorado Commission on Taxation

RAYMOND B. WRABLEY, JR., University of Pittsburgh at Johnstown

ULF ZIMMERMAN, Kennesaw State University

A

AARP AARP, formerly known as the American Association of Retired Persons, is a nonprofit and nonpartisan membership organization that advocates on behalf of its membership. It is considered one of the more powerful lobbying groups in the United States.

The AARP was founded in 1958 by Dr. Ethel Percy Andrus, a retired educator from California. To gain membership in AARP a person must be 50 years of age or older. The latest available information from AARP's 2001 annual report had membership totaling more than 35 million and revenue of $595 million. A third of the members are under the age of 60, 46 percent are 60 to 74 years of age, and 21 percent are 70 years of age or older. About half of all members are working either full- or part-time, and the rest of the members are retired. AARP's motto, spoken by its founder, Dr. Andrus, is to serve, not to be served. The vision of AARP is to excel as a dynamic presence in every community, shaping and enriching the experience of aging for each member and for society.

Efforts of the association are focused on four specific areas: health and wellness, economic security and work, long-term care and independent living, and personal enrichment.

The AARP has a long history of advocacy for people age 50 and older and has gained a reputation as one of the fiercest lobbying organizations on Capitol Hill. In recent years advocacy efforts have been focused on the following issues:

1. Ensuring the solvency of Social Security
2. Protecting pensions
3. Fighting age discrimination
4. Providing prescription drug coverage in Medicare
5. Protecting patients in managed care and long-term care
6. Antipredatory home loan lending

AARP sponsors various programs for its members. The largest programs are the 55 ALIVE driver safety program, AARP Tax-Aide, and the Senior Community Service Employment Program (SCSEP). The 55 ALIVE program provides driver education to older drivers, which can lower the costs of their automobile insurance rates. Tax-Aide provides free tax return preparation primarily for low- and middle-income people age 60 and over.

Approximately 2 million people received assistance with their taxes during the 2001 tax

More than 1,000 members of the AARP rally on the front steps of the Pennsylvania state capitol, seeking expansion of a drug prescription program, on 16 April 2001, in Harrisburg, Pennsylvania.   (WILLIAM THOMAS CAIN/GETTY IMAGES)

season. The Tax-Aide program is staffed by more than 30,000 volunteers. AARP's third-largest program, SCSEP, trains and transitions low-income older persons into paid employment. The placement rate in 2001 was 54 percent. AARP has local offices around the United States that participate in advocacy efforts and offer such programs as summarized above for members.

For more information
AARP. http://www.aarp.org

Jamie Green

accountability   Accountability is an essential concept for all democratic governments as it underpins the processes by which people, elected as politicians or appointed to public office,

demonstrate that they are acting responsibly. The trust and confidence in governments provided by robust accountability processes explain why communities and individuals allow themselves to be governed in a free society.

There are various definitions of accountability in the public sector, but there appears to be general agreement that an essential element is external scrutiny. Scrutiny occurs when politicians, public officials, or agencies charged with specific responsibilities are called to explain their actions or decisions to a person or body with authority (for example a minister reporting to Parliament), or to the community directly, and to accept appropriate sanctions or directions. Scrutiny to demonstrate accountability can occur in three ways.

Political accountability ultimately occurs through the ballot box. Although elections are a clear test of the collective accountability of governments, politicians, and their parties, elections are sometimes considered only partly effective as an accountability mechanism because they are infrequent and do not explicitly consider all issues for which governments are responsible. Parliaments or legislatures are a primary accountability mechanism where individual ministers are questioned on their actions, their policies are debated, and in particular, their management of public finances closely examined. Scrutiny by the media, industry bodies, unions, and increasingly, special interest groups (for example Amnesty International and Greenpeace) is also now a significant part of the political accountability process.

Managerial accountability has risen in importance in recent years as public administration has increasingly adopted concepts largely drawn from the private sector. Managerial accountability is important in terms of defining the trail of authority from public agency staff through agency chief executives to ministers and then to Parliament and the community. However, managerial accountability is limited in that it only focuses on the individual relationships without considering the overall accountability of public officers to the community they serve. A particularly difficult area is that of ensuring adequate accountability for public services provided by the private sector through contracts or privatization.

Legal accountability reflects the requirement that governments and public officials must work within the law, which defines not only the things that can or cannot be done but, in many cases, also how things must be done. While governments may seek to change laws, this is not always possible due to political constraints, and they must therefore act within existing legal requirements and processes. Many jurisdictions now also provide for more direct public accountability through an ombudsman, "freedom of information" and "whistle-blower" legislation, and through administrative appeals tribunals.

Other definitions include individual accountability in terms of professional requirements, codes of conduct and personal ethical standards, the controls of peer pressure and social norms, responsiveness to the needs of citizens, and the requirement for community consultation. While useful in understanding the various ways in which politicians and other public officials are expected to act and respond, it is important that these other definitions do not detract from the core concept of external scrutiny.

Not surprisingly, accountability comes at a cost. These costs include the cost of elections, the protocols required for parliamentary inquiries, and the extensive documentation required to support public works and procurement processes. Accountability processes also sometimes lead to minor reductions in efficiency in the provision of public services. However, the real or perceived costs of public accountability are a small price to pay for the demonstration of transparency and honesty in democratic governments. A major challenge for public administrators is therefore to provide cost-effective services while also meeting appropriate accountability requirements.

For more information

Hughes, Owen E. *Public Management and Administration: An Introduction,* 2d ed. New York: Macmillan, 1998.

Richard Muncey

Addams, Jane (1860–1935) *social worker, philanthropist* Jane Addams was a U.S. philanthropist, social worker, Progressive politician, and Nobel Prize winner at the end of the 19th and the beginning of the 20th centuries.

(Laura) Jane Addams (6 September 1860–21 May 1935) is widely credited as the founder of the modern discipline of social work, but she could also be regarded as a sociologist of the so-called Chicago school. It is in Chicago that she also was most active as a social philanthropist and Progressive politician. A local social service foundation that she opened in 1889 on the Chicago West Side, Hull-House, still exists today.

Addams's political activities included service on Chicago's Board of Education (starting in 1905), presidency of the National Conference of Charities and Corrections (starting in 1909), and delegacy at the Progressive Party convention in 1912, where she seconded Theodore Roosevelt's nomination as its presidential candidate. More broadly, it has been said that Addams, as an early advocate of urban social renewal, was indirectly involved in "every major social reform between 1890 and 1925."

Finally, Addams was a foremost advocate of feminist thought, perhaps best known for her suffragette pamphlet "Why Women Should Vote" (1915) and as a pacifist and international-ist. In the last of these capacities, she came out in opposition to the U.S. entry into the First World War, and participated as delegate at the 1915 International Congress of Women con-vened at The Hague. She was then to be recog-nized as the first American woman to receive the Nobel Peace Prize in 1931. This illustrious career had modest if predictive beginnings. She was born in Cedarville, Illinois, the eighth of nine children, as the daughter of a mill owner and local political leader. Because of a congenital spinal defect and later heart trouble, Jane was plagued by poor health throughout her life but became better after her spinal difficulty was remedied by surgery.

After college studies and extensive traveling in the 1880s, Addams went on to found the phil-anthropic social service foundation of Hull-House on Chicago's West Side in 1889. The services offered to poor people ranged from kindergarten sessions to continuing adult educa-tion. Cultural and recreational facilities, as well as an employment exchange, were added later. The broader civic and political activities Addams pursued were to follow as her reputation grew. Unable to attend the Nobel Prize ceremony, she died in 1935 of a combination of heart trouble

and cancer and was interred in her birthplace of Cedarville after a farewell ceremony in the court-yard of Hull-House.

Addams was herself ambiguous, even criti-cal, toward welfare voluntarism, also advocat-ing a strong role for government action. Thus her life included local government service as well as private social involvement and support to trade unionism. This was evident not least in her personal participation in the (ultimately defeated) campaign to save the Italian-Ameri-can anarchist labor activists Sacco and Vanzetti from execution. Addams was arguably also opposed to liberal individualism, since she emphasized community-based social integra-tion. Finally, beyond suffragism, Addams's femi-nism has remained relevant also for present-day gender struggle. Residents of Hull-House were instrumental in bringing family-planning serv-ices to Chicago and in opposing withholding of abortion services, elements in a fight for repro-ductive rights that still divides America today.

For more information

Addams, J. *The Second Twenty Years at Hull-House.* New York: Macmillan, 1930.

Addams, J. *Twenty Years at Hull-House.* New York: Macmillan, 1910.

Addams, Jane. "Why Women Should Vote." In *Woman Suffrage: History, Arguments, and Results,* edited by F. M. Borkman and Annie G. Poritt, 131–150. New York: National Woman Suffrage Publishing, 1915.

Elshstain, Jean Bethke. *Jane Addams and the Dream of American Democracy: A Life.* New York: Basic Books, 2002.

Fischer, M. "Philanthropy and Injustice in Mill and Adams." *Nonprofit and Voluntary Sector Quarterly* 24, no. 4 (1995): 281–292.

Haslett, D. C. "Hull-House and the Birth Control Movement: An Untold Story." *Affilia—Journal of Women and Social Work* 12, no. 3 (1997): 261–277.

"Jane Addams, Mother of Social Work." http://www.execpc.com/~shepler/janeaddams.html.

Jane Addams Hull House Association. http://www.hullhouse.org/.

Selmi, P. "Social Work and the Campaign to Save Sacco and Vanzetti." *Social Service Review* 75, no. 1 (2001): 115–134.

Siegfried, C. H. "Socializing Democracy: Jane Addams and John Dewey." *Philosophy of the Social Sciences* 29 no. 2 (1999): 207–230.

Eero Carroll

administrative discretion Administrative discretion refers to the power of administrative officials to make decisions based upon their judgement of what is the best course of action in a particular case.

Discretion is the liberty or power a person has to decide or act according to his or her own judgement. Discretionary authority is necessary in government because not all actions can be decided based upon general rules. Government officials must therefore have some flexibility in deciding how or when a rule ought to be applied.

There is some tension between the ideal of the rule of law and the granting of discretionary powers to government officials. The rule of law means that all government authority is derived from and limited by law. Discretionary authority, however, grants power to an official to decide on a course of action based upon his or her view of what is best in the situation. It is for this reason that discretionary authority is normally limited by law and open to review by the courts. A government official may be empowered by legislation to exercise discretion within particular circumstances, but the decisions must still be impartial and reasonable. There are always legal limits to the freedom given administrative officials to make discretionary decisions.

The discretion given to government officials to implement policies decided upon by elected officials is one of the gray areas in which the distinction between politics and administration is blurred. While we normally think of politics as the area in which policy is determined, how the policy is subsequently implemented can have important political implications. While a policy may set out rules that govern how an administrative agency is to proceed, the interpretation of those rules is often left to the agency. Moreover, the power to make and enforce regulations is often delegated to administrative agencies. The statute granting such power may be of such general language that the government agency in question is then allowed to exercise substantial discretion in the formulation and application of the regulations. In recent years, this issue has been most pressing in the areas of environmental regulation and policing.

The essential problem posed by administrative discretion is to find the proper balance between giving nonelected governmental officials too much power to make public policy, and restricting the discretionary power of such officials to the point where they lack the flexibility necessary to make decisions appropriate to specific circumstances.

For more information

Barth, Thomas. "The Public Interest and Administrative Discretion." *American Review of Public Administration* 22 (1992): 289–300.

Dickinson, John. *Administrative Justice and the Supremacy of Law in the United States.* New York: Russell and Russell, 1927.

Lowi, Theodore J. *The End of Liberalism,* 2d ed. New York: Norton, 1979.

Patrick N. Malcolmson

administrative ethics Administrative ethics refers to the ethics or morality in public service organizations, distinct from ethics in the political and business spheres.

Features of an ethical bureau include freedom from corruption (using official resources or power for private purposes), natural justice (all supplicants receive a fair, unbiased hearing), availability of employment to all citizens (not just an elite class) on merit, good work value given for salaries paid, and avoidance of waste.

Economic efficiency, narrowly defined, is not necessarily a criterion. An overriding obligation is to serve the public interest and the well-being of society. Due diligence in data gathering, consultation, analysis, mature reflection, and peer review are also necessary: slipshod work habits are unethical.

The search for methods of ensuring the honesty of officials dates back as far as recorded history. For example, the Code of Hammurabi (Babylonia, 1729 B.C.E.) includes rules for judges and military officers. China introduced merit-based examinations for entrance to an independent, nonpartisan public service in 622 C.E., more than 1,200 years before the West (1854 in Britain, 1883 Pendleton Act in the United States). But it is to Aristotle and the ancient Greeks that the West owes its conception of citizenship, the high ethical duty of a citizen to serve the city-state, and the separation of private from public activity.

Administrative ethics are important for several reasons. First, in politics, it is easy to fall into the habit of regarding one's own cause as noble and one's opponents as the personification of all that is wrong with the country. Administrative ethics is a bulwark against dramatization of issues. Although civil service operations can be separated from partisan activity, there is an intensely value-laden dimension to a great deal of a bureau's functions. Profoundly ethical questions of who benefits from the resources and power of the state arise during both policy formulation and delivery of street-level services. The theoretical notion that politicians make policy and hand it down to robotic functionaries to implement is simply unrealistic and does not acknowledge the service's primary role in originating good policy.

The worth of an ethical civil service is acutely obvious when it is absent, for without it a government cannot even undertake reform. This applies to both totalitarian and democratic régimes. An unethical service loses effectiveness and the capacity to actually implement government decisions.

Across the English-speaking world, the respect that the community holds for governmental institutions declined in the final decades of the 20th century. The symptoms can become the disease, as the failures of a compromised bureaucracy lead to pressure to reduce it further, leading in turn to a reduced institutional capacity to cope with the problems confronting society. In particular, lapses in ethical conduct by leaders dent the credibility of the institutions they represent. A public servant or a bureau may be completely ethical yet still make dramatic mistakes that damage the community's well-being for a long time.

Approaches to administrative ethics can be classified in several ways. One way is to distinguish normative or objective approaches, which set out some ideal standards of behavior with which officials are expected to comply, from positivist, relativist, or subjective approaches, in which situations are judged on their merits by participants at the time: good ends can justify unethical means. The positivist approach is less of a defense against "whatever it takes" behavior by an official's superiors.

An alternative classification contrasts principled with procedural approaches. By the principled approach, civic virtue is the goal of public administration, and the best method of achieving it is to appoint only people of upright character as leaders. In this view, public life is seen as too fluid to rely on written regulations.

The procedural approach emphasizes observance of laws and codes of ethics. It assumes that the absence of wrongdoing constitutes good administration. This legalistic or mechanistic approach has its roots in behaviorism, the theory that humans act mainly in response to external stimuli: punishment and reward. It emphasizes technical efficiency in achieving ends handed down from outside. This approach is stronger in the behaviorist United States than in Europe or the Commonwealth's parliamentary systems. The fatal flaw in this pragmatic approach is that the concept of ethics without an underlying moral purpose is a hollow shell. It can amount to motivation to do the right thing only because of the risk of being caught doing wrong. It can lead to technical compliance (observing the letter of the law while evading its spirit). It does not remedy wrongs that result from acts of omission. Codes do, however, help even the highly principled to know just what their rights and duties are: not every ethical situation is clear-cut.

Ethics do not arise in a vacuum. A bureau's ethical outlook is derived from five main intertwined sources:

First there is personal morality, or the motives that drive individuals. Modern economics claims that bureaucrats are essentially selfish and continually seek to increase their own wealth, status, and position. As a generalization, in the long-established democracies, this assertion is plainly false. So many studies have shown that civil public servants are not motivated solely by pay and conditions that it is a puzzle that anyone could imagine otherwise. Personal morality derives from several sources, including: human genetic inheritance, upbringing and environment (children soak up family attitudes, teenagers imitate peers, employees absorb their workplace's culture), religion, and reason (an ethical life brings life satisfaction).

Second, there are values that come from the professions. These are the standards upheld by one's trade or profession, which can include public administration. Standards can be unwritten traditions, advisory codes, conditions of membership, or regulatory codes that qualify a person to practice. A skilled employee brings contacts and ethical obligations deriving from their membership in a network of trained specialists.

Third, there are procedures, i.e., the bureau's internal procedures and culture. Features conducive to ethical conduct include: leaders who consistently behave ethically; a structure that assigns accountabilities clearly; appointment procedures that are based upon equity and merit, encourage diversity (to resist "groupthink"), mar-

ginalize those who behave unethically, and offer fair pay differentials; a culture that respects inclusion, consultation, and compassion (so-called feminine values) to offset the more usual competitive, hierarchical, and individualist (masculine) values; and a "code of ethics" outlining cherished values or principles, perhaps distinguishable from a more prescriptive "code of conduct," which outlines expected behaviors and invites compliance. The ethical standards of an organization are the responsibility of the entire organization, not just the corrupt individuals in it. Apples go bad most readily when the barrel is contaminated.

Fourth, the Constitution defines a code of conduct because it is the external governmental structure within which the bureau operates. Features conducive to ethical conduct include: a benign constitutional framework; effective machinery-of-government arrangements that uphold the dignity of government; and a core of adequately remunerated, nonpartisan civil servants with security of tenure, separated from the noise and interests inherent in the political sphere.

Finally, a community sets ethical values through the expectations regarding the conduct of their governments. High expectations can lead to high performance, and low expectations will become self-fulfilling. Individuals expect their governments to act in the interest of the community and vote accordingly.

It would be wonderfully inspiring if these five dimensions all reinforced each other; but this does not universally happen. The potential for conflict is clearly visible in the traditional axiom that describes a civil servant's duty: to protect the public interest while serving the government of the day.

An ethical service is continually exposed to politicization and undermining from those who stand to gain from improper conduct. Repeated restructuring, a shift from tenured to contract employment, and a focus on financial measures of performance can compromise traditional ethical values. The worldwide trend since the early 1970s to deregulation, outsourcing, and private-public joint ventures has blurred the fundamental differences between public and commercial organizations and has given rise to some notorious scandals. Clouded accountability and secrecy in commercial transactions tend to lead to conflicts of interest and then corruption.

Although unethical conduct is corrosive, an individual of upright character and conscience can still achieve ethical results while all around others are serving only themselves. The Nuremberg defense ("I was only obeying orders") is not a valid defense.

Ethics can be learned. Knowledge of ethics can help civil servants to resolve conflicts and observers of government to recognize and applaud ethical behavior when they see it.

Who is responsible for holding officials to account for meeting ethical standards? Every citizen. This includes customers who use government services, media who demonstrate that they know the difference between ethical and unethical behavior, and electors who do no more than vote every few years.

For more information

Committee on Standards in Public Life. http://www.public-standards.gov.uk.

Cooper, Terry. *Handbook of Administrative Ethics.* New York: Marcel Dekker, 1994.

Singer, Peter. *How Are We to Live?: Ethics in an Age of Self-interest.* Melbourne, Victoria: Text Publishing, 1993.

Wilson, Edward O. *Consilience: The Unity of Knowledge.* New York: Alfred Knopf, 1998.

Geoff Edwards

administrative law judge   An administrative law judge is a government official who presides over a dispute between two parties, one of which is usually an administrative agency, in a government decision or action.

Administrative law judges, commonly referred to as ALJs, are similar to judges. ALJs preside over hearings in which an individual or group contests an agency decision or rule. Much like a judge in court, the ALJ serves as an independent and impartial reviewer of the agency actions and the claims made by those contesting the agency's actions. Again, like a judge, an ALJ usually has a legal background and has served in some capacity as an attorney or legal adviser. Unlike a judge, however, ALJs may work within the agency itself, but they often must maintain their independence to judge the agency's actions.

ALJs in the United States are required to conduct their hearings according to the federal ADMINISTRATIVE PROCEDURE ACT (APA), particularly sections 554, 556, and 557. Most ALJs perform their work in adjudication, or trial-type hearings. Under the sections of the APA, these trial-type hearings must be performed within certain guidelines. For example, under section 554, individuals who contest an agency action must: be informed of the time, place, and nature of the hearing; and have an opportunity to submit facts and have them considered. Moreover, the presiding individual may not consult a person or group on a fact in question unless all the interested groups are involved as well.

During the course of a hearing, an ALJ may do a number of activities, including: administering oaths and affirmations, issuing subpoenas, passing judgment on "offers of proof" or evidence, regulating the course of the hearing, keeping the records of the hearing, and holding conferences for the "settlement or simplification of the issues" between the contesting parties. Once the ALJ makes her ruling on a matter, that ruling is considered to be the decision of the agency. The agency or the other party may appeal the ALJ's ruling in the matter to the agency head or to a court of law.

ALJs can be at the center of a conflict within their professional responsibilities, and scholars have noted two competing ideas centering on ALJs' responsibilities. Because ALJs are independent and impartial judges of an agency's actions, they are guided by the ideas of fairness and acceptability toward the private parties who challenge an agency's action (the judicial mode of ALJs). However, because many ALJs work within an administrative agency, adjudication is part of an agency's policy-making process. As part of the policy process, ALJs should be guided by accuracy and efficiency toward the agency's mission (the institutional mode of ALJs).

For more information

Asimow, Michael R., Ronald M. Levin, and Arthur Earl Bonfield. *State and Federal Administrative Law.* St. Paul, Minn.: West Group, 1998.

J. Michael Bitzer

Administrative Procedure Act   The Administrative Procedure Act (APA) is designed to ensure uniformity and openness in the procedures followed by federal agencies. The basic purpose of the APA is to ensure that the general public, businesses, and other organizations have access to information about federal agencies and agency regulations and other policies and procedures that may affect them. The APA is the major source for federal agency administrative law. State agencies' administration and regulation are governed by comparable state laws.

Federal regulatory agencies, such as the ENVIRONMENTAL PROTECTION AGENCY, are empowered by Congress to make and enforce regulations (also called rules) that have the full force and effect of law. Generally, such regulations are based in statute and are issued by regulatory agencies in order to implement specific statutory requirements.

The APA includes specific requirements related to this process, often called the rule-making process. One important requirement is that all proposed rules must be published in the *Federal Register.* The public must be given the opportunity to comment and suggest changes before a rule takes effect. The new rule cannot take effect until a minimum of 30 days has elapsed. Some rule making may also include public hearings, if specified in the underlying statute.

In addition to requirements related to the federal rule-making process, the APA includes other provisions. It requires federal regulatory agencies to make available to the public information concerning their functions, policies, and procedures. For example, when a federal agency is reorganized, a description of the new organizational structure must be published in the *Federal Register.* The APA also requires descriptions of and information on the availability of forms necessary to comply with agency requirements to be issued. Agency manuals and procedures must be made available to the general public. It includes provisions governing access to agency information and records, conditions under which an agency can refuse to provide information, and agency record-keeping and reporting requirements related to withholding information.

For more information

U.S. Gov Info/Resources. Administrative Procedures Act. U.S. Code. Title 5, part I, chap. 5. Available online. URL: http://usgovinfo.about.com/library/bills/blapa.htm.

Mark Ragan

administrative searches   Administrative searches are searches permitted by statute that are normally used by government agencies to measure compliance with rules or for health or public safety. The most common administrative search most Americans are familiar with is the search of carry-on luggage at an airport. Other administrative searches might include a game warden inspecting a hunter's vehicle and pack for game birds or animals, or a building inspector inspecting a building for compliance with appropriate building and safety codes.

Administrative searches are not required to meet the burden of probable cause that a law enforcement officer has to meet to conduct a search. Using the examples above, by taking a hunting license or by buying a ticket from an airline, the individual has been placed on notice that he/she is subject to search for safety in the case of airlines and bag limits in the case of the hunter.

Administrative searches sometimes produce criminal evidence. For example, if your bag is inspected at the airport for explosives and weapons, but the search reveals drugs or other contraband, you could be arrested because you in effect "gave permission" for the search by presenting the bag at the security checkpoint. You give up some privacy in order to ride the commercial airliner. If criminal evidence is discovered, courts have ruled that the search is valid and the evidence can be used in a criminal trial. The choice in this case is either submit to the search or do not ride the airliner.

Another form of administrative search often used in criminal justice is the search of a person or his/her house if that person is under parole or probation supervision. Here again the expectation of privacy is reduced for the probationer or parolee. Probation and parole officers can search their clients because of the need for effective supervision and to maintain public safety (in this case to prevent the offender from committing new crimes).

The issue, then, is the expectation of privacy, and the Fourth Amendment right to be free from searches without warrant is diminished when there is a public interest—such as fish and game bag limits, airline safety, or offender supervision—that has been authorized by the legislature or by administrative rule. The history of administrative searches suggests that the courts have found such searches to be "reasonable" and thus not prohibited by the Fourth Amendment of the Constitution.

For more information

Black's Law Dictionary, 7th ed. St Paul, Minn.: West, 1999.

Holtz, Larry E. *Contemporary Criminal Procedure,* 2d ed. Binghamton, N.Y.: Gould Publications, 1992.

Bruce L. Bikle

administrative theory Administrative theory establishes the principles, processes, and arrangements by which the activities of government are administered and controlled. The group of people undertaking these tasks is usually described collectively as the public or civil service (and individually as public officials, public servants, or civil servants) and is usually considered as separate from other groups of people serving the state such as the armed forces, judges, or the police.

From the ancient Egyptian, Roman, and Greek civilizations onward, administrative systems have existed to manage the affairs of state. The early administrative systems had important differences from those of today, as they were based on the loyalty of the individual official to a particular person such as a king, emperor, or minister rather than loyalty to an organization and the state itself. Appointments to positions as public officials were often made on the basis of personal relationships, such as family members or friends, or by buying positions for personal gain.

The positions were often only part-time, undertaken in addition to other sometimes conflicting interests. These early administrative systems were often criticized because they were open to corruption and personal gain by the individual public official. They were often also not very efficient or effective, as there was uncertainty or inconsistency in an approach based on individual interpretation rather than one derived from an agreed collective body of knowledge.

The development of the modern professional public service traces its origins to mid-19th-century reforms in Britain, the United States, and earlier reforms in Europe. These reforms introduced major changes in public administration, removing patronage and introducing merit-based selection for appointment of public officials. They also led to a set of principles for the organization of public administration that had widespread acceptance by the start of the 20th century and continued to dominate thinking on public administration until quite recently. Two major influences on the development of this now-traditional model of public administration were Woodrow Wilson in the United States and the German sociologist Max Weber. Wilson held that government strategy and policy should be developed by politicians separate from its implementation by public officials. Weber described the key principles of a bureaucratic structure, which could apply in either public or private organizations, but was most developed in the public sector. Public-sector bureaucracies reflecting these principles have specific external and usually legislatively defined responsibilities; operate within a rational set of rules and procedures applying to all public officials; are structured as a formal hierarchy so that an individual's authority derives from position and not personal circumstances; keep written documents as records; and have officials in full-time roles requiring specialized training. As a result of the general acceptance of this model of public administration, public services during this time were usually characterized by formal hierarchical bureaucracies directly providing services to the community; a culture emphasizing process rather than outcomes; and politically impartial career public servants with generally lifetime tenure to ensure provision of advice to politicians "without fear or favor."

However, the experiences of the 1930s onward showed that many of the principles of the traditional or classical model of public administration, as it is sometimes called, were inconsistent with observed behaviors. In particular, the view that public administration was separate from the political process was challenged as the development and analysis of public policy, with its implicit value judgments, increasingly was undertaken by the public service. By the 1970s, the traditional model of public administration was increasingly under attack, as was also the very role and scope of government and its activities that established the nature of the public service. Financial constraints on governments challenged the efficiency of direct service provision. Increasing market competition from globalization highlighted the significance of public-sector effectiveness on overall economic performance. Changing attitudes to government were largely driven by political and economic theory, in particular neoliberalism (sometimes called economic rationalism) and public choice theory, and by new approaches in organizational and management thinking that reflected private sector practices. Together these influences challenged the view that an impartial hierarchical bureaucracy was the most efficient way of delivering public services. From the late 1970s onward, many Western democratic governments, led by the United States and Britain, restructured their public services by privatizing or contracting out many services and introducing management concepts into public service agencies that drew largely on private-sector practices. This "new public management," or "managerialism," is now generally characterized by the development of professional managers with defined responsibilities for specific activities and clear accountability for effective use of resources; explicit statements of goals, targets, and performance measures; organizational arrangements structured around specific products or services; a focus on results rather than procedures; and increased competition through contracting and tendering for services.

While the new public management has now largely replaced the traditional public administration in the public services of most Western democracies, it is not without its critics. The recognition of the interdependence and interaction between the public service and politicians raises important questions of accountability for the values and judgments underlying public management decisions, and also for the control of services now delivered by private suppliers on behalf of government. A key strength of the traditional public administration model was its focus on ethical behavior and impartiality. Real tensions exist for public service managers who try to improve efficiency in service delivery through greater use of market mechanisms but at the same time need to demonstrate honesty and use of equitable selection processes. Representation of the public as "customers" or "clients" of public-sector agencies has been criticized as limiting the different types of relationships a community should have with its government. Increasing calls for a more collaborative form of policy development and implementation of public services is now occurring, drawing on the efficiencies of the new public management model but also recognizing the unique role of the public service that separates it from the commercial world. In the future, there appears to be a move away from a "one size fits all" approach in the provision of public services to a pluralist approach that changes over time, location, and context. Increasingly, the scope and nature of public services are tailored to the nature of the service provided and the specific needs and circumstances of the community served, but they are also consistent with the underlying philosophy of the government of the day.

For more information

Hughes, Owen E. *Public Management and Administration: An Introduction,* 2d ed. New York: Macmillan, 1998.

Osborne, David, and Ted Gaebler. *Reinventing Government: How the Entrepreneurial Spirit Is Transforming the Public Sector.* Reading, Mass.: Addison-Wesley, 1992.

Richard Muncey

advisory opinion   An advisory opinion is a judicially issued opinion as to the legality of a proposed piece of legislation or administrative policy upon request by a particular branch of government or administrative agency.

In the United States, the federal courts are prohibited from issuing advisory opinions based on the Constitution's requirement of a case or controversy as well as its doctrine of separation

of powers. The case or controversy mandate, or what has come to be known as justiciable issues, is found in Article III, section 2 of the U.S. Constitution. This development by the framers of the Constitution was a sharp break with the traditional English legal system of the 18th century, which regularly issued advisory opinions upon request. The framers were highly concerned with keeping the powers of the three branches separate and distinct.

The Constitution's division of powers among the three branches of government bolstered the cases-and-controversies prohibition against advisory opinions. The first chief justice of the United States, John Jay, denied Secretary of State Thomas Jefferson's request for advice on the legality of the Neutrality Proclamation that kept the United States out of the French Revolution. In a letter addressed to President George Washington, Jay wrote that the separation of powers instituted by the Constitution "create[s] strong arguments against the propriety of our extrajudicially deciding questions alluded to [in Jefferson's letter requesting advice], especially as the power given by the Constitution to the President, of calling on the heads of departments for opinions, seems to have been *purposely* as well as expressly united to the executive department." Throughout its history, the federal judiciary has strictly followed Jay's reasoning that constitutional design forbids advisory opinions.

However, advisory opinions are not unheard of within the United States. Many state constitutions, such as those of Michigan, Colorado, and Florida, presently permit their courts to advise the legislature and/or executive on pending legislation. Additionally, administrative agencies at the state and federal level have begun to issue advisory opinions interpreting their rules and regulations in advance of any controversy or legal action. However, in all cases, advisory opinions are usually narrowly tailored to address a specific piece of legislation or regulatory rule rather than hypothetical issues and are nonbinding in nature.

Internationally, the practice of court-issued advisory opinions still flourishes. The International Court of Justice, the judicial branch of the United Nations, regularly issues advisory opinions on international law when requested to do so by authorized agencies.

Bradley D. Hays

affirmative action   Affirmative action involves policies that attempt to enhance educational and employment opportunities for particular individuals within society who traditionally have been denied these opportunities due to reasons beyond those of merit. Historically, these individuals have not been provided equal educational or employment opportunities for reasons based on issues of race, color, religion, gender, national origin, and socioeconomic factors. While the public sector has taken the lead in developing and implementing affirmative action policies and programs, many private institutions and organizations have voluntarily also become increasingly active in this area.

Affirmative action initiatives are developed and implemented usually for some of the following reasons: (a) to redress of past discriminatory actions; (b) to enhance hiring, promotion, or admission opportunities; and (c) to create a representative workforce to enhance organizational performance. It is important to understand affirmative action as an antidiscrimination policy to distinguish it from passive nondiscrimination policies. President John Kennedy established the term *affirmative action* in 1961 when he asked government contractors to expand employment opportunities. In general, affirmative action policies attempt to support basic individual freedoms as embodied in the Bill of Rights and the CIVIL RIGHTS clause of the Fourteenth Amendment of the U.S. Constitution.

Contemporary civil rights policies have their beginnings in the Civil Rights Act of 1964, Public Law 88-352 (2 July 1964), which prohibits dis-crimination in public employment and accommodations, particularly in the case of black Americans. Consequently, federal agencies and contractors are required to develop "affirmative action plans" to show their intent to expand opportunities for underrepresented individuals. Later amendments to the Civil Rights Act of 1964 more broadly define the responsibilities and duties of the EQUAL EMPLOYMENT OPPORTUNITY COMMISSION (EEOC), established by the act, toward implementing and enforcing these policies. Originally, affirmative action policy pertained only to the federal government, but following Supreme Court review of these policies, they now include

University of Cincinnati student gathers with several hundred other protesters, from a group calling themselves "By Any Means Necessary," to rally in favor of affirmative action on 23 October 2001 in downtown Cincinnati.   (GETTY IMAGES)

state and local government. Critics of affirmative action contend these policies violate the principal of equality under the law, while advocates respond that discrimination is, by definition, unfair treatment of people because they belong to a certain group. It is in this area where the debate over "goals and timetables" versus "quotas" arises.

Following President Johnson's issuance of Executive Order 11246 (1965) ordering government contractors to set "goals and timetables" to ensure equal employment opportunities for all citizens, the debate over these measures begins and intensifies. According to the principle of affirmative action, a "goal" is a reasonable objective enacted to expand opportunities to target populations within the context of the merit system of employment. In contrast, a "quota" restricts employment or development opportunities to members of particular groups by establishing a required number of proportionate representation that organizations are obliged to attain regardless of merit system requirements. According to this view, "quotas" are incompatible with merit-based public administration. The Employment Standards Administration's Office of Federal Contract Compliance Programs (OFCCP) is the federal government agency that monitors and enforces the development and implementation of these "goals and timetables" standards.

The history and development of affirmative action is best understood by reviewing Supreme Court decisions concerning this matter. For instance, *Regents of the University of California v. Bakke,* 438 U.S. 265, 387 (1978), addresses the issue of qualification versus minority preference. In *Bakke,* the Court decided that universities could consider minority status regarding admissions due to the unique characteristics of institutions of higher education.

However, in *Bakke,* the Court was badly split over exactly how race could be considered in admissions. Four justices ruled that race should never be considered in admissions and therefore would have declared all affirmative action programs to be unconstitutional. Another four justices would have upheld the use of race in admissions as a remedial measure to make up for past discrimination. In the middle was Justice Lewis Powell who struck down admissions policies that solely used race in admissions, but he permitted race to be used as one of several factors considered by schools admissions decisions. Critical to his argument was that promoting a diverse educational environment was a compelling interest that permitted schools to adopt affirmative action programs.

As a result of the *Bakke* decision, schools continued to employ affirmative action and consider race when making admissions decisions. However, because the *Bakke* decision was so split, there were questions regarding whether promoting diversity really was grounds enough to support the constitutionality of affirmative action. In 2003, the Supreme Court resolved this question in two decisions: *Gratz v. Bollinger,* 123 S.Ct. 2411 (2003), and *Grutter v. Bollinger,* 123 S.Ct. 2325 (2003).

In *Gratz,* the Supreme Court declared unconstitutional an undergraduate University of Michigan admissions policy that automatically gave African Americans, Hispanics, and Native Americans an extra 20 points out of a scale of 150 points in a "Selection Index" that was used to decide who would be admitted to the school. The Court argued that the automatic assignment of these 20 points did not allow for individualized consideration in admissions decisions and therefore unfairly benefited some on the basis of their race.

Meanwhile, in *Grutter,* the Supreme Court upheld a law school admissions policy for the University of Michigan that used race as one of several factors to be positively considered when making acceptance decisions. Writing for the majority, Justice Sandra Day O'Connor agreed with much of Powell's decision in *Bakke* that promoting a diverse educational environment was a compelling government interest and that so long as race was not the sole factor in making an admissions decision, this type of affirmative action policy was permissible. O'Connor also stated that she hoped that in 25 years affirmative action would no longer be needed because of the progress made in moving the United States toward a more racially neutral and equal society.

As a result of these two decisions, affirmative action is now permitted in two situations: First, to remedy past discrimination and, second, to promote diversity in a school setting. What impact these decisions will have in other settings, such as in the workplace, remains to be seen.

For more information

Edley, Christopher. *Not All Black and White: Affirmative Action and American Values.* New York: Noonday Press, 1998.

Rubio, Philip F. *A History of Affirmative Action, 1617–2000.* Jackson: University Press of Mississippi, 2001.

Maurice C. Sheppard

agenda setting   Agenda setting is a requisite step of policy making and is practiced by a range of people—for example, from ordinary citizens, interested groups, elected representatives, lobbyists, up to the president.

From the policy and public administration perspectives, an agenda is a series of problems, questions, or concerns to which governmental officials and their political associates give their attention. After the problem on the agenda is examined, alternatives are discussed, a choice is made (e.g., a congressional vote), the decision is formalized (e.g., a bill becomes public law), and the decision must be implemented (e.g., a regulatory agency writes the administrative rules and oversees the implementation).

After individuals, politicians, or administrative officials identify a problem or set of problems that they believe should be addressed by policy makers with the goal of changing public policy, they must employ a variety of steps and methods to ensure that government officials find the issue(s) on their agenda. For instance, people may lobby their elected representatives about the need to pay attention to a certain problem; the president may approach congressional members or agency heads in an attempt to advance his agenda; or academics may propose or critique policy formulation.

John Kingdon advances three explanations of how governmental agendas are set: problem recognition, developments in the political sphere, and the visibility of participants. The first explanation is problem recognition; that is, when the government or policy makers recognize a certain condition as a problem that the government should address and resolve, it has a better chance of first appearing on and then moving through the policy agenda. Kingdon's second explanation has to do with the political environment; that is, while the power of lobbyists is not insubstantial, if they are lobbying for policy that goes against the national mood and goals of elected officials, that policy is unlikely to appear on the policy agenda. Last, a policy or problem is more likely to appear on the agenda when it is advanced by visible policy participants—for instance, the president, close presidential aides, or elected officials. Policy participants with less political visibility include, for instance, academics and bureaucrats.

The ability of a group to set a problem on a policy agenda and then to ensure the policy is addressed and results in a legislative decision depends on an array of factors, including the persistence of nongovernmental actors (e.g., interest groups) and events outside the control of government. For instance, violence against women was a problem long before Congress passed the Violence against Women Act in 1994. Nonetheless, certain events in the 1990s (e.g., the 1992 sexual assault of both female naval officers and female civilians by navy pilots at the Tailhook Convention) and the unrelenting activism of national interest groups (e.g., the National Coalition against Domestic Violence) kept the issue of domestic violence in national attention.

For more information

Kingdon, John W. *Agendas, Alternatives, and Public Policies,* 2d ed. New York: Longman, 1995.

Linda K. Shafer

Aid to Families with Dependent Children

Aid to Families with Dependent Children (AFDC) was the primary U.S. welfare program until 1996. Initially enacted in the 1930s as the Aid to Dependent Children program, it was part of the landmark legislation that created the Social Security program. The program was intended to provide income support for children deprived of parental support due to the incapacity or absence of a parent, replacing widely varying programs in the states. Other provisions of the Social Security Act, notably benefits for families in which a wage earner died or became incapacitated, served as the basic social insurance program for working families. The Aid to Dependent Children program would provide for children who lost the support of a parent who had not contributed sufficiently to the Social Security program to provide coverage for the family.

Over the next four decades, the program remained basically unchanged. Notable expansions during this period included the addition of benefits for an adult in the family, and the option to include benefits to two-parent families, the AFDC Unemployed Parent program.

Under the AFDC program, the federal government provided matching funds for state expenditures, based on a formula that took into account state per-capita income. The federal portion of funding varied from 50 to 80 percent of the costs of the program. The program was administered in most states by a state agency, though in a number of the more populous states, the program was supervised by a state agency but

administered by counties. The federal government established rules under which the program was administered and required states to submit plans that described the program and the options chosen.

The regulatory framework included federal rules for establishing conditions of eligibility, for counting income and resources, and for providing due process protections for applicants and recipients. On the other hand, states had flexibility when it came to the amount of AFDC payments. States established "need standards," the amount of money that a family of a given size would need in order to pay for basic needs, such as shelter and clothing. In addition, the computation of the amount of the benefit varied from state to state. Some states provided the full amount of the gap between the need standard and the family's income, others a percentage of the gap. Still other states had separate payment standards. Thus, payment amounts varied significantly from state to state.

Although AFDC benefits were intended to be temporary, the number of recipients and the length of time that they remained on the welfare rolls grew steadily over time. Social scientists suggest that in combination with other societal factors, such as an increase in the percentage of illegitimate births, an unintended effect of the AFDC program was the creation of a "culture of poverty," in which families remained on the AFDC rolls from one generation to the next. They also suggest that the limitation of benefits to families where one of the parents was absent discouraged marriage and increased illegitimacy. In 1996, approximately 4.5 million families received AFDC; total federal and state expenditures in that year exceeded $24 billion.

These and other factors led to major efforts to reform the program in 1988 and again in 1990. In 1988, the Family Support Act added work requirements, created the Job Opportunity and Basic Skills training program, and for the first time provided significant funding for child care. But these changes did not have the intended effect. By 1996, a consensus of national politicians, state governors, and program administrators came together to radically redesign the program. AFDC was replaced by the TEMPORARY ASSISTANCE FOR NEEDY FAMILIES program, a block grant to states that emphasizes work and family self-sufficiency.

See also WELFARE REFORM.

For more information
Department of Human Services. http://aspe.hhs.gov/hsp/
AFDC/afdcbase98.htm.

Mark Ragan

alternative dispute resolution Alternative dispute resolution, commonly known as ADR, covers a wide range of activities other than full-scale litigation—including fact-finding, mediation, arbitration, minitrials, and other techniques—to end a dispute.

ADR almost always uses one or more independent and impartial third parties who do not have a stake in the outcome of a dispute. They help resolve disputes in various ways. The major ways are: (1) as experts who determine a particular point of fact or scientific standard [fact finders]; (2) as process managers helping the disputants seek a voluntary resolution [mediators]; (3) as investigators who respond to employee grievances or customer complaints [ombudsmen]; and (4) by offering binding decisions akin to magistrates or judges [arbitrators].

The basic similarity of ADR processes is that they are not contested hearings before a judge, and they seek to expedite a resolution to a suit, dispute, grievance, or problem.

ADR dates back centuries in diplomacy and law, as well as in other cultural, religious, and community-based ways to resolve disputes. More recently, ADR in the United States dates to federal labor-management legislation of the 1920s and 1930s. ARBITRATION was created as a way to promptly resolve shop-floor and other workplace disputes so as to avoid labor unrest.

One common form of arbitration is state government "lemon laws" covering consumer–auto dealer disputes over alleged defects in new cars.

A second wave of U.S. ADR dates from the 1960s and 1970s. Social movements of the 1960s stressed the dissatisfaction or disdain for traditional courts and a greater interest in less formal, grassroots, and more collaborative approaches for resolving disputes. Civil justice reformers embraced ADR as a needed response to an overburdened judiciary. However, ADR techniques such as arbitration of commercial contract disputes and mediation of neighborhood conflicts had been in use much earlier. A wider range of ADR methods became prominent, with some reformers envisioning a "multi-door courthouse" where ADR finds the right "fit for the fuss." Consequently, some recast ADR as appropriate dispute resolution, changing the focus from what ADR is not (i.e., litigation and judicial hearings) to a philosophically better way to resolve disputes.

Fact finding provides for experts selected by the disputants to research or examine a particular aspect of a problem and make a specific finding or recommendation. It does not resolve the whole dispute, but rather settles a question of fact. A similar, evaluative form of ADR is early neutral evaluation (ENE). Unlike arbitration, ENE does not call for formal, extensive presentation of fact and law, instead offering a preview of the contours of the dispute. The evaluator comments on points of law, and important or unclear facts, and may offer a nonbinding opinion. The minitrial or summary jury trial ranges from half-day exercises of lawyers' basic arguments to the hearing of witnesses and a judgment rendered by a surrogate judge or jury. A minitrial proceeds with less time and expense than a court hearing as a way to assist disputants' negotiations. Conciliation and MEDIATION are where the impartial intervener does not offer opinions about an outcome for the dispute but may make suggestions. Some processes combine methods, such as med-arb, where the mediator, if unsuccessful, provides an arbitrated outcome.

Issues about ADR include whether the purported savings of cost and time are realized, since the large majority of lawsuits never go to trial. Also, some see ADR as "second-class justice" with less protection of individual rights. ADR's informality may allow for exploitation of less experienced or powerful parties by those of greater wealth or knowledge. Finally, variations on separate ADR methods, such as med-arb, raise concerns about a disputant's understanding of the process and appropriate standards of practice.

For more information

Peacemakers Trust. http://www.peacemakers.ca/ bibliography/bib2ADR.html.

John B. Stephens

American Association of Retired Persons

See AARP.

American Federation of State, County, and Municipal Employees (AFSCME)

The American Federation of State, County, and Municipal Employees (AFSCME) is a labor union that represents employees of state, county, and municipal governments, public and private hospitals, school districts, universities, and nonprofit agencies. With 1.3 million members in 2002, AFSCME is the largest union affiliated with the American Federation of Labor–Congress of Industrial Organizations (AFL-CIO). AFSCME represents members in contract negotiations and grievance and arbitration hearings; lobbies political officials; conducts research on issues of interest to members; provides education to members and leaders; and organizes new members and bargaining units.

AFSCME was first chartered as an independent member of the AFL in 1936. Arnold Zander was elected as AFSCME's first international president. The union emerged out of the efforts of

Wisconsin state employees to protect the state's civil service system, under which employees held jobs on the basis of merit rather than political connections. Throughout the 1930s and 1940s, AFSCME lobbied state and local governments to pass or strengthen civil service laws. During this period, AFSCME competed with the communist-influenced State, County, and Municipal Workers Association (SCMWA) to organize public employees. There was little precedent for unions of public employees, and many states made union activities difficult. By the 1950s, AFSCME had become more militant in pressing for public workers' rights and collective bargaining as a means to improve their working conditions. In 1958, New York City mayor Robert Wagner signed an executive order granting collective bargaining rights to unions representing city employees, and in 1961 President John Kennedy issued a similar executive order legitimizing collective bargaining for federal employees. A more favorable climate for public-sector unions had been created, and AFSCME's membership soared. In the 1960s, under the leadership of President Jerry Wurf, AFSCME worked closely with the Civil Rights movement. In 1968 Dr. Martin Luther King, Jr., traveled to Memphis, Tennessee, to support AFSCME's efforts to organize black sanitation workers. Following Dr. King's assassination in Memphis, the city agreed to recognize the workers' union, AFSCME Local 1733.

AFSCME is a democratically run union governed by a constitution. AFSCME's biennial convention is the highest decision-making body in the union. Convention delegates adopt policies and set the direction for the union. Below the international level, "councils," "locals," and "affiliates" are also governed by constitutions and conventions of elected delegates.

AFSCME is active in state and national politics and is regarded as a major supporter of liberal causes. In 2002, AFSCME was by far the biggest political contributor among public-sector unions. It contributed almost $5 million to political candidates, 99 percent of them Democrats. Besides its political contributions, AFSCME employs full-time lobbyists who testify in Congress and lobby members of the House of Representatives and Senate. It also conducts voter registration and get-out-the-vote drives and uses radio, television, and print media to publicize AFSCME's goals and positions on issues. AFSCME has supported increases in the minimum wage and has opposed privatization of Social Security. It has criticized free-trade agreements like NAFTA (NORTH AMERICAN FREE TRADE AGREEMENT) and GATT (GENERAL AGREEMENT ON TARIFFS AND TRADE) and has opposed efforts to contract out government services (use more private contractors to perform government services).

For more information

American Federation of State, County, and Municipal Employees. http://www.afscme.org.

Raymond B. Wrabley, Jr.

American Society of Public Administration (ASPA)

The American Society of Public Administration (ASPA), founded in 1939, developed in response to major changes in the way the administration of public entities and bureaucracies was being directed and operated. The ASPA organization currently strives to establish and promote professionalism in public administration as well as the fostering of concepts that aid in the progression of the theory and the research of administration. In addition, ASPA promotes advocacy for public administration and for public service in general. Generally speaking, the mission of ASPA is to advance excellence in the field of public administration through the linking of theory and practical application.

It is a mild point of controversy as to what spurred the creation of ASPA, but some tenets are generally accepted as the probable developments that assisted in the rise of the organization. The field of public administration and ASPA both gained strength as aspects of the progressive-reform movement and from emerging research. Some have tied the growth of both to the popularity of MAX WEBER and his idealized concepts of the public bureaucracy. In America, Woodrow Wilson's call for the reform of bureaucracy through the elimination of the spoils system called other scholars to the field. Darrell Pugh, a noted historian who chronicled the history of ASPA, believed that some contributory development of ASPA could be traced to the development of the public administrative network that evolved in the 1930s in Chicago with the Public Administration Clearing House (PACH) and its relationship with ASPA. Still others believe that Franklin D. Roosevelt's Brownlow Committee and the Reorganization Act of 1939 were instrumental precipitating accelerants to the formation and establishment of ASPA.

As ASPA developed over the years, the science of public administration followed the rise of the bureaucracy. ASPA was at the forefront of this development, harnessing many scholars over the years, which in part contributed to identification of ASPA as the most dynamic of the administrative organizations. In 1942, ASPA established the Public Administration Review (PAR) as its literary forum for the expression of public administrative ideas. The prestige of the organization grew with such notable thinkers in the PAR editor-in-chief position as Leonard D. White, Frederick C. Mosher, DWIGHT WALDO, Chester Newland, Lewis Gawthrop, Charles R. Wise, and David Rosenbloom.

ASPA has matured into a multipurpose organization. ASPA promotes various aspects of administrative success through the presentation of its public administrative awards and in the recognition of inventive administrative concepts. The modern trend for ASPA has been directed toward even more expansion of service to the practitioners of public administration. The ASPA website (www.aspanet.org) has proposed volunteerism, offered on-line access to organizational documents, provided members the tools to research historical articles in the PAR, provided nationally recognized awards, acted as a marketer by chronicling the details of conferences, fostered careers in administration through the provision of guidance via their leadership council, and even offered insurance for its members.

ASPA acts as a conduit for the needs of new professionals, for scholars, and for modern practitioners of administration by providing internship opportunities, scholastic writing opportunities, and a job-seekers database. The organization offers prestige for its members and continues today in its original mission of bringing professionalism through recognition and skill development in order to assist administrators in their development and in the efficient and effective delivery of public administration, although this assistance is usually restricted to its membership.

For more information

American Society of Public Administration. http://www.aspanet.org.

Public Administration Review (PAR), published quarterly by the American Society of Public Administration (1942–   ).

Ernest Alexander Gomez

Americans with Disabilities Act of 1990

(ADA)   The Americans with Disabilities Act of 1990 is a comprehensive federal law prohibiting discrimination on the basis of disability. The ADA protects individuals with disabilities against discrimination in public and private employment, public and private services and accommodations, transportation, and telecommunications.

The ADA (PL 101-336) is composed of five sections:

1. Title I deals with unlawful discrimination in employment. Under this section, both public- and private-sector employers with 15 or more employees are barred from discriminating against a qualified individual with a disability in any employment decision or job action.

Also, employers are further obligated under this section to make certain job changes or provide other adaptations—called reasonable accommodations—if such actions are necessary to aid an employee with a disability in performing his or her job, unless doing so would impose an undue hardship.

2. Title II deals with unlawful discrimination in the administration of public programs and services and in the provision of public transportation. Under this section, state or local governments and their instrumentalities, as well as national commuter authorities, are prohibited from discriminating against a qualified individual with a disability in the provision of any type or form of service available to the public. Covered entities are required to follow accessible building standards in new construction or alterations of existing facilities. Entities are further required to make any changes that are needed to make public programs, services, and information accessible to people with sensory and other disabilities as necessary, unless doing so would impose undue burdens or fundamentally alter the nature of the program being provided.

3. Title III deals with unlawful discrimination in the provision of services or goods by private businesses or nonprofit service providers. Under this section, private entities are prohibited from discriminating against an individual with a disability in the benefits, services, goods, facilities, privileges, advantages, or accommodations it offers to the public.

4. Title IV deals with requirements placed upon common carriers engaged in interstate communication (such as telephone companies) to create telecommunications relay systems in order to make their services functionally equivalent for individuals with speech or hearing disabilities.

5. Title V deals with various additional issues. It includes a prohibition of retaliation against individuals who exercise their rights under the act, a statement affirming that states are

People prepare to board an Amtrak train.   (JOE RAEDLE/GETTY IMAGES)

not immune to actions brought against them in federal courts for violating the act, a provision requiring several federal agencies to develop technical assistance plans for covered entities, a provision requiring federal agencies to promulgate guidelines for accessible building design, a provision requiring the initiation of certain studies related to disabilities, a statement defining the extent to which the act applies to Congress and the agencies of the legislative branch, and addresses a number of other miscellaneous concerns.

For more information

Blanck, Peter D., ed. *Employment, Disability, and the Americans with Disabilities Act: Issues in Law, Public Policy, and Research.* Chicago: Northwestern University Press, 2000.

Young, Jonathan M. *Equality of Opportunity: The Making of The Americans with Disabilities Act.* Washington, D.C.: National Council on Disability, 1997.

Steve Noble

Amtrak (National Railroad Passenger Corporation)   Founded in 1971, Amtrak is a federal corporation that was created to consolidate several independent railroads in order to provide the public with a more comprehensive transportation network.

Amtrak began service in May 1971 with a train route from New York to Philadelphia. Soon it was servicing 314 destinations with 184 trains. Amtrak took over all but three of the nation's train operations and eventually, as those routes went out of business, Amtrak took those over also. Amtrak was recently shown to service over 500 stations in 46 states, and to employ almost 24,000 people, up from the initial 25. The expansive duties of Amtrak include operating trains on more than 22,000 route miles of track. On those routes that Amtrak does not own, it rides on freight lines. In 2001, Amtrak ridership peaked at an all-time high of more than 23.5 million riders. In addition to these numbers, Amtrak is the nation's largest provider of contract commuter service for state and local authorities. This brings an additional 61.1 million riders to the trains Amtrak runs, for a total figure closer to 85 million riders per year.

Amtrak more recently has focused on expansion of its rail services to include high-speed trains in designated corridors of service. These corridors are typically between two major cities that both have high populations. One such example has been the creation of the high-speed rail train between Washington and Boston. This train cuts down the travel time between the two cities immensely and has been a boon to the many political ties Amtrak has developed on the East Coast of the United States. Moreover, with this increase in efficiency, Amtrak has been able to compete for some of the consumers that have, in the past, been more likely to fly. Since the 11 September 2001 incidents, Amtrak has seen a rise in train travelers.

Shortly after the tragedies of September 11, the political lobby for the airline industry argued for and was granted financial support. The general climate in the Congress was one of support for any and all of the ailing transportation systems. Prior to the September 11 attacks, the railroad industry did not have as strong a lobby as the airlines and, in consequence, did not receive the same support. Later, the attitude in Congress changed and Amtrak did receive some support for operations. This was a major change in domestic policy toward Amtrak.

For years politicians, most notably the Democratic Party presidential candidate Michael Dukakis, attempted to make Amtrak part of the nation's infrastructure for transportation but with no positive results. The belief that the United States had fallen behind other nations in its rail transportation system was fostered in the mid-eighties with the emergence of Japan's high-speed rail system and France and England's joint development of their train systems. This more recent understanding of the possibilities associated with Amtrak gives the company a larger political bargaining chip than in the past. Yet, there is some hidden political history unrelated to Amtrak that some believe has been playing out since the early nineties and that can be understood by briefly revisiting early U.S. transportation history.

Shortly after the industrial revolution, the main mode of transportation was by rail. These rail companies grew into large monopolies that dictated not how just their industry operated, but others as well. The political climate allowed this to happen because railroad development facilitated the growth of the nation as a whole and because the railroad lobbies were strong. As new sources of energy were tapped and other modes of transportation developed, the railroad industry became more regulated, which in essence shut down the competition in the industry even more and led to fractionalization and the collapse of the industry's profits. Years later, this gave Amtrak the opportunity to engulf the many remnant companies. Many saw the fall of the railroads as a boon to other, more convenient modes of transportation, such as automobiles and airplanes, and their lobbies are very strong. It appears, though, that both Amtrak and the Congress do not want a national railway company, even though support of Amtrak is in the nation's best interests for the future.

For more information

Amtrak. http://www.amtrak.com.

Goodwin, Samuel P., ed. *Amtrak: Background and Bibliography*. New York: Nova Science Publishers, 2002.

Vranich, Joseph. *Derailed: What Went Wrong and What to Do about America's Passenger Trains.* New York: St. Martin's Press, 1997.

Ernest Alexander Gomez

Appropriations Committee   The House of Representatives Appropriations Committee was created in 1865 to assume responsibility for appropriations bills that had previously been under the jurisdiction of the House of Representatives Ways and Means Committee.

The functions of the Ways and Means Committee are often confused with those of the Appropriations Committee. The former focuses on *raising* the money necessary to operate the federal government, while the latter centers its attention on *allocating and spending* federal funds.

A law authorizing expenditure of money must exist before any branch of the federal government can use funds that have been allocated to it. With the exception of the House and Senate Appropriations Committees, each congressional committee can authorize the expenditure of federal funds by enacting legislation that establishes a federal program and enables the program's operation by authorizing the appropriation of a specific sum. However, the appropriated funds cannot be spent, hence the program cannot be effectuated, until the House Appropriations Committee has approved the legislation that authorizes the appropriation.

Currently, the Appropriations Committee has jurisdiction over bills that: appropriate funds to support operation of the federal government; eliminate appropriations where authorized by law to do so; and transfer to another account within an agency unspent funds that were appropriated for that agency. Additionally, after the bills and joint resolutions that create new federal programs are approved by the committees in which they originated, they cannot receive federal funding until approved by the Appropriations Committee. Finally, since the committee is the final arbiter of the sum that each executive department and agency receives, it is expedient that the committee is also responsible for overseeing the organization and operation of each of these departments and agencies.

After receiving a general appropriation bill, the Appropriations Committee must hold hearings and gather information relevant to the bill for at least three days, or for a longer period of time as mandated by the bill or by another law. Upon expiration of this time period, the committee can submit the bill for a vote by the entire House.

Each year, within 30 days after the president submits the nation's budget to Congress, it is mandatory that the Appropriations Committee conduct hearings in an open session, with the entire membership of the House as an audience. The committee members are also required to maintain up-to-the-minute knowledge of federal laws that grant authority to spend funds or provide permanent budget authority. If the committee decides that one of these laws must be modified or terminated, a report and recommendation on this matter must be submitted to the entire House.

For more information

Committee on Appropriations, U.S. House of Representatives. http://www.house.gov/rules/comm_jurisdiction.htm.

———. House Document 104-272, 104th Cong., 2d sess. Available online. URL: http://memory.loc.gov/ammem/amlaw/lawhome.htm.

Legislative terminology: the budget process. http://www.coastalcoalition.org/facts/budgetprocess.html.

Beth S. Swartz

arbitrary and capricious   "Arbitrary and capricious" refers to a manner of decision making by an administrative agency or court that accords with the decision maker's whim, personal preference, or prejudice rather than established rules, settled practice, and relevant evidence or precedents.

Examples would include (1) the selective criminal prosecution of an individual based on his or her race, gender, or the prosecutor's personal animus toward the defendant, and (2) the denial of a building permit or other benefit to an applicant due to the administrator's animus toward the applicant or personal opposition to the applicable criteria for the award.

The term implies that administrators have acted lawlessly and, in many cases, with bad faith. Arbitrary and capricious decision making threatens the rule of law and the uniform, predictable, and fair treatment of persons.

Arbitrary and capricious acts or decisions may be subject to reversal by a higher administrative authority or court.

For more information

Garner, Bryan A., ed. *Black's Law Dictionary*, 7th ed., St. Paul Minn.: West Group, 1999.

Michael Comiskey

arbitration   Arbitration is the settlement of a dispute by the decision of a neutral third party who acts like a judge but with less stringent rules of evidence. Arbitration, often done through private contract, is the oldest form of 20th-century ALTERNATIVE DISPUTE RESOLUTION (ADR) and usually is faster and cheaper than a regular court proceeding.

Arbitration has a history across centuries and many cultures, but its most popular U.S. roots are in labor-management relations. Federal legislation of the 1920s and 1930s created arbitration to prevent labor unrest by promptly and fairly resolving shop-floor and other workplace disputes. Other state statutes use arbitration to resolve consumer–auto dealer disputes over alleged defects in new cars (commonly called "lemon laws").

Nonbinding arbitration yields a recommendation that informs disputants of what is seen as a fair or likely outcome, but negotiations can continue. Binding arbitration offers a resolution with the force of law. Three-person arbitration panels are common, but solo arbitrators are frequent. Usually, arbitrators have expertise in the subject under dispute, unlike lay people serving on juries or judges who must handle a variety of cases.

There are various limits on what kind of decision an arbitrator or arbitration panel can make. Final-offer arbitration (also known as "last-best-offer" or "baseball arbitration") directs the arbitrator to choose between the disputants' positions; no middle position is possible. This format encourages the opponents to moderate their demands, lest their position be rejected. Otherwise, the arbitrator may choose an award at any point between the disputants' positions, based on the evidence, arguments and points of the contract, regulation, professional standards, or law.

Arbitration can be compulsory (set by law) or voluntary. Voluntary refers to the choice of having arbitration of disputes as a part of private contracts, to address grievances, or to express dissatisfaction with goods or services. Commercial arbitration, in the United States and transnationally, is very common. One high-profile example of private arbitration is the determination of salaries of professional athletes in some sports.

Public administrators typically encounter arbitration in personnel laws and policies, construction contracts for public facilities, and through government-run programs of arbitration in the court system, administrative law appeals, etc. There are federal and state government rosters of arbitrators, often separated according to the nature of the dispute. For example, arbitration is used in medical malpractice claims, workplace grievances, workers compensation, as well as for small-claims lawsuits. Arbitration program administrators typically allow parties to choose their own arbitrators. When a three-person arbitration panel is called for, often each party chooses one arbitrator and the two arbitrators choose the third member. The American Arbitration Association (AAA) is one of many sources of arbitration services under contract to businesses, labor unions, and other groups. AAA maintains rosters of arbitrators to respond to requests for substantive expertise and geographic proximity.

Issues in arbitration include how it has become more formalized, time-consuming, and expensive across the 20th century. In fact, many prefer mediation and other ADR methods as alternatives to arbitration. Another concern is that arbitrators are often seen as more favorable to labor or management, plaintiff or defendant, and are sought by parties for their track record rather than for expertise, impartiality, or fairness. With arbitration's roots in the labor-management field, concerns have been expressed about the difficulty of placing women and ethnic and racial minorities on arbitration rosters.

For more information

CRInfo: A Comprehensive Gateway to Conflict Resolution Resources. Available online. URL: http://www.crinfo.org/arbitration/v3-index.cfm.

John B. Stephens

Arrow's Paradox Arrow's Paradox takes its name from the 1972 Nobel Prize winner for economic science, Kenneth Arrow, who was a professor of economics at Stanford University for many years.

The Arrow Paradox stems from his 1951 Ph.D. dissertation, which set out a mathematical proof of the impossibility of social choice. The impossibility theorem, as it came to be known, asserts that it is impossible to mathematically derive social or group choice from individual preferences. The paradox that follows from this is that in any democratic society there is no purely logical way, without the possibility of internal contradictions, to ascertain a preferred collective choice from conflicting individual preferences. The outcome of Arrow's impossibility theorem enunciated in 1950 became the basis of what came to be called social choice theory, which continually seeks to show how social decision making is not rational. This has become a standard economic critique of majority rule, a critique that disturbed Arrow, who spent many years defending democracy by encouraging appropriate civic values and collective morality in public office.

The impossibility theorem is set out in many textbooks and begins with the premise of individual rational choice in the consumption of goods and services (but has also been applied to voting and public goods). The next step in the theorem is to prescribe as a logical standard that individual preferences must be consistent and transitive. As such, if an individual chooses service A over that of B, then she cannot also choose service B over A. For transitivity, the individual who prefers service A to B but also prefers service B to C must also prefer A to C. Arrow argued that social choice did not follow this mathematical transitivity principle. Take the following example as a simple means of understanding this conundrum.

There are three film choices—X (a "guys" movies), Y (a "chicks" movie), and Z (a "kids movie")—and three moviegoers, Alex, Bev, and Chris, have to choose from these options. Following economic rational thought, then each moviegoer will seek to maximize his or her utility, and if all three agree on a choice then there are no logical problems. However, if Alex chooses X to Y and Y to Z; and then Bev chooses Y to Z, and Z to X; and Chris prefers to see Z to X and X to Y, then there is a logical dilemma. That is, while there is a consistency here, it does not extend to single choices. Logically, the three cinema buffs prefer X to Y, in that Alex and Chris both chose X over Y, and they also prefer Y to Z, since Alex and Bev chose Y over Z. The transitivity principle states that film X is preferred to film Z. But as we saw, Bev and Chris prefer to see Z to X, therein violating this principle. It is from this mathematical analysis, albeit more abstract, that Arrow derived his impossibility theorem, arguing that social choice cannot be, in terms of mathematical consistency, derived from individual choice. As such, the paradox is that democracy is not mathematically consistent; nevertheless, we all must make the best of majority rule.

For more information
Arrow, Kenneth. *Social Choice and Individual Values.* New York: Wiley, 1951.
——. *Collected Papers of Kenneth J. Arrow,* 6 vols. Cambridge, Mass.: Harvard University Press, 1983–85.

Gregory McCarthy

auditing   Auditing is the process of providing independent assurance of an organization's operations—most commonly its financial operations—to shareholders or other stakeholders. The main types are external audit and internal audit.

Both types of audit rely on the system of internal controls that an organization should build into its accounting systems. For cost reasons, most audits are risk based and examine only a sample of transactions and balances, so they are unable to provide the absolute degree of assurance that stakeholders often expect. On the other hand, the notable examples of audit failure periodically reported in the media are often attributed to a lack of audit independence from the organization being audited.

In the public sector, external audits are generally carried out by an auditor general or comptroller general who reports to the legislative arm of government. In contrast, the internal audit function reports to the senior management and board of an organization and is carried out either by an in-house unit or a contracted audit firm.

The external audit mandate is a key point of difference between public- and private-sector auditors. In particular, the auditor of a corporation focuses primarily on verifying the organization's financial statements and, in a more limited way, its compliance with legislation. In addition, the independence of auditors in the public sector tends to be better protected than in the private sector by means of more stringent legislation governing the appointment process, tenure of office, and dismissal requirements relating to audit.

With the move within many governments from cash to accrual accounting, reporting, and budgeting, the role of public-sector auditors has evolved in parallel, with the audit opinion or certificate increasingly focusing on whether the organization's financial statements fairly reflect the result of its operations for the year and its financial position at the end of the financial year. At the same time, the traditional public-sector audit continues to focus on certifying compliance with appropriations and other financial management requirements of relevant legislation and rules.

Increasingly, the role and mandate of public-sector audit (external and internal) is expanding to provide an independent appraisal and report on the performance of organizations, functions, or programs subject to audit. These reports can take the form of audit opinions on the reliability and validity of performance measures and indicators reported by the organizations, or they can be in the form of reports with findings and recommendations relating to the organizations' efficiency and effectiveness. In the latter case, the legislative mandate will commonly preclude audit comment on government policy.

For more information
U.S. Government Accounting Office. http://www. gao.gov.

Bob Shead

B

Barnard, Chester Irving (1886–1961) *author, manager* Chester Barnard, a former president of New Jersey Bell Telephone Company, wrote two books—*The Function of the Executive* (1938) and *Organization and Management* (1948)—that stressed the importance of effective leadership in a formal organization.

Born in Malden, Massachusetts, on 7 November 1886, Barnard graduated from Harvard University in 1909. Out of college, he took a job as a statistician for the American Telephone and Telegraph Company in Boston, a subsidiary of the Bell Telephone System. He would spend the next 40 years with the company, rising rapidly through the ranks. In 1922, he became assistant president and general manager of the Bell Telephone Company of Pennsylvania. At the age of 42, he was made president of New Jersey Bell. He retired from that position in 1948.

Barnard was involved in a variety of community activities, including being on the board of managers of the New Jersey Reformatory and a member of the executive committee of the National Probation Association. He was also on the boards of several banks, insurance companies, and businesses. During World War II, he was president of the United Service Organization for Defense and director of the National Fund. After the war he kept his national service up when he was a representative on the Atomic Energy Commission.

Barnard's thought revolved around the understanding that organizations can be active more than individuals. Organizations contain more knowledge, can manage more information, and offer services that an individual cannot. The best way to think of this is as an assembly line for an automobile. One hundred people become more efficient and effective when each works on one aspect of the automobile rather than everyone working on an individual automobile. Thus a formal organization is important to achieve goals. Barnard defined a formal organization as a "system of consciously coordinated activities of two or more persons." An organization is more than the sum of its parts. In other words, an organization is like a stop sign. The word *Stop* conveys more meaning to the individual reading the sign than the individual letters *STOP* that form the word. The organization cannot be broken down to the individuals, but it is more than them.

There are two ways to measure an organization: efficiency and effectiveness. Effectiveness is the degree to which an organization's goals are attained at a minimum of cost. In other words, if the organization's goal is to sell buggies, are they doing it in the best way possible? This means taking into account price, service, supply, community relations, advertising, logistics, and the effectiveness of communication within the company. Efficiency is the individual's personal satisfaction derived from the activity. In other words, are the employees happy in their tasks? This takes into account pay, work environment, and the morality and ethics of the company. The survival of an organization depends on both of these factors. Barnard states, "Effectiveness relates to the accomplishment of the cooperative purpose, which is social and non-personal in character. Efficiency relates to the satisfaction of the individual motives, and is personal in character." An organization cannot hold, attract, or motivate its participants without efficiency, and it needs to be effective to justify its existence.

The executive in an organization must ensure that his organization balances these two goals. The essence of leadership is to create moral codes for others to ensure that the organization prospers. The goals of the organization must be worked into the company's education, training, precepts, and informal organizations. A successful leader must create an organizational morality that overcomes individual interests, gives meaning to common purposes, creates incentive to achieve the goals, and inspires those around him. The best way to achieve this is for the executive to understand what he or she is communicating. In other words, what is he or she saying or projecting to those in the organization? Second, when making a decision, the leader must believe that the decision is consistent with the purpose of the organization. Finally, is the person you are communicating with mentally or physically able to comply with the communication? Barnard offers leaders a practical way to understand their function and evaluate if they are doing a good job.

For more information

Barnard, Chester Irving. *The Functions of the Executive.* Cambridge, Mass.: Harvard University Press, 1968.

Scott, William G. *Chester I. Barnard and the Guardians of the Managerial State.* Lawrence: University Press of Kansas, 1992.

Wolf, William B. *The Basic Barnard: An Introduction to Chester I. Barnard and His Theories of Organization and Management.* Ithaca: New York State School of Industrial and Labor Relations, Cornell University, 1974.

T. Jason Soderstrum

Bill of Rights   The Bill of Rights is the collective term for the first 10 amendments to the U.S. Constitution. These amendments were passed by Congress on 25 September 1789 and ratified by the states on 15 December 1791. In contrast to the Constitution's body, which focuses on the structure and powers of the U.S. government, the Bill of Rights focuses on individual liberties.

When first enacted, the Bill of Rights prohibited only the federal government from infringing upon individual liberties; however, its application was extended to the states with the passage of the Fourteenth Amendment in 1868. Because they were aware of the danger that only the rights specifically stated in the Bill of Rights would be viewed as protected ones, the framers wanted to make clear that the first 10 amendments are an incomplete list of rights. Accordingly, they stated in the Ninth Amendment that other rights are "retained by the people" and in the Tenth Amendment that any right that the Constitution neither delegates to the federal government nor proscribes to the states is "reserved to the States respectively, or to the people."

The central idea behind the Bill of Rights is that some rights are so basic that every individual should have them. However, during the time period in which the Bill of Rights was ratified, not all people were considered individuals, only white men. Consequently, there was little focus on these rights until the mid-1900s, when movement for the extension of CIVIL RIGHTS to all persons began. For example, the Bill of Rights was pivotal to the success of the Civil Rights movement of the 1960s and the women's rights movement of the 1970s, and it is the underlying foundation for the ongoing movements for equal rights by persons with disabilities and members of the gay, lesbian, bisexual, and transgender communities.

As a result of the many movements for the expansion of civil rights, the U.S. government now, by and large, recognizes that all persons are individuals with rights. Accordingly, debate now focuses on which rights are fundamental ones, worthy of absolute protection. There is also debate about balancing fundamental rights in situations where there are conflicts between individuals regarding their rights. For example, although individuals have the right to express their opinions, they do not have the right to force those opinions on others or to intrude into the privacy of others in order to express those opinions.

Modern civil rights laws such as the Fair Housing Act, the Americans with Disabilities Act, and the Equal Employment Act were inspired by the idea central to the Bill of Rights: that every individual has certain rights that no one else, not even the local, state or federal government, can take away. Today the Bill of Rights is undoubtedly the most debated part of the Constitution. Both the Bill of Rights and modern civil rights laws engender discussion about the compromises necessary to have a strong government while protecting individual rights. For example, after the 11 September 2001 "attack on America," there has been much debate about how best to keep citizens safe without curtailing the fundamental liberties guaranteed by the Bill of Rights. There has also been significant debate about whether all individuals within the United States, or only citizens, are protected by the Bill of Rights, in spite of the view of most constitutional scholars that all individuals present within the United States are so protected.

For more information
Constitution Society. http://www.constitution.org.
Rehnquist, William H. "Why a Bill of Rights Is Not Enough." *Wilson Quarterly* 16, no. 2 (1992): 111.

Martha M. Lafferty

block grants   Block grants are a form of grants-in-aid and a means by which the federal government transfers federal aid (i.e., money) to state and local governments (i.e., intergovernmental transfers).

Grants-in-aid replaced the land grants commonly given by the federal government in the 19th century. Grants-in-aid are generally either categorical grants that target a specific project, the recipients of which have little leeway in their use of the funds, or block grants, which consolidate or bundle categorical grants and target a broad program area that the federal government deems to be in the nation's interest (e.g., job training or urban renewal).

Block grants allow the recipient government a lot of leeway in its use of the funds. While the federal government started to use block grants in the 1960s, President Richard Nixon, in his quest to increase efficiency as well as the flexibility of state and local governments, accelerated the use of block grants. Three important block grant programs are rooted in the 1970s, including Community Development Block Grants (CDBG), Comprehensive Employment Training Act (CETA), and Title XX of the Social Security Act. From 1973 to 1982, CETA provided block grants to subnational governments with the goal of improving job training.

Since 1974, the federal government has transferred moneys through CDBGs to revive communities and benefit low- and moderate-income community members. This includes, for example, using grant money to create, improve, or expand affordable housing or community services. Title XX established broad national goals (e.g., assisting people toward economic independence and protecting children from abuse).

Seeking to decrease the size of the federal government and increase subnational government flexibility, under the Omnibus Budget Reconciliation Act of 1981, President RONALD REAGAN consolidated many more categorical grants into block grants, including the Social Services Block Grant and the Preventative Health and Health Services Block Grant. Other grants since 1981 include the Project and Assistance in Transition from Homelessness Block Grant and the 1990 Child Care and Administration and Delivery Block Grant. Since 1981, block grants have accounted for about 11 percent of grant funds transferred from the federal government to state governments.

For more information

Hale, George E., and Marian Lief Palley. *The Politics of Federal Grants*. Washington, D.C.: Congressional Quarterly Press, 1981.

Linda K. Shafer

Board of County Commissioners v. Umbehr

518 U.S. 668 (1996) *Board of County Commissioners v. Umbehr* is a 1996 Supreme Court decision that provides protection against retaliatory termination to contractors who make public statements that offend public officials. It extends First Amendment free speech protection previously benefiting governmental employees to include persons who contract with government.

The facts of *Board of Commissioners, Wabaunsee County, Kansas v. Keen A. Umbehr* are as follows. Keen A. Umbehr was a waste hauler whose contract with Wabaunsee County made him the exclusive hauler of trash for cities in the county. By its terms, the contract between Umbehr and the county was automatically renewed annually unless one of the parties terminated it by giving notice at least 60 days before the end of the year

or a renegotiation was instituted on 90-day notice. Umbehr hauled trash from 1985 to 1991 on an exclusive and uninterrupted basis. At the end of that period the board terminated his contract. He alleged the contract was terminated in retaliation for critical letters he had written to the newspaper and statements he made at the board meetings criticizing the board. The Supreme Court found his complaint stated a cause of action. In making this finding, the Court extended the qualified protection previously only available to employees to include those who contract with government. The decision indicated that the standards previously applicable to employees would now apply to governmental contractors.

The law providing a qualified protection against retaliatory discharge by governmental employers originates with the Supreme Court decision in *Pickering v. Board of Education of Township High School District 205, Will County*, 391 U.S. 563 (1968). In *Pickering*, the Court found that an employee has a qualified protection against retaliatory discharge because of his or her public statements. In deciding whether this protection applies in particular fact situations, the Court promulgated a balancing test. The free-speech interests of the employee to comment on matters of public concern are to be balanced against the interest of the state as an employer in promoting the efficiency of the public services it performs through its employees. In applying this balancing test to employment situations, courts have generally limited the protection given to governmental employees to situations where the employee's speech involved matters of public interest or public concern. Speech relating to the employee's or contractor's employment, but not to issues of general public concern, is to be given little weight as one applies the balancing test. A similar balancing test is to be used in reviewing retaliatory discharge of governmental contractors.

Further, where the employee or contractor is in a policy-making position, or other positions where a service provider's political affiliation or public statements are an appropriate requirement for the effective performance of the task in question, the employee may be terminated for making public statements inconsistent with his job requirements.

On the day *Umbehr* was decided, the Court also decided *O'Hare Truck Service, Inc. v. Northlake* 518 U.S. 712 (1996). The Court in *O'Hare* considered the constitutionality of the decision of Northlake to remove O'Hare Truck Service from the city rotation list of towing service providers in retaliation for the refusal of the company owner to support the mayor's bid for reelection. The owner of O'Hare Truck supported the mayor's opponent. Prior to the decision in *O'Hare*, protection from retaliation based on patronage was limited to employees. *O'Hare* extends limitations on governmental practices, which previously only applied to employees, to include the category of those who contract with government. In extending protection to contractors, the Court adopted a balancing test similar to that adopted in *Umbehr*. The majority opinion provides some guidance with respect to the application of the balancing test, saying that governmental officials should be given substantial discretion with respect to its contractors in order to maintain stability, reward good performance, deal with known and reliable persons, ensure the uninterrupted supply of goods or services, or avoid the appearance of favoritism. Many choices and policy considerations ought to remain open to government officials when deciding to contract with some firms and not others, provided, of course, that the asserted justifications are not the pretext for some improper practice.

For more information

Eckersley, Brent C. "*Board of County Commissioners v. Umbehr* and *O'Hare Truck Service v. City of Northlake:* The Extension of First Amendment Protection to Independent Contractors." *Public Contract Law Journal* 27 (summer 1998).

Nash, Ralph. *Government Contracts Reference Book.* Washington, D.C.: Georgetown University, 1998.

bonds   Bonds are debt securities and a means by which municipalities (as well as federal agencies, corporations, and governments) borrow money. For a variety of reasons (e.g., skyrocketing costs of running a municipality and state legislation limiting property tax rates or local urban spending), municipalities frequently borrow money through bond financing to pay for bridges, roads, hospitals, and other capital improvements and, in limited cases, to meet some financial obligations.

There are several different kinds of bonds, both short term and long term, commonly utilized by municipalities. Tax anticipation notes (TANs) are a common short-term borrowing method generally repaid within a few months out of the city's revenue. TANs are used by cities to remedy, for example, an abnormality in its revenues or expenditures (e.g., meeting employees' pay cycle before the city has collected taxes); cities cannot issue bonds to cover long-term operating deficits. The most common long-term municipal financing instrument is a general obligation (GO) bond. When a city issues a GO bond, it promises (and is under legal obligation) to repay the amount borrowed from future revenue. GO bonds, however, are often subject to state control; often municipalities are required to have a referendum before a city can issue a GO bond. Revenue bonds, another long-term municipal financing instrument, do not require a citizen referendum and thus are a popular means of municipal financing. A revenue bond is used to finance the construction of a specific project, for example a bridge or a stadium. The municipality repays the bond out of the revenue received from the finished project, for example bridge tolls or admission fees. (A real problem arises, however, if the revenue actually collected is less than expected.)

The interest rate offered on municipal bonds is lower than other investment opportunities, but the tax benefits available provide an attractive investment opportunity for some; generally, the interest on municipal bonds is not subject to federal, state, or local income tax. Given the low interest rate but the tax-exempt status of municipal bonds, the most common purchasers of municipal bonds include commercial banks and wealthy people.

Municipalities in the United States are generally rated by Moody's Investors Service, Standard & Poor's Corporation, and Fitch. The ratings (from ΛΛΛ down to B) indicate whether bonds issued by the city would be considered high or low investment grade and also low to high possible yield.

For more information

Aronson, J. Richard, and John L. Hilley. *Financing State and Local Governments,* 4th ed. Washington, D.C.: Brookings Institution, 1986.

Judd, Dennis R., and Todd Swanstrom. *City Politics: Private Power and Public Policy.* New York: Longman, 2001.

Twentieth Century Fund Task Force on Municipal Bond Credit Ratings. *The Rating Game.* New York: Twentieth Century Fund, 1974.

Linda K. Shafer

bounded rationality The concept of bounded rationality, first used by HERBERT SIMON, has to do with the limitations of human rationality in predicting the consequences of actions. It deals with individual actors and their nature as members of a given political, economic, or social system. That is why bounded rationality is relevant to any research activity that depends on human actions. The main idea here is that behavior is governed by culturally transferred norms. Those norms are the result of different experiences that have been gathered over the years. For that very reason, norms allow people to adapt and to act in certain ways, although without having a clear idea about why they do what they do.

The processes used by a person to make choices and to learn from his/her mistakes are the result of his/her limited ability to predict the consequences of his/her actions. What lies behind the inability of a person to consider the results, effects, and impacts of his/her decisions is informational constraints and cultural or ethnic influences.

Political decisions, due to their inherently human nature, are often tied with bounded rationality. For example, when an individual wonders about the implementation of a new economic policy or the building of a new public school, he/she can experience informational restrictions such as not knowing what will be the economic consequences. This lack of information may keep a minister from implementing the policy and may give rise to new and worse unexpected problems. In this sense, the idea of limited or bounded rationality shows why institutional and decisional processes are unpredictable. That is why we recognize that norms, values, and historical processes play a major role when it comes to deciding the final shape and functioning of institutions.

Political processes that involve transactions between individuals or political parties consider decisions and actions that have been carried out without complete knowledge of their impact. Many times, public officials lack full information and consciousness of what they are doing. They cannot forecast the implications of their actions because they are limited by their inability to gather all the relevant information and to compute an optimal solution. The political agents have to discover information (like the strategies of other agents) and constantly adapt their behavior in a learning process that results in better policy decisions and acts, building coalitions with other agents, or forging institutional change.

There is always a certain level of ignorance when a decision is made. That is why the learning process experienced by a person who makes a decision is so important. It does not matter if the decision leads to a failure or a success. The most important thing is to begin a learning process and to accumulate learning experiences.

Those academicians who follow the institutional and the neo-institutional theories have analyzed the relationship between this paradigm and several variables such as the historical evolution of institutions, the organizational behavior of rationally limited actors, and the consequences of an institutional change carried out by people who make inconsistent decisions and act irrationally due to their inherent limitations as human beings.

For more information

Simon, H. A. *Models of Bounded Rationality: Behavioral Economics and Business Organization.* Cambridge, Mass.: MIT Press, 1982.

Mila Gascó and Joan Oriol Prats

Bowsher v. Synar 478 U.S. 714 (1986)

Bowsher v. Synar is an important U.S. Supreme Court case that addressed the powers of the federal government to reduce the federal budget deficit.

In the struggle to control and eliminate the ever-growing federal budget deficit, the 99th Congress passed the Balanced Budget and Emergency Deficit Control Act of 1985, which came to be known as the Gramm-Rudman-Hollings Act, or GRAMM-RUDMAN ACT. The Gramm-Rudman-Hollings Act created a series of regressive spending caps that the annual deficit could not surpass. The act was designed to reduce the federal deficit to zero by the fiscal year 1991. If the federal budget exceeded the established maximums, the act required across-the-board cuts in federal spending to reach the targeted deficit level. To achieve these cuts, the comptroller general, in consultation with the directors of the OFFICE OF MANAGEMENT AND BUDGET and the CONGRESSIONAL BUDGET OFFICE, was to submit a report detailing projected revenues and expenditures and to specify areas of reduction within the budget. The act then compelled the president to issue an order requiring implementation of the reductions posed by the comptroller general.

Several hours after President Reagan signed the act into law, Congressman Michael Synar, later joined by 11 additional members of Congress, filed a complaint seeking to have the courts hold the Gramm-Rudman-Hollings Act unconstitutional. The case was initially heard by a three-judge panel in the U.S. District Court for the District of Columbia, which held that the role of the comptroller general in the deficit reduction process violated the constitutionally imposed separation of powers. The case was then appealed directly to the U.S. Supreme Court.

The Supreme Court upheld the lower court's finding that the Gramm-Rudman-Hollings Act violated the separation of powers doctrine and was thus unconstitutional. Writing for the majority, Chief Justice Warren Burger explained that since the comptroller general was subservient to Congress because the comptroller is removable only by Congress (and not by the president), the powers assigned to the comptroller under the act were of an executive nature (as the comptroller was to execute the budgetary cuts proposed to the president). Thus, Congress had maintained control over the execution of the act by controlling, through threat of removal from office, the individual who was to execute the act.

The Court's ruling had several effects. First, *Bowsher* and other cases like *INS v. Chada*, 462 U.S. 919 (1983), severely curtailed Congress's ability to make structural changes in government through legislation. The structure of much of the federal government comes directly from the Constitution, and thus changes to the constitutional structure must come from an amendment to the Constitution. Neither the executive nor legislative branch can restructure the political process so as to bring about a desired outcome. *Bowsher* left Congress primarily with the option of creating legislation that seeks to control the behavior of individuals or agencies through legal rules rather than by changing the structure of government.

For more information

Aman, Alfred C., Jr., et al. "Symposium: *Bowsher v. Synar.*" *Cornell Law Review* 72, no. 3 (1987): 421–597.

Bowsher v. Synar 478 U.S. 714 (1986).

Bradley D. Hays

Branti v. Finkel 445 U.S. 507 (1980)

Branti v. Finkel extended Supreme Court limitations on patronage politics in an attempt to protect employee freedoms.

In *Elrod v. Burns*, 427 U.S. 347 (1976), the Court had cited the rights of free speech and free association guaranteed by the First and Fourteenth Amendments to overturn a sheriff's decision to discharge certain employees who did not hold confidential or policy making positions. In *Branti,* the Court further extended this decision by upholding two lower federal court rulings that had enjoined and invalidated the partisan firing of two public defenders, who were Republican, by the newly appointed Rockland County, New York, public defender, who was a Democrat.

Justice John Paul Stevens delivered the majority opinion, which was joined by Chief Justice Warren Burger and Justices William Brennan, Byron White, Thurgood Marshall, and Harry Blackmun. Widening the tests of confidentiality and policy making set forth in *Elrod,* Stevens now argued that the important issue was "whether the hiring authority can demonstrate that party affiliation is an appropriate requirement for the effective performance of the public office required." Stevens further decided that a public defender's special responsibilities were not so much to the public at large as to individual clients, specifically noting in a footnote that the case of a prosecutor might be distinguishable. Any need for confidentiality with a client had "no bearing whatsoever on partisan political concerns."

Justice Potter Stewart's dissent portrayed public defenders as confidential employees who did not fall under the *Elrod* rule. Justice Lewis Powell's more vigorous dissent, joined by Justices William Rehnquist and Stewart, portrayed this decision as "the evisceration of patronage practices begun in *Elrod v. Burns.*" Powell pointed both to the long history of patronage in the United States and the value of such patronage in supporting political parties. Powell thought the Court's new standard was vague and argued that elected officials, rather than courts, should decide which individuals should be covered by civil service and which should not. Powell noted that states could evade the decision simply by mandating that assistant public defender positions be elected, as some states had already done. Despite the majority's failure to address the issue, Powell also expressed concern that this decision might have an adverse impact on an attorney general's control over his office.

The tension between broad interpretations of First Amendment rights of speech and association and more practical concerns for efficiency and accountability in government remained the subject of vigorous debate in *Rutan v. Republican Party of Illinois,* 497 U.S. 62 (1990). In that case, the narrow 5-4 majority led by Justice William Brennan further extended the *Branti* doctrine to cover most public employees not only from being fired for partisan reasons but also against other job-related penalties. Justice Antonin Scalia authored a vigorous dissent that could one day provide the basis for modifying or reversing this decision.

For more information

Daniel, Christopher. "Constitutionalizing Merit? Practical Implications of *Elrod, Branti,* and *Rutan,*" *Review of Public Personnel Administration* 12 (January–April 1992): 26–34.

John R. Vile

bribery Bribery is defined as giving something of value (money, services, or goods) to someone in return for some official action. Another category of bribery includes commercial bribery, where the action desired is from a business concern. Cases such as these would include paying a person in one business to do something (or not to do something) that would benefit the person who is offering the bribe. Under federal law and most state codes, bribery is a felony-level crime.

The bribe could be to persuade a government official to take some action. For example, a payment of money or a gift of a trip to Hawaii to a building code inspector to "pass" a building project would be a bribe. Likewise, the bribe might be initiated by a government agent who volunteered to let something pass in exchange for something of value. The bribe could also be to prevent action by a government employee. An example would be a monetary payment to a police officer so that she/he did not write a speeding ticket.

Bribery is clearly an ethical and potentially criminal problem for individuals, government agencies, and corporations, and it can have effects far beyond the intention of the individuals participating in the scheme. For example, a contractor bribes a building code inspector to pass shoddy workmanship that included wiring not installed according to state building code mandates. In the event of a fire, in which people are injured and property is lost, the losses from not doing the wiring correctly in the first place far exceed the gains.

Most bribery activity is fairly low level with goods of low value or small sums of cash changing hands. However large-scale bribery cases are common enough to create the perception through news media that things are not always proper and "straight" in government and business circles. The recent Abscam investigations of a number of U.S. congressmen who accepted bribes for influence or votes is a significant example of the scope of the problem.

Bribery is usually reduced or eliminated by two actions. The first is the speedy investigation and prosecution of people who engage in this behavior. The other means to reduce bribery and corruption in agencies is a function of leadership and management in setting a tone that shows that the behaviors of bribery and corruption are not acceptable. Some government agencies hire a staff of workers or agents, such as inspectors general, who conduct internal affairs investigations and audits of the operation to uncover corruption and bribery.

For more information
Black's Law Dictionary, 7th ed. St. Paul, Minn.: West, 1999.

Bruce L. Bikle

Brownlow Commission The Brownlow Commission was established in 1937 to examine the staff support given to the president of the United States of America. Prior to this time, presidents had little White House staff, and in earlier times presidents were known to deal directly with their own correspondence and telephone calls. In fact, for most of the first century of the presidency, the president operated without even a paid secretary.

The Brownlow Commission was established in response to a change in the nature of the presidency from one of heading a bureaucracy primarily responsible for implementing public policy to one that was also responsible for developing and proposing policy initiatives. This became clear in the New Deal era of the 1930s, during which it became obvious that the president needed more help at his disposal.

The Brownlow Commission was given the mandate to examine the support available to the president and to recommend a structure for matching the support to the demands of the office. The report of the Brownlow Commission resulted in the creation of the White House Office and the EXECUTIVE OFFICE OF THE PRESIDENT

(EOP). After the creation of these offices, the staff serving the president grew substantially, numbering 51 in 1943 and upward of 400 in more recent times.

Different presidents have used varying structures for organizing the White House Office, some relying on a single White House chief of staff to oversee the operations and others preferring a number of assistants, each with full access to the president.

The White House Office provides services to the president at the White House, and key staff are handpicked by the president. The current EOP includes more than a dozen agencies that provide staff services to the president, although they are not physically located in the White House. The heads of most of these agencies are nominated by the president and require Senate confirmation. These include the OFFICE OF MANAGEMENT AND BUDGET and the NATIONAL SECURITY COUNCIL. Historically, the Executive Office and cabinet departments have been the primary providers of policy proposals for presidential consideration, but in more recent years, there has been a trend for presidents to rely more heavily on the White House staff to develop policy proposals. This has created a new relationship dynamic within the structures of the executive branch of government, each vying to influence presidential decisions.

For more information

An Oral History Interview with George M. Elsey. Independence, Mo.: Truman Presidential Museum and Library, July 17, 1969. Available online. URL: http://www.trumanlibrary.org/index.html.

Heritage Foundation. http://www.heritage.org.

Michael Henry

Budget and Accounting Act of 1921 (42 Stat. 18, 1921)

The Budgeting and Accounting Act of 1921 is generally regarded as the first important piece of federal budget legislation—and one of the most critical—because it embraced

the concept of the "executive budget" and centralized budget preparation in the executive branch. It also created two influential federal budget institutions that are still in operation at the start of the 21st century: the Bureau of the Budget (now known as the Office of Management and Budget) and the General Accounting Office.

The executive budget was a key early innovation. Prior to the 1921 act, federal "departments and establishments" submitted appropriations requests (i.e., requests for authority to spend money) directly to Congress, bypassing the president entirely. These uncoordinated agency submissions were compiled in a "book of estimate" for congressional evaluation. But there was no formal timetable for consideration of appropriations by Congress. The 1921 act changed all that.

Under provisions of the 1921 act, federal departments and agencies are required to submit budget requests and estimates directly to the president for transmission to Congress. This effectively strengthened the president's role in national politics by giving him the key budget-making responsibility. Reformers had long favored unifying the federal budget under the president, on the theory that this would enhance accountability by fixing the responsibility for federal spending in the office of the president. Further, as the sole federal official with a national constituency, some believed that he would represent the entire nation in budgetary decision making (a highly dubious proposition).

By vesting so much political power in the president, Congress was sidestepping responsibility for proposing any unpopular fiscal actions (such as tax increases or spending cuts). At the same time, the efficiency of the budget process would be enhanced by unifying the previously fragmented federal budget, thereby enhancing congressional ability to set priorities in a meaningful way. In any case, Congress retained (and still retains) its authority to dispose of new legislation (including budgets) as it sees fit.

In order to assist the president in his new fiscal duties, the 1921 act created a new executive branch institution, the BUREAU OF THE BUDGET (BoB). The BoB was staffed by professionally trained budget examiners who analyzed agency appropriations requests and estimates and made recommendations to the president through the BoB director. Initially situated in the Treasury Department, BoB was moved into the new Executive Office of the President in 1939. BoB was renamed the Office of Management and Budget (OMB) under President Richard Nixon in 1969.

Congress also used the 1921 act to create the GENERAL ACCOUNTING OFFICE (GAO), a legislative branch agency that serves the Congress. The GAO performs the financial audit function for the federal government and supervises the accounting work performed by executive branch agencies. The GAO is headed by the comptroller general of the United States, who is appointed by the president for a single 15-year term, subject to Senate confirmation. In addition to its audit responsibilities, the GAO today emphasizes the evaluation and improvement of government programs and agencies.

For more information

Berman, Larry. *The Office of Management and Budget and the Presidency, 1921–1979.* Princeton, N.J.: Princeton University Press, 1979.

Mikesell, John L. *Fiscal Administration,* 5th ed. Fort Worth, Tex.: Harcourt Brace, 1999.

Mosher, Frederick C. *The GAO: The Quest for Accountability in American Government.* Boulder, Colo.: Westview Press, 1979.

Robert S. Kravchuk

budgeting   Budgeting is the process of allocating scarce or relatively fixed resources among multiple, and sometimes competing, line items and/or programs for some future period.

The word "budget" once meant the leather pouch used for carrying money, but it has now taken on multiple meanings from the technical to the symbolic, from narrow to broad, as has the process of budgeting itself. At the broadest and perhaps most symbolic level, budgeting is about community values and controlling government. A budget is a symbolic representation of what we want from government and what we want for our community. In principle, it is a reflection of community priorities. Budgeting is about what we wish to purchase and who and how we are going to pay for it.

At a narrower and less symbolic level, budgeting in the public sector is similar to budgeting in the private sector or in a home economy. The budgeting process examines where revenue comes from, in what amounts, and whether more or less is needed. Viewed in this way, budgeting is about financial planning. During the process we decide how to allocate our scarce resources across multiple possible expenditures. For example, should we purchase guns or planes or farm subsidies or prescription medication? In addition, budgeting provides some record of how money was spent and whether it was spent for the purpose originally intended. At this level, budgeting is about accountability and management processes (the most narrow and technical level). Here, budgeting is the mechanism for verifying that what was proposed to be spent was in fact spent on what the public and government managers wanted.

In the public sector, the budgeting process consists of budget preparation, discussion, enactment, implementation, and review and audit. During the preparation phase, administrators typically assess future needs, current commitments, and available revenue. During and after budget preparation, opportunities exist for interest groups and citizens to comment on the budget proposal. After public comment, the governing board or appropriate legislative authority enacts the budget through a formal vote, which gives the budget legal standing (in effect becoming a budget "law" or budget ordinance). Once the budget has been enacted, funds can be spent on various programs and line items (e.g., police cars, highway resurfacing, and educational programs) contained within the budget. This process is called budget implementation. Finally, after the budget is implemented, public-sector managers and legislators will review revenues and expenditures to assess whether estimates were accurate, whether guidelines were followed, and whether money was spent as indicated in the budget. Here, programs are often evaluated for their efficiency and effectiveness. For example, questions are asked such as: how many miles of highway were paved? at what cost? how many families traveled on them? is this the best way to spend the public's money?

In the end, budgeting means many things to many people. From overt political symbolism to technical financial accounting practices, budgeting underlies what we choose to spend our money on, who is going to pay for it, and how we are going to accomplish those objectives.

For more information

Nice, David. *Public Budgeting*. Belmont, Calif.: Wadsworth, 2002.

Wildavsky, Aaron, and Naomi Caiden. *The New Politics of the Budgetary Process*. New York: Addison, Wesley, Longman, 2001.

Robert A. Schuhmann

budget stabilization funds Budget stabilization funds are used by governments to finance expenditures during an economic downturn when revenues fall short of budgeted expenditures. Different terminology is used to refer to these funds, including "rainy day funds" and "required ending balances."

Budget stabilization funds are found in 46 states, and some of these states have multiple funds. There are only four states without such funds: Arkansas, Hawaii, Illinois, and Montana. Budget stabilization funds are often used by states to plan the financing of government programs over a longer period than the budget cycle. The funds are also used in some states to address a variety of budgetary issues other than budget stabilization over the business cycle. Some states have incorporated into their funds provisions for targeted or nonrecurring expenditures.

When budget stabilization funds are incorporated in the state constitution, they are generally regarded as more binding constraints. The most stringent funds provide for automatic deposits into the fund based upon a formula, generally using personal income, growth, or some other measure to determine the amount deposited. In some states, deposits into the budget stabilization fund are linked to year-end surpluses. The provisions may require that all or a portion of the surplus be deposited into the fund automatically. In other states, deposits into the fund are through legislative appropriation. The least stringent funds provide for deposits into the fund at the discretion of the executive branch, generally through the state budget or financial officer.

The stringency of budget stabilization funds is most evident in the provisions for withdrawals from the fund. Some states allow the withdrawal of funds only to meet a revenue shortfall that would result in a budget deficit. The withdrawals may be specified by a formula linked to estimates of the revenue shortfall.

A number of states also provide for withdrawal of funds to address emergencies. If the emergency is defined as a natural disaster or unforeseen situation, this provision gives the state a safety valve in using its fund. On the other hand, if the definition of emergency is ambiguous and left to the discretion of the legislative or executive branch, this can erode other constraints on the withdrawal of funds.

In some states, withdrawal of funds requires a supermajority vote of the legislature. In a few states, there are no provisions for the withdrawal of funds or the purpose for which the funds are withdrawn. In some cases, these decisions are left to budget officers and the executive branch.

Fund size reflects the willingness of the legislature to implement its budget stabilization fund. Until recent years, few states had fully funded their budget stabilization funds, and some of these states maintained a zero balance. As a result, budget analysts rightly regarded these funds as insignificant in influencing state finance.

The accumulation of surplus revenue in recent years has enabled many states to build up their budget stabilization funds. Most states had budget stabilization funds in FY 2000 equal to or greater than 3 percent of general fund budgets. The increasing importance of budget stabilization funds reflects the willingness of states to allocate more state revenues to these funds. This link between surplus revenue and budget stabilization funds is not surprising. In a number of states there is an explicit link between surplus revenue and moneys allocated to budget stabilization funds.

Most states have incorporated caps on their budget stabilization funds. The caps are usually expressed as a percentage of general fund appropriations, expenditures, prior-year revenues, or a similar base.

There is also a systematic relationship between budget stabilization funds and taxpayer relief. The recent increases in surplus revenues in most states enabled them to bring their budget stabilization funds to adequate levels. That, in turn, created more incentive for these states to use their surplus revenues for tax relief.

For more information
National Conference of State Legislatures. "State Strategies to Manage Budget Shortfalls." Washington, D.C.: National Conference of State Legislature, 1997.

Brent Smith

bureaucracy   *Bureaucracy* is a common term used to describe the system by which the business of government is carried out by departments, each under the control of a chief. In fact, when citizens transact business with their government, they would consider their point of contact as a bureau, and the person in charge of this bureau as a bureaucrat.

MAX WEBER, the noted German sociologist, defined several of the main characteristics, or attributes, of bureaucratic-type organizations in his book *The Theory of Social and Economic Organization* (1947 translation). These organizational qualities include a high degree of job specialization, a hierarchical authority structure with limited areas of command and responsibility, and impersonality of relationships between and among organizational members. Other important characteristics of bureaucratic organizations include the recruitment of officials based on ability and technical knowledge, and the fact that employees—regardless of their level within the organization—have no personal ownership rights. Under feudal organizations, employees followed rules, but these rules were based on tradition. In a bureaucratic organization, employees follow rules based on public laws and public policies as adopted by officials elected by the citizens they serve.

The downside of bureaucratic organization is that the organization is splintered administratively by separate functions and individual departments, each with its respective department managers and employees. In an era of customer service, it is incumbent upon a chief administrative officer to ensure that all units of the organization work toward a single purpose, serving the public in an objective manner with both professional and timely service. Sometime these organizational goals are lost in a large bureaucracy.

In the final analysis, bureaucratic organizations are not bad, and most large organizations, whether public or private, exhibit many of these bureaucratic characteristics. From a taxpayer's standpoint, it is good that citizens are treated objectively and that rules and regulations are administered impersonally by competent administrators. It is also admirable to hire employees based on their technical abilities rather than politics or nepotism. Also, when someone in a bureaucratic organization quits, the employee merely cleans out his desk, since there are no ownership rights in the organization.

For more information

Barnard, Chester. *Organization and Management*. Cambridge, Mass.: Harvard University Press, 1952.

Brech, E. F., et al. *The Making of Scientific Management*. Bristol, U.K.: Thoemmes Press, 1996.

Caldwell, Lynton. *The Administrative Theories of Hamilton and Jefferson: Their Contributions to Thought on Public Administration*. Chicago: University of Chicago Press, 1944.

Mouzelis, Nicos P. *Organization and Bureaucracy: An Analysis of Modern Theories*. Chicago: Aldine Publishing Co., 1968.

Waldo, Dwight. *The Administrative State: A Study of the Political Theory of American Public Administration*. New York.: Holmes and Meier, 1984.

Roger Kemp

Bureau of the Budget   The Bureau of the Budget (BoB) was created under authority of the Budget and Accounting Act of 1921 (42 Stat. 18, 1921). This act centralized budget preparation in the BoB under the overall direction of the president. The BoB was initially situated in the Treasury Department, but it was moved to the newly established EXECUTIVE OFFICE OF THE PRESIDENT in 1939. This move strengthened the role of the president as the "administrator in chief" of the executive branch. BoB's role was expanded when it was given greater responsibility for improving the management of federal departments and agencies. To signify its new role, the BoB was renamed the OFFICE OF MANAGEMENT AND BUDGET (OMB) under President Richard M. Nixon in 1969, and at the same time the OMB director was elevated to the level of a cabinet secretary.

In order to assist the president in fulfilling his fiscal and financial management duties, the BoB/OMB coordinates the budget preparation and execution process. It has primary responsibility for ensuring overall fiscal control. To fulfill these tasks, from the start the BoB/OMB has been staffed by professionally trained budget examiners whose job is to analyze agency appropriations requests and estimates and to make recommendations to the president through the director. Over the last 20 years, the expertise of OMB staff has greatly broadened to accommodate its expanded responsibilities. These include estimating the budgetary impact of legislation proposed by executive branch agencies (its "legislative clearance" function) and evaluating the costs and benefits of proposed new federal regulations and changes to existing ones (its "regulatory clearance" function), as well as its more traditional responsibilities for monitoring and reporting on federal revenue and expenditure trends, implementing new management initiatives, and promoting the president's budgetary priorities.

With such an expansive and influential role in the process of governing the federal executive branch, the role of the BoB has been increasingly politicized since its evolution into the OMB in the early 1970s. The professional ethic of the BoB was one of "neutral competence," that is, providing sound and objective professional advice to the president. This changed substantially with the election in 1980 of President Ronald Reagan, who increased greatly the numbers of politically appointed OMB staff who were directly beholden to the White House for their jobs. Consequently, OMB staff routinely lobby members of Congress on behalf of the president's legislative proposals. The OMB remains today the focal point for financial management and control of the federal government.

For more information

Berman, Larry. *The Office of Management and Budget and the Presidency, 1921–1979*. Princeton, N.J.: Princeton University Press, 1979.

Mosher, Frederick C. *A Tale of Two Agencies: A Comparative Analysis of the General Accounting Office and the Office of Management and Budget*. Baton Rouge: Louisiana State University Press, 1984.

Tomkin, Shelley Lynne. *Inside OMB, Politics and Process in the President's Budget Office*. Armonk, N.Y.: M. E. Sharpe, 1998.

Robert S. Kravchuk

Bush, George Herbert Walker (1924–)

41st president of the United States   George Herbert Walker Bush, the 41st U.S. president, succeeded Ronald Reagan in the presidency and presided over the end of the cold war.

Born to an affluent and well-connected New England family in 1924—his father, Prescott Bush, would represent Connecticut in the U.S. Senate in the 1950s and 1960s—Bush was awarded the Distinguished Flying Cross for his service as a navy bomber pilot in the Pacific during World War II. After graduating from Yale University with a degree in economics in 1948, Bush moved his family to west Texas to pursue a career in the oil industry. From 1954 to 1964, Bush served as president and co-owner of the Zapata Petroleum Corporation, a pioneer in the construction of offshore drilling platforms. Bush sold his interest in the company for $1 million in 1966.

Bush became increasingly involved in the Republican Party during the early 1960s, serving as chairman of the Harris County Republican Party from 1963 to 1964 and unsuccessfully seeking his party's nomination for a U.S. Senate seat in 1964. In 1966, Bush was elected to the U.S. House of Representatives from Houston's 7th Congressional District, where he would serve on the House Ways and Means Committee for two terms. In 1970, Bush once again sought a U.S. Senate seat but was defeated by his Democratic opponent, Lloyd Bentsen.

With his electoral career seemingly at a standstill, Bush enhanced his political résumé with a series of appointed positions under the Nixon and Ford administrations during the 1970s: U.S. ambassador to the United Nations (1971–73), chairman of the Republican National Committee (1973–74), chief U.S. liaison to China (1974–75), and director of the Central Intelligence Agency (1976–77). In 1980, Bush sought the Republican Party's presidential nomination, but he was defeated in the primaries by former California governor Ronald Reagan. However, at the party's national convention in New Orleans, Bush was selected as Reagan's running mate. The Reagan-Bush ticket soundly defeated the incumbent, Jimmy Carter, in the general election, and Bush would serve as vice president for the entire eight years of the Reagan presidency (1981–89).

Although Vice President Bush served as chairman of presidential task forces on regulatory relief, terrorism, and drug interdiction, he generally kept a low profile during his tenure in the office. However, this approach allowed him to largely avoid the political fallout from the Reagan administration's IRAN-CONTRA affair, and Bush handily won his party's presidential nomination to succeed Reagan in 1988. In a largely issueless campaign, Bush defeated the Democratic nominee, Massachusetts governor Michael S. Dukakis, with 54 percent of the popular vote and 426 electoral votes.

George H. W. Bush and Dan Quayle   (GEORGE BUSH PRESIDENTIAL LIBRARY)

Bush's presidency was characterized by tumultuous change and upheaval in foreign affairs. The brutal crushing of a pro-democracy movement in the People's Republic of China in 1989 elicited international outrage and demands that the Bush administration distance itself from the Beijing government. The Bush administration successfully navigated an end to the previous administration's contentious political battles with Congress over Nicaragua after the defeat of the Marxist Sandinista government in free elections in 1990. More significant was the collapse of the Iron Curtain in late 1989, as the Soviet Union allowed unpopular communist governments to fall in rapid succession throughout Eastern Europe. After a failed coup attempt in 1991, Soviet president Mikhail Gorbachev formally dissolved the Soviet Union and resigned as president, thereby ending the cold war that had dominated American foreign policy for five decades.

Bush also demonstrated a willingness to employ military force to realize foreign policy objectives. In December 1989, U.S. forces invaded Panama to capture General Manuel Noriega, the de facto Panamanian leader and a former U.S. intelligence asset who had been indicted on drug trafficking charges in the United States. Following the Iraqi annexation of Kuwait in August 1990, Bush would deploy more than 500,000 troops to the Persian Gulf and organize an international coalition to repel the invasion. In January 1991, allied forces led by the United States launched Operation Desert Storm, forcing the Iraqis to surrender just five weeks later. Just one month before leaving office, Bush deployed U.S. troops to Somalia to prevent rival clans from interfering with relief efforts.

Despite registering the highest presidential public approval ratings ever measured following the Persian Gulf War, Bush's foreign policy successes proved a liability as the budget deficit skyrocketed and the nation's economy moved into a recession during 1991. Despite some domestic policy achievements—the resolution of the savings and loan crisis, the Americans with Disabilities Act (1990), the Clean Air Act (1990)—Bush had angered conservatives within his party by breaking an anti-tax pledge in 1991, and he was challenged for his party's nomination by conservative commentator Pat Buchanan. In the 1992 general election, Bush was defeated for reelection by Arkansas governor Bill Clinton.

For more information

Duffy, Michael, and Dan Goodgame. *Marching In Place: The Status Quo Presidency of George Bush.* New York: Times Books, 1992.

Greene, John Robert. *The Presidency of George Bush.* Lawrence: University of Kansas Press, 1999.

Mervin, David. *George Bush and the Guardianship Presidency.* New York: Palgrave, 1998.

William D. Baker

Bush, George W. (1948–   ) *43rd president of the United States* George W. Bush was named the 43rd president of the United States following a 2000 Supreme Court decision that effectively halted a recount of disputed ballots in Florida, thereby ending one of the closest and most divisive presidential elections in U.S. history. However, despite the election controversy and the fact that his opponent, Vice President Albert Gore, received a plurality of the popular vote, questions as to Bush's presidential legitimacy were muted after a coordinated series of terrorist attacks on 11 September 2001 stunned the nation and sent the new president's popularity soaring.

Bush, the eldest son of President GEORGE HERBERT WALKER BUSH, was born in New Haven, Connecticut, in 1946 and grew up in Midland and Houston, Texas. After graduating from the exclusive Phillips Academy in Andover, Massachusetts, Bush attended Yale University, where he graduated in 1968; Bush would later earn an M.B.A. at Harvard as well, the first president to hold such a degree. Returning to Texas, Bush served in the Texas Air National Guard, lost a 1978 bid for the U.S. House of Representatives, and pursued a career in the oil and natural gas business during the 1970s and 1980s. Bush left the oil business in 1987 to assist in his father's successful presidential campaign, and in 1989 he put together a group of investors that purchased the Texas Rangers major league baseball team, which he served for five years as the team's managing general partner. In 1994, Bush reentered politics to win the Texas GOP's gubernatorial nomination and went on to defeat the incumbent, Ann Richards, in the fall general election. He was reelected in 1998.

In 1999, Bush announced his candidacy for the Republican presidential nomination, campaigning on a platform calling for Social Security privatization, education reform, major tax cuts, and an end to the political and personal scandals of the Clinton administration. Bush won his party's nomination, raising and spending more money than had any presidential candidate in American history, but lost the popular vote while narrowly winning the electoral college vote in the general election.

Faced with a faltering economy during his first year in office, Bush oversaw congressional passage of a $1.3 billion tax cut, proposed allowing religious groups to receive federal funds to perform social services, crafted an ambitious education reform package with Senate Democrats, and issued an executive order limiting federal spending on stem cell research. He drew criticism for his decision to unilaterally withdraw the United States from the 1972 Antiballistic Missile Treaty, declining budget surpluses, and proposals to open Alaska's Arctic National Wildlife Refuge to oil exploration. However, the September 11, 2001, terrorist attacks on the Pentagon and New York City's World Trade Center forced the Bush administration to shift its focus from domestic and economic policy and to adopt a global campaign against terrorism and a military invasion of Afghanistan.

For more information
Bruni, Frank. *Ambling into History: The Unlikely Odyssey of George W. Bush.* New York: HarperCollins, 2002.
Minutaglio, Bill. *First Son: George W. Bush and the Bush Family Dynasty.* New York: Times Books, 1999.
Mitchell, Elizabeth. *W: Revenge of the Bush Dynasty.* New York: Hyperion, 2000.

William D. Baker

business-to-business electronic commerce (B2B)

B2B commerce refers to business transactions that occur over the World Wide Web or Internet. It is estimated that B2B e-commerce is the real growth area on the Internet. B2B covers a wide range of activities, including electronic data interchange (EDI) with centralized electronic hubs or exchanges, electronic communications, electronic payment provisions, e-procurement, and more. Governments have been major purchasers of B2B services.

B2B brings with it many potential benefits, including less need for warehousing, reduced documentation requirements, more transparent pricing, greater stock control, better interaction, opportunity to identify new trading partners, and improved logistics. Some of the obstacles to greater gains for B2B include:

worries about security
lack of training, project management, and change management
concern that many businesses and governments have made a false start and fallen for the B2B hype
cultural obstacles—people do not want to switch over to a B2B arrangement or embrace collaborative networks

We all have a tendency to think our rules and procedures are the best. Yet B2B demands interdependence, maximum availability, and integration. A B2B system, especially when a government agency is involved, has to be totally secure. Accordingly, significant time must be spent safeguarding the network and infrastructure. The B2B network has to be monitored regularly so that there are no failures.

Other concerns with B2B commerce are that:

failure can occur at the hard drive, software, or network. Data need to be replicated across multiple functions to ensure that analysis, ordering, tracking, invoicing, etc., can continue even after a disaster. Data should also be replicated on the periphery of the network near to where partners or customers are trying to contact the network. Data need to be stored for seven years.

B2B systems require large storage capacity, and the amount is required is increasing dramatically. Data storage requirements are growing at an average of 70 percent a year. The data needs are growing so rapidly that many organizations are looking at outsourcing data storage. But to hand over such sensitive information to a third party is not easily achieved and, in the case of government, may not be authorized.

B2B commerce requires broad bandwidth.

There are also many legal issues that may arise. These range from clear contract provisions, concerns about intellectual property (licensing and technology) ownership, and worries about competition laws. What about the rules of corporate governance in relation to the B2B arrangement? There is also the risk of exposure to the laws of other jurisdictions. Supply-chain structures can be inherently complex, and when they extend across numerous national boundaries, the activity may subject all those in the arrangement to the jurisdictions involved.

For more information

Kalakota, Ravi, and Marcia Robinson. *e-Business: Roadmap for Success*. Reading, Mass.: Addison Wesley, 1999.

Treleaven, Philip, and Charles Birch. *e-Business Start-up*. Elsternwick, Victoria: Wrightbooks, 2001.

Eugene Clark

C

cabinet departments Cabinet departments are part of the executive branch that help enforce the laws and carry out the policies of the federal government. Because the president is the head of the executive branch, he is responsible for administering the laws approved by the legislative branch. Cabinet departments help the president fulfill these responsibilities and provide information for him or her.

With the exception of the attorney general, the head of each of the departments is called a secretary, and they consult the president. They are appointed by the president and confirmed by the Senate. Article 2, sec. 2 of the Constitution briefly mentions the cabinet when it states, "he may require the Opinion, in writing, of the principal officer in each of the executive Departments, upon any subject relating to the Duties of their respective Offices." It does not elaborate or give a definition of what these departments are, how many there should be, or their power and responsibilities.

Yet, early Americans based their understanding of the cabinet on the Privy Council in England, an institution that advised the prime minister. George Washington assembled the first cabinet in 1793 to discuss U.S. neutrality in the French Revolutionary War. James Madison coined the term "president's cabinet" to describe these meetings. The first three executive departments consisted of the War Department, the Treasury Department, and the State Department under the respective leadership of Henry Knox, Alexander Hamilton, and Thomas Jefferson. Each of these cabinet departments would change and expand their duties over time. The attorney general was also part of the early cabinet, but his role was that of an assistant to the president. The State Department performed the tasks currently associated with the Justice Department. It would not be until 1870 that the attorney general would have his own department to provide legal advice for the president and officials of other cabinet departments, represent the federal government in court, and enforce the laws of the nation.

The State Department has bureaus that deal with political affairs. In time, its mission has become more focused on international relations and other aspects of administration and policy. The DEPARTMENT OF THE TREASURY acts as the financial institution of the federal government. Its responsibility is to collect taxes, manufacture and maintain currency, enforce criminal laws regarding finances, account for public money, and supervise the banking system. In 1947, the Department of War combined with the Department of the Navy, added to the cabinet in 1798, to become the DEPARTMENT OF DEFENSE, which held the responsibility of national defense and security. The secretary of war and secretary of the navy ceased to be cabinet officers in 1949.

The position of postmaster general was upgraded to cabinet status in 1829, but it was not until June 8, 1872, that the Post Office Department was made an executive department by order of Congress. The next cabinet department created was the DEPARTMENT OF THE INTERIOR under Zachary Taylor in 1849. Its duties came to be management of public lands, promotion of conservation, development and use of natural and wildlife resources, reclamation of arid lands, administration of national parks, and, after the Grant administration, responsibility for Native American reservations.

In 1889, the DEPARTMENT OF AGRICULTURE was created to help the nation's farmers with scientific research and information. In time it would expand its responsibilities to include consumer issues, environmental issues, and betterment of rural life.

In 1903, Theodore Roosevelt established the Department of Commerce and Labor. This department divided to become the DEPARTMENT OF LABOR and the DEPARTMENT OF COMMERCE under Woodrow Wilson. The Commerce Department promotes programs that encourage business and maintain the economic well-being of the nation. The Labor Department was given the task to "foster, promote, and develop the welfare of the wage earners of the United States, to improve the working conditions, and to advance their opportunities for profitable employment."

Since the Eisenhower administration, six cabinet positions have been added. In 1952, the Department of Health, Education and Welfare, which in 1979 became the DEPARTMENT OF HEALTH AND HUMAN SERVICES, was commissioned with performing administrative, educational, and regulatory functions for welfare, public assistance, and health programs for the American people.

Under Lyndon Johnson in 1965, the DEPARTMENT OF HOUSING AND URBAN DEVELOPMENT was established as part of his Great Society program. Its function was to help improve and develop urban and Indian housing and to offer public assistance where needed. The next year Johnson also commissioned the DEPARTMENT OF TRANSPORTATION to develop an overall transportation policy for the nation. President Jimmy Carter added the DEPARTMENT OF ENERGY in 1977 and the DEPARTMENT OF EDUCATION in 1979. Formed in the midst of the 1978–79 energy crisis, the Department of Energy combined all of the federal energy agencies to better facilitate research and develop a national energy policy. The Department of Education was assigned to administer and coordinate federal funding for education and develop special programs to ensure educational access for children. The DEPARTMENT OF VETERAN'S AFFAIRS was formed as an independent agency in 1930 to help veterans and their families, and George H. W. Bush elevated the Department of Veterans Affairs to cabinet status in 1989.

The current cabinet consists of 15 departments, including the recently created Department of Homeland Security. There have been movements both to add and remove certain departments from cabinet status. A study of the evolution of cabinet departments shows how the executive branch has changed its understanding of its mission and responsibilities over time.

For more information

Hart, John. *The Presidential Branch: From Washington to Clinton.* Chatham, N.J.: Chatham House, 1995.
Goehlert, Robert, and Hugh Reynolds. *Executive Branch of the U.S. Government.* Westport, Conn.: Greenwood Press, 1988.

T. Jason Soderstrum

California v. Cabazon Band of Mission Indians 400 U.S. 202 (1987)

California v. Cabazon Band of Mission Indians was a Supreme Court decision that Native American tribes could offer casinos on their reservations unless the state that surrounds the tribal land consistently treats gambling as either a crime or a violation of the state constitution. If such is not the case, then the state cannot forbid tribes from offering gambling on their lands. Because California offered a great variety of types of gambling such as bingo, card rooms, horse-race betting, and a state-owned and state-operated lottery, the Court ruled that the state could not legitimately claim that the Cabazon's gambling operations were illegal. If California, like Utah and Hawaii, for example, had in its state constitution a ban on multiple forms of gambling, then the state could forbid tribes within its boundaries from offering casino gambling.

This decision crossed ideological lines on the Court. Rehnquist and Brennan, who ideologically had little in common, were both on the side of the tribe. Stevens and Scalia, also a pair with contrasting ideologies, voted in favor of the state. In the end, it was a six-to-three ruling.

In the wake of the *California v. Cabazon* ruling, tribes were free to offer virtually any form of gambling as long as the state that surrounded them had not banned all gambling. States immediately began pressuring Congress for legislation that would prevent all tribes from starting massive casinos on their lands. Congress responded in 1988 with the INDIAN GAMING REGULATORY ACT, which provided a statutory basis for what sorts of gambling could be offered by tribes and for what role states could play in this new economic opportunity granted Native Americans by the Supreme Court. This case and the Indian Gaming Regulatory Act together provide the basis of the public policy on the part of the federal government that underlies all of the legal Native American casinos, bingo halls, etc. that operate around the country.

The *California v. Cabazon* decision is important for an additional reason. It marks yet another instance of the federal government attempting to grant economic self-determination to tribes. This policy on the part of the U.S. government did not begin in earnest until the 1970s. Before that, the federal government varied from the overtly ill treatment of tribes to unsympathetic attempts at assimilation.

For more information

Mason, John Lyman, and Michael Nelson. *Governing Gambling.* Washington, D.C.: Brookings Institution Press, 2001.

Mason, W. Dale. *Indian Gaming: Tribal Sovereignty and American Politics.* Norman: University of Oklahoma Press, 2000.

John Lyman Mason

campaign finance Campaign finance refers to the methods by which candidates obtain the monies needed to fund their quest for elective public office. In the United States there are actually multiple campaign finance systems: one that encompasses federal offices (the presidency and the congress) and those that regulate state and local elections. Not only do campaign finance laws differ state-to-state, but some municipalities have rules governing fund-raising and spending in city elections. This entry focuses on the federal level.

The main predicate of campaign finance rules is the concern that money given to candidates for public office can unduly influence their behavior. In other words, it is feared that contributions could result in a public official acting in the particularistic interest of the donor rather than in the public interest writ large. A great deal of money is spent on election campaigns in the United States. For example, the 2000 electoral cycle saw approximately $3.9 billion spent on campaigns at all levels of government, with about $3.3 billion of that focused on federal offices. Campaigns are expensive for a variety of reasons, not the least of which is the importance (and commensurate expense) of television as a marketing tool. Further, according to the Office of Management and Budget, the FY2002 budget of the United States represented 18 percent of the gross domestic product of the country. The federal government's control over such a large percentage of the economy invites attempts to influence its spending—especially in a society as pluralistic as the United States. Further, the degree to which the Congress can affect a particular industry or a specific ideological position on policy also encourages the participation of interest groups via campaign contributions.

The campaign finance system in the United States has been shaped by a combination of legislation and Supreme Court rulings. Early legislation that focused on controlling contributions includes the Tillman Act of 1907, the Corrupt Practices Act of 1925, the Smith-Connally Act of 1944, and the Taft-Hartley Act of 1947. The Tillman Act forbade contributions to candidates by corporations, although this simply resulted in corporations finding indirect means to support candidates. The Corrupt Practices Act was the main campaign finance law until the 1970s. It required disclosure of receipts and expenses by House and Senate campaigns, but due to the ability of multiple committees to support a candidate, it was nearly impossible to actually account for the funds. Both Smith-Connally and Taft-Hartley forbade contributions to candidates by trade unions. These strictures simply led to the formation of separate committees associated with the unions who could then make contributions. In short, none of these were of great consequence to the raising of money for political campaigns. Also of relevance was the Hatch Act of 1939, which forbade the solicitation of funds by federal employees and was later amended to include contribution caps.

The most significant piece of campaign finance legislation passed in the 20th century was the FEDERAL ELECTION CAMPAIGN ACT of 1971 (FECA) as amended in 1974, 1976, and 1979. Of those amendments, the main rules of campaign finance that are still in operation today came into being via the 1974 legislation—including the creation of the Federal Election Commission (FEC). The Bipartisan Campaign Reform Act of 2002 (BCRA, Public Law 107-155, known colloquially as McCain-Feingold in the Senate and Shays-Meehan in the House) alters and augments the current system and is the first major piece of campaign finance legislation to pass since FECA.

The basic rules of campaign finance are as follows. Money comes from two basic sources: the budgets of candidates or the budgets of independent groups (i.e., interest groups or political parties). Further, the spending of independent groups can be coordinated with the candidate or done without directly consulting with the candidate. As a result, a terminology has developed in regard to the classification of funds donated for the financing of campaigns. "Hard money" is money given directly to candidates and is subject to the restrictions on amounts as dictated by the law. Hard money also includes coordinated expenditures (i.e., money spent on behalf of a candidate but with the express knowledge and/or direction of the candidate). "Soft money" refers to donations made to party committees and interest groups in unregulated amounts and that can be spent on *uncoordinated* expenditures. Soft money came to prominence in the campaign finance system in the 1996 electoral cycle and was the main focus for critics of the system. The BCRA was passed primarily to attempt to limit the influence of soft money. Specifically, it banned the contribution of soft money to national political party committees by corporations, unions, and individuals. Further, groups were banned from airing issue ads (i.e., uncoordinated expenditures) that mention a candidate's name within 60 days of the general election or 30 days prior to the primary.

Federal law makes some important distinctions between funding campaigns for congress and for the presidency. Congressional campaign finance is the most straightforward. Candidates are allowed to directly solicit funds from individuals and groups, with specific limitations in place on those contributions. Contributions are made per election (rather than per annum), which means that a contributor can give both for the primary and for the general election, should their candidate of choice win the primary. Under the original FECA provisions, individuals could donate $1,000 to a candidate, and this amount was raised to $2,000 in 2002 by the BCRA. Groups that wish to contribute must form a political action committee (PAC) for the purposes of fund-raising and dispersal. PACs can give up to $5,000 per candidate per election. Independent groups can also raise soft money and spend it in an uncoordinated way to aid the candidates of their own choosing (which is also true for presidential campaigns), although with the above-mentioned restrictions on campaign ads prior to the election.

The system for fund-raising for a presidential campaign is much more complicated. For primary contests there is partial public financing, and for the general election campaign there is total public financing. During primary election season (essentially January to June), candidates can receive partial public financing if they demonstrate adequate support and agree to spending limits. Adequate support is defined as raising $100,000 in individual contributions of $250 or less, with at least $5,000 coming from 20 different states. At that point, candidates receive matching funds from the federal government for every dollar in individual contributions up to $250. Candidates can receive up to $2,000 from individuals, but every dollar above $250 is not matched. Candidates must abide by a spending cap if they are to receive matching funds. In 2000 the cap was $33.8 million for campaigning and an additional $11.8 million for fund-raising and administrative compliance. Candidates who choose not to receive matching funds, such as George W. Bush in 2000, do not have to adhere to the caps. Bush raised $94.5 million for the 2000 primaries, spending $89.1 million.

The rules change yet again for the general election campaign, as candidates shift from partial to full public financing of their campaigns. Major-party candidates in the 2000 election were awarded $67.6 million for the general election campaign (essentially September, October, and the very beginning of November). Any third-party candidate whose party won 5 percent or more of votes in the prior election was awarded a prorated portion of the full grant, which could be augmented by fund-raising within hard-money guidelines. Candidates may, however, engage in fund-raising to cover administrative costs. It is also noteworthy that political parties and interest groups can spend soft money in support of their candidates, although the BCRA restrictions will ban the use of commercials that mention a candidate by name 60 days before the election starting after the 2002 cycle.

In addition to legislation, the federal campaign finance system has been substantially shaped by the Supreme Court of the United States. There are several key cases that merit attention. The first is *Buckley v. Valeo*, 424 U.S. 1 (1976), which was issued in response to challenges made to the 1974 amendments to FECA. The Court issued several key rulings in *Buckley*, where they upheld the ability of the Congress to limit contributions made to candidates but struck down both mandatory spending limits and limits on spending by independent groups. This latter ruling, which linked money spent on political communication with the free-speech provisions of the First Amendment, was key in the development of soft money and is the most significant obstacle to elements of the BCRA. The issue of soft money was especially bolstered vis-à-vis political parties with the ruling in *Colorado Republican Federal Campaign Committee, et al. v. Federal Election Commission*, 518 U.S. 604 (1996), which allowed political party committees to receive unlimited contributions for "party building," which quickly evolved into uncoordinated spending by the parties in support of their candidates for public office. The Court reiterated a key ruling from *Buckley*,—that contribution limits on monies donated to candidates directly are constitutional—in *Nixon, Attorney General of Missouri, et al. v. Shrink Missouri Government PAC, et al.*, 528 U.S. 1033 (2000). The controversial elements within the BCRA will ensure the continued role of the Court in this area of public policy. A lawsuit in opposition to the new provisions was filed by Senator Mitch McConnell (R-Ky.) immediately after the bill was signed. Interest groups such as the National Rifle Association and the American Civil Liberties Union have either filed complaints or have signaled their intention to do so.

Scandal has normally played a significant role in the passage of campaign finance reform legislation. The Corrupt Practices Act of 1925 was passed in response to the Teapot Dome scandal; the 1974 amendments to FECA were a direct response to WATERGATE; and the BCRA of 2002 would probably not have passed were it not for concerns over the linkage of politicians of both parties to the collapse of the Enron Corporation in early 2002. Also, several specific provisions within the BCRA were aimed at perceived failings within the Clinton administration, including section 302, which prohibited fund-raising on federal property, and section 303, which strengthened existing law banning contributions made by foreign nationals.

For more information

Goidel, Robert K., Donald A. Gross, and Todd G. Shields. *Money Matters: Consequences of Campaign Finance Reform in U.S. House Elections.* Lanham, Md.: Rowman and Littlefield, 1999.

Magleby, David B., ed. *Financing the 2000 Elections.* Washington, D.C.: Brookings Institution Press, 2002.

Maisel, L. Sandy. *Parties and Elections in America: The Electoral Process,* 3d ed. Lanham, Md.: Rowman and Littlefield, 1999.

Sorauf, Frank J. "Politics, Experience, and the First Amendment: The Case of American Campaign Finance." *Columbia Law Review* 94 (1994): 1,348–1,368.

Steven L. Taylor

Carter, Jimmy (1924–　) *39th president of the United States*　James "Jimmy" Earl Carter was born 1 October 1924, in Plains, Georgia. He attended the Naval Academy, graduating in 1946. That year he also married Rosalynn Smith. They eventually had three sons and a daughter.

After graduation from the Naval Academy, Carter served in the nuclear submarine program under Admiral Hyman G. Rickover. Shortly after his father died in 1954, he resigned his commission to return to Plains to operate the family cotton gin and peanut farm.

In 1962 Carter was elected to the Georgia senate. In 1966 he lost the race for governor; however, he was elected in 1970. During his term as governor he instituted many reforms, including reducing the budgets of agencies, increasing their economy and efficiency, and introducing new social programs. He used ZERO-BASED BUDGETING (ZBB) to institute efficiency.

In 1972 Carter began preparing to run for president. In 1974, his travels around the country as Democratic Campaign Committee chairman enabled him to build a political base. In 1975 he won the support of the civil rights coalition. He won 19 out of 31 of the 1976 primaries. His campaign successfully appealed to conservatives and liberals, black and white, poor and wealthy. In the general election of 1976 he defeated incumbent Gerald Ford.

Carter also initiated the CIVIL SERVICE REFORM ACT OF 1978, which has had a lasting impact upon the organization and supervision of federal government employees. He instituted ZBB in federal agencies as he had done in Georgia. He also persuaded Congress (1979) to create a separate Department of Education.

In foreign affairs, he helped negotiate peace between Egypt and Israel at the Camp David accords and took part in the Panama Canal

Treaty and a treaty with China. Carter also worked for arms control and for international protection of human rights, but he was unable to resolve the Iranian hostage crisis.

He was not able to make any Supreme Court nominations, but he did manage to make 265 appointments to federal district and appellate court seats. Many of these appointees were minorities and women.

In 1980 Carter lost to Ronald Reagan in a major electoral college defeat. Carter then returned to Plains to revitalize the family business. He also established the Carter Presidential Center. It includes the Carter Center at Emory University in Atlanta, Georgia, as a center for the discussion of national and international issues. It also contains the Jimmy Carter Library.

In his post-presidential years he worked as a volunteer carpenter for Habitat for Humanity and wrote many books. These include a book of poetry, the story of his senate campaign, a memoir of his presidency, and many others. Carter also helped monitor elections in a number of countries, including Nicaragua, Panama, Haiti, Guyana, and Paraguay. He also traveled to North Korea to help reduce tensions over its suspected nuclear weapons program. In 1994 he traveled to Haiti, where he successfully persuaded the military leaders to restore democracy.

He was the winner of many prizes for his contributions to human development and world peace. In 2002 he won the Nobel Peace Prize for his work at the Carter Center on behalf of peace and human rights.

For more information

Bourne, Peter G. *Jimmy Carter: A Comprehensive Biography from Plains to Post-Presidency.* New York: Simon & Schuster, 1997.

A. J. L. Waskey

case study   A case study is a research design in which the researcher analyzes one or a small number of subjects over an extended period of time. Like other types of social science research, case studies always involve some phenomenon of interest (for example, water use, business location decisions, dropping out of school). Researchers either describe the phenomenon or explain why it exists or occurs. Unlike other social science researchers, case study researchers also investigate the phenomenon's context: the complex set of relationships surrounding it.

Case study research involves four steps. First is *identifying the research question*. Case studies are well-suited for "how" and "why" types of research questions:

- How do barges in the Mississippi River affect the blue catfish?
- Why do some firms locate in Boston's suburbs and others locate downtown?
- Why do teenagers drop out of Thomas Jefferson High School?

All of these questions can be investigated using a case study.

The second step is *choosing the subject or subjects*. Using the dropping-out example, the researcher must decide if he will focus on one student who dropped out, or several. How will the student(s) be selected? Does the researcher want a student who is representative of all the school's dropouts, or the one who has had the most problems?

The third step is identifying what information will be needed to help answer the question. This is the *data collection* stage. Typically, case studies involve collecting background information on the subject(s) and important people or places in the subject's life (for example, his neighborhood [is it urban, suburban, or rural?] and his school [is it big or small?]). Case studies also involve conducting interviews, obtaining important documents and records, and on-site observations. The fourth step is *data analysis*. This is where the researcher assembles the data into some framework so that it "tells the story" about the phenomenon. Finally, the researcher writes the case study. This case study report includes sections on each of the four steps and may include additional information.

One strength of the case study approach is that the researcher understands the context of the phenomenon. Learning about the context is possible because the researcher focuses on a small number of subjects and does so over an extended period of time. Knowing the context enables researchers to explore the complexity inherent in many social research questions.

Because case study researchers learn much about the context, they are well-suited to develop hypotheses about the phenomenon. This is the second strength of the case study design. The researcher can identify what factors are most important in describing or explaining the phenomenon. The researcher studying dropping out of high school might identify a student's perception of poor job prospects as a major reason that the student quit school. The researcher might then hypothesize that students who do not have good job prospects are more likely to drop out than students whose prospects are better.

Case study research faces two limitations when compared with other types of social science research: it is neither generalizable nor objective. One problem with case study research is that the researcher cannot make general statements about the phenomenon. The researcher can only speak about his experience with the one or few subjects he observed. This lack of generalizability puts the researcher at a severe disadvantage over those who conduct research on populations or probability samples from populations. Those researchers are able to make claims about phenomena regarding large groups of people.

A second problem with case study research is that it is subjective, that is, heavily dependent upon the perceptions and judgments of the researcher. Because the researcher is intensely involved in studying one or a few subjects for an extended period of time, it is very difficult to remain detached from the situation. This makes it a highly personal exercise, one that is very difficult for other researchers to replicate exactly.

For more information

Stake, Robert E. "Case Studies." In *Handbook of Qualitative Research,* 2d ed., edited by Norman K. Denzin and Yvonna S. Lincoln, 435–454. Thousand Oaks, Calif.: Sage Publications, 2000.

Yin, Robert K. *Case Study Research: Design and Methods,* 2d ed. Thousand Oaks, Calif.: Sage Publications, 1994.

Jason Palmer

categorical grants   Categorical grants are a form of GRANTS-IN-AID and a means by which the federal government transfers federal aid (i.e., money) to state and local governments (i.e., intergovernmental transfers). Grants-in-aid replaced the land grants commonly given by the federal government in the 19th century. Grants-in-aid are generally either categorical grants (which target a specific project) or BLOCK GRANTS (which consolidate or bundle categorical grants and target a broad program area).

Unlike recipients of block grants, recipients of categorical grants have little leeway in their use of the funds. For instance, a city that receives a categorical grant to renovate an urban park cannot use the money for any other purpose. The U.S. DEPARTMENT OF HOUSING AND URBAN DEVELOPMENT, for instance, offers several categorical grants, including designated-housing-choice vouchers (to assist nonelderly families with disabilities to rent affordable private housing), mainstream vouchers (to enable both elderly and nonelderly persons with disabilities to rent affordable private housing), and housing-choice vouchers (to help low-income families find private housing.)

Categorical grants, which generally have detailed matching requirements, are either project grants or formula grants. Project grants are designed to be used on certain issues or problems targeted by Congress. Subnational governments must submit detailed proposals to apply for project grants and compete for funds; not all applicant governments will receive grants. The U.S.

DEPARTMENT OF ENERGY offers energy-project grants designed to enable communities to explore and implement alternative fuels and energy-efficient technologies. Subnational governments receive formula grants based on a formula that may include, for instance, population, tax base, per capita income, and the number of people in a targeted group (e.g., disabled citizens, children in poverty, etc.). States and communities who seek formula grant funds do not compete with each other, nor do they have to submit grant applications; the amount they receive is formula based. The U.S. DEPARTMENT OF JUSTICE's S*T*O*P (Services, Training, Officers and Prosecutors) Violence Against Women formula grants are not only designed to enable states to develop and/or strengthen their criminal justice systems' response to and handling of violence against women, but recipients are required to use a specific percentage of the funds for various and specific preventive endeavors.

For more information

Hale, George E., and Marian Lief Palley. *The Politics of Federal Grants*. Washington, D.C.: Congressional Quarterly Press, 1981.

Linda K. Shafer

Central Intelligence Agency The Central Intelligence Agency (CIA) is the leading agency in the U.S. intelligence community. On 26 July 1947, President Harry S. Truman signed the National Security Act establishing America's first peacetime intelligence agency. Amendments added in 1949 strengthened the act.

The CIA's mission is to provide intelligence to the president, the NATIONAL SECURITY COUNCIL (NSC), and others responsible for handling national security. It also conducts counterintelligence and performs such other duties as the NSC may direct. The CIA's charter assigns it the task of foreign intelligence and gives domestic intelligence to the FEDERAL BUREAU OF INVESTIGATION (FBI). This division of labor overlaps at times.

The director of central intelligence (DCI) heads the CIA, which is organized into four "teams" (directorates). The DCI, appointed by the president with approval by the Senate, coordinates the intelligence community and manages the CIA with support from two deputy directors.

The Directorate of Science and Technology (DST) is a mission team that gathers information from radio, TV, print media, electronic signals, and satellite data. Most of this information is from publicly available open sources.

The mission of the Directorate of Operations (DO) is to gather information from many sources, but often it is from secret, covert, and illegal sources. Agents recruited by CIA officers in countries around the world provide most of this information. The CIA has at least one CIA officer in every country in the world. The DO is the "agency" that sends out spies on "spook" operations.

The mission of the Directorate of Intelligence (DI) is to develop intelligence briefings, reports, bulletins, and estimates for various consumers from the raw information provided by the two other directorates. The DI produces accurate, timely, and objective intelligence in response to national security questions about the capabilities and intentions of all real and potential foreign enemies.

The final team is the Mission Support Offices. It consists of five diverse offices that are responsible for security, recruiting, supplying spy tools and training, ensuring health, and overseeing the "company's" communications systems.

The budget of the CIA is hidden in various appropriations in the federal budget. A challenge to CIA budget secrecy failed in *United States v. Richardson*, 418 U.S. 166 (1974). However, the CIA, responding to a Freedom of Information suit, reported in 1997 that it had spent $26.6 billion in 1996, but that for reasons of national security that it would not reveal such information again. It is estimated that the CIA has over 20,000 employees.

Congressional oversight is provided through the House Permanent Select Committee on Intelligence (HPSCI) and the Senate Select Committee on Intelligence (SSCI). In addition, the CIA works with the Foreign Relations, Foreign Affairs, Armed Services, and Appropriations Committees, all responsible for authorizing the programs of the CIA.

For more information

Kessler, Ronald. *Inside The CIA.* New York: Pocket Books, 1992.

Richelson, Jeffrey. *The Wizards of Langley: Inside the CIA's Directorate of Science and Technology.* Boulder, Colo.: Westview Press, 2001.

A. J. L. Waskey

charter school   A charter school is a school that has received a charter (a legal right to exist) from a state or local agency. The charter provides public funding to the school for a set period of time and waives many of the regulations that apply to other public schools.

Charter schools are often founded because the school administrator believes that an alternative approach to education will be more effective than current educational practices. However, many government regulations prevent experimentation in schools. In order to avoid possible legal problems associated with new educational practices, a state agency exempts the charter school from many of the state educational laws.

Charter schools are a form of school choice. In fact, anyone is eligible to found a charter school. They must simply follow the state's guidelines. Because charter schools are publicly funded, any student can attend. However, the decision to attend a charter school is entirely voluntary. School districts do not appoint students or teachers to charter schools.

Charter schools are also held accountable for their results. Typically, charter schools use state achievement tests to monitor student progress. If

Students walk by the Mariana Bracetti Charter School in Philadelphia, Pennsylvania.   (WILLIAM THOMAS CAIN)

charter schools do not produce satisfactory results, they often lose funding or their charter.

The rationale for charter schools is the belief that experimentation, ingenuity, and accountability will foster better schools. Advocates of charter schools argue that public schools are prevented from experimenting due to overburdensome regulations, thus ingenuity is often stifled. In addition, advocates also argue that public schools receive funding regardless of whether or not they produce positive results. A charter school must show results or it will cease to exist.

Minnesota enacted the first charter school law in 1991. Since then, 34 other states have passed charter school legislation. Although the number of charter schools is always fluctuating, it currently hovers around 1,700.

Critics of charter schools argue that charter schools decrease funds for public schools; segregate students by disability, class, and race; are rarely held accountable; and are risky. It is true that public school funds are used to pay for charter schools. However, advocates note that the number of students in public schools also decreases when a charter school opens.

"The State of Charter Schools," a recent study by the DEPARTMENT OF EDUCATION, clearly rejects the notion that charter schools discriminate against students of color, or by income or disability. In fact, the data show that students of color are overrepresented in charter schools.

Given that charter schools are such a new phenomenon, there is concern over whether these schools will be held accountable for their educational innovations. Most states have not established clear and effective accountability processes.

For more information

Finn, Chester, Bruno Manno, and Gregg Vanourek. *Charter Schools in Action: Renewing Public Education.* Princeton, N.J.: Princeton University Press, 2000.

Good, Thomas, and Jennifer Braden. *The Great School Debate: Choice, Vouchers and Charters.* London: Lawrence Erlbaum Associates, 2000.

Mathew Manweller

Chevron U.S.A., Inc. v. Natural Resources Defense Council 467 U.S. 837 (1984)

In *Chevron U.S.A., Inc. v. Natural Resources Defense Council,* the U.S. Supreme Court announced a two-part doctrine directing the federal courts to uphold federal agencies' interpretations of federal statutes so long as (1) congressional intent is ambiguous and (2) the agency's interpretation is reasonable. Scholars of law, public administration, and political science consider *Chevron* to be a landmark case in administrative law. The Chevron doctrine has redefined the role of the federal courts in matters of agency decision making, and, by increasing the amount of deference granted to administrative agencies, it indicates a fundamental shift in the balance of power among the three branches of government.

The facts of the case are straightforward. The statutory language in question is contained in the Clean Air Amendments of 1977, which directed states not meeting air quality standards to create permit programs regulating new or modified stationary sources of air pollution. By the late 1970s, the ENVIRONMENTAL PROTECTION AGENCY (EPA) had developed a twofold definition of "stationary source." A source was either (1) an entire plant or factory (the plantwide definition) or (2) each component of the plant or factory, such as a smokestack or furnace (individual component definition). In the early 1980s, the EPA declared that states were to adopt the "plantwide definition" of a stationary source. The Natural Resources Defense Council (NRDC) challenged the EPA's interpretation in the federal courts, arguing that the EPA had contradicted the congressional intent of the Clean Air Amendments. A federal court of appeals agreed with the NRDC and struck down the EPA's declaration. The case was appealed to the Supreme Court.

The Supreme Court reversed the ruling of the Court of Appeals and upheld the EPA's definition of stationary source. More important, they devised a two-part test, now known as the Chevron doctrine, governing how the federal courts should process legal challenges to agency interpretations of statutory language. First, the courts must determine whether or not Congress has spoken directly to the statutory interpretation in question. If congressional intent is clear beyond question, then the agency should implement the statute as written. However, and this is part two of the test, if congressional intent is unclear or if the statutory language is ambiguous or missing, then the federal courts are to uphold an agency's interpretation *so long as it is reasonable or permissible.* In the *Chevron* case, the Court first concluded that the language of the Clean Air Amendments was ambiguous. Second, the Court ruled that the EPA's interpretation of the statute was reasonable, and therefore, it was upheld.

The precise impact of *Chevron* has been intensely debated in law, public administration, and political science circles. *Chevron's* implications concerning the separation of powers are compelling. For example, assume Congress passes, and the president signs, a bill giving the federal government responsibility for providing additional low-income housing assistance to all metropolitan communities in the United States. The law authorizes the DEPARTMENT OF HOUSING AND URBAN DEVELOPMENT (HUD) to implement the objectives. Assume Congress neglected to specify the meaning of "low income" in the statute. Having been granted statutory authority, HUD defines "low income" to mean at or below the national poverty level. If this definition is challenged, the federal courts will uphold HUD's definition (assuming it is reasonable, which it seems to be), since the statutory language is unclear. In the post-*Chevron* era, Congress would have to state explicitly the meaning of "low income" in the statute or risk agencies' interpreting the meaning with a considerable level of discretion. Thus, in matters of statutory construction and interpretation, Congress, the courts, and federal agencies face different incentives and strategies in the light of the *Chevron doctrine*. This implication makes *Chevron* a significant research topic for scholars of administrative law.

For more information

Merrill, Thomas W. "Judicial Deference to Executive Precedent." *Yale Law Journal* 101 (1992): 969–1,041.

Merrill, Thomas W., and Kristin E. Hickman. "Chevron's Domain." *Georgetown Law Journal* 89 (2001): 833–921.

Schuck, Peter H., and Donald Elliott. "To the Chevron Station: An Empirical Study of Federal Administrative Law." *Duke Law Journal* 5 (1990): 984–1,077.

Sunstein, Cass R. "Law and Administration after *Chevron.*" *Columbia Law Review* 90 (1990): 2,071–2,120.

Brandon Bartels

Cigarette Labeling and Advertising Act   The Cigarette Labeling and Advertising Act requires a conspicuous "surgeon general's warning" to be placed on all cigarette packages and advertising.

Amendments to this law in 1971 and 1973 banned the advertisement of cigarettes and little cigars from television and radio airwaves. On 11 January 1964, U.S. Surgeon General Luther L. Terry released the 387-page report of the Surgeon General's Advisory Committee on Smoking and Health. In it, the committee concluded that cigarette smoke is a cause of laryngeal cancer, lung cancer, and bronchitis. Based on over 7,000 studies, it was the first governmental document to state that "cigarette smoking is a health hazard of sufficient importance in the United States to warrant appropriate remedial action."

What this "appropriate remedial action" would be was left to Congress to decide. After a great deal of lobbying by consumer groups and tobacco companies, the legislative branch attempted to "establish a comprehensive Federal Program to deal with cigarette labeling and advertising with respect to any relationship between smoking and health." Enacted in 1965, the Cigarette Labeling and Advertising Act required that a "surgeon general's warning" appear on all cigarette packages. In 1984, the law was amended requiring one of the following labels to appear:

- Surgeon General's Warning: Smoking Causes Lung Cancer, Heart Disease, Emphysema, and May Complicate Pregnancy.
- Surgeon General's Warning: Quitting Smoking Now Greatly Reduces Serious Risks to Your Health.
- Surgeon General's Warning: Smoking By Pregnant Women May Result in Fetal Injury, Premature Birth, and Low Birth Weight.

• Surgeon General's Warning: Cigarette Smoking Contains Carbon Monoxide

Tobacco companies are allowed to somewhat abbreviate this warning on outdoor billboards. They also do not have to put this warning on promotional materials such as clothing, hats, or memorabilia with the company logo or brand name on it. Finally, cigars, pipe tobacco, and roll-your-own cigarette tobacco escaped this legislation and are not required to have such warnings. Warnings on chew, snuff, and smokeless tobacco were authorized in 1986 under the Comprehensive Smokeless Tobacco Health Education Act.

Tobacco companies and importers are required to submit packages and advertisements to the FEDERAL TRADE COMMISSION (FTC) for approval. The warning is to appear in a conspicuous location in the advertisement or package and be clearly legible to the consumer. The company must also assure the FTC that these warning statements will be distributed wherever the product is sold in the United States. Under the law, the FTC is required to report to the Congress annually on advertising practices and promotions by the tobacco industry.

The Office of Consumer Litigation (OCL) of the Justice Department is in charge of enforcement and investigation of the law when it comes to television and radio broadcasts. It also provides consultation and nonbinding advice to promoters and institutions in regard to the law. The OCL is to forward the results of its investigations to the proper Justice Department office. Any company found in violation of the law faces a severe financial penalty. The OCL and tobacco companies have frequently challenged each other on how broadly to interpret the law. For example, in 1995, the OCL obtained a court decree forcing Marlboro to remove its sign next to the scorers' table in Madison Square Garden because of its prominence on television broadcasts. While some critics believe that the Cigarette Labeling and Advertising Act did not go far enough, many of its supporters believe it has been a major success for public health, pointing to the fact that smokers have fallen from 52 percent of the population in 1965 to just 28 percent 30 years later.

For more information

Arno, P. S., et al. "Tobacco Industry Strategies to Oppose Federal Regulation." *Journal of the American Medical Association* 275, no. 16 (April 24, 1996): 1,258–1,262.

Gostin, L. O., P. S. Arno, and A. M. Brandt. "FDA Regulation of Tobacco Advertising and Youth Smoking: Historical, Social and Constitutional Perspectives." *The Journal of the American Medical Association* 277, no. 5 (February 5, 1997): 410–418.

Redman, Eric, and Richard E. Neustadt. *The Dance of Legislation.* Seattle: University of Washington Press, 2001.

T. Jason Soderstrum

Citizens to Preserve Overton Park, Inc. v. Volpe 401 U.S. 402 (1971)

In *Citizens to Preserve Overton Park, Inc. v. Volpe,* the U.S. Supreme Court announced what is now known as the HARD LOOK doctrine, which instructs federal courts to examine and scrutinize thoroughly disputed agency actions when determining whether a federal agency has acted in accordance with the language or intent of a federal statute. Because of the standard of review announced by the Supreme Court, *Overton Park* is often considered a cornerstone case in administrative law. It is perhaps the most widely cited court case, by both administrative law scholars and federal judges, regarding how the federal courts are to process legal challenges to federal agency actions.

The facts of the case center on the secretary of transportation's approval (in 1968) for building an expressway that would intersect Overton Park, a 342-acre park in Memphis, Tennessee. At issue was whether the secretary's actions were in accordance with section 4(f) of the Department of Transportation Act of 1966. Section 4(f) emphasizes that when transportation projects are being considered, special efforts must be made not to interfere with public parks or recreation areas. Projects are allowed to go forward if (1) there is no other viable alternative to using the public park space, or (2) the project minimizes potential damage to the park space. "Citizens to Preserve Overton Park," a small group of Memphis citizens, challenged the secretary's actions in federal court. A federal district court rejected the citizens' claim, and the Sixth Circuit Court of Appeals affirmed that decision. The Supreme Court reversed the court of appeals' holding and ruled that the secretary failed to abide by section 4(f). The DOT, according to the Court, should not grant funding to projects interfering with public park space unless alternatives, designed to avoid public park interference, pose unique problems.

In the opinion, the Supreme Court presented a doctrinal statement providing instruction as to how the federal courts should decide cases involving disputed agency actions. According to the hard-look doctrine, the courts are to determine whether the agency acted with *clear error in judgment*. They must scrutinize the actions of the agency against the language and principles of the federal statute. However, the courts are not to substitute their own judgment for the agency's judgment. Concerning the *Overton Park* question, the Court ruled that the secretary of transportation's actions violated the principles of section 4(f).

By directing courts to examine thoroughly the actions of an agency to determine whether that action is arbitrary and capricious, the hard-look doctrine is a strict standard of review and offers little deference to administrative agencies. Consider the following hypothetical example. Congress passes, and the president signs, a "farmers assistance bill" authorizing the Department of Agriculture to subsidize farmers in Midwestern states plagued by severe droughts. The law implies that the government is to grant federal aid to "significantly affected" farmers such that the aid makes up for a farmer's financial losses due to the droughts.

To determine who is eligible, the secretary of agriculture declares that "significantly affected farmers" are those who lost over half of their usual incomes as a result of the droughts. Under the hard-look standard, the federal courts would have to determine whether the secretary's declaration was in accordance with the general objectives of the statute and whether or not the decision represented a clear error in judgment. If a federal court concluded that the statute's aim was to provide federal aid to farmers regardless of how much income they lost due to the drought, they would strike down the secretary's declaration of eligibility. Under the hard-look standard, then, the courts are not to grant federal agencies unbridled discretion. They must carefully determine whether the agency made clear errors in judgment or violated the general principles of a federal statute.

For more information

Shapiro, Martin. "Administrative Discretion: The Next Stage." *Yale Law Journal* 92 (1983): 1,487–1,522.

Singer, Matthew. "The Demise of Section 4(f) Since *Overton Park* and Its Implications for Alternative Analysis in Environmental Law." *Environmental Law* 28 (1998): 729–753.

Strauss, Peter L. "Revisiting *Overton Park*: Political and Judicial Controls over Administrative Actions Affecting the Community." *UCLA Law Review* 39 (1992): 1,251–1,329.

Brandon Bartels

city managers   City managers are nonelected municipal officials appointed by the city council. The city manager has the responsibility of running the city and is given the necessary administrative authority. The city's various department heads report to the city manager, who has supervisory authority over them. Policy making, legislating, and governmental decisions are retained by the city council. This form of municipal governance is called the city-council plan.

City-council municipalities are most common in mid-sized cities (25,000–250,000 residents). Smaller cities generally do not have the budget to retain a professional city manager, and larger cities simply are too diverse to be effectively overseen by a single manager.

Benefits of the city-council plan of municipal government include the separation of politics from the efficient running of a city and the use of the expertise of a trained professional city manager. On the other side, however, the city manager is not responsible to the residents of the municipality; she or he was hired by the city council, not chosen by the electorate. A question of accountability thus arises, as the authority to hire or fire a city manager is in the hands of the city council.

For more information

Teske, Paul, and Mark Schneider. "The Bureaucratic Entrepreneur: The Case of City Managers." *Public Administration Review* 54 (July/August 1994): 331–340.

Linda K. Shafer

civil liberties   The term *civil liberties* refers to the freedom of a citizen to exercise ordinary rights, as of speech or assembly, without unwarranted or arbitrary interference by the government.

The American system of government is founded on two counterbalancing principles: first, that the majority of the people governs through democratically elected representatives; and second, that sometimes the power of a democratic majority must be limited in order to ensure individual rights. The U.S. Constitution was designed to direct, limit, and constrain the use of power to protect liberty. Majority power is limited by the Constitution's Bill of Rights, which consists of the original 10 amendments ratified in 1791, the three Reconstruction Era amendments (the Thirteenth, Fourteenth and Fifteenth), and the Nineteenth Amendment giving women the right to vote, passed in 1920.

The Bill of Rights guarantees a long list of rights that have been debated, interpreted, and defined in many ways throughout American history. The First Amendment rights include freedom of speech, association, and assembly, freedom of the press, and freedom of religion supported by the separation of church and state.

Our right to equal protection under the law guarantees citizens equal treatment regardless of race, sex, religion, or national origin. Our right to due process ensures fair treatment by the government whenever the loss of liberty or property may be at stake. Our right to privacy guarantees citizens freedom from unwarranted government intrusion into our personal or private affairs.

In a long tradition of defending civil liberties, the American Civil Liberties Union (ACLU) has devoted its mission to the preservation and extension of the rights enumerated in the U.S. Constitution. Founded in 1920, the ACLU grew out of earlier groups that had defended the rights of conscientious objectors during World War I. ACLU projects are geared toward three major areas of civil liberties: inquiry and expression, including freedom of speech, press, assembly, and religion; equality before the law for everyone, regardless of race, nationality, sex, political opinion, or religious belief; and due process of law for all.

ACLU has participated in many major civil liberties cases argued in U.S. courts. Some of these cases include: the Scopes "monkey trial" in Tennessee (1925), *Brown v. Board of Education* school desegregation case (1954), and the defense of the right of a neo-Nazi group to demonstrate in Skokie, Illinois, during the 1970s.

The scope of civil liberties is widely debated and interpreted according to various events in our country and worldwide. Although the United States is the freest country in the world, some argue that American liberties are increasingly violated or limited as the government's influence spreads to various aspects of our society. As the framers of the Constitution predicted, and as has become apparent in modern times, liberty can be restricted by people with good intentions. It is often the case that, when a new federal law is proposed, liberty rights activists from all political spectra examine the law to determine whether constitutional rights will be violated.

Several areas have emerged where the government's intrusion on civil liberties has been questioned. Privacy has been a fundamental right with a long tradition in the United States. The government's efforts to curb child pornography, organized crime (through wiretapping), and a long list of emerging cybercrimes have resulted in invasions of privacy. Mandatory drug and AIDS testing for employment, life insurance, or other health screenings are often viewed as an intrusion into privacy rights. Freedom of speech is often debated. Limits on speech have been questioned in the government's quest to curb campaign spending and the ability of individuals to advance their political ideas. Another threat to free speech is the campaign to outlaw flag burning. In modern times, some members in Congress have pushed for a constitutional amendment to forbid the desecration of the American flag.

The government's war against terrorism raises questions regarding two kinds of rights—the rights governments are required to secure and those they must respect during this process. Additionally, the government has asked for expansive authority to conduct domestic surveillance of citizens, giving officials new access to personal information contained in business and school records. Some groups are arguing that the very liberties we created government to secure are at risk.

Preservation of civil liberties in America requires a constant reevaluation of the powers of the federal government. On a daily basis, new developments require that the government balance the rights of individuals with the goals of maintaining one of the largest and most complex governments in the world. Issues ranging from Internet security to wiretapping to law enforcement require our government to examine the impact on civil liberties and their enforcement.

See also CIVIL RIGHTS.

For more information
American Civil Liberties Union. "Freedom Is Why We're Here." 1999.
Cato Institute. Cato Handbook for 105th Congress, *Civil Liberties in America.* Washington, D.C.: Cato Institute, 2001.
U.S. Constitution Amendments I–X, XIII–XV, XIX.

Cherylyn A. Harley

civil rights   Civil rights are the political, economic, and social rights that are guaranteed under the law to the citizens of a nation.

The U.S. Constitution (1787) guarantees a range of civil rights, including the freedom of speech and assembly, the right to vote, the right to equal protection under the law, and procedural guarantees in criminal and civil trials.

The first 10 amendments of the U.S. Constitution, which are collectively referred to as the Bill of Rights (1791), contain a number of important civil rights. For example, the First Amendment protects the freedom of speech and assembly and the free exercise of religion; the Fourth Amendment protects against unreasonable searches and seizures by the government; and the Fifth Amendment provides, among other things, that a person cannot be deprived of life, liberty, or property without the due process of law. As originally written, the Bill of Rights protected citizens from the actions of the federal government, but these rights were eventually applied against actions of the state governments in a series of cases decided by the Supreme Court between the 1930s and the 1960s.

In its most common usage, the term *civil rights* refers to the rights of racial minorities. After the American Civil War, three amendments—known as the Reconstruction Amendments—were made to the U.S. Constitution. The

Thirteenth Amendment (1865) outlaws slavery. The Fourteenth Amendment (1868) declares that the states must provide equal protection under the law, and that they may not deprive any person of life, liberty, or property without the due process of the law. The Fifteenth Amendment (1870) provides that the right to vote shall not be denied on account of "race, color or previous condition of servitude." The Reconstruction Amendments purported to grant Blacks an equal political and social status.

Despite the existence of the Reconstruction Amendments, basic civil rights were routinely denied to blacks until the Civil Rights movement of the 1950s and 1960s. After the Civil War, Southern states implemented a program of segregation in which blacks were separated from whites in every aspect of life, including housing, transportation, restaurants, education, and employment. The Supreme Court upheld the constitutionality of segregation in *Plessy v. Ferguson*, 163 U.S. 537 (1896). In *Plessy,* the Supreme Court declared that a Louisiana statute that required "separate but equal" accommodations for blacks and whites in railroad cars did not violate the equal protection clause of the Fourteenth Amendment. According to the Court, the Louisiana statute did not stamp "the colored race with a badge of inferiority" unless the "colored race choose to put that construction upon it."

In addition, Southern states adopted numerous tactics, including literacy tests, property qualifications, and poll taxes, to deprive blacks of the right to vote. The Supreme Court did little

A group of African-American students, who were refused service at a luncheon counter reserved for white customers, staged a sit-down strike at the F. W. Woolworth in Greensboro, North Carolina, 1960. (LIBRARY OF CONGRESS)

to protect the black franchise; indeed, it upheld the constitutionality of the poll tax in *Breedlove v. Suttles,* 302 U.S. 277 (1937), and the literacy test in *Lassiter v. Northhampton County Board of Elections,* 360 U.S. 45 (1959).

The Civil Rights movement of the 1950s and 1960s challenged the gross political, social, and economic inequality that blacks faced. Grassroots movements in black communities began to resist segregation in the South. For example, on 1 December 1955, Rosa Parks refused to move from the white section of a bus and was promptly arrested. This incident led to one of the most important events in the early Civil Rights movement—the enormously successful Montgomery bus boycott. In 1960, the "Greensboro four" began "sit-ins" to protest the inequality of public accommodations. Important leaders in the black community, such as Dr. Martin Luther King Jr., rallied their followers to resist the discriminatory practices and institutions that relegated African Americans to the status of second-class citizens. In August 1963, Dr. King gave his famous "I Have a Dream" speech that came to symbolize the need for racial equality. The National Association for the Advancement of Colored People (NAACP) was a key organization that promoted the cause of racial justice. The NAACP was instrumental in pursuing legal remedies to establish and protect the civil rights of African Americans.

In 1954, the Supreme Court finally overturned its decision in *Plessy v. Ferguson,* 163 U.S. 537 (1896). In *Brown v. Board of Education,* 347 U.S. 483 (1954), the Court explicitly rejected the "separate but equal doctrine" as a violation of the equal protection clause of the Fourteenth Amendment. The Supreme Court decided that "separate educational facilities are inherently unequal" because they imbue a sense of inferiority in African-American students. Despite the Supreme Court's ruling, there was hardly any desegregation in the school system even 10 years after the *Brown* decision.

It was only with the involvement of Congress and the executive branch that civil rights became effective. Congress passed the Civil Rights Act of 1964, which banned discrimination on the basis of race. The Supreme Court upheld the constitutionality of the Civil Rights Act in two cases that dealt with racial discrimination in public accommodations. In *Heart of Atlanta Motel v. United States,* 379 U.S. 241 (1964), the Supreme Court held that the Civil Rights Act applied to a motel that refused to rent rooms to blacks. Similarly, in *Katzenbach v. McClung,* 379 U.S. 294 (1964), the Supreme Court held that the Civil Rights Act applied to a restaurant that engaged in racial discrimination.

Congress also passed the Voting Rights Act of 1965, which was a watershed event in the history of voting rights. The Voting Rights Act prohibits the use of any voting qualification or procedure that abridges or denies the right to vote on the basis of race or color. In 1966, the Supreme Court upheld the constitutionality of the Voting Rights Act in *South Carolina v. Katzenbach,* 383 U.S. 301 (1966).

The current controversy in civil rights centers of the constitutionality and desirability of affirmative action programs that take race into consideration in employment decisions and university admissions. Proponents of affirmative action argue that the long history of slavery and discrimination justifies the preferential treatment of racial minorities. Critics of affirmative action argue that even benign racial preferences amount to racial discrimination and that any kind of discrimination on the basis of color is wrong.

In *Regents of University of California v. Bakke,* 438 U.S. 265 (1978), Allan Bakke, a white applicant, claimed that his equal-protection rights were violated when the university, under a racial quota program, accepted minority-group students who had lower test scores and grades than Bakke. In *Bakke,* the Supreme Court decided that racial quotas were unconstitutional but that race could be taken into account as one factor in the admissions process. Since the *Bakke* decision, the Supreme Court has become increasingly hostile toward affirmative action policies.

See also CIVIL LIBERTIES.

For more information

Graham, Hugh D. *The Civil Rights Era: Origins and Development of National Policy 1960–1972.* New York: Oxford University Press, 1990.

Polman, H. L. *Constitutional Debate in Action: Civil Rights and Liberties.* New York: HarperCollins, 1995.

Sullivan, Patricia. *Days of Hope: Race and Democracy in the New Deal Era.* Chapel Hill: University of North Carolina Press, 1996.

Yasmin A. Dawood

Civil Service Reform Act of 1978   The Civil Service Reform Act of 1978 (CSRA 78), along with Reorganization Plan Number Two, was the most comprehensive reform of the federal personnel system since the Pendleton Act of 1883. Together, they abolished the Civil Service Commission and replaced it with two agencies: the OFFICE OF PERSONNEL MANAGEMENT and the MERIT SYSTEMS PROTECTION BOARD, which also contained the Office of Special Counsel; created the SENIOR EXECUTIVE SERVICE, an elite corps of senior career administrators; and required executive agencies to develop and utilize performance appraisal systems. They also established a merit pay system for midlevel career managers that linked salary increases to job performance, not years of service; created the FEDERAL LABOR RELATIONS AUTHORITY to administer the provisions of the Federal Service Labor-Management Relations Statute and oversee labor-management activities pertaining to federal labor unions; and renewed the commitment of the federal government to affirmative action while encouraging experimentation with new management techniques.

Although the Civil Service Reform Act (CSRA) was passed on 13 October 1978, and Reorganization Plan Number Two came about when President Carter exercised his right to reorganize the executive branch, their roots go back many years. When the commission model was adopted in 1883, it was grounded in the notion that having a self-contained entity placed outside the presidential chain of command would be less affected by political influence and would likely result in a more professional and efficient civil service. Over time the thinking in public administration changed, and there was a move toward increasing the ability of the president to run the executive branch while at the same time holding him more accountable for its performance. Still others had taken issue with the structure of the Civil Service Commission, namely, that it violated the principle of separation of powers by allowing one agency to perform the legislative, executive, and judicial functions.

On a separate front, the Second Hoover Commission had made, as one of its many recommendations to promote efficiency and economy in government, the suggestion to establish a "senior civil service." This proposed cadre of top administrators would allow agency heads greater flexibility in attracting and retaining the most qualified individuals for key government positions located just below political appointees by allowing for greater pay and better benefits. These factors, which were coupled with a growing negative perception of civil service in general during the early 1970s, coalesced into the CSRA and Reorganization Plan Number Two.

The creation of the Office of Personnel Management (OPM) centralized the federal personnel function and made the agency directly accountable to the president, while the establishment of the Merit Systems Protection Board (MSPB) allowed for a semi-independent agency to oversee the protection of merit system principles and employee rights. The Office of Special Counsel (OSC) was created to investigate employee complaints involving prohibited personnel practices, and it was authorized to present any evidence of wrongdoing discovered before the MSPB.

The Senior Executive Service (SES) was loosely modeled after the British higher civil service, where administrators are trained to be generalists who can manage any number of differing programs, one of the key elements being that administrators rotate from office to office, gathering experience as they go. The SES was also designed to open higher-level positions to qualified candidates outside of government by allowing individuals from the private sector— who possessed the right skills—to cross over into the public sector without having to work their way up the ladder. This was part of a larger effort to attract the best and the brightest to government service.

Take the U.S. DEPARTMENT OF TRANSPORTATION (DOT), for example, where many of the administrators come from outside the department and even outside of government. Some positions in DOT agencies, such as those with the Federal Railroad Administration and the Federal Aviation Administration, require that candidates possess highly technical knowledge in addition to management skills. Accordingly, the most qualified candidates often come from those industries regulated by DOT, such as the railroads and aviation.

While the CSRA and Reorganization Plan Number Two have received mixed reviews, there seems to be a general consensus that separating the functions performed by OPM from those of MSPB and placing OPM within the presidential chain of command have improved government operations. There also seems to be general agreement that OSC has been a disappointment in the area of employee rights. The SES, on the other hand, has only been somewhat of a disappointment: the concept is usually embraced as a good one, but there seems to be considerable disparity among agencies in implementing it successfully.

Overall, the CSRA provided much-needed reform to an antiquated personnel system. Having come full circle, the legislation increased executive control by concentrating the federal personnel function within the presidential chain of command and allowing for SES appointments from outside of government service. At the same time, it relinquished some of the political neutrality that had been established by the Pendleton Act of 1883, which called for a nonpartisan

Civil Service Commission and advocated merit principles.

For more information

Civil Service Reform Act of 1978. Public Law 95-454. 95th Cong., 2d sess., 11 January 1979.

Van Riper, Paul P. *History of the United States Civil Service.* Evanston, Ill.: Row, Peterson & Company, 1958.

Jonathan Greenblatt

Civil Service Reform League   The Civil Service Reform League was a citizen-initiated organization created in 1877 to fight the excesses of the spoils system and help guide civil service reform in the United States.

First called the New York Civil Service Reform Association (NYCSRA), its first effort was drafting a bill for Congress that would "regulate and improve the Civil Service of the United States." Members of the association took their ideas and critiques on civil service reform legislation to Senator George Pendleton of Ohio, who had been pitching his own civil service reform bill to Congress. Pendleton reviewed the association's ideas and agreed that any revised bill should include many of the provisions suggested by the association and that these ideas would revitalize and renew the bill. Congress finally adopted the new bill as the Pendleton bill.

Membership in the NYCSRA grew rapidly as the association gained popularity through its involvement in the Pendleton bill. The New York association published an appeal to groups across the country in an effort to spur interest in civil service reform. This appeal called people around the United States to mobilize into a concerted national movement. Affiliated societies had formed all over the United States by 1881 and were propelled to action.

Despite the attention that the league received, the efforts to bring about civil service reform may not have come to fruition had it not been for the assassination of President Garfield in July of

1881. President Garfield died at the hands of a disillusioned job seeker who did not gain the office he expected based on the spoils system. This created an environment ripe for civil reform, which the league seized upon.

Within days of the assassination, the league publicized Garfield's views on reform using pamphlets and posters and advertised their cause to an animated public. The Pendleton bill, which had earlier made its debut in front of Congress, was now reintroduced and Congress took 11 months to debate and refine the bill. The Pendleton Act was passed in January 1883. With the passage of the Pendleton Act came the impetus for many states and local governments to adopt similar legislation. Until its demise in 1924, the league worked hard to keep the cause of civil service reform on the national agenda.

For more information

Stewart, Frank M. *The National Civil Service Reform League.* Austin: University of Texas, 1929.

Robert A. Schuhmann

civil service system   The civil service system is the name generally given to the public personnel management system used for most government employee positions in municipal, state, and federal governments. Civil service or merit-based personnel systems developed as a result of abuses in traditional employment practices in government.

Known as political patronage or the spoils system, the former method of doling out government jobs was as a reward to individuals on the basis of their political party membership, campaign support, or political contributions to elected candidates. However, reaction against the political patronage or spoils system by the public grew with evidence of waste and inefficiency in government. Public jobs were no longer seen as just "rewards" for political support or party loyalty but important jobs requiring knowledge, abilities, and skills. Amid growing criticism, the

assassination of President Garfield in 1881 by a dissatisfied job seeker raised national attention to the problems of the patronage system.

As a result, the Congress established the civil service system with passage of the Civil Service Act of 1883. Known as the PENDLETON ACT, the law established the principle of merit in federal government employment and established a Civil Service Commission for administration of the act. The new system established by Congress consisted of a body of rules based on the concepts of merit and political neutrality. Major aspects of the civil service system include the elimination of politics from personnel decisions; the selection of civil service personnel by open, competitive examinations; the appointment of individuals on the basis of merit; and efficient and fair recruitment, selection, and reward systems.

While civil service reform was occurring at the federal level of government, several states developed their own civil service systems (including New York State in 1893 and the state of Massachusetts in 1884). Since 1970 the U.S. government has required each state to establish a state merit-based public personnel system for employees. Appointments in these state systems are also determined on the basis of merit-based competitive examinations without regard to race, religion, color, national origin, gender, or political affiliation.

Since 1883 a number of enacted legislative efforts have been undertaken to improve the original design of the federal civil service system under the Pendleton Act. Most notable of these is the CIVIL SERVICE REFORM ACT OF 1978 (CSRA), which divided the roles of administering and policing policies under the Civil Service Commission by establishing the OFFICE OF PERSONNEL MANAGEMENT for administrative personnel functions and the MERIT SYSTEM PROTECTION BOARD for merit protection and enforcement. As of 2000, more than 2.7 million civilians were employed within the federal government, half of whom work within the DEPARTMENT OF DEFENSE or the

DEPARTMENT OF VETERANS AFFAIRS, and more than 4 million people work within the 50 state governments.

For more information
Kettle, D. F,. et al. *Civil Service Reform; Building a Government That Works.* Washington, D.C.: Brookings Institution Press, 1996.
Mosher, F. C. *Democracy and the Public Service,* 2d ed. New York: Oxford University Press, 1982.

Dahlia Bradshaw Lynn

Clean Air Act   Prior to the 1950s, air pollution was largely a state and local concern. Beginning in 1955, the federal government began researching the problem. The Clean Air Act (CAA) refers to a series of federal laws that attempt to regulate and reduce air pollution in the United States. Congress passed the first CAA in 1963 when it attempted to reduce air pollution by setting emissions standards for stationary sources such as power plants, but it did not set standards for mobile sources, such as cars and trucks. Amendments to the CAA were passed in 1965, 1966, 1967, and 1969 in an effort to set standards for auto emissions, among other things.

Even with these amendments the CAA appeared inadequate. So Congress passed the CAA of 1970, which set new primary and secondary standards for ambient air quality, established new limits on emissions from stationary and mobile sources, and for the first time required enforcement by both state and federal governments. The 1970 CAA gave the newly created ENVIRONMENTAL PROTECTION AGENCY (EPA) the authority to list airborne toxins for regulation. The act also set National Ambient Air Quality Standards (NAAQS) and, for the first time, gave citizens the right to take legal action against anyone, including the government, who violated emissions standards. However, automobile manufacturers found it difficult to meet the standards, and Congress extended the deadlines with

1977 amendments to the act. The 1977 amendments also extended deadlines to meet the ambient air quality standards for cities.

In 1990 Congress acted again to revise the law. The 1990 CAA reinforced the role of states by forcing them to take responsibility for locales that had not met ambient air quality standards, and it allowed states to create deadlines for emissions standards for each source of pollution. To reduce pollution, the act mandated toxic sources to use the best available control technology (BACT) and called for a reduction in the production of chlorofluorocarbons (CFCs) to reduce atmospheric ozone depletion.

Although the 1990 act significantly altered and added to the regulatory requirements of the earlier laws, the basic framework and procedural aspects of the 1970 act and its 1977 amendments have remained constant. However, the 1990 act includes an additional list of 189 hazardous air pollutants that the EPA must regulate. And as with the earlier CAA, states are responsible for implementing much of the law by issuing new air emissions permits, monitoring existing sources, and designing state implementation plans (SIPs) that specify how the state will reduce air pollution. If a state fails to meet federal standards in its SIP, the EPA can take over implementation in that state.

Finally, the 1990 CAA also includes a permit program for larger pollution sources; makes it easier to fine violators; increases the opportunities for citizen participation in the development of SIPs, permitting, and litigation; and for the first time, allows for the use of market-based and economic incentives to reduce air pollution. Although some states and environmental activists have objected to the use of market-based and economic incentives, the programs appear to be working as designed.

For more information
Bryner, Gary. *Blue Skies, Green Politics: The Clean Air Act of 1990 and Its Implementation,* 2d ed. Washington, D.C.: CQ Press, 1995.

Marzotto, Toni, Vicky Moshier Burnor, and Gordon Scott Bonham. *The Evolution of Public Policy: Cars and the Environment*. Boulder, Colo.: Lynne Rienner, 2000.

Donald P. Haider-Markel

Clean Water Act of 1972

The Clean Water Act of 1972 continues to provide a clear path for clean water and a solid foundation for an effective national water program.

In the late 1960s, only a third of the nation's waters were safe for fishing and swimming. Sewage treatment plants served only about half of the nation's population, and nearly 500,000 acres of wetlands were being lost each year. In response to growing public concern for such serious and widespread water pollution, in 1972 Congress enacted the first comprehensive national clean water legislation. The Clean Water Act is the primary federal law that protects our nation's waters, including lakes, rivers, aquifers, and coastal areas.

This was not, however, the first attempt to clean the nation's environment. The Federal Water Pollution Control Act of 1948 was the first comprehensive statement of federal interest in clean water programs, and it specifically provided state and local governments with technical assistance funds to address water pollution problems, including research. However, since water pollution was viewed as primarily a state and local problem, there were no federally required goals, objectives, limits, or even guidelines. When it came to enforcement, federal participation was strictly limited to matters involving interstate waters and only with the consent of the state in which the pollution originated. Throughout the 1950s and 1960s water quality continued to deteriorate. The growing concern of the late '60s and early '70s for the environment set the stage for an entirely new and tougher federal approach to cleaning up the environment.

The Clean Water Act's primary objective is to restore and maintain the integrity of the nation's waters. The act has been termed a technology-forcing statute because of the rigorous demands placed on those who are regulated by it to achieve higher and higher levels of pollution abatement. The act's objective translates into two fundamental national goals: eliminate the discharge of pollutants into the nation's waters, and achieve water quality levels that make the waters fishable and swimmable.

The CWA provides a comprehensive framework of standards, technical tools, and financial assistance to address the many causes of pollution and poor water quality, including municipal and industrial wastewater discharges, polluted runoff from urban and rural areas, and habitat destruction. The act today consists of two major parts, one being the title II and title VI provisions that authorize federal financial assistance for municipal sewage treatment plant construction. The other is the regulatory requirements, found throughout the act, that apply to industrial and municipal dischargers.

For example, the Clean Water Act requires major industries to meet performance standards to ensure pollution control; charges states and Native American tribes with setting specific water quality criteria appropriate for their waters and developing pollution control programs to meet them; provides funding to states and communities to help them meet their clean water infrastructure needs; and protects valuable wetlands and other aquatic habitats through a permitting process that ensures that development and other activities are conducted in an environmentally sound manner.

For more information

Hunter, Susan. *Enforcing the Law: The Case of the Clean Water Acts (Bureaucracies, Public Administration, and Public Policy)*. Armonk, N.Y.: M. E. Sharpe, 1996.

Craig Donovan

Clean Water Act of 1977

The Clean Water Act (CWA) of 1977 is an amendment to the

Federal Water Pollution Control Act (FWPCA) of 1972, the first comprehensive clean water legislation passed in the United States. The FWPCA was enacted as a response to the growing public concern in the 1970s regarding widespread water pollution. Today, the CWA serves as the primary federal law protecting our national waters.

The fundamental objective of the CWA is to restore and maintain the integrity of our nation's surface waters. The act fulfills this mission through five key components. First, it provides a set of minimum national effluent standards for industry. Second, it provides a listing of water quality standards. Third, it sets forth a discharge permit program that serves to enforce the water quality standards. Fourth, it makes provision for special problems like toxic spills and chemicals. Lastly, it provides a revolving construction loan program for publicly owned treatment works.

The CWA allows the U.S. ENVIRONMENTAL PROTECTION AGENCY (EPA) to set effluent limitations for pollutants that can be discharged by industrial plants and municipal sewage plants. The EPA does this in two steps. It first establishes a nationwide, base-level treatment by assessing what is technologically and economically achievable in a particular industry. Next, if necessary, the EPA requires more stringent levels of treatment for certain plants to achieve water quality objectives for a particular body of water into which that plant discharges.

The EPA publishes water quality criteria for lakes, rivers, and streams under the directives of the Clean Water Act. There are two types of information in these directives. The first are discussions of scientific data on the effects of pollutants on public health, aquatic life, and recreation. The second are quantitative concentrations or qualitative assessments of the pollutants in water that generally ensure adequate water quality for specific uses. The criteria are based solely on scientific judgment and data regarding the relationships between environmental/human health effects and pollutant concentrations.

Instead of serving as regulations, the water quality criteria serve as guidelines regarding the environmental effects of pollutants and present scientific data regarding these pollutants. This information is useful in creating regulatory requirements that are based on water quality impacts. The CWA has established a partnership between states and the EPA to control the discharge of pollutants into surface waters from source points. To implement this program, the EPA develops national guidelines based on the "best available technology" that is economically achievable for an industry type. Then, states determine the beneficial uses for their waterways and establish the water quality standards that will ensure that the body of water is clean enough for its designated use.

The primary method that is used to impose the CWA limitations on pollutant discharges is the National Pollutant Discharge Elimination System (NPDES). Under this program, any person responsible for the discharge of a pollutant into U.S. waters from a source point must apply for a permit and obtain one before discharging. These permits are reviewed and renewed every five years to take into account improvements in technology. Thirty-nine states in the United States run this type of program. In states that have the authority to implement a CWA program, the EPA still retains oversight responsibilities. The states, the federal government, or citizens can sue persons or organizations that violate their permits.

For more information

Adler, Robert W., Diane Cameron, and Jessica Landman. *The Clean Water Act 20 Years Later.* Washington, D.C.: Island Press, 1993.

Evans, Parthenia B., ed. *Clean Water Act Handbook.* Chicago: Section of Natural Resources, Energy, and Environmental Law, American Bar Association, 1994.

Houck, Oliver A. *The Clean Water Act TMDL Program: Law, Policy, and Implementation.* Washington, D.C.: Environmental Law Institute, 1999.

Elizabeth Corley

Clinton, William Jefferson (1946–) *42nd
president of the United States* Bill Clinton was
the first U.S. chief executive to be born after
World War II, the first Democratic president after
12 years of successive Republican administrations, and the first to take office following the
end of the cold war. Although his two terms in
office coincided with the longest period of sus-
tained economic growth in U.S. history, the
Clinton presidency saw years of intense partisanship, personal and public scandal, and the
first presidential impeachment since Andrew
Johnson's in 1868.

Clinton was born William Jefferson Blythe
IV in Hope, Arkansas, the son of a nursing student and a traveling salesman who was killed in
an auto accident before his son's birth. Adopting the name of his stepfather, Clinton
attended Hot Springs public schools and as a
high school senior in 1963 was selected as a
delegate to Boy's Nation, where he met Senator
J. William Fulbright and President Kennedy,
fueling a lifelong interest in public affairs. After
high school, Clinton attended Georgetown
University, where he majored in international
affairs, worked in Fulbright's Senate office, and
won a Rhodes Scholarship that allowed him to
study at Oxford University from 1968 to 1970.
In 1970, Clinton enrolled in Yale Law School,
where he met his future wife, Hillary Rodham,
and he spent much of 1972 as the Texas state
coordinator of George McGovern's unsuccessful presidential campaign.

After receiving his law degree in 1973, Clinton returned to Arkansas to join the faculty of
the University of Arkansas School of Law at
Fayetteville. In 1974, the 27-year-old Clinton
won the Democratic Party nomination to challenge Third District Republican John Paul Ham-
merschmidt for his seat in Congress. Although
he lost the congressional race in the general election, Clinton gained valuable experience and
attention that would serve him well in his successful bid for the Arkansas attorney general's
office two years later. In 1978, Clinton was

President William Jefferson Clinton   (GETTY IMAGES)

elected governor, a post he would hold for all but
two of the next 14 years.

In 1991, as public dissatisfaction over the
state of the national economy began to over-
shadow the foreign policy accomplishments of
the GEORGE H. W. BUSH administration, Clinton
announced that he would seek the 1992 Democratic presidential nomination. Despite public
controversy over allegations of extramarital
affairs, past drug use, and his Vietnam War draft
record, Clinton ultimately won his party's nomination and went on to defeat Bush and Texas bil-
lionaire H. Ross Perot in the general election that
fall, with 43 percent of the popular vote and 370
electoral votes. In 1996, Clinton defeated former
Senate Majority Leader Robert J. Dole to win a
second term in office, the first time a Democrat
had been elected to two successive terms since
Franklin Roosevelt in 1936.

The first two years of Clinton's presidency
were tumultuous ones, with the administration
suffering political defeats over national health
care reform, an economic stimulus package, and

a proposal to end discrimination against homosexuals in the military; embarrassing military setbacks in Haiti and Somalia; and investigations into the firing of the White House Travel Office staff and Clinton's relationship with a failed Arkansas savings and loan in the 1980s. However, the Republican Party won control of both houses of Congress in the midterm elections of 1994, and Clinton thereafter moderated his political course, announcing in his 1996 State of the Union address that "the era of big government is over." Nevertheless, in the years that followed, the relationship between Clinton and the congressional Republicans worsened, culminating in House passage of two articles of impeachment arising out of Clinton's efforts to mislead a grand jury about the nature of his relationship with a White House intern. In February 1999, the Senate failed to convict Clinton on either impeachment charge.

Despite the political turmoil of his presidency, Clinton succeeded in compiling an impressive series of legislative accomplishments, including the Family and Medical Leave Act (1993), the Motor Voter Act (1993), the Brady Act (1993), the Americorps Community Service Initiative (1993), the Goals 2000 Education Standards (1994), telecommunications reform (1996), the Health Insurance Portability and Accountability Act (1996), welfare reform (1996), and a new Chemical Weapons Convention treaty (1997). Clinton also placed his vice president, Albert Gore, in charge of his "reinventing government" initiative, which would ultimately streamline the federal bureaucracy by 377,000 employees and reduce federal spending as a share of the economy from 22.2 to 18.5 percent.

The Clinton administration also presided over a period of unprecedented economic growth and prosperity, with some of the lowest unemployment, inflation, and interest rates in decades. Following the passage of a landmark deficit-reduction package in 1993 and a balanced budget agreement with Congress in 1997, decades of persistent federal budget deficits came to an end, and the nation soon enjoyed its first budget surpluses since the 1960s. In foreign policy, the Clinton administration oversaw the passage of the NORTH AMERICAN FREE TRADE AGREEMENT and a new GENERAL AGREEMENT ON TARIFFS AND TRADE; expanded NATO; intervened militarily in Bosnia, Kosovo, and Iraq; and brokered peace negotiations in the former Yugoslavia, Northern Ireland, and Israel.

For more information

Berman, William C. *From the Center to the Edge: The Politics and Policies of the Clinton Presidency.* Lanham, Md.: Rowman and Littlefield, 2001.

Renshon, Stanley A. *High Hopes: The Clinton Presidency and the Politics of Ambition.* New York: Routledge, 1998.

Schier, Stephen E. *The Postmodern Presidency: Bill Clinton's Legacy in U.S. Politics.* Pittsburgh: University of Pittsburgh Press, 2000.

William D. Baker

cloture   Cloture is a procedural rule for ending a filibuster.

Legislatures are deliberative bodies, where debate is essential to producing good legislation. As a deliberative body, the U.S. Senate has adopted rules that allow its members virtually unlimited debate. The Senate is a relatively small body with only two members from each state, so it can afford the luxury of permitting members to speak to issues at length. The House of Representatives, by contrast, has 435 members and is simply unable to afford to allow its numerous members to leisurely debate legislation.

Under the rules of the Senate, members may speak at length on a bill under consideration. However, this privilege can be used to stymie the legislative process by organizing a filibuster. From the first Congress in 1789 until 8 March 1917, the only way to stop a filibuster in the Senate was by means of a unanimous consent resolution, which is a method that can still be used. In the lame-duck session of the 64th Congress (1915–17), a dozen progressives used a filibuster to defeat President Woodrow Wilson's desire to arm American merchant vessels. In response Wilson called Congress into special session to deal with the filibustering issue. The result was Rule XXII of the Senate. It provided for cloture by allowing 16 senators to sign a cloture petition, which would be filed with the presiding officer of the Senate. Two days later a cloture vote would be taken. To be successful, the cloture would need at least two-thirds of those present and voting to win.

In 1975 the growing workload of the Senate required a more efficient system because sessions were now lasting the whole year. In response, Rule XXII was changed to three-fifths of the membership (those duly chosen and sworn) of the Senate. The change allows a filibuster to be stopped by a vote of 60 or more senators instead of by the previous 67. If a cloture is invoked, each senator may speak on the bill for no more than one hour. A total of 30 hours may be spent in postcloture debate; afterward the bill must be voted upon by the Senate.

The change in the rule applied to measures before the Senate, but not to the rules of the Senate itself. To invoke cloture if the debate involves changing a rule of the Senate still requires a two-thirds vote of the Senate.

Invoking cloture is difficult and requires strong bipartisan support. Some senators are reluctant to vote for cloture because the right of extended debate is such an integral element of Senate history and procedure.

For more information

Bach, Stanley. "Filibusters and Cloture in the Senate." In *Congress of the United States: Powers, Structure, and Procedures,* edited by N. O. Kura. New York: Nova Science Publishers, 2001.

Bird, Robert C. "The Cloture Rule." In *The Senate 1789–1989: Addresses on the History of the United States Senate.* Vol. 2. Washington, D.C.: U.S. Government Printing Office, 1989.

A. J. L. Waskey

Commission on Civil Rights The Commission on Civil Rights is a federal agency established under the Civil Rights Act of 1957 that is charged with investigating and collecting information relating to discrimination on the basis of race, color, religion, sex, age, disability or national origin.

The U.S. Commission on Civil Rights is an independent, bipartisan federal agency that was established in order to collect information with respect to the denial of equal protection of the laws and discrimination. The commission also investigates incidents in which citizens believe that they are being deprived of their rights to vote on account of their race, color, religion, sex, age, disability, or national origin. In addition, the commission submits reports and recommendations to the president and the Congress as well as issuing announcements to the general public to discourage discrimination.

The Commission on Civil Rights does not act as an advocate for those individuals whose civil rights have been violated. In addition, the commission has no power to enforce remedies in the cases it investigates. The commission does have the power to hold hearings and issue subpoenas in order to assist its fact-finding mandate. The commission consults with local, state, and federal governments and private organizations and refers complaints to those bodies where appropriate. The commission also runs the Robert S. Rankin Civil Rights Memorial Library in Washington, D.C., which houses over 50,000 reference works on the subject of CIVIL RIGHTS.

The Commission on Civil Rights is led by eight commissioners, four of whom are appointed by the president and four of whom are appointed by Congress. The selection of the commissioners does not require confirmation by the Senate. At any given time, no more than four commissioners may belong to the same political party.

Since 1957, the Commission on Civil Rights has published over 160 reports on civil rights issues and over 70 statutory reports that provide recommendations to the president and Congress. For example, the commission published a report entitled *Voting Irregularities in Florida during the 2000 Presidential Election* (2001). The commission concluded that violations of the Voting Rights Act had occurred, leading to an extraordinarily high level of voter disenfranchisement "with a significantly disproportionate impact on African American voters."

The commission has published reports on a diversity of topics, including employment discrimination in state and local governments, racial and ethnic tensions in the Mississippi Delta, police practices, the practical effects of the Americans with Disabilities Act, the health status of minorities and women, educational opportunities for the disabled, the impact of the Federal Fair Housing System, the enforcement of the Indian Civil Rights Act, discrimination on the basis of age, and the effect of the Immigration Reform and Control Act of 1986. These reports are available to the public.

For more information

Dulles, Foster R. *The Civil Rights Commission, 1957–1965*. East Lansing: Michigan State University Press, 1968.

"The Rise and Fall of the United States Commission on Civil Rights," *Harvard Civil Rights-Civil Liberties Law Review* 22 (1987): 449.

Yasmin A. Dawood

committee system   The committee system is a set of working groups within a legislative body that consider bills relating to specific areas of public policy.

Committees typically have three main responsibilities: conducting public hearings on important national issues, amending and approving legislation, and providing legislative oversight. Through these activities, committee systems, which exist at both state and federal levels, serve a variety of purposes within a legislature. Most practical among these is the ability of committees to increase the efficiency of the legislature. While legislators can only address one bill at a time during floor debate, a number of highly specialized committees—each consisting of a few members—can meet at the same time and examine more pieces of legislation.

Committees also create legislative experts. Since each committee typically has jurisdiction over one area of public policy, committee members can become very knowledgeable about a particular issue. This specialization produces experts within the legislative body who can offer information to their colleagues. During floor debate on a bill, when all members of the legislative body have an opportunity to debate and vote on a piece of legislation, committee members often lead debate on the issue. This power is enhanced by the fact that, since committees have the ability either to report out or hold legislation, they act as gatekeepers, setting the policy agenda for the larger legislative body.

State and federal committee systems will typically contain one or more of four main types of committees: standing, select, special, and joint. Standing committees are permanent committees that typically cover a single, substantive, broad policy area, such as agriculture or health and human services. Standing committees may further comprise a system of subcommittees, which are smaller groups that explore a narrower area of policy within the larger jurisdiction of the standing committee. Taken together, standing committees and subcommittees coordinate activity on the majority of legislation introduced by the members of a legislative body. In 2002 the U.S. Senate contained 16 standing committees, while the U.S. House contained 19 standing committees.

Select and special committees, by contrast, are generally not permanent. They are fact-finding bodies that are initiated to explore one narrowly focused policy concern—such as the U.S. Senate's Select Committee on Aging—and they typically lack the ability to take action on a piece of legislation. Joint committees allow members of both houses to work together, often on issues related to the administration of government, such as, in 2000, the Joint Committee on Inaugural Ceremonies. Other joint committees deal with policy-related matters, such as the Joint Committee on Taxation.

Membership of legislative committees is typically divided proportionally among members of the political parties represented in the legislature. Legislators usually select the committees in which they would like to be members, and party caucuses hammer out the final membership lists. The types of committees that members choose are often relevant to the interests of their district. For example, a member of Congress from a midwestern state might request membership on the Agriculture Committee in order maximize his involvement in issues that are important to his constituents. In other cases, legislators might request membership on more prestigious, high-profile committees. The two principal leadership positions in committees—the chairperson and the ranking minority member—are held by members of the majority party and minority party, respectively.

Standing committees of the U.S. House include:

Committee on Agriculture
Committee on Appropriations
Committee on Armed Services
Committee on the Budget
Committee on Education and the Workforce
Committee on Energy and Commerce
Committee on Financial Services
Committee on Government Reform
Committee on House Administration
Committee on International Relations
Committee on the Judiciary
Committee on Resources
Committee on Rules
Committee on Science
Committee on Small Business
Committee on Standards of Official Conduct
Committee on Transportation and Infrastructure
Committee on Veterans Affairs
Committee on Ways and Means

Standing committees of the U.S. Senate include:

Committee on Agriculture, Nutrition and Forestry
Committee on Appropriations
Committee on Armed Services
Committee on Banking, Housing and Urban Affairs
Committee on the Budget
Committee on Commerce, Science and Transportation
Committee on Energy and Natural Resources
Committee on Environment and Public Works
Committee on Finance
Committee on Foreign Relations
Committee on Governmental Affairs
Committee on the Judiciary
Committee on Health, Education, Labor and Pensions
Committee on Rules and Administration
Committee on Small Business
Committee on Veterans' Affairs

For more information

Davidson, Roger H., and Walter J. Oleszek. *Congress and Its Members,* 8th ed. Washington, D.C.: Congressional Quarterly Press, 2002.

Kreihbel, Keith. *Information and Legislative Organization.* Ann Arbor: University of Michigan Press, 1997.

Schickler, Eric. *Disjointed Pluralism: Institutional Innovation and the Development of the U.S. Congress.* Princeton, N.J.: Princeton University Press, 2001.

Smith, Steven S., and Christopher J. Deering. *Committees in Congress.* Washington, D.C.: Congressional Quarterly Press, 1984.

Tracy McKay Mason

community action agencies (CAAs)   Community action agencies (CAAs) are nonprofit, private, and public organizations established under the Economic Opportunity Act of 1964. Established to help people achieve economic self-sufficiency, CAAs were part of President LYNDON BAINES JOHNSON's Great Society programs that were designed and billed as America's War on Poverty.

The Economic Opportunity Act and the Federal Office of Economic Opportunity were designed to implement a guarantee of equal opportunity through a mandate that pledged: "Although the economic well-being and prosperity of the United States have progressed to a level surpassing any achieved in world history, and although these benefits are widely shared throughout the Nation, poverty continues to be the lot of a substantial number of our people. The United States can achieve its full economic and social potential as a nation only if every individual has the opportunity to contribute to the full extent of his capabilities and to participate in the workings of our society. It is, therefore, the policy of this Nation to eliminate the paradox of poverty in the midst of plenty in this Nation by opening to everyone the opportunity for education and training, the opportunity to work, and the opportunity to live in decency and dignity. It is the purpose of the Act to strengthen, support, and coordinate efforts in furtherance of that policy."

Economic opportunity offices at the state level were created in order to provide funds and technical support that enabled local citizens to create CAAs, grassroots-based organizations designed to meet the problems and needs of the poor in their area. The law stated that programs would be "developed, conducted, and administered with the maximum feasible participation of the residents of the areas and members of the groups served." It called for community action programs to mobilize resources that could be used in a direct attack on the roots of poverty. This is an early example of the federal government distributing control of public program decisions to lower levels of government. This change was part of the realization that local issues of poverty, education provision, health, and welfare varied dramatically at the local level, and federally mandated programs designed to address such issues could not be designed to respond to the unique demands experienced by each local government.

One of the early foci of the CAA was the educational system and how the delivery of education was inequitable with respect to children from low-income families. The idea behind the movement was to shift power from teachers and administrators over to the local inhabitants. Along with the school and district administration, the community would share in the decision-making power and contribute to the programs for the school. The significant policy-making power was now extended to the citizens in order to influence the schools' personnel, curriculum, and budget levels. The purpose of community control was to increase community participation in the making of school policy, especially by the poor and those who were not previously involved. This allowed for greater political accountability among educators. Today CAAs continue to provide support and to serve as a voice for low-wealth citizens and their communities in both urban and rural settings.

Today there are approximately 1,000 community action agencies in the United States serving 96 percent of the nation's counties. These agencies are connected by a comprehensive network that includes national, state, and regional associations; a national lobbying organization; and the association of Community Service Block Grant (the core funding for CAAs) administrators.

CAAs are a primary source of support for the more than 34.5 million people who are living in poverty in the United States. The majority of CAA clients are extremely poor, with incomes below 75 percent of the federal poverty threshold, or $9,735 for a family of three (the average family size for the client population). CAAs as a network serve approximately 10.9 million individuals per year, of which 3.9 million are family members. Additionally, 54 percent of CAAs are in rural areas, 36 percent of CAAs are in areas considered both urban and rural, and 10 percent of CAAs are located in urban areas. The average population of a CAA's service area is approximately 300,000 people. The average number of low-income people within these service areas is 37,600.

CAAs are found in nearly every dimension of daily activity, with an extensive array of community services including: networking services such as the creation of community coalitions and community needs assessments; emergency services ranging from cash assistance, intervention in child/spousal abuse cases, and emergency and natural disaster response and assistance; education programs like Head Start, child care, support for working families, and alternatives for at-risk youth; support for federal food and nutrition programs such as WIC (Women, Infants, and Children) and USDA (U.S. Department of Agriculture) communities distribution programs; family development; employment training programs supporting on-the-job training, skill development, and job placement; housing assistance for first-time home-buyer programs, homeless services, and home-repair services; economic development programs that foster micro-enterprise development, local business investment, and asset-building programs for low-income people; local health-care support for prenatal care, maternal and infant care, immunization, treatment for substance abuse, and low-cost pharmaceutical programs; income management for at-risk households; and transportation support for medical, employment, and child care services.

For more information

Murphy, Joseph, and Lynn G. Beck. *School-Based Management as School Reform: Taking Stock.* Thousand Oaks, Calif.: Corwin Press Inc., 1995.

Brent C. Smith

comparable worth   Comparable worth is the concept that men and women should be compensated equally for work requiring comparable skills, tasks, and effort.

This theory, also referred to as sex equity or pay equity, was introduced in the 1970s in an attempt to correct inequities in pay for occupations traditionally held by men and women. The U.S. Department of Labor, Bureau of Labor Statistics, reports that in 1999 the 57 million women employed in the U.S. workforce earned only 72 cents for each dollar earned by working men. Furthermore, women earned less than men in 99 percent of all occupations for which Bureau of Labor Statistics data were available. This discrepancy between the salaries of men and women has come to be known as the "gender gap," and the principal remedy proposed to correct the inequity is a job-evaluation method designed to compensate for gender bias and other conditions that have led to inequities in the wage levels of women and men workers. According to this theory, workers' salaries should be calculated on a scale of socioeconomic value that transcends traditional supply and demand. The system would develop a wage scale that would replace that determined by the freely operating labor market.

Even after passage of the Equal Pay Act (1963), which declared that men and women would receive equal pay for equal work, wages for occupations traditionally held by women continued to lag behind those for jobs predominantly held by men. Efforts to correct such discrepancies through legislation have met with resistance from business groups and others who state that the job-evaluation methods interfere with the operation of a free market. In *American Federation of State, County and Municipal Employees v. State of Washington* (1981), the state of Washington was ordered to provide raises and compensatory back pay to female state employees, who were found to be earning 20 percent less than their male coworkers. Although the decision was overturned on appeal, the case brought the issue of comparable worth to political prominence in the 1980s. Pay equity laws have since been enacted in Europe and in a number of states and municipalities in the United States. Conservative and business groups continue to oppose the implementation of pay-equity programs.

For more information

Gregory, J., R. Sales, and A. Hagewisch, eds. *Women, Work and Inequality.* New York: St. Martin's Press, 1999.

Kelly, R. M., and J. Bayes. *Comparable Worth, Pay Equity, and Public Policy.* New York: Greenwood Press, 1988.

Killingsworth, M. R. *The Economics of Comparable Worth.* Kalamazoo, Mich.: W. E. Upjohn Institute, 1990.

Sharon Timberlake

conference committee A conference committee is a legislative working group found in bicameral legislatures whose task is to work out different versions of a bill passed by each house.

Before a bill can be sent to the president for his signature, both the U.S. House of Representatives and U.S. Senate must approve the bill in the same form. Similarly, the houses in a bicameral state legislature must work out any differences that exist before the bill can be offered to the governor. This compromise can occur if the houses adopt amendments that bring the two bills into line. If this is not successful, conference committees comprising members of both houses are appointed to resolve discrepancies that remain in the two versions of a bill.

Membership of a conference committee is typically chosen among the members of the original committees or subcommittees that had jurisdiction over the measure, as well as the sponsor of the bill. Seniority, political party representation, and the expertise of conferees on the issue can also be important. Depending on the size and complexity of the bills, conference committees may be further divided into subconferences that negotiate smaller sections of the entire bill.

Legislators often have the opportunity to "instruct" their house's conferees, when they can request that the conferees take certain stands at the houses' conference. In some states, conferees have the opportunity to consider the bill in its entirety. However, House and Senate conference committees are only directed to negotiate the differences that exist between the bills as passed by their respective houses; similar provisions should not be open for debate during the conference. Despite this, bills resulting from the conference sometimes include new material or significant changes.

The members of the conference committee must conclude the process by reaching agreement on all points of contention. These agreements are compiled in a document called a conference report, which is a final version of the bill that will be sent to each house for approval. The conference report must be approved by a majority of each house's conferees in order to be adopted. Once the report reaches the floor, legislators must either approve or reject the report in its entirety and do not have an opportunity to vote, except on some appropriations-related measures, on individual components of the agreement. Conference reports are not amendable, which helps maintain the integrity of the negotiation process. If approved by each house, the new compromise bill is forwarded to the president for his signature; otherwise, the houses may begin the conference process anew or start fresh with a new piece of legislation.

For more information

Davidson, Roger H., and Walter J. Oleszek. *Congress and Its Members,* 8th ed. Washington, D.C.: Congressional Quarterly, 2002.

Shepsle, Kenneth A., and Barry R. Weingast. "The Institutional Foundations of Committee Power." *American Political Science Review* 81 no. 1 (1987): 86–104.

Thomas: Legislative Information on the Internet. http://thomas.loc.gov.

Vogler, David J. *The Third House: Conference Committees in the U.S. Congress.* Chicago: Northwestern University Press, 1971.

Tracy McKay Mason

conflict of interest *Conflict of interest* is a term that refers to circumstances that may compromise the independence (though not the intellectual capacity) of a lawyer, judge, fiduciary, accountant, mediator, arbitrator, journalist, physician, or other professional. A conflict of interest may violate professional ethical standards and raise legal issues where there is either an actual conflict or a potential one. Thus, the appearance of a conflict is sufficient to raise the issue.

The question of how a conflict arises and whether it may be resolved presents in a variety of circumstances. A professional might have a conflict of obligation, where he or she cannot satisfy one obligation without failing in another. Alternatively, a direct conflict of interest occurs when a professional has an interest or a stake that he or she cannot fulfill without simultaneously failing to fulfill professional obligations to the individuals or entities he or she is employed by or otherwise obligated to serve.

As a matter of propriety, it is essential in professions such as those to avoid any conflict of interest by separating private interests from professional obligations. In addition, in fields such as law, it is professionally inappropriate to represent two clients with competing interests. For a judge, a mediator, or an arbitrator, it is a violation of ethics to sit on a case where he or she has a relationship to one of the parties by blood, economic interest, or other part-time employment.

In some situations, conflicts can be resolved by promptly and fully informing all of the clients or parties of the interest that gives rise to the conflict. Then the clients should have the opportunity to either knowingly and voluntarily waive the conflict (consent to continued involvement with the full knowledge of the conflict of interest) or to choose to have the individual with the conflict withdraw from representation, participation, or consideration. However, in many situations the conflict cannot be resolved because disclosing the conflict of interest would breach a duty to the other client or party with the conflicting interest. In such cases, the only proper remedy is self-removal or recusal of the individual who has the conflict of interest.

From an institutional standpoint, conflicts of interest in the workplace might involve hiring, assessment, and promotion (or demotion). Large organizations frequently implement guidelines and protocols to provide for disclosure of potential or actual conflicts and to protect the integrity of the institution and its processes.

Ultimately, whether the conflict is in an institutional setting or a smaller professional circumstance, the purpose of protections against undisclosed conflicts of interest is to prevent (or minimize) power imbalances, ensure fair competition or fair judgment, and preserve the rights of those involved.

For more information

Davis, Michael, and Frederick A. Elliston. *Ethics and the Legal Profession.* Amherst, N.Y.: Prometheus Books, 1986.

LeClair, Debbie Thorne, O. C. Ferrell, and John P. Fraedrich. *Integrity Management: A Guide to Managing Legal and Ethical Issues in the Workplace.* Tampa, Fla.: University of Tampa Press, 1998.

Demetra M. Pappas

Congressional Budget Office The Congressional Budget Office (CBO) is an independent nonpartisan office in Congress created under the Congressional Budget and Impoundment Act of 1974 (CBIA) (2 U.S.C. 621 et seq.) and designed specifically to assist Congress and its committees (House and Senate Budget Committees first, followed by the House and Senate Appropriations Committees, the House Committee on Ways and Means and the Senate Committee on Finance, then other standing committees) with economic, budget, and policy analyses during the budget process.

To aid the Budget Committees in formulating Congress's annual budget resolution, CBO issues a Budget and Economic Outlook report (updated midyear) containing spending and revenue projections based upon economic assumptions (including inflation and mandatory program and discretionary spending workloads) over the next 10 years. This "baseline" is seen as the amount that would be raised or spent without new legislation; any legislation that would change revenue or spending projections is "scored" for its budgetary impact. CBO assists the Senate Appropriations Committee by analyzing the president's revenue and spending proposals from the OFFICE OF MANAGEMENT AND BUDGET (OMB) against CBO budget projections. Once the budget resolution is adopted, CBO provides outlay estimates for House and Senate appropriations bills prior to passage. Under CBIA and the Unfunded Mandates Reform Act of 1995, CBO must provide five-year budget estimates and federal mandate direct-cost estimates (plus the economic assumptions and analytical methods used) for all bills reported by a full committee of either house, which become part of each bill's committee report. CBO performs its "scorekeeping" function by regularly supplying the Budget and the Appropriations Committees with measurements of the extent to which pending legislation (including draft proposals, floor amendments, conference reports) or approved legislation may impact the budget based upon baseline revenue and spending projections.

The CBO director is jointly appointed by the Speaker of the House and the president pro tempore of the Senate, upon House and Senate Budget Committees' recommendations, for a four-year term. There is no limit on subsequent terms, but the director can be removed by Senate or House resolution. The director appoints the deputy director and other professional staff on merit only. Alice M. Rivlin, CBO's first director,

separated the staff by function into four program divisions and three budgetary divisions; this structure remains unchanged. The program divisions—Long Term Modeling, Microeconomic and Fiscal Studies, Health and Human Resources, and National Security Divisions—make up about one-third of CBO's current 232 full-time staff and provide policy and program analysis related to both long-range issues (e.g., Social Security) and numerous other legislation areas. The Budget Analysis Division prepares bill cost estimates, budget projections, and baseline spending analysis; the Macroeconomic Analysis Division produces economic forecasts and short- and long-term economic projections; and the Tax Analysis Division makes tax revenue estimates (assisted by Congress's Joint Committee on Taxation) and tax revenue projections. Despite its best efforts, the validity of CBO projections often becomes the focus of criticism by the executive branch, some congressmen, and other economists in and out of government.

Writing of its early history in *Congress and the Budget* (Bloomington: Indiana University Press, 1978), Joel Havermann described CBO as a "one of a kind" institution serving 535 "masters" and noted how nonpartisanship was essential to its credibility and to its central role of computing "the costs of possible courses of policy, and the advantages and disadvantages of each" while not recommending any particular policy over another. Such neutrality was in direct contrast to the OMB that, up until 1974, had been Congress's sole source of budgetary information on departments and agencies as well as a major "public advocate" for presidential policies and programs. Despite the volatile political climate in which it operates, CBO has remained independent and "steadfastly maintained its reputation as a supplier of objective facts" since 1975.

For more information

Committee on the Budget: Majority Caucus. *Basics of the Budget Process: A Briefing Paper.* U.S. House of Representatives. February 2001.

Congressional Budget Office. http://www.cbo.gov.

House Budget Committee. http://www.house.gov/budget.

Penner, Rudolph. "The Uncertainty of Budget Estimates." *Business Economics* 36 (July 2001): 20.

Schick, Allen. *The Federal Budget: Politics, Policy, Process.* Washington, D.C.: Brookings Institution Press, 2000.

U.S. Senate Budget Committee. http://www.senate.gov/~budget.

Kathleen M. Simon

constituency Constituency refers to any group of people, voters, or organizational members to whom policy makers can be held accountable for their actions, or whose support policy makers aim to win. Often the term is used to refer to the support base of policy makers serving in the specific capacity of representatives in legislative assemblies, who also have a formal mandate to represent a given constituency.

Formally, such legislative constituencies are almost always geographically defined. In this sense, a constituency can be seen as a "de jure apportionment of space for the purpose of electing representatives of people living in the territorial limits of a democratic state." However, countries vary widely precisely with respect to how the limits of constituencies are defined and, thus, with respect to what a "constituency" is understood to be. Variations are produced by and affect the role of political parties in candidate selection and apportionment procedures, the ethnic and social structure of the population, and electoral laws governing who is entitled to vote and on what terms.

Thus, with respect to party involvement in candidacies, constituencies are to varying degrees purely geographical or politically partisan. The United States is in one sense closest to having "merely" geographical constituencies, in that political parties are weak, the constitution is federal, and the electoral system is majoritarian. The winning candidate in a given constituency is formally expected to represent the interests of all people living within her district, regardless of the candidate's or voters' party affiliations. At the other end of the scale, in Scandinavia, electoral systems are proportional, constitutions are unitary, and the parties are stronger. Seats are apportioned among political parties rather than individual candidates on the basis of shares of popular votes that party lists have received at the national level. Here the "constituencies" that politicians are expected to represent are viewed as less localist and more strictly national and partisan in nature.

However, political parties can also play differing organizational roles with respect to the actual process of deciding where constituency borders are drawn. Here, countries vary with respect to what their constituencies can become. In this respect the United States and India are at one end of a scale, with politicians deeply involved in deciding where the limits of geographical constituencies are drawn. At the other end, in Britain and in Sri Lanka, constituencies are defined more neutrally, without the substantial involvement of those who may benefit. In systems where constituency borders are determined by politicians, districts where they are to compete can be divided so that safe support bases are carved out for given parties, or so that electoral districts acquire constituent populations that are ethnically or socially unrepresentative. The process whereby constituency borders are manipulated for party gain is in the U.S. literature referred to as "gerrymandering." In cross-national literature, it is referred to as "malapportionment," whereby the allocation of seats among representatives becomes unequal to the distribution of votes across parties, and the representation of given constituencies becomes correspondingly biased.

The degree of malapportionment that can be said to prevail depends crucially on what measures and assumptions of representative fairness are used, a subject of ongoing and contentious debate. Recent Supreme Court decisions against state-level attempts to prevent racial gerrymandering in the United States in 1996 have been controversial also among U.S. conservatives, in the sense that the decisions have imposed new burdens on states and limited the scope of state action in determining apportionment.

In a broader and less formal sense, constituencies can be viewed as any social group that decision makers can be called upon to represent. Thus, constituencies can be based in gender, ethnicity, sexual orientation, economic interests, and many other bases of social affiliation. Concerns that ethnic minorities and women have not been fairly represented as constituencies through any existing formal channels have led to the founding of entirely new political parties and formal interest groups. Examples are as various as the Black Panther Party founded in the United States in 1966 and (on a nonparty basis) the European Women's Lobby in the European Union. In recent studies on Australian politics, members of Parliament from ethnically plural constituencies were found to make policy interventions in Parliament that refer to ethnic issues more often, in apparent attempts to represent home-district ethnic constituencies without a formal mandate to do so.

Finally, constituencies can also in some sense be created to support policies that policy makers wish to see implemented and actively seek to create opinion for. In one recent work on policy activism for preventive mental-health policies, "creating a constituency" for this policy is variously held to involve attracting grassroots support, building coalitions, identifying and developing allies, and skillfully utilizing the media to identify issues and raise public awareness. Some constituencies, not least those united by common economic interests, may also attempt to influence government policy by "capturing" the administrative authorities attempting to regulate their activity. This can be viewed as less than legitimate, in that regulatory bodies are formally not supposed to represent the interests of any constituencies or to do anything other than execute government orders and laws. Tripartism, empowering public-interest groups to advocate their interests in centralized forums, has been advocated as one way of lessening the risks for clandestine and harmful "regulatory capture."

For more information

Ayres, I., and J. Braithwaite. "Tripartism: Regulatory Capture and Empowerment." *Law and Social Inquiry: Journal of the American Bar Foundation* 16, no. 3 (1991): 435–496.

Johnston, R. "Manipulating Maps and Winning Elections: Measuring the Impact of Malapportionment and Gerrymandering." *Political Geography* 21, no. 1 (2002): 1–31.

Long, B. B. "Developing a Constituency for Prevention." *American Journal of Community Psychology* 20, no. 2 (1992): 169–178.

Lowenstein, D. H. "You Don't Have to Be Liberal to Hate the Racial Gerrymandering Cases." *Stanford Law Review* 50, no. 3 (1998): 779–835.

Rush, M. E. "The Variability of Partisanship and Turnout: Implications for Gerrymandering Analysis and Representation Theory." *American Politics Quarterly* 20, no. 1 (1992): 99–122.

Samuels, D., and R. Snyder. "The Value of a Vote: Malapportionment in Comparative Perspective." *British Journal of Political Science* 31 (2001): 651–671.

Singh, C. P. "A Century of Constituency Delimitation in India." *Political Geography* 19, no. 4 (2000): 517–532.

Zappala, G. "The Influence of the Ethnic Composition of Australian Federal Electorates on the Parliamentary Responsiveness of MPs to Their Ethnic Subconstituencies." *Australian Journal of Political Science* 33, no. 2 (1998): 187–209.

Eero Carroll

consultant A consultant is someone who provides compensated and specifically defined public administration–related services for clients but is not a member of the client organization. In public administration, clients typically include organizations such as government agencies, nonprofit organizations, and businesses. Consultants usually work full-time for consulting companies, which compete with each other for clients, or they are self-employed, hired directly by the client.

The role of consulting in public administration has grown considerably since the 1960s, both in terms of the number of consulting companies and of self-employed consultants. An important reason for this increase is that the use of consultants offers several advantages to government agencies, nonprofit organizations, and businesses.

First, in order to accomplish their missions, organizations often require certain services or specific products that they cannot develop in-house because they lack the expertise or the resources. Rather than put all the time and effort into developing the necessary expertise, organizations often find it preferable to hire consultants who already understand how to do the work to complete the task. For example, the U.S. Air Force requires high-performing aircraft to fulfill its responsibilities, but it does not build the planes itself. Instead, the air force hires companies whose expertise is in building planes.

Second, actual and perceived objectivity for some activities and services is a necessity. Thus, to achieve this objectivity, organizations turn to consulting firms or consultants to perform this kind of work. For example, Congress requires that many federally funded programs be evaluated every so often. An evaluation by the agency administering the program may lack credibility because the agency would be evaluating itself. Therefore, agencies often hire consultants to conduct evaluations because the consultants not only have the expertise to conduct a useful evaluation, they also are objective, which is very important for the evaluation to have credibility with Congress and others outside the agency.

Finally, the competition among consulting firms and among consultants may lead to high-quality services for the client, because consulting firms and consultants who want business must deliver good services. Otherwise the client will hire someone else next time. For example, if a firm hired to conduct an evaluation completes it late and overspends, the client will likely choose another firm to do the next evaluation.

Some in public administration view the growth in the use of consultants negatively. The reasons for these views include problems with oversight, the development of monopolies, and the costs. Concerning oversight, critics believe that if a government agency is charged with performing a service, it should do it itself for reasons of accountability. Monopolies are a danger as well. As indicated above, the concept of competition is an important justification for the use of consultants. A lack of competition removes a major performance incentive for consultants. Finally, some believe that consultants cost more than the value they provide.

Despite these objections, it appears that consulting firms and consultants will continue to be an important and valuable part of the public administration field. Their expertise, commitment to service, and overall advantages offer much to government, nonprofit organizations, and other businesses.

For more information

Osbourne, David, and Ted Gaebler. *Reinventing Government*. New York: Penguin Books, 1992.

Zaino, Gene. "New Options for Engaging Today's Independent Workforce." *PA Times* (December 2001): 1, 6.

Todd Stephenson

Consumer Product Safety Commission

The Consumer Product Safety Commission (CPSC) is an independent federal agency that Congress established in 1972 to prevent injuries related to commonly used consumer products by developing and enforcing uniform, nation-wide safety standards for these products. The CPSC also is intended to ensure public access to current information about frequently used consumer goods in order to allow consumers to evaluate the comparative safety of products. Empowering consumers to make wise choices in the marketplace is particularly important, since the CPSC is prohibited from recommending products because to do so would interfere with commerce.

CPSC has jurisdiction over approximately 15,000 types of products that may be powered by electricity or batteries and are used regularly, by both children and adults, in or near their homes, offices, or schools. They include large home appliances, such as refrigerators and washing machines; small home appliances, such as coffee makers, electric razors, and electric drills; landscaping equipment, such as lawnmowers, leaf blowers, and hedge trimmers; and all toys, from the smallest Matchbox series automobile to dollhouses to the most elaborate playground equipment.

Every business that manufactures, imports, distributes, or sells a product under CPSC's jurisdiction must comply with all CPSC rules and regulations related to that product. In cases of noncompliance, CPSC can impose a penalty of up to $5,000 per violation, with each day of an ongoing violation considered to be a separate offense. The maximum penalty for an ongoing violation is $12.5 million. This maximum penalty can also be imposed on a business that knowingly manufactures, imports, distributes, or sells a product that CPSC has banned or considers hazardous or that does not conform to CPSC rules. However, CPSC can reduce a penalty if this action is appropriate, considering the type of defect, the number of defective products distributed, the severity of injury, or in relation to the size of the noncompliant business.

CPSC does not have jurisdiction over all consumer products. Instead, other federal agencies that have expertise in certain consumer goods

are authorized to regulate the safety of those products. These non-CPSC consumer watchdog agencies include: National Highway Traffic Safety Administration, which works with auto manufacturers to regulate the safety of on-road motor vehicles; ENVIRONMENTAL PROTECTION AGENCY, which creates and enforces standards to reduce risk of injury to consumers through use of pesticides or exposure to toxic waste; Federal Aviation Administration, which maintains safe commercial air transportation; and FOOD AND DRUG ADMINISTRATION, which tests food and cosmetics for purity and consistent quality, and tests drugs for purity, effectiveness, and lack of dangerous side effects.

Despite the similarity between the names of the CPSC and the Bureau of Consumer Protection, the latter is an agency within the FEDERAL TRADE COMMISSION that protects consumers from unfair, deceptive, or fraudulent acts or practices. This type of protection focuses on reducing the possibility of damage to an individual's finances or credit, a function that is fundamentally different from that of the CPSC and the other product-oriented watchdog agencies, all of which aim to minimize the risk that an individual will suffer bodily harm.

When a business involved in manufacturing, importing, distributing, or retailing consumer goods discovers that one of its products is unsafe, the party who discerned the problem must notify the CPSC. The "whistle blower" then has a choice of: waiting, with the possibly unsafe product off the market, until CPSC's staff has time to create rules and regulations; or taking a proactive approach, with the hope that this action may result in a shorter interruption of the stream of commerce. The proactive approach requires that the business cooperate with and contribute to CPSC's analysis of the possibly unsafe product, sharing the workload until the business and the CPSC have completed "voluntary standards," or mutually agreeable measures that will ensure consumer safety. Thereafter, these voluntary standards can be granted the full force and effect of rules and regulations that were drafted by CPSC without input from the business community, with the result that CPSC has authority to mandate industry-wide compliance with these voluntary standards.

For more information

CPSC Publication 178. Washington, D.C.: Consumer Product Safety Commission, March 2001. Available online. URL: http://www.cpsc.gov/cpscpub/pubs/178.html.

Beth S. Swartz

consumer protection on the Internet

High on most countries' e-commerce agenda is the development of effective approaches to consumer protection. This will ensure that work in the area of business-to-consumer electronic commerce is compatible with that taking place in other areas, including business-to-business electronic commerce and the provision of government services online.

No doubt an international standard will eventually emerge with the United States, Europe, and other regions playing a key role in its development. The global nature of the problem is exemplified by the OECD Guidelines for Consumer Protection in Electronic Commerce, which were strongly influenced by U.S. developments in this area as well as those such as the European Union's Distance Selling Directive.

The Guidelines for Consumer Protection in Electronic Commerce do not, however, proffer a set of enforceable laws, but instead seek to have the outlined principles govern the development of industry rules or codes of practice regarding electronic commerce. The 12 principles are:

1. **Protection**
   Consumers using electronic commerce should be entitled to at least the same levels of protection provided by the laws and practices that apply to existing forms of commerce.

2. **Identification**
   Consumers should be able to establish the identity and location of businesses with whom they deal. These include company numbers and location of their registered or official office, location, telephone number, and industry affiliations.

3. **Information**
   Consumers should have readily available clear and comprehensive information before and after any purchase of goods or services. This information should include:

   The seller's legal identity and physical location
   The total price of the goods, including any delivery charge for which the consumer would be liable under the contract
   Where known, supplementary charges such as handling, postage, taxes
   Credit offered in accordance with the National Uniform Consumer Credit Code
   The monetary exchange rate and conditions being used
   Any restrictions, limitations, or conditions on purchase including warranties or guarantees
   Details of any cooling-off period
   Delivery arrangements
   Refund arrangements and costs for return of goods
   Length of the validity of the offer
   How and where complaints are handled
   Parental/guardian approval of requirements for minors

4. **Clarity**
   Sellers should state the contract terms in clear, simple language. This means avoiding the use of jargon and the adoption of well-accepted retail terminology. Important terms should be defined.

5. **Confirmation**
   Sellers should ensure they receive confirmed meaningful consent from consumers for a

purchase of goods and services. It is recommended that this entail a three-step process confirming:

An interest in buying
Full price, terms, and conditions of payment
Agreement to purchase

Sellers should make reasonable efforts to confirm the buyer's identity, for example, in the case of minors.

6. **Payment**
Consumers should be entitled to receive clear information about the types of payment that are accepted by the merchant or the payment provider. This should include any fees associated with payment and details regarding the security of payment methods. This principle should be read in conjunction with other developments regarding encryption.

7. **Complaints procedure**
Consumers should have their complaints and inquiries dealt with fairly and effectively. In making complaints, consumers should provide as much detail as possible and keep an electronic record. Sellers should demonstrate a commitment to handling complaints promptly and fairly.

8. **Dispute resolution**
Sellers should provide information to consumers about affordable and effective dispute resolution arrangements, where they are available. The dispute resolution schemes should meet the standards of: (a) accessibility, (b) independence, (c) fairness, (d) accountability, (e) efficiency, and (f) effectiveness.

9. **Privacy**
Sellers must respect customer privacy. In doing so they should adhere to the National Principles for the Fair Handling of Personal Information. Based on the OECD's Guidelines Governing the Protection of Privacy and Transborder Flows of Personal Data (1980), these principles establish a bench-mark for the handling of personal information and provide guidelines about the collection, use, disclosure, quality, security, access, and correction of personal information. Businesses should adopt specific guidelines regarding issues like the use of cookies (small pieces of information sent to a consumer's computer to identify repeat customers, tracking the way people navigate through a website, and so on). The principles suggest that sellers clearly offer consumers the alternative of rejecting cookies and, where possible, provide an opt-in arrangement by which the consumer explicitly consents to their use.

10. **Code compliance**
Industry code-administration bodies must closely monitor the application and effectiveness of their codes and be able to correct any deficiencies that are identified.

11. **Confidence**
Each code operating body should strive to maintain and promote consumer confidence in the global marketplace. This means ensuring that consumers have ready access to effective information about their rights and entitlements; that such bodies have a website containing the full text of the industry's code and details of current members subscribing to the code; and that the website provide links to other information and an e-mail facility allowing consumers to contact code administrators in relation to further information, complaints, and assistance.

12. **Regulation**
Governments should actively develop their consumer protection responsibilities. This can be done by actively pursing disreputable businesses who breach the laws in relation to electronic trading, by seeking harmonization of the laws governing electronic commerce, by encouraging self-regulatory schemes, and by applying appropriate consumer protection legislation and the like.

These 12 principles have been highly influential and are reflected in both the legislation and court decisions of most OECD countries.

For more information

Wilhelmsson, Thomas, Salla Tuominen, and Heli Tuomola. *Consumer Law in the Information Society.* The Hague, Netherlands: Kluwer Law International, 2000.

Eugene Clark

contractualism　Contractualism is the use of contracts in a range of arenas to control and define the behavior of individuals and organizations subject to them. This approach has become more prevalent as the political economic wave of neoliberalism and globalization has rendered other means of control less effective.

Examples of contractualism include contracts between unemployed people and financial support agencies, employment contracts, and the provision of essential services. For many, this step was an obvious one, and the resultant efficiencies undisputed. However, this has proven not to be the case in every instance.

Market failure occurs in a number of cases. It might become apparent that it is not possible to provide particular goods or services at a price that is competitive. There may not be sufficient interest or numbers of contenders to generate a field of competitors for the provision of the goods or services. Although analysis is in its early stages, it appears that the expected cost savings have not always come about, yet contractualism persists in these areas. This may be because of an abiding belief in the benefits of contractualism, but it might also be because the loss of infrastructure has made reversal of this step difficult or impossible.

Some have argued that the moral dimension of some contracts, for example between a welfare recipient and a government agency, is questionable. There is clearly an enormous power imbalance between the two parties to this type of contract, with little room for negotiation. The contract then becomes a means of changing a social relationship into a legal one that is rigid in structure and intent. It is manifestly not likely to be a relationship into which both parties have entered and negotiated freely.

Advocates of contractualism claim that it is not only effective, but it is likely to result in more appropriate and accessible goods and services, provided in a flexible and responsive way. It is clear that contractualism has the capacity to empower those involved in contractual relationships, but this is highly dependent on the parties beginning negotiations from a position of equal or comparable power. Nevertheless, in an era of increasing globalization in which neoliberalism and contractualism are gaining momentum—and other means of regulating relationships are losing favor—contracts are becoming routine.

For more information

Alford, John, and Deidre O'Neill, eds. *The Contract State.* Melbourne, Victoria: Centre for Applied Research, Deakin University, 1994.

Davis, Glyn, Barbara Sullivan, and Anna Yeatman, eds. *The New Contractualism?* Melbourne, Victoria: Macmillan, 1997.

Phillips, David. "Contractualism and Moral Status." *Social Theory and Practice* (summer 1998): 183–205.

Megan Alessandrini

control　The term *control* can refer to a cause or a process. As a cause, control means initiating an action. As a process, control means meeting some objective. The critical difference is that initiating an action is separate from obtaining feedback information on the effect of the action.

For example, opening the throttle on a land vehicle controls the amount of fuel going to the engine. However, this does not control its speed, which depends on its initial speed and the slope of the terrain. To control speed, the driver needs feedback information to make adjustments, and this process is described as regulation. Mechanisms can be designed to automatically make the adjustments, like governors on steam trains or a cruise controller on an automobile. These allow the driver to control by setting a speed without the need to receive feedback information or make adjustments, which are done automatically. This illustrates how the two meanings of the word are intimately connected and why it is useful to have a different word (regulation) to describe the process of control.

In social organizations, according to writers like A. S. Tannenbaum, control is "any process in which a person or group of persons or organization of persons determines, i.e., intentionally affects, what another person or group or organisation will do." Control in this sense does not require either a standard to be established or feedback information on whether the standard has been achieved. For example, establishing a budget to control costs may not work if unbudgeted costs arise. An increase in profit may be sought by controlling expenditures, but expenditure control may not control profits without adjustments if there are costs from redundancy or litigation or if there are reduced sales.

However, many other writers use the word *control* to mean meeting an objective. This requires setting a standard, measuring variations from the objective desired, and making necessary corrections. Details of the standard might not be defined, as when referring to a manager controlling a subordinate. The objective of control may be only to prevent certain outcomes, like preventing antisocial behavior.

The context of using the word *control* may make its use clear. However, clarity in the meaning of the word becomes important when applying the science of governance to evaluate social institutions. In this situation, the process of achieving an objective would be described as regulation, not control.

For more information

Ashby, W. R. *An Introduction to Cybernetics.* London: Methuen, 1968.

Tannenbaum, A. S. *Control in Organizations.* New York: McGraw-Hill, 1962.

Shann Turnbull

co-optation   Co-optation is a mechanism that organizations use to deal with potential adversaries in their environments. The concept was developed by sociologist Phillip Selznick in his study of the Tennessee Valley Authority during the 1930s. In its formative years, the agency was faced with carrying out its mission of flood control and agricultural development while competing against established organizations in its environment. Selznick concluded that organizational environments are indifferent or even hostile, presenting an especially critical problem for new organizations seeking to establish themselves.

According to Selznick, co-optation involves sharing of power, symbolically or in fact, with important actors in the environment in order to secure support or to minimize resistance. It represents an important means of organizational adaptation. However, it is less a strategic action by organizational leaders than an inevitable process rooted in the very act of organizing. In Selznick's analysis, co-optation is the price organizations pay to reduce potential environmental threat.

Co-optation can be either formal or informal. Formal co-optation occurs when an organization needs to absorb external elements. As Selznick notes, formal co-optation "involves the establishment of openly avowed and formally ordered relationships." These relationships can include signed contracts or agreements, the establishment of new organizational elements designed to provide access, or they can extend as far as appointments to official positions within the initiating organization.

Formal co-optation occurs under two circumstances. First, when the legitimacy of an organization's governing group is called into question, informal co-optation provides a means of reinforcing that legitimacy by getting established actors to indicate their support for the organization by joining it, thus lending their credibility and legitimacy to the initiating organization. The second circumstance that can lead to formal co-optation occurs when the initiating organization requires participation by outside groups for administrative purposes. It allows the leaders to establish the form of self-government, though not necessarily the substance, since the leadership of the initiating organization does not intend any actual transfer of meaningful power. Instead, the power-sharing arrangement is more symbolic than real.

An example of informal co-optation occurred with the 2002 meeting of the World Economic Forum in New York City. Previous meetings of this body, as well as other international development organizations, had been the targets of aggressive protests by antiglobalization activists. In Seattle, Genoa, and Quebec, meetings were disrupted and attendees faced crowds of unruly and sometimes violent protesters seeking to draw attention to issues ranging from environmental degradation to exploitation of workers by international corporations. In earlier meetings, representatives of these dissenting groups were excluded, and security forces were used to maintain some semblance of control. In contrast, organizers of the New York World Economic Forum conference invited these groups in as participants. Pro-labor representatives, religious leaders, and environmental activists were all included on panels and in discussions. As a result, the tactics used by protesters were far less disruptive than had been the case with previous international conferences. In fact, news reports indicated that police officers and journalists outnumbered protesters many times over at some of the organized protest rallies.

In contrast to formal co-optation, informal co-optation is a response to specific centers of power that may be able to deny resources needed by the initiating organization. In informal co-optation, representatives of other organizations are actually granted participation in the co-opting organiza-tion's decision-making processes. Unlike formal co-optation, informal co-optation involves the transfer of substantive power rather than simply its form. Since informal co-optation represents capitulation to specific interests that may not be consistent with the interests of the general community, such arrangements are generally not acknowledged publicly.

The lack of acknowledgement that characterizes informal co-optation makes it more difficult to recognize. Under Selznick's definition, only the leaders of the organizations involved in the arrangement would be aware that a deal had been made. Selznick's primary example of informal co-optation, the transfer of control over TVA's fertilizer program to representatives of the land-grant universities, is based on a subjective interpretation of the motives of those involved.

The consequences of co-optation, especially informal co-optation, include modification, or even sacrifice, of some organizational goals and programs in order to purchase freedom to pursue other goals deemed more important. The costs can be considerable. These adaptive responses generate conflicting commitments among organizational participants, and the organization changes in ways unforeseen by its founders and leaders. Thus, while essential for survival, co-optation inevitably leads to unanticipated consequences for the organization that constrain future action.

For more information

Selznick, Philip. *TVA and the Grass Roots: A Study of Politics and Organization.* Berkeley: University of California Press, 1949.

David Edwards

copyright   Copyright refers to the body of legal rights protecting creative literary, dramatic, artistic, or musical works and other forms of intellectual property. Copyright gives to the creator, or to the assigned copyright owner of a work, the sole right to produce or further reproduce the work. In U.S. law, these rights have been codified under Title 17 of the U.S. Code. The most recent extensive revision of the U.S. copyright laws was the Copyright Act of 1976 (PL 94-553).

The historical origins of copyright as a legal concept can be found in Europe not long after the invention of the printing press in the mid 1400s. By the next century, ruling powers in various countries began to grant national printing patent monopolies and gave publishers the ability to turn print information into a tightly controlled commodity. It was not until the 18th century, however, that any government sought to codify the concept of copyright. In 1710 the Statute of Queen Anne did just that, but beyond simply recognizing copyright, this law went further to establish the rights of authors to control their works and supported the philosophy that authors had a "natural right" to their works that is based in common law.

Early in U.S. history, Congress was given the constitutional power to "promote the Progress of Science and useful Arts, by securing for limited Times to Authors and Inventors the exclusive Right to their respective Writings and Discoveries." (U.S. Const., art. I, sec. 8, cl. 8). Congress exercised this power for the first time in 1790, when the first federal copyright statute was passed, which followed the lead of many state statutes already in existence at the time. U.S. copyright law has been amended many times over the years, mostly to extend protections to a greater variety of creative genres and production media, such as sound recordings and movies. The most recent clarification of extension to new media occurred in 1998 with the passage of the Digital Millennium Copyright Act, or DMCA (PL 105-304). The DMCA strengthened protections against infringements of intellectual property rights to digitally encoded information and made it illegal to circumvent encryption locks or other digital rights management (DRM) tools used by computer software and digital video producers.

One important limit over complete control of copyright to any work is known as "fair use." Fair use defines the common rights of users of copyrighted works, and it is based on the premise that there may be some circumstances in which the information contained in works covered by copyright may be used to accomplish a social good without needing permission from or compensation to the copyright owner. Fair use as a legal right was primarily defined within judicial doctrine rather than statutory language, until it was finally incorporated in statutory language in 1976 within Section 107 of the Copyright Act (codified in 17 U.S.C. 107). Among other things, Section 107 granted express statutory limitations on copyright that had been developed previously under case law. Since fair use is generally determined on a case-by-case basis, this statute included language intended to provide guidance on determining when a fair-use claim could be made.

For more information

Bettig, Ronald V. *Copyrighting Culture: The Political Economy of Intellectual Property.* Boulder, Colo.: Westview Press, 1996.

Lawrence, John Shelton. "Copyright Law, Fair Use, and the Academy: An Introduction." In *Fair Use and Free Inquiry: Copyright Law and the New Media,* 2d ed., edited by J. S. Lawrence and B. Timberg, 3–19. Norwood, N.J.: Ablex, 1989.

Steve Noble

corporate social responsibility   Corporate social responsibility (CSR) is a theoretical perspective that requires corporations not only to conform with the law and its regulatory obligations but, at the same time, perform to a higher standard than that which is required by the law.

Being a good corporate citizen and abiding by government and professional compliance codes and requirements is no longer sufficient, say the CSR theorists and practitioners, to justify a company's license to operate in the marketplace. Companies must display an elevated level of quality in all that they do. This, so the theory goes, requires cultivation of an organizational "culture of mindfulness," a vigilant and constant awareness of the possibility of wrongdoing, a personal ethic of care, and an assumption of individual responsibility for the consequences of one's actions.

According to CSR advocates, corporate directors will often make broad statements and universal generalizations regarding their responsibilities, such as "we will do no harm" and "we will act ethically." In practice, these standards are likely to translate into relativities such as "minimize risk" and "act in conformity with prevailing social norms." Corporate social responsibility, in contrast, is a broader notion, going beyond these tenets to place upon corporations an obligation to contribute actively to the common good of society as a whole.

CSR theorists believe that, to a large degree, financial responsibility to shareholders is dependent, in the long term at least, on factors such as responsible environmental management, safety, and responsiveness to societal needs and demands. This is not an entirely new approach. The idea that corporations are responsible to more than just shareholders has been gaining momentum for some time. For example, the Turnbull Report on the Combined Code of Corporate Governance, developed in the United Kingdom, introduced the notion of "stakeholder capitalism." The report of the Treadway Commission in the United States into fraud control had also previously recommended that public companies should develop and enforce written codes of corporate conduct in order to foster a

Demonstrator holds a sign protesting corporate greed during an AFL-CIO rally on the steps of Federal Hall in New York City. (STEPHEN CHERNIN/GETTY IMAGES)

strong ethical climate, to open channels of communication, and to help protect against criminal activity generally.

Allied with CSR is the notion of "corporate obligation." This obligation is justified as a fair return for society granting corporations the legal protection of limited liability and according them the social permission to operate freely in the marketplace. CSR advocates insist that corporations should *earn* their "social licence to operate."

The concept of corporate social responsibility involves motivating governments and industries alike to encourage and reward moves toward harmonization of standards and the building of a corporate culture of risk management. Through incentives, governments and industry associations can encourage risk-prevention propriety in business affairs. By providing appropriate reporting mechanisms, CSR advocates may convince business leaders that the pursuit of sustainability does not necessarily carry financial risk; in fact, it may enhance propriety and hence profitability.

For more information

Institute of Chartered Accountants in England and Wales. Turnbull Report. Available online. URL: http://www.icaew.co.uk.

Rick Sarre

corporatization Corporatization is a process in which a public-sector unit is removed from public administration and incorporated to be an independent limited company or an incorporated joint-stock company.

During the last 15 years, corporatization has been fairly popular in many countries as a method of reforming public-sector enterprises and business activities. Public utilities and services like mail, railways, telecommunications, and property management have been corporatized out of the government sector. Local governments and cities have corporatized harbors, waterworks, public transport, public housing, and even cul-

tural institutions like theaters and orchestras, and health facilities like laboratories and hospitals.

The general intention of corporatization is to enable the unit to have more autonomy and liberate the management of the unit from the control of day-to-day politics and the accountability for public budgets. Public-sector units have to operate in accordance with public law, but incorporated companies operate under company law, enabling more flexible organization and faster decision making.

At the time of corporatization, the public sector usually makes additional reforms. An object of policy makers is to introduce or increase competition, and to achieve this objective, the incorporated units are often put in competitive markets with private firms by removing barriers to entry, subsidies, restrictions of production and special privileges. In some cases, the new companies are forced to compete for finance and skilled labor on an equal footing with private firms, and the former public managers assume virtually the same powers and incentives as private-sector managers.

Whether corporatization is the same as privatization is an interesting question. Privatization is a complex concept that can be defined in many ways. Sometimes privatization is defined to refer to the application of private-sector management and financing principles to public administration. This kind of privatization includes a wide range of initiatives, like deregulation and liberalization measures that promote competitive tendering practices, externalization of public services by using outsourcing services, and lowering of taxes and collecting more user fees. In that sense, corporatization is a kind of privatization measure because it entails the risk of bankruptcy, and the corporatized units have to adopt the decision-making procedures used by private companies, developing a basic structure of organization and operating as a self-financing entity.

If privatization is defined only as the sale of a publicly owned asset, then we have to make a clear distinction between corporatization and

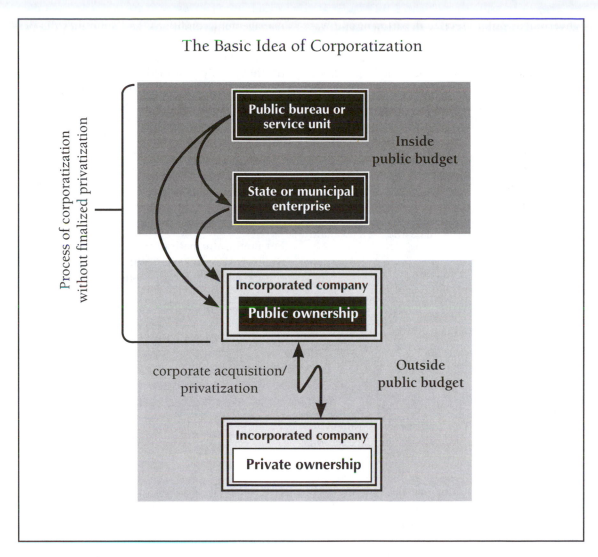

The Basic Idea of Corporatization

The basic idea of corporatization.

privatization. In the case of corporatization, the owner of the incorporated company is still the public sector, and pure corporatization does not assign any property rights to private investors. The public sector can appoint the board of directors of the corporatized unit, which ensures continuing control over the company. However, in some cases, especially in transition economies, corporatization is only a halfway solution, with many governments seeing it as a first step in the process of real privatization. At the same time, some governments think that total privatization is not needed at all, and the incorporated companies are seen to have an important role to play as a part of mixed economies and in the competitive quasi-markets of public services.

A successful example of corporatization is the New Zealand Post Office. It was formerly a government public service department and was corporatized in 1987 as a limited liability company. New Zealand Post Ltd. streamlined its activities and made personnel cuts from 12,000 to less than 7,000. During the 10 years after corporatization, the costs of sending a letter dropped approximately 30 percent. In 1994 New Zealand Post Ltd. was chosen Company of the Year in the Deloitte/Management Magazine Top 200 Company Awards. Originally, the aim of the New Zealand government was to privatize the post company by selling it to private investors, but later the plan was abandoned. Only a very few cases are as successful as the New Zealand Post Office.

In many cases corporatization has not caused any dramatic changes. The city of Lahti in Finland, with 96,000 inhabitants, corporatized its waterworks in 1993. The main reason for this was that during the economic recession, cuts in public spending were required in every service bureau and department, including the waterworks. The management of the waterworks saw the cuts as a very unwise policy, because the waterworks was a self-financed unit and it did not need the taxpayers' money at all. The management wanted to avoid the cuts, and it forced through the decision to corporatize in the city council. Since corporatization there have not been any dramatic changes in its activities, but the management of Lahti Water Ltd. is further away from the problems of the city budget, its management environment is stable, and it can concentrate on pure management issues regardless of political trends. Local politicians are only annoyed that if the company makes annual profits after corporatization, it will have to pay taxes to the state government before it can pay dividends to the owner, the city. If a public bureau makes a profit, all the surplus is tax free for the city.

Many arguments have been stated for and against corporatization in the literature. Advocates of corporatization have argued that it improves the efficiency of the unit, facilitates cooperation with the private sector, creates better management conditions, and simplifies the personnel administration of the unit. Nevertheless, on the other hand, it has been said that corporatization is only a cosmetic reform because it cannot totally break the link between politicians and the unit. Advocates of democratic values have stated that corporatization is contrary to democratic principles, because the incorporated companies are outside democratic decision-making procedures. Corporatization has also been criticized in a juridical framework, reminding everyone that corporatization weakens the legal protection of citizens.

For more information

Griffiths, Alan, and Stuart Wall, eds. *Applied Economics, Introductory Course,* 8th ed. New York: Longman, 1999.

Shirley, Mary M. "Bureaucrats in Business: The Roles of Privatisation versus Corporatization in State-Owned Enterprise Reform." *World Development* 27, no. 1 (1999): 115–136.

Toime, Elmar. "New Zealand Post—Creating a Benchmark Organization." *International Journal of Strategic Management, Long Range Planning* 30, no. 1 (1997): 11–20.

Pekka Valkama

cost-benefit analysis Cost-benefit analysis provides the core of a business case to justify an allocation of resources to a program or a proposed investment. In the public sector, it is also used in developing regulatory impact statements to assess the costs and benefits of a government's regulatory options.

The objective of a cost-benefit analysis is to support more-efficient resource-allocation decisions by identifying which option, including the no-change option, best achieves the outcomes sought. By requiring all of the variables and assumptions on the costs and benefits of each option to be specified, it aims to provide a more objective and transparent approach to how these decisions are made.

In the public sector, the costs and benefits being analyzed are not restricted to those that accrue to the entity making the decision, as is generally the case with a business. In particular, a public-sector cost-benefit analysis aims to capture the economic costs that are borne by businesses, such as traffic delays or restricted trading hours, as well as the social costs that are borne by the community, such as the cost of environmental damage or personal injury. Similarly, it will also consider benefits that spill over to external parties, such as increases in land values or in workforce skills.

However, in practice, it is often difficult, if not impossible, to reliably value many costs and benefits. In the absence of a market price, economists can estimate, for example, the value that society would place on access to a national park by measuring visitors' travel costs and the value of their leisure time foregone in making such a visit. These contingent valuation techniques are generally preferred to the alternative of surveying users on their willingness to pay an entry fee, as the latter approach is likely to overestimate the benefits. Where there is significant uncertainty about key variables, such as the level of demand, the cost-benefit analysis should include a sensitivity analysis that assesses the impact of changes in those variables. For example, if visitor numbers are taken to be 25 percent lower or higher than the most likely estimate, the sensitivity analysis would show the impact on the net benefits.

Where a benefit or cost cannot be reliably quantified at all, it should not be ignored but accounted for in a qualitative way. This could be in the form of a table that specifies the relevant stakeholder groups affected and the types and extent of the likely impacts on each of them. In this approach, the decision criterion will not be the simple question: Does the benefit-cost ratio exceed the threshold? Instead, the decision maker will need to assess the quantified impacts together with the unquantified ones.

There will generally be a time dimension to the assessment of the net benefits of particular options. Because the decision maker (and the community as a whole) will tend to have a preference for immediate benefits over ones that are delayed (and vice versa for costs), as well as a preference for lower-risk options over higher-risk ones, cost-benefit analysis requires that, for each option, the net benefits accruing in future years be discounted back to their present value.

The discount rate to be used in this present-value calculation will depend on:

- Whether the costs and benefits have been measured in real (inflation-adjusted) or nominal terms
- The assessed level of risk associated with the particular option
- Whether taxes are included in the costs
- The benefits foregone from the next-best use of the funding

In the private sector, the benefits foregone from the next-best use of funding can be estimated from capital market returns. However, in the public sector, consideration of the next-best use will depend on which role government is playing and whether the alternative use of funds would be to reduce (or not increase) taxes or to spend those funds on another program. For public-sector cost-benefit analyses, the risk-free interest rate on government securities, reduced by the expected inflation rate, is often used as the base discount rate, with higher rates being included in a sensitivity analysis.

For more information

U.K. Treasury. *Green Book*. Available online. URL: http://www.hm-treasury.gov.uk/mediastore/otherfiles/96.pdf.

Bob Shead

cybernetics   Norbert Wiener created the word *cybernetics* for the title of his 1948 book to describe "the science of control and communication, in the animal and the machine." The word is derived from the Greek for to "steer" or "govern." Cybernetics is the science of governance.

This more general definition provides a basis for applying the science of information and control to social organizations.

The truths of cybernetics are not conditional on their being derived from some other branch of science. Cybernetics has its own foundations. It started off as being closely associated with physics, but it depends in no essential way on the laws of physics or on the properties of matter. However, its laws are mathematically based.

Cybernetics is about the way machines, animals, and social systems can behave. It is not limited to the study of explaining the function or behavior of any particular machine, animal, or social system, but seeks to explain all possible types.

Cybernetics provides design criteria for building self-regulating machines, biological structures, and social organizations. The ability of any of these types of systems to be self-regulating and sustainable depends upon their possessing operating properties discovered by the pioneers of information and control science. The integrity of cybernetics laws is confirmed by the structure of living things that have evolved from the survival of the fittest.

The success and survival of social organizations is likewise dependent upon their possessing an information-and-control system that best follows cybernetic laws. There are three basic laws of requisite variety that need to be considered for firms, government departments, and nonprofit organizations.

The mathematician John von Neumann showed that errors in decision making using unreliable components could be reduced as much as desired by utilizing a requisite variety of decision makers. Another mathematician, Shannon, showed that errors in communication could be reduced as much as desired with a requisite number of information channels. These results are intuitively consistent with the idea of cross-checking. A medical researcher, W. R. Ashby, explained that control of many variables is not possible without a requisite variety of control agents. This is intuitively consistent with the need for opposing teams in body-contact sports to each possess the same number of players. A corollary of the law of requisite variety of control agents is the impossibility of directly amplifying regulation to control numerous variables. To extend regulation, an indirect approach of introducing supplementary regulators is required.

These insights have profound implications for public administration and public policy, especially as the complexity of society increases. The failure of centralized systems of socialism can be explained in terms of the lack of a requisite variety of decision makers, communication channels, and control agents. Privatization introduces greater variety, but corporations, like government departments, are commonly organized as a centralized command-and-control system that limits requisite variety. The growing complexity of society is increasing the number of variables that need to be controlled.

Cybernetics laws indicate that as the complexity of society increases, new organizational forms will emerge to allow private and public organizations to introduce supplementary controllers of the variables that they need to regulate. The trend is evident from the emergence in the new technology industries of network governance that expands the variety of decision makers, communication channels, and control agents.

For more information

Ashby, W. R. *An Introduction to Cybernetics.* London: Methuen, 1968.

Turnbull, S. "Stakeholder Governance: A Cybernetic and Property Rights Analysis." In *Corporate Governance: The History of Management Thought,* edited by R. I. Tricker, 401–413. London: Ashgate Publishing, 2000. Available online. URL: http://cog.kent.edu/lib/turnbull6/turnbull6.html.

———. *A New Way to Govern.* London: The New Economics Foundation, 2002.

Shann Turnbull

D

Dahl, Robert (1915–) *political scientist*
Robert Dahl is an American political scientist who was born in Inwood, Iowa. After serving in the army, he entered Yale University in 1946, where he graduated, obtained his Ph.D., and became one of the most outstanding political scientists in the world. After retiring, he also taught at Yale as a Sterling professor of political science emeritus, focusing on the concept of democracy, its value, its dynamics, and its challenges.

Best known for his studies in democratic theory, Dahl has also analyzed the role citizenship plays in avoiding tyranny, war, torture, or other forms of social control. However, his most important contribution is the concept of polyarchy, which he completes with other interesting ideas such as: an excellent review of democracy theories, the goals and essential attributes of an ideal democracy, the political institutions that really matter to democracy nowadays, and the underlying conditions that support today's democracy.

The concept of polyarchy (a word that Hegel had already used and that, in Greek, means "rule by the many") is widely developed for the first time in Dahl's book *A Preface of Democratic Theory* (1957). In that book, he explains that there are two requirements for democracy to be optimized: political equality and popular sovereignty. These two conditions are further explained in another of his books, *Polyarchy: Participation and Opposition* (1971). There he links political equality to public debate (or political competition) and popular sovereignty to effective participation. And using those two new concepts, he says that, given a limited amount of ideal democracy, it is possible to evaluate how a political system really works. He, therefore, establishes that the closer the analyzed political system is to the ideal one, the better. The political system that performs the best, considering political equality and sovereignty, is called a polyarchy. In this sense, for Dahl, the U.S. system is not a democracy. It is a polyarchy.

There are three other important issues in Dahl's works: fragmentation, consensus, and political activity. For Dahl, fragmentation can lead to improved conditions for the strongest minorities. On the other hand, democratic institutions must answer citizens' requests, and in doing so they have to guarantee that they are able to solve those demands while obtaining the needed consensus to govern legitimately. Finally, in order to keep the rulers accountable for their actions and to build consensus, the civil society must play an active political role.

In Robert Dahl's latest book, *On Democracy* (1998), he goes through the history of democracy and studies the relationships between the economic and social performance of different countries and their democratic status. For example, Dahl shows that India, which is a socially fragmented country, has a firm democracy because its political institutions have fostered consensus and have been accountable for their actions.

The pioneering work of Dahl sets an analytical framework that takes political and social institutions into account. That is new and important because it means that society matters.

For more information

Dahl, R. *A Preface to Economic Democracy.* Berkeley: University of California Press, 1957.

———. *Polyarchy: Participation and Opposition.* New Haven, Conn.: Yale University Press, 1971.

———. *On Democracy.* New Haven, Conn.: Yale University Press, 1998.

Mila Gascó and Joan Oriol Prats

delegation doctrine   The delegation doctrine pertains to allocations of legislative authority to administrative agencies. It is rooted in Anglo-American political philosophy and constitutional tradition. Ironically, although American courts have interpreted the doctrine to legitimate such allocations, it is typically referred to as the nondelegation doctrine.

John Locke, in Chapter 11 of his *Second Treatise of Government*, argued that "transfer" of legislative power ran counter to the social contract: "For [legislative power] being but a delegated Power from the People, they, who have it, cannot pass it over to others." Locke's view to the contrary notwithstanding, as law professor Kenneth Culp Davis wrote in 1975: " . . . the non-

delegation doctrine to which the Supreme Court has in the past often paid lip service is without practical force."

Practical governmental realities have trumped Lockean logic. As early as 1813 the Supreme Court opined: "[W]e can see no sufficient reason, why the legislature should not exercise its discretion [to delegate authority to the president], either expressly or conditionally, as their judgment should direct" (*The Brig Aurora,* 7 Cranch 382.) In 1825, Chief Justice John Marshall unequivocally supported the delegation of legislative power. In *Wayman v. Southard,* 10 Wheaton 1, Marshall observed: "Congress may certainly delegate to others, powers which the legislature may rightfully exercise itself." And he specified a line distinguishing legitimate from illegitimate delegations: " . . . those important subjects, which must be entirely regulated by the legislature itself, [are different] from those . . . in which a general provision may be made, and power given to those who are to act under such general provisions to fill up the details."

The devil is in the details. Throughout the latter half of the 18th and into the first third of the 20th centuries, as the United States became an urban, industrialized society, courts struggled with what statutory standards, if any, should accompany legislative delegations of authority to administrative agencies. This question has been addressed in terms of separation-of-powers doctrine. The only two cases in which the Supreme Court voided legislative delegations of authority—*Panama Refining Co. v. Ryan,* 293 U.S. 388 (1935), and *A. L. A. Schechter Poultry Corp. v. United States,* 295 U.S. 495, 530 (1935)—turned on how delegation in the absence of legislative standards "is delegation running riot . . ." (Justice Benjamin Cardozo concurring in *Schechter*).

Courts were responding to the late-19th-century experiments by states that pioneered the modern pattern of economic regulation. Seeking to govern railroad rates, legislatures created boards or commissions to which they delegated authority to exercise the functions of all three branches of government. Congress created the Interstate Commerce Commission in 1887 to regulate the rates and practices of railroads with respect to interstate commerce "in the public interest."

The contemporary judicial understanding of delegation was articulated by the Supreme Court in *Mistretta v. United States,* 488 U.S. 361 (1989): "[O]ur jurisprudence has been driven by a practical understanding that in our increasingly complex society, replete with ever changing and more technical problems, Congress simply cannot do its job absent an ability to delegate power under broad general directives."

Not everyone agrees with this formulation. Some scholars contend the post–New Deal formulation advanced "the decline of Congress, the decline of independence among regulatory agencies, the general decline of law as an instrument of control. . . ." And on the Supreme Court, Justice Thomas recently suggested: "On a future day . . . I would be willing to address the question whether our delegation jurisprudence has strayed too far from our Founders' understanding of separation of powers" (Concurring in *Whitman v. American Trucking Associations, Inc.,* 99-1257 [2001]).

For more information

Cahill, Lisa A., and J. Russell Jackson. "Nondelegation after *Mistretta:* Phoenix on Phaethon?" *William and Mary Law Review* 31 (1990): 1047.

Davis, Kenneth Culp. "A New Approach to Delegation." *University of Chicago Law Review* 36 (1969): 713.

Lowi, Theodore. *The End of Liberalism: The Second Republic of the United States,* 2d ed. New York: Norton, 1979.

Schoenbrod, David. *Power with Responsibility: How Congress Abuses People through Delegation.* New Haven, Conn.: Yale University Press, 1993.

James C. Foster

Dennis v. United States 341 U.S. 494 (1951)

Dennis v. United States is a First Amendment case in which the Supreme Court upheld the conviction of suspected communists for conspiring to advocate the violent overthrow of the U.S. government.

During the Second World War, Congress responded to the fears of an international communist threat by enacting the Smith Act in 1940. The most important case that arose under the Smith Act was *Dennis v. United States,* 341 U.S. 494 (1951). In *Dennis,* the defendants were convicted under the Smith Act for conspiring to advocate the overthrow of the government of the United States by force and violence, and of conspiring to organize the U.S. Communist Party. A majority of the Supreme Court upheld the convictions.

At issue in *Dennis* was whether the First Amendment of the Constitution protects radical political speech. The First Amendment states that "Congress shall make no law . . . abridging the freedom of speech or of the press." If Congress passes a law that restricts speech, and if the law is challenged, then a federal court has the power to determine whether the law is constitutional under the First Amendment.

Prior to *Dennis v. United States,* the Supreme Court decided that Congress could pass laws that restrict speech, provided that certain circumstances were present. In *Schenck v. United States,* 249 U.S. 47 (1919), Justice Holmes articulated the "clear and present danger" test. Under this test, speech could be restricted by Congress if the speech created a "clear and present danger" that the illegal act would come about. Speech could not be restricted, however, if there existed a remote likelihood of danger. For example, a false cry of "Fire!" in a crowded theater was not constitutionally protected speech because it would cause mayhem and endanger the public. Justice Holmes used the example of falsely crying "Fire!" in a theater to demonstrate his claim that not all speech was constitutionally protected.

In *Dennis v. United States,* the Supreme Court applied the "clear and present danger" test in such a way that provided very little First Amendment protection to political speech. The Court, in an opinion by Justice Vinson, held that the defendants' conspiracy to organize the Communist Party and to teach and advocate the overthrow of the U.S. government constituted a "clear and present danger." The justices stated that the evil being advocated by the defendants (i.e., the violent overthrow of the government) was so great that their speech could be restricted, even though the likelihood of an overthrow actually occurring was remote. For this reason, a majority of the justices concluded that the defendants were constitutionally convicted for violating the Smith Act.

Two justices dissented from the Supreme Court's opinion. Justice Black argued that the First Amendment had been "watered down" to the point that it was simply an admonition to Congress rather than a strict constitutional requirement. The other dissenter, Justice Douglas, argued that the "clear and present danger" test had been misapplied by the Court majority. Justice Douglas believed that Congress could restrict speech only if the danger was so imminent that there was "no time to avoid the evil that the speech" threatened.

Dennis v. United States is generally viewed as a case that greatly narrowed the scope of the First Amendment protections of radical political speech. Some commentators suggest that in times of war (and during the communist scare), the Supreme Court was less protective of political speech. It is in these times, however, that the greatest protection for subversive advocacy is required, because such speech would always seem threatening to the national welfare. The Supreme Court has moved away from its holding in *Dennis v. United States* and today provides far greater protection for political speech.

For more information

Bollinger, Lee C. *The Tolerant Society: Freedom of Speech and Extremist Speech in America.* New York: Oxford University Press, 1986.

Shapiro, Martin M. *Freedom of Speech: The Supreme Court and Judicial Review.* Englewood Cliffs, N.J.: Prentice Hall, 1966.

Stone, Geoffrey R., et al. *The First Amendment.* New York: Aspen Law & Business, 1999.

Yasmin A. Dawood

de novo hearing   The term *de novo* is used, in the context of administrative law, in the phrase "trial de novo," which refers to a hearing, conducted in a court of law, for the purpose of appealing an unsatisfactory determination in an administrative hearing. To allow consideration of the law and facts of the case without bias related to the previous disposition of the matter, the trial de novo court is generally instructed to disregard the record and outcome of the hearing. Since the court must then, in effect, treat the matter as if no administrative hearing had been conducted, it is appropriate to use the Latin phrase *de novo,* meaning "afresh," or "as if for the first time," to describe the perspective from which the court of law must examine the case.

A trial de novo is necessary when an administrative agency's hearing reaches an incorrect conclusion because of misunderstanding or misapplication of law, acting beyond the scope of its authority, failing to follow required procedures, or reaching a conclusion unsupported by the evidence presented in the case.

Except for factual material that can be verified only by consulting the record of the administrative hearing, the court in a trial de novo examines every issue of law and fact as if that prior hearing had never been conducted. The reviewing court's independent interpretation of the issues is crucial to avoiding reenactment of the prior hearing's errors.

For a majority of federal agencies, decisions of administrative hearings are subject to de novo review by U.S. district courts. However, a small number of agencies have statutory authority to conduct an in-house, appellate-level administrative hearing. In these agencies, the initial hearing before an administrative law judge or hearing examiner cannot be appealed to the court, but only to the higher-level administrative tribunal. However, U.S. district courts have jurisdiction over appeals from these in-house, appellate-level decisions.

For more information

Code of Federal Regulations, Title 20, sec. 655.11, 2001 ed.

Title 5 U.S. Code, Part I, chaps. 5 and 7.

West's *Encyclopedia of American Law,* 1998 ed., s.v. "de novo."

Beth Simon Swartz

Department of Agriculture The United States Department of Agriculture (USDA) is a department in the executive branch that aids and supports the agricultural segment of America. Established on 15 May 1862, it was commissioned to "acquire and to diffuse among the people of the United States useful information on subjects connected with agriculture in the most general and comprehensive sense of the word." More specifically, the department was to conduct experiments, improve seeds and plants, collect pertinent data and statistics, and publish an annual report and other reports that could help improve agriculture.

The bill directed that a commissioner (appointed by the president) rather than a secretary with cabinet status was to head the department. Isaac Newton was sworn in as the first commissioner of agriculture on 1 July 1862. Under his guidance and until the late 19th century, the department's focus was on helping farmers improve their productivity. The education and research concentration began to change in the 1880s as the department started to become more regulatory.

In light of public hostility and concern over manufactured products like oleomargarine, the USDA began to examine food processors. In response, it created the Division of Chemistry,

headed by Harvey W. Wiley, with the mandate to examine adulterated foods. It gained even more regulatory power as Americans battled livestock diseases, Texas fever, and hog cholera. The Bureau of Animal Industry was established in 1884 to prevent the importation of diseased livestock and determine the causes. In the 1890s, its mission continued to grow as Congress ordered the department to inspect livestock and meat that were shipped interstate. The building and improvement of rural roads also became a concern of the USDA during this period, as did institution of a policy to establish and expand foreign markets.

As the department increased its scope and responsibilities, agricultural concerns wanted the USDA elevated to cabinet status to increase their voice in government. On 9 February 1889, President Grover Cleveland signed such legislation and appointed Norman J. Colman as the first secretary of agriculture. He was quickly replaced by the new president Benjamin Harrison with Jeremiah McLain Rusk on March 6.

One of the most important secretaries of agriculture was James "Tama Jim" Wilson, appointed in 1897. Under his 16-year administration, the USDA extended its scientific and regulatory responsibilities. He was responsible for establishing several new bureaus, including the Bureau of Plant Industry, the Bureau of Forestry, and the Bureau of Entomology. The most important of these new bureaus might have been the Bureau of Chemistry (1901), which acquired the responsibility of examining manufactured or processed foods to see whether they contained harmful chemicals and whether the contents of the food were what manufacturers claimed them to be. In 1914, the Smith-Lever Act created an official extension service—operated jointly by the USDA, agricultural colleges, and local government—to make farmers aware of the most useful and scientific ways of improving their operations.

Yet, the federal government again changed the mission of the USDA when President

Franklin Roosevelt took office on 4 March 1933. The department began to create programs and policies to give farmers financial assistance in the wake of the Great Depression. Henry A. Wallace was appointed as secretary. Roosevelt tried to address the problem of low prices and surplus production. The Agricultural Adjustment Administration (AAA) was created on 12 May 1933 to pay farmers to reduce production of certain products and keep certain lands idle. Although it was later declared unconstitutional, it helped farmers survive during the height of the depression. During the 1930s, other programs were set up to help farmers economically, including the Soil Conservation and Domestic Allotment Act, Resettlement Administration, Farm Security Administration, Soil Conservation Service, Federal Crop Insurance Corporation, and a second AAA program.

In the post–World War II years, the USDA continued to look for solutions for overproduction and low prices and expanded its research. Public Law 480, known as the Food for Peace Program, in 1954 commissioned the USDA to ship food to foreign nations. By 1970, the department had fed over 47 million children across the world. It also helped developing nations to improve their agriculture, nutrition, health, and standard of living. The department also has sought to improve the health and the standard of living of American consumers through the actions of the Food and Nutrition Service (FNS). The USDA has also become increasingly concerned with the environment. All of this has led critics to charge that the USDA has divided loyalties and is no longer as concerned with helping small farmers. Rather, large farmers and consumers seem to be the beneficiaries of their programs. While the USDA receives some criticism, it has been of untold benefit to American farmers.

For more information

Hurt, R. Douglas. *The Department of Agriculture*. New York: Chelsea House Publishers, 1989.

Rasmussen, Wayne D., and Gladys L. Baker. *The Department of Agriculture*. New York: Praeger, 1972.

Terrell, John Upton. *The United States Department of Agriculture: A Story of Food, Farms and Forests*. New York: Duell, Sloan and Pearce, 1966.

T. Jason Soderstrum

Department of Commerce   The Department of Commerce (DOC) became a federal executive department in 1913.

Currently, its goals of economic growth, job creation, improved standard of living, and maintenance of a competitive edge in the world marketplace remain very similar to those at its inception nearly 90 years ago. However, to achieve maximum productivity while maintaining a serious effort to reach those goals, the DOC has inevitably grown, and it is constantly evolving to accommodate the changing needs of the general population and to efficiently use its own highly skilled and educated staff and the information technology that allows these specialists to do their best work. Of necessity, DOC has developed a complex infrastructure, with the secretary of commerce at the helm, and is ultimately responsible for managing, inspiring, and coordinating the efforts of approximately 30,000 employees distributed among 11 operating units.

The International Trade Administration, one of DOC's 11 operating units, promotes U.S. exports of manufactured goods and nonagricultural commodities and services, and it participates in formulating and implementing U.S. foreign trade and economic policies. The International Trade Administration comprises four divisions. The main function of one unit is investigation of dumping complaints to determine whether foreign goods are being sold in the United States at less than fair value. The second division provides U.S. businesses with industry-specific analysis and advice on trade and investment issues. The third unit maintains commercial offices around the world to improve

U.S. businesses' access to foreign markets and to ensure compliance with the United States's more than 200 trade agreements. The fourth and final division operates a network of 100 U.S. and 140 worldwide export assistance centers. These offices are staffed with specialists who help businesses to enter promising new markets with currently popular and competitively priced goods, and help U.S. businesses secure financing for international trade ventures.

The Bureau of Export Administration is responsible for encouraging and regulating the growth of U.S. exports while implementing and enforcing federal statutes aimed at halting proliferation of weapons of mass destruction. This operating unit is also the U.S. licensing agency for dual-use commodities, enforcing rules and regulations that affect them.

The Economics and Statistics Administration produces, analyzes, and disseminates important economic indicators via a round-the-clock dial-up bulletin board, monthly compact discs, and the Internet (at www.stat-usa.gov). This unit of DOC is also responsible for collecting census data.

The National Oceanic and Atmospheric Administration (NOAA) is the administrative agency that oversees five divisions, including some fairly familiar agencies such as the National Weather Service, Office of Oceanic and Atmospheric Research, and the National Marine Fisheries Service. NOAA also includes two little known, but vitally important, agencies. The first is the National Environmental Satellite, Data and Information Service, which operates U.S. environmental satellites and manages the world's largest atmospheric, geophysical, and oceanographic database, a resource of vital national security information. The second is the National Ocean Service, the agency that operates U.S. underwater national parks and advocates protection of wetlands, water quality, beaches, and wildlife. It also restores marine areas harmed by pollution and provides scientific expertise during major oil spills and the cleanup operations that follow.

The Technology Administration, the DOC's youngest agency, was created in 1988 to work with private-sector businesses to foster economic growth by developing and applying new technology. This agency also funds high-risk research that may benefit the U.S. economy and employs scientists to engage in research that will result in development of advanced technologies. In an effort to stimulate improvements to U.S. technological competitiveness, this agency awards the Malcolm Baldrige National Quality Award and the National Medal of Technology. The Technology Administration also promotes development of international agreements to increase U.S. access to foreign science and technology.

The National Technical Information Service collects, maintains, and disseminates information about U.S. government research conducted by and for the U.S. government, as well as for additional public and private sources worldwide. Most important in the 21st century is this agency's operation of an online information-dissemination system, FedWorld, which offers the broadest possible access to government information.

The National Telecommunications and Information Administration advises the president, Congress, and regulatory agencies on diverse technical and policy questions pertaining to regulation of the telecommunications industry. This agency also offers matching grants to nonprofit organizations, for innovative, practical technology projects within the United States, and to businesses involved in construction or improvement of noncommercial public telecommunications facilities.

The Economic Development Administration provides grants to economically distressed communities to generate new employment, help retain existing jobs, and stimulate industrial and commercial growth; operates a program that helps to fund construction of public works; and awards grants for research on emerging economic development issues.

The Minority Business Development Agency promotes growth and competitiveness of the nation's minority-owned businesses by providing management and technical assistance, financing, and improved access to international markets.

The Office of Business Liaison serves as the primary point of contact between the Commerce Department and the business community.

The Patent and Trademark Office, created in 1790, is the oldest operating unit of the DOC. Since its inception, this agency has continually collected applied technical information, and it now has the world's largest collection of this material. By providing patent protection, this office has encouraged inventors to develop their ideas. Trademark protection has stimulated the economy by protecting businesses' individuality and identity. The Patent and Trademark Office examines applications for patents, grants patents on inventions, publishes and disseminates patent information, maintains files of U.S. and foreign patents for public use, and supplies copies of patents and official records to the public. It performs similar functions for trademarks.

For more information

Department of Commerce. http://www.usdoc.gov/pubinfo/intro.html.

Microsoft Encarta Encyclopedia, 2000 ed., s.v. "Department of Commerce."

Beth Simon Swartz

Department of Defense   The Department of Defense is the largest department in the federal executive branch, and its primary responsibility is to ensure the security of the United States. Established under the National Security Act of 1947, it was given its present name under the amended legislation of 1949. The new department's purpose was to improve coordination of the armed services.

According to Article II, Section 2, of the Constitution, the president was the "Commander-in-Chief of the Army and Navy." For the first 150 years of this nation's history, the Department of Defense's activities were served by two different departments, the War Department and the Department of the Navy. The War Department was created in 1789 to assist the president in his military decisions. The secretary of war was mainly concerned with land operations of the army. Nine years later, due to pirates on the Barbary Coast making naval operations more important, the Department of the Navy was formed. The two departments only coordinated their activities on operations that affected both services. The president was forced to settle any dispute that arose between the two. Because the army and navy's missions seldom overlapped, the president's job of coordinating the two was not time consuming.

Yet by World War I, this lack of coordination began to result in serious waste of resources, money, and time. The rising cost of military spending, the increasing size of each service, national security concerns, and the success of combined army-navy-air force operations in World War II highlighted the need for a single cabinet department.

On 17 September 1947, James Vincent Forrestal was sworn in as the first secretary of defense. This new department was originally called the National Military Establishment (NME). Its purpose was to be "a comprehensive program for the future security of the United States."

This notion of "national security" led to a new level of coordination between civilian and military officials. Not only did the secretary of defense have to deal with his own department, but three newly created agencies as well—the NATIONAL SECURITY COUNCIL (NSC), the CENTRAL INTELLIGENCE AGENCY (CIA), and the National Security Resources Board (NSRB). The act also gave statutory recognition to the JOINT CHIEFS OF STAFF (JCS) within the department, who were to advise the secretary of defense, the president, and the NSC. The JCS was also to coordinate the three services, preparing strategic plans, assessing logistic responsibilities, and establishing unified commands in strategic areas.

While one of the goals of establishing the Department of Defense was to end interservice squabbling and overlap, the result has not been perfect, and the department has undergone a number of organizational changes. The department maintained military readiness during the cold war and afterward, and it has coordinated the services in a number of conflicts and near-conflicts, including Berlin, Korea, Cuba, Vietnam, the Persian Gulf, and Afghanistan.

The DOD is the largest executive branch department, with a budget of over $330 billion in 2002, and is responsible for the management and direction of nuclear weapons, weapons effects, and weapons testing. In a changing world, the Department of Defense constantly adapts itself to preserve the security of the nation.

For more information

Borklund, C. W. *The Department of Defense.* New York: Frederick A. Praeger, 1969.

Cohen, Andrew, and Beth Heinsohn. *Department of Defense.* New York: Chelsea House Publishers, 1990.

Cole, Alice C., et al., eds. *The Department of Defense: Documents on the Establishment and Organization 1944–1978.* Washington, D.C.: Office of the Secretary of Defense Historical Office, 1978.

T. Jason Soderstrum

Department of Education   The U.S. Department of Education is a cabinet-level department of the federal executive branch. As of January 2002, the department employed 4,900 people in its central and 10 regional offices. The Department of Education is divided between its operational divisions (e.g., Office of General Counsel and Office of Legislation and Congressional Affairs) and its program areas (e.g., Office of Elementary and Secondary Education and Office for Civil Rights). The FY2001 budget for the Department of Education was approximately $42 billion (out of the federal government's $1.9 trillion budget).

The department was created in 1980, but its history dates back to 1867, when Congress established the non-cabinet-level Department of Education. The purpose of the department at that time was to collect and disseminate information and statistics on the condition of education and to increase the effectiveness of schools. The first commissioner, Henry Barnard, quickly ran into trouble with Congress. The department was then turned into the Office (and then the Bureau) of Education and placed within the Department of the Interior, where it stayed until 1939. Then, the Bureau of Education was moved to the newly established Federal Security Agency (FSA). FSA became the Department of Health, Education, and Welfare (HEW) in 1953, and the Office of Education stayed at HEW until the Department of Education was created by Congress in 1979 (Department of Education Organization Act, PL 96-88) and began operations 4 May 1980.

The department exists today to ensure equal access to educational opportunities for individuals, to improve the quality of education, and to support research on education. It accomplishes these goals through dozens of policies and programs. The largest of these programs administers federal grants: Title 1 grants to local school systems, special education grants to states, and Pell grants for lower-income families to assist students in attending college or university. These three programs account for over one-half of the Department of Education's budget. The department also oversees the federal student-loan programs that in FY2001 amounted to about $47 billion. Title 1 refers to the Title 1 of the Elementary and Secondary Education Act of 1965 (ESEA, reauthorized in 1994 and 2002). This program provides financial assistance to school systems in high-poverty areas. Special education grants are provided to states to assist them in providing educational services to students with disabilities. Pell grants are awarded to students from lower-income families who are entering or continuing in college. Federal students loans are also available for undergraduate, graduate, and professional-school students.

The department faces many political and management challenges. Among these are long-standing tensions between supporters of public education (for example, the National Education Association) and those who favor school-choice reforms such as charter schools and vouchers. Additionally, the management of the federal student-aid programs has come under criticism for waste and fraud. Despite calls for reform (e.g., *A Nation at Risk* and *America 2000: An Education Strategy*) and years of increased funding and research, America's students still perform at or below average when compared with students from other countries.

Between managing its daily operations, handling the pressures of a politically tense environment, and implementing recent reauthorization of the ESEA, the Department of Education will continue to be a focus of attention and an active organization.

For more information

America 2000: An Education Strategy. Washington, D.C.: Department of Education, Government Printing Office, 1991.

A Nation at Risk. Washington, D.C.: Department of Education, Government Printing Office, 1983.

Radin, Beryl A., and Willis D. Hawley. *The Politics of Federal Reorganization: Creating the Department of Education.* Elmsford, N.Y.: Pergamon Press, 1987.

U.S. Department of Education. http://www.ed.gov.

Jason Palmer

Department of Energy The Department of Energy (DOE) has its roots in the Manhattan Project of World War II, which created the first atomic bomb. It was formed originally as the Atomic Energy Commission (AEC) in 1947, created by President Truman under the Atomic Energy Act of 1946, and given responsibility for all atomic energy activities in the United States. This included development of plutonium and uranium for weapons. President Eisenhower signed the Atomic Energy Act of 1954 establish-ing a civilian nuclear power program, with the AEC in charge. President Ford abolished the AEC in 1974 under the Energy Reorganization Act, which led eventually in 1977 to the Department of Energy as a cabinet-level department. This period also saw the split between the Department of Energy and the Nuclear Regulatory Commission, intended to separate issues of promoting nuclear power and ensuring safety of reactors.

The DOE mission today is "to foster a secure and reliable energy system that is environmentally and economically sustainable, to be a responsible steward of the Nation's nuclear weapons, to clean up our own facilities and to support continued United States leadership in science and technology." To meet this mission, the DOE forms partnerships with a wide range of organizations with goals of:

- Promoting secure, competitive, and environmentally responsible sources of energy that meet the needs of the public

- Supporting national security, promoting international nuclear safety, and reducing the risk from weapons of mass destruction in the United States and elsewhere

- Supporting improved environmental quality by cleaning up the waste from nuclear weapons and civilian nuclear research and development programs, minimizing future waste generation from nuclear activities, safely managing nuclear materials, and permanently disposing of the nation's radioactive wastes

- Creating advancements in science and technology that are essential for the DOE mission and for maintaining the nation's science base

- Carrying out information collection, analysis, and research on energy data such as availability, use, and prices to help policy makers ensure long-term energy supply

- Increasing the efficiency and productivity of energy supplies, while reducing environmental impacts from production of energy

The DOE carries out much of its mission through a network of national laboratories. Some of these (such as Oak Ridge, Brookhaven, Argonne, and Lawrence Livermore) have very broad programs of research and development on energy supplies, the environment, and health protection. Others (such as the Environmental Measurements Lab in New York) have more specialized tasks that support specific activities within the DOE, such as monitoring for nuclear fallout. The Office of the General Counsel is responsible for DOE's work in policy and law related to energy policy and environmental protection. The science, engineering, and policy sides of the DOE, including its Office of the Secretary of Energy, work closely to help the nation identify effective energy policies that are consistent with the goal of environmental protection, and to clean up past environmental damage from energy and weapons programs.

For more information

Tuggle, Catherine, and Gary Weir. *The Department of Energy (Know Your Government)*. Broomall, Pa.: Chelsea House Publishers, 1989.

Douglas Crawford-Brown

Department of Health and Human Services

The Department of Health and Human Services is an executive agency managed by the secretary of health and human services, a member of the president's cabinet. In addition to acting as the chief operating officer of the Department of Health and Human Services (HHS), the secretary is obligated to inform and advise the president on the federal government's programs related to health and welfare.

HHS is the successor to the Department of Health, Education and Welfare (HEW), which Congress created in 1953. In 1979, Congress created a separate Department of Education and renamed the former HEW as the Department of Health and Human Services. Today, HHS has two main branches: the Division for Human Services and the Public Health Service.

The Division for Human Services includes three operational divisions: the Administration on Aging, the Administration for Children and Families, and the Centers for Medicare and Medicaid Services.

Congress created the Administration on Aging (Older Americans Act, 42 U.S.C.A. §§3001 et seq.) to provide services and programs that would enable older citizens to remain in their own homes and communities, despite inconveniences and infirmities related to their age. HHS allocates funds to state governments for the purpose of promoting the best possible quality of life for older Americans. States must use these funds to establish and operate state and local programs providing group meals, social events, and legal and protective services for older citizens.

The Centers for medicaid and medicare Services administer the MEDICAID AND MEDICARE health care programs, which benefit approximately 25 percent of the U.S. population. Medicare provides health insurance for more than 40 million elderly and disabled Americans. Medicaid, funded and administered jointly by the federal and state governments, provides health care for approximately 20 million children and covers the cost of nursing-home care for more than 10 million low-income elderly. Additionally, the Centers for Medicare and Medicaid Services oversee the Children's Health Insurance Program, through which state-approved insurance plans issue health-insurance policies to more than 2 million children throughout the United States.

The Administration for Children and Families (ACF) oversees and provides funding for more than 60 programs designed to promote the economic and social well-being of families, children, individuals, and communities. One of these programs, commonly known as "welfare," and officially called TEMPORARY ASSISTANCE TO NEEDY FAMILIES, provides short-term financial subsidies to ensure the well-being of children and families. ACF also provides funds for

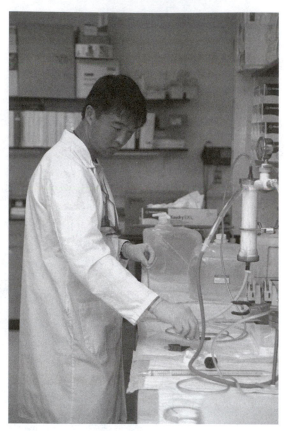

A biologist performs tests on water samples in the Parasitic Diseases Laboratory at the Centers for Disease Control and Prevention, Atlanta, Georgia. (GAVIN AVERILL/GETTY IMAGES)

programs that subsidize child-care costs for low-income families, supports state-operated foster-care systems, and assists state programs that place abandoned and foster children in adoptive homes. Additionally, ACF administers the vitally important National Child Support Enforcement System. By locating parents who have avoided their obligations to pay child support, and by then mandating that these parents pay a portion of children's living expenses, this system has significantly reduced the number of single-parent families receiving funds from the Temporary Assistance to Needy Families program.

ACF also oversees and funds Project Head Start, a well-established and well-regarded early-intervention program that is concerned not only with teaching educationally disadvantaged preschool-age children, but also with maintaining the health of the children and their families. Head Start serves meals to each child attending the program and provides any additional social services necessary to ensure each child's educational and personal success. ACF also encourages the private and voluntary sectors to establish and maintain youth programs such as Boys' and Girls' Clubs.

To enable and encourage developmentally disadvantaged individuals to achieve their full potential, ACF also administers programs that provide these individuals with the best possible education as well as all necessary, complementary services, such as physical, speech, and occupational therapy. ACF also manages programs that provide social and financial assistance for Native Americans.

The Public Health Service—the second branch of HHS—includes eight operational divisions: Agency for Healthcare Research and Quality, Centers for Disease Control and Prevention, Food and Drug Administration, Health Resources and Services Administration, Indian Health Service, National Institutes of Health, Public Health Service Commissioned Corps, and Substance Abuse and Mental Health Services Administration.

The Agency for Healthcare Research and Quality supports research designed to: improve the quality of, reduce the cost of, and broaden access to essential medical services; improve patient safety; and address medical errors. The statistical data collected by this agency provide health-care policy makers with the information they need to plan for improvements in the quality of health-care services.

The Centers for Disease Control and Prevention (CDC) are responsible for administering national programs to prevent and control communicable and vector-borne diseases, reduce environmental pollutants that cause health problems, and improve workplace safety. CDC is also responsible for conducting epidemiological research, directing quarantine activities, consulting internationally on the topic of controlling preventable diseases, and collecting and maintaining national health statistics.

The FOOD AND DRUG ADMINISTRATION (FDA), established in 1906, has responsibility for protecting public health by ensuring that foods are safe and pure, food additives and colorings are not harmful, cosmetics are harmless, other chemical substances such as pesticides and household cleaners are not injurious to health, and pharmaceutical products and medical devices are safe and efficacious. The FDA uses the prior-evidence-of-safety test to determine whether a substance presents a hazard. For example, if a manufacturer asks FDA to test a new cosmetic, the researcher first uses the item on the skin of test animals. If the researcher performs the tests repeatedly without inducing adverse reaction in the test animals, the FDA may allow human volunteers to test the substance. After testing a substance, FDA allows marketing only if the material meets the FDA standards of safety.

The Health Resources and Services Administration creates partnerships with, and then provides funding for, state and community organizations that provide essential health services for people who would otherwise be without health care due to poverty, uninsured status, or residence in an area lacking access to health-care providers. This agency funds more than 3,000 health centers that provide comprehensive health care, including prenatal care and supportive treatment for HIV, to approximately 9 million patients annually.

By maintaining facilities and staffing at 37 hospitals, 60 health centers, and 46 health stations, the Indian Health Service provides health care for approximately 1.5 million Native Americans, including those who live in urban areas as well as those who live on Indian reservations throughout the United States.

The National Institutes of Health (NIH) conduct and support biomedical research focused on discovering causes and cures, as well as methods of preventing diseases. This agency maintains its own laboratories and awards grants and contracts to universities and other private research facilities. NIH also maintains internationally renowned research centers focused on: cancer; heart, lung, and blood diseases; allergy and infectious diseases; and human genome research.

The Public Health Service Commissioned Corps (PHSCC) is a uniformed service administered by the surgeon general. This agency's staff includes a variety of health-care professionals, including physicians, surgeons, veterinarians, dieticians, and registered nurses. Corps members are responsible for prevention of disease and injury, identification and correction of environmental health hazards, assurance regarding the safety and efficacy of drugs and medical devices, provision of health services to medically underserved populations, and provision of health expertise in time of war or other national or international emergency.

The Substance Abuse and Mental Health Services Administration collaborates with state substance-abuse agencies to improve the quality and availability of information on prevention of substance abuse, addiction treatment, and accessibility of general mental-health services. This agency also funds a nationwide drug-abuse prevention program conducted by local police departments and directed at elementary and middle-school students.

For more information

U.S. Public Health Service. http://www.usphs.gov/html.

West's Encyclopedia of American Law, Vol. 6. Saint Paul, Minn.: West Publishing Company, 1998.

Beth Simon Swartz

Department of Housing and Urban Development (HUD)   The federal Department of Housing and Urban Development (HUD) is a cabinet-level agency that implements and enforces national housing and community development

policies. In 1965 President LYNDON BAINES JOHNSON authorized HUD's establishment to revive inner-city neighborhoods and develop a response to the urban housing crisis. The new agency centralized and consolidated myriad federal departments that had previously dealt with housing policy.

By 1940 a majority of the U.S. population resided in urban areas. The transformation to an urban nation continued throughout the following decades, but governments and communities were slow to face this trend and the growing problems created by dense settlement. Massive housing shortages as well as decay of infrastructure and residences in the inner cities prompted congressional intervention in shelter issues. The Great Depression generated emergency housing needs that were the impetus for the first federal shelter legislation. In 1937 Congress provided funds for building low-income housing and slum clearance projects. Over the next 25 years Congress expanded community development and redevelopment programs with moderate success. Additional legislation was passed to stabilize private home mortgages and provide assistance to developers who built rental homes for defense workers. When HUD was belatedly established in 1965, its first charge was to dispense funds and administer programs created by these earlier actions.

President John F. Kennedy originated the campaign for HUD's establishment to provide centralized management of housing policy and generate prestige for housing and urban development programs. President Johnson later carried out Kennedy's intention to appoint America's first African-American cabinet member, Robert C. Weaver, as the department's head.

HUD's mission was and is to provide a decent, safe, and sanitary home and suitable living environment for every American. In part HUD acts as a middleman, brokering between political leaders, home builders, and low-income citizens in need of housing assistance. HUD creates opportunities for home ownership for low-income people with subsidies and federally backed mortgages, provides rental assistance, and enforces

affordable housing laws. HUD also provides incentives for cities and developers to build public and private low-income housing. However, HUD is also charged with rejuvenating declining neighborhoods through economic stimulation and the creation of job opportunities, improving transportation facilities and public areas, protecting open space, and generally helping local communities meet their development needs. Finally, HUD provides funds to shelter and care for urban homeless and enforces fair-housing laws. To carry out its mission HUD transfers federally allocated funds to state and local governments as well as to nonprofit organizations.

To implement housing and development policy HUD is currently organized with six program teams, including the Office of Housing, Community Planning and Development, Public and Indian Housing, the Government National Mortgage Association (Ginnie Mae), and Multifamily Housing Assistance Restructuring Office. The heads of these programs report to HUD's secretary, who is appointed by the president and is supported by an undersecretary. The secretary also oversees HUD's 17 support offices, the Office of Federal Housing Enterprise Oversight, the inspector general, and 10 regional offices organized similarly to the national agency.

For more information

Willman, John B. *The Department of Housing and Urban Development*. New York: Fredrick A. Praeger Publishers, 1967.

Jessica L. Hills

Department of Justice   The Department of Justice (DOJ) was formally created by an act of Congress signed by the president on 22 June 1870. This act of Congress created not only an administrative agency but also unified governmental legal administration under the titular control of a single individual, the attorney general of the United States. This newly created office was to be in control of all governmental litigation and was empowered to argue any case in which the government had an interest in any court of the United States.

Since its inception, the Department of Justice has fulfilled several roles in government. It has acted as the primary litigation specialist for the United States, particularly in cases before the Supreme Court. It has become an important cabinet-level adviser to the president through the person of the attorney general. It has become an important component of the executive bureaucracy, and it has operated as the chief law enforcement agency in the United States.

From an office of essentially four officers in 1870, the Department of Justice has grown enormously. It now employs more than 80,000 people. Its original simple divisions have grown to more than 30 divisions, bureaus, and offices. Its budget has ballooned from almost nothing, with most attorneys paid on a part-time or contract basis, to almost $8 billion annually.

The transformation of the Department of Justice from a small office charged simply with litigating in the name of the United States to a major player in the federal bureaucracy mirrors the growth of government more generally. This transformation has its roots in the transition from a national government of limited powers to one that exercises strong positive regulatory functions. As the government has attempted to regulate and control additional aspects of life in the United States, it has been the Department of Justice and its officers who have been charged with enforcing those new laws.

The Department of Justice oversees some of the most recognizable and important components of the American legal bureaucracy. The FEDERAL BUREAU OF INVESTIGATION (FBI) was added to the DOJ in 1924 and remains one of the largest and most powerful of its subunits, operating largely independently as the national investigative service of the United States. The Bureau of Prisons, which operates and oversees the entire federal prison system, has been part of the DOJ since 1930. The Immigration and Naturalization Service (INS), responsible for all immigration and naturalization law enforcement, was transferred from the DEPARTMENT OF THE TREASURY to the DOJ in 1940. The Civil Rights Division of the DOJ created in 1957 is responsible for enforcing the provisions of the 1957, 1960, and 1964 Civil Rights Acts as well as the 1965 Voting Rights Acts. The DRUG ENFORCEMENT ADMINISTRATION was added to the department in 1973 to enforce narcotics and controlled-substances law.

The history of the DOJ is a history of consistent growth over time. The growth has been budgetary but also growth in importance. From a small office of four people, the Department of Justice has become one of the most important political and legal institutions in the government, overseeing some of the largest and most powerful components of the federal bureaucracy.

For more information

Clayton, Cornell. *The Politics of Justice: The Attorney General and the Making of Legal Policy.* Armonk, N.Y.: M. E. Sharpe, 1992.

Huston, Luther A. *The Department of Justice.* New York: Praeger, 1967.

David A. May

Department of Labor The Department of Labor was born when President William Howard Taft signed the Organic Act of the Department of Labor into law on 4 March 1913. The chair of the Department of Labor is appointed by the president and approved by the Senate and is one of the president's cabinet members. The first woman appointed to serve in a presidential cabinet was Frances Perkins, appointed in 1933 by President Franklin Delano Roosevelt as chair of the U.S. Department of Labor.

The Department of Labor (DOL) describes its role: it "fosters and promotes the welfare of the job seekers, wage earners, and retirees of the United States by improving their working conditions, advancing their opportunities for profitable employment, protecting their retirement and health care benefits, helping employers find workers, strengthening free collective bargaining, and tracking changes in employment, prices, and other national economic measurements. In carrying out this mission, the department administers a variety of federal labor laws including those that guarantee workers' rights to safe and healthful working conditions; a minimum hourly wage and overtime pay; freedom from employment discrimination; unemployment insurance; and other income support."

On 5 March 1920, in response to both women's increasing presence in the labor force and as political actors, Congress created the Women's Bureau in the DoL. It was originally established to collect information about women in the labor force and to advocate government action (e.g., protective labor legislation) focusing on the status of women wage earners.

As the United States grew and the role and place of labor and business have changed, the DOL has had to evolve to meet those needs as mandated by legislative and executive decisions. For example, in 1938 the Fair Labor Standards Act established the Wage & Hour Division; in 1965 an executive order established the Office of Federal Contract Compliance; and in 1970 the Occupational Safety and Health Act created the Occupational Safety & Health Administration in the Department of Labor. Further, Congress has rested oversight authority of several acts with the DOL, including the Migrant and Seasonal Agricultural Worker Protection Act of 1983 and the Family and Medical Leave Act of 1993.

For more information

U.S. Department of Labor. http://www.dol.gov.

Linda K. Shafer

Department of the Interior   The Department of the Interior (DOI) is the home of many of the nation's conservation agencies. The department is responsible for the management, protection, and operation of more than 400 million acres of federal land and their resources. It also carries out the U.S. government's trust responsibilities to American Indians and Alaska Natives and coordinates federal policy in many U.S. territories.

The DOI was created in 1849 to administer the nation's lands acquired through the Louisiana Purchase, the Mexican War, and the acquisition of the Oregon Territory. In contrast to the State Department, which was responsible for foreign affairs, the DOI was originally designed to be the "Home" Department. Several departments that were created later, such as Agriculture, Education, and Labor, originally resided in the DOI.

Not all U.S. conservation agencies are located in DOI. The Forest Service and the National Resource Conservation (formerly the Soil Conservation Service) are located in the Department of Agriculture. The Army Corps of Engineers is part of the U.S. Army.

DOI contains nine principal agencies, each with its own mission and purpose. The National Park Service (NPS) manages the 80-million-acre National Park System. The system contains not only national parks, but also national monuments, seashores, recreation areas, lakeshores, urban parks, cultural areas, and military sites.

The U.S. Fish and Wildlife Service (FWS) conserves and protects migratory birds, endangered species, freshwater and anadromous fisheries, and certain marine mammals. It operates the National Wildlife Refuge System which includes more than 500 units encompassing more than 90 million acres.

The Bureau of Land Management (BLM) manages approximately 270 million acres of public land that possess diverse resources, including energy and minerals, timber, livestock forage, fish and wildlife habitat, scenic and recreation resources, wilderness areas, and archaeological and historic sites. BLM also manages an additional 570 million acres of subsurface mineral rights reserved by the federal government and held in trust for public benefit.

The Bureau of Reclamation (BOR) was initially a developer of water projects. It now manages those projects' water, land, and biological

Cars fill a parking lot near Yosemite Falls in Yellowstone National Park, California. Yellowstone is managed by the National Park Service, which is an agency of the Department of the Interior. (DAVID MCNEW/GETTY IMAGES)

and cultural resources. BOR is the nation's largest wholesale supplier of water and the sixth largest electric utility in the West.

The Bureau of Indian Affairs (BIA) administers federal programs for federally recognized Indian tribes. It protects the trust assets of Indian tribes and Alaska Natives. BIA also provides government services for Indian tribes, including law enforcement, social services, education, housing improvements, loan opportunities for Indian businesses, and leasing of land.

The U.S. Geological Survey (USGS) is the federal government's largest earth sciences and civilian mapmaking agency. Each year, USGS publishes about 3,000 reports and maps.

The Minerals Management Service (MMS) accounts for and manages the public's mineral resources. It also manages the Outer Continental Shelf's mineral resources.

The Surface Mining Reclamation and Enforcement (SMRE) division works with states and tribes to ensure lands are reclaimed after mining.

The Office of Insular Affairs (OIA) coordinates federal policy for the territories of American Samoa, Guam, the U.S. Virgin Islands, and the Commonwealth of the Northern Mariana Islands. It provides financial and technical assistance to help these governments attain locally determined economic, social, and political goals.

For more information

U.S. Department of the Interior. http://www.doi.gov.

Robert W. Malmsheimer

Department of the Treasury The Department of the Treasury is a cabinet-level office of the United States responsible for the management of the federal government's finances, including the collection of taxes, regulation of banks, and the development of economic policy. The Treasury Department is one of the United States's two oldest cabinet departments. It was created by an act of Congress in 1789, along with the Department of War (now the Department of Defense). The head of the former department is known as the secretary of the Treasury; Alexander Hamilton served as the first Treasury secretary under President George Washington.

The Treasury Department consists of two parts. There are the department offices, which are primarily responsible for the development of economic policy and for the management of the cabinet agency as a whole, and the bureau offices, which amount to about 98 percent of the Treasury's staff, and carry out the primary enforcement duties of this cabinet agency. There are several bureaus within the Treasury Department. The Bureau of Engraving and Printing (created in 1862) designs and produces U.S. money and currency. The U.S. Mint (created in 1792) designs and manufactures coins. The Bureau of Public Debt (created in 1921) borrows money for the government by selling savings bonds and Treasury bills (T-bills). The Community Development Financial Institution makes credit and money available to help economically distressed communities. The Financial Management Service keeps track of the government's accounts and monies. The Financial Crimes Enforcement Network monitors and tracks domestic and international financial crimes. The Internal Revenue Service (IRS), created in 1862, enforces the federal tax code and collects federal taxes. The Alcohol and Tobacco Tax and Trade Bureau (TTB) regulates and enforces laws covering the use, sale, and consumption of alcohol and tobacco products. And the Offices of Controller of the Currency and Thrift Supervision regulate national and state banks and financial institutions, respectively.

The Treasury Department also used to be the home to the U.S. Customs Service (created in 1789), the Federal Law Enforcement Training Center (created in 1970), and the U.S. Secret Service (created in 1865). The latter is best known for providing protection to the president since 1901 when President McKinley was assassinated. All of these functions were transferred to the new Department of Homeland Security in 2003. Also, in 2003, the Bureau of Alcohol, Tobacco and Firearms (ATF), created as a separate office mainly responsible for enforcing the criminal law regarding these three products, was transferred to the Justice Department, leaving the TTB in the Treasury Department. The Bureau of Immigration, created in 1891, used to be in the Treasury Department, and its job was to operate Ellis Island in New York, which served as a major port of entry for immigrants to the United States.

The main personnel in the Treasury Department include the Secretary of the Treasury, who is the head of the entire cabinet department. That person is appointed by the president, subject to confirmation by the United States Senate. Easily confused with the Treasury secretary, is the treasurer of the United States. The latter office, created in 1777 before the entire department was established, was originally responsible for the collection and management of government funds. Michael Hillegas was the first person to hold this position, with Ivy Baker Priest, the first female treasurer, appointed by President Eisenhower in 1953. For most people, the only way they might recognize the two offices as distinct is when they look at the paper currency—the signature of both the secretary of the treasury and the treasurer of the United States appear on all United States paper money. Another important position is the inspector general, who is responsible for auditing and investigating the Treasury Department.

Throughout its history the Department of Treasury has been very important. Alexander Hamilton issued a series of landmark reports in 1790 charting a path to build the United States into a major financial and manufacturing power. Hamilton also endorsed the creation of the first Bank of the United States in 1791. Creation of the first Bank and, after its charter expired, a second in 1816, raised major constitutional questions regarding whether Congress had the power to create such an institution. President Washington asked Thomas Jefferson and Alexander Hamilton for their opinions on its constitutionality, with the former arguing that its creation was unconstitutional because there was no explicit language in the Constitution that said Congress could create it. The controversies surrounding the creation of the first and second national banks raised many questions about the power of the federal government, and there were many political, and legal battles that flowed from their existence. However, the two banks were powerful tools that helped solidify national power.

In 1814 during the War of 1812, the British burned the main Treasury building and dined by its light across the street in Rhodes Tavern. By 1839 a new main Treasury building was ready for partial occupancy and since then it has become a historical landmark.

In 1920 Prohibition went into effect, and the Internal Revenue Service was given primary responsibility for its enforcement. During the depression in the 1930s, the Treasury Department proclaimed a bank holiday to slow down withdrawals from financial institutions, and in 1932 the Reconstruction Finance Corporation was formed to lend money to stimulate economic recovery.

Overall, while most people seldom pay much attention to the operations of the Treasury Department, it is perhaps one of the most important government offices in the United States.

David Schultz

Department of Veterans Affairs

The Department of Veterans Affairs is the federal department that has the responsibility of providing services and support for the men and women who have served in the U.S. armed forces. The armed forces include: the U.S. Army, the Marine Corps, the U.S. Air Force, the U.S. Navy, the Coast Guard, the National Reserves, and the National Guard.

The Department of Veterans Affairs (VA) was established as a cabinet-level position on 15 March 1989. However, the practice of caring for our veterans dates back to the Pilgrims' time at Plymouth Rock in 1620. The Pilgrims saw that a law was needed that would protect the welfare of all American veterans by stating that disabled soldiers must be supported by the colony.

The Continental Congress of 1776 sought to encourage enlistment into the Revolutionary War by promising to provide lifelong medical care and pensions for soldiers who became disabled during the hostilities. In 1811, the federal government established the first hospitals to serve veterans, and in the 19th century, the veterans assistance program was modified to allow for benefits and pensions to include widows and dependents. The government also established nursing homes and long-term-care facilities after the Civil War. In fact, the government has led the way in terms of hospitals, medical care, and long-term care, and the private health-care facilities have followed that model. The quality of care that veterans have received over the last 200 years has reflected the value that our society has placed upon the men and women who served in our armed forces.

Before World War I, Congress established a new system of veterans benefits to include programs for disability compensation, insurance, and vocational rehabilitation for the disabled. During the 1920s, these benefits were separately administered by three different agencies: the Veterans Bureau, the Bureau of Pensions of the Interior Department, and the National Home for Disabled Volunteer Soldiers. Eventually, these three separate agencies were incorporated into the Veterans Administration.

The Department of Veterans Affairs succeeded the Veterans Administration and has been assigned the responsibility of administering all federal benefits in many areas to veterans, their dependents, and their survivors. The department is housed under the cabinet in the executive branch of the federal government and is headed by the secretary of veterans affairs. It is the second largest of the 14 cabinet departments, serving approximately one-third of our nation's population, around 70 million people. The department has the responsibility of providing nationwide programs, including: compensation and pensions, education and training, medical care, psychological and readjustment counseling, insurance, vocational rehabilitation for disabled veterans, survivor benefits, home loan assistance, research, and national cemeteries.

The Department of Veterans Affairs provides the following time line describing the history of government action in support of U.S. veterans:

1930 The Veterans Administration was created by Executive Order 5398, signed by President Herbert Hoover on July 21.
1944 On June 22, President Franklin Roosevelt signed the Servicemen's Readjustment Act of 1944 (Public Law 346, passed unanimously by the 78th Congress), more commonly known as the "The GI Bill of Rights," offering home loan and education benefits to veterans.
1953 The Department of Veterans Benefits was established, succeeded in 1989 by the Veterans Benefits Administration.
1988 Legislation to elevate VA to cabinet status was signed by President Reagan.
1989 On March 15, VA became the 14th department in the president's cabinet.

For more information

Department of Veterans Affairs. http://www.va.gov.

Lesele H. Rose

deregulation Deregulation means cessation of governmental price control on a commodity. Subsequent to deregulation, the price of the commodity is established by the interaction of supply, demand, and competition, without governmental influence or intervention.

The U.S. economy is predicated on the existence of free markets, in which government cannot interfere with a vendor's choice of the selling price of goods or commodities. Yet, during the past century, the federal government has regulated prices in several vitally important industries, including electrical and natural gas service; airline tickets; and cellular, local, and long-distance telephone service. Since it is completely inconsistent with the concept of the free-market economy, how did the government justify imposition of this type of governmental control? Although all of the industries in the above list followed similar patterns of nonregulation followed first by regulation and later by deregulation, the importance of regulation and deregulation of the electrical power industry in the 21st century allows it to serve as a relevant and convenient case in point.

At the turn of the 20th century, when less than 5 percent of all U.S. homes were electrified, most of that small number of households generated their own power. Between 1905 and 1925, electrical industry pioneers realized that the high unit cost of power created by single household generators priced electricity out of the range of the vast majority of individuals. Instead, they demonstrated that electricity could be generated far more efficiently and inexpensively by using very large generators to create unprecedented amounts of power, which could then be delivered to many households through a network of transmission and distribution lines. Local and state governments effectively prohibited competition to guarantee the success of individuals willing to make the substantial investment necessary to purchase and install equipment for a community electrical generating facility. This was accomplished by dividing counties into "franchise" areas, within which only one company was authorized to generate, transmit, and distribute electricity. The ease of interesting investors, coupled with the public interest in electrified homes, allowed the percentage of electrified households to rise from 5 percent in 1905 to 53 percent in 1925.

The Sherman Antitrust Act of 1870 prohibited, as a "vertical monopoly," the most efficient method of developing and operating community electrical facilities, which involved common ownership of the generating, transmission, and distribution equipment. To eliminate this impediment to electrification, Congress legalized the efficient type of electrical system by amending the Sherman Act to: (1) define this system as a permissible "natural monopoly," rather than a prohibited vertical monopoly; and (2) allow the continued existence of a "natural monopoly" utility only if it agreed to adhere to price schedules established by the federal government and to provide, on request, electrical service for anyone living within the utility's geographical area. The revised law also mandated that the price schedules provide a fair rate of return for those who invested in the utility.

This historical information clarifies that the government's motivation for establishing price controls was to prevent monopolistic electrical utilities from overcharging consumers. It is then somewhat puzzling that the conservative politicians who in the early 1970s began to question the constitutionality of any government regulation of commercial enterprises completely ignored the consumer protection aspect of price regulation. These politicians argued that excessive regulation stifled initiative, prevented emergence of new suppliers and patterns of service, and denied consumers the benefits of choice and competition. Congress must have found this reasoning persuasive, because in 1978, long-distance telephone service became the first of several industries to be deregulated. During the next 20 years, the federal government also curtailed its participation in rate setting for commercial passenger airlines, electric and natural gas utilities, local telephone service, cable service, and broadband providers.

Despite the conservative rhetoric alleging that price regulation harms consumers, deregulation has not always benefited these individuals. When separate local and long-distance telephone service were made available, the price of long distance plummeted, but the price of local service continued to rise. Airline fares tumbled after deregulation was enacted.

Deregulation of the electrical power industry has not yet benefited any consumers. California's brownouts during 2001, events that had an adverse impact on millions of individuals, were directly related to deregulation. Cessation of federal involvement in rate setting precipitated the notorious Enron bankruptcy in 2002, a fiasco that involved so much money that it not only damaged the finances of thousands of investors, but also adversely impacted the entire U.S. financial market. Finally, consumers throughout the United States have dealt with the financial strain of the continually increasing price of electricity.

Natural-gas deregulation has resulted in major price fluctuations, caused in part by the manipulation and eventual failure of businesses that tried to generate income by trading natural gas, and also in part by the bankruptcies of ventures that attempted to profit by retailing natural gas in competition with existing utilities. As in the case of electricity, the effect of natural gas deregulation has not reduced the financial burden on the consumers. Instead, the price of natural gas continues to rise.

In the United States, although pro-consumer forces instigated the trend toward deregulation, the results of the removal of government price controls have been unpredictable. Only one trend is clear: as a general rule, deregulation helps businesses that are on sound financial footing and harms those that are undercapitalized.

For more information
Federal Energy Information Administration. http:// www. eia.doe.gov/cneaf/electricity/chg_stru_update/ toc.html.

Scott, David L. *Wall Street Words: An Essential A to Z Guide for Today's Investor.* Boston: Houghton Mifflin, 1998.

U.S. Department of Energy. http://www.energylawnet.com/restructuring.html.

Beth S. Swartz

descriptive representation   Descriptive representation occurs when political representatives in the national legislature accurately reflect the composition of the general society.

A central concept in democratic theory, descriptive representation stands for the proposition that a legislative body must resemble or "mirror" the people in order to be truly representative. Descriptive representation is concerned with the composition of the legislature and how accurately that composition reflects society.

A typical exposition of the concept of descriptive representation is found in John Adams's *Thoughts on Government,* which he wrote during the American revolutionary period. Adams states that a representative assembly "should be in miniature an exact portrait of the people at large. It should think, feel, reason, and act like them. That it may be the interest of this assembly to do strict justice at all times, it should be an equal representation, or, in other words, equal interests among the people should have equal interests in it."

The concept of descriptive representation is particularly important to proponents of proportional representation. A legislature is proportionally representative if it includes the same proportion of each relevant group that is present in the nation. Relevant groups are usually defined by race, class, or gender.

The central policy issue that is raised by the concept of descriptive representation is whether historically disadvantaged groups in society are better represented by members of their own groups. For example, should blacks be represented by black representatives or by white representatives? Should women be represented by female representatives or by male representatives? Those in favor of descriptive representation argue that representatives who resemble their constituents in terms of racial identity or gender are best suited to understand the perspectives and promote the needs of their constituents. In addition, the presence of women and blacks in a representative assembly provides legitimacy to the democratic system because important subgroups are not excluded from the political process.

Those opposed to descriptive representation for disadvantaged groups argue that it is more important to focus on what the representative *does,* rather than what he or she *looks like.* For example, empirical studies have shown that female representatives do not necessarily promote the interests of women. Critics of descriptive representation contend that it is far more important for representatives to promote the substantive interests of their constituents, rather than to resemble their constituents.

Various institutional mechanisms are used to ensure descriptive representation. In some states, district lines are drawn to create majority black districts. The creation of majority-minority districts encourages the election of candidates from historically underrepresented groups. Legislatures in other countries set aside a certain number of seats for members of relevant subgroups, such as women, racial minorities, and religious minorities. These institutional devices are often the subject of intense controversy, given the diverse views on the advantages and disadvantages of descriptive representation.

For more information

Mansbridge, Jane. "Should Blacks Represent Blacks and Women Represent Women? A Contingent 'Yes.'" *The Journal of Politics* 61 (August 1999): 628–657.

Pitkin, Hanna F. *The Concept of Representation.* Berkeley: University of California Press, 1967.

Yasmin A. Dawood

digital divide The "digital divide" refers to the gap between the information technology (IT) haves and have-nots. This gap may involve the contrast between groups within a particular country as well as between countries or regions of the world.

Some argue that one consequence of the Information Age is a growing gap between the digital haves and have-nots. For example, the United States has more computers than the rest of the world. South Asia has 23 percent of the world's population but less than 1 percent of its Internet users. A typical computer will cost a person in Bangladesh more than eight years of income, in contrast to one month's salary for a person in the United States. Moreover, English is the dominant language of this new form of commerce. More than 80 percent of websites are in English, yet less than 10 percent of the planet speaks English as their first language.

At a country level, if the digital divide is not addressed, we will have lost the opportunity to use new telecommunications advances to strengthen the community network and build upon our social capital. Internationally, groups like the United Nations need to be more proactive in redressing this imbalance. We also have to be clever in getting the most out of existing technology.

The causes of the digital divide relate to barriers to IT access and can take many forms.

- Linguistic barriers, given the Internet is mostly in English. Even in English-speaking countries such as the United States, Canada, and Australia, there are many who do not speak English.
- Financial barriers. People cannot afford a computer or Internet access
- Old age and infirmity can be a barrier for some. This will become greater with the aging of the population.
- Gender can be a barrier. Note the evidence in many countries of fewer girls taking computer studies in school.
- Geography can be a barrier, with IT infrastructure being considerably better in the major cities as opposed to small regional communities
- There is a knowledge barrier. If people are illiterate, the Information Age can be especially terrifying
- There are legal barriers. Concerns about insurance and uncertainties about privacy are just two examples of major constraints
- There can be technical barriers. How do we achieve sufficient bandwidth?
- Disability can be a barrier, for example if you are blind or hard of hearing.
- There are psychological barriers, with some people having an IT phobia Barriers are not confined to individuals. In many cases the groups that seek to help the disadvantaged are themselves disadvantaged. Some individuals have multiple barriers. For example, the homeless are often illiterate, poor, in rural areas, etc.

Just as the problems are multifaceted, so is the range of solutions. Many governments, for example, have passed legislation that ensures a minimum level of technology to disadvantaged groups. An example is special IT infrastructure for the rural areas. Governments have also assisted schools in providing computers and IT education in the hopes that such measures will open up new possibilities to disadvantaged groups.

Disability legislation in countries such as the United States and Australia has mandated that websites be sensitive to the fact that the Internet is often a vital communication tool to those with blindness and other disabilities. Websites need to be accessible to these groups. In some cases, new technology is part of the answer in empowering disadvantaged groups to have access to the Internet. An example is the adoption of multilevel channels of communication, in recognition that some people will not be able to access information in digital form.

The private sector has also been increasingly aware of its duty to society to ensure that the benefits of this new technology do not leave out key sectors of society. For example, the Bill and Melinda Gates Foundation has given away hundreds of millions of dollars. Internationally, too, wealthier countries as well as major private companies are beginning to be proactive in making technology available to those countries that otherwise could not afford it.

For more information

Cohn, T., S. Fraser, and S. McBride. *Power in the Global Era: Grounding Globalization.* New York: Macmillan Press, 2001.

Ebo, B. *Cyberimperialism? Global Relations in the New Electronic Frontier.* New York: Praeger Publishers, 2000.

Hundt, Reed E. *You Say You Want a Revolution: A Story of Information Age Politics.* New Haven, Conn.: Yale University Press, 2000.

Eugene Clark

Dillon's Rule More than 100 years ago, Judge John F. Dillon of the Iowa Supreme Court wrote a judgment that has affected the relationship between municipalities and states to the present time. In 1872 Judge Dillon declared: "It is a general and undisputed proposition of law that a municipal corporation possesses, and can exercise, the following powers, and no others; First, those granted in express words; second, those necessarily or fairly implied in, or incident to, the powers expressly granted; third, those essential to the declared objects and purposes of the corporation—not simply convenient, but indispensable."

What does that mean? It is a rule that limits the powers of local governments, i.e., cities and towns are creatures of their respective states. It is the state that has the power to command the cities by passing laws that affect the cities, while the cities are very limited about what laws they can pass to govern themselves. Local power is derived from the state constitution and state laws.

It is generally believed that during the first 100 years of this country's history, towns and cities were free to rule themselves, with little interference from their states. But times change, and by 1872 state legislators were asserting their powers for several reasons. First, state legislators were dominated by rural interests, and rural interests were not interested in aiding the cities. Second, state legislators were increasingly nervous watching the stream of immigrants coming into the cities and voting in such numbers that immigrants were gaining positions of power in the largest cities. Increasingly, municipal government appeared to be spending extravagantly. Third, the post–Civil War period was one of industrialization, and with industrialization there was increasing demand by many citizens for governments to step in and help regulate the increasing complexity of city life.

The stage was set for Dillon's Rule. After Judge Dillon issued his ruling, judges in other states used his ruling in their cases, and over the years, the rule became quite popular with the states although not as popular with local governments. When courts had cases about the legality of a local government action, they often resolved that action in favor of that state. Examples of how this affects municipalities abound. If a local government wishes to charge a sales tax, that municipality has to ask the state's permission. If two local governments wish to merge, they must ask the state's permission.

There are a few states that have refuted Dillon's Rule. Alaska proclaimed that the state believed in maximum local control and was not interested in ruling the detailed life of any municipality. As a result, municipalities in Alaska have a great deal of discretion.

Lynne A. Weikart

discretion Discretion entails freedom to choose and to act of one's own accord. Administrative discretion pertains to government officials' relatively autonomous ability to exercise power by engaging in rule making and adjudicative action. Administrative discretion is essential to governing a complex, postindustrial society. Nevertheless, controversy continues over both the nature and the extent of legitimate administrative discretion. When American government officials exercise discretion, questions about accountability often follow. Most pejoratively, Americans suspect administrative discretion to be bureaucratic power wielded arbitrarily by faceless functionaries.

The tension between exercising and checking government officials' discretion is played out in the practice of—and debated in the literature about—American government and politics. This nervousness goes hand-in-hand with the historical development of the American administrative state. In what historian Henry Steele Commager termed a "commercial republic," Americans privilege the private ordering of economic relations over state regulation. Prior to the New Deal era, the legal foundations of administrative discretion were frail. Throughout the latter half of the 19th century, and well into the 20th, state and federal courts interpreted constitutional provisions (especially due process) as proscribing government involvement in market relations. The Great Depression swept such prohibitions away. As Chief Justice Charles Evans Hughes stated of the New Deal view in *NLRB v. Jones and Laughlin*, 301 U.S. 1 (1937):

> The fundamental principle is that the power to regulate commerce is the power to enact 'all appropriate legislation' for its 'protection or advancement' . . .; to adopt measures 'to promote its growth and insure its safety' . . .; 'to foster, protect, control, and restrain.' . . . That power is plenary and may be exerted to protect interstate commerce 'no matter what the source of the dangers which threaten it.'

Despite decisions like *NLRB v. Jones and Laughlin* establishing the legal foundation for government officials to exercise administrative discretion, the political basis for regulatory power remains fragile—fragility fueled by a normative opposition to "excessive" government regulation and a cultural commitment to the rule of law. Americans are suspicious of "big government" to begin with; we fear unchecked government most of all. Consequently, over the past 75 years, a welter of approaches to controlling administrative discretion have been devised. These have ranged from institutional checks, such as judicial review and executive or legislative oversight of administrative decisions, to internal restraints derived from managerial and professional standards, and modes of public involvement.

In the scholarly literature of administrative law, these controls are hotly debated. Complicating realization of the goal of accountability are two facts. First, well over 80 percent of discretionary administrative action is informal. Second, of those relatively few decisions that are reviewable, 99 percent are not reviewed. This means that most administrative discretion is exercised "in the shadow of the law," out of sight and out of reach. This circumstance aggravates lingering doubts about the legitimacy of the administrative state.

For more information

Davis, Kenneth Culp. *Discretionary Justice: A Preliminary Inquiry.* Urbana: University of Illinois Press, 1971.

Lowi, Theodore. *The End of Liberalism: The Second Republic of the United States,* 2d ed. New York: Norton, 1979.

Pierce, Richard J., Jr. "Political Accountability and Delegated Power: A Response to Professor Lowi." *American University Law Review* 36 (1987): 391.

Skowronek, Stephen. *Building a New American State: The Expansion of National Administrative Capacities, 1877–1920.* New York: Cambridge University Press, 1982.

James C. Foster

discrimination   *Discrimination* is a term with meanings in both psychology and the law.

In psychology, discrimination refers to an ability to perceive and respond to a variety of stimuli. In the law, discrimination ordinarily carries the sense of a difference in the treatment between persons variously situated. *Black's Law Dictionary,* for example, defines discrimination as the effect of a law or established practice that either confers or denies privileges to a certain class of persons because of certain noted traits. Among these personal traits are race, age, sex, nationality, religion, handicap, sexual orientation, and others of a similar nature.

People and nations have forever discriminated against others. The United States is no exception, and examples of discriminatory practices have been around at least as long as there has been a nation. For example, the Constitution of the United States, as ratified, treated slaves differently from other persons. A slave was counted, for purposes of apportioning seats in the House of Representatives, as only three-fifths of a person. Many states enacted similarly discriminatory measures that were applied to both slave and nonslave minority populations.

These forms of discriminatory practices continued with little serious questioning until the years following the Civil War (1861–65). The Civil Rights Act of 1875, part of a series of progressive steps addressing the discriminatory treatment of the then-freed slaves, prohibited discrimination in certain public accommodations. This statute was, however, declared unconstitutional by the U.S. Supreme Court in a celebrated 1883 decision known as the Civil Rights Cases. At the heart of the Supreme Court's decision was a determination that the Thirteenth Amendment to the Constitution didn't authorize the Civil Rights Act, since the amendment was intended only to abolish slavery. The Supreme Court determined that the equal access to public accommodations measures were not incident to the abolition of slavery.

Over the years since 1875, the discriminatory effects of federal and state laws have expanded or contracted in part due to social and cultural influ-

ences. In 1896, the Supreme Court, in its ruling in *Plessy v. Ferguson,* held that the Thirteenth Amendment had only addressed fundamental rights of citizenship and was not enacted to ensure equality in mere social rights. The Supreme Court's affirmation of the principle of "separate but equal" stood as the law of the United States until 1954. In that year, the Supreme Court reversed its *Plessy* decision and expressly repudiated the "separate but equal" principle in the landmark case of *Brown v. Board of Education.*

The modern era of civil rights law, and the accompanying efforts to correct the discriminatory effect of social and cultural practices, can be said to begin with the enactment by Congress of the 1964 Civil Rights Act. In this legislation, Congress granted new authority to the federal government to regulate discrimination found in the practices of both public and private entities. This major civil rights law has been followed by the later passage of legislation such as the Voting Rights Act of 1965, the Fair Housing Act of 1968, and more recently, the Americans with Disabilities Act of 1990. Each of these later measures was intended by Congress to address in a more narrow way the effects of certain discriminatory practices.

For more information

Lee, David W. *Handbook of Section 1983 Litigation.* New York: Aspen Publishers, 2001.

Peller, Gary. "Civil Rights." *Encyclopedia of the American Constitution,* 2d ed., vol. 1. New York: Macmillan Reference, 2000.

Smolla, Rodney. *Federal Civil Rights Acts,* 3d ed. St. Paul, Minn.: West Group, 1994.

Jerry E. Stephens

distributive policy   Distributive policy is policy that confers direct benefit upon one or more groups without hurting or taking away from other groups. This policy involves certain decisions by government regarding limited resources on "who gets what, when, and how." In the focus of government, distribution might cover material goods such as money, taxes, and houses, or services such as education and medical care to individuals, groups, or communities.

Distributive policy is aimed at promoting private activities that are argued to be desirable to society as a whole which would not or could not be undertaken without government support. The distributive policy, for example, exists in the school lunch program because this program could not exist without assistance from the government. Examples of distributive policies include Federal Aid to Education, Financial Aid to Students, Federal Aid to Disabled, Medicaid, or Medicare. Another example of this policy would be pork-barrel legislation by congress. "Pork barrel" came into use as a political term in the post–Civil War era. It comes from the plantation practice of distributing rations of salt pork to slaves from wooden barrels. When used to describe a bill, it implies the legislation is loaded with special projects for members of Congress to distribute to their constituents back home as an act of generosity, courtesy of the federal taxpayer. Distributive policies allow them to focus policy benefit directly in their congressional districts.

The distributive policy, however, is very individual in its impact and is at the heart of public-policy controversies, whether it is distribution of goods and services, wealth and income, health and illness, or opportunity and disadvantage.

The proponents and opponents of distributive policy base their arguments on distributive justice. The normative principles of distributive justice—designed to allocate goods in limited supply relative to demand—vary in numerous dimensions. For instance, they vary in what goods are subject to distribution (income, wealth, opportunities, etc.) or on the nature of the recipients of the distribution (natural persons, groups of persons, reference classes, etc.). In addition, government has to decide on what basis the goods should be distributed (equality, according to individual characteristics, according to free-market transactions, etc.). Moreover, the government faces a number of challenges in the process of distribution through lotteries (e.g., distribution of government jobs), competition, and elections because it has to maintain fairness. Conflict sometime arises when people do not agree on relevant characteristics of recipients and items.

For more information
Lasswell, Harold. *Politics: Who Gets What, When and How,* 2d ed. New York: McGraw-Hill, 1936.
Stone, Deborah A. *Policy Paradox and Political Reason.* New York: HarperCollins Publishers, 1988.

Raissa Muhutdinova-Foroughi

double dipping   *Double dipping* is a nickname for the practice of simultaneously drawing a pension while also earning a salary from the government.

The formal name for double dipping is *dual compensation.* Double dipping may be done, for example, by a military retiree who is drawing a pension, and who has also gained employment as a civilian employee with the federal government. This individual would then receive two incomes. The first would be from the military pension, and the second would be from the civil service job.

Attitudes toward dual compensation vary. Some have found it very acceptable, while others consider it to be patently objectionable. Those who are opposed to double dipping usually argue that somehow the "double-dipper" is getting paid twice for the same work. Or that somehow it is like nepotism, or a sinecure. Those who favor the practice of double dipping see it as a way to retain people with skills and experience. As a consequence, double dipping at the federal, state, and local levels is a practice that is at times prohibited, permitted, or promoted.

The CIVIL SERVICE REFORM ACT OF 1978 tried to prevent the practice of double dipping by military personnel who retired at, or above, the rank of major or lieutenant commander unless the officer in question was disabled. Current federal regulations (5 CFR 553) permit a limited amount of double dipping by exempting those deemed essential or by permitting limited work for a salary that amounts to about half of the retirement pension.

Double dipping may be promoted at times to retain talented and experienced people when labor shortages appear due to retirements. In Ohio, for example, a state law allowing double dipping was passed to encourage recently retired teachers to return to teaching for a regular salary while also drawing a pension. The policy goal was to fill a critical teacher shortage.

Many politicians promote the hiring of federal civilian and military retirees to work in state government, business, or nonprofit organizations for a full salary while drawing full pension. This practice is encouraged as a way to gain experienced and skilled employees. State government employees sometimes improve their retirement benefits by working in two or more jurisdictions.

The nickname *double dipping* is taken from the image of an ice cream cone with two scoops, perhaps with two different flavors. The term has spread to other areas of both public and private life. For example, it is applied to some social security benefits cases and to the most widely used approach to valuing a sole practitioner's practice in family court. For the purpose of establishing alimony in a divorce case, a common complaint is that when applying the excess earning method—used to calculate the value of the community property in a professional practice — the estimates of the value are counted twice, or "double dipped."

For more information
5 Code of Federal Regulations, Part 553 (1-1-02).
5 USCS Section 5527, Dual Pay and Dual Employment, subchap. IV, sec. 5531.

A. J. L. Waskey

Drug Enforcement Administration The
Drug Enforcement Administration (DEA) is the arm of the federal government of the United States charged with the enforcement of the country's controlled-substances laws. The DEA focuses on stopping both distribution and production (whether cultivation or manufacture) of illicit substances.

As per its mission statement, the DEA is responsible for criminal investigations, intelligence gathering, and the seizure of forfeited assets related to narcotics trafficking, as well as coordinating drug enforcement activities with federal, state, local, and foreign law-enforcement and policy-implementing entities. The agency operates out of 21 domestic divisions and has 78 offices in 56 foreign countries. As of fiscal year 2001 there were 4,601 special agents in the field and a total of 9,209 employees in the organization.

The DEA was created by President RICHARD NIXON in 1973 via Presidential Reorganization Plan Number Two. This plan merged the Bureau of Narcotics and Dangerous Drugs, the Office of Drug Abuse Law Enforcement, and the Office of National Narcotics Intelligence within the Justice Department with the Drug Investigations unit within the U.S. Customs Service. The main legislative focus of the DEA is the enforcement of the Controlled Substances Act, which was originally passed as part of the Comprehensive Drug Abuse Prevention and Control Act of 1970. The CSA assigns the attorney general the job of enforcing the nation's laws on controlled substances, which can be delegated to any officer or agency of the federal government. The Justice Department's main tool for enforcing the Controlled Substances Act is the Drug Enforcement Administration.

While the DEA is the chief federal law-enforcement agency focused on illicit substance control, it is by no means alone in terms of drug policy. It is, rather, one of numerous parts of a vast network of governmental bureaucracies that plan, enforce, and evaluate U.S. drug policy. This "narco-enforcement complex" (as Bertram et al. dub it) consists of more than 50 federal agencies across 11 cabinet-level departments and other federal entities, as well as state and local law enforcement. The DEA itself accounts for only 7.9 percent of the FY2001 National Drug Control

Budget and 17.7 percent of the Justice Department's allocation of that budget.

For more information

Bertram, Eva, et al. *Drug War Politics: The Price of Denial.* Berkeley: University of California Press, 1996.

Drug Enforcement Administration. *DEA Briefing Book.* Washington, D.C.: Department of Justice. Available online. URL:http://www.usdoj.gov/dea/briefingbook/index.html.

Office of National Drug Control Policy. *Summary: FY 2002 National Drug Control Budget.* Washington, D.C.: U.S. Government Printing Office, 2001.

Steven L. Taylor

drug policy   In the debate over drug policy there are three main schools of thought: prohibition, legalization, and decriminalization.

The current operative paradigm in U.S. policy making is prohibition, based on both moral arguments against the consumptions of illicit substances and public-health concerns as to the widespread ramifications of easy access to such materials. However, a substantial policy-oriented debate is ongoing in regard to legalization or decriminalization. Those who seek either legalization or decriminalization argue that the current prohibitionist policies are responsible for the organized-crime elements of the narcotics world, and therefore argue that the solution is to remove the huge profits associated with the drug trade from the equation.

Legalization arguments range from specific drugs (such as marijuana) to total repeal of antinarcotics laws—normally substituting a new regulatory scheme as currently exists for licit drugs. Decriminalizers argue for significant reductions in penalties for personal possession of small amounts. The objections to prohibition are based on a variety of arguments, ranging from the inefficacy of the current policies to market-based arguments to libertarian personal freedom. Despite the intensity of such debates, the clear public sentiment is for the continuation of the prohibitionist paradigm.

Antinarcotics policy in the United States is based on attacking both supply and demand. Primarily the focus is on the supply-side of the equation, which translates into attacking productive and distributive capabilities as well as focusing on pushers and users. Attempts at demand side reductions, such as education and treatment in lieu of imprisonment, are also in place. The FY2001 National Drug Control Budget allocated 31 percent of its funding for the demand side (drug abuse treatment, education/prevention, and research—with treatment and prevention receiving the lion's share by far). On the supply side, 52 percent went to domestic law enforcement, and international efforts garnered 17 percent. The supply side of the equation, therefore, receives roughly 69 percent of the monies allocated for drug policy. (Of course, law enforcement aimed at users also has a demand-side component insofar as fear of prosecution deters some users or potential users.)

The legislative origin of U.S. narcotics policy is the Harrison Narcotics Act of 1914, which was the first major piece of drug control legislation passed by Congress. The administration of the law was handled by the Treasury Department, first by the Bureau of Revenue, then by 1920 under the jurisdiction of the Narcotics Division of the Prohibition Unit. The rationale for federal regulation of drug distribution under this act was based on the right to tax (as was also the case with the Marijuana Tax Act of 1937). Later laws would base the right to regulate illicit substances on interstate commerce grounds. Since the passage of the Harrison Act, numerous pieces of legislation and various executive orders have been issued in regard to the illicit drugs question. Of these, three that are vital to any understanding of the basics of current U.S. drug control policy are: the Controlled Substances Act of 1970, the Anti-Drug Abuse Act of 1988, and the Office of National Drug Control Policy Reauthorization Act of 1998.

The Controlled Substances Act of 1970 (CSA) (a portion of the Comprehensive Drug Abuse Prevention and Control Act of 1970) is the main legal underpinning of current U.S. drug policy. This law classifies controlled substances into five schedules, ranging from Schedule I substances, which are deemed highly addictive and lacking in medical value, to Schedule V substances, which may create physical or psychological dependence but have clear and accepted medical value. Factors used in scheduling of substances include (but are not limited to): likelihood of abuse, historical patterns of abuse, medicinal value, and public health concerns. Ultimately, the main two variables are abuse potential and medical use. Schedule I drugs are totally prohibited, even for research purposes. Substances on Schedules II through V are regulated, but on a sliding scale of strictness from II to V.

The 1988 and 1998 legislation dealing with the Office of National Drug Control Policy (ONDCP) focused on the administration and coordination of drug policy. The first piece of legislation created the ONDCP (whose head is colloquially known as the "drug czar") which functions out of the executive office of the president. This office serves as a central clearinghouse for drug policy coordination as well as a means of providing policy advice to the president.

The overall nexus of actors involved in drug policy enforcement is vast. The FY2002 proposed National Drug Control Budget provides over $19.1 billion to agencies in 11 cabinet-level departments, as well as other federal government entities. State and local law enforcement also play a key role in this vast set of actors that Bertram et al. call the "narco-enforcement complex."

Drug policy contains substantial foreign-policy elements, given that such significant substances as marijuana, cocaine, and heroin come from abroad. This affects U.S. foreign policy vis-à-vis such countries as Colombia, which is the world's main producer of cocaine (as well as being a significant source of heroin) and Mexico, which given its border with the United States, serves as a conduit for all manner of illicit substances. Even the events of

September 11 had ties to drugs, given that the Taliban regime in Afghanistan was a producer and exporter of heroin.

Crop eradication has been a lynchpin of U.S. antidrug policy in the Western Hemisphere since the 1970s (first with marijuana, and then with coca). President GEORGE H. W. BUSH's "Andean Initiative" was aimed at the eradication of coca leaf in Bolivia, Colombia, and Peru in the late 1980s. Policy goals were reached primarily through aerial spraying of known coca fields, although crop substitution programs and other activities were included. This policy was of great success in Bolivia and Peru, where coca cultivation plummeted. However, the growth of the plant simply shifted to Colombia, which had significantly trailed Peru in numbers of hectares under cultivation prior to the implementation of the policy. By the end of the 1990s, Colombia had become the source of approximately 90 percent of the world's cocaine. This is a clear example of what has been called the "balloon effect" vis-à-vis crop eradication—squeeze a balloon and the air bulges out opposite where pressure is being applied, squeeze the new bulge and force the air out of it, and a new bulge appears, etc. Indeed, increased pressure on Colombian coca farmers appears to be forcing some cultivation back into Peru.

For more information

Bertram, Eva, et al. *Drug War Politics: The Price of Denial*. Berkeley: University of California Press, 1996.

MacCoun, Robert J., and Peter Reuter. *Drug War Heresies: Learning from Other Vices, Times, and Places*. Cambridge, U.K.: Cambridge University Press, 2001.

———. *The National Drug Control Strategy: 2001 Annual Report*. Washington, D.C.: U.S. Government Printing Office, 2001.

———. *Summary: FY 2002 National Drug Control Budget*. Washington, D.C.: U.S. Government Printing Office, 2001.

Steven L. Taylor

E

earmarked revenue Earmarked revenue is a type of revenue that emerges from a specific source that will then be used for a specific purpose. One of the most common earmarked revenues are motor-fuel taxes, which are paid by motorists when they purchase gasoline or diesel fuel and are then reserved for highway and bridge construction, repair, or maintenance. Unlike general revenues, earmarked revenues cannot be transferred to any other programs or funds beyond that for which they are earmarked.

Critics believe that earmarking funds limits budgetary discretion and ties specific revenues to specific programs whether those funds are needed or not. In short, opponents believe that earmarking funds ties the hands of chief executives and legislators. On the other hand, supporters believe that earmarking revenues provides program stability and has large-scale voter support.

For more information

Axelrod, Donald. *Budgeting for Modern Government.* New York: St. Martin's Press, 1995.

Robert A. Schuhmann

earned-income tax credit The earned-income tax credit is a means-tested federal program that is generally stigmatized as a public assistance program. Howard Jacob Karger and David Stoesz, however, note that the earned-income tax credit (EITC) lies somewhere between a tax reform program (because it "moderates the regressive social security tax for low-income workers"), a public assistance program (because "it supplements the wages of low-income households"), and a social insurance program ("in that only people actively participating in the workplace are eligible"). The EITC—working like a negative income tax—allows people meeting certain income and family criteria to receive a federal tax rebate.

In order to qualify for the EITC, at the most basic level, taxpayers (single or married) first must be residents or citizens with valid social security numbers and have earned income. Their tax credit depends on their gross income and family status. For instance, according to the Internal Revenue Service in 2002, working parents who earn less than $32,121 can claim an EITC; their tax credit depends on the number of qualifying children. A childless single taxpayer between 25 and 65 years old whose income is less than $10,710 may also qualify for an EITC. In neither case can the taxpayer have investment income over $2,450.

The Internal Revenue Service estimates that taxpayers claimed $31.3 billion in EITC credit in 2000. Though the EITC has helped millions of people in the United States, it does not help all poor. For instance, a citizen/resident who is so poor that he or she does not have to file a tax return does not receive the EITC. Further, it is not a very well-known program, and thus many eligible poor families do not claim it.

For more information

Karger, Howard Jacob, and David Stoesz. *American Social Welfare Policy: A Pluralist Approach,* 4th ed. New York: Allyn & Bacon/Longman, 2001.

U.S. Internal Revenue Service. http://www.irs.gov.

Linda K. Shafer

e-government   E-government involves the transformation of government functions from a paper-based to an electronic environment. In most countries, government has played a major role in the promotion of e-commerce and has sought to lead the way by example.

The move to e-government has involved the transformation from a model of industrialized government (centralized, bureaucratized, paper-based, impersonal, rule-based, and organized into departments) to that of an information-based government (decentralized, digital, personalized, client focused, interconnected, and organized in new ways).

It is generally recognized that there are four major stages in the evolution to the delivery of government services over the Internet. In the first stage, the agency has a website that publishes information about itself and its services. In stage 2 the agency allows Internet users to access the agency database(s) and to browse, explore, and interact with the data. Agencies at stage 3 allow users access as in stages 1 and 2 and also permit them to enter secure information and engage in transactions with the agency. In stage 4, in addition to the level of access permitted at stage 3, the agency, with the user's prior approval, shares with other government agencies relevant information provided by that user with a view to providing a whole-of-government integrated service.

While most government agencies are at stage 1, the most significant gains for e-government will come when agencies move from automation of existing government services to using telecommunications technology to reengineer government itself.

Significant impediments remain to government adoption of e-commerce, especially in relation to legislative reform. These impediments include: concerns about the legal status of electronic documents; development of standards and procedures to implement legislation that would legalize electronic signatures and documentation; development of methods of archiving and protecting government records; implementation of procedures to deal with fraud; and privacy and security concerns.

Government plays several roles in the development of e-commerce. In the traditional sense, government is a regulator. It passes laws that affect citizens and business. One of the most important objectives is to build a legal and regulatory framework that secures the confidence of all citizens; provides at least the same level of protection for consumers engaged in electronic commerce as is provided for other forms of commerce; favors market-based regulation; and conforms with agreed international positions.

Government can also be an enabler of e-commerce. Through the setting of best-practice standards and the promotion of technology (whether it be through the development and implementation of a high-level policy or by simply providing money to the right industry sector), the government can try to ensure leadership in this important area.

E-government developments cannot occur in isolation. The global dimensions of information technology are such that a U.S. policy or a European Union (EU) policy alone is not sufficient. The information society is by its nature global, and thus, as regards many issues, it requires global answers. Recent developments of the EU in harmonizing its information technology laws and the importance that the EU placed on the protection of intellectual property rights, together with U.S. amendment of its intellectual property laws to comply with its obligations under THE GENERAL AGREEMENT ON TARIFFS AND TRADE (GATT) and the World Intellectual Property Organization (WIPO), are obvious examples of a growing harmonization of laws and the move toward an international legal regime.

As globalization continues and the global economy grows, the United States remains an active proponent of e-business/commerce in various international fora such as the World Trade Organization, the United Nations, the Organization for Economic Cooperation and Development, the Asia Pacific Economic Cooperation Forum, and the World Customs Organization.

For more information

Clark, Eugene, George Cho, and Artur Hoyle. *E-Business: Law and Management for the 21st Century.* Canberra, Australia: Info-Sys Law International Publications, 2001.

UNCTAD. *E-commerce and Development Report.* New York and Geneva: United Nations, 2001. Available online. URL: http://www.unctad.org/en/pub/ps1ecdr01.en.htm.

Eugene Clark

Elrod v. Burns 423 U.S. 347 (1976)

Elrod v. Burns was a 5-3 decision of the U.S. Supreme Court declaring that discharge or threats of discharge of non–civil service government employees from jobs being satisfactorily performed, solely because of their political beliefs, violated the First and Fourteenth Amendments to the Constitution.

In accord with Illinois political practice, Democrat Richard Elrod, upon assuming the office of sheriff of Cook County in December 1970, ordered the discharge of numerous non–civil service employees who had worked for his Republican predecessor. Three discharged employees (floor supervisor John Burns, process server Fred Buckley, juvenile court bailiff/security guard Frank Vargas) and one about to be discharged (office employee Joseph Dennard) filed suit in federal district court against Richard Elrod, Richard J. Daley, the Democratic Organization of Cook County, and the Democratic County Central Committee of Cook County, claiming that their removal, "solely because they did not support and were not members of the Democratic Party and had failed to obtain sponsorship of one of its leaders," was in violation of the Constitution and several federal civil rights laws. At the time the department employed about 3,000 people, half of whom held protected merit positions and the rest occupied patronage appointments. Illinois law allowed for such dual hiring practices.

Five justices agreed with the Court's judgment to condemn all but confidential, policy-making patronage dismissals, but only Justices White and Marshall joined Justice Brennan in a plurality opinion. Justices Stewart and Blackmun objected to the plurality's broad discussion of the "constitutional validity" of political party hiring practices (the patronage system) in order to decide the narrow dismissal question. Justice Stevens took no part in the case. The plurality and the dissenting justices (Powell, Burger, Rehnquist) determined that this case involved a question of constitutional interpretation appropriate for the Court to decide, and did not concern a political question (better left to Congress or the president) or a separation-of-powers issue. Thus the Court must determine whether the state has shown that the restrictions it has placed on an individual employee's First Amendment freedoms of political belief and association "further some vital government end by a means that is least restrictive" of these freedoms "in achieving that end, and the benefit gained must outweigh the loss of constitutionally protected rights."

In applying the test, the plurality concluded that the state had failed to show how patronage dismissals were a least-restrictive means to achieve ends such as (1) ensuring effective government, the efficiency of public employees, and the availability of employees highly accountable to the public; (2) ensuring that representative government is not undercut by the failure of employees to implement new policies; and (3) preserving the democratic process and the party system upon which it relies. Less drastic means were available to achieve the same results. These included dismissal for insubordination and poor job performance, limiting patronage dismissals to policy-making positions, and preventing the "entrenchment of one or a few parties to the exclusion of others," which "retards the elective process." In contrast, Justice Powell's dissent recognized the strength of the state's interests, particularly for local elective offices, since "unless the candidates for these offices are able to dispense the traditional patronage that has accrued to the offices, they also are unlikely to attract donations of time or money from voluntary groups" to pay for publicity and disseminate political information to the public, as well as to enable the ongoing activities of local party organization between elections.

Burns was followed by *Branti v. Finkel* (1980), *Rutan v. Republican Party of Illinois* (1990), and *O'Hare Truck Service, Inc. v. City of Northlake* (1996)—the collective impact of which was to severely restrict state and local government political patronage systems—as the Court attempted to protect the First Amendment rights of public employees and contractors while ensuring an efficient and productive government workforce in the public's interest.

For more information

Hamilton, David K. "The Continuing Judicial Assault on Patronage." *Public Administration Review* 59 (January 1999): 54.

Vinzant, Janet C., and Thomas H. Roback. "Dilemmas of Legitimacy: The Supreme Court, Patronage, and the Public Interest," *Administration and Society* 25 (February 1994): 443.

Kathleen M. Simon

eminent domain   Eminent domain refers to the power of the government to take private property for public use, including instances where the owner of the property does not willingly consent to the transfer of the property to the government. In the United States, the governmental right to take property is limited by many state constitutional provisions and the taking clause of the Fifth Amendment to the U.S. Constitution, which in pertinent part provides as follows:

> No person shall be . . . deprived of life, liberty or property, without due process of law; nor shall property be taken for public use without compensation.

The above Constitutional provision imposes two requirements on both state and national governments. First, the owner of the property must receive compensation for the property taken. Second, the property may only be taken for a "public use." The compensation required is equal to the market value of the property at the time the property is taken. If the state and property owner can not agree on the market value, a trial is held and a judge or jury determines the value of the property taken.

The "public use" requirement has been interpreted very broadly. The courts have found that the "public use" requirement is satisfied where property is taken because land ownership was extremely concentrated in only a few owners, and the government wanted to convey it to a larger number of owners (*Hawaii Housing Authority v. Midkiff*, 467 U.S. 229, [1984]). Similarly, the "public use" requirement is satisfied where blighted property is taken so that it can be redeveloped for use in the private sector (*Berman v. Parker*, 348 U.S. 26 [1954]). The "public use" requirement is also satisfied in situations where the property is taken so that it can be conveyed to a privately owned utility.

The reach of the "taking clause" is not limited to situations where the government actually takes property, but extends to situations where government regulations diminish the value of property or allow entry onto the property without the consent of the owner. For example, when a New York statute gave permission for a cable TV provider to install its cable within a building without the consent of the owner in order to serve tenants desiring cable service, the Court held that the law constituted an unlawful taking of the apartment owner's property (*Loretto v. Teleprompter Manhattan CATV Corp.*, 458 U.S. 419 [1982]).

Similarly, when the use or economic value of property is diminished by a regulation, the Court will find an unlawful taking if the use restriction frustrates the reasonable investment-backed expectations of the property owner (*Penn Central Transportation Co. v. New York*, 438 U.S. 104 [1978]). When a regulation eliminates virtually all the economically beneficial uses of the property, the Court will find a taking unless the effect of the regulation is no greater than the result under the common law of nuisance (*Lucas v. South Carolina Coastal Council* 505 U.S. 1003 [1992]).

For more information

Epstein, Richard. *Takings: Private Property and the Power of Eminent Domain.* Cambridge, Mass.: Harvard University Press, 1989.

Mandelker, Daniel. *Land Use Law.* New York: Lexis Law Publishing, 2001.

Scott Peters

Employee Retirement Income Security Act of 1974

The Employee Retirement Income Security Act of 1974 (ERISA) was passed by Congress to overcome many of the deficiencies of private-sector defined-benefit retirement plans. Defined-benefit plans are those that promise a given income level upon retirement based on age, number of years of service with the company, and sometimes level of salary attainment. A president's commission report in 1965 highlighted many weaknesses in plan funding, design, reporting, and disclosure. Also, as documented by the commission report, it was not uncommon for employees to be denied their pension rights because of employer bankruptcy, company acquisition by another firm, termination of a plan, or other denial of promised benefits.

Not covered by the law are defined-contribution retirement plans. The latter do not promise a specified benefit, only a level of contribution. Exceptions are employee savings and thrift plans, deferred profit-sharing plans, employee stock-ownership plans, and money purchase plans, all of which are classified as defined-contribution plans but are still covered under ERISA. The law does not govern public-sector defined-benefit plans, although there have been numerous attempts to extend ERISA requirements to government sponsored plans.

The law governs six important areas.

- Reporting and disclosure. Employees and beneficiaries must be informed of their entitlements and rights under covered plans.
- Fiduciary standards. These are protections of plans against mismanagement and misuse of assets.
- Plan participation rules. In most cases, eligibility for participation cannot be denied beyond the time an employee reaches age 21 and completes one year of service. Participation must follow within six months of meeting these requirements.
- Vesting. After meeting certain requirements, a participant will retain a right to benefits accrued, or some portion of them, even if employment with the plan sponsor terminates prior to retirement.
- Funding rules. Funding must be determined, monitored, and adjusted by actuaries (statisticians who compute risk and life

expectancy) to assure the beneficiary's payout is there when promised. Regular contributions must be made, and past liabilities (such as a history of underfunding) or plan improvements must be amortized (spread) over 30 years or less.

- Plan termination insurance. If a plan is terminated before it is fully funded, ERISA provide a system of pension plan termination insurance under a separate government agency, the Pension Benefit Guaranty Corporation (PBGC).

For more information

"ERISA Remembered." *Employee Benefit Plan Review* 39 no. 2 (1984): 11.

McCaffery, Robert M. *Employee Benefit Programs, A Total Compensation Perspective,* 2d ed. Boston: PWS-Kent Publishing Co., 1992.

Gilbert B. Siegel

Enron and the Wall Street scandals   See SARBANES-OXLEY ACT OF 2002.

enterprise zones   Enterprise zones were first advanced in the United States by both President RONALD REAGAN and President GEORGE W. BUSH. Enterprise zones were federal experiments with urban economic renewal and revitalization, creating partnerships between state, local, and federal governments.

Proponents of enterprise zones believed that creating zones with less government interference and increased economic incentives would encourage businesses to relocate to or expand in these zones. To that end, companies in enterprise zones could avail themselves of an array of incentives, including business property depreciation, employer tax credits for new hires, and lower corporate tax rates. Municipalities had to deregulate and provide an array of incentives, including, for instance, relaxing or even waiving zoning rules and building codes, exempting state utility taxes, and providing an array of tax abatements from an array of taxing districts.

The Clinton administration revised the enterprise zones, renaming them "empowerment zones." The main difference was a focus on economic redevelopment in distressed communities. President Bill Clinton also believed that the federal government should take a proactive role in these zones and so awarded zones on a competitive basis to local governments that advanced the best plans for economic revitalization of distressed communities. Most of the zones were created in the most distressed communities. Businesses were still eligible for an array of tax credits, but the zones were also eligible for grant money to be used to provide needed services (e.g., child care) to the area's residents. The Clinton administration's intent was to ensure that the bulk of the zone benefits would go to the area's residents.

Enterprise zones, despite their promise, face many criticisms. For instance, businesses with historically rapid employee turnovers that provide neither living-wage jobs nor careers (e.g., the fast-food industry) receive employer tax credits. Further, enterprise zones are not limited to areas in need of economic revitalization, nor have enterprise zones in distressed areas resolved unemployment. In addition, many people argue that businesses can leave one community for another to take advantage of the benefits of the enterprise zone while economically hurting the first community.

The federal offices that oversee enterprise zones include the U.S. DEPARTMENT OF HEALTH AND HUMAN SERVICE's Office of Community Services, the U.S. DEPARTMENT OF AGRICULTURE, the U.S. DEPARTMENT OF HOUSING AND URBAN DEVELOPMENT, the U.S. DEPARTMENT OF COMMERCE, the U.S. DEPARTMENT OF EDUCATION, the U.S. DEPARTMENT OF TRANSPORTATION, the U.S. DEPARTMENT OF JUSTICE, the ENVIRONMENTAL PROTECTION AGENCY, and the SMALL BUSINESS ADMINISTRATION.

For more information

Gittell, Marilyn, et al. "Expanding Civic Opportunity: Urban Empowerment Zones." *Urban Affairs Review* 33, no. 4 (1998): 552–555.

Green, Roy, and Michael Brintnall, eds. *Enterprise Zones*. Newbury Park, Calif.: Sage Publications, 1991.

Linda K. Shafer

environmental impact statement

An environmental impact statement (EIS) is a public document prepared by a federal agency when it proposes a major action that significantly affects the environment. An EIS allows federal decision makers to understand the environmental consequences of their proposals and to consider environmental factors in their planning and decision making, just as they consider economic, political, and other factors when they make decisions.

The National Environmental Policy Act (NEPA) requires federal agencies to prepare an EIS whenever their proposals will have significant environmental impacts. Unlike other environmental laws, NEPA does not regulate one particular area of the environment, such as air, water, or land. Instead, NEPA imposes a mandatory procedural obligation on every federal agency to investigate the potential environmental effects of all major proposals before proceeding. More important, NEPA does not impose substantive requirements on agency decision making. It is a procedural statute. Once a federal agency has complied with NEPA's procedures, the agency can proceed with its proposed action, even if the action will cause environmental harm.

NEPA requires the preparation of an EIS whenever a federal agency proposes a (1) major (2) federal action (3) that significantly affects (4) the quality of the human environment. If an agency's proposal meets all four of these criteria, it must prepare an EIS. If one or more of these requirements are not met, the agency does not need to prepare an EIS.

While some agency actions always require the preparation of an EIS and an EIS is specifically excused for other actions, an agency often needs more information to determine whether its proposal triggers an EIS. In this case, an agency will prepare an Environmental Assessment (EA) to determine whether or not its proposal meets all four EIS criteria. If an agency concludes that any of the EIS criteria are not met, it issues a "finding of no significant impact" (FONSI). The FONSI describes why the proposed action does not trigger the need for an EIS. If the EA reveals that the proposed action does meet the EIS requirements, then the agency must prepare an EIS.

The first step in the EIS process is called scoping. Scoping allows other agencies and the public to help the agency determine the scope of the EIS and significant issues that must be discussed in the EIS. After scoping, the agency prepares a draft EIS (DEIS) that discusses: (1) the purpose and need for the proposed action, (2) the affected environment, (3) reasonable alternatives to the action (including no action), (4) the possible and unavoidable environmental impacts of the proposal and the alternatives in comparative form, (5) appropriate possible mitigation measures, and (6) the agency's preferred alternative. The DEIS is then released to relevant federal, state, and local agencies and to the public for comments. After reading and considering these comments, the agency can alter the proposal or prepare a final EIS (FEIS). In the FEIS, the agency must respond to each comment, modify its analyses where necessary, and cite authority for its final determination. After the FEIS is circulated to interested parties, the agency has approximately 30 days to make its final decision on the proposal.

Some commentators criticize EIS litigation and correctly point out that the judicial remedy for incorrectly following the EIS procedure is simply for the agency to correctly prepare the EIS. However, the EIS requirement has caused federal agencies to modify numerous projects to reduce their environmental impact and abandon many environmentally unjustifiable projects.

For more information
Bass, Ronald E., Albert I. Herson, and Kenneth M. Bogdan. *The NEPA Book: A Step-by-Step Guide on*

How to Comply with the National Environmental Policy Act, 2d ed. Point Area, Calif.: Solano Press Books, 2001.

Robert W. Malmsheimer

Environmental Protection Agency (EPA)

The Environmental Protection Agency is the U.S. federal agency responsible for protecting human health and safeguarding the natural environment—air, water, and land—upon which life depends.

The EPA was established as an independent agency by Reorganization Plan No. 3 of 1970. It resulted from a consolidation of the Federal Water Quality Administration, Department of the Interior; the Federal Radiation Council, an independent agency; Environmental Health Service (Environmental Control Administration and National Air Pollution Control Administration); Public Health Service (PHS); and Department of Health, Education and Welfare (HEW).

There were numerous predecessor agencies to the EPA, and it is interesting to see the diverse agencies that were consolidated to create this new single agency that coordinates federal action to reduce environmental pollution. These predecessors included: Federal Radiation Council (1959–70); in the Public Health Service, the Federal Security Administration (FSA, 1949–53); HEW (1953–70); Division of Water Supply and Pollution Control (DWSPC, 1949–65); Federal Water Pollution Control Administration (FWPCA, 1965–66, to Department of the Interior); Bureau of Disease Prevention and Environmental Control (BDPEC, 1966–68); Consumer Protection and Environmental Health Service (CPEHS, 1968–70); PHS, HEW, and Environmental Health Service (EHS, 1970); Environmental Control Administration (ECA, 1968–70); National Air Pollution Control Administration (NAPCA, 1968–70); Federal Water Pollution Control Administration (1966–70); and the Federal Water Quality Administration (1970).

EPA gives "leadership in the nation's environmental science, research, education and assessment efforts." The agency coordinates with other federal agencies, state and local governments, and Indian tribes to develop and enforce regulations under existing environmental laws. EPA is also "responsible for researching and setting national standards for a variety of environmental programs and delegates to states and tribes responsibility for issuing permits, and monitoring and enforcing compliance."

Since its activities are very broadly based and its regulatory authority significant, the EPA is often seen as quite intrusive in the functioning of businesses, industry, agriculture, and many areas of life in the United States (i.e., "over-regulating"). On the other hand, those seeking stronger action by the EPA at times blame the agency for "getting in bed with the polluters."

One of the policy-centered problems facing EPA has been a shifting regulatory and political environment, resulting in profound "mission creep" and an inability of the agency to focus and manage itself effectively. It has been called "a conglomerate of offices" trying to administer numerous regulatory laws that have been written, often without regard to each other and thus at cross-purposes. Under the Clinton administration, an effort at "reinventing EPA" was launched. Its purpose was to create a model regulatory system in which a command-and-control approach to environmental regulation would be replaced by a more efficient and pragmatic model. One of the most promising of these reforms has been the Common Sense Initiative (CSI). This pushed the EPA, states, and regulated industries to seek new, faster, more innovative, and less punitive solutions to pollution control and prevention.

However, Congress has resisted changing the statutory environment and fundamentally redesigning the approach to environmental regulation, preferring to tinker with the existing framework. This, as well as federalism—which dilutes the agency's authority into 10 regional offices dealing with 50 state governments that

A farmworker handles common pesticide used in food production. The Environmental Protection Agency is responsible for the regulation of pesticides.   (PHOTO BY USDA)

take responsibility or are participants in the environmental policy process—further disperses the agency.

For more information

Landy, Marc K., et al. *The Environmental Protection Agency: Asking the Wrong Questions from Nixon to Clinton*, expanded ed. New York: Oxford University Press, 1994.

Quarles, John. *Cleaning Up America: An Insider's View of the Environmental Protection Agency*. New York: Houghton Mifflin Co., 1976.

Steffen W. Schmidt

Equal Employment Opportunity Act   The
Equal Employment Opportunity Act (EEOA) refers to Title VII of the Civil Rights Act of 1964, Public Law 88-352 (2 July 1964) and amendments that make it illegal to intentionally discriminate against individuals based on race, color, religion, gender, or national origin in the area of employment.

Title VII also makes it illegal for employers to undertake unintentional discriminatory practices that have the effect of intentional discrimination against individuals. Unintentional discriminatory practices might include the following: hiring and firing; compensation, promotion, job advertisements; recruitment, testing, training, and apprenticeship programs; and pay. All private employers, state and local governments, and education institutions that employ 15 or more individuals must comply with these regulations.

In addition, this act also covers private and public employment agencies, labor organizations, and joint labor-management committees controlling apprenticeship and training. According to this act, employers must post visible notices within the work area that advise all employees of their rights under Title VII.

An important feature of the EEOA is the establishment of the EQUAL EMPLOYMENT OPPORTUNITY COMMISSION (EEOC) as the independent federal regulatory agency. The EEOC provides oversight and coordination of all federal equal employment opportunity regulations, practices, and policies. The EEOC is composed of five commissioners and a general counsel appointed by the president and confirmed by the Senate. The commissioners are appointed for five-year staggered terms and have authority to establish equal-employment policy and provide the general counsel with the necessary approval to conduct litigation. Headquartered in Washington, D.C., the EEOC provides enforcement, education, and technical assistance activities through its 50 field offices across the United States.

Individuals who believe they have experienced employment discrimination can file an administrative charge with the EEOC. The EEOC mediation-based alternative dispute-resolution (ADR) program encourages all parties, with the assistance of a neutral mediator, to voluntarily participate in confidential deliberations that resolve discrimination issues in appropriate cases. While the act covers discrimination in federal employment, different procedures are used to process these charges.

Despite the valuable functions that the EEOA performs as a legal instrument for articulating and structuring the protection of employee rights in the public and private sectors, its interpretation and enforcement have come under increasing criticism over time. Specifically, there are charges that the EEOC has, on occasion, misinterpreted the law and failed to keep pace with the expanding scope of the agency's responsibilities as employment and socioeconomic issues become increasingly complex. For instance, as the annual number of complaints filed with the EEOC over time have increased substantially, agency staffing continues to increase only marginally. This gap between the administrative agency's politically delegated duties and agency resources illustrates a broader issue in public administration—the constraints facing public organizations trying to meet expanding demands with relatively fewer resources.

For more information

Buckley, John F. *Equal Employment Opportunity Compliance Guide 2001.* New York: Aspen Publishers, 2001.

Twomey, David P. *Equal Employment Opportunity Law,* 3d ed. Mason, Ohio: South-Western Publishing Co., 1994.

Yasmin A. Dawood

Equal Employment Opportunity Commission   The Equal Employment Opportunity Commission is a federal agency, established by Title VII of the Civil Rights Act of 1964, that is mandated to eliminate illegal discrimination in the workplace.

The U.S. Equal Employment Opportunity Commission (EEOC) enforces a number of statutes that prohibit employment discrimination on the basis of race, color, religion, sex, national origin, age, or disability. The laws enforced by the EEOC include the Civil Rights Act of 1964, the Age Discrimination in Employment Act of 1967, the Equal Pay Act of 1963, the Americans with Disabilities Act of 1990, and the Civil Rights Act of 1991.

Any person who believes that he or she has been discriminated against in the workplace has the right to file an administrative charge with the EEOC. Once the EEOC is satisfied that there are sufficient grounds to believe that discrimination has occurred, it attempts to conciliate between the employer and the employee in order to reach a voluntary resolution. If conciliation fails, the EEOC may decide to bring suit in federal court.

The EEOC is aided by 90 state and local fair-employment-practices agencies (FEPAs) that help process discrimination charges.

The EEOC receives approximately 75,000 to 80,000 administrative charges per year. It also files a number of lawsuits every year on behalf of victims of employment discrimination. For example, the EEOC filed 327 suits and resolved 428 suits in 2000. In addition, the EEOC files amicus curiae briefs to provide support in other cases where employment discrimination is being addressed.

The EEOC is run by five commissioners, who are appointed for five-year terms, and a general counsel who is appointed by the president and confirmed by the Senate.

In its early years, the EEOC only had the power to engage in conciliation, education, and outreach. In 1972, Congress significantly expanded the role of the EEOC when it granted the Commission its ability to litigate cases and enforce antidiscrimination statutes. The Equal Employment Opportunity Act of 1972 provided the EEOC with the authority to sue both governmental and nongovernmental employers.

One of the greatest challenges facing the EEOC is processing the tremendous backlog of claims that has developed over the years. For example, there was a backlog of 94,700 unresolved charges by 1977. Part of the difficulty is that the EEOC is responding to individual complaints as well as attempting to redress systemic patterns of discrimination that affect large numbers of employees. The large number of existing claims and the continued influx of new claims has led some commentators to suggest that the EEOC has not been effective in eliminating discrimination in employment.

For more information

Munroe, Maurice E. R. "The EEOC: Pattern and Practice Imperfect." *Yale Law and Policy Review* 13 (1995): 219.

Selmi, Michael. "The Value of the EEOC: Reexamining the Agency's Role in Employment Discrimination Law." *Ohio State Law Journal* 57 (1996): 1.

Yasmin A. Dawood

equal protection clause   The equal protection clause is the provision of the Fourteenth Amendment to the U.S. Constitution that prohibits the states from denying persons within their territorial and legal jurisdiction "the equal protection of the laws." The objective of equal protection is to ensure that people will be treated alike in like circumstances, thus securing to all persons within the state's boundaries the full enjoyment of their personal and civil rights. This guarantee is one way to redress the unequal balance of power between the state and its citizens, and it applies only to "state action," that is, to the actions of the state and all its entities and agencies.

In order to carry out its many functions, the state must be able to classify its citizens and treat them in different ways. For example, the state must determine who is eligible to drive a car, practice medicine, or receive a liquor license. It is not arbitrary, capricious, or discriminatory to decide that seven-year-olds may not drive a car or that only a person who has received a medical degree may practice medicine. However, when the classifications are designed to include or exclude people from a class based on characteristics such as race, religion, or national origin, the state is seen to be overstepping the limits of its legitimate power unless it can show good reasons for its discriminatory treatment. Although the Fourteenth Amendment was originally intended to protect the freedom of recently emancipated African Americans, it applies to all persons within a state's jurisdiction. Basically, equal protection means that state law must treat all people similarly situated in the same way, giving them the same rights and imposing the same duties. This does not mean that a state may not lawfully treat people differently. Equal protection allows differential treatment when it is reasonable and not arbitrary, and people in different circumstances can be treated differently. However, the equal protection clause of the Fourteenth Amendment prohibits "invidious discrimination," a wholly arbitrary and capricious treatment of similarly situated persons in an unequal manner.

More than a century of case law has shaped the nature and limits of equal protection. Equal protection is intended to protect the exercise of fundamental constitutional rights, such as the right to marry, to have children, to exercise free speech, to vote, to engage in interstate travel, and to engage in a lawful business. The protections of the Fourteenth Amendment have been found to cover all the fundamental rights guaranteed under the U.S. Constitution.

Persons who claim denial of equal protection must challenge the validity of the state action in court. The purpose of such a lawsuit is to secure judicial review of the statute alleged to be discriminatory and obtain redress, if warranted. Courts review statutes alleged to violate equal protection according to a two-tiered standard. Most economic and social legislation must meet the test of bearing "a rational relationship to a legitimate state interest or purpose," a test that tends to favor the state. However, when it is alleged that the statute involves a "suspect classification," the law is subjected to the much more rigorous standard of STRICT SCRUTINY. This means that, in addition to showing the usual rational relationship, the state must show the existence of a "compelling state interest" to justify the statute, which puts a heavy burden of proof on the state. Suspect classifications include those based on race and national origin, religion, alienage (foreign citizenship), sex, and nonresidency. For example, in 1967, in *Loving v. Virginia* (388 U.S. 1), the U.S. Supreme Court struck down a law banning interracial marriage. However, many other classifications are not considered "suspect," even though unequal treatment results. For example, age, illegitimacy, and having a criminal record are not considered to be suspect classifications. A number of states punish habitual offenders much more severely than first-time criminals, but this differential treatment does not violate equal protection. And the state can still discriminate on the basis of an otherwise suspect classification, such as national origin, when it appears that there is a compelling interest to do so. Accordingly, in 1944, in *Korematsu v. United States* (323 U.S. 214), the U.S. Supreme Court upheld a civilian exclusion law aimed at Japanese Americans during World War II.

The equal protection clause of the Fourteenth Amendment only applies to actions by the states. Discriminatory actions by the federal government are regulated by the due process clause of the Fifth Amendment.

For more information
Legal Information Institute. http://www.law.cornell.edu/topics/equal_protection.html.

Celia A. Sgroi

Ethics in Government Act   The Ethics in Government Act, also known as the Independent Counsel Act, was passed in order to promote public confidence in public officials through independent investigations, financial disclosures, and restrictions on post-governmental employment. It was signed into law on 26 October 1978 as Public Law 95-521 by President James Carter. In the aftermath of the Nixon administration's WATERGATE scandal, congressional leaders sought to create a law that would restore the American people's faith in their federal government and prevent further bribery, graft, or conflicts of interest. It has been amended a number of times since its enactment, with the most significant revision being the Ethics Reform Act of 1989.

The act mandates that all senior officials, political appointees, agency heads, managers, and high-ranking officers in the military must publicly declare their sources of income and document their assets. These officials are also required to make public the assets of their spouses and dependent children as well. This is to include stocks, bonds, mutual funds, pensions, real estate, noninvestment income, and honoraria. Officials must also document any gifts, including food, lodging, and entertainments they receive from a nongovernmental source such as private individuals, lobbying groups, media, or social clubs. Almost 20,000 individuals in the executive branch are required to file such reports.

These reports are sent to the OFFICE OF GOVERNMENT ETHICS (OGE). Established under the law, it is an independent agency in the executive branch whose job is to prevent conflict of interest from occurring and to resolve those conflicts of interest once they are uncovered. There, ethics officials review the reports and identify potential conflicts of interest. Once this process is over, these reports are made public and can be viewed by anyone upon request. For example, through media requests to the OGE, the American people learned that President Clinton had received $190,000 worth of gifts from supporters before leaving office. Questions regarding the appropriateness of some of the contributions caused the Clintons to return almost half of these gifts.

The act puts limitations on post-governmental employment to prevent government officials from cashing in on their government service. After leaving office, individuals often go to work for special interests who sought favor from them while they were in office. This not only allows for potential misconduct on the part of the official, but gives unfair advantage to the special-interest group. Federal officials cannot be involved in lobbying efforts for at least one year after leaving office and at least two years on matters that the individual supervised while in office. There is a lifetime ban in specific instances where the official used his personal influence while in office.

The most controversial aspect of the act is the establishment of an independent counsel. The Congress was trying to prevent another "Saturday night massacre," wherein Nixon tried to fire Archibald Cox in order to stop his investigation. Under the act, if the attorney general receives information that a high-ranking official has committed a crime, he or she has 30 days to determine whether the information is reliable. If so,

the attorney general has 60 more days to begin a preliminary investigation and decide if further investigation is needed. If so, a federal three-judge panel—appointed every two years by the chief justice of the Supreme Court—decides whether an independent counsel is needed and the range of his or her activities. The independent counsel has the full authority of a federal prosecutor and full access to the Justice Department. The independent counsel can only be removed from office by the attorney general, and "only for good cause, physical or mental disability . . . or any other condition that substantially impairs the performance of such independent counsel's duties." The most famous independent counsel is Ken Starr, who was commissioned to investigate alleged misconduct by President Bill Clinton.

The Ethics in Government Act has not been the panacea Congress hoped it would be. Many government officials feel that the full-disclosure laws are in some instances impossible to meet. The revolving door between government service and special interests has not stopped. Finally, many of the original supporters of the independent counsel have started to believe that changes needed to be made after the investigations of Presidents Reagan and Clinton. In the aftermath of their scandals, Congress allowed the special prosecutor provision to expire. With the special prosecutor costing the government millions of dollars and with both major parties feeling the sting of the law, there is little chance the special prosecutor law will be revived in its current form. The Ethics in Government Act is a work in progress that continues to be fine-tuned and changed over time as Congress tries to assure the American people of their government's honesty.

For more information

Anechiarico, Frank, and James B. Jacobs. *The Pursuit of Absolute Integrity.* Chicago: University of Chicago Press, 1996.

Garment, Suzanne. *Scandal: The Culture of Mistrust in American Politics.* New York: Anchor Books, 1992.

T. Jason Soderstrum

European Union   The European Union (EU) is the result of a process of cooperation and integration that began in 1951 among six countries (Belgium, Germany, France, Italy, Luxembourg, and the Netherlands). Today, it can be viewed as a supranational institution formed by the following 15 European countries: Austria, Belgium, Denmark, Finland, France, Germany, Greece, Ireland, Italy, Luxembourg, Netherlands, Portugal, Spain, Sweden, and United Kingdom.

The main objectives of the European Union are: (1) to promote economic and social progress (the single market was established in 1993; the single currency in 2002), (2) to assert the identity of the European Union on the international scene (through European humanitarian aid to non-EU countries, common foreign and security policies, action in international crises and common positions within international organizations, (3) to introduce European citizenship (which does not replace national citizenship but complements it and confers a number of civil and political rights on European citizens), (4) to develop an area of freedom, security, and justice (linked to the operation of the internal market and more particularly to the freedom of movement of persons), and (5) to maintain and build on established EU law (all the legislation adopted by the European institutions, together with the founding treaties).

The European Union is built on an institutional system that is the only one of its kind in the world. The member states delegate sovereignty for certain matters to independent institutions that represent the interests of the union as a whole, its member countries, and its citizens. A commission traditionally upholds the interests of the union, while each national government is represented within the council, and the European Parliament is directly elected by citizens. Democracy and the rule of law are therefore the cornerstones of the structure.

This institutional triangle is flanked by two other institutions: the Court of Justice (ensuring compliance with the law) and the Court of Audi-

tors (responsible for auditing the accounts). The following five bodies make the system complete: the Economic and Social Committee and the Committee of Regions (they help to ensure that the positions of the EU's various economic and social categories and regions, respectively, are taken into account), the European Ombudsman (who deals with complaints from citizens concerning maladministration at the European level), the European Investment Bank (an EU financial institution), and the European Central Bank (responsible for monetary policy in the euro era).

The European Union does not have a formal constitution. Instead, it has been built through a series of treaties that represent binding commitments by the member states signing them. The first three are the founding treaties: (1) the Treaty establishing the European Coal and Steel Community (Paris, 1952), (2) the Treaty establishing the European Community (Rome, 1958), and (3) the Treaty establishing the European Atomic Energy Community (Rome, 1958).

These have been amended on several occasions. There have also been three more far-reaching reforms bringing major institutional changes and introducing new areas of responsibility for the European institutions: (1) the Single European Act (Luxembourg and The Hague, 1987), (2) the Treaty on European Union (Maastricht, 1993), and (3) the Treaty of Amsterdam (1999). Furthermore, the Treaty of Nice, agreed at the European Council in December 2000 and signed in February 2001, amends the existing treaties. It will enter into force once it has been ratified by the 15 member states in accordance with their respective constitutional procedures.

For more information
European Union. http://europa.eu.int/.

Mila Gascó

events of 11 September 2001   The events of 11 September 2001 were the terrorist hijacking of four commercial airplanes in the United States. Two crashed into and destroyed the World Trade Center Towers in New York City; one plane crashed into the Pentagon; and one crashed in rural Pennsylvania. Overall, more than 3,600 people died as a result of these events. The importance of the events of 11 September 2001 (often referred to the "events of September 11" or the "9/11" or "911" events), is evidenced by their dramatic impact upon domestic and foreign policy in the United States and upon the world. Domestically, it led to a host of new security laws and the creation of a new federal cabinet department, while in foreign affairs it has made the elimination of terrorism a major goal of the United States.

On the morning of 11 September 2001, four jets were hijacked by members of the al-Qaeda terrorist organization, a group whose origins could be tied to parts of the Arabic and Islamic world. American Airlines flight 11 out of Boston was crashed into the north tower of the World Trade Center in New York City, and then United Airlines flight 175 out of Boston was crashed into the south tower. Subsequently both towers collapsed and over 3,000 people died. On the same day, al-Qaeda terrorists crashed American Airlines flight 77 into the Pentagon, killing several hundred people, and then United Airlines flight 93 crashed in Somerset County, Pennsylvania, after passengers on the airplane fought with the terrorists, thus preventing it from perhaps being crashed into another building.

The crash of these four airplanes had a dramatic effect on the United States and the world in several respects. First, this was the largest terrorist attack ever on the United States. Second, the damage to New York City and to Wall Street stock markets was extensive, contributing to economic problems for the former and exacerbating an already ongoing economic recession in the United States. Third, New York City, as well as the Pentagon, had to address significant cleanup and rebuilding efforts.

Yet the most important aspects of the 9/11 events were their impact on President George W.

Bush and American domestic and foreign policy. The president's response to the terrorist attacks was to launch an invasion against Afghanistan and its Taliban leaders, who were hosting Osama bin Laden, the head of the al-Qaeda group. Within weeks the Taliban were ousted from power. In undertaking this military response, President Bush enjoyed over 90 percent support from the American public, revising a presidency that seemed to be aimless.

In addition, the events of 11 September led to a short-term change in American attitudes toward government. For about 30 or 40 years prior to 9/11, Americans had become increasingly distrustful of government. Yet the terrorist attacks

Smoke billows from the World Trade Center's twin towers after they are struck by commercial airliners that had been hijacked by terrorists.   (SHAW/GETTY IMAGES)

seemed to reverse that, at least temporarily, in that the public now wanted more government intervention. These terrorist attacks, along with economic scandals that were occurring on Wall Street at the same time, signaled an important turning point in American politics, as it suggested renewed demands for an activist government.

Among the responses that 9/11 produced were efforts to create a new Department of Homeland Security and a proposal to make this new department into a cabinet-level bureau. This new department would take over the functions of many different agencies in an effort to improve security within the United States. Another response was to replace private security workers at airports with federal employees, while a third was the creation of special loans to the airlines to pay for the economic losses associated with 9/11. There were initial calls for other security measures in the country, including the easing of rules on wiretapping and surveillance, as well as demands to require national identification cards. Others called for the use of racial profiling or the special searches of Arabic-looking individuals who were boarding airlines, and many groups with ties to the Arabic and Islamic worlds were scrutinized to see if they had any terrorist contacts. Critics argued that many of these measures violated the U.S. Constitution.

Finally, the events of 11 September changed American foreign policy. In one speech, the president described a war on terrorism, while in another he described several nations, including Iran, Iraq, and North Korea, as part of an "axis of evil." The importance of these speeches seemed to place renewed emphasis upon the United States using military power to address terrorism around the world. Critics claimed that such a strategy would isolate America in the world, while supporters described these policies as essential to making the United States and the world more safe.

As of this writing, it is difficult to assess the entire impact that the events of 11 September had upon America and the world. Yet in many ways, they changed and challenged American domestic and foreign policy, and they forced tremendous changes in how public agencies and administrators performed their duties.

For more information
White House. Department of Homeland Security. http://www.dhs.gov/dhspublic/index.jsp

David Schultz

excise tax   Excise taxes are traditionally defined as taxes imposed by reason of the performance of an act, engagement in an occupation, or enjoyment of a privilege. Common excise taxes include gas taxes and taxes on the use of telephone communication services. The term encompasses an extraordinarily broad selection of separate taxes that are generally unrelated to federal or state income taxes or to generally applicable state and local sales taxes. As a result, excise taxes now constitute something of a miscellaneous category of taxes.

Excise taxes can be calculated in one of many different ways, such as with reference to the quantity of goods purchased, the frequency of an act, or the duration of a right or privilege. Excise taxes generally are not calculated with respect to a person's wealth, income, total consumption, or ability to pay. Excise taxes are sometimes similar to user fees when they are applied to compensate the government for costs associated with a certain activity. An example of this type of tax would be the tax applied to the sale of heavy trucks under section 4051 of the Internal Revenue Code, or the tax applied yearly under section 4481 of the Internal Revenue Code on the use of heavy trucks.

The primary purpose of some types of excise taxes is to raise revenue, while the purpose of other excise taxes may be to discourage the performance of an act or the consumption of a good. Examples of the latter are common. For instance, the gas-guzzler tax provided in section 4064 of the Internal Revenue Code applies a tax in an amount between $1,000 and $7,700 per automobile sold that has a fuel economy less than specified amounts. Another example is the tax on ozone-depleting chemicals found in section 4681 of the Internal Revenue Code, which applies a tax calculated with reference to the number of pounds of certain specified chemicals sold or used by a producer or importer, and also applies a tax on imported products that require the use of one or more specified chemicals in their production.

A few excise taxes are designed to encourage compliance with income tax rules. An example of this would be taxes that apply to investments that jeopardize the charitable purpose of private foundations, as provided in section 4944 of the Internal Revenue Code. These taxes are imposed on both the foundation and the management of the foundation where a private charitable foundation invests funds in an improper manner. Other examples include taxes that are imposed when certain requirements that apply to pension and other employee benefit plans are not followed, as provided in sections 4971 et seq. of the Internal Revenue Code.

For more information

Internal Revenue Code, sections 4001–5881.

Brian Derdowski, Jr.

executive leadership system   The executive leadership system is an approach to managing the federal bureaucracy in which the president exercises leadership to formulate policy and employs management skills to direct policy implementation with tools such as the budget.

After the patronage system was reduced radically by the civil service merit-system reforms, new problems arose. The merit system as envisioned by various theorists sees the members of the bureaucracy as political eunuchs who dutifully carry out policies without personal input. However, the merit-system model for implementing policy is staffed by human beings who often have their own agendas. In addition, the quadrennial changes or reaffirmations of presidential leadership mean that civil service personnel are charged with implementing policies with which they may not agree. Or they may be unresponsive to the need to develop new policy initiatives, including changes to improve efficiency and effectiveness to give greater flexibility in managing the ever-growing and ever-changing bureaucracy.

To counter these problems, a new system of executive leadership has been developed. Improvement in presidential control of the budget process was suggested by the BROWNLOW COMMISSION as early as 1939. The president also was authorized to reorganize the organs of government with congressional approval. The goal was to reduce duplication and to strengthen the chain of command. The president also was authorized to develop the EXECUTIVE OFFICE OF THE PRESIDENT to oversee agency activities and to assist in developing and implementing new policy programs.

The executive leadership system has produced its own set of problems. In the usual budget battles between the president and the Congress, the goal of executive leadership could destroy other values. This is probably the effect of Richard Nixon's attempt to impound funds. The action—while intended to curb inflationary spending—violated the constitutionally donated congressional power of the purse.

The executive leadership system seeks to allow the president to manage the system with personnel of his own choosing. The vast majority of civil service employees do not owe the president political allegiance, so implementation of presidential policies may be met with resistance or inadequate enforcement. Second, there are only a relatively small handful of patronage appointments available to the president. To assist the president in implementation of policy initiatives, a system of senior executive service (SES) personnel has been developed (Civil Service Reform Act of 1978). SES personnel are not merit employees, but they can be put into top jobs or moved about in the system at presidential discretion. They are usually highly trained, skilled, and experienced. They are paid more, but if relieved of duty, they return to their original civil service grade.

For more information

National Commission on the Public Service. *Leadership for America: Rebuilding the Public Service/The Report of the National Commission on the Public Service and the Task Force Reports to the National Commission on the Public Service,* Paul A. Volcker, chairman. Lexington, Mass.: Lexington Books, 1990.

Waterman, Richard W. *Presidential Influence and the Administrative State.* Knoxville: University of Tennessee Press, 1989.

A. J. L. Waskey

Executive Office of the President

Franklin D. Roosevelt brought major changes to the role and perception of the office of the president of the United States. Roosevelt was a transitional president in many ways, and significant federal growth occurred during his administration.

In recognition of the increased expectations and responsibilities of the executive branch, Roosevelt established the Executive Office of the President by executive order under the Reorganizations Act of 1939. The creation of the EOP was for the purpose of giving the president an official staff of advisers to help him carry out the increasingly difficult job of being president. It was official recognition that a president has great reliance on the people with whom he surrounds himself.

Currently, this administrative unit is made up of 11 separate offices or councils. The people appointed to these offices are the president's closest advisers and serve at his pleasure. That is, he can fire the individuals in these positions at his own discretion.

The people who have the most day-to-day contact with the president are found in the White House office. High-profile positions within this office would include the chief of staff, the national security adviser, and the White House press secretary. These positions tend to have the highest profile, and White House staffers are closely associated with the president by the press and the public. For example, the press secretary is frequently seen on the nightly news, and the chief of staff often represents the president on the Sunday talk shows. Because of their high profile, they are also most vulnerable to dismissal. Most administrations have to make replacements in White House staff positions, if for no other reason than to show that the president is making a necessary "shake-up" in response to bad publicity or poor approval ratings.

While it is not possible to give a comprehensive list here, other significant offices organized under the Executive Office of the President are:

- Office of Management and Budget—has the primary task of helping the president in budget preparations.
- Council of Economic Advisers—is responsible for providing economic analysis and advice for the formulation of economic policy.
- National Security Council—consists (typically) of the president, the vice president, the secretary of state, the secretary of defense, the director of the central intelligence agency, and the chairman of the Joint Chiefs of Staff. The National Security Council advises the president on matters of national security, both at home and abroad.

Over the years, advisers within the Executive Office of the President and members of the cabinet have had conflicts over administration policy. In general, this has occurred because executive office advisers' sole interest is assisting the president, while cabinet members have the dual role of advancing the presidential agenda and also protecting the interests of the department they lead. Sometimes the roles of a cabinet member can come into conflict and create resentment among White House staffers.

The Executive Office of the President has greatly changed the operation of the presidency and will continue to play a major role in the development of policy.

For more information

Botterweck, Michael C., and Mary Kate Hiatt. *People and Politics: An Introduction to American Government,* 8th ed. Wheaton, Ill.: Gregory Publishing, 1999.

Richard P. Davis

Executive Order 10988   Presidential Executive Order 10988 was created by President Kennedy to create a unified pattern of procedures between the federal government and the many labor unions representing federal workers.

The history of labor law in this country is long and oftentimes violent. Union membership and activity among federal government employees can be traced to the early days of this country. Employees of naval shipyards and army arsenals organized into unions sometime in the early part of the 19th century. The first federal government employee work stoppage occurred in 1835 and 1836, when employees at the Washington and Philadelphia Navy Yards struck for the 10-hour day and for general redress of their grievances. Their resistance was met with force.

The first formation of national unions of federal civil service employees began in the late 19th century. The National Association of Letter Carriers was established in 1889 as the first national postal union. In 1935, Congress passed the National Labor Relations Act (Wagner Act) and created the NATIONAL LABOR RELATIONS BOARD (NLRB) to administer it. This act established for the first time the policy that "employees shall have the right to organize and bargain collectively." However, this law applied only to private-sector employees.

World War II ended in 1945. The postwar period was marked by inflation in the private sector—new jobs, higher pay—and unrest among public employees. City employees struck in a number of municipalities. Reaction to the discontent was swift, and by the end of 1947, eight states had passed laws that would penalize striking public workers.

Also in 1947, the U.S. Congress passed the TAFT-HARTLEY ACT, which restricted labor unions in private industry. Despite this opposition, unions for government employees continued to grow. By 1955, the year of the AFL and CIO merger, membership passed the 200,000 mark. The attitudes of government employees were changing as well during this time. Many of the union's new members came from big cities that had strong trade-union roots and traditions. At labor conventions in the mid and late 1950s, union members began stressing public workers' rights and collective bargaining as a means to improve their working conditions. In 1958, New York City mayor Robert Wagner signed an executive order that granted collective-bargaining rights to unions representing city employees.

Collective bargaining in the federal service began in earnest in the 1960s. In 1961, President Kennedy appointed a commission to study labor-management relations within the federal government. It found that there was no overall pattern and that various agencies had adopted a chaotic set of arrangements to deal with unions. The Kennedy administration responded in January 1962 with Executive Order 10988. An executive order is an order issued by the president (or a state governor) that applies to the agencies within the executive branch of government.

Executive Order 10988 gave federal employees the right to join unions. It also represented the first government-wide policy on collective bargaining in the federal government and marked a major reversal of policy toward unionism in the federal sector. The scope of bargaining (those issues on which the parties were allowed to "meet and confer") was carefully restricted. EO 10988's most interesting feature was a three-level arrangement. If an employee association or labor union represented a majority of the employees in an agency (with at least 60 percent of the employees voting), it was granted "exclusive recognition." If it had between 10 and 50 percent, it received "formal recognition," and if less than 10 percent, "informal recognition." This contrasts sharply with almost all other industrial relations laws in the United States, where only exclusive recognition is allowed.

The result of this system was that competing minority unions could and did exist in many federal agencies, and membership grew rapidly in the years following. By 1970 the federal work force was 48 percent unionized. EO 10988 was substantially enlarged upon by President Nixon in 1969 with EO 11491, which expanded the representational rights of unions and employees and ended the three-tier system. It also established the Federal Service Impasse Panel, the assistant secretary of labor management relations, and the Federal Labor Relations Council (FLRC) to administer the labor relations program.

For more information

Zieger, Robert H. *American Workers, American Unions (The American Moment)*. Baltimore: Johns Hopkins University Press, 1994.

Craig Donovan

executive privilege   Executive privilege is the power of the president and high-level executive officers to withhold information from Congress and the courts. It protects the president from disclosing details pertaining to military and foreign policy, pending criminal investigations, or other confidential deliberations. The privilege does not protect the president or other officials against revealing embarrassing or incriminating information about wrongdoing in the administration.

President George Washington first invoked the privilege, although the term was not coined until the 1950s. Administrations commonly use other phrases such as confidential communications or cite other powers such as the separation of powers to justify denying Congress or the courts information. Early presidents followed Washington's lead, notably Thomas Jefferson and James Madison, and the 1803 decision in *Marbury v. Madison,* 1 Cranch (5 U.S.) 137, acknowledged the president's need for confidential discussions with his advisers. The Eisenhower administration sought to expand the privilege to all executive branch members. Presidents since Eisenhower have affirmed the traditional understanding that the privilege is the president's only. President Richard Nixon asserted that the privilege was an absolute one. However, the Supreme Court in *United States v. Nixon,* 418 U.S. 683 (1974), held that it is a qualified one that may be overcome by the public's compelling interest in fair criminal trials. The courts also rejected the Clinton administration's efforts to expand the privilege to the first lady and to the secret service agents guarding the president.

Executive privilege poses the conflict between the president's need for confidentiality and the Congress's and public's right to know what the president is doing and thus to hold him accountable for his actions. Supporters of the privilege argue that presidents require the forthright advice of their advisers and that this would be compromised if private conversations and documents were made public without good cause. Critics such as Harvard Law School Professor Raoul Berger argue that the privilege is unconstitutional. The Constitution does not explicitly grant the president such a power, and some presidents such as Nixon have abused it.

Since the WATERGATE scandal, presidents have been reluctant to assert executive privilege, fearing the taint of being identified with Richard Nixon's excesses. Some scholars and politicians fear that the denial of executive privilege may prevent the president from accomplishing important tasks. There seems to be no historical instance, however, where Congress or the courts forced the president to divulge confidential materials that harmed national security or stifled candid discussions for his successors. The courts and

Congress have sought to accommodate presidents when secrecy rather than publicity is crucial.

The separation-of-powers system, with its political process of debate and compromise, gives Congress ample power to challenge a president's assertion of executive privilege. Congress can apply public pressure on the administration through congressional hearings; it can hold administrators in contempt of Congress; it can litigate through the courts; and it can impeach the president. Congress's reluctance to reject all executive-privilege claims demonstrates its recognition of the need for some degree of confidentiality in administering government.

For more information

Berger, Raoul. *Executive Privilege: A Constitutional Myth.* Cambridge, Mass.: Harvard University Press, 1974.

Rozell, Mark J. *Executive Privilege: The Dilemma of Secrecy and Democratic Accountability.* Baltimore: Johns Hopkins University Press, 1994.

Timothy J. O'Neill

ex parte   *Ex parte* is a Latin phrase used frequently in the context of both judicial and administrative proceedings. However, neither forum utilizes this phrase for its literal meaning of "by or for one party" or "by one side only." Additionally, administrative regulations and judicial interpretation attribute significantly different meanings to *ex parte.*

> In the context of administrative law, "ex parte communication" means an oral or written communication not on the public record with respect to which not all of the parties received reasonable prior notice (5 U.S. Code §551).

In addition to the U.S. Code provisions regarding ex parte communication, the rules of federal agencies (Code of Federal Regulations) include an extensive list of permissible oral or written ex parte communications, including: matters that an administrative law judge or manager or director of an agency has statutory authority to decide; matters that all of the parties agree, or an agency official rules, may be accomplished; proposal of settlement of all of the issues involved in a hearing; request for a status report on a case; or matters generally significant to administrative practice not specifically related to any pending agency proceeding.

In the judiciary, the term *ex parte* usually refers to a situation in which one party appears before the judge and asks to be heard, either in the absence of the adversary or after purposely neglecting to give the adversary notice of the hearing. In the legal context, this situation is problematic. An ex parte, or unilateral hearing with a judge is strictly contrary to the Fifth Amendment's concept of "due process," which is rooted in the necessity of giving fair notice to all parties who may be affected by a legal proceeding.

However, despite an ex parte hearing's ideological conflict with the Constitution, adequate notice of judicial proceedings may irreparably harm one of the parties to the lawsuit. For example, in a domestic violence case, the battered party may appear before the judge to ask that the abusive spouse be prohibited from stalking. Although an ex parte hearing does not provide due process, in this situation, few judges would balk at granting the threatened party a temporary injunction. However, a temporary injunction is a very-short-term solution. Civil law requires that as soon as possible after a temporary injunction is granted, the hearing officer or administrative law judge convene a hearing with all parties present to consider a permanent injunction.

An ex parte hearing may gain judicial approval only in two other situations: first, when a plaintiff makes an ex parte request for an order to extend the time to serve a summons on the defendant; or when a plaintiff makes an ex parte request for dismissal prior to the defendant's answer or appearance in a lawsuit. In both cases, such requests will probably be granted. In the first situation, the defendant will not be harmed if the plaintiff and judge meet ex parte, because the defendant, having not yet received a summons, in all likelihood does not know that the plaintiff will soon sue him. In the second situation, if the judge conducts the ex parte hearing and then grants the dismissal sought by the plaintiff, the parties who met ex parte have saved the defendant from a trip to the courthouse.

For more information

5 U.S. Code, Sections 550 through 559.

'Lectric Law Library's Lexicon. FindLaw. Available online. URL: http://www.alllaw.com.

West's Encyclopedia of American Law. St. Paul, Minn.: West, 1998.

Beth Simon Swartz

ex parte Curtiss 299 U.S. 304 (1936) Ex parte Curtiss (United States v. Curtiss-Wright Exporting Corporation) is the leading U.S. Supreme Court case addressing the power of the president to conduct the foreign affairs of the United States. The opinion held that control of foreign relations is exclusively within the power granted by Article II of the Constitution to the president. Furthermore, the opinion of the Supreme Court established the principle that the president does not need an express grant of authority from the Constitution in order to control the foreign relations of the United States.

The Curtiss case arose after the 1932 war fought between Paraguay and Bolivia. In response to the fighting, Congress authorized the president to prohibit shipments of war supplies to these two nations if the president determined that a boycott would advance the causes of peace. President Franklin D. Roosevelt's administration did determine that such a boycott was warranted. The Curtiss-Wright Exporting Corporation was then indicted by the federal government on a complaint of conspiring to violate the terms of the embargo. The U.S. District Court, however, found for Curtiss-Wright and dismissed the indictment.

The opinion of the Supreme Court was written by Associate Justice George Sutherland. This opinion has been frequently termed a "ringing endorsement" of the independent authority of the president in the field of foreign relations. But the opinion has just as frequently been criticized. In an article in the Yale Law Journal, Charles Lofgren has written that "attempting to assess Curtiss-Wright's impact is hazardous." He notes, for example, that much of Justice Sutherland's opinion is dicta, or language not necessary to resolve the exact issue presented to the Supreme Court. That specific issue was limited to one regarding the constitutionality of the delegation of power over foreign relations to the president by the Congress. Lofgren also questions whether the Founding Fathers had the same understanding of the extent of constitutional powers that should be granted to the president that the Supreme Court concluded were warranted here. It is probably fair to conclude that the Curtiss opinion appealed to proponents of an expanded presidential authority to conduct foreign affairs at a time when the United States sought to broaden its interests in the modern world.

For more information

Lofgren, Charles A. "United States v. Curtiss-Wright Export Corporation: An Historical Reassessment." Yale Law Journal 83 (1973): 1–32.

Jerry E. Stephens

externalities Externalities are commonly referred to as spillovers from production and consumption activities, where the initial entity (producer, consumer) does not take into account the effect of its actions on others.

Externalities can either have positive or negative effects on economic well-being. If individuals receive satisfaction from a neighbor's landscaping, this represents added well-being to others from an individual's actions and is an example of a positive externality. The classic example of a negative externality is that of pollution. Here a firm does not take into account the waste or by-product from the process of producing goods, which is discharged into the environment. These discharges typically have adverse effects on the environment and on natural and living resources, such as mankind, thus imposing a cost on society in terms of cleanup and/or losses in economic well-being. These losses could comprise added health costs or the value associated with detrimental health effects, a decrease in enjoyment from recreational activities at polluted sites, a decrease in well-being due to actual reductions in recreational participation at polluted sites, and losses from detrimental effects on living and natural resources. In some cases losses can include nonuse values such as decreases in existence value (a value that individuals who do not use a site are willing to pay to preserve that site).

Economic theory uses the occurrence of externalities as an example of market failure, where the benefits and costs generated from private actions differ from benefits and costs generated to society. In the case of negative externalities, added costs or burdens are placed on society, and the economic well-being generated from the initial production/consumption action on society is less than that generated from the marketplace. In particular, we say the social costs are greater than private costs or that social benefits are less than private benefits. In this case, society would prefer to have fewer units of the good produced/consumed. Considering positive externalities, society receives additional benefits from the initial production/consumption action, and we say that social benefits exceed private benefits. Here society would prefer to have more of the good produced/consumed.

Government policies are related to externalities in many different ways. One basic idea that comes from economic theory is to design a policy so that the initial producer/consumer that causes the externality takes responsibility and changes its behavior. If it is a negative externality, a policy that would cause fewer units to be produced/consumed is desirable, and if it is a positive externality, just the opposite. Policy options include taxation, pollution charges, and imposition of environmental standards (ambient standards), discharge limits (using end-of-pipe technology, e.g., scrubbers on smokestacks), or discharge permits (setting limits on discharges by industry and allowing the trade or sale of these permits between firms that discharge less than the limit and firms that discharge more than the limit).

For more information

Mishan, E. J. *Cost-Benefit Analysis.* New York: Praeger, 1976.

Ofiara, D. D., and J. J. Seneca. *Economic Losses from Marine Pollution: A Handbook for Assessment.* Washington, D.C.: Island Press, 2001.

Douglas D. Ofiara

F

fact-finding   Fact-finding is the second step in the problem-solving model, a method that analyzes how people solve problems. The approach includes the following series of six steps, which are effective in solving problems and discovering opportunities: (1) objective finding, (2) fact-finding, (3) problem finding, (4) idea finding, (5) solution finding, and (6) acceptance finding.

The purpose of the second stage of the process is to list all the data, questions, and feelings that give a clear picture of the situation as it exists at the moment. At this stage, the goal is to make a long list of the facts that are related to the situation being investigated in order to gather all the essential data. Some of the questions that need to be answered are: Who is involved? Who might gain if this situation is resolved? What is known about this situation? What is unknown? What is a brief history of the situation? What has already been tried or thought? What are some of the obstacles encountered? How long has this situation been a concern? What would an ideal outcome be?

In order to gather the key data about the situation, researchers recommend proceeding in two phases. First, it is necessary to gather as much data as possible about the situation: facts, feelings, or questions. This activity is called diverging. During this phase, the fact finder avoids unwarranted assumptions, examines the situation from a wide variety of points of view, listens to and accepts others' versions of the facts, extends effort to dig out hidden information, and shows no reluctance to ask simple questions. Second, since some data are more important than others, the data must be reviewed to select the key information and the most-relevant facts. This second step is known as converging.

Since, from our point of view, a public policy is a decision made in the public context, the problem-solving approach is of great importance. Even more, in order to properly diagnose the problems that need to be addressed with a specific public policy, fact-finding must be conducted.

For example, if the government wants to design a public policy on education, it will have to know who is involved (teachers, students, parents), what is known about the situation (85 percent of the population finishes high school; there are not many qualified teachers; there is a lot of violence in schools), what is unknown (why people do not want to attend university; what the students' expectations are; what other things students would like to do during school hours), or what some of the obstacles encountered are (there is no budget; student's attendance in school is dropping).

The efficiency of this fact-finding process is such that this method of acquiring relevant information about a problem or a situation has been adopted by political scientists and entrepreneurs, giving rise to what has been called fact-finding missions.

In the political field, fact-finding missions are meant to gather information on a specific issue within a field of reference (e.g., justice, economic issues, or agricultural policy). Many times, fact-finding missions have been initiated with the idea of making them serve as an immediate response and reaction to crucial issues, such as those related to human rights. International organizations such as the United Nations have also used them as a means for the peaceful settlement of disputes, for verifying the execution of international agreements and treaties, or for preventive diplomatic activities.

Fact-finding missions related to the opening of markets are exploratory missions designed to expose companies to developing markets. Therefore, each mission features access to local industry experts, business development officials, and potential local business partners. Fact-finding missions are tailor-made to meet individual company needs and goals.

For more information
Jones, Charles O. *An Introduction to the Study of Public Policy.* New York: Thompson Publishing, 1997.

Mila Gascó and Fran Equiza

Fair Labor Standards Act   The Fair Labor Standards Act (FLSA), enacted by the federal government in 1938, established fair labor standards. There are four provisions of the FLSA: minimum wage, child labor, overtime, and record keeping.

The FLSA guarantees that workers are paid a minimum hourly wage for their labor. Since 1938, the law has been amended multiple times to increase the minimum wage. The 1996 amendments increased the minimum wage to $4.75 an hour on 1 October 1996 and to $5.15 an hour on 1 September 1997. The current minimum wage remains at $5.15 an hour, although a bill (the Fair Minimum Wage Act of 2001) was introduced in the Senate in May 2001 to raise the federal minimum wage to $5.75 an hour. States may also have a minimum wage law to account for variations in the cost of living.

As with most legislation, there are exceptions to today's prevailing minimum wage. Tipped employees, youth under age 20, full-time students, vocational education students, and disabled workers fall under a different minimum-wage scheme. Tipped employees, like waiters/waitresses, may be paid $2.13 an hour if they receive more than $30 a month in tips. If these employees' tips and $2.13 an hour do not equal the minimum hourly wage, the employer must make up the difference. Youth under the age of 20 receive a minimum wage of $4.25 an hour for their first 90 consecutive calendar days on the job.

In addition to setting a youth minimum wage, the FLSA includes child-labor provisions. The FLSA limits the hours of work a minor (a person under the age of 16) can perform. It also prohibits minors from working in hazardous occupations. Minors who work in agriculture still have restrictions placed upon them, but to a lesser extent than minors employed in nonfarm jobs.

According to the FLSA, employees who work over 40 hours a week must be paid one and one-half (1.5) times the regularly contracted hourly wage for every hour over 40. This is commonly referred to as "overtime." Not all types of businesses have to pay their workers a minimum wage or overtime. Certain computer-related occupations, sales employees, and some farm workers are examples of employee sectors who receive some exemptions to the minimum-wage and overtime regulations.

It is important to understand that the minimum-wage laws are not universally accepted and remain a subject of public debate. Supporters not only favor the use of a minimum wage, but also often advocate for an increase in the hourly pay. Advocates believe that the minimum wage should reflect the current cost of living and that the current $5.15 an hour is not enough for people to live on. The minimum wage also prevents discrimination in pay. Certain types of jobs in the service and retail sector are often more likely to pay less than the minimum wage. People with less education and minorities often fill these types of jobs, like hotel housekeeping staff. Without a minimum-wage law, it is likely that certain people would receive less money for the work they perform and end up in poverty. Opponents of the minimum wage law believe that requiring businesses to pay a set hourly wage to their employees places an economic hardship on businesses, especially if the minimum wage is increased. If a business is required to pay its workers more, it is likely that the business may not be able to absorb the increase in labor costs and have to lay off some of its workers or close entirely. The other scenario is that the business passes the increased cost of its labor onto the consumer. The minimum wage could in turn raise the cost of goods, and in turn, the cost of living for everyone. Additionally, setting a minimum wage for certain types of work may lead to increased wages for all workers. People in jobs that require more advanced skills or education often demand a higher wage for their work. If the base pay for all work increases, these people would likely demand an increase in their wages as well. This could lead to the scenarios previously discussed, namely laid off workers or higher costs of goods and services.

The FLSA also requires employers to keep records on wages, hours, and other items specified by the DEPARTMENT OF LABOR. The records do not have to be in a specific format, and employers usually maintain the information requested anyway. For these reasons, record keeping has not been debated like the minimum wage.

For more information

Nordlund, Willis J. *The Quest for a Living Wage: The History of the Federal Minimum Wage Program.* Westport, Conn.: Greenwood Press, 1997.

U.S. Department of Labor. http://www.dol.gov/dol/topic/wages/index.htm.

Sharon Friedrichsen

faith-based initiatives Faith-based initiatives are movements to use government tax revenue to fund religious charity efforts. President GEORGE W. BUSH has made faith-based initiatives the centerpiece of his welfare proposals.

President Bush is not the first politician to support faith-based initiatives. Several states had a history of collaborating with religious charities before 1996. The Personal Responsibility and Work Opportunity Reconciliation Act of 1996, signed into law by President Bill Clinton, prohibited public officials from discriminating against religious social service providers that wished to compete for government contracts and allowed religious organizations to express their religious views while providing social services. President Bush, a Republican, seeks to expand this program so that religious charities can directly receive federal funds to support their efforts in providing after-school programs, drug treatment counseling, meal assistance, and other work.

Supporters of faith-based initiatives argue that religious organizations are more efficient and effective in delivering social services to the needy than the federal government and its endless bureaucracy can ever hope to be, and that providing federal funds would allow them to greatly expand their efforts. These initiatives would also continue the devolution of the provision of social services to the local level, which many argue leads to social programs that are more responsive to the needs of particular communities.

Opponents of these initiatives offer several arguments against them. The most often cited objection is that providing government funds to religious organizations is a violation of the constitutional guarantee of the separation of church and state. Many liberals worry that the federal government will deem certain belief systems (such as Wicca, Scientology, or the Church of Satan) as "illegitimate" religions and refuse to fund their charitable efforts. Such a system of classification may threaten to favor groups with Judeo-Christian beliefs and marginalize all others. Others fear that federal funds will go to groups that do not meet antidiscrimination laws, resulting in state endorsement of groups that discriminate by race, ethnicity, gender, or sexual orientation. Religious leaders and some conservatives worry that religions will be forced to de-emphasize their religious teachings to conform to these antidiscrimination laws, thereby placing religion under the control of the government and compromising the very thing that makes faith-based charities effective in the first place.

For more information

"Pros & Cons of Faith-Based Initiatives." Available online. URL: http://altreligion.about.com/library/weekly/aa020701a.htm.

Schnurer, Eric B., and Jennifer Kolker. "Faith Based Initiatives: More than Meets the Eye, or Less?" Center for National Policy. Available online. URL: http://www.cnponline.org/Issue%20Briefs/ State-lines/statelin0301.htm.

Brien Shelley

Family and Medical Leave Act   The Family and Medical Leave Act (FMLA) is a 1993 federal law signed by President Bill Clinton that permits employees to take time off from work at periods in their lives when they need respite of this sort. They might have developed an illness that necessitates weeks of treatment, adopted a baby, or had one of their own. Or they might feel obligated to devote all their energies to caring for an ailing relative.

The FMLA was opposed by organizations such as the National Federation of Independent Business, and an earlier version had been vetoed by President George H. W. Bush. It covers all agencies of national, state, and local government (including public schools), and most private-sector firms with 50 or more employees. It requires that all these organizations grant their help up to 12 weeks of unpaid leave during any 12-month period for any one of the following purposes.

1. To care for a newborn or newly adopted child.
2. To care for an immediate family member (spouse, child, or parent) who has a "serious health condition."
3. To enable the employee to get treatment and rest when he/she is unable to work because of a "serious health condition."

To qualify for the rights granted under the act, a staffer must have worked for her/his establishment for at least 12 months and worked at least 1,250 hours during that time span. The law places one direct financial burden on the firm, requiring it to keep in force any health insurance it was offering the leavetaker before his/her departure. And, when she/he comes back, she/he is entitled to her/his original post or one that is similar and carries equivalent pay.

Until the FMLA's enactment, the United States was the only country out of 100 surveyed by the International Labor Organization whose national government did not require employers to grant parental leave, i.e., time off to care for a newborn or newly adopted child. (However, before the FMLA, many American states did have their own—usually relatively weak—parental leave laws.) Even today, the parental-leave measures of most industrialized countries are more generous than the FMLA, mandating payment during the period the staff member is out, setting that period at considerably more than 12 weeks, and covering smaller firms.

Between New Year's Day 1999 and mid-October of 2000, about 14 million to 16 million workers who met the FMLA's coverage and eligibility requirements took leave for one of the reasons listed in the act, though significantly less than 50 percent of these men and women formally invoked the measure when asking for their break. About 38 percent of these 14 million to 16 million people took the time off because they themselves were sick; and 98 percent of them returned to work for the same employer after their leave was over. Fifty-four percent of the individuals (some of whom worked in noncovered jobs) staying out for one of the reasons mentioned in the FMLA were away for 10 or fewer days, and only 10 percent were absent for more than 60 days. Millions more would like to use the benefits of the law but feel they cannot afford to do so because they will not be paid while away. Thus President Clinton had the U.S. Labor Department issue a regulation in 2000 allowing states to utilize any surplus in their unemployment insurance funds to pay for FMLA leaves. Bills have been introduced in over a dozen states to permit this.

About a third of the covered businesses do find it difficult to comply with the paperwork the act requires. Especially troublesome for administrative purposes are breaks taken intermittently rather than all at once. However, some firms voluntarily grant their staff more than the 12-week maximum the FMLA demands, and some accord full or partial pay to workers who are out for one of the reasons the act specifies. The work of just about everyone who goes on FMLA leave is performed by a colleague and/or by a temporary replacement hired from the outside.

For more information

Kramer, Daniel C. *Workplace Sabbaticals: Bonus or Entitlement.* Westport, Conn.: Quorum Books, 2001.

Rosenberg, D. "We Have to Sacrifice." *Newsweek* 27 (August 2001), 46.

U.S. Department of Labor. *Balancing the Needs of Families and Employers: Family and Medical Leave Surveys.* Washington, D.C.: U.S. Department of Labor, 2001.

Daniel C. Kramer

Farm Credit Administration   The Farm Credit Administration (FCA) is an independent agency of the executive branch that supervises the Farm Credit System (FCS), which provides financial resources for those engaged in agriculture. In other words, because farm income varies from season to season, year to year, the FCA provides loans to help the farmers get by and improve their operations. It provides short- and long-term credit to farmers and cooperatives and was designed to help farmers buy property, refinance, and get through periods of seasonal need. Its loans are secured by liens on livestock and warehouse receipts for crops.

The FCS was established in 1916. Its roots date back to the 1908 Country Life Commission, which examined the problems facing the rural areas. Farmers were the poorest segment of the American population at the time. The commission's report noted that there was not enough credit available to farmers. Agricultural loans were difficult to obtain from commercial banks, and high interest rates made repayment a hardship. Over the next eight years, several executive and legislative bodies tried to figure out how to address the issue. In 1914, a Joint Committee on Rural Credits was created to come up with legislation. Two years later, the Congress created a mortgage credit system of 12 regional Federal Land Banks (FLB). While the federal government would invest the initial $125 million, it would ultimately be financed by farmers and investors.

In 1923, under the Agricultural Credits Act, Congress added 12 Federal Intermediate Credit Banks (FICBs) to help extend aid to farmers. Yet, flaws in the system and the 1929 stock market crash led to loan delinquencies and a decline in farm values. Many farmers became hostile to the credit system as it foreclosed on thousands of farms and became more conservative in its loan policies.

In order to save the failing FCS, Congress and the president had to reorganize the system. In 1929, the Congress passed the Agricultural Marketing Act, which stabilized farm prices and financed the development of cooperatives. Four years later, Franklin Roosevelt issued an executive order that unified all existing federal agricultural-credit organizations into the Farm Credit Administration (FCA). Congress also refinanced the land banks with $189 million and cut interest rates under the Emergency Farm Mortgage Act. It also passed the Farm Credit Act, which established 13 banks for cooperatives and established a new production credit system for farmers through credit associations. In 1939, the FCA was transferred to the Department of Agriculture for better management and remained under that agency's oversight until 1953.

The next four decades, the 1940s through the '70s, was a time of prosperity for American agriculture. By 1947, the land banks were able to reimburse the federal government its seed money. The other institutions in the system were able to follow suit 21 years later. With FCS now completely owned by farmer/investors, in 1969 the Nation Services Commission on Agricultural Credit was established to plot the future of the FCS. Its recommendations became the Farm Credit Act of 1971. This act reorganized the FCA and expanded the services that institutions could provide to farmers to include home mortgages, leasing services, and utility lending.

Yet the FCA again faced financial problems during the 1980s farm crisis. Congress stepped in to insure the system stability. The system has decreased in size since the 1980s, when 37 banks and 1,000 lending institutions were involved, to its present size of six FCS banks and slightly more than 200 lending institutions. Yet, the importance of the FCA in maintaining a stable agricultural segment of American society can not be underestimated.

For more information

Benedict, Murray R. *Farm Policies of the United States, 1790–1950: A Study of Their Origins and Development*. New York: Twentieth Century Fund, 1953.

Harl, Neil E. *The Farm Debt Crisis of the 1980s*. Ames: Iowa State University Press, 1990.

Hurt, R. Douglas. *American Agriculture: A Brief History*. Ames: Iowa State University Press, 1994.

T. Jason Soderstrum

featherbedding Featherbedding is a union practice designed to increase union employment and guarantee job security by requiring employers to hire unnecessary workers or to limit production according to union rules or safety statutes.

The term *featherbedding* first came into use during the 1940s, when unions required railroads to retain firemen on trains even after diesel locomotives had replaced steam engines and firemen were no longer needed to shovel coal. Other examples concern union contracts that require the hiring of an apprentice along with a journeyman electrician or plumber whether the apprentice is needed or not, and musicians' union contracts that stipulate the hiring of a specific number of musicians regardless of need. Unions defend the practice as a means to protect the jobs of union members that might be threatened by technological advances.

The U.S. Congress attempted to abolish the practice of featherbedding through the TAFT-HARTLEY ACT OF 1947. Section 8(b)(6) of the act declares that union demands for payment for services not performed constitutes an unfair labor practice. The provisions of the law have been interpreted narrowly in the courts, and as a result only the practice of paying union members who do not work is prohibited, i.e., in instances where excessive union labor is required and hired but does not perform actual work. The courts have ruled that unions may require payment of wages for work that is unnecessary or of no value to an employer as long as the work is actually performed. In addition, payments can be made to workers who perform no work as long as they remain willing to work. The existence of featherbedding is usually disputed and depends on the interpretation of what constitutes a reasonable labor requirement.

Featherbedding is regarded to be a nonproductive method of increasing demand for labor and wages of union members. By increasing these components of production costs, featherbedding tends to ultimately increase prices. The practice is most often found among craft unions, where technological changes are more likely to make jobs obsolete, rather than in industrial unions, where changes in technology may actually benefit some segments of union membership.

For more information

Leiter, R. D. *Featherbedding and Job Security.* New York: Twayne Publishers, 1964.

Douglas D. Ofiara
Sharon Timberlake

Federal Bureau of Investigation (FBI)

The Federal Bureau of Investigation is the chief law-enforcement agency within the U.S. DEPARTMENT OF JUSTICE. Mandated to investigate most federal crimes, the FBI has jurisdiction over 200 different matters, including bank robbery, espionage, interstate transport of stolen property, and fraud against the U.S. government. The agency's response to the 11 September 2001 terrorist attacks reinforced its role in responding to threats against national security, a function it first assumed during World War II. Other major areas for investigation include crimes using the Internet, certain "white collar" or corporate violations, and activities of organized criminal enterprises.

Besides its investigative function, the FBI is authorized to provide services to other police agencies. For example, the FBI academy provides training for police officers worldwide. The agency also maintains computerized databanks of fingerprint and DNA records from known criminals around the world that police use in attempts to solve crimes. Police departments also send evidence from crime scenes to the FBI crime laboratory for expert analysis. The behavioral sciences unit, popularized in movies and books, assists police with investigations of unusual violent crimes, particularly serial murder and rape. The FBI also gathers statistics on offenses known to police and summarizes them in the annual *Crime in the United States: The Uniform Crime Reports.*

The agency was initially created as the "Bureau of Investigation" in 1908 to conduct investigations for the U.S. attorney general. In 1924, J. EDGAR HOOVER was appointed director, an office he would hold for 48 years. Although Hoover was controversial, he is credited with instituting reforms that increased the professionalism of the agency. Hoover also was adept at using publicity to enhance the stature of the FBI as tough and incorruptible "G-men" and to enlist the help of citizens. For example, he instituted the "top ten wanted fugitives" list in 1950 to get tips that might aid in capturing criminals on the run. Renamed the Federal Bureau of Investigation in 1935, the agency saw its reputation enhanced by stopping infamous mobsters in the 1930s, such as John Dillinger, Baby-Face Nelson, and Ma Barker.

The history of the FBI highlights the growing responsibility of the federal government. For example, following the kidnapping of the famous aviator Charles Lindbergh's son, kidnapping cases involving interstate travel were made a federal offense, and the FBI assumed investigative authority. The 1964 Civil Rights Act also placed violations of these laws under the bureau's jurisdiction.

As its scope has grown, so has its size. The FBI has grown from a small band of 30 agents in 1908 to over 11,000 at the start of the 21st century. Administrative and professional staff that support the special agents now number over 16,000. Over two-thirds are assigned to 56 field offices and more than 40 liaison offices in foreign nations. The director of the FBI is now appointed by the president pending confirmation by the U.S. Senate, with a term that cannot exceed 10 years.

U.S. flags fly over the Federal Bureau of Investigation building in Washington, D.C.   (ALEX WONG/GETTY IMAGES)

For more information

Federal Bureau of Investigation. www.fbi.gov.

Schmallenger, Frank. *Criminal Justice Today.* Englewood Cliffs, N.J.: Prentice-Hall, 1991.

Theoharis, Athan. *The FBI: An Annotated Bibliography Research Guide.* New York: Garland Publishers, 1994.

Anthony Petrosino

Federal Deposit Insurance Corporation

The Federal Deposit Insurance Corporation (FDIC) is an independent agency of the federal government that was created by Congress in June 1933 during the height of the Great Depression. Between the October 1929 stock market crash that initiated this financial disaster and the March 1933 beginning of President Franklin Delano Roosevelt's first term in office, more than 9,000 banks in the United States failed.

As a result of the bank failures, many Americans who had entrusted their savings to banks lost their money. As their friends' and relatives' savings disappeared, even the individuals whose funds were in solvent banks began to lose confidence in the banking business in general and began to withdraw their money. Consequently, very little business was transacted, even by the few capable banks.

When the financial industry became paralyzed by the combination of lost funds and lost confidence, Congress created the FDIC to reestablish public trust and thereby stabilize the banking system. Since 1934, FDIC has maintained an unblemished record of keeping every cent of its insured funds safe from bank failure.

Because FDIC guarantees that customers' bank deposits of up to $100,000 each will be safe and available for withdrawal on demand, the public continues to trust U.S. banks and savings and loan associations.

Although the U.S. banking system is very stable, it is inevitable that a small number of banks will be unable to stay in business. FDIC is responsible for helping each failing institution to untangle its finances using methods that are the least costly to the insurance fund and least disruptive for customers.

To promote the safety and soundness of the banks it insures, and of the U.S. financial system in general, FDIC identifies, monitors, and takes action to reduce or eliminate risks to insured funds. Additionally, FDIC regulates the financial affairs of all banks that are members of the FEDERAL RESERVE SYSTEM while also regulating about 6,000 state-chartered nonmember banks, which are commercial and savings banks that are not members of the Federal Reserve System.

To remain capable of fulfilling its mission of protecting customers' deposits, FDIC administers two federal deposit insurance funds, both of which are backed by the full faith and credit of the U.S. government. The Bank Insurance Fund guarantees deposits in most commercial banks and in federally chartered savings banks. The Savings Association Insurance Fund, created in 1989 as the successor to the Federal Savings and Loan Insurance Corporation (FSLIC), insures deposits up to certain limits at certain savings and loans and at state-chartered savings banks.

Congressional appropriations provide the budget necessary for FDIC to manage the FSLIC Resolution Fund, created by Congress in 1989 help alleviate financial problems caused by the 1980s' thrift industry crisis. FDIC performs all of its other functions without congressional appropriations, relying only on its modest operating budget, which is derived from deposit insurance premiums that banks and savings associations pay to FDIC, and from earnings on FDIC's investments in U.S. treasury securities.

The FDIC is managed by a board of five directors who are appointed by the president, subject to confirmation by the Senate. To insure that the FDIC is as careful with its funds as its member banks must be with their depositors' money, FDIC's ledgers are subject to congressional oversight and also to regular audits by the General Accounting Office.

For more information

Federal Deposit Insurance Corporation. http://www. fdic.gov/about/learn/symbol/index. html.

West's Encyclopedia of American Law, vol. 4. St. Paul, Minn.: West, 1998.

Beth Simon Swartz

Federal Election Campaign Act   The Federal Election Campaign Act (FECA) regulates the raising and spending of money by candidates for federal office. The provisions of the law have evolved through a series of amendments and Supreme Court decisions over several decades. FECA was originally passed in 1971 in response to increasing concern about skyrocketing campaign costs and the political influence of "fat cat" donors and special interests. Critics argued that access to federal office was increasingly limited to wealthy candidates or those willing to become beholden to the wealthy.

The FECA of 1971 established limits on spending for advertising by candidates for Congress and the presidency; required broadcasters to sell candidates air time at low rates; strengthened requirements that candidates publicly report their campaign contributions and expenditures; limited the amount of money that a candidate or his family could contribute to his own campaign; and authorized the use of labor union dues or corporate funds to set up and administer special political action committees (PACs). A separate law, passed in 1971, established a presidential election fund to finance presidential elections. The fund would be created from voluntary taxpayer contributions, but its implementation was delayed until after the 1972 presidential election at the insistence of President Richard Nixon.

Partly as a consequence of the stricter reporting requirements of FECA, serious campaign finance abuses were exposed in the 1972 Nixon reelection campaign. These abuses and the related Watergate scandal prompted calls for further campaign finance controls. In 1974, Congress passed amendments to FECA that created the most far-reaching campaign finance regulations in U.S. history. The new law established limits on contributions to candidates for federal office and limits on spending by those candidates. It also imposed stricter requirements for public disclosure of campaign contributions and expenditures while creating a system for public financing of presidential elections.

Under the law, individuals can only contribute $1,000 to a candidate per election; organizations and state parties can only contribute $5,000 to a candidate per election; and strict limits are placed on the amount a candidate or his family can contribute to his own campaign. Overall spending limits were imposed on candidates for the presidency and the Congress. One of the most significant provisions was for public subsidies for candidates seeking their party's presidential nomination and public financing of the presidential campaigns in the general election. The law created the Federal Election Commission (FEC) to implement and enforce the new regulations.

FECA supporters hoped the new law would limit the influence of large donors and special interests, broaden the base of financial support for candidates, and level the playing field in federal campaigns so that money would not be the main determinant of election outcomes. Critics, liberal and conservative, argued that the limits on contributions and expenditures violated free speech and association rights protected by the First Amendment. The public financing of presidential elections was also criticized for shifting campaign costs to taxpayers and for discriminating against minor-party candidates.

In 1976, the Supreme Court ruled in *Buckley v. Valeo*, 424 U.S. 1 (1976), that the spending limits imposed on House, Senate, and presidential candidates violated the First Amendment. Limits on "independent expenditures" made by individuals or organizations that were not coordinated with a candidate were also ruled unconstitutional. In both cases, according to the Court, spending limits restrained the quantity and diversity of political speech. However, the Court ruled that presidential candidates who accept public financing could be required to abide by spending limits. Limits on contributions to candidates and parties were also upheld.

In 1979, FECA was amended again in response to complaints by state and local parties that limits on their contributions to candidates had severely reduced their legitimate role in presidential elections. They also complained that spending limits forced candidates to devote most of their spending to television and cut back on traditional grassroots efforts, including the distribution of buttons, bumper-stickers, and yard signs. The 1979 amendments authorized state and local parties to raise and spend money with few limits if the money was used for "party-building" activities, voter registration drives, or get-out-the-vote efforts.

FECA has remained controversial over the decades, especially the "soft money" loophole that was being vigorously exploited by the 1990s. The 1979 amendments, along with favorable interpretations of the law by the FEC and the courts, have allowed the parties and federal candidates to divert hundreds of millions of dollars of unregulated contributions—"soft money"—to the state parties. This money is then spent primarily on television "issue ads" that are described as "party-building" efforts, but that are clearly intended to promote the campaigns of federal candidates. Critics argue that this loophole allows presidential candidates who accept public financing to violate spending limits. Corporate, union, and wealthy donors who are barred from direct contributions to candidates are able to gain undue political influence through their soft-money contributions, according to the critics.

In 2002, Congress passed the McCain-Feingold bill as an amendment to FECA. This law, officially called the Bipartisan Campaign Reform Act (BCRA) OF 2002, banned, among other things, soft money contributions; restricted state political party election activity in federal races; and clarified the line between issue and express advocacy. The law was immediately attacked as unconstitutional by several groups, and in *McConnell v. Federal Election Commission* 251 F.Supp. 2d 176 (D. D. C. 2003) a special three-judge panel declared portions of BCRA unconstitutional. The judges issued three separate opinions totaling 1,638 pages, and it was unclear even to experts what remained valid law as a result of the opinion. The United States Supreme Court halted enforcement of this opinion and scheduled a hearing on the case for September 2003 in order to clarify the law on campaign finance before the presidential and congressional races of 2004.

For more information
Corrado, Anthony, et al., eds. *Campaign Finance Reform: A Sourcebook*. Washington, D.C.: Brookings Institution Press, 1997.

Raymond B. Wrabley, Jr.

Federal Executive Institute   The Federal Executive Institute (FEI) is a training and development facility for senior executives in the federal government.

The FEI was created by President Lyndon B. Johnson in May 1968. In a memorandum to the Civil Service Commission, Johnson directed the formation of an organization with a mission to offer training classes designed to sharpen the management ability of top executives in the federal government. Johnson requested the commission to locate the institute in Charlottesville, Virginia. Johnson envisioned specific benefits from the Charlottesville location. It was anticipated that the relatively convenient 50-mile travel distance from Washington, D.C., would promote participation by federal executives. In addition, there was a belief that the institute

would benefit from academic collaboration with the University of Virginia at Charlottesville.

The FEI occupies a 14-acre campus and provides facilities for residential living, education, and recreation. Participants in FEI classes and programs stay in private guest rooms and have access to a fitness center. Education takes place in on-site classrooms or the Susan B. Anthony Library.

The curriculum offers two major study programs. Leadership for a Democratic Society courses are designed to enhance program performance and interagency cooperation. Exchanging information and developing positive work relationships are key components in this area of study. The Center for Executive Leadership classes develop skills to improve team building and organizational growth. Institute classes are taught by a small number of resident faculty and a large number of adjunct faculty.

Enrollment for courses is limited to executives from the senior executive service (SES) or executives who have reached grade GS-15. The limitation is deliberate in meeting the objective of targeting the highest management levels of the federal government.

There is no appropriated money directed to the operation of the FEI. Funding is generated entirely from tuition paid by participants. Therefore, it is incumbent upon FEI to provide classes that add value to participants.

In addition to the FEI at Charlottesville, training centers for federal employees are located in Denver, Colorado, and Shepherdstown, West Virginia.

For more information
Federal Executive Institute. www.leadership.opm.gov/fei/.

Richard J. Van Orden

federalism   Federalism is a constitutional principle referring to the division of power between the national government and the states, as embodied in the Tenth Amendment. "The powers not delegated to the United States by the Constitution, nor prohibited by it to the States, are reserved to the States respectively, or to the people." The national government and the states are limited sovereigns. The Constitution attempted to balance the need for stronger central government with a desire to retain some power for the states.

The powers of the national government, known as delegated powers, include (1) enumerated powers, those listed in the Constitution, and (2) constitutionally implied powers, those identified by the Supreme Court as naturally flowing from the enumerated powers. The identification by the Supreme Court of implied constitutional powers has greatly expanded its national authority. Implied constitutional powers were first established for the Supreme Court in *Marbury v. Madison*, 5 U.S. (1 Cranch) 137 (1801), for Congress in *McCulloch v. Maryland*, 17 U.S. (Wheat.) 316 (1819), and for the presidency in *in re. Neagle*, 135 U.S.1 (1890). A long line of cases decided by the Supreme Court, particularly those decided during the Great Depression, has continued to expand the implied constitutional powers of the national government.

The powers belonging to the states are known as reserved powers. Although national authority has expanded over the years, the Supreme Court has protected state power in a variety of contexts. For example, a state retains the power to decide where its capital is located (*Coyle v. Smith*, 221 U.S. 559 [1911]), to be free from performing congressionally mandated background checks (at state expense) for gun control (*Printz v. U.S.*, 117 S.Ct. 2365 [1997]), to be free from the congressional requirement to take ownership of toxic waste (*New York v. United States*, 505 U.S. 144 [1992]), and to be free from federal court intervention into an ongoing state prosecution (*Younger v. Harris*, 401 U.S. 37 [1971]).

The Civil War amendments, specifically aimed at limiting state power after the war, had a profound effect upon the Union/state relationship. The Thirteenth Amendment outlawed states from legalizing slavery; the Fourteenth Amendment required the states to give due process and equal protection; the Fifteenth Amendment prohibited states from denying the right to vote on account of race. The due process clause of the Fourteenth Amendment has been used by the Court to apply most of the protections in the Bill of Rights, which apply directly only against the national government, against the states. This has greatly enhanced national authority, particularly that of the Supreme Court, over the authority of the states.

Later amendments enhanced national power by authorizing a national income tax (Sixteenth), prohibiting states from using gender as a criterion for voting (Nineteenth), prohibiting use of a poll tax in federal elections (Twenty-fourth), and protecting the right to vote for 18-year-olds (Twenty-sixth). National authority was greatly strengthened by these amendments. The Eleventh Amendment enhanced state power by protecting states from suit by citizens of another state.

James Madison in *The Federalist Papers* considered federalism, along with the principle of separation of government into three branches, to be a double protection of our liberties. He defined tyranny as the concentration of power and viewed the division of governmental power as a way to prevent tyranny over our liberties. Congress, the president, and the Supreme Court would each be a check on the power of the other, as the states and national government would each be a check on the power of the other. Federalism became an experiment in democracy, complicated and ever changing.

For more information
Walker, David. *The Rebirth of Federalism*, 2d ed. New York: Chatham House, 2000.

Carol Tebben

Federal Labor Relations Authority   The Federal Labor Relations Authority (FLRA) is the independent federal government agency charged with the responsibility for overseeing labor-management relations between the federal government and its 1.9 million civilian employees worldwide, excluding postal workers.

Approximately 1.1 million federal workers are represented by unions in 2,200 bargaining units. The FLRA's mission is to resolve disputes that arise under Title VII of the CIVIL SERVICE REFORM ACT OF 1978, also known as the Federal Service Labor-Management Relations Statute. This includes adjudicating cases regarding the negotiability of collective-bargaining agreement proposals, hearing appeals concerning unfair labor practices and representation petitions, and ruling on exceptions to grievance arbitration awards.

The FLRA was established by the Civil Service Reform Act of 1978 and is based in Washington, D.C. Modeled on the NATIONAL LABOR RELATIONS BOARD, the Office of the Chairman and Members has three board members, including the chairman, who are appointed to serve five-year terms by the president with the advice and consent of the Senate and the Office of the General Counsel. The chairman of the authority also serves as the chief executive and administrative officer of FLRA. He also serves on the National Partnership Council, which was created during the Clinton administration to encourage greater labor-management cooperation among federal employees. Finally, the chair heads the Foreign Service Labor Relations Board and chooses its two other members.

The authority includes six offices: the aforementioned Office of the Chairman and Members; the Office of Administrative Law Judges, which hears cases and makes recommendations involving unfair labor practices; the Collaboration and Alternative Dispute Resolution Office, which attempts to resolve disputes using dispute-resolution techniques; the Office of the Solicitor, which represents the FLRA in court proceedings and also provides legal advice in intra-agency disputes; the Office of the Executive Director, which manages the FLRA's programs, including budget, personnel,

and procurement; and finally, the Office of Inspector General, which is responsible for carrying out audits and investigations and promoting more-efficient administrative practices.

Besides the authority, the FLRA includes the Office of the General Counsel, which investigates and prosecutes violations. The general counsel is appointed to serve a five-year term by the president with the advice and consent of the Senate. The general counsel also administers cases arising out of the FLRA's seven regional offices. Administrative law rulings of the FLRA can be appealed to the U.S. Court of Appeals and the Supreme Court.

The FLRA is probably best known for its adjudication of the Professional Air Traffic Controllers Organization (PATCO) strike in 1981. When President Reagan ordered the Federal Aviation Administration to fire the 11,000 striking air-traffic controllers represented by PATCO, rather than bargain with them, the FLRA's chief administrative law officer upheld their termination and the breaking of the union on the grounds that public employees do not have a statutory right to strike.

For more information
Broida, Peter B. *A Guide to Federal Labor Relations Authority: Law and Practice, 1979–1988*. Washington, D.C.: Dewey Publications, 1988.

Northrup, Herbert R., and Amie D. Thornton. *The Federal Government as Employer: The Federal Labor Relations Authority and the PATCO Challenge*. Philadelphia: Industrial Research Unit, Wharton School, University of Pennsylvania, 1988.

Round, Michael A. *Grounded: Reagan and the PATCO Crash*. New York: Garland Pub., 1999.

Vernon Mogensen

Federal Maritime Commission   The Federal Maritime Commission (FMC) was established in 1961 as an independent government agency responsible for the regulation of shipping and maritime commerce in the foreign trade of the United States.

Among other things, it certifies the financial responsibility of vessels that carry oil and other hazardous material to cover the cost of cleaning spills in navigable waters. The predecessor agencies to the FMC were the U.S. Shipping Board (1917–34); the U.S. Shipping Board Bureau, Department of Commerce (1934–36); the U.S. Maritime Commission (1936–50); and the Federal Maritime Board (1950–61).

The commission is made up of five members who are appointed by the president with the advice and consent of the Senate.

According to the official commission report, it has eight functions and responsibilities.

- Protects shippers, carriers, and others engaged in the foreign commerce of the United States from restrictive rules and regulations of foreign governments and from the practices of foreign-flag carriers that have an adverse effect on shipping in U.S. trade
- Investigates—upon its own motion or upon filing of a complaint—discriminatory, unfair, or unreasonable rates, charges, classifications, and practices of ocean common carriers, terminal operators, and freight forwarders operating in the foreign commerce of the United States
- Receives agreements among ocean common carriers or marine terminal operators and monitors them to assure that they are not substantially anticompetitive or otherwise violative of the Shipping Act of 1984
- Reviews tariff publications under the access and accuracy standards of the Shipping Act of 1984
- Regulates rates, charges, classifications, rules, and regulations contained in tariffs of carriers controlled by foreign governments and operating in U.S. trades to ensure that such matters are just and reasonable
- Licenses U.S.-based international ocean-transportation intermediaries (OTIs)
- Requires bonds of U.S.- and foreign-based OTIs

- Issues passenger-vessel certificates showing evidence of financial responsibility of vessel owners or charterers to pay judgments for personal injury or death or to repay fares for the nonperformance of a voyage or cruise.

The FMC's jurisdiction includes many areas of maritime industry. The areas over which it has no jurisdiction are "vessel operations, navigation, vessel construction, vessel documentation, vessel inspection, licensing of seafaring personnel, maintenance of navigational aids or dredging. These activities are handled by other federal, state and local agencies."

One of the most important regulatory issues handled by the agency in recent years has been the deregulation of the shipping industry. The Ocean Shipping Reform Act of 1998 (OSRA) amended the Shipping Act of 1984 and became effective in May of 1999. It was a compromise between those in Congress who wanted "minimal or no legislative reform and those seeking more or even complete deregulation."

Although many of the agency functions seem arcane—they are certainly very technical—the shipping industry is in many respects the most significant lifeline that connects the United States with overseas markets and those markets with the United States. In recent years, with the astronomical increase in cruise lines and cruise ship passengers, the FMC has also had a huge impact on the leisure/tourism industry. Looming financial difficulties and even bankruptcies in the cruise business in the late 1990s have made its functions for this sector even more important. Shipping licensing and regulation, and the consequences of these policies in terms of costs and safety, have a huge impact on every American consumer and business and thus make this lesser known federal regulatory agency quite important.

For more information
Federal Maritime Commission. *U.S. Federal Maritime Commission Handbook.* Armonk, N.Y.: International Business Publications, 2001.

Federal Maritime Commission, National Archives and Records Administration. http://ardor.nara.gov/fmc/fmc2.html.

Steffen W. Schmidt

Federal Mediation and Conciliation Service

The Federal Mediation and Conciliation Service (FMCS) is an independent agency of the U.S. government, created by Congress in 1947 to resolve disputes between labor organizations and employers to ensure the free flow of interstate commerce. Broadened since the agency's inception, it is currently mandated to encourage development of stable labor-management relations through training in and utilization of constructive joint processes; improve employment security and organizational effectiveness; and provide mediation and conflict resolution services to private enterprises and to local, state, and federal government agencies.

The FMCS employs approximately 200 full-time mediators, based in 78 field offices located throughout the United States. A mediator's first step in achieving a positive outcome to a labor-management dispute is to communicate effectively so that both labor and management comprehend that the quality of their relationship affects both the quality of the enterprise's products and the productivity of its employees. These two measures of success have a direct impact on profitability, which is necessary for employment security. When labor and management understand that they can achieve their interrelated goals of profitability and job security only if they work as a team, rather than as adversaries, the mediator can help the parties to progress toward these goals.

After establishing good communication, the mediator analyzes the relationships among or between the parties and identifies deficient aspects of the workplace, such as decreased employee morale, decreased productivity, excessive numbers of grievances or complaints of unfair labor practices, or poor communication between union leadership and management. After discussing these negative factors with the parties, the mediator usually recommends that the parties enroll in specific training classes that will enable them to remedy their problems. The training may focus on topics such as consensus decision making, effective negotiation, team building, or roles and responsibilities of union and management. Alternatively, the mediator may recommend one of the more formal, comprehensive training programs offered by FMCS. The FMCS course in win-win bargaining is one of the most popular of these formal programs. It teaches labor and management techniques for utilizing a nonadversarial, joint problem-solving approach to negotiation. Participants learn negotiation methods that enable them to transform their dispute into a win-win outcome and to implement this outcome by replacing labor-management antagonism and suspicion with a working relationship based on mutual goals.

In addition to dispute mediation, FMCS offers preventive mediation services that seek to improve the labor-management relationship by teaching both parties methods for: managing pre- and post-contract negotiation problems, jointly solving problems, resolving grievances, managing changes and decisions, overcoming barriers to quality and productivity, and collaboratively enhancing employee job satisfaction and employment security.

In lieu of the more expensive, time-consuming options of formal litigation, agency adjudication, or agency rule making, FMCS often recommends ALTERNATIVE DISPUTE RESOLUTION for labor-management disagreements. In most cases, a neutral third party helps the disputing parties reach mutually acceptable solutions. Government agencies often enlist a mediator's assistance to design systems for dispute resolution or develop agency-specific programs of education, training, and mentoring. FMCS mediators are also frequently requested to assist government agencies in settling problems related to public policy, or in negotiating new or enforcing existing laws or rules. Finally, mediators also help government agencies to settle disputes related to equal opportunity, education, and regulatory negotiations.

FMCS also utilizes the services of arbitrators who are independent contractors, chosen from FMCS's list of highly qualified individuals. An arbitrator functions as a judge by hearing evidence and making decisions or awards based on that evidence. If an FMCS arbitrator is asked to assist when a conflict arises between an employer and an employee organization during the term of a contract, the parties to the dispute choose the arbitrator they prefer from a panel composed of several arbitrators from FMCS's list. Instead of confronting one another in an adversarial process conducted in a courtroom, it is easier for both labor and management to resolve problems under the guidance of the arbitrator, in the nonintimidating setting of their own offices.

FMCS is authorized by the Labor-Management Cooperation Act of 1978 to choose the projects that will receive grants to fund projects that seek to (1) create or continue labor-management committees in the public sector or in the private sector, at either the plant level or on an area- or industry-wide basis; or (2) encourage innovative approaches to collaborative labor-management relations and problem solving. The organizations that are authorized to apply for FMCS grants are state and local units of government; certain private, nonprofit corporations; labor-management committees; and labor organizations or private businesses applying jointly with each other.

For more information

Federal Mediation and Conciliation Service. http://www.fmcs.gov/aboutfmcs.htm.

Federal Mediation and Conciliation Service. *Building Labor-Management Relationships: A Winning Combination.* Available online. URL: http://www.fmcs.gov/pubinfo/Brochures/Build%20LM%20Relationships.htm.

Beth S. Swartz

Federal Register The *Federal Register* is the daily regulatory newspaper of the executive branch of the federal government. It is through this newspaper that rules and other public notices relating to the administration of much of the federal government are first published. On a typical day, the *Federal Register* may include many of the following items: (1) presidential documents, (2) rules and regulations, (3) proposed rules and regulations, and (4) notices of meetings and other agency activities.

The need for the *Federal Register* arose with the increased number of federal governmental agencies in the 20th century. This need for such a regular administrative news source was given dramatic emphasis during the 1930s litigation attacking New Deal legislation regulating the oil industry. It was discovered during appeals to the Supreme Court that the regulations on which the litigation was based had been revoked. None of the parties to the litigation had known of this revocation.

A famous 1934 article by Erwin Griswold in the *Harvard Law Review* had stated the case for better and more systematic publication of executive branch matters. Griswold had described the current governmental situation as "government in ignorance of the law." This article graphically described the documentary chaos of the early New Deal legislation. The Federal Register Act of 1935 was designed to remedy this situation by providing for the systematic publication of any administrative rule or regulation having general administrative or legal effect.

While the *Federal Register* does provide an improved system of notice about the existence of or the proposal to enact administrative rules and regulations, research ordinarily does not begin with this daily newspaper. A companion publication, the *Code of Federal Regulations,* provides a means by which administrative rules and regulations currently in legal effect can be examined. In the *Code of Federal Regulations,* rules and regulations are grouped together by the administrative agency issuing the regulatory material. This approach, furthermore, provides a simple subject arrangement. The first edition of the *Code of Federal Regulations* was published in 1939 and contained all regulations in force as of 1 June 1938. The *Code of Federal Regulations* is now regularly revised each year.

For more information

Office of the Federal Register. *The Federal Register: What It Is and How to Use It.* Washington, D.C.: Office of the Federal Register, National Archives and Records Administration, 2002.

Jerry E. Stephens

Federal Reserve Board　The Federal Reserve Board is the governing body and ultimate overseer of the FEDERAL RESERVE SYSTEM and the banking industry in the United States and was established as a federal government agency on 23 December 1913, when the Federal Reserve Act was signed into law by President Woodrow Wilson.

The board is composed of seven members appointed by the president of the United States and confirmed by the U.S. Senate, and these members serve a term of 14 years. The chairman and vice chairman of the board are also appointed by the president and confirmed by the Senate, and each serves a term of four years. The current chairman is Alan Greenspan, who succeeded Paul Volcker. The general responsibility of the Federal Reserve Board is to oversee the conduct of the monetary and financial system and of banking and financial operations. All banks and other financial institutions must comply with actions and policies of the board. This is the entity that meets and decides on appropriate monetary policy actions, establishes regulations that affect the banking and financial institutions and markets, and initiates actions that address the conduct of banking and finance.

To fulfill these responsibilities the board must conduct research on domestic and international finance as well as on economic development and growth. The board is also responsible for supervising and regulating the overall operations of the U.S. banking system. This includes oversight of the Federal Reserve banks' services to banks and other financial institutions as well as examination and supervision of various banking institutions. Each of the 12 Federal Reserve banks must submit its annual budget to the board for approval. They have further responsibility over the nation's payment system and administer many of the nation's laws regarding consumer credit protection.

Members of the Board of Governors are in continual contact with other policy makers in government and frequently testify before Congress. The board must also submit a report biannually to the Congress about the economy and status of monetary policy as required under the Humphrey-Hawkins Act. The board also meets frequently with members of the President's Council of Economic Advisors and other key officials, and the chairman meets with the president and the secretary of the treasury. The board publishes detailed statistics on the economy and on banking and financial operations in serials such as the monthly *Federal Reserve Bulletin* and in announcements of board actions.

Federal Reserve Board chairman Alan Greenspan testifies on the state of the U.S. economy before a Joint Economic Committee in Washington, D.C. (ALEX WONG/GETTY IMAGES)

The ultimate policy action the Federal Reserve Board undertakes is the use of monetary policy to affect the business cycle of economic activity. It does this by expanding the money supply if cyclical activity is contracting, as during recessions and depressions, or by contracting the money supply if cyclical activity is expanding too fast and there is a threat of inflation. The tools of monetary policy available to the Federal Reserve Board and the Federal Reserve System include: (1) open market operations (buying and selling of U.S. government securities in the open market), (2) changes in the discount rate (the interest rate charged banks and financial institutions on loans), (3) changes in reserve requirements (reserves or currency that banks and other financial institutions must hold against deposits), (4) changes in margin requirements (percentage of the purchase of stocks or equities that must be paid in cash), and (5) moral suasion (written or verbal comments on undesirable practices). Responsibility of open market operations is given to the Federal Open Market Committee (FOMC) composed of the seven members of the Board of Governors and five of the 12 Federal, Reserve bank presidents. The chairman of the Board of Governors acts as the chair of the FOMC, and the president of the Federal Reserve Bank of New York serves as the vice chair of the FOMC. The Board of Governors has ultimate authority over changes in reserve requirements and discount rates and must approve changes in the discount rate.

See also MONETARY POLICY.

For more information

Board of Governors of the Federal Reserve System. *The Federal Reserve System: Purposes and Functions.* Washington, D.C.: Government Printing Office, 1994.

Ekelund, R. B., Jr., and R. D. Tollison. *Macroeconomics: Private Markets and Public Choice.* Reading, Mass.: Addison-Wesley Longman, 1997.

Douglas D. Ofiara

Federal Reserve System   The Federal Reserve System encompassing the Federal Reserve bank known also as "the Fed," is the central bank of the United States, the regulatory body of commercial banking and finance in the United States, and is referred to as the banker's bank. The Federal Reserve System was created by Congress in 1914 following the formal passage of the Federal Reserve Act signed by President Woodrow Wilson on 23 December 1913. At that time its purpose was to provide a safer, more flexible, and more stable monetary and financial system. Over time its functions have grown.

Today, it is the bank that oversees all banking institutions and operations in the United States and serves as the final voice on banking affairs. The Fed sets and administers policies and regulations that the U.S. banking system has to comply with. In the United States, banks are chartered or licensed by either state governments or the federal government. If chartered by the federal government, banks are known as federal banks and must belong to the Federal Reserve System. Presently, two-thirds of all banks are not members of the Federal Reserve System; however the regulatory powers and policies of the Federal Reserve System now apply to all banks and other financial institutions.

The Fed is the lender of last resort to promote safety and credibility of the banking system. It does this by assisting banks and other financial institutions in times of need (banking panics) by providing short-term loans or extra currency. At first this was only available for member federal banks, but since 1980 this privilege has been extended to all depository institutions as long as they satisfy minimum levels of currency or reserve holdings set by the Fed—hence the designation of the Fed as a banker's bank. If minimum reserves are not met, banks must either deal with federal banks or other large banks for assistance. The Federal Reserve System controls the money supply of the United States from direction by the FEDERAL RESERVE BOARD and the Federal Reserve chairman.

MONETARY POLICY actions are designed to affect the economic business cycle, i.e., cyclical economic activity in the United States. The Federal Reserve System is the only legal entity authorized to create and issue currency or legal tender in the United States. The currency issued is known as Federal Reserve notes, which are legal tender for all debts, public and private. This means that the federal government, by accepting federal reserve notes for payments, also expects private businesses to do likewise. Hence, Federal Reserve notes, or paper money, are known as fiat money—certified by government decree or fiat to be money or legal tender. Fiat money such as Federal Reserve notes is not backed by a commodity such as gold or silver, as once was the case, and are intrinsically worthless. It is only because the American public has full faith and confidence in the federal government, acting as an agent through the Federal Reserve Board, that we accept Federal Reserve notes as money.

The Federal Reserve System is not old, relative to other central banks such as the Bank of England, created in 1694, or the Bank of Japan in 1882. It was created in 1914 after two failed starts to create a national or central bank in the United States, the first in 1791 (the Bank of the United States, referred to as the First Bank of the United States) and the second in 1816 (the Second Bank of the United States). The reason for such a central bank in general is to facilitate and reduce the costs of transactions and trade through the use of a single or universal currency. In the days of early banking in the United States, trade and transactions were hampered by hundreds and even thousands of currencies (over 9,000 individual currencies around 1860), which had to be individually verified and authenticated before a transaction could take place. This slow process increased the cost of doing business and limited economic growth in general.

The Federal Reserve System is composed of 12 Federal Reserve banks located throughout the United States in 12 regions or Federal Reserve districts controlled or governed by the Federal Reserve Board in Washington, D.C. The Federal Reserve banks and their districts are as follows: district 1 contains the Boston Fed, district 2 of the New York Fed, district 3 the Philadelphia Fed, district 4 the Cleveland Fed, district 5 the Virginia Fed, district 6 the Atlanta Fed, district 7 the Chicago Fed, district 8 the St. Louis Fed, district 9 the Minneapolis Fed, district 10 the Kansas City Fed, district 11 the Dallas Fed, and district 12 the San Francisco Fed. Of these Federal Reserve banks, the Federal Reserve Bank of New York has the most important function to perform, that of open market operations, a tool of monetary policy.

It is through the New York Fed, based on directions from the Federal Open Market Committee and the Federal Reserve Board, that U.S. government securities (usually Treasury bills, short-term bills sold at discounted rates in units of $10,000 to $1,000,000) are bought or sold in order to affect the money supply. All monetary policy, however, is developed by the Federal Reserve Board concerning expansions or contractions of the money supply through a variety of monetary policy tools. (For example, additional reserves were made available for increased perceived demands for currency in the new millennium.)

For more information

Board of Governors of the Federal Reserve System. *The Federal Reserve System: Purposes and Functions.* Washington, D.C.: Government Printing Office, 1994.

Ekelund, R. B., Jr., and R. D. Tollison. *Macroeconomics: Private Markets and Public Choice.* Reading, Mass.: Addison-Wesley Longman, 1997.

Douglas D. Ofiara

Federal Trade Commission The Federal Trade Commission (FTC) is an independent regulatory agency of the U.S. government that was created by Congress in 1914 for the primary purpose of promoting fair competition in interstate commerce. As used in the legislation that created the FTC, the phrase "promoting fair competition" includes, but is not limited to: forbidding creation of monopolies, and dismantling of already existing monopolies in any type of business; preventing false advertising regarding food, drugs, and cosmetics; and gathering data about economic conditions to use this information to encourage the free flow of interstate commerce. Congress envisioned the FTC as a watchdog agency that would monitor commerce in order to maintain competition among businesses, since fair competition invariably results in self-regulation of business practices and prevents development of monopolies.

The FTC is composed of five commissioners whom the president, with the approval of the Senate, appoints to seven-year terms. No more than three commissioners may belong to the same political party.

President Woodrow Wilson proposed creation of the FTC as part of a program intended to check the growth of monopolies and preserve competition as an effective regulator of business. This president recognized that in the late 19th and early 20th centuries, providers of an assortment of essential consumer goods and services took advantage of deficiencies in then-existing law. These vendors were acting within the existing law when they monopolized sectors of the marketplace by entering into exclusive dealing contracts, engaging in price-fixing and discrimination, acquiring stock in their competitors' businesses, and creating interlocking directorates. Elimination of competition allowed monopolies to raise prices to unreasonable levels, since consumers were able to purchase their essential goods or services only from the monopolistic business. By passing the legislation that created the FTC, Congress effectuated many of President Wilson's procompetition ideas.

Congress granted the FTC jurisdiction over all interstate businesses except for banks and businesses involved in interstate transport of consumer goods, over which other federal agencies had jurisdiction. Congress also authorized the FTC to define "unfair methods and practices." FTC interpreted this phrase to include false advertising, mislabeling, fraudulent actions, and misrepresentation of quality, guarantee, or terms of sale.

The FTC has three major subdivisions, one of which is the multifaceted Bureau of Competition. While the entire bureau adheres to the concept that fair competition among small and mid-sized companies is necessary to create an equitable balance between consumer prices and business profits, the bureau's specific responsibilities include many diverse aspects of commerce.

The Bureau of Competition acts according to a statutory mandate that it engage in research and propose policies on competition-related issues. An additional facet of the bureau's duties is to investigate allegations that a business is engaged in activities that restrict competition. If an administrative hearing determines that a business is actually involved in anticompetitive practices, an administrative law judge has authority to enjoin the unlawful activity. However, the administrative body has no jurisdiction over enforcement of a "cease and desist" order. Only a court of law has authority to fine or otherwise penalize a business for noncompliance with an injunction.

The duty of the FTC's Bureau of Consumer Protection (BCP) is to prevent businesses from exposing consumers to unfair, deceptive, or fraudulent practices. The BCP is fundamentally different from the similarly entitled CONSUMER PRODUCT SAFETY COMMISSION in that the BCP seeks to protect consumers from unlawful business activities, while the Consumer Product Safety Commission focuses on protecting consumers from businesses' unsafe, potentially injurious products. A business that continually exhibits noncompliance with a "cease and desist" order cannot be fined by BCP. Only a court of law has this authority.

Each of the BCP's five divisions specializes in one type of consumer protection:

The Division for Advertising Practices aims to protect consumers from deceptive and unsubstantiated advertising. Its efforts are concentrated on three types of promotional campaigns: advertisements for tobacco, alcohol, energy-saving products, foods, over-the-counter drugs, and allegedly environmentally safe products; television infomercials; and marketing materials that make claims that consumers are unable to evaluate or substantiate.

The Division of Enforcement works with the U.S. DEPARTMENT OF JUSTICE and U.S. district courts to ensure compliance with administrative and judicial orders issued in consumer protection cases and to enforce consumer protection laws, rules, and guidelines. Additionally, this FTC division is responsible for investigating and participating in civil litigation intended to prevent fraudulent, unfair, or deceptive advertising.

The BCP's Division of Financial Practices enforces consumer credit statutes that forbid discrimination in lending and debt collection.

The Division of Marketing Practices works with federal district courts to enjoin recently contrived, fraudulent marketing practices. Additionally, this division is required to obtain compensation for scam victims and to prevent scam artists from continuing their schemes in other venues.

The Division of Planning and Information collects and analyzes data about enforcing consumer protection laws, educates consumers about their legal rights under the FTC Act, and assesses the impact of the FTC's activities on the economy and on the general public.

When so ordered by the president or Congress, or on its own initiative, the FTC has authority to: investigate the practices of an individual company or an entire industry; participate in other federal agencies' rulemaking proceedings; or seek an injunction in an administrative law court.

The Bureau of Economics assists the FTC in evaluating the economic impact of its actions. One of the bureau's responsibilities is to provide economic analysis and support for rulemaking, and also for antitrust and consumer protection investigations. The FTC Act mandates that the Bureau of Economics provide Congress, the executive branch, and the public with analyses of the impact of government regulation on competition and consumers, and also of market processes related to antitrust, consumer protection, and regulation.

During the last two decades, the rapid pace of technological advancements has resulted in the development of methods and created situations that existing law has been unable to classify as legal or illegal. In response to this problem, the FTC has given high priority to a project that aims to reestablish the boundary between lawful and unlawful behavior, and then to publish industry-specific booklets containing guidelines that clarify the applicability of existing laws to new concepts and practices. FTC's long-term goal for this project is to publish booklets about many different fields of endeavor, thereby enabling individuals employed in a wide variety of industries to make sound business decisions.

The FTC has authority to issue an advisory opinion in situations where the information in its industry-specific booklets is inadequate to enable a business to determine the legality of instituting a new practice or of initiating the use of a new method to accomplish a preexisting task.

For more information
Federal Trade Commission. http://www.ftc.gov/be/index.htm.

Beth Simon Swartz

fiscal policy   Fiscal policy consists of the use of government spending, income transfers, and taxation by the federal government to affect the macroeconomy. These policies are also practiced by state governments.

The purpose of fiscal policies is to correct for imbalances in employment or economic growth. To appreciate the role of government in the overall economy, it is useful to consider ideas from national income accounting. Here the economy is composed of four components or sectors: households, firms, government, and foreign countries. In each of these sectors money is spent on goods and services, and there is a flow of money back to the sector. The first approach is referred to as the flow of expenditures, and the return flow is the flow of income or earnings.

For a simple economy, this can be thought of as a flow of money from consumers to firms for goods, with a matching return flow from firms to consumers for wages. By the principles of national income accounting, both flows must match. Hence, measures of gross domestic product (market value of all final goods and services produced in an economy over time from domestic resources) can be determined either way. Using the expenditures approach, one would sum the spending by households on final goods and services (consumption spending); spending by private firms on inputs and machines (investment spending); spending by the government on goods and services such as public roads, schools, national defense (government spending); and spending on foreign exports less spending on imports by foreign residents (net exports) to obtain gross domestic product (GDP) if the final goods are produced using resources located within country. The distinction changes if resources located outside a country are included and becomes gross national product (GNP).

On the basis of national income accounting, government spending is a component of GDP measures. The government's array of fiscal policy tools includes other actions. The government also transfers income from individuals more fortunate to individuals less fortunate, referred to as income transfers. Both government spending and income transfers can be thought of as leakages, money is being paid out.

To finance such activity, the government uses taxes. Hence, government spending, income transfers, and taxation are referred to as fiscal policy. These three components comprise a government's budget. Here a balanced budget occurs when money out equals money in or when spending plus income transfers equals tax revenues. In the real world the government's budget is more complicated, with financing from government bonds and other leakages and injections.

Fiscal policy works to stimulate the economy by increasing government spending or by reducing taxes. Both work in different directions. Government spending causes an increase in the overall demand for goods and services, causing firms to use more resources (the most important being labor) and produce more goods and services. The intended effect is to increase overall output or the productive capacity of the economy and reduce unemployment. Government spending is referred to as an "aggregate demand policy." The effect of taxes affects the aggregate supply curve, a concern of SUPPLY-SIDE ECONOMICS.

For more information
Ekelund, R. B., Jr., and R. D. Tollison. *Macroeconomics: Private Markets and Public Choice.* Reading, Mass.: Addison-Wesley Longman, 1997.

Douglas D. Ofiara

flat tax   "Flat" tax refers to a tax policy whereby everyone pays the same rate. The flat tax concept invokes the notion of replacing the current U.S. income tax system with a flat-rate consumption tax. Although our current tax structure is referred to as an income tax, it actually contains elements of both an income and a consumption-based tax.

The term "flat tax" is often associated with a proposal advocated by Robert E. Hall and Alvin Rabushka, two senior fellows at the Hoover Institution at Stanford University. In 1981 they proposed the replacement of the federal individual income tax and the federal corporate income tax with a flat-rate consumption tax. Over the years, members of Congress, presidential candidate Steven Forbes, policy analysts, academics, and business leaders have advocated various forms of a flat tax.

The Hall and Rabushka concept maintains that tax simplification would make the economy more efficient and increase private savings. The continued complexity of the federal individual and corporate income tax systems creates excessive administrative and compliance costs. Additionally, a consumption tax would allow individuals to be taxed on what they take out of the economy (consuming) rather than what they produce (working and saving). Finally, the flat tax proposal allows for a more efficient use of resources, resulting in higher economic growth and a rise in living standards.

Others argue that our current, though imperfect, tax code ensures that people with similar incomes pay similar amounts in taxes, and people with higher incomes pay more in taxes. Opponents also claim that the flat tax proposal allows too much money to escape tax and that it taxes labor disproportionately, as opposed to the claim that the flat tax would tax all labor and capital income at once. For individuals, the flat tax taxes only labor, because the tax base is only wages, salaries, and pension benefits. For businesses, taxable profits include a return to labor and capital; therefore, labor is unable to escape all taxation at the business level.

Flat tax advocates maintain that by eliminating the individual tax on capital source income, future savings and investment will increase. Flat taxes exempt from tax not only income from future savings and investment, but also income from existing saving and investment, thereby resulting in added tax benefits to current investors, who might already comprise the top 5 percent of the income distribution.

There are broad economic policy issues affecting the flat tax proposal and its effect on the national economy. The flat tax would be shifted backwards onto owners of equities (old capital) and wage earners. The current income tax system is progressive, therefore, the impact of the flat tax across all income levels is still unknown. The flat tax would also reduce the tax burden on the young but increase it on older individuals. Other policy issues surround the impact on specific industries including businesses, charitable organizations, housing, and state and local governments—all entities with differing levels of tax implications. Finally, simplicity is a constantly debated topic among government leaders, economists, and taxpayers, who are all interested in alleviating the complexity of the current system.

For more information

Hall, Robert E., and Alvin Rabushka. *The Flat Tax,* 2d ed. Stanford, Calif.: Stanford University, Hoover Institution Press, 1995.

Hammond, M. Jeff. *The Failings of the Flat Tax.* Washington, D.C.: Progressive Policy Institute, 1996.

Cherylyn A. Harley

Follett, Mary Parker (1868–1933) *social reformer, activist* Mary Parker Follett believed that all avenues of human engagement prepared and trained people for citizenship and, as such, were closely related to democracy. She was particularly concerned with the role of democracy in everyday life and, especially, saw business administration as another part of human existence and, as such, also related to democracy.

Follett attended Radcliffe College and Cambridge University and first applied her training by working in Boston neighborhoods. At the turn of the century, few professions welcomed or even admitted women. At a time when there were few to no government-provided social provisions to meet the changing needs of a growing citizenry, it is not surprising that educated and upper-class women found their niche in social work, a field that was new, open, and not yet understood to be the province of government. Given the unique training and knowledge of settlement workers and social workers, President Franklin D. Roosevelt, in designing his New Deal program, turned to them and drew from their expertise. Follett's experience in neighborhood schools, however, served as a springboard away from hands-on social work and toward political science, business management, and organizational theory.

Follett, together with the Women's Municipal League of Boston, first worked to make schools into centers for neighborhoods, not simply buildings that were open for a limited period during the day for classroom work. Steven Skowronek notes that in doing so, she "developed a set of ideas and principles about the group basis of democracy and the foundations of social interaction. At the heart of this theorizing was her concept of 'integration'. . . a process by which individuals from very different backgrounds could encounter one another in small groupings and re-create themselves through their interactions in ways that transcended both conflict and compromise."

Follett's work and ideas set the groundwork for further exploration of the political theory of pluralism, i.e., that power is dispersed through an array of groups (e.g., organized interest groups, grassroots organizations, civic groups, etc.), which compete for the ability to influence political and policy choices and outcomes. In her book *The New State* (1918), Follett "applied her conception of neighborhood organization and human interaction to questions of industrial organization, political organization, national organization, and international organization."

Starting out in social work, she became a prolific author and lecturer on business organization and administrative theory. These too, Follett believed, were necessary components for a strong, healthy democracy.

For more information

Graham, Pauline, ed. *Mary Parker Follett—A Prophet of Management: A Celebration of Writings from the 1920s.* Boston: Harvard Business School Press, 1995.

Linda K. Shafer

Food and Drug Administration   The Food and Drug Administration (FDA) is the executive branch department that conducts research on the safety of, and oversees federal laws regarding, the manufacture, transportation, and sale of foods, drugs, cosmetics, and other items. Part of the Department of Health and Human Services, it regulates the supply of drugs and assures the safety of processed and manufactured foods. Its history is one of reorganization and increasing responsibility.

The roots of the agency date back to 1862 when Abraham Lincoln appointed chemist Charles M. Wetherill to head the Bureau of Chemistry in the newly formed DEPARTMENT OF AGRICULTURE (USDA). Wetherill and his fellow scientists were concerned with food alterations and chemical preservatives. By 1873, they published reports on the adulteration of milk and the problems for human beings of using arsenic and copper as fertilizers. Food alteration, particularly oleomargarine, became a major concern in the American population during these years.

Harvey W. Wiley, known as the "crusading chemist" and the "father of the Pure Food and Drugs Act," began to address these fears. A gifted public speaker, Wiley enlisted the help of consumers' groups and women's clubs to turn public opinion toward a "pure food" bill. National magazines like *Collier's Weekly, Ladies' Home Journal,* and *Good Housekeeping* carried on the USDA's cause. In 1902 Wiley shocked the nation with his use of a "poison squad" of young men who voluntarily agreed to ingest chemical preservatives and show how dangerous they were to people's health. Officially called the "Hygienic Table," these experiments went on for five years. As a result, the first Food and Drug Act was passed on 30 June 1906, prohibiting interstate commerce in misbranded and adulterated foods, drinks, and drugs. On the same day, the Meat Inspection Act was passed, allowing for the inspection of sanitary conditions in meat-packing plants.

The Bureau of Chemistry enforced these laws until 1927, when it was reorganized into the Food, Drug, and Insecticide Administration. In its reorganization, it lost its law-enforcement function. Four years later, it was renamed the Food and Drug Administration (FDA). In 1940, officials began to worry about conflicts of interest between the FDA and the USDA, with the former representing the needs of consumers and the latter interested in helping farmers. Consequently the FDA was transferred to the Federal Security Agency. In 1953, this agency became the Department of Health, Education, and Welfare and, later, the DEPARTMENT OF HEALTH AND HUMAN SERVICES.

By 1933, FDA officials recognized that the 1906 Food and Drug Act was obsolete. Known as the "Tugwell bill," for Roosevelt's assistant Rexford Tugwell's interest in the law, it was defeated. For five years, the Roosevelt administration attempted to fashion a consumer protection law and finally succeeded with the Federal Food, Drug, and Cosmetic (FDC) Act. This act extended FDA control to cosmetics and therapeutic devices. It required that new drugs be shown safe before marketing, thus starting new systems of drug regulation. It also required that safe levels of tolerance be established for unavoidable poisonous substances. On 25 June, 1938, President Roosevelt signed the new law into being.

With the new law on the books, the FDA's workload expanded during World War II. In 1945, the Penicillin Amendment required the FDA to test and certify the safety and effectiveness of penicillin products and other antibiotics. Three other amendments over the next 15 years

further sharpened the focus of the FDA. The Pesticide Amendment in 1954 spelled out the procedure for setting safety limits for pesticides and residue on agricultural products. In 1958 the Food Additives Amendment required manufacturers of new food additives to establish their safety. The Delaney proviso prohibited any food additive that could be shown to induce cancer. Finally, the Color Additive Amendment, two years later, required manufacturers to establish the safety of color additives in foods, drugs, or cosmetics. In other words, no substance can be introduced into the food supply unless given prior approval.

During the 1960s, FDA medical officer Frances Kelsey was instrumental in keeping thalidomide off the U.S. market. This drug was later shown to cause birth defects in infants. Public concern led to the Drug Amendment of 1962, which tightened control over prescription drugs. Drug companies were required to send adverse-reaction reports to the FDA. This new policy of preventing harm also concerned medical devices. In 1976, the Medical Device Amendment required manufacturers to register with the FDA and follow quality control procedures. Thus devices such pacemakers and surgical implants must be proved safe before being marketed. The safety mandate of the FDA was also extended to babies with the Infant Formula Act of 1980, which established standards for the nutritional content of baby food.

The Food and Drug Administration was created "to promote honesty and fair dealing in the interest of consumers." It has endeavored to protect the American people ever since.

For more information

Heimann, Clarence Fredrick Larry. *Acceptable Risks: Politics, Policy, and Risky Technologies.* Ann Arbor: University of Michigan Press, 1997.

Patrick, William. *The Food and Drug Administration.* New York: Chelsea House, 1988.

T. Jason Soderstrum

food stamps Food stamps supplement the incomes of poor families by providing coupons and electronic benefits transfer (EBT) cards to eligible families and individuals.

Food stamps were born in 1964, when Congress passed the Food Stamp Act as part of President Lyndon B. Johnson's War on Poverty. Because the food stamp program existing before 1964—a pilot program started two years earlier—was an outlet for farmers' surpluses, the 1964 act gave authority for administration and oversight of the food stamp program to the U.S. Department of Agriculture. Since 1964, the act has been subject to frequent revision, most recently by the Personal Responsibility and Work Opportunity Reconciliation Act of 1996.

As with most social assistance programs in the United States, the food stamps program is means tested. The dollar amount of food stamps that a recipient receives is based on a variety of factors, including income level and family size, savings account ceilings (no more than $2,000 if under 60 years old), and market value of recipient's automobile (no more than $4,650), though various deductions are allowed. To apply, applicants must contact their local food stamp office (which could be listed under a variety of names), fill out the requisite forms, and go through a personal interview to determine qualification.

Not all foods can be purchased with food stamps or the EBT cards. For instance, alcohol and tobacco products are disallowed, as are non-food items, vitamins and medicines, hot foods, and foods that will be eaten in the store.

For more information

Food and Nutrition Service, U.S. Department of Agriculture. http://www.fns.usda.gov/fns/.

Noble, Charles. *Welfare as We Knew It: A Political History of the American Welfare State.* New York and Oxford: Oxford University Press, 1997.

Linda K. Shafer

foreign policy

Rational actor model

The "rational actor model" of foreign-policy decisions represents a framework for decision making based on assumptions that people and nations act rationally to achieve desired goals. This model is one of three perspectives that were identified by Graham Allison in the 1971 book *Essence of Decision.* The rational actor model explains foreign-policy making by reviewing the aims and calculations of nations or governments. The model assumes that nations that are part of the international system are rational, calculating actors. The concept of rationality is premised on the view that human behavior can be understood and predicted. This perception is widely accepted in the social sciences.

For example, in economics it is assumed that choices are rationally made among alternatives. The preferred alternative will maximize output for a given amount of input or minimize the amount of input for a given output. Economists assume that consumers purchase the mix of goods that maximize their utility and that firms maximize their profit by setting marginal costs relative to marginal revenue. In statistical game theory, a rational-decision problem consists of selecting among a set of alternatives. Each alternative is assumed to have a measurable set of consequences. Consequences are ranked in order of preference, and decision makers select the alternative whose consequences are preferred. This provides a blueprint for the rational actor model.

In formulating the rational actor model, Allison noted that governments choose actions that maximize strategic foreign-policy goals such as national security. Governments choose from among various options. Decision makers and analysts estimate the consequences of each option. Action is then chosen in response to strategic problems. Threats and opportunities that confront the nation are evaluated. In this model, decisions follow the sequential process:

(1) strategic goals are formulated, (2) a range of options are described, (3) benefits and costs of each of the options are identified, and (4) the alternative whose cost-benefit mix ranks the highest is selected.

In addition to this basic design, variations of the rational actor model are also described by Allison. One variation of the model emphasizes national character as opposed to emphasizing the strategic goals and objectives of a nation. In this variation, psychological tendencies of a nation as well as values shared by citizens are studied. It is believed that knowledge about national character can be quite useful in evaluating alternatives and consequences. Another variation of the rational actor model focuses on an individual leader or leadership clique. It is assumed that those individual leaders or leadership cliques wish to maximize their personal preferences. Knowledge about the preferences of leaders (rather than national character) is used to predict goals, alternatives, costs, and benefits of alternatives. For example, it is believed that new foreign-policy calculations had to be made following the fall of the shah of Iran and the transfer of power in Iran to a fundamentalist Islamic group. New alternatives and options could rationally be considered given such new information about leadership changes.

The rational actor model presents a systematic framework for analysis. This model is characterized by a clear statement of goals, identification of options, measurement of costs and benefits, and choice of the highest-ranking alternative. It is a dominant model in the field of public administration, a discipline that is grounded in the view that efficiencies can be rationally identified and applied to the government sector. The rational-actor framework can also be applied to a multitude of foreign-policy decisions such as how to respond to terrorist attacks.

Organizational process model

The "organizational process model" of foreign-policy decisions explains decision making from the perspective of organizational behavior. It was popularized by Allison in *Essence of Decision*.

In the organizational process model, government behavior is viewed less as a matter of deliberate choice (as in the view of the rational process model) and more as an output of large organization deliberations. Allison believed that outputs of large organizations were influenced by factors such as the types of organizational procedures that were in place. Under the perspective of the organizational process model, decisions of leaders are constrained by the capacities and limitations of organizations. For example, Allison notes that presidents rarely, if ever, make foreign-policy decisions by themselves without input from powerful organizations. Choices of executives are colored by the information provided and the options presented by officials of these influential organizations.

According to Allison, the many facets of foreign affairs require problems to be parceled out to relevant organizations. For example, in the organizational structure of the U.S. government, the Department of State has primary responsibility for diplomacy. The DEPARTMENT OF DEFENSE (DOD) has responsibility for military security, and the CENTRAL INTELLIGENCE AGENCY (CIA) has responsibility for intelligence. Each of these organizations has distinctive norms and values that shape its organizational outputs.

The organizational process model's power derives from its ability to uncover organizational routines and predict an organization's position on issues based upon analysis of those routines. In producing foreign-policy outputs, organizations are influenced by their goals, standard operating procedures, and repertoires. Organizational expectations influence the size and funding for the organization. Such expectations relate to statutory authority for the organization, demands of citizens, and interest-group behavior. Standard operating procedures (SOPs) are grounded in the norms of the organization and the basic operating styles of members. Standardized procedures provide direction for the performance of tasks such as writing reports and preparing budgets. Standard operating procedures establish rules of thumb that facilitate coordinated action by large numbers of individuals. Rules are usually simple enough to allow for easy learning and unambiguous application. Without standard operating procedures it is difficult to perform tasks. However, standard operating procedures can also lead to organizational rigidity, sluggishness, and an inability to adapt to new environments.

The organizational process model looks at the relative power of organizations when analyzing foreign-policy outputs. Allison used information about the relative power of organizations in the former Soviet Union to explain some of their foreign-policy outputs. He contended that the force posture (production and deployment of certain weapons) of the former Soviet Union was determined by the particular interests of large military and research organizations. For example, the weak position of the Soviet air force within the larger Soviet military establishment was said to explain the Soviet Union's failure to acquire a large bomber force in the 1950s. The slow buildup of Soviet intercontinental missiles was attributed to its placement within another hierarchy (Soviet ground forces) that had little interest in the development of an intercontinental missile system.

The organizational process model in essence asserts that knowledge about how organizations act and think can be very helpful in explaining foreign-policy decisions. The model is important to public administration and organizational theory in that it prioritizes the role of organizations in the decision-making process.

Government politics model

The "government politics model' of foreign-policy decisions is grounded in the perspective that policy is an outcome of political conflict between actors within the government. It is based on the view that government officials compete with each other to gain influence and make foreign policy.

This is the third model (Model III) of various perspectives of foreign-policy making laid out by Allison in *Essence of Decision*. According to Allison, decisions of governments are not necessarily the result of rational deliberations (Model I) or outputs of organizations (Model II) but can be viewed as the outcome of "pulling and hauling" (bargaining and negotiating) between government players who vie for political influence.

The government politics model builds upon previous research by scholars and Kennedy administration insiders Richard Neustadt and Roger Hilsman. Neustadt helped to develop the view that participants in government had independent bases of power and shared decision-making responsibility with many other actors. He contended that prior to ultimate policy choices, decisions followed certain processes or regularized channels. Bargaining continually occurred along these regularized channels. The role of the president of the United States was important, but his authority guaranteed only extensive "clerkship." The real power of the president was seen by Neustadt as the power to persuade. Presidents share governance responsibilities with others who are not always entirely responsive to the president's command. Presidents therefore must use the formal powers of office to induce, cajole, and persuade particular department heads, congressmen, or senators to endorse specific policies.

Roger Hilsman similarly viewed government decision making from the perspective of acts of political pressure. Hilsman argued that the political process of making decisions exhibited three basic characteristics. These were: (1) a diversity of goals and values that must be reconciled before a decision can be reached, (2) the presence of competing clusters of people who are identified with each of the alternative goals and policies, and (3) the relative power of groups of people who are relevant to the final decision. Hilsman concluded that policy making should be seen as a process of conflict and consensus building. He noted that battles over national foreign policy were common in the Kennedy administration.

Building upon these insights, Allison's Model III stated that decisions of governments should be viewed as "intranational political resultants." These "resultants" of political negotiations reflected the outcomes of political conflicts between government officials who have different personal interests and different perceptions of their roles in the policy-making process. Allison contended that foreign-policy choices emerged from intricate, simultaneous, and overlapping games between players within government. Players in the games did not act upon consistent sets of strategic objectives but according to their own conceptions of national, organizational, and personal goals. A "pulling and hauling" ensued that determined policy.

The principal value of the government politics model is its ability to predict policy decisions based upon analysis of political conflicts within government. Knowledge of the key players, their bases of power, their perceptions, their goals, their views of the stakes involved, and their channels of communication in the decision-making process are used in predicting decisions. It is assumed that players have different goals, bases of power, and perceptions of the national interest. These players engage in political battle to implement their desired visions. This model does an excellent job in explaining the political intricacies of how public policy is formulated. It supplements other perspectives in the field of public policy.

For more information

Allison, Graham. *Essence of Decision*. Boston: Little, Brown and Company, 1971.
Dunn, William. *Public Policy Analysis,* 2d ed. Englewood Cliffs, N.J.: Prentice Hall, 1994.
Halperin, Morton H. *Bureaucratic Politics & Foreign Policy*. Washington, D.C.: The Brookings Institution, 1974.
Hilsman, Roger. *To Move a Nation*. Garden City, N.Y.: Doubleday, 1967.
Neustadt, Richard. *Presidential Power.* New York: Wiley, 1960.

Steven Koven

formal hearing   A formal hearing is a trial-type setting in which a resolution is sought between two parties— one of which usually is an administrative agency, regarding a policy or decision made by an administrative agency—while due process is protected.

Formal hearings are required when the U.S. Constitution, the creating and/or authorizing statutes, or the ADMINISTRATIVE PROCEDURE ACT (APA) call for them. Under the U.S. Constitution's Fifth Amendment—and through the Fourteenth Amendment for the states—governments must afford their citizens the due process of the law or the insurance of fairness of procedure to the persons affected. Generally, formal hearings are the most extensive and detailed in nature, with requirements for the hearings dictated by either law or the courts.

Within rule making, the courts have recognized that formal hearings are not necessary to ensure the fair and due process of the law for individuals. (See INFORMAL HEARINGS.) However, when adjudication (or a court-like hearing process) of a "substantial interest" of an individual or group is conducted, the U.S. Supreme Court requires that an agency must follow certain guidelines. A "substantial interest" may include the termination of benefits, for example. The U.S. Supreme Court has held that there are three factors that must be balanced when due process is required in a hearing: (1) a private interest that is affected by an official action, (2) the risk to the individual of diminishing that interest and the value of granting additional safeguards in the procedures against denying that interest, and (3) the interest of the government, particularly when it comes to fiscal and administrative burdens that may be imposed by granting extra procedures (*Mathews v. Eldridge,* 424 U.S. 319 [1976]).

The components that guarantee due process within a formal hearing are usually considered to be timely and adequate notice; the confrontation and cross-examination of adverse witnesses; the oral presentation of arguments and evidence; the right to retain an attorney; the use of the record of activities of the hearing as the determination of the results; a statement of reasons for the judgment, along with the evidence used in reaching the judgment; and an impartial decision maker to preside over the hearing (see *GOLDBERG V. KELLY,* 397 U.S. 254 [1970]).

The APA sets out the features of a hearing for a federal agency, found in Sections 554, 556, and 557. However, unless the agency is required to conduct a formal hearing (usually the law says "on the record," thus triggering the requirement for formal hearings), the APA may not mandate that agencies conduct formal hearings, particularly in regard to rule-making procedures. Thus, many administrative agencies may have greater discretion in their policy making by rule making, due to the fact that agencies do not have to follow the strict and explicit guidelines set out in the APA.

For more information
Cooper, Phillip J. *Public Law and Public Administration.* Itasca, Ill.: F. E. Peacock Publishers, Inc., 2000.

J. Michael Bitzer

Freedom of Information Act The Freedom of Information Act (FOIA) was passed in 1966 as an effort to make government accountable to its citizenry.

Prior to the FOIA, the ADMINISTRATIVE PROCEDURE ACT (APA) of 1946 asked agencies to publish administrative procedures in the FEDERAL REGISTER in an effort to keep up with the growing administrative state. (An agency is defined as "a governmental organization, such as a department, bureau, office, commission, board, administration, advisory council. . . .") Since APA merely asked agencies to publish in the *Federal Register* and did not have the authority to require them to do so, many did not. This led to the creation of the FOIA. The FOIA makes it a requirement for agencies to preserve and publish administrative procedures concerning rule making, adjudication, inspecting, and licensing in the *Federal Register.*

Enacted in 1966 as Public Law 89-487, the FOIA replaced the public information section of the APA. The FOIA legislates what documents governmental agencies must make available to citizens upon request. The FOIA acts as a checks-and-balance system because it keeps agencies accountable to the citizens. Agencies must keep records of their organization's function(s), policies, procedures, decisions, and all essential transactions. The FOIA allows citizens to request these documents and specifies a timeline for agencies to fill the request. (All requests must be made in writing.) Originally, agencies had 10 days to respond to a request. The FOIA Amendment of 1996 has extended this period to 20 working days (excluding Saturdays, Sundays, and legal holidays). If a request is denied and this decision is appealed, the agency has an additional 20 days to respond.

Each agency has the discretion of collecting fees to cover the costs of the document search and document duplication. Fees are collected in advance only when the cost exceeds $250. The 1996 amendments to the FOIA have created a three-tiered fee structure. (1) Commercial users are charged the cost of document search, duplication, and review. (2) Educational or noncommercial institutions and the news media are only charged for the cost of duplication. (3) All other requesters are charged for document duplication and search.

Congress passed the Electronic Freedom of Information Act (EFOIA) in 1996 to address materials published online. The EFOIA makes it clear that computerized records fall under the guidelines set forth in the FOIA of 1966. The EFOIA requires agencies to publish their policies and rules on the Internet. Previously, agencies were required to publish the agency's description, function, and procedures in the *Federal Register*. Under EFOIA, agencies must publish this information on the Internet and make it available in an "electronic reading room." The EFOIA also stipulates that agencies must search all materials, those published in print as well as on the Internet, to fill a request. The agency has to supply the materials in any format requested, including print, compact disc, etc.

Only agencies fall under the guidelines of the FOIA. The president does not fall under this act, nor does any departmental entity whose sole function is to advise and assist the president. This is known as the sole-function test. If an entity has any other duties in addition to advising the president, then it is deemed an agency and must comply with the FOIA. Another area of restriction concerns entities funded by the government that are not an actual government agency or department, such as the Corporation for Public Broadcasting. These entities do not have to release information, since they are not under the guidelines of the FOIA. Even if that entity performs research for an actual agency, the research is not under the guidelines of the FOIA because the agency did not do the actual research and can say it accepted the information with consent of confidentiality.

For more information

Botterman, Maarten, et al. *Public Information Provision in the Digital Age: Implementation and Effects of the U.S. Freedom of Information Act.* Santa Monica, Calif.: RAND, 2001.

Foerstel, Herbert N. *Freedom of Information and the Right to Know: The Origins and Applications of the Freedom of Information Act.* Westport, Conn.: Greenwood Press, 1999.

McClure, Charles R., Peter Hernon, and Harold Relyea, eds. *United States Government Information Policies: Views and Perspectives.* Norwood, N.J.: Ablex, 1989.

La Loria Konata

free rider *Free rider* is a concept used to describe a person or institution that receives a benefit or a good without paying for it. For example, if a person uses a public park funded by city taxpayer dollars while paying no taxes to support that park, that person is a "free rider."

The concept of a "free rider" is usually characterized as a free-rider *problem*. That is, if a good is provided (e.g., a city park) whether or not any particular individual in question pays, why should anyone contribute to paying the cost? People are believed to be rational actors, and if they know that something will be provided whether or not they contribute, people have little incentive to pay. Here, any amount the single individual would contribute would be negligible relative to the cost of the park. Therefore, the amount missing would be tiny and would probably not be missed. All of this is, of course, true. The free-rider problem emerges when everyone begins to think this way. If everyone reasoned in a similar way, then the good would not be provided (no one would contribute). Hence, the free-rider problem.

In the end, free riders and free-rider problems exist when people consume "PUBLIC GOODS." A public good is one that all members of a group benefit from, even if it is provided for only one member of the group. For example, clean air is a public good. If one person works hard to convince government that clean air is a good thing and then government helps to provide it, not only does the person who asked for cleaner air receive the benefit, but those who did not work to support clean air receive the benefit as well. Those who did not write letters to their congresspersons and who did not otherwise expend effort to receive the clean air benefit just as much as those who did.

This is one of the reasons that governments are asked to provide public goods. Governments have the power to coerce citizens to contribute through taxes and fees, thus spreading the cost of this good to all those who benefit, which minimizes the free-rider problem.

For more information
Bickers, Kenneth N., and John T. Williams. *Public Policy Analysis: A Political Economy Approach.* New York: Houghton Mifflin, 2001.
Stiglitz, Joseph E. *Economics of the Public Sector.* New York: W. W. Norton, 2000.

Robert A. Schuhmann

G

gambling policy   Gambling is one of the most heavily regulated industries in the United States, largely because it is believed to have the potential to cause social harm. Gambling policy is set primarily by the states, and it was perhaps the fastest changing area of state policy in the late 20th century. In 1960, only one state allowed casino gambling, no states ran lotteries, and even charity bingo was illegal in 40 states. In 1960, 24 states banned all forms of gambling. Today, some form of casino gambling is legal in 11 states (plus the many others that have casinos on Native American lands within their borders), bingo and pari-mutuel betting on horse and dog racing are commonplace, and 37 states are directly in the gambling business with their own lotteries. Only two states (Utah and Hawaii) continue to ban gambling completely.

Gambling policy takes several forms—legalizing particular forms of gambling, setting up strict rules about specific gambling activities, taxing gambling, and even running gambling games as a state operation (state lotteries). There are four major categories of gambling that state policy deals with: bingo, pari-mutuel racetrack betting, lotteries, and casinos. There are varia-tions within these categories, such as differences between betting on dog and horse races and between high- and low-stakes casinos, but these four categories of gambling have unique histories, and they are treated largely as distinct from one another in public policy.

Gambling is not new in the United States, nor is government policy to regulate and even promote it. Government-run lotteries were used to fund such early capital-intensive projects as the Erie Canal, Harvard University, and even the settlement of Jamestown, Virginia. Government and private lotteries flourished in the 18th and early 19th centuries, but after many scandals, they came into disrepute and were banned in every state by the 1880s. Other forms of gambling, such as betting on horse races, dice and card games, and so forth, were also banned by the states in the Progressive Era of the late 19th and early 20th centuries. During the Great Depression, a few states legalized pari-mutuel betting both to generate jobs and to raise revenue by taxing bets. In 1931, the sparsely populated and isolated state of Nevada legalized casino gambling with an eye toward both economic development and state tax revenue. In 1964, New Hampshire

Gamblers playing craps at Caesars Palace Hotel and Casino in Las Vegas, Nevada.   (ROBERT MORA/GETTY IMAGES)

launched the nation's first state-run lottery of the 20th century in an attempt to fill its coffers without resorting to a sales or income tax. In 1988, the federal government instigated the process of opening casinos and bingo parlors on Native American lands by passing the INDIAN GAMING REGULATORY ACT (IGRA). These lands are seen as sovereign and exempt from state law, and IGRA set up a process through which states and Indian tribes could work out gambling compacts.

Gambling contributes a moderately important amount to state government revenue, especially in some states, such as Nevada. However, it is difficult to determine the total impact of gambling activity on state government revenue because much of it is hidden in sales taxes on betting, alcohol, food and hotel sales, and excise taxes (at and around casinos and racetracks),

income taxes on those working in the gambling industry, and so forth. The most important direct state gambling revenue is lottery income. In 1999, the 37 states that ran lotteries had a combined $33.9 million in lottery sales. However, 57.8 percent of this money went to lottery prizes, and 5.9 percent went to lottery administration. This left a total of $12.3 million for state revenue, ranging from $1.4 million in New York to only $7,205 in Montana. But even in New York, this represented only 1.6 percent of the state's total general revenue. Most state gambling revenue goes into general revenue and can be spent for any state expenditure, but some state lotteries have provisions that require their proceeds to be spent on education. However, even in these states it is not clear that education benefits disproportionately from lottery revenue.

While the details of the policy arguments about gambling vary with the type of gambling and policy being considered and with the political context, clear themes have emerged in the debate. Those opposed to the expansion of gambling argue that it leads to various social ills and that the burden of gambling taxes (including the implied taxes of lottery ticket sales) is unfairly distributed. Gambling is said to be associated with organized and petty crime, problem gambling, alcohol and drug abuse, family breakup, and personal financial problems. Opponents also argue that those who gamble are disproportionately economically disadvantaged, and thus taxes on gambling are regressive. Gambling opponents tend to be Protestant church leaders and social service advocates.

Gambling proponents tend to be those in the gambling industry and business people generally. While a libertarian progambling argument exists (why should the government establish this "victimless crime"?), the proponents' main arguments are economic. First, gambling is seen as a politically painless source of state revenue, either as direct revenue through a state-run lottery or as a new tax base, as in casino gambling. It is argued to be a voluntary tax (or even a "tax on stupidity"). Chambers of commerce and local government officials also lobby for legalizing pari-mutuel and casino gambling as a way to enhance the economic development of impoverished areas. It is argued that a casino or racetrack brings jobs, both directly for those working at these institutions and indirectly for those working at businesses who cater to gamblers (hotels, restaurants, tour operators, etc.).

As state gambling policy has become increasingly lenient over the past 40 years, the tenor of the policy debate has evolved. In the early years of the changes in gambling policy (pre-1970), gambling opponents won much more often than they lost in state legislative gambling policy debates, and legal gambling spread slowly. But in the late 1970s and early 1980s, as the states struggled to find revenue in tough economic times and as gambling appeared not to be so threatening in the several states that had already legalized it, gambling proponents began to win the day much more frequently. By the 1990s, economic-development arguments and the national acceptance of legal gambling led to even the most reluctant states with the strongest antigambling Protestant factions to liberalize their gambling laws, such as when Mississippi established casino gambling and Georgia established a lottery. By the late 1990s, the furious pace of state gambling policy change had died down considerably, both as states achieved the types of gambling their citizens were comfortable with, and as gambling revenues and taxes stabilized and even fell with the profusion of legal gambling outlets.

For more information

Mason, John Lyman, and Michael Nelson. *Handling Gambling*. New York: The Century Foundation Press, 2001.

National Gambling Impact Study Commission. *Final Report*. Washington, D.C.: National Gambling Impact Study Commission, 1999.

Christopher Z. Mooney

Gantt, Henry Laurence (1861–1919) *inventor, writer*   Henry Laurence Gantt was an early pioneer of scientific management and inventor of the GANTT CHART.

Henry Laurence Gantt was born in 1861 on a plantation in Maryland near Baltimore. When he was 12 his father was dead and the family was impoverished. Fortunately he was admitted to the Baltimore McDonogh School, where he flourished. After graduating from McDonogh he attended and graduated from Johns Hopkins University. He then studied at the Stevens Institute, from which he graduated in 1884 with a degree in mechanical engineering. After working in industry, he taught for a year at the McDonogh School.

In 1887 he joined Frederick W. Taylor at the Midvale Company. Their 14-year association would continue at Bethlehem Steel Company and elsewhere. During these years Taylor was developing his system of work and payment—a differential piece-rate system. It was an attempt to improve the efficiency of labor and to reward the increased production. However, it was somewhat punitive because those who were unable to meet the production quota were penalized. Gantt in the meanwhile developed a similar system that was much more humane. Gantt's system was a task-and-bonus system. It was instituted with systematic training, continued with encouragement from management. The system helped workers to achieve higher production rates and to receive appropriate financial rewards as well. This system reflected Gantt's educational experiences at the McDonogh School.

During these years Gantt took out several patents. He invented an improved mold for steel ingots that was widely used in American industry. However, most of Gantt's important contributions were in the area of industrial management rather than mechanical engineering. After 1895 Gantt worked as a consulting engineer specializing in improving plant efficiency.

In 1888 Gantt joined the American Society of Mechanical Engineers, where he held numerous positions during his career. He also published frequently in the society's journal. In all, there are over 150 extant addresses, papers, reports, and books in Gantt's literary corpus. His most important books were *Work, Wages, and Profits* (1916) and *Organizing for Work* (1919).

Gantt made at least four major contributions to management practices. His task-and-bonus system was to be implemented widely. A second important contribution was to see the manager as a teacher of workers rather than a taskmaster driving them. Gantt also emphasized the responsibility of companies to render service to the community rather than focusing on profits alone.

Gantt's most important contribution was the Gantt chart, developed over many years while working at different companies. It was perfected during World War I while he worked for the army. His Gantt chart greatly aided management of manpower and matériel, with a resultant increase in productivity.

In 1919 Gantt was suddenly stricken with a digestive disorder and died at his home in Montclair, New Jersey, on November 23.

For more information

Alford, L. P. *Henry Laurence Gantt: Leader in Industry.* New York: The American Society of Mechanical Engineers, 1934.

A. J. L. Waskey

Gantt chart   The Gantt chart is a powerful graphic managerial tool for planning and control.

Gantt charts enable managers to plan production schedules, projects, sales campaigns, and many other activities. Control can be exercised over the work completed by charting actual progress against the planned schedule. The graphic display in a Gantt chart enables the manager to quickly see how work is progressing toward completion of the plan.

The Gantt chart was developed by HENRY LAURENCE GANTT to improve industrial operations. During his career as a management consultant, Gantt developed charts to display various data. In the late 1800s at Bethlehem Steel, Gantt developed a task-and-bonus system that he graphed. In the years that followed he developed a "daily balance chart" (American Locomotive Company), a "red-and-black bonus chart" (Brighton Mills), the "percentage chart" (Saylesville Bleacheries), a "production-cost chart" (Remington Typewriter), the "idleness-expense chart" (Chaney Brothers), and the Gantt chart at the Frankford Arsenal.

The Gantt chart has been widely adopted because of its advantages. It forces the manager to create a clear plan, easily understood by all. It compares what will be done with what has been done and when. It is easy to read and to draw, and the upkeep of the plan requires simple clerical effort. The chart reveals when performance has fallen short, enabling quick remedial action to be taken. And the chart is quite compact and can be recorded on a single sheet of paper.

To make a Gantt chart, all that is needed is a plain sheet of paper—letter size or larger—and a lead pencil. Down the left side are recorded the jobs, or phrases, or machines, or work of a department, or events of some project, or a production activity. Across the top of the page in columns is recorded a time scale—hours, days, weeks, and months are the units of time commonly used. The time to accomplish tasks, jobs, or activities is represented with straight thin lines. As these are completed a heavy line is drawn underneath. Symbols can be used on the chart for many purposes, such as a triangle to mark a project milestone.

The Gantt chart is a dynamic operating chart because it furnishes information for action. It creates a plan for the future; it provides information about current operations; and it creates a record of past achievements.

There are versions of the Gantt chart that are not called by Gantt's name but are nevertheless derived from the Gantt chart. There are also mechanical charts, such as schedule boards or wall charts, that used mechanical pegs or strings or tapes to record production.

Computer programs for project management are widely available. The most common view in these programs is the Gantt chart, showing time values for tasks, related costs, human assignments, and resource assignments.

For more information

Gantt, Henry L. *Organizing for Work.* 1919. Reprint, New York: Easton Hive Publishing Co., 1974.

Mingus, Nancy. Chap. 11 in *Alpha Teach Yourself Project Management in 24 Hours.* Madison, Wis.: CWL Publishing, 2002.

A. J. L. Waskey

garbage-can model The garbage-can model is a concept used to help understand organizations and, more recently in a revised version, the policy process. Although originally used to help us understand the organizational decision process, the garbage-can model has also become an important way of understanding when and why some policies emerge on government's agenda.

According to this model, four separate streams run within every organization: problems, solutions, participants, and choice opportunities. Each stream operates independently, unrelated to the others. In this image, an opportunity is a "garbage can" into which participants dump various kinds of problems and solutions as they emerge. Thus, the decision or outcome in an organization depends upon the mix in the garbage can at any particular time and how participants process it. The decision also depends on how many garbage cans there are, what type of garbage is being produced, how they are labeled, and how quickly each can is removed from the scene. In this view, decisions depend on the independent interaction of participants, problems, solutions, and opportunities. At any given time the garbage-can "mix" can be different, which will result in a different outcome.

In terms of the development of public policy, the model posits that a similar series of events unfolds. Here, the policy process (similar to the decision process noted above) consists of several independent streams: the problem stream (various problems that have gained the community's or government's attention), the policy stream (community of specialists including bureaucrats, interest groups, and academics), and the politics stream (national mood, public opinion, election results). Like the earlier description, these streams operate independently of one another within the "garbage can." When these separate streams become coupled, we see the greatest policy change. For example, according to the garbage-can model, when a particular problem connects to a group of specialists and the national mood is receptive, we get the greatest chance for policy development or policy change. Depending on what the problem is, who is involved, and the spirit of the times, an entirely different policy could emerge from the "garbage can."

Overall, both garbage-can models help to describe and explain the seemingly chaotic nature of organizational decision making and public policy making.

For more information

Cohen, Michael D., James G. March, and Johan P. Olsen. "A Garbage Can Model of Organizational Choice." *Administrative Science Quarterly* 17 (March 1972): 1–25.

Kingdon, John W. *Agendas, Alternatives, and Public Policies.* New York: HarperCollins, 1995.

Robert A. Schuhmann

Garcia v. San Antonio Mass Transit Authority **469 U.S. 528 (1984)** The Supreme Court decided in *Garcia v. San Antonio Mass Transit Authority* that Congress has the constitutional authority to require states to pay their employees a minimum wage.

Garcia had a significant effect upon the constitutional division of authority between the national government and the states. The decision is important because the Court allowed Congress to determine the limits of its own commerce-clause power on the issue of minimum wage. *Garcia* overturned a previous case, decided eight years earlier, which had declared that Congress did not have the constitutional authority to require states to pay their employees a minimum wage.

The earlier case, *National League of Cities v. Usury,* 426 U.S. 833 (1976), involved the wages of local police, firefighters, and sanitation workers. For purposes of the Constitution, local governments are included under the category of state government. Under the commerce clause, Congress has the authority to regulate commerce among the states. The Court reasoned in *National League of Cities* that because the wages of city workers was an in-state matter, and interstate commerce was not involved, the wages of

city workers was an issue of state authority. The *Garcia* case, involving the wages of city mass-transit workers, overruled *National League of Cities.*

In *Garcia* the Supreme Court expanded the commerce-clause powers of Congress to include the regulation of the wages of city employees. It reasoned that protecting cities in their "traditional governmental functions" was becoming unworkable and mentioned that the national government heavily funded local mass transit. The *Garcia* decision explained that judges should not interfere with the requirement that cities pay workers a minimum wage because state power would instead be protected by the structure and process of American government. According to the *Garcia* decision, Supreme Court protection of state power was considered to be interference with the democratic process.

In dissent Justice Powell asserted that the *Garcia* decision had abandoned the principle of federalism. He argued that difficulty in drawing a line between traditional and nontraditional activities of local government does not justify abandonment of the effort. Justice Powell observed that providing federal funding does not imply the constitutional authority to regulate. He challenged the Court's assertion that because members of Congress are elected in the states, they would automatically protect state decision-making power. Citing a footnote in *National League of Cities,* he compared this argument to an assertion that because members of Congress are individuals, they will automatically protect individual rights. Justice Powell said the contest in *Garcia* is not democracy versus judicial intervention but, rather, democracy at the national level versus democracy at the local level.

Justice O'Connor dissented that the *Garcia* decision was against the spirit of the Constitution. Justice Rehnquist, author of the *National League of Cities* opinion, dissented that *Garcia* would someday be overturned. Congress responded to *Garcia* by amending the law to add flexibility for state compliance with minimum wage requirements, but Congress continues to regulate the way states pay their employees.

For more information

Tebben, Carol. "Is Federalism a Political Question? An Application of the Marshallian Framework to *Garcia*." *Publius* 20 (winter 1990): 113–122.

Carol Tebben

General Accounting Office   The General Accounting Office (GAO) is the investigative arm of Congress, and it studies programs and expenditures of the federal government. That is, GAO examines how the federal government spends taxpayer dollars and provides advice on how it can become more effective and responsive.

GAO is an independent and nonpartisan agency that works for Congress and the American people. It is one of the most outstanding controlling organizations, as stated by many world scientists working in the fields of program evaluation and auditing of public institutions. Its roles include (1) evaluating how well government policies and programs are working, (2) auditing agency operations to determine whether federal funds are being spent efficiently, effectively, and appropriately, (3) investigating allegations of illegal and improper activities, and (4) issuing legal decisions and opinions.

When GAO reports its findings to Congress, it recommends actions. Its work leads to laws and acts that improve government operations and save billions of dollars. For example, addressing terrorism, GAO has recently issued several reports on this topic where the organization evaluates the preparedness of the country in order to confront new attacks. Some of the issues addressed in these reports are security in federal buildings, mail sanitization, and intergovernmental cooperation.

The GAO was born in 1921 as a result of the Budget and Accounting Act, which was aimed at improving federal financial management after World War I. By that time, the president had a lot of power to manage the budget, and there was a need to counterbalance that power. That is why the Congress required a tool independent of the executive branch that could investigate how federal funds were spent.

Although the agency has always worked for good government, its mission and organization have changed a great deal since 1921 in order to keep up with congressional and national needs. The GAO has evolved in three stages.

During the first period (1921–50), the GAO's main task was focused on legally and formally controlling vouchers, which were forms used by executive branch administrative officials and disbursing officers to record information on spending. (This early period of GAO's history has often been called the voucher checking era.)

Later, from 1950 to 1967, and as a result of the Accounting and Auditing Act, the office shifted from checking individual vouchers to conducting more-comprehensive audits of federal spending. This emphasis on examining the economy and efficiency of government operations in the postwar era marked the first major evolutionary change for GAO, not only because of the transformation of its role, but also because of the change of its organizational structure, which was downsized from 15,000 to 4,000 workers.

In 1967, GAO broadened its scope and moved into program evaluation. This major shift, although as essential as the previous one, was not as traumatic to the organization. Again, new norms led to legislation that sanctioned the new tasks: the Legislative and Reorganization Act in 1970 and the Congressional Budget and Impoundment Control Act in 1974.

During the 1980s and early 1990s, GAO examined high-risk areas in government operations, paid close attention to budget issues, and worked to improve federal financial management. Today the modern GAO serves the nation by carrying out a broad range of financial and performance audits and program evaluations related, particularly, to social policies.

The current GAO structure has about 5,000 workers, many of whom are specialists in the public administration and public policy fields, with emphasis on evaluation, law, economics, or accounting. The agency has always been headed by a comptroller general, who is appointed to a 15-year term. The long tenure of the comptroller general gives GAO a continuity of leadership that is rare within government.

The Congress is the main client of the GAO. This means that its main responsibility consists of supporting the Congress's job of controlling the activities of the executive branch. The GAO's core values are accountability, integrity, reliability, independence, objectivity, and transparency. Those principles assure its institutional credibility, which is essential to the accomplishment of its goals.

For more information

General Accounting Office. http://www.gao.gov/.

Mila Gascó and Fran Equiza

General Agreement on Tariffs and Trade

The General Agreement on Tariffs and Trade (GATT) was established after World War II as one of the measures designed to increase international economic cooperation (along with the World Bank and the International Monetary Fund).

Twenty-three countries initially signed the agreement that initiated a series of negotiations to reduce trade tariffs between the countries. The first round of negotiations resulted in 45,000 tariff concessions affecting about one-fifth of the world's trade at the time. This first round of negotiations began in 1946 and concluded with the GATT coming into effect in January 1948.

Although the basic text and format of the agreement stayed in place for almost five decades, there were a number of voluntary membership changes, agreements, and other efforts to reduce tariffs. The most significant gains in trade liberalization through GATT were realized through a series of "trade rounds," where intensive negotiations on a wide range of tariffs were held under the auspices of the GATT. These rounds had an advantage over issue-by-issue negotiations as they allowed for a balancing of concessions and gains between the players.

The first of these "trade rounds" is referred to as the Tokyo round. By the time this round was held between 1973 and 1979, 102 countries had agreed to take part in the negotiations. The round succeeded in reducing tariffs by an average of one-third in the world's nine major industrial markets. Key gains were made in the manufacturing sector, while the agricultural sector saw minimal gains in trade liberalization. However, this is the first round where significant progress was made in the harmonization of practices between governments, leading to more standardized legislation, regulations, and policies affecting international trade.

The Uruguay round began in 1982 and was intended to focus on creating a new multilateral system of trade. The initial attempts failed, largely due to agricultural issues. However, another meeting was held four years later (1986) in Punta del Este, Uruguay, resulting in an agreement to launch the Uruguay round.

A further meeting in 1988 in Montreal, Canada, brought an agreement for a second phase of negotiations and a framework for settling disputes. The round continued past the original time frame of 1990 until a final draft text was agreed to in December 1991. A complete agreement was reached in December 1993 and signed in April 1994.

The GATT 1994 agreement continued to exist until 1995, when it was superseded by the founding of the World Trade Organization (WTO). The amended GATT is an integral part of the WTO agreement. The WTO agreement is the beginning of the first permanent institution to administer world multilateral trade agreements, including a faster and more automatic dispute-resolution system.

For more information

General Agreement on Tariffs and Trade. http://www.gatt.org.

Hoda, Anwarul. *Tariff Negotiations and Renegotiations under the GATT and WTO: Procedures and Practices.* New York: Cambridge University Press, 2001.

World Trade Organization. http://www.wto.org.

Michael Henry

general-obligation bond   A general-obligation bond is one of two types of long-term debt issued by state and local governments that are backed by the full faith and credit, or taxing power, of the government that issues the securities. This means that the issuing government is obligated to pay the debt from any and all available revenue sources in order to meet interest and principal commitments.

The second type of long-term bond available for issue by state and local governments is the revenue bond. Revenue bonds are repaid with forecasted revenue from a specific source. If the revenues are not sufficient to pay the interest or principal fully, then the bondholders suffer the loss.

Bond investors (individuals, funds, and institutional lenders) view the commitment of all necessary revenue sources as a reduction of risk that increases the likelihood of payment of interest and repayment of principle. Thus general-obligation bonds typically bear lower interest rate charges than equivalent revenue bonds.

Long-term debt financing of public capital projects can be justified on the basis of the benefit principle. Because capital expenditures by state and local governments involve the construction of facilities (roads, public institutions, wastewater treatment, and other structures) that will provide a stream of public services to future citizens of the state or municipality, it is reasonable to finance such expenditures through debt.

Long-term debt is differentiated from short-term debt by the repayment period (short-term is typically repaid in less than one year), which is typically 10, 20, or 30 years. Long-term debt accounts for more than 90 percent of state-local total outstanding debt. This is because state legislation and state constitutions allow debt to be issued for nearly every purpose except to finance cash flows.

General-obligation bonds, which rose from approximately $70 billion in 1980 to almost $350 billion in 1999, accounted for approximately 30 percent of the total long-term debt of local governments. This percentage represents an increasing trend in state-local debt toward the use of revenue bonds, as states and localities have expanded the purposes for which they borrow. As late as 1977, 56 percent of the long-term debt was in the form of general-obligation bonds. The rise in revenue-based bonds is closely tied to the rise in quasi-public services undertaken by state and local governments, including local development corporations, senior-housing corporations, public/private utility providers, etc. These organizations provide what were previously considered private-sector services, and the financing and operation of these organizations is often maintained separately from the general government budget. As such, debt issuance is isolated and backed by the individual organization's revenue.

The fundamental economic characteristic that makes state-local government bonds attractive investments is that the federal government does not tax the interest income received by investors. Typically, states will also exempt the interest income paid to residents from bonds issued by that state or its localities. This affords state-local bonds the role of a tax shelter or tax-favored investment for lenders. The primary economic effect of the tax exemption is to allow lower interest rates for state-local bonds than similar taxable bonds issued by corporations. As a result, the tax exemption serves to subsidize both state-local governments, through lower borrowing costs, and investors in state-local bonds, through higher net (after-tax) returns. As a result, state-local government bonds often carry lower interest rates (the amount paid by the government entity to borrow the money) than comparable private-sector or U.S. government bonds because of the tax exemption. This relationship between federal tax policy and interest charges can be tied back to the interest level of investors. For example tax-law changes can induce higher or lower demand for state-local bonds by investors, thereby lowering or raising interests costs to state-local governments and increasing or decreasing the intensity with which governments issue bonds. This was evident in the mid 1980s when the planned tax-law changes of the 1986 Tax Reform Act reduced the attractiveness of bonds to investors.

There is a formal and consistent process that results in a state-local government bond issue. First, the issuing government employs the services of a number of financial intermediaries in the actual process of selling bonds. These include bond counsel (attorneys), who examine the legality of the issue, assure the prospective investors that the government has taken all required and appropriate legal steps in order to sell the bonds, and who work to ensure that the interest will be exempt from federal income tax; and a financial adviser and underwriter (possibly from the same firm as the bond counsel), who advise on the structure of the bonds, prepare the necessary financial documents, and market the bonds to investors.

Second, state-local governments bonds are usually given a credit rating by at least one of the two major private rating firms, Moody's Investor Service or Standard and Poor's. The credit rating (denoted AAA, AA, A, BBB, and so on) is intended to provide information to potential investors about the perceived risk of the bonds and thus evaluates the economic and fiscal health of the issuing government and the specific purpose or project for the borrowed funds.

Finally, there is generally an active market for investors to buy or sell existing state-local tax-exempt bonds, through mutual funds if no other way. This means that some investors may be able to sell state-local government bonds to other investors, thereby receiving returns of the principal before the term of the bond is up.

For more information

Fisher, Ronald. *State and Local Public Finance,* 2d ed. Chicago: Irwin, 1996.

Kaufman, George C., and Philip Fischer. "Debt Management." In *Management Policies in Local Government Finance,* edited by John Aronson and Edward Swartz. Washington, D.C.: International City Management Association, 1987.

Mikesell, John. *Fiscal Administration: Analysis and Applications for the Public Sector,* 5th ed. Fort Worth, Tex.: Harcourt Brace College Publishers, 1999.

Brent C. Smith

general revenue   General revenue is money regularly collected by a government that has not been earmarked for a special purpose and is not an unusual windfall.

Revenue, categorical and general, includes all the money accepted by some part of the government from sources outside the government during a fiscal year. However, not all governmental receipts can be counted as revenue. Excluded are refunds, borrowings, sales of investments, transfers between agencies, or trust-fund transactions. Also not counted as revenue are unsettled tax disputes, noncash gifts or bequests or receipts-in-kind, and noncash transactions, such as receipt of technical services.

There are four major types of general revenue: taxes, intergovernmental revenue, current charges, and miscellaneous general revenue. What is counted as general revenue versus categorical revenue varies between the localities, states, and the federal government.

Taxes are compulsory exactions that governments impose for public purposes on wealth or income. General revenue from taxes can include penalties and interest as well. General-revenue tax receipts can come from personal or corporate income taxes, corporate filing fees, estate taxes, beverage taxes and licenses, taxes on tobacco, documentary stamps, gambling taxes, excises, sales taxes, severance taxes, tariffs, intangible taxes, medical-hospital fees, and other taxes. In addition, revenues from fees for hunting, fishing, vanity car tags, or other such activities produce general revenue.

Excluded from general revenue are taxes supporting retirement and medical care systems (e.g., Social Security and Medicare), or previously dedicated taxes such as federal gasoline taxes for the highway trust funds.

The second type of general revenue is intergovernmental revenue. This category contains those monies received from other governments, including grants, shared taxes, and contingent loans and advances for support of particular functions or for general financial support. State and local governments receive great sums in this category.

The third category of revenue counted as general revenue is current charges. This category comprises charges for services or charges for the sale of products in connection with general government activities—national or international. For example, general revenue may come from charges for military materiel, publicly owned commercial concessions, cemeteries, airport hangar fees, landing fees, postal insurance fees, court filing fees, or charges for documents. The Census Bureau's accounting practices treat revenues reported as current charges on a gross basis without offsetting the cost to produce or buy the commodities or services sold. For the federal government, this category includes revenue from premiums related to non-social insurance programs such as crop insurance, farm mortgage insurance, and home mortgage insurance. Also it can include service charges applied to another government acting as its collection agency.

The fourth type of general revenue is miscellaneous general revenue. These are items that do not fall into one of the above categories, for example, cash gifts.

The Census Bureau treats liquor store, utility, or insurance trust operations as revenue other than general revenue.

For more information

U.S. Census Bureau. "Revenue." Chap. 7 in *Federal, State, and Local Governments: Government Finance and Employment Classification Manual*. Washington, D.C.: U.S. Government Printing Office, 2002.

A. J. L. Waskey

general schedule *General schedule* is the term that identifies the compensation and job classification system for white-collar jobs in the federal government.

This classification system organizes jobs according to a numerical occupational structure. Within the general schedule (GS), related jobs are organized by 100-level occupational categories. Examples include accounting and budget, GS-500; engineering and architecture, GS-800; and general administrative, clerical, and office services, GS-300. Specific occupational jobs are further subdivided by series. Examples include the accounting series, GS-510, and the secretary series, GS-318.

Within each job series, individual jobs are assigned a general schedule grade. Grades vary according to levels of responsibility and difficulty. Jobs in the general schedule are assigned a numerical grade that ranges from GS-1 to GS-15, with the higher number indicating greater responsibility and greater pay. Within each of the 15 general schedule grades, there are 10 pay steps. For example, the general schedule in 2002 pays a GS-12 public utilities specialist $49,959 annually at step one and $61,614 at step seven.

According to the general schedule classification structure, entry-level professional work is generally considered to be GS-5 and GS-7. Management level responsibility is typically graded at GS-13 to GS-15. Positions above GS-15 are outside the general schedule and are included in the SENIOR EXECUTIVE SERVICE (SES).

Classification standards are developed by the OFFICE OF PERSONNEL MANAGEMENT (OPM) and implemented by federal agencies. Classification standards are intended to encourage consistency and equity salary among federal agency employees who perform substantially equal work. In theory, an electrical engineer who designs electrical wiring drawings for the Department of Energy should be classified the same and receive the same pay as an electrical engineer who is designing electrical wiring drawings for the Bureau of Reclamation.

The classification standards program for positions in the general schedule was established by the Classification Act of 1949, which is codified in the U.S. Code, Title 5. The statute defines each grade in the general schedule and establishes the principle of equal pay for substantially equal work. In 1999, 72 percent of federal civilian employees were working under the general schedule.

For more information
U.S. Code. Title 5.
United States Office of Personnel Management. http://www.opm.gov.

Richard J. Van Orden

General Services Administration The General Services Administration, more commonly referred to as GSA, is a federal government agency. On 1 July, 1949, the Federal Property and Administrative Services Act was signed into law by President Truman, authorizing the establishment of GSA. This legislation was passed to avoid senseless duplication, excess cost, and confusion in handling supplies and providing space to the federal government.

GSA is headquartered in Washington, D.C., and has 11 regional offices around the United States. GSA provides oversight in the following areas:

Workspace, security, and furniture
Equipment, supplies, tools, computers, and telephones
Travel and transportation services
Federal motor vehicle fleet
Telecommuting centers and federal child-care centers
Preservation of historic buildings
Management of a fine arts program
Development of, advocation for, and evaluation of government-wide policy

According to GSA's most recent strategic plan, the mission of GSA is to help federal agencies better serve the public by offering—at best value—superior workplaces, expert solutions, efficient acquisition services, and innovative management policies. GSA has six goals:

Provide best value for customer agencies and taxpayers
Achieve responsible asset management
Operate efficiently and effectively
Ensure financial accountability
Maintain a world-class workforce and a world-class workplace
Conscientiously carry out social, environmental, and other responsibilities as a federal agency

GSA's current assets include more than 8,300 government-owned or leased buildings, over 170,000 vehicles, and technology programs and products ranging from laptop computers to systems that cost over $100 million. An interesting fact about GSA is that only 1 percent of the agency's total budget is provided by Congress. The majority of GSA's budget comes from the fees they charge for the services and products they provide. GSA currently employs over 14,000 people.

For more information
General Services Administration. *U.S. General Services Administration Strategic Plan.* Washington, D.C.: U.S. Government Printing Office, 2003.
General Services Administration. http://www.gsa.gov.

Jamie Green

Gilbreth, Frank Bunker, and Lillian Evelyn Moller Gilbreth (1868–1924 and 1878–1972) *industrial engineers* Frank Bunker Gilbreth and Lillian Evelyn Moller Gilbreth were industrial engineers who pioneered in the field of motion study and scientific management.

Frank Gilbreth was born 7 July 1868 in Fairfield, Maine. Educated at Andover and the Rice Grammar School, he prepared for MIT. Although he passed the qualifying exams, he chose instead to enter the contracting business. Starting as an apprentice bricklayer, he noticed that the men teaching him how to lay bricks used different motions in their work. Observing that wasted motion increased worker fatigue, he wondered which motions were most efficient. He soon reduced bricklaying to a simple few motions and at the same time was able to nearly triple the number of bricks laid.

In 1904 Gilbreth married Lillian Moller, born on 24 May 1878, the daughter of a German-immigrant sugar refiner. She was a recent graduate of the University of California at Berkeley with degrees in English. After their marriage Lillian earned a Ph.D. in psychology to better complement Frank's work.

The Gilbreths used many devices and techniques to study work motions. They were the first to use the new motion-picture camera to study the repetitive motions of work. They invented the microchronometer clock to time motions studied in films.

Frank Gilbreth also invented the "white list" card system, which was an early appraisal form for workers and a forerunner of merit-rating systems. The Gilbreths developed the process chart and the flow chart. They also undertook studies in worker training, work environments, health, worker fatigue, and tools. Together they wrote many books, including *Fatigue Study* (1916) and *Applied Motion Study* (1917).

The life of the Gilbreth family before the death of Frank Gilbreth was told by two of their children in the book *Cheaper by the Dozen* (1948), later made into a movie. They describe their home as a school for scientific management, filled with process and work charts and with many chores the subject of filming and motion analysis.

In 1907 Frank met Frederick W. Taylor, and the two became admirers and collaborators. Taylor's book, *Scientific Management*, devoted several pages to describing Gilbreth's bricklayer studies. Taylor called his method "time study," while Gilbreth called his "motion study."

During World War I Gilbreth joined the U.S. Army as an efficiency expert with the rank of major. Motion studies were made of many of the army's activities, including field stripping machine guns and rifles. The Gilbreths also studied how to retrain amputees. Lillian helped General Electric redesign home appliances for disabled homemakers. They also lobbied Congress for vocational rehabilitation.

Frank died 14 June 1924 from a heart ailment. After her husband's death, Lillian decided to go to London and Prague to present his papers at previously planned meetings. She spent the remainder of her life working as an efficiency expert.

For more information

Gilbreth, Frank B., Jr., and Ernestine Gilbreth Carey. *Cheaper by the Dozen.* 1948. Reprint, New York: Thomas Y. Crowell Company, 1963.

A. J. L. Waskey

goal displacement Goal displacement is when the goals of individuals or groups do not align with the goals of the overall organizations to which they belong.

Organizations are often quite specific about the procedures that individuals and groups should follow and about the objectives that they should achieve. Organizations then often motivate them to follow the specified procedures and achieve the specified objectives by applying rewards and sanctions. However, assumptions about the end results of following certain procedures and achieving certain objectives can be flawed, and so the actual results produced by individuals and groups may not align with the desired results of organizations. Goal displacement occurs when individuals and groups are not allowed enough discretion to alter their behavior and activities in response to their unique, emerging, and changing circumstances and to determine for themselves how they can best advance the organizations' goals.

One way that goal displacement can occur is when the means become the ends. Organizations often specify that individuals and groups should follow certain procedures, and then use rewards and sanctions to motivate individuals and groups to adopt the specified means in their daily activity. Adopting the specified means becomes their goal.

Specifying means can have the benefit of preventing behavior that is fraudulent or inefficient. Organizations can set the goals of individuals and groups to promote accountable and efficient behavior, which in turn often advances organizations' overall goals. Organizations must limit the discretion that individuals and groups have over the means they adopt in order to limit behavior that runs counter to the overall goals. However, the policy and administrative environments of public organizations are typically very fluid and diverse. As a result, those who specify means typically cannot predict all the situations that individuals and groups will find themselves in, and thus they cannot know exactly what behavior would best advance the overall goals of the organization.

By limiting the discretion that individuals and groups have over the means they adopt, organizations may also limit the ability of individuals and groups to respond to unique, emerging, or changing information. Without such discretion, individuals and groups do not have the option of selecting innovative means that might better advance the overall goals. The more detailed the specification of the means, and the greater the motivation to adopt those means, the more likely it will be that individuals and groups will treat that goal-driven behavior not as a means to an end but, rather, as an end in itself. Goal displacement occurs to the extent that the end result of such behavior varies from the end result desired by organizations.

An example of means becoming ends can be found in government purchasing policies. For program objectives to be fully met, program officials must spend their resources as economically as possible. However, officials are sometimes incapable of or uninterested in properly determining the relative economy of alternative uses of resources and selecting the most economical use. Governments thus often require, through policies on the purchase of goods and services, that: (1) managers scrutinize and authorize the purchases of their officials before they are made, weeding out those that appear wasteful; (2) auditors examine the books and "paper trails" for instances where purchases were made without the proper scrutiny and authorization; and (3) sanctions are levied against officials and managers who do not follow the purchasing policy. Here, governments use the means of managerial oversight and audit to promote the end of economical spending in support of program objectives.

Unfortunately, officials may not be certain of their need for a good or service until very close to the time when they should actually use it, and managers may be too busy to scrutinize purchase requests with minimal delay. As a result, obtaining managerial authorization for a purchase can take so long that the need for it has expired by the time the good or service is received. When this happens, the good or service either is not used for its intended purpose or is not used at all. In either case, the good or service is received too late for the full value to come from its purchase. Another possibility is that officials, predicting the slowdown, either do not bother to request a purchase in the first place, or they obtain different goods or services through different means. When these things happen, the good or service that would provide the greatest value is not obtained and used by the official.

In many different ways, then, following the purchasing policy can cause officials to not use their resources to purchase goods and services that provide maximum value and thus do not fully achieve the objectives of the programs they deliver. When officials and managers are sanctioned for any deviation from this specified process of managerial oversight and audit, the means become their ends, and they may comply with the policy even when it is obvious that compliance is preventing them from achieving the real ends, i.e., the program's objectives. To the extent that managerial oversight and audit does not lead to economical spending and ultimately to the full achievement of program objectives, the goals of officials and managers will not align with the goals of the government—and the greater the incentive for officials and managers to achieve their goals, the greater the amount of goal displacement.

Another way that goal displacement can occur is when the ends that individuals and groups seek do not combine or aggregate to produce the ends that an organization as a whole seeks. Organizations often identify a number of components of their desired ends, assign responsibility for their achievement to various individuals and groups, and then use rewards and sanctions to motivate individuals and groups to achieve the specified ends. Achieving the specified ends becomes their goal.

This application of MANAGEMENT BY OBJECTIVES can help ensure that individuals and groups pursue only goals that, when combined with those of others, advance the overall goals of the organization. Organizations must limit the discretion that individuals and groups have over the ends they seek in order to limit activities that do not contribute the most to the overall goals. However, the goals of public organizations can be vague and contentious, and the ways that policies and programs actually produce results are often poorly understood. As a result, those who specify ends typically cannot fully understand how the overall goals of the organization may best be broken down into individual- and group-specific goals. Furthermore, since the quantity and quality of ends may be difficult to quantify, it can be difficult to determine how best to measure the achievement of those goals. By limiting the discretion that individuals and groups have over the ends they seek, organizations may also limit their ability to respond to unique, emerging, or changing information about how individual and group activities could contribute to organizational objectives by undertaking activities that contribute the most.

The more detailed the specification of the ends, the more likely it will be that the goals that individuals and groups pursue have captured either more or less than they should; and the greater the motivations to seek those ends, the more likely it will be that individuals and groups will either undertake activities that are not needed, or not undertake activities that are needed. Goal displacement occurs to the extent that the end result of the activities they do undertake varies from the end result desired by the organization.

An example of individual and group ends not combining to produce organizational ends concerns policing. Increased public safety is one end that police forces typically pursue, and this end can be furthered by stopping and ticketing those who drive in ways that pose a threat to public safety. However, police officers are sometimes incapable of or uninterested in properly determining how many tickets should be issued and actually issuing those tickets. Police forces thus often: (1) analyze the incidence and consequences of unsafe driving in their districts; (2) require, through the use of quotas, that some of their police officers issue a specified number of tickets over a specified time period; and (3) apply rewards or sanctions, depending on whether those officers meet or fail to meet their quotas. Here, police forces make issuing tickets the end of some of their members in an effort to promote the organizational end of increased public safety.

Unfortunately, it is difficult to tell just how much issuing tickets contributes to the result of public safety, as well as how much other police activities contribute to that end. As such, it is difficult to determine the particular number of tickets that would prompt police officers to spend either so little time issuing tickets that dangerous drivers continue to pose large threats to public safety, or so much time issuing tickets that other threats to public safety go unaddressed. When the quota is set too high, some of the time that police officers spend issuing tickets could be spent—with greater impact on public safety—either addressing other threats or addressing the same threat through different activities (e.g., prevention). At the same time, other quotas, assigned to other police officers undertaking other activities, would be set too low, since the marginal contribution to public safety of those activities would be greater than that of issuing tickets.

In different ways, then, meeting quotas can cause police officers to spend their time on activities that collectively do not increase public safety as much as another mix of activities would, and so do not fully achieve the objectives of their police forces. When police officers as individuals and groups are rewarded for meeting their quotas or sanctioned for not meeting their quotas, they will often do their best to meet them, even when it is obvious that the police force's ends could be better promoted by undertaking different activities. To the extent that issuing tickets does not lead to safer driving and as much of an increase in public safety as would other police activities, the goals of police officers will not align with this goal of the police force—and the greater the incentive for police officers to achieve their goals, the greater is the amount of goal displacement.

Many of the current performance-management reforms in Western countries involve decreasing specificity over desired means and increasing specificity over desired ends. These reforms rely on the maxim that "what gets measured, gets done." However, they may only prompt individuals and groups to simply "manage for the measures," rather than for the overall objectives of their organizations. One form of goal displacement may replace another.

Organizations can never perfectly align their goals with the goals of individuals and groups because the means and ends of individuals and groups that would best serve the interests of the organization can never be fully and precisely predicted, specified, and motivated. To avoid goal displacement, organizations must not attempt to fully and completely specify the goals of individuals and groups, but rather the organization should allow them discretion over both their means and their ends so they can respond to unique, emerging, and changing circumstances. However, discretion has its own drawbacks: individuals and groups may not know any more than do organizations what means and ends would best serve the interests of the organization, and individuals and groups may be tempted to ignore the interests of the organization altogether, focusing instead on their own interests. In both cases, the behavior and activities that individuals and groups would choose for themselves could be even worse, from the perspective of the organization, than the behavior and activities the organization would choose for them.

Organizations should seek to limit goal displacement by allowing individuals and groups some discretion. On the other hand, organizations risk goal displacement if they allow individuals and groups more discretion than they are able and willing to use properly.

For more information

Merton, Robert K. "Bureaucratic Structure and Personality." *Social Forces* 17 (1940): 560–568. Reprinted in *Reader in Bureaucracy,* edited by Robert K. Merton. New York: Free Press, 1952, 361–371.

Wilson, James Q. *Bureaucracy: What Government Agencies Do and Why They Do It.* New York: Basic Books, 1989.

David I. Dewar

Goldberg v. Kelly 397 U.S. 254 (1970)

Goldberg v. Kelly was a key decision by the U.S. Supreme Court involving procedural due process.

Residents of New York City who were receiving welfare payments, provided under the Aid to Families with Dependent Children program, brought suit concerning the process by which such aid was terminated. The residents claimed that the notification and hearing process violated due process rights under the Fourteenth Amendment to the U.S. Constitution. Under the Fourteenth Amendment a state government cannot deny life, liberty, or property except by due process of law. Procedural due process concerns the protection of citizens against arbitrary actions by public officials.

American federalism has evolved into a system where delivery of many public services requires cooperation between the national government and those at the state and local levels. This system is often referred to as "cooperative federalism." Local and state governments are responsible for implementing the procedures for payment of entitlement programs such as AID TO FAMILIES WITH DEPENDENT CHILDREN. Qualified citizens are guaranteed payment under programs such as this (AFDC no longer exists and has been replaced by multiple state programs), and when these benefits are terminated, litigation in the federal court system often follows.

As with most cases involving due process rights, the U.S. Supreme Court had to balance the needs of the state with the need to protect individual rights. The states have a legitimate need to control welfare fraud and prevent abuse of the system. In this case the commissioner of social services of the City of New York, Jack R. Goldberg, had terminated the benefits of those recipients deemed no longer eligible. This is a typical state action involving the enforcement of administrative rules. However, since it does involve "state" action, as opposed to "private" action, civil liberty protections can often be invoked. Individuals, according to the Court, must be provided the opportunity to "make their case" to those who would terminate welfare benefits.

The Court ruled that procedural due process requires that a pretermination evidentiary hearing be held for welfare recipients before benefits are terminated. That is to say, people in danger of losing their benefits have a right to a hearing before the official who is making the termination decision. While the hearing does not have to resemble a trial, it should provide procedural safeguards, such as adequate notice, ability to make an oral presentation, right to confront witnesses, right to retain an attorney, and a decision based on rules and evidence.

The Court has refined and narrowed the scope of pretermination hearings since *Goldberg v. Kelly,* but the ruling was significant because it recognized that welfare payments were a right rather than a privilege.

For more information

Rosenbloom, David. *Public Administration: Understanding Management, Politics, and Law in the Public Sector,* 4th ed. New York: McGraw-Hill, 1998.

Richard P. Davis

Goldwater-Nichols Department of Defense Reorganization Act of 1986   The

Goldwater-Nichols Department of Defense Reorganization Act of 1986 was a major piece of legislation aimed at increasing the efficiency of the U.S. military by strengthening the chairman of the Joint Chiefs of Staff and weakening the power of the individual service branches (the army, navy, and air force). It is widely believed to be the most effective of a long series of military reforms dating back to World War II.

The NATIONAL SECURITY ACT OF 1947 created the modern U.S. military structure, with a secretary of defense as head of the National Military Establishment, a small agency that coordinated the cabinet-ranked Departments of the Army, the Navy, and the Air Force. A 1949 amendment abolished the service departments as separate entities and merged them into an enlarged DEPARTMENT OF DEFENSE. The secretary of defense was given full control over the whole department and the Office of the Secretary of Defense was enlarged to assist him. Further amendments were added in 1953 and 1958, removing the services from the chain of command and creating a chairman of the Joint Chiefs of Staff. All these moves were aimed at creating a single, harmonious military planning framework and ending a century of interservice rivalry and inefficient allocation of resources. By most accounts, these moves failed.

A series of military failures in the 1970s and early 1980s (most notably the Mayaguez incident, the botched rescue of the American hostages in Iran, the massacre of 241 marines in Beirut, and the hapless Grenada invasion) brought renewed pressure from Congress for reform. Barry Goldwater and Bill Nichols, the chairmen of the Senate and House Armed Services Committees, respectively, were the chief architects of the reform effort, along with Senator Sam Nunn, who succeeded Goldwater as chairman when the Democrats took control of the Senate.

After two years of hearings and blue-ribbon-panel studies, these leaders concluded that better coordination among the military services was essential. For example, in Grenada, the army and air force were literally unable to communicate with each other because of incompatible radios. In one famous incident, a soldier had to call in an air strike by use of his personal long-distance calling card.

Goldwater-Nichols gave more power to the JOINT CHIEFS OF STAFF, especially its chairman; created a vice chairman to ensure that the chairman's preferences would be carried out when he had to leave Washington; created a "procurement czar" to oversee all equipment purchases; created an assistant secretary of defense for special operations and low-intensity conflict to give more emphasis to those missions; and required a quadrennial report to Congress on roles and missions. Additionally, it created career incentives for offi-

cers to serve in so-called joint or purple-suit assignments where, for example, an army officer would serve a tour in an air force headquarters.

The legislation has been successful in many ways. In the 1991 Gulf War, General H. Norman Schwarzkopf was able to control all forces under his command, not just those in his own army, without going through the internecine bickering so often seen in past operations. In a break with tradition, the air war was conducted according to Schwarzkopf's judgment of what worked best operationally, rather than divided up equally between the air force, navy, and Marine Corps.

Despite the act's successes, however, serious problems remain. While the system is designed to operate in a top-down fashion, most decisions are made at much lower levels, without substantial guidance from above. This means that, in reality, the services are still largely left to their own devices with regard to formulating strategy and doctrine. In the absence of strong direction from above, the services remain the dominant forces in shaping annual force programs and defense budgets. Also, the mandated quadrennial defense reviews have met with nearly universal skepticism. Most analysts believe the reports merely serve to justify the budgeting and procurement desires of the military services rather than reflecting dispassionate analysis of the defense needs of the nation.

For more information

Caraley, Demetrious. *The Politics of Military Unification: A Study of Conflict and the Policy Process.* New York: Columbia University Press, 1966.

Goldwater-Nichols Department of Defense Reorganization Act of 1986. Public Law 99-433. 1 Oct. 1986. 100 Stat. 992.

Lederman, Gordon Nathaniel, and Sam Nunn. *Reorganizing the Joint Chiefs of Staff: The Goldwater-Nichols Act of 1986.* Westport, Conn.: Greenwood, 1999.

Sarkesian, Sam C. *U.S. National Security: Policymakers, Processes, and Politics,* 3d ed. Boulder, Colo.: Lynne Reiner, 2002.

Wolfe, Steven A. "Leaving Key West: The Struggle to Rationalize Roles and Missions." In *The American Military in the Twenty-First Century*, edited by Barry M. Blechman et al. New York: St. Martin's Press, 1993.

James H. Joyner, Jr.

Goodnow, Frank J. (1859–1939) *professor, writer* Frank J. Goodnow is often called "the father of American administration," and his thoughts and writings helped change the face of municipal government by stressing the hiring of experts for jobs previously held by elected officials or political appointees. He was born on 18 January 1859 in Brooklyn, New York. Goodnow received his A.B. degree from Amherst College in 1879. He then attended law school at Columbia University, where he also took classes from the School of Political Science. Graduating in 1882, he worked for a law firm in New York City for a short period. He then studied at the École Libre des Sciences Politiques in Paris and at the University of Berlin in 1883–84.

Returning to America, he took a previously offered position at the political science department at Columbia in October 1884, where he was eventually elevated to professor of administrative law in 1891 and Eaton professor of administrative law and municipal science in 1903. While at Columbia, he was commissioned to be part of the committee to draft a new charter for greater New York by Governor Theodore Roosevelt and sat on the federal Commission on Economy and Efficiency. In 1912, he became an adviser to the Chinese government on constitutional matters.

He was named president of Johns Hopkins University on 1 October 1914, a position that he maintained until 1929. During his years in office, the university moved to Homewood, Maryland, in 1916. In his most controversial move, he proposed discontinuing undergraduate work at the institution in 1925. Known as the Goodnow Plan, the proposal was supported by the board of trustees, but ultimately failed. The latter part of his tenure in office was marked by his efforts to establish the school's law department, which only lasted one year before the financial pressures of the Wall Street crash forced it to close in 1929. He died on 15 November 1939.

Goodnow wrote several books on public administration, including *Politics and Administration* (1900), *Principles of Constitutional Government* (1916), *The Principles of the Administrative Law of the United States* (1905), *Social Reform and the Constitution* (1911), *Politics and Administration: A Study in Government and Municipal Government* (1919). The subject he had the greatest influence on was city/municipal government. Goodnow believed that it was almost impossible to have a democratic government in a city and to have it run efficiently. The very conditions of city life and character made democracy difficult. In turn, the best way to improve efficiency was to introduce experts into certain positions. Goodnow frequently quoted F. C. Winkler, "where you want skill, you must appoint; where you want responsibility, elect." In his opinion, there was no reason to have elections beyond the council and mayoral positions. He wrote, "Many elective officers produce a boss ridden city and an inefficient administration." The problems of the modern city were beyond the capacity of legislators with limited experience and were best left to knowledgeable individuals.

Goodnow stressed that while there must be a general popular control over the execution of the law, there was a large part of administration that was unconnected with politics and should be left as such. This notion became the popular reform known as "the short ballot movement." Several municipal governments and commissions based the restructuring of their city's government on Goodnow's ideas.

For more information

Blassingame, Lurton W. "Frank J. Goodnow: Progressive Urban Reformer." *North Dakota Quarterly* 40 (summer 1972): 22–30.

Goodnow, Frank J. *Municipal Problems.* New York: Macmillan, 1897.

T. Jason Soderstrum

Government Performance and Results Act of 1993

The Government Performance and Results Act of 1993 is a law requiring federal government agencies to establish standards and report on achievement of results. The purpose of this act was to shift the federal government's focus from activities to results.

The act specified six main purposes. The first was to improve the confidence of the American people in the capability of the federal government by holding federal agencies accountable for achieving program results. The second purpose was to initiate program performance reform with a series of pilot projects in setting program goals, measuring program performance against those goals, and reporting publicly on their progress. The third and fourth purposes included promoting a new focus on results, service quality, and customer satisfaction; and helping federal managers improve service delivery by requiring that they plan for meeting program objectives and by providing them with information about program results and service quality. The fifth purpose of the act was to improve congressional decision making by providing more-objective information on achieving statutory objectives and on the relative effectiveness and efficiency of federal programs and spending. The final purpose was to improve internal management of the federal government.

The Government Performance and Results Act (GPRA) requires all federal agencies to submit multiyear strategic plans, annual performance plans, and annual performance reports. GPRA also contains provisions for PERFORMANCE BUDGETING, i.e., linking organizational activities to costs represented in the budget. Excluded from the act's requirements are the legislative and judicial branches of the government, the Central Intelligence Agency, and the Panama Canal Commission. The Postal Service has separate requirements.

The strategic plan provides the framework for the GPRA requirements. It should include a comprehensive mission statement and a description of general goals and objectives. Identification of key factors that could effect achievement of the general goals and objectives is required. A description of program evaluations used and a schedule of future evaluations should also be included. Program evaluations are defined as assessments, through objective measurement and systematic analysis, of the manner and extent to which programs achieve intended objectives.

Performance plans are submitted with an agency's budget request in September. A revised plan is then prepared to reflect the president's budget. These plans are to be linked with the strategic plan currently in effect, providing detailed and year-specific content based on the broader strategic plan. The performance plan should include the performance goals and indicators for the fiscal year and a description of the processes and skills, technology, human capital, and information or other resources that will be needed to meet the goals. Finally, a description of how the results will be verified and validated should be submitted with the performance plan.

The third requirement under GPRA, the performance report, should assess and review the results of the previous year's performance goals. An evaluation of the performance plan for the current year in comparison to last year's successes or failures is required, as well as an explanation for any failures. Summaries of program evaluations completed during the preceding year should also be included.

GPRA also sought to increase managerial accountability and flexibility by allowing agencies to include in performance plans proposals to waive certain administrative procedural requirements and controls. A portion of the act also specified the use of performance budgeting where levels of performance, including outcome-related performance, would result from different budgeted amounts.

Pilot programs were used to begin the process of implementing the Government Performance and Results Act. As specified in the act, at least five agencies were designated as pilot programs for submission of performance plans and reports, managerial accountability and flexibility, and performance budgeting. Beginning in September of 1999, GPRA specified that strategic plans were required for submission to Congress and the Office of Management and Budget. By October of 2000, all federal agencies were required to complete performance plans and reports.

Full implementation of this law and the successes of government agency strategic plans, performance plans, and performance reports are somewhat varied. For example, some would argue it is easier for the Department of Transportation to make a connection between highway safety programs and decreasing traffic deaths; in comparison, it would be harder to connect the Department of Health and Human Services funding of basic research to improvements in Americans' everyday health. Such examples illustrate the difficulties and complexities of judging the successes of this law.

Organizations interested in analyzing the success of performance plans and reports usually find mixed results across agencies. Most evaluations have focused on the clarity and availability of the plans and reports. From such evaluations, success is varied across agencies. For example, the 2000 performance report from the Department of Veterans Affairs is credited with having accomplishments clearly stated. However, the reports from the Department of Health and Human Services and the Nuclear Regulatory Commission were missing necessary data or were not easily found.

There has been little success related to GPRA's performance-budgeting provisions. Many believe performance budgeting is the most important part of GPRA and is where the incentive exists to truly perform because it is related to receiving money. Attempting to link budgets to performance and results is certainly not a new issue for government, but GPRA is the first time a law has required performance budgeting. Without true incentives to encourage increased performance, it is not surprising when government agencies do not achieve results. It is the hope of many that eventually achievement and reporting of results will one day be linked to the budget allocation process.

For more information
Government Performance and Results Act. http://www.ombwatch.org/gpra/gpratext.html.
Ingraham, Patricia W., et al. *Transforming Government Lessons from the Reinvention Laboratories*. San Francisco, Calif.: Jossey-Bass, 1998.

Jamie Green

Grace Commission   The Grace Commission was established in 1982 to examine the federal government's operations from a business perspective. The commission made a vast number of recommendations to enhance government efficiency and cost-effectiveness, but because most of these recommendations would have required congressional action and political change, they proved generally incapable of implementation.

Formally named the President's Private Sector Survey on Cost Control (PPSSCC), the Grace Commission was established by President RONALD REAGAN and chaired by J. Peter Grace, long-time chairman and chief executive officer of W. R. Grace & Co.. It is significant partly for its sheer and wholly unprecedented magnitude, compared with its numerous forerunners, from Taft's 1912 Commission on Economy and Efficiency and, since World War II, the two Hoover Commissions and the Ash Council. A 161-member executive committee guided the efforts of 2,000 volunteer executives from a wide array of industries. Its research yielded 47 volumes, summarized in a two-volume final report that contained 2,478 recommendations for cutting costs, enhancing revenues, and otherwise improving the efficiency of the federal government, with a promised savings of $424 billion in three years. Grace himself published a more popularly accessible 190-page version, *Burning Money*.

While there were some good recommendations, the fact that nearly three-quarters of them would require congressional action made their implementation unlikely. A government-sponsored charge card for travel was a useful idea, but then closing 7,000 small post offices and almost two-thirds of Social Security branch and district offices, which would indeed save money, would also make government ever more remote to its citizens. And it probably went too far in recommending the repeal of the Davis-Bacon Act and giving the president a line-item veto.

The savings promised by the commission were deemed gross exaggerations by GAO (GOVERNMENT ACCOUNTING OFFICE) and CBO (CONGRESSIONAL BUDGET OFFICE) studies, which came up with an outside maximum of $98 billion. On the other hand, many of the commission's recommendations—which might have resulted in cost savings 10 to 15 years later—would have cost huge sums up front, which naturally made their implementation politically all the more unlikely. A chief such recommendation was to update the federal government's computer systems, which were far behind those of the business world. Moreover, the system was to be centralized so that all the government's computers could "talk to one another" and share time. This was not only ironic in an era when the business mantra was decentralization and delegation, but also problematic in that it would undermine the security and confidentiality agencies like the Department of Defense, the FBI, and the IRS require.

The commission also did not bother to acquaint itself with the recommendations of its many predecessor commissions, thus repeating many of their findings without ever examining the real underlying problem. A further irony lies in the presumption that government is run less efficiently than business, despite the fact that countless government agencies have, historically, been managed by individuals who had distinguished themselves as outstanding managers in the business world (Robert McNamara, William Simon, Roy Ash, Michael Blumenthal, George Romney, George Shultz, Caspar Weinberger, et al.).

And while Grace described his commission members as the "best and brightest," "the top business and managerial talent in America," an analysis by George Downs and Patrick Larkey showed that 37 of the affiliated companies (whose executives served on the commission) "finished dead last in their respective industries in terms of five-year return on equity," and 65 of these firms were below median in performance and far below the best performers in their industry on the same criterion.

Grace was also at great pains to claim that all this cost the government absolutely nothing. (A private nonprofit foundation provided approximately $3.5 million in cash and in-kind contributions.) However, one should consider (1) the millions foregone in revenue when task force members deducted their work as charity or business expense and (2) the amount of government work not done because government employees were working with commission staffers.

For more information

Downs, George W., and Patrick D. Larkey. *The Search for Government Efficiency: From Hubris to Helplessness.* New York: Random House, 1986.

Goodsell, Charles T. "The Grace Commission: Seeking Efficiency for the Whole People?" *Public Administration Review* 44, no. 3 (1984).

Grace, J. Peter. *Burning Money: The Waste of Your Tax Dollars.* New York: Macmillan, 1984.

Kelman, Steven. "The Grace Commission: How Much Waste in Government?" *The Public Interest* 78 (winter 1985).

Levine, Charles H., ed. *The Unfinished Agenda for Civil Service Reform: Implications of the Grace Commission Report.* Washington, D.C.: Brookings, 1985.

Ulf Zimmermann

Gramm-Rudman Act   The Gramm-Rudman Act is the shorthand name for the Gramm-Rudman-Hollings Act, also known as the Balanced Budget and Emergency Deficit Control Act of 1985.

In 1985, in an attempt to combat the growing federal budget deficit, Congress passed and President Reagan signed this bill. To get government spending in line with government revenues, Gramm-Rudman established "maximum deficit amounts" for the years 1986 to 1991. If, during any of those years, the federal deficit exceeded the maximum deficit amount, the act required across-the-board federal spending cuts. By specifying deficit targets in the legislation, the bill's sponsors—Republican senators Phil Gramm of Texas and Warren Rudman of New Hampshire and Democratic senator Ernest F. Hollings of South Carolina—designed the act to balance the federal budget by 1991.

In addition to setting maximum deficit amounts, Gramm-Rudman made quite a few changes to the congressional budget process. These changes all aimed to provide enforcement of the maximum deficit amounts and to strengthen congressional budget enforcement generally.

When it was passed, Gramm-Rudman represented a significant departure from previous budget reforms. That is because the act was the first binding constraint on federal spending. It concentrated on creating a specific budget outcome, while previous reforms had attempted to solve budget problems by manipulating institutional relationships in government and the information-providing component of the budget process.

Critics of Gramm-Rudman accused the legislation of having two major problems. First, they charged that the act had too much of a short-term view. Since, under Gramm-Rudman, all that mattered was the single year for which the budget was being made, Congressmen were likely to ignore a long-term picture. That encouraged Congressmen to try to comply with the annual budget targets through short-term fixes and gimmickry, which might only make budget problems worse in the long run.

Second, critics argued that a major provision of Gramm-Rudman was unconstitutional, and in 1986 the Supreme Court agreed. In a 7-2 decision in *Bowsher v. Synar,* the Supreme Court ruled that Gramm-Rudman's delegation of budget-cutting authority to the comptroller general violated the principle of separation of powers by vesting executive branch authority in a legislative branch official. Because the comptroller general, the director of the General Accounting Office, can by law be removed only by Congress, the Court ruled that the comptroller general is "subservient" to Congress and cannot be entrusted with executive powers.

The Court let the rest of Gramm-Rudman stand, asking Congress only to correct its one constitutional flaw. In 1987, Congress did so by passing the Balanced Budget and Emergency Deficit Control Reaffirmation Act. That act assigned budget-cutting responsibilities to the Office of Management and Budget, which is part of the executive branch, and extended the system of maximum deficits amounts until 1992.

Though the act did curtail the growth rate of federal spending, the federal deficit did not disappear as Gramm-Rudman's proponents had envisioned. By 1993, the deficit was over $200 billion, larger than it had been in 1985.

For more information

Gilmour, John B. *Reconcilable Differences? Congress, the Budget Process, and the Deficit.* Berkeley: University of California Press, 1990.

White, Joseph, and Aron Wildavsky. *The Deficit and the Public Interest: The Search for Responsible Budgeting in the 1980s.* Berkeley: University of California Press, 1989.

Susan McWilliams

grants-in-aid   Grants-in-aid are allocations of money from the federal government to states or localities for different purposes.

Federal grants are of two types: categorical and block. CATEGORICAL GRANTS can only be spent by state and local governments for very special purposes, spelled out by the law and by the granting agency. There are many categories of projects supported by this type of grant. They are issued by different federal agencies, which have considerable discretion to decide who will receive the aid and how it will be spent.

There are two types of categorical grants: project and formula. Project grants can be for physical projects such as dams. Project grants can also be for programs such as a grant to a college or university for faculty development. The projects supported by project grants are very well-defined and managed with detailed supervision by the federal agency issuing the grant.

The second type of categorical grant is the formula grant. In this type of grant, federal funds are automatically awarded to state and local governments on the basis of criteria spelled out in a formula drafted by Congress. They are different from project grants because a formula gives federal agencies no discretion in determining how the grant-in-aid funds are to be awarded. Interstate highway funds from the Highway Trust Fund are issued on a formula basis. Usually the formula is 75 percent federal funding and 25 percent state funding.

Many other projects and programs are funded as formula grants. Programs to support Head Start programs or local centers are often of this type. This type of program requires the commitment of state or local matching monies in order to get the grant. To get the project money, communities must raise matching funds, sometimes from private or religious donors. One reason for this type of grant is the belief that if the local government or citizenry is not willing to commit their own money to the project, then this is a sign that they do not believe in it and, therefore, the prudent course is to abandon the proposed project.

The other type of federal grant is the BLOCK GRANT. This type of grant allocates federal aid in huge blocks for broad purposes and gives state governments considerable discretion to decide how those funds will be spent. They are the opposite of categorical grants.

Federal grants have been issued from the beginning of the republic. However, with the Franklin Roosevelt administration, grants-in-aid multiplied enormously. Block grants developed from opposition to the enormous growth of the federal government. The intention was to devolve some power to the states.

REVENUE SHARING was like block grants, only broader. A fixed sum of money was turned over automatically to the states and local governments (local governments only after 1980) to be spent as they saw fit. It was a program that originated under President Nixon in 1972 and lasted until abolished by President Reagan in 1986.

For more information
Reagan, Michael, and John Sanzone. *The New Federalism*. New York: Oxford University Press, 1981.

A. J. L. Waskey

Gulick, Luther (1892–1993) *scholar* Luther Gulick was one of the foremost scholars of public administration. So important was his influence on the development of public administration that Lyle Fitch, a biographer of Gulick, asserts that most of the important works published in public administration during the latter half of the 20th century bear Gulick's imprint.

Gulick graduated with a Ph.D. from Columbia University in 1920. He served for several years with the New York Bureau of Municipal Research (later renamed the Institute of Public Administration). From 1931 to 1942, Gulick was professor of municipal science and administration at Columbia. Gulick also served as city administrator of New York City and was instrumental in the founding or development of several major professional associations, including the International Management Association, the Public Administration Clearing House, the

Brookings Institution, the American Society for Public Administration, the National Academy of Public Administration, and the National Planning Association.

Over his lifetime Gulick authored several works, including *Evolution of the Budget in Massachusetts* (1920), *Administrative Reflections from World War II* (1948), *American Forest Policy* (1951), and *The Metropolitan Problem and American Ideas* (1962). He is best known, however, for his *Papers on the Science of Administration* (1937), a volume of papers coedited with Lyndall Urwick. This edited collection was an attempt by leading scholars to summarize the state of knowledge of administration and management at the time. Gulick's chapter, "Notes on the Theory of Organization," provides what was then considered to be some of the most innovative insights into managerial principles and techniques. For example, in terms of the work relationship between managers and subordinates, Gulick urged managers to employ optimal spans of control while cautioning managers against employing too wide a span of control, that is, having too many subordinates under one superior.

Gulick also noted the need for organizations to adhere to the principle of unity of command, meaning that subordinates should not receive orders from more than one manager within a given position in an organization's hierarchy. To do otherwise would only invite confusion among subordinates regarding which directive to follow; this would be particularly troublesome if the orders were contradictory in nature. Gulick emphasized that it was important for managers to adhere to these principles if they wanted to achieve optimum performance. Gulick is also known for coining the acronym, POSDCORB, which stands for the seven major functions of management: planning, organizing, staffing, directing, coordinating, reporting, and budgeting.

Besides these accomplishments, Gulick served as a key member of President Franklin D. Roosevelt's Committee on Administrative Management from 1936 to 1937. The report that resulted from this effort called for a fundamental strengthening of the president's hand over managing the executive branch. The report recommended a major reorganization of the executive branch and ultimately led to congressional passage of the Reorganization Act of 1939. Two of the more salient recommendations were the creation of an EXECUTIVE OFFICE OF THE PRESIDENT and the transference of the Bureau of the Budget (the precursor to the present-day OFFICE OF MANAGEMENT AND BUDGET) into the Executive Office of the President.

For more information

Fitch, Lyle C. *Making Democracy Work: The Life and Letters of Luther Gulick, 1892–1993.* Berkeley, Calif.: University of California, Institute of Governmental Studies, 1996.

Gulick, Luther, and Lyndall Urwick, eds. *Papers on the Science of Administration.* New York: A. M. Kelley, 1937.

Patrick G. Scott

H

hard look "Hard look" is a policy of strict review adopted by judicial courts when examining administrative agency actions or decisions.

As adopted by the U.S. Supreme Court in a 1971 case, *Citizens to Preserve Overton Park v. Volpe* (410 U.S. 402), and a 1983 case, *Motor Vehicle Manufacturers Association v. State Farm Mutual Automobile Insurance Co.* (463 U.S. 29), the concept of a "hard look" review addresses how deferential a court should be toward an agency decision. When a court seeks to review an agency decision or the process by which it made the decision, the court will scrutinize the records and evidence that the agency used to make its decision. When judges invoke the "hard look" review of an agency decision, the courts are looking for detailed explanations by the agency as to why it made the decision.

In the *State Farm* case noted above, the National Highway Traffic Safety Administration (NHTSA), in a 1972 ruling, required that cars produced after 1982 be equipped with passive restraints, either airbags or automatic seatbelts. In 1981, the NHTSA, citing the lack of evidence that passive restraints would produce significant safety benefits, rescinded its 1972 rule.

Insurance companies challenged the NHTSA's reversal, and the U.S. Supreme Court found that the NHTSA's actions had been "arbitrary and capricious" when it rescinded its 1972 ruling. The Court held that in changing its mind, the agency needed to give "a reasoned analysis for the change" by showing "the evidence which is available, and must offer a 'rational connection between the facts found and the choice made.'" The NHTSA had not considered that while drivers could disengage the automatic seatbelts, making them useless, the airbags could not be disengaged, and the agency had failed to take that evidence into account.

By invoking a "hard look" into an agency's explanation and the evidence that supported the decision, the courts have required that agencies address all of the factors and present all of the evidence. However, some scholars believe that the courts are seeking to substitute their judgments for those of the agencies. Judges are not often experts in technical and detailed matters, unlike administrators. When a judge second-guesses the actions of an administrator, the court is substituting its own judgments and values for that of an administrative official. On the other hand, some scholars argue that judges must "check" administrative officials and their decisions; otherwise, administrators may act unreasonably, carelessly, or inconsistently.

For more information

Breyer, Stephen. "Judicial Review of Questions of Law and Policy." *Administrative Law Review* 38 (1986): 363–398.

Cooper, Phillip J. *Public Law and Public Administration.* Itasca, Ill.: F. E. Peacock Publishers, 2000.

Melnick, A. Shep. "Administrative Law and Bureaucratic Reality." *Administrative Law Review* 44 (1992): 245–259.

J. Michael Bitzer

Hatch Acts   The Hatch Acts are a series of federal laws passed in 1939 and 1940 that placed restrictions on the political activity of federal employees. The purpose of these restrictions is (1) to ensure that public employees are not using public resources for partisan purposes and (2) to help maintain the political neutrality of the government. Both principles are deemed critical to maintaining citizen confidence in the administration of government programs.

In 1939 there were fears in Congress and among the general public that President Franklin Roosevelt would use the expansion of the size of the federal government under the New Deal for personal and political purposes. With over 40 percent of the federal workers not covered or protected by civil service laws, the president had significant authority to use the staffing of the government for patronage purposes. These fears were heightened by Roosevelt's efforts in 1939 to purge opponents of the New Deal from the Democratic Party.

The Hatch Acts, found in 5 United States Code, section 7324, make it illegal for federal employees to engage in certain political activities, such as running for office, campaigning, fund-raising, or soliciting funds for other candidates. Violation of the Hatch Acts can result in dismissal or other sanctions.

The Hatch Acts apply not only to federal employees, they also extend to individuals who receive a portion of their compensation from federal funds. This means that state and local employees may also be "hatched," or covered by the Hatch Acts. Many state and local governments also have their own version of the Hatch Acts (known as "little Hatch Acts") that apply to their employees, even if they are not receiving federal funds.

Several arguments have been given in defense of the Hatch Acts. First, the acts are described as a perfect example of a Progressive Era reform. One goal of Progressives was to separate politics from the administration of the government to ensure that administrators were making decisions based upon their best technical expertise and not upon political factors. These twin goals are referred to as the political/administration dichotomy and neutral competence. The belief was that promoting the political neutrality of the federal bureaucracy would improve its efficiency and eliminate corruption.

A second defense of the Hatch Acts is that allowing public employees to engage in certain types of political activities could undermine public confidence in the government. If citizens saw workers campaigning, running for office, or otherwise involved in partisan activity, it could lead the public to question whether the workers were acting in the best interests of the people or simply serving their own interests. Finally, the acts have been defended as a way of preventing elected officials and federal workers from pressuring other public employees to get involved in politics.

The Hatch Acts make it harder for public employees to use government resources to further their political advantages. Thus, these laws can be seen as a way to limit the use of government as a source of spoils or patronage. These laws also help to level the political playing field between those who work in government and those who do not.

Many have argued that the Hatch Acts violate the First Amendment rights of public employees. However in both *United Public Workers v. Mitchell*, 330 U.S. 75 (1947), and *United States Civil Service Commission v. Letter Carriers*, 413 U.S. 548 (1973), the U.S. Supreme Court upheld the laws, stating that the restrictions were necessary to promote efficiency, public confidence, and eliminate corruption.

Since their passage, public labor unions have pressed for repeal of the Hatch Acts. In 1993 President Clinton signed a bill modifying several provisions of the Hatch Acts, yet leaving in place the basic bans on political campaigning.

For more information

Schultz, David A., and Robert Maranto. *The Politics of Civil Service Reform.* New York: Peter Lang Publishing, 1998.

David Schultz

health maintenance organization A health maintenance organization is an arrangement for the delivery of managed health care to specific groups of people. These organizations are popularly known as HMOs.

The idea of the HMO emerged in the United States in the late 1920s and 1930s as an experiment for providing low-cost health care to the poor. It was not until the 1970s, in the face of consumer concern over the rising cost of health care, that the Congress enacted legislation to stimulate the growth of managed care. By the late 1990s, the managed-care model had become the device of choice for using the marketplace and the profit motive to control medical costs in the United States.

Health maintenance organizations generally restrict medical coverage to care from medical providers who cooperate within the plan's network of providers. HMOs further require that specialty care be recommended by the individual member's primary-care physician. This primary-care physician acts as a gatekeeper, regulating the delivery of other and more-specialized medical care. In addition, as part of controlling the costs of patient care, most managed-care plans have adopted utilization review procedures that determine whether the primary-care physician's proposed course of medical treatment and proposed location of medical service are necessary, based on established clinical criteria.

Health maintenance organizations have been widely criticized. In part, this criticism reflects a general public perception that managed health-care providers offer too little care for their customers. This may be due to restrictions set by the various health plans on the delivery of certain types of medical care. In addition, many believe that adequate methods of appeal and review are lacking. Such appeal and review procedures would be helpful in determining the propriety of the HMO's medical-care decisions.

The perception that managed health care has failed to provide appropriate service for its customers has energized a movement for protective legislation. Proposals for consumer-protection legislation include a statement for a "Patient's Bill of Rights." These issues—as well as the momentum toward managed care as the employer's preferred method of paying for health care—have focused attention on the adequacy of mechanisms whereby HMO enrollees can raise and resolve disputes.

For more information

Hughes, Alana. "The Road Once Taken: Socialist Medicine in Southwestern Oklahoma." In *"An Oklahoma I Had Never Seen Before": Alternative Views of Oklahoma History*, edited by Davis D. Joyce. Norman: University of Oklahoma Press, 1994.

Rees, Alan M. *Consumer Health Information Source Book*, 6th ed. Westport, Conn.: Oryx Press, 2000.

Regan, Alycia C. "Regulating the Business of Medicine: Models for Integrating Ethics and Managed Care." *Columbia Journal of Law and Social Problems* 30 (1997): 635.

Rosenfeld, Isadore. *Power to the Patient: The Treatments to Insist on When You're Sick.* New York: Warner Books, 2001.

Jerry E. Stephens

Heckler v. Chaney 470 U.S. 821 (1985)

Heckler v. Chaney is a significant development in administrative law. The Supreme Court interpreted §701 of the federal ADMINISTRATIVE PROCEDURE ACT (APA) (5 U.S.C. 501 et seq.), which pertains to the scope of judicial review. The legal question in *Heckler v. Chaney* is: When is administrative inaction subject to review by courts?

Chaney and other respondents in this case had been convicted of capital offenses in Oklahoma and Texas and sentenced to death by lethal injection of drugs. They had petitioned a federal government agency, the FOOD AND DRUG ADMINISTRATION (FDA). First, they maintained that using these drugs for capital punishment violated the federal Food, Drug, and Cosmetic Act (FDCA). Second, they asked the FDA to attach warning labels to all the drugs stating that they were unapproved and unsafe for human execution. Third, they asked the FDA to: inform the drug manufacturers and prison administrators that the drugs should not be used in executions, adopt procedures for seizing the drugs from state prisons, and recommend the prosecution of all those in the chain of distribution who knowingly distribute or purchase the drugs with intent to use them for human execution. The FDA refused their requests.

Justice Rehnquist, writing for a unanimous Court, upheld the FDA's refusal to act. His point of departure was APA §701(a)(2). That section specifies an exception to the susceptibility of agencies to judicial review "[when] agency action is committed to agency discretion by law." Citing cases dating back to 1869, Justice Rehnquist observed that "[t]his Court has recognized on several occasions over many years that an agency's decision not to prosecute or enforce . . . is a decision generally committed to an agency's absolute discretion." *Heckler v. Chaney* adheres to this line of decisions. The Court concluded "that an agency's decision not to take enforcement action should be presumed immune from judicial review under 701(a)(2)." Thus, the *Heckler* court read §701(a)(2) as creating a rebuttable presumption, i.e., an assumption capable of being refuted by offering opposing evidence and arguments of unreviewability.

Commentaries on *Heckler v. Chaney* have raised several concerns. First, the decision disregarded APA §706(1), which specifies that courts shall "compel agency action unlawfully withheld or unreasonably delayed," and the §551(13) definition of agency "action" to include "failure to act." Second, the *Heckler* Court's sharp distinction between "action" and "inaction" has been called into doubt by the practical realities of the regulatory state. Third, while maintaining that administrative agencies have scarce resources and are not able to act in all situations, *Heckler* is silent about circumstances under which courts may oblige an agency to act. Finally, *Heckler* immunized administrative agencies, enabling them to shield significant legislative and judicial judgments from scrutiny under the screen of executive discretion, or, as Bhagwat put it, "playing, as it were, a game of three-branch monte."

For more information

Bhagwat, Ashutosh. "Three-Branch Monte." *Notre Dame Law Review* 72 (1996): 157.

Levy, Donald M., and Delora Jean Duncan. "Note, Judicial Review of Administrative Rulemaking and Enforcement Discretion: The Effect of a Presumption of Unreviewability." *George Washington Law Review* 55 (1987): 596.

Sunstein, Cass R. "Reviewing Agency Inaction after *Heckler v. Chaney.*" *University of Chicago Law Review* 52 (1985): 653.

James C. Foster

home rule   Home rule refers to the power of local governments to adopt ordinances and conduct activities without statutory enabling acts. It is an exception to the more common rule that local governments may not take any action or adopt any ordinances that are not authorized by the state legislature. In many states, the home rule provision is part of the state's constitution, in others, the basis for home rule is statutory. Usually, home rule is limited to municipalities. A few states also provide home rule authority for counties. Home rule is generally not provided for special districts or townships.

Home rule is based on a theory of local self-government that local people are best suited to administer their own local affairs. In the broadest sense, home rule may not only allow local governments to exercise authority, but also allow local voters to choose the character of municipal organization, the nature and scope of municipal services, and all local activity.

Traditionally, authority of local government is subject to DILLON'S RULE, which provides that—absent explicit authority—units of local government cannot act. Dillon's Rule further provides that a state's enabling acts must be construed narrowly. Absent an explicit home rule provision in a state's constitution, local governments are political subdivisions of the state, and the state legislature has absolute control over the number, nature, and duration of the powers and the extent of the territory over which they may exercise authority. The great weight of authority denies the existence of any inherent right of local self-government that is beyond the control of the legislature.

Usually, home rule is limited to the local government's own affairs and does not extend to matters that may impact beyond its borders. For example, courts have invalidated home rule ordinances that limited the noise made by intrastate and interstate railroads. Similarly, attempts by local units of government to change the state's property laws are often invalidated.

The principle of home rule, or the right of local self-government with respect to local affairs, was first implemented in the United States in 1875 when Missouri adopted a constitutional amendment providing home rule for municipalities. Since then, some type of home rule authority has been adopted by a majority of the states.

For more information
McQuillin, Eugene. *Municipal Corporations Section 1. 40–1.43.* St. Paul, Minn.: West Publishing Co., 1999.

Scott Peters

Hoover, J. Edgar (1895–1972) *FBI director*
J. Edgar Hoover served as the director of the FEDERAL BUREAU OF INVESTIGATION (FBI) for 48 years, from 1924 to 1972.

Hoover was born in Washington, D.C., in 1895. He earned two law degrees through evening courses at George Washington University while working during the day at the Library of Congress. After finishing his advanced law degree in 1918, he went to work for the U.S. DEPARTMENT OF JUSTICE and quickly became the assistant to the attorney general. In 1924, Attorney General Harlan Fiske Stone appointed Hoover as the director of the Justice Department's Bureau of Investigation, the agency that later came to be known as the Federal Bureau of Investigation or FBI. Hoover served as the director of the FBI until his death in 1972.

The FBI is the agency responsible for investigating and apprehending violators of federal crimes such as bank robbery, kidnapping, and other offenses that violate criminal laws enacted by Congress. Most crimes, such as burglary and murder, are violations of state criminal laws, so the FBI focuses its attention on a limited list of offenses. Under Hoover's supervision, the focus of the FBI's investigations expanded to include counterintelligence and counterespionage. Thus the FBI took the lead in hunting for German and Japanese spies during World War II and spies from communist countries during the cold war from the 1940s to the 1980s.

Hoover is credited with introducing training and procedures that applied scientific methods to the investigation of crimes. Under Hoover, the FBI created and maintained a centralized file of fingerprints that law enforcement agencies throughout the country relied upon in seeking to identify lawbreakers. The FBI also opened a crime laboratory that used scientific techniques to analyze evidence. He ended previous hiring practices that had enabled unqualified political appointees to become federal agents. Instead, he required FBI agents to have educational backgrounds in law or accounting. In addition, agents had to undergo background checks, interviews, and physical fitness tests. Hoover opened the National Police Academy in 1935, which later became known as the FBI Academy, to provide training programs for FBI agents as well as law enforcement officers from state and local agencies around the nation. Hoover's emphasis on training, qualifications, and scientific methods professionalized the FBI. The FBI became a role model for other law enforcement agencies that had traditionally been guided by political appointees and partisan politics.

Although Hoover made significant contributions to the professionalization of law enforcement and justice administration, he also misused his position and power during his long tenure in office. He ruled the agency with absolute power. Personnel within the FBI knew that they could not question his policies or actions without losing their jobs. Hoover's long tenure in office and powerful position in Washington stemmed, in part, from his use of FBI agents to gather information about the private lives of politicians and public figures. Government officials hesitated to question Hoover's use of power because of the possibility that he would reveal embarrassing information about them or their families and associates. Hoover also used FBI resources to investigate and harass political dissenters within the United States, such as African-American civil rights activists and opponents of the Vietnam War. For example, Hoover's agents secretly followed and tape-recorded private conversations of Martin Luther King, Jr., because Hoover wanted to convince government officials that King's tireless work for racial equality should be dismissed as the work of a "communist." Many people who worked on behalf of civil rights for African Americans during the 1960s came to believe that they could not rely on the FBI to protect them, even when they were subjected to violent attacks by the Ku Klux Klan and local law enforcement officials.

J. Edgar Hoover is regarded as an innovative public administrator whose professionalization of the FBI set a standard that influenced the improvement of law enforcement agencies throughout the country. However, Hoover's 48-year tenure as director of the FBI is also regarded as illustrating the risks of abuse that may follow from giving a single individual too much unchecked authority within a powerful government agency.

For more information

Garrow, David J. *The FBI and Dr. Martin Luther King, Jr.* New York: Viking Press, 1983.

Powers, Richard Gid. *Secrecy and Power: The Life of J. Edgar Hoover.* New York: Free Press, 1988.

Christopher E. Smith

Hoover Commission   The dramatic increase in the size of the federal government bureaucracy during the New Deal raised concerns about whether the president could properly control the many new agencies and employees. The 80th Congress in 1947 formed the Hoover Commission to study the executive branch and to present recommendations for reorganizing the bureaucracy.

The commission was named after Herbert Hoover, the 31st president of the United States, who served in that office from 1929 to 1933. Hoover, the last Republican president, was seen by the Republican-controlled Congress as the most qualified to lead such an important commission. Hoover and the members of the commission took more than two years to examine the many agencies in the executive branch, their organization, their budgeting, and how they performed their jobs. The commission's report was presented in 1949 and included scores of suggestions about how the executive branch could be better run.

The Hoover Commission noted that during the 1930s and 1940s, the president had been overwhelmed by the number of agencies reporting directly to him. To combat that problem, the commission suggested that the various agencies be placed under the control of departments. This would allow the agency to report to the secretary of a particular department, who would then report directly to the president. Many decisions would be made by the cabinet secretary without the involvement of the president, which would prevent him from being overwhelmed by requests.

Hoover and his commission also wanted to give agency officials greater power to make decisions on their own. The many rules and regulations created by Congress prevented many agencies from deciding on how to spend their money and carry out the tasks assigned to them. By giving discretion to agencies, Hoover hoped that better and faster decisions would be made.

Hoover proposed that agencies be given larger staffs to implement policy and argued for the creation of a central office for the storage of paperwork rather than having each agency keep its own files. The commission suggested different ways of budgeting so that agencies could keep track of what money they spent and where. The commission also made suggestions on how different departments could be reorganized to make them more efficient.

Overall, the Hoover Commission estimated that their suggestions, if used by the federal government, would save several billion dollars a year, or about 5 percent of the budget. Both Congress and President Harry Truman used the Hoover Commission's report to improve how the federal government functioned.

The success of the first Hoover Commission prompted President Dwight Eisenhower, a Republican, to form another after his election in 1953. Unlike the first commission, though, the Second Hoover Commission was more involved in the political controversies of the time. Hoover and his supporters on the commission criticized many of the spending programs backed by members of Congress and called for their elimination. Splits occurred within the second commission, and its suggestions were mostly ignored by Congress and the president.

For more information

Nash, Bradley, and Cornelius Lynde. *A Hook in Leviathan.* New York: Macmillan, 1950.

Smith, Richard Norton. *An Uncommon Man: The Triumph of Herbert Hoover.* New York: Simon and Schuster, 1984.

Doug Clouatre

House Ways and Means Committee   The Ways and Means Committee was first established in 1789 to determine how much revenue the federal government needed to raise to cover the expenses it expected to incur. After shouldering this responsibility for eight weeks, the House of Representatives dissolved the Ways and Means Committee, and ordered that matters concerning federal expenditures be referred to the secretary of the treasury.

In January 1802, realizing that the secretary of the treasury had progressively increased his power by making decisions about monetary matters that should have been debated in Congress, the House reclaimed its authority by appointing a permanent, standing House Ways and Means Committee. This committee was responsible for decisions concerning the judicial, executive, and legislative branches' revenues, expenditures, and public debt matters, as well as the federal agencies' revenues and expenditures. Additionally, the committee was authorized to audit congressional and federal agency budgets. Hence, overnight, the committee was re-created and assigned an utterly overwhelming amount of work.

In 1865, the creation of the standing Committees on Appropriations and on Banking and Currency allowed the Ways and Means Committee to relinquish some its excessive burden. Concurrently with the creation of new committees and the reassignment of some of the committee's previous work, Congress reaffirmed the committee's importance by authorizing that it fulfill the Constitution's mandate that the House originate all legislation intended to raise revenues. The Committee retained a major responsibility. Today, 135 years later, the basic subject matter of its jurisdiction remains unchanged. However, the current complexity of the federal government means that a much greater volume of far more complicated legislation falls under the committee's purview.

Currently, 40 members of Congress serve on the committee. Because the committee has broad responsibilities, the full committee meets only to deal with tax issues. For other topics, the 40 members split into six subcommittees: Social Security, Trade, Oversight, Health, Human Resources, and Select Revenue Measures.

The jurisdiction of the Ways and Means Committee in the 21st century includes the revenue-raising and government-borrowing legislation mentioned specifically in the Constitution, and which will continue to be essential for proper functioning of the federal government. Revenue-raising legislation is that which requires payment of funds to the federal government. The major revenue-raising categories are individual and corporate income taxes, excise taxes (special taxes on nonnecessities such as cigarettes and liquor), and estate and gift taxes.

The Ways and Means Committee is responsible for legislation relating to tariffs, import trade, and trade negotiations. While tariffs and duty payments collected by U.S. Customs agents were a major source of revenue when the committee was first created, their importance has decreased in the last century. However, during the same time period, trade legislation has become far more complex. The committee is the origination point for legislation on unfair trade practices, agricultural restrictions, international commodity agreements, textile restrictions, and finally— an area of enormous importance since the terrorist attacks of 11 September 2001—national security.

Another type of legislation that must originate in the committee authorizes the secretary of the treasury to manage the government's borrowing of money. The secretary is currently authorized to issue bonds and sell Treasury notes, up to a statutory limit of approximately $6 trillion.

One major category of legislation that was not anticipated in the Constitution, and which must be introduced through the committee, finances several programs established by the Social Security Act. The most expensive of these programs provides income for elderly and disabled individuals. This program sends the monthly Social Security checks and costs nearly $400 billion annually. Also originating in the committee is the legislation that funds Medicare, the second-most-expensive Social Security program. This program provides hospital insurance for elderly and disabled persons at an annual cost of more than $200 billion per year.

Additional programs created by the Social Security Act are: Supplemental Security Income, which provides income for certain elderly or very young individuals and for many disabled individuals, costs more than $30 billion per year; aid to low-income families, formerly known as welfare benefits, requires an annual expenditure of more than $17 billion; and unemployment compensation, home services for disabled individuals, and foster-care programs that cost about $30 billion annually.

To become a law, legislation of the varieties noted above must first be introduced, and then passed, by the Ways and Means Committee. The next step in the sequence is passing the House of Representatives by winning a majority vote. Continuing through the sequence, the legislation is sent to the Senate, which must also vote affirmatively. Thereafter, the legislation becomes a law if approved and signed by the president.

The House Ways and Means Committee's responsibilities are vast. Despite the staggering number of pieces of legislation that pass through the committee each year, none of them can be ignored or even treated lightly, because of both the enormous sums of money involved and the importance of the subject matter to the nation's economy and national security. Because of the weight of the duties incumbent upon the members of this committee, they are well trained to assume the duties of higher offices, as evidenced by the eight presidents and eight vice presidents who have been members or chairmen of the House Ways and Means Committee.

For more information

National Archives and Records Administration, Center for Legislative Archives. http://www.nara.gov/nara/legislative/house_guide/hgch21.html.

U.S. House of Representatives, Ways and Means Committee. http://waysandmeans.house.gov/history.htm.

Beth Simon Swartz

housing policy Housing policy refers to programs developed by the U.S. government that help provide shelter to poor individuals and families, promote private home ownership, redevelop communities, and stimulate the economy through housing construction. Federal intervention in housing issues has been historically driven by these four broad goals.

The first federal foray into housing came in 1892 when Congress provided $20,000 to investigate slum conditions in large cities. The resulting report described poor housing conditions in four cities, but no further action was taken. In 1913, when Congress implemented the first federal income tax, it provided a tax credit for home mortgage interest payments. This policy had the dual purposes of reducing the burden of the new income tax and promoting home ownership with a federal subsidy.

When the United States entered World War I, war workers faced housing shortages as they moved closer to industry and wartime jobs. The federal government authorized loans to real estate companies willing to build rental homes for these workers. World War I would be the first of three national emergencies precipitating federal housing policy, followed by the Great Depression and World War II.

As part of the National Industrial Recovery Act of 1933, designed to lift the country out of depression, Franklin Roosevelt authorized slum clearance and the construction or repair of low-income housing. The physical condition of inner-city business districts and residential neighborhoods had deteriorated, and the depression left many people without the means to pay rent. The program offered developers loans to build low-income housing. The program faltered because few developers found such projects a profitable or attractive enterprise without raising rents higher than what low-income residents could pay. The government then turned to grants to local governments as a means to build federally owned public housing for the needy. While this program constructed 22,000 low-income housing units, even more units were destroyed in slum clearance. In many cities the public housing authority had close ties to the construction and real estate industries. Federal funds were often used by local governments to buy slum lands from private owners at inflated prices, while no new housing was planned.

The Public Housing Act of 1937 used the administrative blueprint of the 1933 program to provide shelter for low-income people. The federal government provided loans and grants-in-aid to local housing authorities to clear slums and build housing for people unable to afford safe and sanitary dwellings. Because residents still paid rent for public housing, the very poorest people were not aided by these projects.

A second prong of Roosevelt's housing policy was aimed at invigorating the housing construction industry by creating opportunities for home ownership. The National Housing Act of 1934 enabled savings-and-loan institutions to invest in the housing market by securing individual bank accounts. Additionally, the act created a basic home mortgage program through the Federal Housing Administration (FHA). By federally backing mortgages, this act enabled lending institutions to provide loans with small down payments and 25–35-year payoff plans with relatively little risk. Later, in 1938, the Federal National Mortgage Association (FNMA or Fannie Mae) was created to lend money to private institutions for building moderate-income housing. Both programs have been incredibly successful at promoting home ownership.

When workers streamed into cities for jobs created by World War II, federal and local governments rapidly built more than 2 million rental units to house wartime laborers, which were later sold on the private market. At the end of the war, home-buying opportunities were provided to thousands of returning veterans though low-priced, long-term, federally backed loans similar in nature to those authorized in 1934. The 1944 Veterans Administration (VA) Servicemen's Readjustment Act, with no-down-payment requirements, helped thousands of low- and moderate-income families to purchase homes.

After World War II, public attention was again turned to inner-city slums. A diverse coalition of interests came together to push for federal action in revitalizing the inner city physically and economically. The Housing Act of 1949 was the culmination of this coalition's efforts. It provided for the elimination of slums and blight, decent housing for low-income residents, and a commitment to rebuild the nation's cities. The act empowered local governments to remove slums and subsidized private developers to purchase cleared land at low costs. Redevelopment funds were to be used predominantly for residential building. However, in many cities, local polit-

ical and economic elites focused federal funds on reversing the economic decline of the inner city. This resulted in an increasingly commercial skew to redevelopment (or urban renewal) programs, with little attention paid to the housing needs of those displaced by slum clearance.

Hundreds of thousands of low-income, inner-city residents were victims of this policy. In a number of cities, the displaced were predominantly African-American. The removal of low-income housing by slum clearance and the presence of restrictive covenants and blatant prejudice prevented many African Americans from entering the private housing market. Consequently, poor African Americans became concentrated in substandard inner-city residences and public housing.

The segregation of African Americans in the inner city was exacerbated by the federal home-ownership programs, FHA and VA loans. In both programs, loans were predominantly funneled to suburban areas and were made off-limits to African Americans who might have been able to afford a mortgage. Also contributing to the decay and segregation of minority communities was the practice of redlining, refusing to insure or extend a mortgage to certain geographical areas because of the racial or ethnic composition of the neighborhood. Beginning in the 1930s, the Federal Housing Administration encouraged local officials to draw color-coded maps indicating the creditworthiness of neighborhoods. The term *redlining* refers to the act of drawing a red line around areas considered poor insurance and mortgage risks. Officials took into consideration the condition of the property in a neighborhood but also made the explicit assumption that the presence of black and other minorities lowered property values. In addition to being refused federal aid for the promotion of home ownership, redlined African-American communities also faced discrimination by private insurers and lenders. Federal segregationist policy was not changed formally until the 1968 Fair Housing Act prohibited discrimination in the sale, rental, advertising, or financing of housing.

Public housing resulting from the 1949 Housing Act was condemned as fundamentally flawed, contributing to the drastic segregation of poor and minorities in large cities. Federally authorized public housing suffered from insufficient funding, which meant units were often unattractive and uncomfortable. Additionally, federal funds were not allocated for ongoing maintenance until 1970. Decisions about the location of public housing sites were left to local officials, many of whom were not willing to take the political risk of building low-income housing in middle-class, often white, neighborhoods. These restrictions combined to create dense inner-city communities of very poor people, isolated from the rest of society. Due in part to the high price of inner-city land, cities chose to build low-cost, high-rise apartment complexes plagued by vandalism and crime. However, it is important to note that these units provided higher-quality housing than many of the low-income residents could afford on the open market. Even today, dilapidated public housing has 1-to-3-year-long waiting lists for people in need of reduced rents.

Throughout the 1960s various attempts to amend earlier housing policy were implemented. The predominant change in housing policy was a shift from federally built and owned public housing to the provision of federal subsidies for privately owned low-income housing. Direct subsidies were provided for both construction and rental of low-income properties. These changes helped families that had previously been too poor to rent public housing by making up the difference between the market rate of the rental property and 25 percent of the residents' income. Additionally, Congress implemented more-stringent low-income housing requirements for the receipt of redevelopment moneys. In 1965 a cabinet-level agency was created to address the nation's housing needs. The DEPARTMENT OF HOUSING AND URBAN DEVELOPMENT (HUD) was authorized in an attempt to centralize housing policy

and reinvigorate a commitment to provide shelter for the needy as part of President Johnson's Great Society programs. During the 1960s federal grants to local governments for urban development increased tremendously. A total of 240 new grant programs more than doubled federal expenditure on transfers to local governments.

By the 1970s the focus of federal housing policy had changed once again. In 1973 President Nixon declared a moratorium on housing and community development assistance. In an effort to reform public housing and urban redevelopment policy, the 1974 Housing and Community Development Act consolidated a variety of programs into the Community Development Block Grant (CDBG) program, thus returning federal housing policy to local discretion. With CDBG funding, municipalities received blocks of federal moneys to spend on community development as they saw fit, rather than for specific purposes as the earlier grant programs required. Section 8 of the 1974 act increased subsidies for privately owned low-income housing and provided up to 40-year contracts guaranteeing renters for participating landlords.

Since the late 1970s, the net number of new federally subsidized housing units has been in decline. By 1980 the number of public housing units had grown to 1.2 million, but this has remained largely stagnant since that time. During the 1980s, federal grant programs to local governments declined both in number and amount. In 1987, the first federal policy to help communities deal with homelessness was implemented. To revitalize aging public housing structures, Congress allocated funds for modernization and rehabilitation between 1980 and 1992. Two significant recent developments in housing policy were the 1990 HOME Investment Partnerships program and the 1993 Home Ownership and Opportunity for People Everywhere (HOPE VI) program. HOME provides block grants to local governments to increase the supply of low-income housing and opportunities for home ownership. The HOPE VI program provides funds to improve distressed public housing projects.

For more information

Mitchell, J. Paul, ed. *Federal Housing Policy and Programs: Past and Present.* New Brunswick, N.J.: Center for Urban Policy Research, 1985.

Weicher, John C. *Housing: Federal Policies and Programs.* Washington, D.C.: American Enterprise Institute for Public Policy Research, 1982.

Jessica L. Hills

Hull-House

Hull-House was a settlement house founded in 1889 by JANE ADDAMS and Ellen Gates Starr in a rundown mansion in a poor, immigrant neighborhood on the West Side of Chicago.

Hull-House was destined to become the most famous settlement of its kind in the United States and the locus for numerous social welfare studies and programs. It was unlike the organized charity or mission societies of the late 1800s that provided the urban poor with relief or assistance, and it was distinct from settlement houses that operated in a religious context or focused on immigrant Americanization or on the specific needs of the black emigrant urban dwellers. According to its charter, the object of Hull-House was "to provide a center for a higher civic and social life; to institute and maintain educational and philanthropic enterprises, and to investigate and improve the conditions in the industrial districts of Chicago."

Inspired by a visit to London's Toynbee Hall and the university settlement ideas of Samuel Barnett, Addams and Starr believed they had come upon a way for college-educated individuals to mutually benefit themselves and society, beyond the traditional avenues available at the time. They solicited money and support from church and women's groups for what magazine and newspaper articles called their "Toynbee experiment," and they leased the so-called Hull's House from Helen Culver, business part-

ner and heir of Charles J. Hull, who had built the house in 1856. College friend and lawyer Julia Lathrop joined them in 1890, and what started as an invitation to neighbors to hear about and view art objects grew within a few years to include a reading group, art gallery, kindergarten, a music school, the first public playground and public bath, a bookbindery, craft shop, plus a variety of evening classes, social clubs, and lectures.

Residents, volunteers, and supporters were drawn to the settlement almost immediately. Residents typically worked at outside jobs, paid to live in a "cooperative" setting (private room with communal dining facilities), and assisted with settlement activities or conducted research. According to Addams, what came to be known as Hull-House was an "experimental effort to aid in the solution of the social and industrial problems which are engendered by the modern conditions of life in a great city." Once physically "settled" in this locale, settlement residents could more easily overcome the "differences of race and language," begin to communicate with people in the area, and, without preconceived notions of their own, "arouse and interpret public opinion of their neighborhood."

After needs were identified by these cross-class/cross-cultural exchanges, Hull-House could respond with appropriate clubs, classes, and programs, or the residents could use the information "to furnish data for legislation" and "use their influence to secure it." The latter approach led to investigations of child labor, the sweating system (garment sweatshops), tenement conditions, ethnic-group population rates, wage rates, and immigrant infant mortality by residents such as socialist/trade unionist Florence Kelley, labor leaders Alzina Stevens and Mary Kenney, Alice Hamilton, social reformer Robert Hunter, and city planner George Hooker. As leaders in the Progressive movement at the local, state, and national levels, Hull-House reformers were involved in the creation of the Illinois Juvenile Court, protective associations for juveniles and for immigrants, state and national child labor laws, city school improvements, public playground and recreation center development, better housing and public health services, and other policies to improve social conditions and make government more responsive and efficient.

Within its first 20 years the settlement grew to 13 interconnected, centrally heated buildings occupying a city block on property leased from Culver, adding a courtyard; coffee house; gymnasium; kindergarten; nursery; labor museum; theater; men's and working women's residences; clubs for men, women, and boys; and a dining hall. Support and maintenance of Hull-House and its operations depended upon gifts from wealthy benefactors and residents of means (which included Addams herself), sales, and rents.

For years Addams traveled and lectured extensively, which brought increased renown to Hull-House. This attracted more funds and supporters, including visitors from many professions and with varied philosophies who not only publicized the settlement activities but often stayed on or returned to give lectures and volunteer their time. This ongoing propensity to welcome the free exchange of ideas sometimes led to negative publicity and discontinuance of support from those who opposed trade unions, socialists, radicals, progressive reformers, and particularly Addams's pacifist stance during World War I. Eventually Culver donated the leased block property to Hull-House, but financial difficulties were an ongoing concern.

Addams was resident director from 1889 until her death in 1935, and few would dispute the extent of her influence upon the success of the Hull-House experiment. The settlement continued to respond to its community's changing needs over the next three decades by first working with the New Deal agencies, then hiring social workers, and emphasizing social services. Urban renewal programs soon displaced the West Side neighborhoods, and Hull-House was forced to sell its buildings in 1963 to make way

for the University of Illinois Chicago campus. The original Hull mansion, now a museum and designated a national historic landmark in 1967, remains on the site along with the restored settlement dining room. The work of Hull-House continues through several community centers located throughout Chicago that make up the Hull House Association.

For more information

Addams, Jane. *Twenty Years at Hull House*. New York: Macmillan, 1910.

Bryan, Mary Lynn McCree, and Allen F. Davis, eds. *One Hundred Years at Hull House*. Bloomington: Indiana University Press, 1990.

Crocker, Ruth Hutchinson. *Social Work and Social Order*. Urbana: University of Illinois Press, 1992.

Hull House Association. www.hullhouse.org.

Jackson, Shannon. *Lines of Activity*. Ann Arbor: The University of Michigan Press, 2000.

Kathleen M. Simon

human relations Human relations or the human relations "school" is the name applied to a framework of ideas or theories about organizational management focusing on the human dimension in organizations. These ideas focus on the social and psychological factors affecting the job behavior of people in the workplace. Much of the research concerning the connection between the productivity of employees and the way they are treated in the workplace is attributed to this particular group of concepts.

In 1932, research at Western Electric's Hawthorne Works factory by Elton Mayo became, for its time, the most significant demonstration of the importance of social and psychological factors in the workplace linking human relations with productivity. Prior to the work of Elton Mayo and others, the management of workers was based on an approach that focused on getting the most possible work out of employees with little regard for individual employee needs and concerns. A strong emphasis by managers and supervisory personnel on control, authority, and discipline—and an impersonal approach to employees—was seen as necessary to reduce the effect of individual personality and force workers to do their jobs.

Early work by human relations theorists such as MARY PARKER FOLLETT argued that the ability to get workers to be more productive rested on the ability to include employees in decision making and to focus on individual and group needs of workers. Follett reasoned that rather than being a detriment to the organization, the human element was the key to organizational success and worker productivity. However, there was little research to support the idea that paying attention to human relations would increase production.

In 1924 the Hawthorne Works of the Western Electric Company and the National Research Council began a project to investigate the workplace environment and worker productivity. The Hawthorne studies had tremendous impact. The investigation ultimately provided evidence that those interpersonal relationships, particularly those between employees as well as involving supervisors and employees, influence self-esteem and self-confidence of workers, and ultimately impact the output or productivity of an individual worker. Elton Mayo's research confirmed the importance of human relations in organizations and established the connection between how workers were treated and the quality of their work. The findings of the Hawthorne studies and the work of other human-relations theorists firmly established the human factor as an important element in organizational effectiveness and operations, and showed managers that workers had to be considered greater than the machinery they operated.

Many of the early theories expressed by the human-relations researchers are evident in modern management strategies and programs such as participatory management, TOTAL QUALITY MANAGEMENT, team building, and employee development programs. All of these are designed to ensure that employees are recognized for their contributions and involved in their organization's development and growth.

For more information

Rainey, H. G. *Understanding and Managing Public Organizations,* 2d ed. San Francisco: Jossey Bass, 1997.

Rieger, B. J. "Lessons in Productivity and People." *Training and Development* 49 (1995): 56–59.

Dahlia Bradshaw Lynn

Humphrey's Executor v. United States 295 U.S. 602 (1935)

Humphrey's Executor v. United States was an important Supreme Court case that considered whether the president of the United States has an unqualified removal power for members of independent regulatory commissions.

Congress created independent regulatory agencies as a body of experts to discharge duties independent of the executive. Members of independent regulatory commissions act in both a quasi-legislative and quasi-judicial manner to establish decisions concerning U.S. regulatory power. The executive can select members for these commissions, and they are approved with the advice and consent of Congress. Congress establishes both fixed terms of service and the partisan composition of these agencies. In the 1930s President Franklin Roosevelt sought to strengthen his control over the management of government agencies to make them give greater accountability to the executive. If the president can remove such agency officials at will, there would be substantially greater executive than legislative control over administrative authority.

In this case, President Franklin Roosevelt removed William E. Humphrey, a Republican conservative member of the FEDERAL TRADE COMMISSION appointed by President Hoover, in an attempt to gain partisan control over this agency, which enforces national antitrust laws and investigates competitive practices in the economy. The commission has rule-making authority on these economic matters. Humphrey died prior to the filing of the lawsuit, and the litigation was brought by his executor for wrongful removal and back pay. The U.S. Supreme Court unanimously ruled that the president's assertion of an unqualified removal power violated the separation-of-powers doctrine. If the principle asserted by the president were supported, the president could threaten the independence of regulatory agencies, and Congress had established these agencies as independent from the executive. The Court argued that the president could only remove this type of commission member for good cause, such as neglect of duties or malfeasance in office.

This decision overruled *Myers v. United States,* 272 U.S. 346 (1926), which had granted broad presidential authority to remove at will those officials, i.e., postmasters, who are one of the units of the executive department and whose activities are confined to executive duties. *Wiener v. United States,* 357 U.S. 349 (1957), supported the *Humphrey's Executor* analysis and expanded it to another type of administrative unit, the War Claims Commission. The *Humphrey's Executor* analysis demonstrates that constitutional provisions do not allow the executive to exercise coercive influence over congressionally created administrative units.

For more information

Burgess, Susan R. *Contest for Constitutional Authority.* Lawrence: University Press of Kansas, 1992.

Fisher, Louis. *Constitutional Dialogues: Interpretations as Political Process.* Princeton, N.J.: Princeton University Press, 1988.

Steven Puro

I

Immigration and Naturalization Service (INS) v. Chadha 462 U.S. 919 (1983) In *Immigration and Naturalization Service (INS) v. Chadha,* the Supreme Court ruled that the legislative veto is an unconstitutional violation of separation of powers.

After 1900, Congress began to delegate legislative power to the executive branch. In the 1930s, Congress adopted the legislative veto as a way to control presidential use of executive orders and other exercises of presidential power.

In the 1960s, President Johnson's Great Society programs rained a flood of new legislation, much of it regulatory in nature. Administrative rules and regulations issued by the executive branch grew enormously in the administrations that followed. In response to various interests, Congress increasingly used the legislative veto to control both the president (e.g., War Powers Act of 1973) as well as the executive branch's agencies and the administrative rules and regulations they issued. By the 1980s the legislative veto was a part of over 200 acts of Congress. Jagdish Chadha—subjected to a legislative veto—appealed it as unconstitutional.

Jagdish Chadha was born in Kenya, at that time a British colony, of Indian parents. In the mid-1960s he came to the United States to study under a British passport. After graduating from Bowling Green University, he found that neither Great Britain nor Kenya would let him return. With an expired student visa, and lacking permanent residency status, Chadha, though qualified, could not get a job. Chadha then applied for permanent residency status in the United States. After a lengthy INS (Immigration and Naturalization Service) hearing, Chadha's application for permanent residency was approved. However, on 16 December 1975, nearly two years later, the House of Representatives vetoed the INS decision. Chadha faced deportation.

By the time Chadha experienced a legislative veto, both the executive branch and many activist public-interest groups had come to opposed the legislative veto. Alan Morris, chief litigator for consumer activist Ralph Nader, took Chadha's case as an opportunity to have the legislative veto declared unconstitutional. Soon lawyers from the Justice Department and the INS also joined the case.

The case was decided on 23 June 1983 by a vote of 7-2 in the Supreme Court. Chief Justice Warren Burger wrote the Court's opinion. He held that the Constitution requires that a bicameral Congress must present to the president legislation for enactment that has followed the steps specified by the Constitution. Legislative vetoes bypass these steps and are unconstitutional.

Justice Lewis Powell's concurring opinion argued that the case should have been decided by balancing the legislative veto's utility against its potential for intrusion into another branch's rightful domain. Justice Byron White's dissent defended the legislative veto as a virtually indispensable political invention that allowed the Congress to exercise oversight of the executive branch's enforcement of the law.

At one blow, the Chadha decision overturned more congressional enactments than all other such decisions in the entire history of the republic combined.

For more information
Craig, Barbara Hinkson. *Chadha: The Story of an Epic Constitutional Struggle.* Berkeley: University of California Press, 1990.

A. J. L. Waskey

implementation Implementation is the process of putting into practice the decision to act on a particular preferred policy option, and it is considered the sharp end of policy because it involves coordinating the resources (budgetary and human) associated with that practical process into an action plan.

Implementation is always part of the policy development process and is the phase that turns chosen policy into action. Implementation is therefore the practical process of policy. It is a way of translating policy into action and ensures that the money and other resources of government are put into actual programs of service. For example, when government decides to build a new motorway, this happens because of a decision to accept a particular policy direction, based upon analysis of all the factors involved in the idea to build one.

Some of the factors that would need to be considered when implementing a policy decision to build a motorway, for example, are impact related. That is, how much will the motorway cost and where will the money come from, and is there enough to ensure that any unforeseen problems can be funded? To this end, the implementation phase is largely dependent upon having a flexible policy to begin with so that the motorway can be built regardless of any changes. Another factor is the population and whether it is expected to grow or change in profile. The most important factor in the implementation phase is, however, politics and in particular which party is in power and what other influential groups are around to influence whether and how the motorway will be built. Many motorway ideas have been stopped because people have formed action groups to prevent the building or to delay the processes while environmental studies are done. Implementation is therefore the practical nexus between politics and the public and is therefore the phase in policy most affected by changes in politics or power.

An important link in the implementation phase is the plan. This is the design phase and identifies barriers, clarifies cooperatives and resources, and then sets timelines. This is the most logical phase of the policy implementation process as it plots out what has to happen in order to build the motorway. People are the biggest resource in the process, and it is easy to gloss over this aspect of implementation and assume that it is merely a function of public organizations, but more commonly it is outsourced to nongovernment agencies. Governments build motorways by engaging private contractors to build them, and in this way the contractors implement policy on behalf of government. The reliance on external agencies has required greater expertise in the management of contracts and has potentially added to the cost of policy processes for governments worldwide.

Policy failures are often attributed to the implementation phase, and to some extent this is appropriate because it is the sharp end of the policy process and reflects the planning throughout. One way organizations have tried to prevent failure is to construct implementation structures that take into consideration the complex interconnections between programs. Implementation structures work because they take into consideration what is required to change or stay the same in order to succeed as effective examples of policy implementation.

For more information

Hogwood, B. W., and B. Guy Peters. *The Pathology of Public Policy.* Oxford and New York: Oxford University Press, 1981.

Sturgess, G. "1997 Policy Advice in a Virtual State." *Canberra Bulletin of Public Administration* 84 (May 1997): 84–92.

impoundment Impoundment occurs when the president refuses to spend the funds that have been allotted to a federal department or agency.

The first impoundment occurred fairly early in the nation's history, during the presidency of Thomas Jefferson. But impoundments were used sparingly until the early 1970s, when President Richard Nixon precipitated a political crisis over disagreements with Congress about domestic policy priorities. The president refused to spend some $12 billion allocated to highway, health, education, and environmental purposes, arguing that they were unnecessary and a waste of the taxpayers' money. Nixon argued that impoundments were included under the president's executive powers under Article II of the Constitution.

From the start, the constitutionality of impoundments has been challenged as a basic violation of the president's duty to see that the "laws are faithfully executed." Agency appropriations and authority to spend are matters of federal law, which the president is obligated to make available. The 1974 Congressional Budget and Impoundment Control Act (Public Law 93-344, 12 July 1974) affirmed the president's obligation to spend money allotted to agencies under federal law, but the act permitted the president to impound funds subject to congressional approval. Under the 1974 act, impoundments take one of two forms: "rescissions" and "deferrals."

Rescissions are essentially cancellations of budget authority previously provided, prior to the time that the budget authority expires. In this case, unless Congress agrees with the president and rescinds the funds within 45 days (measured as congressional session days, rather than calendar days), then the president is obligated to make the funds available to be spent. In recent administrations, around one-third of all rescissions have been accepted by Congress. Deferrals are temporary delays in the obligation and expenditure of funds previously provided. Deferrals generally cannot be made for purely policy reasons, but only in order to promote savings, efficiency, or to deal with emergencies. Unlike rescissions, deferrals may be put into effect upon notification of Congress through a deferral message that explains the circumstances for deferring spending. However, there is a clear understanding that the funds eventually will be spent. Unless Congress specifically rejects the president's request for deferral, it is presumed to be approved. Congress routinely accepts over 99 percent of all deferrals.

It is generally recognized that the impoundment process created under the 1974 Budget Act represented a reasonable compromise between management flexibility and legal obligation. Under the process in place after 1974, the president can refuse to spend money, but only if Congress specifically agrees. In other words, the law must be executed as it has been enacted. The president can defer spending largely at his discretion; however, should Congress disagree with his reasons, it can compel him to make the funds available immediately. In this case, a delay in spending may take place, provided that it makes good management sense. If not, then Congress obliges the president to execute the budget as it was enacted into law. As a direct consequence of the impoundments process established in 1974, impoundments have not precipitated a political crisis since that time.

For more information

Lynch, Thomas D. *Public Budgeting in America,* 4th ed. Englewood Cliffs, N.J.: Prentice-Hall, 1995.

Schlesinger, Arthur M., Jr. *The Imperial Presidency.* Boston: Houghton Mifflin Company, 1973.

Robert S. Kravchuk

income tax   An income tax is a tax on the annual income of individuals, corporations, or other entities assessed for the purpose of collecting revenue for the government or to further some economic or regulatory purpose.

For almost the first 100 years of American history there was no federal or state income tax. However, to pay for the financing of the Civil War, President Lincoln imposed an income tax. This tax was challenged in court, but was upheld in *Springer v. United States,* 102 U.S. 586 (1881). Subsequently in *Pollock v. Farmers' Loan & Trust Company,* 202 U.S. 107 (1895) the Supreme Court declared a tax on income to be unconstitutional, leading eventually to the passage of the Sixteenth Amendment in 1913, which empowered Congress to impose an income tax.

A tax on income can be structured in several ways. A progressive income tax is one where individuals who earn more money pay a higher portion of tax than those who earn less. For example, individuals earning more than $100,000 a year may pay approximately 31 percent of the income in tax, while individuals making less than $25,000 may pay 20 percent or less of their income in tax. The philosophy behind a progressive income tax is based on the ability to pay. That is, those who make more money can better afford to pay taxes than those who make less. In addition, a progressive income tax is often justified on the belief that those who earn more money derive more benefits from society

and therefore should contribute more. Finally, some support a progressive income tax as a way of equalizing incomes between the rich and the poor.

A second type of income tax is a flat tax. A flat tax is one where all income levels are treated the same and everyone pays, say, for example, 5 percent of their income towards support of the government. Some people believe flat taxes are more fair than progressive taxes because they treat all taxpayers the same.

The primary purpose of an income tax is to generate revenue for the government so that it can perform its basic services, such as providing for defense, roads, schools, and other programs. However, an income tax can also serve other social or regulatory functions. For example, taxes are often used as ways to induce or encourage certain activities in the economy. In cases of recession, economists who call themselves Keynesians (named for John Maynard Keynes, a famous 20th-century economist) argue that an income tax cut is a way to stimulate economic demand. By cutting income taxes, taxpayers will have more money to purchase goods, thereby increasing economic output and the hiring of people to produce these goods. Using the tax cut to stimulate demand in this case is referred to as a *fiscal policy.* Others argue that cutting taxes, especially for the wealthy and businesses, gives both of them more money to invest in the economy. Advocates of this position are often referred to as *supply-siders,* because they adhere to an economic theory called supply-side economics.

Besides using them as a way to help the economy, taxes could also be used to discourage certain types of behavior. For example, the government could label certain types of activities as nontaxable, such as the purchase of municipal bonds, to encourage people to buy them. In other cases, certain types of activities, such as contributions to charity or a retirement account, may constitute deductions that lessen or decrease taxpayers' income tax liability. Such an exemption or deduction creates an incentive for people to give to charities or plan for their old age.

In the United States, the federal tax code is enacted by Congress and it describes what types of income count for the purposes of a tax. For example, under federal law, taxpayers must report their income from illegal activities and pay income taxes on it. The tax code also describes different tax rates and it provides for the Internal Revenue Service (IRS) to be the primary agency involved in the collection of federal income taxes. The IRS also has the power to make it own rules. Of the 43 states that have individual income taxes, there are departments of revenue responsible for enforcing the state's tax code.

Many Americans appear to hate income taxes and claim they are overtaxed. However, compared to the income tax rates in western European nations and to the rates that existed in America in the 1950s, contemporary income tax rates in the United States are quite low. One of the critical issues that elected officials face is that citizens want lots of services from the government but appear unwilling to pay taxes for them. Striking a balance between providing government programs and convincing people to pay their share of taxes is a major public policy issue, not only in the United States, but in most countries around the world.

For more information

Nordhaus, William D., and Paul Samuelson. *Macroeconomics.* New York: McGraw Hill/Irwin, 1997.

David Schultz

incremental budgeting   Incremental budgeting is a system of allocating resources to organizations, or to organizational units, based on their allocations in the preceding budget period (normally the previous year). It contrasts with ZERO-BASED BUDGETING in which the budget is developed from "a clean sheet"—based on a fresh assessment of the level of activities required and their costs.

Under incremental budgeting, the previous budget is used as the starting point for the following budget. Additions are made for new or expanded expenditure items (which can comprise programs, functions, outputs, or expenditure types). These incremental costs can be funded from growth in the revenue side of the budget or from the deletion or scaling back of existing expenditure items.

Often, the previous budget will classify items to identify whether and how they roll forward into the subsequent budget. A classification of "base" and "special" items separately identifies those costs that are taken to be permanent from those that have a limited life (such as activities funded by a multiyear research grant). A second way of classifying costs that is commonly used to determine budget increments divides them as "labor" and "nonlabor." In this case, separate increments can be determined according to the levels of wage inflation and price inflation and, where applicable, according to the number of additional staff approved.

A further classification of costs can be used where an agency administers the payment of benefits in accordance with legislation or government policy. For budgetary purposes, it is useful to classify these administered costs separately from the controlled costs of the agency, which would be subject to closer scrutiny.

Systems of incremental budgeting are much simpler to administer than zero-based budgets. However, they tend to compound the problem of lock-in, where it becomes difficult to reallocate resources to match changes in customer needs and government priorities or to take advantage of advances in technology. Therefore, incremental budgets are often supplemented by periodic reviews or performance audits aimed at assessing the efficiency and effectiveness of existing activities. Increasingly, governments are also encouraging and requiring agencies to report ongoing measures of efficiency and effectiveness to better inform the resource allocation process.

For more information
National Association of State Budget Officers. http://www.nasbo.org.

Bob Shead

incrementalism Incrementalism is the "science of muddling through," in the words of its principal advocate, Charles E. Lindblom. This perspective on the making of public policy in the United States argues that policy is made in relatively small steps, in an evolutionary rather than a revolutionary fashion. As a theory of public policy making, incrementalism stresses the fact that intelligence is limited and information is incomplete and that, given our system of pluralistic power and multiple access (or veto) points, policy makers do not master or solve public policy problems, such as crime, welfare, education, or national security, so much as they cope with them.

Incrementalism, again in the hands of theorists like Lindblom, calls our attention to the salient fact that policy making is not and cannot be rational, in the sense that one knows all the policy options and their consequences as one tries to solve a public problem. Moreover, incrementalism, as "the intelligence of democracy," contends that policy makers pursue their own particular versions of the public good, versions often determined or at least strongly influenced by the organizational culture and/or bureaucratic position within which policy makers operate. Budgeting, for example, in spite of various other theoretical approaches, is, from the standpoint of incrementalism, a process of taking the previous year's budget as the base and adjusting it incrementally through the method of successive limited comparison.

Public policy making, as understood by incrementalism, emphasizes the fact that organizational cultures are relatively stable; that bureaucratic processes are strongly ingrained; and that procedures and priorities change gradually, based in large measure on the record and understanding of past experiences and the "bounded rationality" of decision makers. Thus, in the making of public policy, one finds adjustment at the margins, as opposed to a fully rational, comprehensive method of policy making, where one knows all the policy options, all their consequences, and therefore, is able to choose the "best" policy. The mosaic of public policy, from the vantage point of incrementalism, entails the making and remaking of public policy; policy is made endlessly and *not* once and for all.

Incrementalism highlights the fact that, in the words of Lindblom, "Making policy is at best a very rough process." Organizational structures, bureaucratic policies and procedures, and policy history all demonstrate that while policy makers often have overlapping and mutual (if not common) interests, there is, by virtue of the structure and performance of our system, no one chief or central coordinator. Ours is a system of public policy making in which persuasion or bargaining is more effective than mere command and in which, due to common interests and values, there is the requisite interdependence and coordination of policy makers without the existence of one central coordinator at the apex of the system.

For more information
Lindblom, Charles E. "The Science of Muddling Through." *Public Administration Review.* 19 (spring 1959): 79–88.
———. *The Intelligence of Democracy: Decision Making through Mutual Adjustment.* New York: Basic Books, 1965.

Stephen K. Shaw

Indian Gaming Regulatory Act The Indian Gaming Regulatory Act (IGRA) of 1988 refers to a federal law that specifies the right that Native American tribes have to offer some forms of gambling and the right that tribes have, with the negotiated consent of their states, to offer casino gambling.

The U.S. Congress, in response to the Supreme Court's decision in CALIFORNIA V. CABAZON BAND OF MISSION INDIANS, which authorized that any tribe could offer gambling (of any sort) on its lands unless the state surrounding the tribe treated gambling like a crime, passed the Indian Gaming Regulatory Act. The legislation states that its purpose was to "provide a statutory [clear and legal] basis for the operation of gaming by Native American tribes as a means of promoting tribal economic development, self-sufficiency, and strong tribal governments."

The law requires that the tribes themselves (not individual members of the tribe) actually own their gambling facilities and that these facilities be on tribal lands. Further, IGRA specifies that the revenues from gambling facilities be used primarily to fund tribal government operations and programs, the general welfare of the tribe and its members, and tribal economic development, including education, health, and improvements to infrastructure.

Tribal lands, the law defines, are any lands that the tribe owned and controlled at the time that IGRA was passed. Tribes can purchase land and open gambling facilities on it only if the secretary of the interior and the governor of the state involved agree.

IGRA divided gambling on tribal lands into three general classes. Class I gambling includes tribal games and social games played for prizes of nominal value. Class II gambling includes bingo, lotto, punch cards, and other games that are legal in most states and are not played against the house. Both of these types of gambling can be offered by almost any tribe in the United States and, for the most part, are regulated only by the tribe. A Native American tribe in Alabama, for example, offers high-stakes bingo among other games under the auspices of these provisions in the IGRA.

IGRA also specifies Class III gambling, which includes casino gambling, pari-mutuel (horse and dog, usually) racing, jai alai, card games played against the house, and video poker. Class III gambling is governed by compacts negotiated between individual states and individual tribes. States can get from tribes some fees to cover the infrastructure and expense (electrical and sewer lines, police and fire protection, expanded and improved roadways) of having casinos within their borders. Tribes can sometimes get from states, as California tribes have gotten from that state, exclusivity agreements that prevent the states from allowing commercial (private) casinos such as Harrah's.

For more information

Mason, John Lyman, and Michael Nelson. *Governing Gambling*. Washington, D.C.: Brookings Institution Press, 2001.

John Lyman Mason

Individuals with Disabilities Education Act

The law now known as the Individuals with Disabilities Education Act (IDEA) was originally enacted by Congress as the Education for All Handicapped Children Act of 1975 (PL 94-142). Congress changed the name of the act in 1990 as part of PL 101-476.

IDEA has seen a number of amendments over the years, the last significant revision being in 1997 as PL 105-17. Although the law has seen many technical revisions over time, the primary purposes of the law have remained essentially intact. The IDEA statute promotes two goals: (1) access and inclusion by requiring public schools to provide a free appropriate public education to children with disabilities in the least restrictive environment; and (2) effective education for children with disabilities by setting up special education and related services designed to meet their unique needs and prepare them for employment and independent living.

IDEA establishes the responsibility of states and localities to educate children with disabilities and protects the rights of these children to appropriate and inclusive education. This concept is a further extension of prohibitions against disability discrimination in federally funded programs first utilized in Section 504 of the Rehabilitation Act of 1973 (PL 93-112), which itself was modeled after Title VI of the Civil Rights Act of 1964 (PL 88-352), which prohibited discrimination under federally funded programs on the basis of race, color, or national origin. The premise for IDEA, therefore, is the concept that the right of every child with a disability to be educated is grounded in the equal protection clause of the 14th Amendment to the U.S. Constitution—a conclusion affirmed by the Supreme Court in two landmark cases three years before the passage of PL 94-142, *Pennsylvania Association for Retarded Citizens* [PARC] *v. Pennsylvania*, 343 F.Supp. 279 (Pa. 1972), and *Mills v. Washington, D.C., Board of Education*, 348 F.Supp. 866 (D.C. 1972).

Secondly, IDEA establishes a system of special education and related services designed to ensure that the education being received is effective in meeting the individual needs of each student with a disability. IDEA also provides a funding formula by which the federal government supports states in providing these services, contingent on congressional appropriations. A crucial component in providing these services that is central to the support services authorized under IDEA is the Individual Education Plan (IEP). As required under this statute, all students who receive services under IDEA must have an IEP designed to ensure that the services being received are effectively designed and administered. The IEP includes behavior and academic goals and objectives to be achieved stated in measurable terms, and it lists the supporting services and accommodations (including assistive technologies and media services) that will be used to help meet these goals and objectives.

For more information

Legislative History. *United States Code Congressional and Administrative News 1975*. 1432.

Rothstein, L. *Special Education Law*, 3d ed. New York: Longman Publishing Co., 2000.

Steve Noble

informal hearing   An informal hearing is a process that does not follow explicit guidelines or that may not necessarily ensure complete due process protection for the individual or group appealing an administrative action or decision; it does, however, allow for resolution of a dispute.

When an important government action does not impact a substantial interest (for example, termination of benefits) on an individual or group, informal hearings may be utilized to resolve the dispute. Informal hearings do not adhere to strict guidelines for their procedures. Instead, these hearings try to resolve the dispute without the adversary aspects of a formal hearing. ALTERNATIVE DISPUTE RESOLUTION (ADR) hearings are one such example. Within these hearings, the parties involved try to arrive at a mutually acceptable decision, so that there is no clear-cut "winner" or "loser" within the proceeding, but both parties are satisfied with the outcome.

Other types of informal hearings may be classified as either "paper" or "oral" hearings. Like ADR hearings, these hearings do not have the same trial-type aspects as a formal hearing, but are either based on written arguments submitted by the parties ("paper") or based on an oral presentation by both sides to a decision maker.

The ultimate goal is to resolve the dispute without having to use strict procedures. However, some disputes involve such serious matters to a party that only a formal hearing will ensure the protection of their rights of due process.

For more information

Cooper, Phillip J. *Public Law and Public Administration*. Itasca, Ill.: F. E. Peacock Publishers, 2000.

J. Michael Bitzer

institutional reform litigation Institutional reform litigation is brought on behalf of individuals with little ability to influence the political process through conventional means. The litigants hope that because federal court judges are appointed for life and do not have to run for public office, they will be more willing to respond to their demands. The litigation is largely characterized by class-action suits, typically brought on behalf of groups—such as racial minorities, prisoners, poor children, or inhabitants of mental institutions—who are relatively few in number and lack the political clout to compel public officials to respond to them. The litigation is based on the belief that, unlike elected officials who are fearful of jeopardizing their political careers, the appointed judges will be more likely to order states to allocate resources for their benefit.

In the 1970s and 1980s, the nation's public-interest attorneys increasingly sought to enlist the power of the federal courts to compel state and local governments to reform public institutions and public services. Because they believed that the political process was not likely to respond to the demands of their politically powerless clients, reformers turned to class-action litigation. In part, these reformers followed the example of public-interest lawyers for the CIVIL RIGHTS movement in the 1960s and 1970s, who had turned to the federal courts for relief in their battle against racial discrimination in schools, housing, and employment. Many of the issues brought to the courts in the civil rights litigation efforts resurfaced in the lawsuits over institutional reform. And in deciding the latter cases, the federal court judges often mirrored the results of the earlier civil rights cases.

Known also as "public law litigation," "remedial decree litigation," "systemic litigation," and "structural reform litigation," institutional reform litigation involves plaintiffs who claim that the government deprives them of their rights. On behalf of their clients, legal-rights advocates argue that the plaintiffs are denied constitutional rights, primarily pointing to the "cruel and unusual punishment" clause of the Eighth Amendment and the due process clause of the Fourteenth Amendment of the U.S. Constitution as the source of these rights.

The federal courts have long been a preferred arena for systemic reform efforts, with litigants attempting to compel schools and public housing projects to desegregate in the 1950s and 1960s and attempting to secure relief against state institutions, such as state and local prison systems, mental hospitals, police departments, and child welfare systems, in the 1970s and 1980s. As a consequence of such lawsuits, federal court judges have played an important role in public policymaking for the last several decades.

These lawsuits sought to reform mental institutions, public school systems, correctional institutions, and child welfare systems, naming as defendants the head of the prison system, mental health system, child welfare system, or educational system. As the lawsuits developed, they typically involved intense bargaining between the parties over the implementation of the decree or settlement and continuing judicial involvement, with judges retaining jurisdiction over the case—sometimes for decades—because, as the plaintiffs (and to some extent, the judges) were to learn, a judicial finding that the system was out of compliance with constitutional standards did not signal the end of the case.

Such cases as *Wyatt v. Stickney,* 325 F. Supp. 781 (1971); *Hobson v. Hansen,* 327 F. Supp. 844 (1971); *Ruiz v. Estelle,* 503 F. Supp. (1980); *United States v. City of Parma,* 494 F. Supp. 1049 (1980); and *B. H. v. Johnson,* 715 F. Supp. 1387 (1988) exemplify the institutional reform litigation of the 1970s and 1980s. Brought into the courtrooms of such federal judges as Frank Johnson, Skelly Wright, William Wayne Justice, Frank Battisti, and John Grady, the suits frequently led to negotiated settlements or judicial orders to the defendants to reform the public institutions involved in the lawsuits.

The litigants often succeeded in obtaining far-reaching orders detailing the minimum number of square feet in prison cells, enumerating the number of psychiatrists required in state hospitals, designating specified numbers of low-income housing units, ordering equalization of public school teachers' salaries, providing for "rehabilitation" or "habilitation" for prisoners and the mentally ill, and designating caseworker-client ratios in child welfare agencies. In their supervisory roles during the course of the litigation, the work of the federal court judges ranges from overseeing the decisions of the prison, hospital, or child welfare administrators, to consulting with the appointed monitors or special masters, to becoming involved in the day-to-day decisionmaking of the institutions.

There has been more than two decades of scholarship on structural reform litigation, focusing on the role of the federal courts in the modern administrative state. Most studies examine suits against large-scale institutions, primarily state prison systems, and show how these institutions become transformed by the federal judiciary following the onset of the litigation. Conditions in the Arkansas prisons, as well as those in Texas, Colorado, California, Ohio, and Illinois, set the stage for suits that sought to end the horrific living conditions and brutality in the prisons, often resulting from inept or corrupt officials and strong overtones of racial discrimination. Because of the trigger provided by such lawsuits, beginning with the pathbreaking Arkansas case, *Holt v. Sarver,* in 1965, able public-interest lawyers and, often, sympathetic judges together ultimately produced widespread changes in state and local penal institutions.

Other studies have focused on suits to reform child welfare systems around the nation. Because abused children, unlike prisoners, are sympathetic plaintiffs, they are more likely to get the support of the public and the media. In cases such as *B.H. v. Johnson,* attorneys for children in foster care sought to protect the children who were separated from their biological families from being further victimized by asking for lower caseloads for child welfare workers, better training of supervisory personnel and agency staff, increased protection for the children in care, and better health care. As a consequence of these lawsuits, federal court judges played an important role in the child welfare policy-making process by placing many of them under court supervision.

The proliferation of institutional reform cases spawned a debate among scholars over the role of the courts in social policy decision making and the ability of federal judges to reach sound policy results. The debate arose in part because, by requiring the courts to weigh the extent of the state's obligation to the plaintiffs, these suits expanded the judicial role in public policy making and raised questions about federal court decrees triggering a redistribution of state resources. As a result of the lawsuits, state and local governments were often forced to commit funds to public institutions and, consequently, were sometimes required to raise state or local taxes or cut services to pay for the court-ordered resources. Not surprisingly, states resisted these demands for reform and characterized the court's interference in their fiscal and managerial authority as an unwarranted intrusion into their sovereignty.

These concerns about FEDERALISM and state autonomy have motivated many to question the wisdom of federal court judges engaging in the policy-making process. Reflecting in part this concern for state autonomy, states' rights advocates and judicial scholars have questioned the propriety of nonelected and nonaccountable federal court judges ordering reform of government institutions at the state and local level. In particular, they dispute the court's ability to make determinations of liability and award proper relief to litigants. These opponents of social reform litigation claim that in requiring state legislatures to commit funds to institutions that are targeted by the litigation despite competition for those funds elsewhere, courts ignore practical budgetary constraints and impose unrealistic demands on state and local governments.

Additionally, they stress their concern about the federal judiciary interfering in the administration of state institutions, as well as its capacity for overseeing the results of the changes ordered in public bureaucracies. In raising questions about the court's effectiveness in carrying out social reform, they contend that the courts lack the expertise to implement their decisions, and they object to judicial orders that intrude into the work of government officials who have the needed expertise and experience in administering public institutions.

Supporters of institutional reform litigation believe that the federal courts are the proper arenas for such cases because litigants without political power, such as prisoners, children, or people with mental disabilities, have difficulty making their voices heard by elected officials. Because they are often subject to the state's control—in prisons, hospitals, or foster care institutions—they are unable to utilize the normal political channels of power to influence policy makers. Moreover, advocates of institutional reform litigation argue that the debate is moot because courts are required to accept cases that are properly brought before them and do not have the legal authority to dismiss such cases. And, they maintain, it is precisely because they are nonelected and nonaccountable that federal court judges have the freedom to pursue unpopular policies. Additionally, they deny that judges are required to have the expertise to administer the state institutions because they are frequently assisted in crafting the decrees by special masters and monitors, agency heads, and the street-level workers. Finally, they insist that the judges are not solely responsible for the outcome of the litigation because state officials, including legislators and chief executives, and the litigants themselves are all typically engaged in the process of implementing the decree or settlement agreement.

Scholars also differ over the success of institutional reform litigation. Although critics argue that the federal courts are largely ineffectual in producing social policy reform, others note that there is often a catalytic effect of litigation on public policy reform. Litigation that succeeds in changing the policy of a single bureaucracy often serves as a stimulus to further litigation that can result in changes in bureaucratic policy in other jurisdictions. However, even if the litigation by itself does not produce immediate and sweeping results, it can function as part of an effective political strategy for achieving social reform in a number of ways. First, by securing greater access to the policy-making process by traditionally unrepresented groups, it may mobilize the litigants themselves to make demands on the democratically elected institutions. Second, the litigation often receives publicity that can sway public opinion and mobilize public support for the goals of the litigants. And ultimately, by creating public pressure on the political bodies to fulfill the goals of the litigants, the litigation may lead to passage of reform legislation in the state legislatures or city councils. Thus, scholars argue, it is shortsighted to view the results of the litigation narrowly rather than as part of a broader strategy for social reform policy.

As scholars have noted, social reform is a lengthy and complex process with many setbacks and slow advances. In the battle for social reform, litigation is often an effective tool, with the federal judiciary playing an important role and serving as a reminder that the federal courts can protect the rights of individuals in the modern administrative state. However, for a variety of reasons, there is also concern that involving federal court judges in the public policy-making process over the long run is contrary to the rules of a democracy, where the majority is supposed to rule and elected officials are normally charged with making public policy.

It seems clear that as long as such plaintiffs turn to the courts for help, and as long as the courts continue to maintain oversight of government institutions, the debate between the detractors and advocates of institutional reform litigation will continue.

For more information

Haar, Charles M. *Suburbs Under Siege: Race, Space, and Audacious Judges.* Princeton, N.J.: Princeton University, 1996.

Mezey, Susan Gluck. *Pitiful Plaintiffs: Child Welfare Litigation and the Federal Courts.* Pittsburgh: University of Pittsburgh Press, 2000.

Schultz, David A., ed. *Leveraging the Law: Using the Court to Achieve Social Change.* New York: Peter Lang, 1998.

Susan Gluck Mezey

intergovernmental relations   The term *intergovernmental relations* refers to the interactions between levels of government in a single political system. In the United States, this involves sharing of power and policy responsibilities, as well as communications between the federal government and state and local governments.

In any federalist political system, subnational governments share power with a national government. The U.S. federalist system attempts to balance the power and responsibilities of the national and state governments by allotting certain powers and responsibilities to each while also providing each with powers to check the actions of others. Additionally, state governments have created local governments that include city and county governments, school districts, and a host of other local governing bodies. The power of local government is only as extensive as the state government allows. These local governments share power and policy responsibilities with state governments and even the national government. But in a very real sense, states can coerce local governments to do whatever they want; state governments can mandate that localities take specific policy actions.

Governments in the American political system have become increasingly interdependent over time, especially in terms of sharing jurisdiction in policy areas and in terms of revenue sharing. For example, in the area of environmental protection, state governments foot most of the bill and have most of the responsibility for implementing and enforcing federal environmental laws. States have come to rely on revenues from the federal government, and local governments often rely on funds and grants from state government as well as the national government. Indeed, local governments have created organizations that lobby state and national government and manage relations between these levels of government, while states have created their own organizations to represent state interests in Washington, D.C.

Throughout most the 20th century, the national government increased its power and responsibility relative to the states. Traditionally the national government had been responsible for defending the country and for services such as mail, leaving primary responsibility for policies such as education and social welfare to the states. But beginning in the 1930s, the national government became increasingly involved in social services and public works, such as interstate highway construction. In addition the national government increasingly mandated that the states take specific policy actions or face the loss of federal funds, among other actions. By the 1970s, a movement to devolve power back to state and local governments began, which continues today.

As citizens and elected officials have struggled to define the proper role of government in American society—as well as the specific roles of national, state, and local governments—the issue of cooperation between levels of government and relations between levels of government have become increasingly important. And as concerns over disparities in economic and social justice across states become more apparent, intergovernmental relations will continue to rise in importance. Nevertheless, even as state and local governments have created agencies to address intergovernmental relations, the national Advisory Commission on Intergovernmental Relations was disbanded in 1996 after 37 years of activity.

For more information

Anton, Thomas J. *American Federalism and Public Policy: How the System Works.* New York: Random House, 1989.

Conlan, Timothy. *From New Federalism to Devolution: Twenty-Five Years of Intergovernmental Reform.* Washington, D.C.: Brookings Institution Press, 1998.

Derthick, Martha. *Keeping the Compound Republic: Essays on Federalism.* Washington, D.C.: Brookings Institution Press, 2001.

O'Toole, Laurence J., Jr., ed. *American Intergovernmental Relations,* 3d ed. Washington, D.C.: CQ Press, 2000.

Donald P. Haider-Markel

Iran-Contra   Iran-Contra is the name given to a series of events in the presidency of RONALD REAGAN that, in their collectivity, constituted a major political scandal and a grave constitutional crisis in the 1980s. At the center of these events one finds the selling of military weapons to the government of Iran in exchange for the release of American hostages held by that country, with some of the profits from the brokering of arms being used to support the allegedly covert war against the Sandinista regime that came to power in Nicaragua in the summer of 1979.

The crisis erupted when the operation, which worked out of the White House and the NATIONAL SECURITY COUNCIL, led largely by Lt. Col. Oliver "Ollie" North, was made public by a Lebanese newspaper in Beirut in mid-November 1986. The story revealed that, contrary to its own consistent public statements of denial and to the spirit if not the letter of congressional statute, the Reagan administration was trading arms for hostages to aid the counterrevolutionaries, or "contras," in

Central America. The plan, often referred to simply as "the enterprise," was hatched because the administration of Ronald Reagan, from the Oval Office down, was committed to stemming a perceived Marxist communist flood in Central America, emanating from the Sandinistas in Nicaragua. The Reagan administration firmly believed that a communist "beachhead" was unacceptable and that U.S. foreign policy, with or without the explicit support of the Congress, must assist the contras.

Central to an understanding of Iran-Contra is the Reagan administration's capacious conception of executive power, if not executive prerogative. According to this view of presidential power, the president is the sole organ of U.S. foreign policy, and if he finds himself facing a skeptical, recalcitrant Congress, his powers as commander in chief, along with inherent executive authority, permit—even require—that he take any unilateral action deemed necessary in the face of a particular threat, especially in the realm of national security policy.

Thus, covert operations from the National Security Council staff in the White House, and not the CENTRAL INTELLIGENCE AGENCY (CIA), were justified as essential to protecting American vital interests, and, absent supportive congressional action, could be pursued and implemented beyond the scrutinizing eye of the legislative branch and the American public. The Iran-Contra affair is a child of the perspective that views Congress with contempt and considers constitutional principles, such as checks and balances and statutory safeguards—such as the Boland Amendment of 1984—as merely admonitory in nature. The result was a secretive, unaccountable foreign policy venture that became a fiasco and almost brought down a highly popular president in infamy.

After the scandal erupted in the fall of 1986, and for approximately the next six months, President Reagan publicly and consistently denied the allegations of trading arms for hostages and aid to the contras, but in 1987 he finally acknowledged, in a nationally televised address, that "mistakes were made." Congressional hearings and judicial proceedings ensued, but the full story of this sordid affair is yet to be known.

For more information

Draper, Theodore. *A Very Thin Line: The Iran-Contra Affairs*. New York: Touchstone, 1991.

Koh, Harold H. *The National Security Constitution: Sharing Power after the Iran-Contra Affair*. New Haven, Conn.: Yale University Press, 1990.

Stephen K. Shaw

iron law of oligarchy   The iron law of oligarchy is a principle that claims that no matter how democratic any movement, group, organization, or government is when it begins, it eventually becomes an oligarchy (a government controlled by a small group).

The claim—that all organizations are naturally oligarchic—was developed by the sociologist Robert Michels (1879–1936) in his major work *Political Parties*. Other elite theorists include Vilfredo Pareto (1848–1923) and Gaetano Mosca (1858–1941).

Michels taught at the Universities of Turin, Basel, and Perugia. Prior to World War I, Michels studied German Social Democratic parties, which were believed to be the most democratic organizations in the world at the time. However, Michels argued that these ideologically antiaristocratic institutions demonstrated the inevitability of oligarchic rule. For example, despite often very humble beginnings, leaders of Germany's Social Democrats would inevitably acquire elite skills and knowledge for controlling a bureaucracy that was ever less democratic. For Michels, "Whoever says bureaucracy says oligarchy."

Elitist applications of the iron law of oligarchy conclude that democracy is an impossible illusion. This conclusion is often joined with a second political assertion—that democracy is undesirable because it means rule by the unfit masses.

The iron law of oligarchy is probably a true principle. Any organization, large or small, will need to perform a variety of management functions—planning, goal setting, budgeting, division of labor, execution, supervision, and evaluation. These functions could all be done after democratic debate, in the fashion of a New England town meeting. This inefficient method for decision making would likely engender the organization's demise. It is more efficient for organizational leaders to assign tasks to the members. However, the inevitable result is that some people come to have more power than others, lines of authority develop, and an organization becomes bureaucratic.

Several implications arise from the iron law of oligarchy. First, within a bureaucracy, the iron law may mean that there is a formal official who is less powerful than an officially subordinate individual who has risen to be the informal leader of the office or work group. Second, while bureaucracies in modern mass society are by nature oligarchic, a variety of mechanisms can be instituted to ensure a democratic process for decision making. Third, the iron law of oligarchy need not be fatal to democratic rule because universal education in statecraft—political skills and knowledge needed by rulers—can be taught to everyone.

Finally, elite theory has a critical flaw because it dismisses differences between elites and leaders with the view that elites are born and cannot be made. Command is the main view of power in elite theory. Democracy believes the opposite. Leaders are made, not born. Democratic leaders may use power in many styles of leadership. Consequently, the iron law of oligarchy is not necessarily fatal to democracy.

For more information

Meisel, James, ed. *Pareto & Mosca: Makers of Modern Social Science*. Englewood Cliffs, N.J.: Prentice-Hall, Inc., 1965.

Michels, Robert. *Political Parties: A Sociological Study of the Oligarchical Tendencies of Modern Democ-*

racy. 1915. Reprint, New York: The Free Press, 1962.

A. J. L. Waskey

iron triangles   The term *iron triangle* refers to three participants—an executive agency, a congressional committee or subcommittee, and a special-interest group—all associated with a particular public program. During the mid-1900s, one way to describe who makes policy was with the phrase "iron triangles." The alliance is called "iron" because the relationship among the three participants endures over time for the mutual benefit of everyone in the alliance.

In the pluralist model of democracy, interest groups represent a form of public participation that was thought to be a more accessible and open process through the mobilization of interests. However, through the study of iron triangles, it became clear that interest groups are not necessarily effective at enhancing public participation in the policy-making process. In fact, these iron triangles exclude other interests and can make it difficult to change public policy over time.

The relationship among the parties in the tripartite work group often supported special projects of interest to all the parties involved. For instance, congressional committees were key players because they had funding and oversight jurisdiction over an agency's programs. These committees could control the creation, expansion, or elimination of the agency's programs. In return, committee members have projects administered by these agencies that help satisfy their constituents and campaign funders. Committee members are aware that constituents are more likely to support their reelection if they are provided with projects and services from agencies that are funded by the congressional committee. In addition to constituent services, agencies also help congressional committees by providing information to help them understand the program. Another key player is the special-interest group that represents members who benefit from an agency's programs. Therefore, these interest groups have a vested stake in the continued support of the agency and also have electoral support for the congressional committee members who continue to support the agency programs of interest to the group's members.

Each of the participants has overlapping interests with the others, which results in a strong, mutually supportive alliance that endures challenges to its position over time. The three members of the iron triangle remain constant in their policy-making role, which means that over time they tend to dominate other interests in the policy area by not allowing outsiders to control the policy. Before the 1960s and 1970s, there were no large interest groups or committees that could challenge these tightly controlled iron triangles. Today—with the increased number of interest groups and congressional committees and a more active media—iron triangles no longer explain policy making.

There have been some well-known iron triangles in the policy areas of agriculture, wetlands, environment, smoking, nuclear energy, and pesticides, to name a few. For example, in agricultural policy, the Senate Committee on Agriculture, the U.S. DEPARTMENT OF AGRICULTURE, along with the farmers and agricultural chemical companies, were the three major sides in the iron triangle. Another example is nuclear energy, with the Joint Committee on Atomic Energy in Congress, the Atomic Energy Commission, and the nuclear energy companies. Today many of the iron triangles of policy making have been collapsed over time by outside challengers.

By the late 1900s, the notion of iron triangles was refined to explain the more complex interaction of how policy making takes place. Concepts like issue networks, policy entrepreneurs, and issue monopolies better describe the larger diversity of participants and fluidity of relationships among the participants involved in policy making. In these explanations, no one participant appears to totally control the policies and issues, and challenges can come from a variety of sources like national events, disasters, public opinion, the media, science and technology, competing congressional committees, and interest groups. Studies now focus more on how issues get onto the agenda and how these issues are framed and redefined over time to impact policy changes.

While today there are clearly some issue monopolies that can have more influence over policy than others, rarely can a traditional iron triangle manage to remain the dominant policymaking participant over long periods of time as it did in the past.

For more information

Baumgartner, Frank R., and Bryan D. Jones. *Agendas and Instability in American Politics*. Chicago: University of Chicago Press, 1993.

Heclo, Hugh. *Issue Networks and the Executive Establishment*. Washington, D.C.: American Enterprise Institute, 1978.

Tzoumis, Kelly. *Environmental Policymaking in Congress: The Roles of Issues Definitions in Wetlands, Great Lakes, and Wildlife Policies*. New York: Taylor and Francis, 2001.

Kelly Tzoumis

J

Jackson, Andrew (1767–1845) *seventh president of the United States*   Andrew Jackson, the seventh U.S. president, was famous for his political battles with Congress and for firmly establishing the spoils system.

Born of Scots-Irish ancestry on the Carolina frontier in 1767, Jackson had no formal education, family connections, or inherited wealth. He relied on his own wits and initiative to establish himself as a wealthy planter and lawyer in Tennessee, as a military hero in the War of 1812, and as an Indian fighter in the First Seminole War of 1817–18. Jackson embodied the new democratic spirit that had begun to develop during the 1820s and proved to be the most forceful and energetic president since Jefferson, dominating the presidency with the sheer force of his personality and aggressively expanding the powers of the office.

In his first term as president, Jackson sought to reform the appointment process for federal officeholders. He established the spoils system, providing government jobs to party loyalists while removing the appointees of the defeated party. In practice, however, Jackson's reform of the civil service was more style than substance, and only one-fifth of federal officeholders were replaced during his administration.

As president, Jackson won considerable support in the South and West as a result of his Indian policies, because pressures to remove Native Americans had been building there since the War of 1812. Jackson sided with the states and proposed to Congress that the Indians be forced to emigrate beyond the Mississippi River. Congress acted on Jackson's proposal in the Indian Removal Act of 1830, appropriating $500,000 to negotiate new treaties with the civilized tribes in which they would surrender their lands in the Southeast and relocate to present-day Oklahoma. Most Native Americans had left the eastern United States by 1838, and thousands died en route from cold, disease, and hunger, in what the Cherokee called the Trail of Tears.

In the nullification crisis of 1832, Jackson's policies precipitated the most serious sectional crisis since the Missouri debates of 1819–20. Southerners were angry over federal tariffs that had been increasing steadily since the 1810s. The outcry was loudest in South Carolina, where cotton prices remained low following the Panic of 1819 and where the tariffs were seen as an

In this cartoon, President Andrew Jackson refuses to renew the charter of the Bank of the United States. Pandemonium ensues amid "The Downfall of Mother Bank." (LIBRARY OF CONGRESS)

unconstitutional extension of national powers over the states, as well as a possible precursor to the federal emancipation of slaves.

The antitariff forces in South Carolina called themselves the nullifiers, a name derived from Vice President and South Carolinian John C. Calhoun's theory that a state had the sovereign power to declare an act of the national government null and inoperative within the borders of that state. With Calhoun's approval, a South Carolina convention in November 1832 nullified the federal tariffs of 1828 and 1832, and it was announced that South Carolina would no longer collect the federal tariff after 1 February 1833. In January 1833, Jackson asked for and Congress passed the Force Act, authorizing the president to put down nullification through military force

if necessary. To defuse the crisis, Jackson also supported a new tariff that would cut duties by half within two years, but his political enemies in Congress pushed through their own Compromise Tariff of 1833, lowering duties to 20 percent but extending the reductions over 10 years. Frightened by the Force Act and enticed by the Compromise Tariff, the South Carolina nullifiers backed down, but not before they had also nullified the Force Act.

The centerpiece of Jackson's presidency came in his battle against the Second Bank of the United States, which Jackson saw as a corrupt tool of Eastern financial interests. The Bank War erupted in 1832 when, presented with draft legislation to recharter the bank, Jackson chose to veto it instead. When Congress failed to override his veto, Jackson then set out to destroy the bank itself, ordering his treasury secretary to remove federal deposits from the bank in 1833.

By destroying the Second Bank of the United States and rejecting the attempts of South Carolina to nullify a national tariff, Jackson firmly established the Democratic Party as the enemy of special privilege, the friend of the common man, and the defender of the Union. Even when Jackson left the presidency, the Democratic Party was so identified with the interests of the people that it was able to elect Martin Van Buren to the presidency in 1836, even though he had none of Jackson's charisma and appeal.

For more information

Remini, Robert V. *The Life of Andrew Jackson.* New York: Perennial, 2001.

Schlesinger, Arthur M., Jr. *The Age of Jackson.* Boston: Little, Brown, 1988.

William D. Baker

job specialization   Job specialization is the assignment of duties and responsibilities in a bureaucracy based on the nature of work and possession of human competencies for its performance. The goal of job specialization is to produce the most efficient means to accomplish tasks.

Job specialization can be understood relative to its components: *job* and *specialization*. Before defining them, however, it is necessary to understand the design of work in formal organizations. Work is performed in flows through series of steps to produce outputs such as products and decisions. The steps are usually referred to as tasks and have various requisites for their performance. The latter may be hardware (computers or other machinery) or software (standard operating procedures, performance specifications, computer programs). Human requirements for performance of tasks are competencies. Human competencies are various areas of: knowledge (learned formally or by experience), skill

(e.g., physical or verbal), abilities (e.g., intelligence, aptitudes), and personal characteristics (e.g., motivation, attitudes). These are abbreviated as KSAPs.

In designing a process flow, use of machinery and technology are considered, along with tasks performed by humans. The tasks and related technology are grouped in clusters to create *positions.* A position is the work of one person that is specialized in the performance of its tasks. The position, with its component tasks and requisite KSAPs, becomes a formal element of the organization. Positions might be constructed from tasks of various flow processes with different outputs. Formalization and specialization of the position are usually reflected in a position description.

The following illustrates the flow of tasks in trials carried out by a person in the position of deputy city attorney: (1) in jury trials, waits for witnesses to arrive and the trial to commence; (2) prepares and delivers opening statements; (3) presents case (witnesses, evidence); (4) rebuts witnesses; (5) prepares and delivers closing argument; (6) waits for verdict or information requests from jury. These are a flow that results in a trial output (e.g., verdict). However, the deputy city attorney also performs tasks that are part of other flows, but which are combined in the attorney's position because of the specialized KSAPs required. These tasks are: reviews criminal cases filed and the prefiling documentation; decides on strategy of prosecution (e.g., charges); prepares legal opinions on civil, criminal, and municipal matters; reads professional materials (e.g., appeals, supreme court cases, law journals).

Jobs are groups of positions that perform the same, similar, or related tasks and require common KSAPs. While tasks and positions are the building blocks of organization and are most important in day-to-day management and performance of work, jobs simplify human resource management. They aid in recruitment, selection, assignment, and compensation of personnel. Large organizations may consist of tens of thousands of positions but as few as 100 different jobs. The job description is the counterpart (for jobs) of the position description. It provides the same type of information, but synthesized for many positions with the same job title. Often, language used to describe tasks in the job description is more generalized and referred to as duties and responsibilities. This is to facilitate inclusiveness of multiple tasks from many positions.

Job evaluation systems, such as position classification and factor point systems, are used to translate pay policies and market compensation information to the organization's pay plan. The pay matrix, usually consisting of pay grades and steps, is the basis of internal fairness in base rates of compensation in the organization. Jobs are valued or weighted differently, and all that are weighted the same are allocated to the same pay range in the matrix.

Recruitment, selection, and assignment of a small number of persons for essentially the same position usually use information from the position description. Both task and KSAP information can be used to assess qualifications of candidates or present employees. Recruitment and selection of large numbers of persons for the same job, as is often the case for police officer, may rely on the job description supplemented by studies to develop assessment strategies for various KSAPs.

Finally, job specialization is an important element of public administration for at least four reasons. First, it provides the legal-rational basis for design and standardization of work in public bureaucracies. Second, it formalizes authority and responsibility of the public work force. Third, it is an important basis for holding public servants accountable to the public. Last, it is the source of inferences about competencies required to perform the work of the public service.

For more information

Guest, Robert H. "Job Enlargement—A Revolution in Job Design." In *Classics of Personnel Management*, edited by Thomas H. Patten, Jr. Oak Park, Ill.: Moore Publishing, 1979, 291–297.

Siegel, Gilbert B. "Work Management and Job Evaluation Systems in a Government Environment." Chap. 28 in *Handbook of Human Resource Management in Government*, edited by Stephen E. Condrey. San Francisco: Jossey-Bass Publishers, 1998.

Siegel, Gilbert B., and Robert C. Myrtle. "Work-Systems Design." Chap. 4 in *Public Personnel Administration: Concepts and Practices*. Boston: Houghton Mifflin, 1985. Reprint, Lanham, Md.: University Press of America, 1989.

Gilbert B. Siegel

Johnson, Lyndon Baines (1908–1973) *36th president of the United States* Lyndon Baines Johnson, the 36th U.S. president, was responsible for one of the most ambitious domestic and social agendas of any American president. In just over five years in office, the Johnson administration was responsible for the passage and implementation of the Civil Rights Act of 1964, the Voting Rights Act of 1965, Medicare, Medicaid, and a myriad of housing, education, environmental, and consumer protection initiatives. However, his domestic successes were ultimately overwhelmed by an increasingly unpopular and seemingly intractable war in Vietnam that would ultimately destroy Johnson's presidency.

Born to a poor but politically prominent family in the Texas hill country, Johnson taught at a predominantly Hispanic public school before graduating from Southwest Texas Teachers College in 1930. Johnson worked as secretary to Democratic representative Richard M. Kleberg of Texas during 1931–34, and in 1935 he was appointed Texas's National Youth Administration Director, a post he would hold until 1937. In 1937, Johnson won a special congressional election for Texas's 10th District, a seat that he would hold until 1949. In 1948, Johnson defeated Governor Coke Stevenson in Texas's Democratic Senate primary by just 87 votes, earning him the nickname "Landslide Lyndon." Johnson would serve in the Senate until 1961, eventually rising to become the youngest Senate majority leader in

U.S. history in 1955. A leading candidate for the Democratic presidential nomination in 1960, Johnson was passed over at the party's national convention for Senator John F. Kennedy and was convinced instead to accept his party's vice-presidential nomination.

Johnson was unexpectedly catapulted into the presidency with the assassination of President Kennedy on 22 November 1963. As president, Johnson enunciated his vision of a Great Society, a broad legislative agenda encompassing the War on Poverty, civil rights legislation, MEDICAID AND MEDICARE, environmental protection, and consumer safety programs. In the election year of 1964, Johnson used the legislative skills he had honed over two decades in persuading Congress to pass a number of key pieces of legislation. The Economic Opportunity Act of 1964 established the Office of Economic Opportunity to administer and fund a number of new federal antipoverty programs, including the Job Corps, Volunteers in Service to America (VISTA), Head Start, Upward Bound, and government-subsidized work training, daycare, and legal assistance for the poor, while the Civil Rights Act of 1964 barred discrimination in employment and public accommodations and authorized the attorney general to initiate desegregation lawsuits.

In August, Johnson was nominated for president by acclamation at the Democratic National Convention in Atlantic City, New Jersey, and the following November he won 61 percent of the popular vote and 486 electoral votes to defeat the Republican candidate, Barry Goldwater, the greatest margin ever recorded in a contested presidential election. With strong Democratic majorities now in place in both the House and the Senate, Johnson had the political capital with which to realize his vision of a Great Society. In the years that followed, Johnson would pressure Congress into passing a variety of pieces of legislation, including the Voting Rights Act of 1965 (prohibiting literacy tests for voting and authorizing federal supervision of state election procedures), the Water Quality Act of 1965, the Clean Air Act of 1965, The Clean Water Restoration Act of 1966, the Fair Packaging and Labeling Act of 1966, The National Traffic Safety Act of 1966 (setting mandatory safety standards for automobile manufacturers), the Highway Safety Act of 1966, the Wholesome Meat Act of 1967, the Air Quality Act of 1967, and the Civil Rights Act of 1968 (barring discrimination in federal housing programs). Johnson also signed legislation creating the Medicare program to provide medical insurance for those 65 years of age and older, and the Medicaid program to provide medical benefits for the poor.

Johnson's narrow victory over Eugene McCarthy in the 1968 New Hampshire Democratic primary illustrated the degree to which public support for the war in Vietnam had dissipated, and in late March Johnson dramatically announced that he would not seek reelection in 1968.

For more information

Dallek, Robert. *Flawed Giant: Lyndon B. Johnson, 1960–73*. New York: Oxford University Press, 1998.

Goodwin, Doris Kearns. *Lyndon Johnson and the American Dream*. St. Martin's Press, 1991.

Unger, Irwin, and Debi Unger. *LBJ: A Life*. San Francisco: Wiley, 1999.

William D. Baker

Joint Chiefs of Staff The Joint Chiefs of Staff (JCS) are the senior military officers in the United States, consisting of a chairman, vice chairman, the army chief of staff, chief of naval operations, air force chief of staff, and Marine Corps commandant. A larger planning body known as the joint staff works for the JCS and assists their efforts.

The JCS was first assembled to coordinate military decision making for World War II and functioned as a military command headquarters for U.S. forces. The Joint Chiefs of Staff were removed from the chain of command in 1953 and have subsequently been responsible only for administration and planning. They lost further prestige with the GOLDWATER-NICHOLS DEPARTMENT OF DEFENSE REORGANIZATION ACT OF 1986, which made the chairman the sole adviser to the president on military matters, removing the service chiefs from the process.

The chairman of the JCS is by law the senior uniformed member of the armed forces, outranking all other generals and admirals but without command authority. The position was created in 1949 to improve interservice cooperation and was given voting power in 1958. The chairman is appointed by the president, subject to Senate confirmation, for a two-year term that begins on October 1 in odd-numbered years. He may be reappointed for an additional two terms, or a total of six years, during peacetime and without limit during wartime. The law also directs that the individual selected as chairman have previous experience as vice chairman, service chief, or commander of a unified or specified command, but it permits the president to waive this requirement if he deems it in the national interest.

The chairman is the chief adviser to the president and secretary of defense on all military matters. He is given statutory authority, subject to the authority and direction of the president and secretary of defense, over strategic direction and planning, preparedness, assessment, budgeting, doctrine, and training for the armed services. He is also directed to prepare a report for the secretary of defense on the roles and missions of the armed forces "not less than once every three years." The report focuses on changing threats, unnecessary duplication within the military, and changes in technology that can be applied to warfare.

Among the more notable chairmen were General Omar Bradley (1949–53), the first chairman, and General Colin Powell (1989–93), who was the first African-American chairman and also the youngest person ever appointed to that office.

For more information

Goldwater-Nichols Department of Defense Reorganization Act of 1986. Public Law 99-433. Oct. 1, 1986. 100 Stat. 992.

Lederman, Gordon Nathaniel, and Sam Nunn. *Reorganizing the Joint Chiefs of Staff: The Goldwater-Nichols Act of 1986.* Westport, Ct.: Greenwood, 1999.

Snow, Donald M., and Eugene Brown. *United States Foreign Policy: Politics beyond the Water's Edge,* 2d ed. New York: Bedford/St. Martin's, 2000.

James H. Joyner, Jr.

judicial review of administrative action

Judicial review of administrative action is the process by which the courts examine agency decisions, including rule making and adjudications, to ensure that they comply with standards and procedures established by law.

Administrative agencies are subject to restraint by all three constitutional branches of government. Legislatures may control agencies through oversight, policy direction, and budgetary powers, while the executive generally does so through appointments and executive orders. These political controls are proactive, setting an agency's future direction. In contrast, courts are reactive institutions that limit agency action by reviewing decisions after they have been made. Judicial review of administrative action is limited by the existence of internal appeals processes within many agencies, the necessity of an aggrieved party, the need for a grievance recognized by the law, the considerable time and expense involved, and legal restrictions on courts' jurisdiction over certain types of administrative action. Nevertheless, the courts remain an essential check on the discretion of administrators and set many of the standards that guide their work.

The courts do not consciously or systematically set policy, but they review agency action to ensure that it has complied with the requirements established by the relevant legal regimes.

Those requirements are drawn from a variety of sources, including the Constitution, statutes, the agency's published regulations, and the agency's internal procedures and guidelines; in addition, courts often consider the basic rationality of an administrative rule or the evidence supporting an administrative order. The constitutional issues in judicial review may concern whether the agency is exercising power that properly belongs to the branch in which the agency is housed. For example, executive branch agencies may not exercise legislative powers without general guidelines first established by the legislature, nor may legislative agencies possess enforcement powers. More commonly, constitutional questions are raised when an action allegedly contravenes a person's constitutional rights established in case law, such as equal protection or due process.

Courts look to statutes to determine whether administrators have acted within their proper range of authority, whether proper procedures were followed, and whether the agency has properly interpreted its legislative mandate. Because agencies are extraconstitutional, they derive all of their authority from the legislation that established them or authorized the programs that they administer. Courts must consider whether the legislature has properly delegated authority to the agency, whether the agency action falls within the sphere of that delegation, and whether the procedures required by statute have been observed. In reviewing administrative actions, the courts check to ensure that the agency has interpreted the statute authorizing its activities in a reasonable manner and has not acted in an "arbitrary or capricious" manner.

A court may also review any agency action to ensure that its decision is based on "substantial evidence." When an aggrieved party litigates a decision, the court may review the decision to ensure that it was made in a deliberate manner based on all the information on the record and was not based on insufficient information or information that was not properly entered into the record. However, courts generally defer to agency judgments that are based on technical expertise or administrative experience, and they provide administrators with substantial discretion to choose different policies or procedures. Although the standard of review for whether the ultimate decision is reasonable and based on substantial evidence does not change according to whether the agency uses more or less formal proceedings, the degree of formality affects the extensiveness of the record produced and the due process to which parties may be entitled.

For more information

Breyer, Stephen. "Judicial Review of Questions of Law and Policy." *Administrative Law Review* 38 (1986): 363–398.

Chevron v. Natural Resources Defense Council, 467 U.S. 837 (1984).

Schuck, Peter, and E. Donald Elliott. "To the Chevron Station: An Empirical Study of Federal Administrative Law." *Duke Law Journal* 1990 (1990): 984–1077.

Daniel Levin

jurisdiction, governments, and the Internet

Jurisdiction refers to the power of a government or one of its agents (e.g., a court) to exercise legal authority. Given that the Internet flows readily across state and national boundaries, it is often difficult to determine which of many possible laws may apply.

It is often difficult to locate a content provider. Even when the location is determined, the digital nature of the Internet means that a business can shift locations in a matter of hours. Locating a server is not the same thing as finding the legal identity behind the machine. At the same time, allowing Internet users to sue content providers in the local court of each user means that the content provider can be sued in multiple jurisdictions at the same time for essentially the same act.

All that can be said for the moment is that the law on these issues is unsettled. Individual governments are waiting on international developments. These jurisdictional issues must be resolved soon. Otherwise they will threaten the viability of online commerce. As international transactions increase, the present case-by-case approach will prove to be dysfunctional. Ebay, for example, has had to work closely with authorities in each jurisdiction to ensure that its online auction complies with local laws. This has worked, but it has been very time consuming.

Most of the reported cases involving jurisdiction in an Internet environment emanate from the United States. U.S. courts have traditionally applied a three-part analysis to establish jurisdiction. There must be sufficient (at least minimum) contacts with the forum, or the defendant must have purposely availed itself of the benefits of conducting business in the forum. The claim must have arisen out of these contacts; and the exercise of jurisdiction must be reasonable.

The problem is that these traditional jurisdictional tests are proving to be outmoded. The much-cited sliding-scale test proposed in *Zippo Manufacturing v. Zipo Dot Com Inc.* (952 F.Supp. 1119 [WD Pa 1997]) is seen by many as no longer workable. In that case the court based its finding of jurisdiction on whether the site was "active" or "passive."

The problem with the active-versus-passive-site test is that, with modern technology, a site that looks active may be passive, whereas a site that looks passive may be active. Perhaps a better test is the "target" test. If the activities of the website were "targeted" at a particular jurisdiction, then jurisdiction should be found. Other commentators point to the importance of contract provisions that limit the site's application to a particular jurisdiction, for example by a click agreement executed by users of the site. Unfortunately, it is not clear that legal authorities in all jurisdictions would recognize the validity of such contractual provisions. Yet another solution may be found in the development and adoption of technologies that would limit a site's exposure to particular geographic boundaries.

Countries are thus struggling with the question of whose law will apply to these transactions. The fear for international business is that countries will tend to take an "expansive" view that will protect their national interests in the short term but harm the overall viability of global trade by making it less certain in legal outcome and more expensive to comply. This fear is heightened by the passage of the Brussels regulation, which is operational from March of 2002. As a "regulation" this new jurisdictional rule will be binding on all countries. This contrasts with a "convention," which is negotiated between the countries, or a "directive," which is implemented individually by each member state. The Brussels regulation provides that the courts of the consumer's home country will have jurisdiction over a foreign defendant if the latter "pursues commercial or professional activities in the Member State of the consumer's domicile or, by any means directs such activities to the Member State . . . and the contract falls within the scope of such activities."

In light of these developments, what will have to emerge is an international treaty and perhaps some sort of administrative structure to handle such issues. Such a world body would require countries to be less sensitive to their own sovereignty and more sensitive to the need to have the appropriate infrastructure to facilitate world trade. Yet, a loss of control could mean a loss of revenue for particular countries.

For more information

American Bar Association. Cyberspace Law Committee and Business Law Section Report. "Achieving Legal and Business Order in Cyberspace." Available online. URL: http://www.abanet.org/buslaw/cyber.

"Hague Convention on Jurisdiction and the Recognition and Enforcement of Foreign Judgments in Civil and Commercial Matters." Available online. URL: http://www.hcch.net/e/workprog/judgm. html.

Eugene Clark

K

Keynesianism Keynesianism refers to economic theory and policies that follow from the teachings of John Maynard Keynes, a famous British economist who taught at Cambridge University in England.

The theory that is referred to as Keynesian theory in macroeconomics was a response to the failure of the macroeconomic system following the Great Depression (where financial markets around the world collapsed, sending the economy into a severe and lengthy period of depressed economic activity). Keynes advanced his theories in the book *The General Theory of Employment, Interest, and Money* (1936) that accounted for situations of protracted depressed economic activity.

Keynes rejected the current Classical theory, which held for a self-adjusting or self-regulating economic system that assumed fully flexible prices and wages. His theory accounted for price or wage "stickiness," whereby prices and wages did not automatically adjust on their own. Something caused them to be inflexible or rigid or sticky. This critical assumption could then cause an aggregate economy to "hang up," resulting in low economic activity accompanied by unnatural levels of unemployment. The economy would linger at this state (or equilibrium) until all prices and wages slowly adjusted. After some time, the economy would return to a balance characterized by high levels of economic growth and low levels of unemployment.

Research in the past three decades based on Keynesian Macro Theory is referred to as New Keynesian Macro Theory and revolves around the basic idea of a price or wage rigidity that can culminate in effects felt at aggregate or macroeconomic levels. Some examples involve the presence of wage/labor contracts that cause wages (nominal wages, or wages unadjusted by inflation) to change slowly, depending on the time period the contract covers, e.g., every three years. The idea here is that if large employers use labor contracts, it is possible that wages in these contracts will not change quickly and will not change at the same time. So there is a period of slow adjustment in wage rates, depending on economic activity.

In addition, producers may not change prices on a regular basis but may do so a few times each year. The idea here is that price changes for large firms that produce many products take time and cost money. Constant price changes are also hard to coordinate throughout all product lines and store outlets. Catalog companies, such as L. L. Bean, announce prices in their fall catalog, for example, but do not change the price during the fall if the economy expands or contracts. This is the same for automobile manufacturers and most firms. Hence, prices are also slow to change and only change if product lines do not sell or if depressed economic activity reduces the discretionary income of individuals, among other reasons. This slow response to changes in both wages and prices conforms to the ideas of Keynes and can account for macroeconomic systems that do not automatically adjust.

For more information

Eklund, R. B., Jr., and R. D. Tollison. *Macroeconomics: Private Markets and Public Choice.* Reading, Mass.: Addison-Wesley Longman, 1997.

Keynes, J. M. *The General Theory of Employment, Interest, and Money.* London: Macmillan, 1936.

Douglas D. Ofiara

L

law Law is derived from the idea that a society or nation needs to protect the rights of its citizens. The form of that protection is theoretically based on the concept of a social contract by which the members of the society agree to abide. That is, we must provide a common set of rules that will assure, as much as possible, equality and justice.

The current structure of the law centers on our system of nation-states and international organizations. A rule of conduct is developed for and accepted by these governing authorities and enforced by court systems. This, however, has not always been the case. Law has not always been tied to particular territories. Law has also been associated with clans, tribes, and nations of people. Among early nomadic tribes, rules of law only applied to those within the tribe. For instance, there would not necessarily be any rule prohibiting stealing from someone outside of the tribe. As modern territorial boundaries began to be set, laws were recognized as having legitimacy within these borders. Another area of development has been international law that helps define the actions of the governments of these nation-states.

Essentially, the law governs relations between peoples and governments and informs them of the code of conduct in advance. Democratic governments distinguish themselves by implementing a system of law. In the United States people take pride that the "rule of law" governs our actions, in opposition to the "rule of man" imposed by totalitarian regimes. These regimes provide no consistency in the law but rather depend on the judgment or whim of the current ruler.

Law can be derived from myriad sources, including:

Constitutions—the U.S. Constitution provides the general rights and liberties that U.S. citizens enjoy. Constitutional law provides vague guidelines that often require judicial interpretation. Because context matters, the courts must provide specific guidelines as to the application of these rights. For instance, the exercise of free speech cannot endanger others. The time, place, and manner of free speech rights have been defined by the courts.

Statutes—legislative bodies at all levels of government are responsible for writing and implementing statutory law. The idea of representative democracy is best symbolized by our legislative branches. The "will of the people" is represented in the statutes passed by these bodies. However, under a system of law, the popular sentiment cannot override the basic principles of the law. That is why in the United States, statutory law cannot violate the U.S. Constitution.

Judicial decisions—also referred to as common law or judge-made law. When the judicial branch interprets the law, that interpretation sets a standard known as legal precedent. Future courts abide by the precedent as a way of providing consistency in the law.

Administrative rules—most of the legal decisions in the United States are made by bureaucrats. Administrative law refers to the complex system of rules and regulations that government agencies have developed for providing public services.

For more information

Friedman, Lawrence W. *A History of American Law,* 2d ed. New York: Simon and Schuster, 1985.

Richard P. Davis

Law Enforcement Assistance Act   The Law Enforcement Assistance Act (LEAA) was created as a part of the 1968 Safe Streets and Crime Control Act. Impetus for the passage of the act was the report *Challenge of Crime in a Free Society* produced by the President's Commission on Crime and Administration of Justice in 1967.

The LEAA worked with a broad mandate to foster system change and improve law enforcement effort through federal assistance and contributions to leadership. Four areas of emphasis were undertaken by the LEAA. The first was the effort to improve comprehensive criminal-justice planning at the state level. Second was the provision of financial and technical assistance to criminal-justice agencies to strengthen

their operations. The third area was the conduct of program evaluations and research and developmental project grants to improve the operations of criminal-justice agencies. The fourth area was to develop new methods and activities that could improve the ability of state and local governments to reduce crime, apprehend and rehabilitate offenders.

Over its 14-year history the LEAA provided approximately $7.5 billion to state, local, and county law enforcement agencies to upgrade their operations. LEAA funds also were spent to provide universities and community colleges with funds to establish criminal-justice programs to train future public safety personnel. Funds were also granted to allow colleges and universities to provide in-service training and college degrees to officers who were employed by criminal-justice agencies.

There were a number of significant programs that were started with the assistance of the LEAA, including:

Career criminal programs that focused on the prosecution of repeat offenders

Improvements in the management of prosecutor's offices

STING programs that created police-operated fencing operations where burglars and thieves would "fence" their stolen goods and later be apprehended

Treatment Alternatives to Street Crime (TASC) drug and alcohol treatment programs designed to reduce recidivism The LEAA also contributed to a significant change in the culture of law enforcement and criminal justice. Professional criminal justice managers now expect to be able to find research on problems, collaborate on new ideas and emerging issues that confront them, and find funding sources to develop new initiatives.

The LEAA was discontinued due to lack of funding by Congress in 1982. The reasons were many and complex, but several stand out. First, in spite of the large investment of federal dollars, the crime rates continued to rise. Second, while many of the LEAA programs were exceptionally well administered, there were some perceived abuses by agencies that were more interested in technology and military-style equipment, or that failed to deliver expected performance reports or research results.

In spite of the demise of the LEAA, several federal programs continue to provide similar services. The Byrne Grant program of the Department of Justice provides states with funds for criminal-justice improvement. The Office of Justice Assistance and the Office of Justice Programs of the Department of Justice continue to provide a number of program and research grants, and publish a large volume of research findings and reports for the use of academics, criminal-justice and government agencies, and the general public.

For more information

Feeley, Malcolm, and Austin Sarat. *The Policy Dilemma: Federal Crime Policy and the Law Enforcement Assistance Administration, 1968–1978.* Minneapolis: University of Minnesota Press, 1980.

Bruce L. Bikle

leadership The concept of leadership can be thought of as the ability or capacity of an individual to influence others to take some type of action. In the context of an organization, leadership is based on the ability of an individual with power or authority to influence people in work units to achieve certain organizational goals and objectives. Leadership can also be thought of as the ability to inspire a shared vision among a group of individuals, to enlist the support of others to help make projects happen, to set standards by personal example, and to encourage and reward success.

A number of theories have been developed to determine the characteristics or traits that make an individual an effective and successful leader. Among the first theories that tried to explain leadership was the idea that all successful leaders share a group of common traits or personal characteristics that are common among them. These traits included physical attributes such as height, intellectual characteristics such as academic achievement, and personality characteristics such as determination and loyalty. While a number of important traits characterizing leaders were identified as a result of this research, ultimately it was recognized that there are no traits universally shared by all leaders. Leaders come in all shapes and sizes.

A number of other leadership theories have been advanced that attempt to describe leadership along several other dimensions. These include aspects such as the concern for relationships with subordinates, emphasis on productivity and performance, the relationship between leadership style and the organizational setting, and the balance between concern for people and concern for production. Two ideas currently receiving a substantial amount of attention include transformational leadership and the relationship between leadership and organizational culture.

Transformational leaders have the ability to motivate others toward the achievement of higher aspirations or goals for the benefit of a community or political cause beyond their own self-interests as members of a particular group or organization. Transformational leadership is based on a desire and capacity to move individuals in organizations and groups to higher goals by working within the core values or cultures of their organizations. Mother Teresa and Martin Luther King are examples of transformational leaders who sought not only support from individuals, but also called for a new society, one based on fairness, compassion, and service. Many individuals inspired by their efforts contributed time, resources, and effort to these ideas. Even with their deaths, their visions continue to this day throughout the world.

Transformational leaders also place a strong emphasis on managing certain aspects of culture within their organizations. Leaders can create or change culture, enhance culture, as well as improve culture in organizations. The development of an effective culture is linked to key strategies, including the encouragement of certain values and behaviors, the use of criteria for granting awards, developing new work processes to reflect new cultural standards, and the development of formal value statements promoting the organization's principles. In today's modern organization, effective leadership emphasizes the importance of learning, communication, information sharing, participatory decision making, flexibility, and the commitment to an organizational vision.

For more information

Hickman, G. R., ed. *Leading Organizations: Perspectives for a New Era.* Thousand Oaks, Calif.: Sage Publications, 1998.

Dahlia Bradshaw Lynn

Legal Services Corporation   The Legal Services Corporation is funded by the federal government to ensure access to the civil legal system for individuals who cannot afford to hire an attorney.

This private nonprofit corporation was established in 1974 when Congress passed the Legal Services Corporation Act, 42 U.S.C. §2996 et seq. The Legal Services Corporation (LSC) funds state and local offices that provide a variety of legal services to individuals across the country. Only individuals with household incomes that are less than 125 percent of the poverty threshold are eligible for representation by such offices. The policy underlying the creation of LSC is that legal services are a basic right to which everyone is entitled. The LSC only provides civil legal services because the Fifth Amendment already acts as a guarantee that indigent criminal defendants will be provided an attorney.

The LSC is governed by an 11-member board of directors. The board members are appointed by the president of the United States, and the board is required to be nonpartisan in that no more than six board members can be from the same political party. From its inception through the mid-1990s, LSC-funded organizations began representing clients in a number of high-profile class-action lawsuits that challenged actions of state, local, and federal government. Consequently, the LSC became a target of funding cuts and even faced the possibility of receiving zero federal funding in 1996. As a result of significant funding cuts, the LSC has scaled back its controversial challenges and now focuses on more essential legal services. As a result, a majority of the agency's current clients are women seeking restraining orders to protect them from abusers.

Because the Legal Services Corporation is funded by the federal government, there have always been restrictions on the actions of the state and local organizations funded by it. For example, legal services offices are prohibited from lobbying; using funding to support political candidates; accepting legal fees; participating in litigation involving nontherapeutic abortions, secondary school desegregation, military desertion, or violations of the selective service statute; and participating in class-action lawsuits unless specifically authorized by the corporation. Such restrictions illustrate the tension between the policy of providing legal services for those who cannot afford their own attorney and the idea that there are some things tax money should not be used to fund. But there are limits on the restrictions that Congress can place on the LSC. For example, in 1996, Congress prohibited the LSC from funding litigation that had the purpose of challenging existing welfare law. However, the Supreme Court held that prohibition unconstitutional because it violated the First Amendment rights of LSC attorneys and clients. See *Legal Services Corporation v. Velasquez,* 531 U.S. 533 (2001).

For more information

Houseman, Alan W. "Civil Legal Assistance for the 21st Century: Achieving Equal Justice for All."

Center for Law and Social Policy. Available online. URL: http://www.clasp.org.

Palmer, Elizabeth A. "Legal Services Corporation's Future Appears Secure, Agency's GOP Detractors Concede." *CQ Weekly* 59, no. 24 (16 June 2001).

Martha M. Lafferty

legislative oversight   Legislative oversight is a process, employed by state legislatures and Congress, to ensure that governmental agencies carry out the law and administer programs in a way that conforms with legislative intent.

This monitoring function is increasingly important at the federal level as Congress continues the trend of delegating authority to the executive branch. Legislatures often pass laws that are deliberately vague or general. To carry out these laws, governmental agencies often must draft rules and regulations that clarify the meaning of laws or that provide day-to-day guidelines on how to manage programs established by statutes. One purpose of legislative oversight is to ensure that government is held accountable for enforcing the spirit and letter of the law. Oversight consumes a lot of legislative time and energy. A focus on congressional oversight reveals a variety of oversight tools.

Congress can pass laws to give it oversight leverage. The Government Performance and Results Act of 1993, for example, was passed by Congress to promote cost-effective federal spending by requiring agencies to submit annual performance plans and reports, thus pressuring agencies to implement their goals within a specific time frame. Also, the Congressional Review Act of 1996 allows members of Congress to review and disapprove of executive agency rules and regulations. Used since 1933, the legislative veto is yet another way for one or both houses of Congress to block executive action. The legislative veto is a statutory enactment that allows the president or executive agencies to take actions that may later be approved or rejected by one or both houses of Congress.

Other types of oversight involve an investigative role. Frequently, Congress launches investigations probing for governmental waste, fraud, inefficiency, and corruption. Among the most famous were the Teapot Dome inquiry (1923), the Watergate hearings (1973–74), the Iran-contra investigation (1987), and the 1997–98 investigation of violations of campaign finance laws. As part of these investigations, hearings are held, which allow members of Congress to ask detailed, sometimes embarrassing questions of agency directors.

The power of the purse is an important legislative oversight tool. Congress can cut, bar spending, or reduce funding for governmental agencies. This may lead to a reduction in staff for the agencies, prevent agencies from carrying out certain functions, or even curtail their programs. In June 2000, for instance, Congress passed legislation that prohibited the OCCUPATIONAL SAFETY AND HEALTH ADMINISTRATION (OSHA) from using federal moneys to formulate new ergonomics regulations that seek to prevent repetitive-motion injuries among workers. After the space shuttle *Challenger* explosion of 1986, NASA's budget was cut as members of Congress saw firsthand the problems in shuttle safety. At the same time, Congress can also express approval of an agency by increasing its budget, sometimes beyond what the administration requested, such as the 2002 increase in national defense spending, which went far above President George W. Bush's request. The appropriations process is probably the most effective legislative oversight mechanism.

The inspectors general offices, created by Congress in 1978, provide another means of oversight. The inspectors general report directly to Congress on their attempts to end waste, fraud, and abuse. Inspectors general meet often with legislative officials and are often asked to conduct specific audits and investigations. Another watchdog agency, the GENERAL ACCOUNTING OFFICE (GAO), actually conducts audits and investigates executive agencies at the request of members of Congress. For example, a 2000 GAO report highlighted 61 federal programs that could be reduced in scope or terminated to save money.

The U.S. Senate confirmation process of high-ranking presidential appointees provides the Senate a direct oversight role. For instance, in 2001, two Defense Department nominees were placed on hold as key Republican senators perceived that Defense Secretary Donald H. Rumsfeld was unresponsive to the queries of congressional leaders. The Senate confirmation may inquire into the qualifications, independence, and policy predispositions of presidential appointees to the Cabinet and the federal judiciary. Some confirmation hearings have been very controversial, such as the nominations of Robert H. Bork (1987) and Clarence Thomas (1991) to the U.S. Supreme Court. The confirmation hearings may result in a public record of an appointee's policy stances, for which they may also be held to account at a later date.

Legislative oversight occurs informally on an everyday basis. Legislators may use telephone calls, letters, personal contacts, and informal understandings to influence administrative decisions and to formulate their statements in committee reports, hearings, and debates. A variety of factors heighten interest in legislative oversight, such as public and elected-official skepticism toward government and its ability to function effectively; the growth of government programs and regulations that affect the lives of citizens, who in turn inform elected officials of any governmental red tape they may encounter; more investigative reporting by mainstream and fringe media organizations; increased public distrust of government in the wake of abuses of power by governmental officials; and the increased availability of resources that permit greater scrutiny of governmental activities. Even with these factors, oversight is often viewed as counterproductive or unsystematic. It can produce a blame game in which no one takes responsibility when things go wrong. No one, for

example, stepped up to take responsibility for the savings and loan crisis in the 1980s. Much finger-pointing occurred and oversight existed, but to no avail—the savings and loan industry bailout had to go forward and imposed great costs on American taxpayers. Oversight undoubtedly will continue. The ability of legislatures to use it effectively is debatable.

For more information

Davidson, Roger H., and Walter J. Oleszek. *Congress and Its Members*. Washington, D.C.: CQ Press, 2002.

Oleszek, Walter J. *Congressional Procedures and the Policy Process*. Washington, D.C.: CQ Press, 2001.

Ruth Ann Strickland

legislative veto   The legislative veto is a procedure employed by one or both houses of Congress requiring executive agencies to submit their regulations or actions for approval. Often included in a bill, legislative vetoes state that before executive branch actions, regulations, or decisions take effect, they can be blocked or modified by one or both houses of Congress by a majority vote after a designated period of time has elapsed. As a congressional oversight mechanism, the legislative veto is appealing because it allows Congress a second chance to review executive actions and to keep federal administrators in touch with their concerns and interests. At the same time, executive agencies appreciate the procedure because it gives them more decision-making authority than they might otherwise have.

The legislative veto was first exercised in 1932, when Congress responded to President Herbert Hoover's request for authority to reorganize the national administrative system by giving itself the legislative veto power. During the 1960s and 1970s, Congress used the legislative veto in over 200 laws. It became particularly popular in the 1970s as Congress sought to reassert itself after the Watergate scandal and the Vietnam War. Members of Congress felt compelled to place more controls on the discretion of the executive branch. Attempting to confront what some called the "imperial presidency," Congress used the legislative veto to regain power it may have lost by delegating authority to the executive branch. In the 1970s, a variety of agencies were subjected to legislative veto, including the FEDERAL TRADE COMMISSION, the National Highway Traffic and Safety Administration, and the FOOD AND DRUG ADMINISTRATION. Some questioned whether the legislative veto was an effective mechanism for controlling executive agency discretion, claiming that it was merely symbolic and not a substitute for periodic oversight or for congressional policy guidance to agencies. Others have argued that legislative vetoes were most helpful in generating congressional consensus behind statutes already enacted into law, such as consumer protection laws.

In the early 1980s, the U.S. Supreme Court, in *IMMIGRATION AND NATURALIZATION SERVICE V. CHADA* 462 U.S. 919 (1983), struck down the legislative veto as unconstitutional, claiming that it violated the principle of separation of powers between the legislative and executive branches. In *Chadha*, the Supreme Court specifically struck down a statute that allowed one house of Congress to veto a decision of the Immigration and Naturalization Service allowing a deportable alien to stay in the United States. Holding that a bill requires passage by a majority of both houses of Congress, the Court stated that the legislative veto exercised in *Chadha* violated the principle of bicameralism. The Court also ruled that legislation passed by both houses of Congress should be presented to the president for his signature or veto. Despite this Supreme Court ruling, the legislative veto is still in use. Between 1983 and the end of the 105th Congress, more than 400 new legislative veto provisions were enacted into law. Its use continues because both branches—executive and legislative—see it in their best interests. The executive agencies get some flexibility when implementing laws, while Congress gets to exercise authority over executive actions, if it chooses. This sense of mutual benefit has probably prevented other challenges that might have emerged over the legislative veto.

For more information

Craig, Barbara Hinkson. *Chadha: The Story of an Epic Constitutional Struggle.* New York and Oxford: Oxford University Press, 1988.

Foreman, Christopher H., Jr. *Signals from the Hill: Congressional Oversight and the Challenge of Social Regulation.* New Haven and London: Yale University Press, 1988.

Korn, Jessica. *The Power of Separation: American Constitutionalism and the Myth of the Legislative Veto.* Princeton, N.J.: Princeton University Press, 1996.

Ruth Ann Strickland

Lincoln, Abraham (1809–1865) *16th president of the United States*   Abraham Lincoln was the 16th U.S. president and shepherded the nation through its most devastating crisis, the American Civil War, profoundly expanding the powers of the office in the process.

Born in 1809 to an illiterate farmer in Hardin County, Kentucky, Lincoln grew up poor in Kentucky and Indiana before his family settled in Illinois when Lincoln was a young man. Lincoln had very little formal schooling and was largely self-educated. He worked at a number of jobs as a young man—Mississippi River flatboat operator, general store clerk, postmaster—before being admitted to the state bar and establishing a law practice in Springfield, Illinois, in 1836. He enlisted in the Illinois militia and was elected a captain during the 1832 Black Hawk War, but he never saw combat.

After an unsuccessful race in 1832, Lincoln was elected to the Illinois state legislature as a Whig in 1834, where he served until 1842. He was elected to the U.S. House of Representatives in 1846, where he was a vocal opponent of the Polk administration's Mexican War and served on the Post Office and Post Roads Committee and the War Department Expenditures Committee. However, discouraged by his lack of influence in Washington, Lincoln returned to Springfield in 1849 and resumed his law practice after just one term in Congress.

His political career seemingly over, Lincoln emerged as one of the most successful corporate lawyers in Illinois during the early 1850s. However, the nation's increasing polarization over the issue of slavery eventually drew Lincoln back into the political realm. He was elected to the state legislature again in 1854 but chose instead to mount an unsuccessful campaign for the Senate. Strongly opposed to the extension of slavery into the territories, Lincoln abandoned the divided Whig party for the new Republican party in 1856. He was considered but passed over for the Republican vice-presidential nomination in 1856.

In 1858, Lincoln won his party's nomination to challenge Illinois's Democratic senator Stephen Douglas, a powerful national figure who had spearheaded the controversial Kansas-Nebraska Act, which had for the first time opened up the territories to slavery. Although Douglas ultimately won reelection, Lincoln garnered national attention as a result of an unprecedented series of debates between the two candidates over the issues of the day, primarily the spread of slavery. When the Republicans held their national convention to select a presidential candidate in Chicago in 1860, Lincoln emerged as the favorite-son candidate, ultimately defeating several well-known and better qualified hopefuls to win the nomination.

With the Democratic Party divided into Northern and Southern wings, and with a third-party candidate drawing votes from border states, Lincoln won 180 electoral votes and 40 percent of the popular vote, the smallest percentage of the popular vote ever garnered by a successful presidential candidate. In the Deep South, where Lincoln's name had not even appeared on ballots, the election of the Republican ticket was met with scorn and outrage. Before Lincoln could even take office, South Carolina seceded

from the Union, followed by Alabama, Georgia, Louisiana, Mississippi, and Texas, and in February 1861, the rebellious states formed the Confederate States of America with former Mississippi senator Jefferson Davis as its president. Following South Carolina's attack on the federal installation at Fort Sumter in Charleston harbor, the border states of Virginia, Tennessee, and Arkansas seceded as well, and the Civil War had begun.

Despite its superiority in population and industrial might, the North fared poorly during the first two years of the war, and Lincoln grew increasingly frustrated with the quality and hesitancy of his generals. The South, on the other hand, had many experienced and effective military leaders, as well as the advantage of fighting a largely defensive campaign on its own territory. Eventually, however, the North's advantages proved decisive, and the Confederacy, diplomatically isolated and unable to secure the supplies and armaments necessary to continue the war, surrendered at Appomattox Courthouse in Virginia in April 1865.

In his efforts to preserve the Union, Lincoln expanded the powers of the presidency as no previous chief executive ever had, unilaterally expanding the size of the army, spending unappropriated funds from the U.S. Treasury, restricting civil liberties, and suspending the writ of habeas corpus in areas under military jurisdiction. In September 1862, Lincoln issued the Emancipation Proclamation, freeing slaves in those states still at war on 1 January 1863, although it was not clear that he had that constitutional authority as president. Although Congress largely approved of Lincoln's exercise of emergency powers after the fact, the Supreme Court would rule in *ex parte Milligan* (1866) that his use of military tribunals in areas not under military rule was unconstitutional. The war did not consume all of the administration's attention, however. Major pieces of legislation adopted during the Lincoln presidency included the Homestead Act (1862), granting 160 acres of public lands to those willing to settle and improve it for five years, and the Morrill Act (1862), appropriating public lands to the state to finance agricultural and mechanical-arts colleges.

With the war drawing to a close, Lincoln defeated former Union general George McClellan to win reelection in 1864, and in his second inaugural address in April 1865 he called for national reconciliation with the conquered South. However, just a week after the Confederate surrender at Appomattox, Lincoln was fatally wounded by a Southern sympathizer at Ford's Theater in Washington, D.C. He died the following morning, April 19, 1865.

For more information

Donald, David Herbert. *Lincoln.* New York: Touchstone, 1996.

McPherson, James M. *Abraham Lincoln and the Second American Revolution.* New York: Oxford University Press, 1992.

Oates, Stephen B. *With Malice toward None: A Life of Abraham Lincoln.* New York: Perennial, 1994.

William D. Baker

Lindblom, Charles E. (1917–) *political scientist, economist*   Charles Lindblom is a professor of economics who is most noted in public administration circles for his 1959 article "The Science of 'Muddling Through,'" which challenged the rational-comprehensive method of decision making by suggesting that decision makers instead perform a series of successive limited comparisons among a relatively small number of alternatives.

Building on the concepts introduced by HERBERT SIMON, Lindblom argued that decision makers ordinarily make small incremental decisions that are largely influenced by short-term political forces because (1) all of the information affecting a particular decision is rarely, if ever, available, and (2) humans would lack the capacity to process it even if it were.

During the 1950s, Lindblom, along with other members of the Yale school of political science, began to study how decision makers actually behaved as opposed to how they were supposed to behave. This new approach to research led to the development of a school of thought that challenged the prevailing philosophies of decision making as being rational-based and paved the road to modern decision theory. Lindblom contended that decision makers are heavily influenced by the environmental factors surrounding decisions and, along with Herbert Simon, developed the notion of incremental adjustment—where policy makers choose among alternatives that are similar and vary only slightly.

In his most notable publication "The Science of 'Muddling Through,'" Lindblom compares the rational-comprehensive method to successive limited comparison using the analogy of roots to branches, with the former as roots and the latter as branches. Lindblom refers to the rational-comprehensive method as roots because this approach "starts from scratch" by considering all of the relevant factors affecting a given decision. Successive limited comparisons, on the other hand, are like branches because they do not require the decision maker to start at the beginning when making a decision.

Lindblom's approach to decision making can be illustrated by considering the example of a park district administrator who has been charged with the responsibility of implementing a new after-school program for children in the community. According to the rational-comprehensive approach, she should decide what factors might be important in a program such as this, make a list of all of the potential programs that could contain these factors, assign costs and benefits to all of the factors, and select the program that maximizes benefits while minimizing costs. In other words, she should visualize all of the potential alternatives and then rank them in terms of costs and benefits. Lindblom on the other hand, would expect her to look at two or three viable alternatives—perhaps programs that are currently operating in other nearby park districts—and compare them with each other. Thus the administrator would only consider a small number of alternatives, eventually selecting the one that best met the needs of the community.

Lindblom has been criticized for downplaying the importance of decision making by referring to it as "muddling through." Critics have also taken issue with Lindblom and other incrementalists placing decision theory at the center of public administration. Nonetheless, Lindblom's ideas remain influential in public administration circles and he is often associated with his pragmatic insight: that synoptic analysis may be preferred in theory, but incremental adjustment is more prevalent in practice.

For more information

Lindblom, Charles E. "The Science of 'Muddling Through.'" *Public Administration Review* 18 (winter 1959): 1.

Lindblom, Charles E., and Edward J. Woodhouse. *The Policy-Making Process.* Englewood Cliffs, N.J.: Prentice Hall, 1992.

Jonathan Greenblatt

lobbying Lobbying is the attempt to influence legislation by persuading policy makers to support a particular position.

The term *lobbying* has its origins in 17th-century England, where advocates would plead their cases in informal meetings with members of Parliament in the large antechamber, or lobby, outside the House of Commons, England's principal legislative assembly. Lobbying has since evolved into a complex and powerful component of contemporary American policy making. The direct lobbying of political decision makers occurs in all three branches of government (executive, legislative, judicial) and at all levels of governance (federal, state, local).

Lobbying can take many forms. Signing a petition, meeting with the town councilor,

donating to a political organization, and writing a letter to the editor are all common ways interested citizens attempt to influence public policy. Such individual actions, however, are not normally powerful enough to sway politicians. For truly effective lobbying, concerned citizens must coalesce into interest groups—organizations of like-minded individuals that unite in the pursuit of shared public-policy goals.

There are currently tens of thousands of interest groups in the United States representing almost every imaginable concern. Among the most powerful on Capitol Hill are the AARP (American Association of Retired Persons), the National Rifle Association, the AFL-CIO, the Christian Coalition, the American Medical Association, the Chamber of Commerce, and the National Association of Manufacturers.

The right of concerned citizens to petition their government for political change through these groups is both a fundamental right and a key ingredient of American democracy; the public lobbying efforts of interest groups have indeed played a vital role in the improvement of American government. At the same time, lobbying has often been criticized for allowing "special interests" to buy access to decision makers and thus exert undue influence on the policy making process.

Interest groups draw not only on their extensive memberships to persuade policy makers; they also count on a highly sophisticated set of lobbying techniques. First, interest groups engage in the direct lobbying of policy makers through the provision of expert testimony at committee hearings, personal meetings with legislators, direct communications with government offices, assistance in drafting legislation and administrative procedures, and frequent informal and chance meetings off Capitol Hill. These activities are normally directed at key members of relevant House and Senate committees.

Interest groups also engage in indirect lobbying, which involves the attempt to influence policy makers by mobilizing public support on an issue. When this mobilization genuinely springs from local, community efforts, it is called grassroots lobbying. However, when elite special interests (e.g., "big tobacco") are surreptitiously behind the effort to mobilize the public, it is often ironically labeled "astroturf" (i.e., artificial grassroots) lobbying.

Interest groups are increasingly turning to the services of the more than 12,000 registered professional LOBBYISTS in the D.C. area. The elite lobbyists on Capitol Hill are former politicians and bureaucrats who are able to capitalize on their inside knowledge and extensive contacts. The prestigious K Street law firms are also powerful players in Washington's "influence industry." Beyond direct and indirect lobbying, these firms have found that the threat of class-action and amicus curiae litigation is a powerful lobbying device.

The final ingredient in successful lobbying is money. In addition to $1.45 billion in reported annual lobbying expenditures (1999), interest groups exert enormous pressure on legislators through donations to their political campaigns. Some critics have decried the potentially corrupting influence of money and have responded with reform movements to tighten 1995's Lobbying Disclosure Act and to close the so-called soft-money loophole that has allowed virtually unregulated donations to political parties.

For more information

Berry, Jeffrey M. *The Interest Group Society,* 3d ed. New York: Longman, 1997.

Center for Responsive Politics. http://www.opensecrets.org.

Smucker, Bob. *The Nonprofit Lobbying Guide,* 2d ed. Washington, D.C.: Independent Sector, 1999.

Gregory D. Saxton

lobbyist *Lobbyist* is a term referring to a person who makes representations, usually to government, on behalf of another organization or individual.

Lobbyists are increasingly finding niches of opportunity to represent clients at all levels of government throughout the world. Lobbyists and lobbyist techniques have grown from the need to better communicate and have recognized the needs of business groups, the different levels of government, community groups, and the general public. LOBBYING can be directed to the processes of government and decision makers responsible for policy and outcomes, or it can be targeted more generally at the environment and public relations aspects of different social groups, particularly the press and public opinion.

Lobbying has arisen because the consumers and users of government have become more professional and better organized. Traditional approaches that relied on bureaucratic intervention and public-interest concepts of public service have become less appropriate and less trusted than in earlier years. Trust in the public sector to remain sensitive and recommend adjustment to policy and processes has lessened. In some contexts, it has become recognized that reliance on the public service for adjustment of policy and procedures has proven too narrow and too specifically defined by the requirements of established interests, especially those well served by the system of political parties in each country, which are very often dictated to by the widely recognized limitations of electoral cycles and lowest-common-denominator approaches to policy development in order to satisfy the majorities required to sustain democratic government.

Lobbying has also been found to be important where policy development has been inferior or less than perfect, especially in cases where not all the policy effects of a government or legislative decision were foreseen or taken into account. Lobbying can mean that policy, when implemented, is adjusted in terms of more-direct relevance to consumers of government services and policy, and the final result is more efficient and effective for all concerned.

Lobbying involves considerable effort at representation to executive and political agents and can thus mean that better explanation and criticism is given of government policy, particularly of entitlements and rights envisaged in a program or policy. The process of representation often takes the form of formal submissions and letters to those responsible for policy development. It can also involve direct personal communication with senior politicians, senior public servants, or their representatives in meetings that can be highly structured, informal, or occasional, or simply a phone call.

There is no universal background for being a lobbyist. Political awareness and excellent communication skills are paramount if the lobbyist is to be a success. Projects can be short term, as in the case of organizing government monetary support for a particular project or activity. The projects undertaken can also be tactical and long term, as might be the case when a particular sector lobbies for economic policy reform and the payoff or fee is dependent on much longer-term considerations. Lobbyists are sometimes employed within corporate or sectoral settings. Increasingly, many newer entrants to the lobbying sector are organized as small businesses offering diverse support for business, some levels of government, and community groups. Some are reputedly better equipped than traditional government and political structures to develop policy and satisfy the public interest.

For more information

Birnbaum, Jeffrey H. *The Lobbyist: How Influence Peddlers Get Their Way in Washington.* New York: Times Books, 1992.

Moloney, Kevin. *Lobbyists for Hire.* Brookfield, Vt.: Dartmouth Publishing, 1996.

Stephen Kendal

locality pay   Locality pay is used to compensate employees for geographical cost-of-living differences between their regular pay schedule and prevailing rates in the private sector. The federal government has the most extensive and centrally organized plan for this differential payment. Some states also apply differentials, but none is as comprehensive as the federal system. For example, the state of California pays for the cost-of-living differences, but it varies on a decentralized basis by department and by occupation. Locality pay also gets confused with incentives to work in areas perceived to be undesirable locations. Accordingly, this discussion will focus on the federal system.

The Federal Employees Pay Comparability Act of 1990 (FEPCA) was passed to overcome recruitment and retention problems created by differences between federal-government and private-sector salary levels in high-cost-of-living metropolitan areas. Employee annual pay adjustment is in two parts: (1) a national, across-the-board increase, and (2) a locality-based pay adjustment. The law was implemented over a nine-year period to bring federal pay to within 5 percent of prevailing rates for similar jobs in a locality.

The locality-pay determination procedure starts with ongoing studies designed to calculate the pay gaps in each of the (currently) 32 designated pay localities plus the rest of the United States on which the raises are based. These surveys are done by the U.S. Bureau of Labor Statistics of more than 100 occupational levels for pay comparability between federal and nonfederal employment.

Each year the Federal Salary Council, a group made up of labor union representatives and compensation experts, submits recommendations on local pay gaps to the president's pay agent, which consists of the secretary of labor, director of the OFFICE OF MANAGEMENT AND BUDGET, and director of the OFFICE OF PERSONNEL MANAGEMENT. The pay agent decides the pay areas and reports on pay gaps to the president, recommending raises. The president then formally announces the raises.

Eligibility for locality pay is based on where the employee works, not on where the worker lives. Locality pay does not transfer with an employee who moves from one pay zone to another. Relocating employees will receive the rate of pay applying in their new work location. Locality pay applies only to general-schedule employees in the contiguous 48 states. The general schedule consists of pay rates and ranges in annual amounts under which most white-collar federal employees are compensated. Locality pay does not apply to overseas or to Alaska or Hawaii. Federal employees in these locations receive geographic pay adjustments based on cost-of-living measurements.

For more information

Federal Employees Almanac 2000. Reston, Va.: Federal Employees News Digest, Inc., 2000, 10–16.

Gilbert B. Siegel

M

magnet schools Magnet schools are a form of school choice that is often used to facilitate racial integration.

Magnet schools provide opportunities for parents to select where they will send their children to school, and, like all forms of school choice, magnet schools are intended to encourage innovation as a way of improving public education. A key feature of magnet schools is their unique curriculum designed to develop a content area or teaching methodology that is not offered anywhere else in the district. For example, many magnet schools specialize in science or the arts or adopt a one-of-a-kind teaching philosophy. However, magnet schools are a form of school choice with a unique mission. Most magnet schools are established in urban areas to promote racial diversity.

Magnet schools were developed to provide an alternative to busing as a remedy for school segregation. In *Morgan v. Kerrigan,* 530 F.2d 401 (1st Cir 1976), the courts concluded that magnet schools are a legal method of desegregation. Magnet schools act to desegregate school districts because they are intended to be high-quality schools located in urban areas. Because these high-quality schools offer a unique educational experience, the children of affluent suburban parents will be drawn in, resulting in a less segregated environment. Some evidence suggests the program is working. Over 75 percent of magnet schools have more applicants than available slots. Moreover, white students comprise approximately 32 percent of enrollment in magnet schools located in predominantly black districts.

In 1972, the DEPARTMENT OF EDUCATION used the Emergency School Aid Act (ESAA) to provide funds for magnet schools. In 1985, magnet-school funding returned with the Magnet Schools Assistance Program (MSAP). A total of $739 million has been spent on magnet schools since 1985.

Critics of magnet schools focus on two issues—accountability and representation of at-risk students. Critics argue that magnet schools are not held accountable to most federal and state educational objectives. Although the Department of Education has established standards for magnet schools, these standards are not always measured or enforced. In addition, some reports suggest that special-education students, low-English-proficiency students, and low-income students are underrepresented in magnet schools.

For more information

Barr, Robert, and William Parrett. *How to Create Alternative, Magnet and Charter Schools That Work.* Bloomington, Ind.: National Education Service, 1997.

Smrekar, Clair, and Ellen Goldring. *School Choice in Urban America: Magnet Schools and the Pursuit of Equity.* New York: Teachers College Press, 1999.

Mathew Manweller

management by objectives   Management by objectives (MBO) is a management technique that involves a collaboration between management and staff in the design of organizational goals.

The management-by-objectives concept was introduced by Peter Drucker in the early 1950s. From Drucker's perspective, organizational goals are not always reflected in the work efforts of smaller work units within an organization. Organizational subgroups may duplicate or counteract the work of other groups. A lack of communication and coordination results in organizational inefficiencies.

The purpose of MBO is to align work goals across an organization. With an MBO approach, managers meet with staff to develop work objectives that are consistent with the larger organizational goals. Documentation of the objectives allows the organization to identify inconsistencies or points of friction across the organization. Budgets and other resources required to achieve the objectives must be identified. The time period to accomplish the objectives is typically set for a 12-month period. At the end of the year it is important to assess the level of achievement associated with the objectives. This review is the starting point for the creation of the next year's objectives.

The MBO discussions between manager and staff create opportunities for improving the sense of community in an organization. Although the MBO focus is on organizational output and production, the collaborative process associated with MBO gives the approach an organizational development dynamic. If properly conducted, the communication component of MBO can build levels of trust and rapport in an organization in addition to facilitating the production of the enterprise.

Although the intent of MBO is to create opportunities for managers and staff to mutually discuss and agree on organizational objectives, MBO is not always applied appropriately. The administration of President Richard Nixon believed that MBO would be helpful in aligning the political agenda of the White House with the budgets and performance of federal agencies. In a presidential memorandum in May 1973, Richard Nixon mandated the use of MBO for most federal agencies. However, the Nixon administration learned that the political impacts on many federal agencies were not immediate or obvious. As a result, the Nixon administration abandoned MBO after two years.

When properly implemented, MBO applies communication and coordination as a means of enhancing the efficiency and effectiveness of an organization's performance.

For more information

Drucker, Peter. *The Practice of Management.* New York; Harper & Row, 1954.

Odiorne, George S. *Management by Objectives: A System of Managerial Leadership.* New York: Pittman, 1965.

Sherwood, Frank P., and William J. Page, Jr. "MBO and Public Management." *Public Administration Review* 36 (January/February 1976): S-11.

Richard J. Van Orden

management information system   A management information system (MIS) is a system that acquires, stores, retrieves, and relates data and then converts those data into information or reports designed to assist decision makers. There are as many definitions of MIS as there are experts writing about it.

One definition is: "Management Information Systems (MIS) is the study of the design, implementation, management and use of information technology applications in organizations." Yet another definition is: "Management information systems can be defined as information systems that provide reports which assist the managerial monitoring and control of organisational functions, resources or other responsibilities."

These definitions do not clarify the meaning of MIS for the average nontechnical person. In fact, even those with much technology experience find this term somewhat muddy. We can tell from these two definitions that an MIS involves use of technology or systems within organizations. Does MIS involve studying the application of information technology, or is it the provision of reports that assist in managing organizations? The fact is that MIS encompasses both these ideas and more.

The notion of information systems (IS) is older than the use of computer technology. Before there were computers, organizations had information to control and monitor. And before there were computers, designing methods of organizing, retrieving, distributing, and securing information was a key concern of organizations both big and small. Government's role in handling information is critical because it maintains records of some kind on just about all citizens, including information about a person's health, finances, residence, and family. Clearly, managing information is not a new challenge. However, what is new is the intensification of accessing, sorting, retrieving, and distributing information made possible through the use of computer technology.

Computers have been used to help with the management of information since the late 1950s. Initially, computers were relied upon to relieve workers of repetitive, routine tasks like motor vehicle registration and tax processing. As computing has evolved, so has the use of computing technology for information management. In fact, the most commonly used term for computers today is information technology—a clear acknowledgement that their most basic function is the management of information.

An MIS in the public sector is referred to by many as public management information systems, or PMIS. This is intended to distinguish between the uses of MIS in the commercial sector and its unique and complex uses in the public or government sector. For public sector managers, how a particular technology is used is more significant than which technology is used.

As described by David Andersen and Sharon Dawes, public managers must analyze information management problems using "four critical lenses": organizational, technological, economic, and political. They are all important, but the political lens is unique to public-sector organizations. For public administrators, managing information systems effectively requires knowledge and understanding of both internal organizational politics and the external political environment. Above all else, management information systems in the public sector must be designed to assist with the unique decision-making needs of public administrators. Those systems, while managing information, must also support government's important role of serving the public well. This means that issues of data security and privacy are of paramount concern.

Management information systems vary in terms of specific hardware, software, connectivity, and applications from organization to organization. This is appropriate because an effective MIS meets the unique needs of the organization for which it was constructed. Public agencies must strike a balance between promoting efficient service provision to their constituents while protecting their individual privacy. An MIS must operate in a secure environment, but some segments of it must often be publicly accessible. For example, a system that enables online voter registration through the World Wide Web must, at the same time, ensure that the data storage system operating in the background severely restricts access to those voter records. This is a delicate balancing act made more difficult by the dynamic nature of the underlying technological infrastructure.

There is much excitement today about e-government and its promise for a better-served and more-engaged citizenry. It is important to note that an e-government application is dependent upon a well-designed MIS at its core. The future of e-government will certainly be affected by the rapid growth of wireless technologies. Currently, these services are huge security risks and present enormous challenges for data protection. As wireless technologies become more pervasive, it is imperative that public-sector information-technology decision makers proceed cautiously to ensure that citizen privacy rights are not sacrificed on the altar of technological advancement.

Management information systems, whatever their configuration, are as essential to governmental operations as the elected officials and public administrators upon whom we depend for making and implementing policy. It is critical that an MIS be well designed, strategically implemented, and regularly evaluated.

For more information

Anderson, D. F., and S. S. Dawes. *Government Information Management: A Primer and Casebook.* Englewood Cliffs, N.J.: Prentice Hall, 1991.

Garson, G. D., ed. *Information Technology and Computer Applications in Public Administration: Issues and Trends.* Hershey, Pa.: Idea Group Publishing, 1999.

Gupta, U. G. *Management Information Systems: A Managerial Perspective.* Minneapolis: West Publishing, 1996.

Heeks, R. "Public Sector Management Information Systems." Institute for Development Policy and Management. Available online: URL: http://idpm.man.ac.uk/idpm/ispswpf5.htm.

———. "Management Information Systems in the Public Sector." In *Information Technology and Computer Applications in Public Administration: Issues and Trends,* edited by G. D. Garson. Hershey, Pa.: Idea Group Publishing, 1999, 157–173.

Holden, S. "The Evolution of Information Technology Management at the Federal Level: Implications for Public Administration." In *Information Technology and Computer Applications in Public Administration: Issues and Trends,* edited by G. D. Garson. Hershey, Pa.: Idea Group Publishing, 1999, 62–80.

Marchand, D. A. "Information Management: Strategies and Tools in Transition." *Information Management Review,* 1 (summer 1985): 27–34.

Carole Richardson

Maslow, Abraham Harold (1908–1970)

psychologist Abraham Maslow was an existential psychologist who developed one of the most influential theories about human needs and motivation, which is commonly referred to as Maslow's hierarchy of needs. Born to uneducated Jewish immigrants from Russia on 1 April 1908 in Brooklyn, New York, Maslow was the first of seven children. He was pushed toward academics and earned B.A., M.A., and Ph.D. degrees in psychology from the University of Wisconsin during the 1930s.

First appearing as an article entitled "A Theory of Human Motivation," Maslow's theory is based on the following premises: all humans are motivated by needs; human needs can be summarized in five hierarchical levels, ranging from the most elementary needs to the highest level of self-fulfillment; individuals must satisfy lower-level needs before moving to higher ones; and once a need has been satisfied, it no longer acts as a motivator.

The most significant aspect of Maslow's theory for public administration is the hierarchy of needs, which groups human needs into five categories. The first is physiological needs and includes our most fundamental and basic necessities such as oxygen, water, food, physical health, and comfort. The second category contains safety needs, that is, to be safe from danger or the fear of attack. The third group is made up of love and belonging needs—where individuals look to develop positive social relationships with friends and family. Next come esteem needs, which include the desire for strength, confidence, and self-respect, as well as the need to feel valued by others. The final level is self-actualization, or the need to fully develop and realize one's potential.

The following example illustrates Maslow's hierarchy of needs. A student recreation supervisor at a local university has two employees: worker A and worker B. Worker A is a full-time student who is working part-time to achieve a sense of belonging and self-respect, while worker B is a part-time student working full-time in order to put food on the table. The supervisor, who is familiar with Maslow's theory, understands that she is going to have to spend more time on career development with worker A because worker A is motivated by higher-level needs and accordingly brings a different set of expectations to the job. Worker B on the other hand is motivated by survival needs and, at least for the time being, requires less attention.

Maslow's concepts were very influential during the emergence of the Human Relations period of public administration, from the 1940s through the 1960s, which challenged the scientific management notion that workers were predominantly motivated by economic incentives and instead suggested that they were also influenced by social forces. Maslow, whose early understanding was influenced by the Hawthorne experiments of the 1930s, in turn influenced others such as Douglas McGregor, Chris Argyris, and Frederick Herzberg. For example, McGregor, who called for management to organize tasks so that workers could meet their needs and organizational objectives simultaneously, based his theory firmly upon Maslow's hierarchy.

Maslow's theory, however, has not gone without criticism: it has been attacked for its lack of empirical evidence and criticized for oversimplifying the complex nature of human needs. Even so, Maslow's work continues to be influential in the realm of motivation and organizational behavior theory, and it is widely used for training managers in both the public and private sectors.

For more information

Bolman, Lee G., and Terrence E. Deal. *Reframing Organizations.* San Francisco: Jossey-Bass, 1997.

Maslow, Abraham H. "A Theory of Human Motivation." *Psychological Review* 50 (1943): 370–396.

Jonathan Greenblatt

mediation   Mediation is a form of assisted negotiation where an impartial and independent party without the power to render a decision helps disputants communicate better and consider possible solutions for their dispute. The most popular version of ALTERNATIVE DISPUTE RESOLUTION over the last 20 years, mediation is becoming more common by statute, ordinance, and discretionary practice in many public agencies.

A mediator is skilled in handling the emotions, issues analysis, and interpersonal relations of difficult negotiations. Many mediators set ground rules for discussion as one way to reduce tension and improve understanding between antagonists. Mediators encourage disputants to see the other side's perspective and consider a voluntary settlement of their problem.

Mediation has a long history, but its more formal U.S. roots are in labor-management relations. For example, the National Mediation Board was established in 1934 to facilitate harmonious labor-management relations within the railroad and airline industries. The Federal Mediation and Conciliation Service, with a wider range of workplaces to cover, dates from 1947. State and local government public-personnel systems often provide for mediation as one step in their grievance procedures. Public-construction contracts have included mediation clauses more recently.

In international diplomacy, nongovernmental organizations and nation-state officials are often called mediators, but they are less likely to be truly impartial. Instead, they tend to bring other considerations to a conflict, including the ability to provide financial, military, or other resources, which makes their involvement more of a multilateral negotiation than mediation. A U.S. community-based mediation movement dates from the 1970s, with city or neighborhood centers offering free or low-cost mediation for neighbor-neighbor, tenant-landlord, and other everyday civil and minor criminal kinds of problems. Local mediation centers are often supported, in part, by funding from local government agencies, from the courts, and from civic, religious, or other community organizations.

The community mediation model often includes a two-person mediation team, whereas the majority of mediators in other fields work solo. Many levels of the civil justice system use mediation, ranging across small claims, criminal misdemeanor, and divorce cases. Since the 1970s, mediation has been extended to regulatory and policy issues, with the U.S. Environmental Protection Agency taking the lead in developing regulatory negotiation, which involves a mediator/facilitator. A set of competencies for complex public policy mediation has been established by a professional association, the Association for Conflict Resolution.

Mediation sessions include both face-to-face meetings and caucuses, which allow a mediator to meet privately with only one disputant. A mediator chooses to caucus as one tool to reduce tension, to encourage opponents to consider new proposals, to do "reality-testing" of a party's position, and sometimes to make suggestions. Caucuses are confidential, and the mediator meets with one party and then the other. Any information gathered from a caucus is not shared unless the disputant tells the mediator to transmit a proposal, raise a new idea, or query the other disputant on some point. Some mediators rarely or never caucus. They believe caucus-ing undercuts the disputants working out the problem directly and places too much power in the mediator.

For more information
Association for Conflict Resolution. http://www. acresolution.org/.
Mediate.com. http://www.mediate.com/.

John B. Stephens

Medicaid and Medicare Medicaid and Medicare constitute, respectively, the United States's foremost old age health-care insurance program and general medical assistance program at the federal government level.

The twin programs of Medicaid and Medicare were created under the Social Security Amendments of 1965. As such, they are among the more important pieces of social legislation passed in the United States. The Medicare program is essentially an (in principle) universal health-care insurance program for persons aged 65 or older, while the Medicaid program is an income-tested medical assistance program for children and the working-age population of limited means. The programs have undergone numerous legislative changes since their creation.

The Medicare bill was first signed by President Lyndon B. Johnson on 30 July 1965 in the presence of former president Harry Truman, who had proposed this legislation as early as 1945. Besides most elderly (excluding some who have not paid contributions while of working age), the program today also covers some people with disabilities under age 65, as well as people suffering from permanent kidney failure. The Medicare program is twofold. The so-called Part A benefits cover hospital insurance and do not have to be paid for by most, while Part B benefits constitute medical insurance (available for a monthly premium). The hospital insurance benefits are either provided upon admittance to any participating doctor or hospital, or to private companies sometimes called HEALTH

MAINTENANCE ORGANIZATIONS (HMOs), Part B benefits cover doctors' services, outpatient care, and some other services not covered by Part A, such as physical and occupational therapy and some home health services.

The Medicaid program was introduced under the same Social Security amendments of 1965 and involves federal-state subsidies. It is today the third-largest source of health insurance in the United States, after employer-based coverage and Medicare, and is the largest in the federal safety net of public assistance programs. In 1998, it covered 41.4 million low-income children, their families, elderly people, and individuals with disabilities—approximately 12 percent of the total U.S. population. The program has expanded over its first 35 years to include preventive services for children and has come to provide more freedom for states to provide coverage. From 1984 to 1990, Congress enacted a series of mandates that expanded eligibility for low-income children by gradually delinking Medicaid eligibility from welfare eligibility, a process arguably completed by the 1996 welfare reform.

Enrollment rates have however fallen since 1996, with the largest declines occurring in families with the very lowest incomes. Though the expansion of Medicaid has had demonstrably equalizing effects both for women's use of obstetricians' services and on ethnic differences in enrollment rates, the use of services through Medicaid remains stratified by differences in the political strength of the system's various constituencies, as well as by social class.

For more information

Currie, J., and J. Gruber. "Public Health Insurance and Medical Treatment: The Equalizing Impact of the Medicaid Expansions." *Journal of Public Economics* 82, no. 1 (2001): 63–89.

Deortiz, C. M. "The Politics of Home Care for the Elderly Poor: New-York-City Medicaid-Funded Home Attendant Program." *Medical Anthropology Quarterly* 7, no. 1 (1993): 4–29.

Department of Health and Human Services. *Your Medicare Benefits.* Washington, D.C.: HHS, 2001.

Hakim, R. B., et al. "Medicaid and the Health of Children." *Health Care Financing Review* 22, no. 1 (2000): 133–140.

Health Care Financing Administration. "Medicare and You." Publication No. HCFA-10116. Baltimore: HCFA, 2001.

Kronebusch, K. "Children's Medicaid Enrollment: The Impacts of Mandates, Welfare Reform and Policy Delinking." *Journal of Health Politics, Policy and Law* 26, no. 6 (2001): 1,223–1,260.

Kronebusch, K. "Medicaid and the Politics of Groups." *Journal of Health Politics, Policy and Law* 22, no. 3 (1997): 839–878.

Provost, C., and P. Hughes. "Medicaid: 35 Years of Service." *Health Care Financing Review* 22, no. 1 (2000): 141–174.

Racine, A. D., et al. "Differential Impact of Recent Medicaid Expansions by Race and Ethnicity." *Pediatrics* 108, no. 5 (November 2001): 1,135–1,142.

Eero Carroll

merit system   The merit system refers to the staffing of government agencies and departments based upon individual technical knowledge and expertise and not upon politics or party affiliation.

The idea of hiring individuals based upon merit was introduced into the U.S. federal government in 1883 with the passage of the PENDLETON ACT. Prior to 1883, individuals were mainly hired or promoted on the basis of their political affiliation or because they knew someone in government who had hiring authority. This system, known as the spoils or the patronage system, often resulted in numerous problems, including the hiring or promoting of unqualified people, the exchange of jobs for political support, and pressures upon government employees to take politics into consideration when performing their duties. As a result, the spoils system opened the staffing of the government to charges that it was inefficient and corrupt.

Public administration scholars and reformers as diverse as Woodrow Wilson and Max Weber contended that the spoils system was an inferior way to organize the government. Instead, hiring individuals on the basis of merit would accomplish several goals. First, it would ensure that the most qualified person would be hired for a job. Second, it would help remove politics from administration and promote the goal that government workers were performing their jobs based upon their expertise and the public interest. Third, it would promote efficiency and consistency in the performance of administration.

Both Wilson and Weber, as well as other advocates of the merit system, argued that one of the best ways to assure merit in hiring and promotions is through the use of examination process, such as standardized tests. These would be objective tests, and as generally implemented, the applicants receiving the top scores on the exam would be interviewed and considered for the job. Another aspect of the merit principle is the idea that once hired, individuals would receive civil service protections. This means that they would be guaranteed their jobs and could not be fired except for cause.

Many of these ideas were embodied in the 1883 Pendleton Act as well at the state and local level. Over the years, the merit system has been extended to cover a greater percentage of government positions, such that it is now the primary way to staff the public sector. Yet there are several exceptions to the merit system.

First, individuals who are hired at the senior level of the government are often not covered by the merit principle. Instead, elected officials are given the ability to hire close advisers and policy makers based upon numerous personal factors. The reason for this is that it is believed that elected officials should be free to hire people who agree with them politically. A second exception to the merit principle gets at the issue of what merit is. Does merit necessarily mean the person who scores the highest on a test, or does it refer to persons who have the most education, or who have worked the hardest? How to measure merit is difficult. Third, in the last 40 to 50 years, demands to diversify the civil service have introduced the concept of affirmative action, which some critics claim compromises hiring based on merit. Fourth, the introduction of unions into the public sector along with principles such as seniority have forced a readjustment in hiring and promotion practices. Finally, demands to make the government more flexible and capable of rapid change have led to demands to abandon the civil service tenure system, as in the state of Georgia. Losing this protection may perhaps make it more difficult to enforce the merit system.

For more information

Pfiffner, James P., and Douglas A. Brook, eds. *The Future of Merit: Twenty Years after the Civil Service Reform Act.* Washington, D.C.: Woodrow Wilson Center Press, 2000.

Schultz, David A., and Robert Maranto. *The Politics of Civil Service Reform.* New York: Peter Lang Publishing, Inc., 1998.

David Schultz

Merit Systems Protection Board The U.S. Merit Systems Protection Board (MSPB) is an independent, quasi-judicial agency in the executive branch that serves as the guardian of the federal MERIT SYSTEMS.

The board's mission is to ensure that federal employees are protected against abuses of merit principles. Though there is a long history of controversy over what is meant by the term *merit*, the Civil Service Reform Act of 1978 defined its principles:

Recruitment from all segments of society
Selection and advancement on the basis of ability, knowledge, and skills, under fair and open competition

Fair and equitable treatment in all personnel management matters without regard to politics, race, color, religion, national origin, sex, marital status, age, or handicapping condition

Regard for individual privacy and constitutional rights

Equal pay for work of equal value, considering both national and local rates paid by private employers

High standards of integrity, conduct, and concern for the public interest

Efficient (economic) and effective (achieving objectives well) use of the federal work force

Retention of employees who perform well, correction of the performance of those whose work is inadequate, and separation of those who cannot or will not meet required standards

Performance improvement through effective education and training

Protection of employees from arbitrary action, personal favoritism, or political coercion

Protection of employees against reprisal for lawful disclosures of information

Various other direct prohibitions on federal managers that implement these principles

MSPB has a statutory mandate to review and decide upon appeals from personnel actions (appointments, removals, assignments, suspensions) for the federal government and for some state and local government employees in federally funded positions.

The board consists of three members with no more than two appointed from the same political party. Members are appointed by the president and confirmed by the Senate. They serve overlapping, nonrenewable, seven-year terms.

The board's Office of Special Counsel processes most appeals though its own procedures, and the office can bring them to the board for final decision. These appeals brought by the special counsel may be concerned with individual rights, charges of abuse of merit systems, or political activity violations. It also may bring to the board certain proposed actions against administrative law judges (administrative law governs the powers and procedures of administrative agencies that affect the rights of private parties) and requests to review a regulation or implementation of the U.S. Office of Personnel Management by a government agency.

The MSPB conducts studies of the civil service (all employees of government who are not in military service) and merit systems in the executive branch to determine whether they are free of prohibited personnel practices. It also oversees significant actions and regulations of the U.S. Office of Personnel Management to determine whether they are in accord with the merit system principles. The U.S. Office of Personnel Management is the president's central personnel agency.

For more information

U.S. Merit Systems Protection Board. *Celebrating 20 Years, Building a Foundation for Merit in the Twenty-first Century, a Twenty Year Retrospective of the U.S. Merit Systems Protection Board 1979–1999.* Washington, D.C.: Government Printing Office, January 1999.

Gilbert B. Siegel

Minnowbrook Conference The Minnowbrook Conference was a meeting organized in 1968 by DWIGHT WALDO to solicit the views of public-administration scholars under the age of 35 on the field's future in relationship to the turmoil of the late 1960s. From a historical perspective, the conference served as the beginning of the NEW PUBLIC ADMINISTRATION movement, a significant development in the world of public administration.

Waldo organized the conference at a time when there was a great deal of unrest in the country because of the Vietnam War, Civil Rights movement, and a general hostility toward institutions and traditional values by a vocal and aggressive group of student radicals. He wanted to know how his younger colleagues believed public-administration practitioners and scholars should respond to these challenges and opportunities.

The assembled participants held a variety of views on these issues, with many sympathetic and supportive of the efforts by student radicals and others to change American society. During the Minnowbrook Conference, the majority of the scholars argued for a public administration focused on achieving social equity by attacking economic, social, and other problems while reaching out to the people it serves in a caring and humane manner. The majority staunchly opposed the notion of a cold bureaucracy carrying out the policies of others, such as politicians. Rather, they argued for public administrators to take the initiative in tackling what they viewed as society's ills and saw the fight against these problems as public administration's primary function. Frank Marini, one of the participants, described the main ideas discussed at Minnowbrook as morality, ethics, values, social equity, client focus, and elimination of social and political repression. Minnowbrook resulted in further meetings, articles, and books focusing on these topics, culminating in the development of the new public administration movement.

Critics of the meeting were upset that Waldo did not invite more-experienced scholars who may have been able to provide some perspectives that were not represented by the participants. In addition, other critics opposed some of the ideas generated at the conference, such as administrators becoming more active to solve social problems instead of following the lead of elected officials.

Despite these criticisms, the ideas stemming from the Minnowbrook Conference and the activities that followed it influenced a generation of scholars and practitioners, and they continue to impact the field today in both practice and academe. Participants organized a second Minnowbrook Conference in 1988 to assess the progress of the previous 20 years.

For more information
Lowery, George. "Dwight Waldo Putting the Purpose in P.A." *Maxwell Perspective* (spring 2001). Available online. URL:www.maxwell.syr.edu/perspective/spr01_waldo_main.htm.Downloaded June 2003.
Marini, Frank. *Toward a New Public Administration: The Minnowbrook Perspective.* Scranton, Pa.: Chandler Publishing, 1971.

Todd Stephenson

monetary policy   The term *monetary policy* refers to a collection of policies that the Federal Reserve can employ to regulate the upward and downward swings in the economy.

The Federal Reserve has a significant amount of power to influence the national economy by its ability to increase or decrease the nation's money supply via changes in the discount rate, open-market operations, or the reserve requirement. A monetary policy designed to increase the amount of money available to consumers and investors, and therefore to increase economic growth, is an expansionary monetary policy. A monetary policy designed to restrict economic growth is a contractionary monetary policy.

The Federal Reserve comprises several components. There are 12 district banks across the nation, and each has its own president. In addition to the district presidents, there are seven governors, appointed to 14-year terms by the president of the United States, known as the Board of Governors. Presiding over the Board of Governors is the Federal Reserve chairman, also appointed by the president. Probably the most important component of the FEDERAL RESERVE SYSTEM is the Federal Open Market Committee (FOMC), made up of the seven governors and five of the bank presidents. This committee has the important job of determining the monetary policy for the nation.

The Federal Reserve controls the money supply using three economic tools. The Federal

Reserve has the power to control open-market operations, alter the reserve requirement, and change the discount rate.

The Fed's open-market operations involve the buying and selling of public government bonds. When the Federal Reserve sells bonds to a bank, the bank must use its resources to purchase the bond. In doing so, the bank has less money to loan out to individuals and businesses. When the banks have less money to loan out, consumption and investment fall, and the economy contracts. Conversely, when the Federal Reserve buys government bonds from the banks, money is injected into the economy. In such a transaction, the Federal Reserve receives a bond back from the bank, and the bank receives cash from the Federal Reserve. The bank uses the cash as excess reserves and loans the reserves to individuals and businesses. This increases consumption and investment which in turn cause an increase in the GDP (gross domestic product).

The Federal Reserve requires banks to keep a portion of the money they receive in deposit available at all times. This is called the reserve requirement. If the Federal Reserve increases the reserve requirement, banks are required to keep more money on hand and therefore have less money to loan out. Increases in the reserve requirement result in smaller economic growth, while decreases have the opposite result—economic growth.

Finally, the Federal Reserve controls the interest rates that banks are charged to borrow money from the Federal Reserve. This is known as the discount rate. If the discount rate is low, banks will borrow a lot of money; if the discount rate is high, banks are discouraged from borrowing money. The more money banks have, the more money they can loan to individuals and businesses. Therefore, the Federal Reserve's control over the discount rate can affect economic growth rates.

Unfortunately, the effects of monetary policy are not instantaneous. It takes several months for changes in the interest rate to work through the economy and have an effect on investment. These delays—called time lags—make the Federal Reserve's job very difficult. In addition to the uncertainty caused by time lags, the Federal Reserve is also unsure about how much it needs to alter the money supply in order to get a particular change in total output. Sometimes the Federal Reserve increases the money supply too much, sometimes not enough. The end result is that sometimes monetary policy is implemented with good intentions but ends up destabilizing the economy.

See also FEDERAL RESERVE BOARD.

For more information

Morris, Irwin. *Congress, the President, and the Federal Reserve: The Politics of American Monetary Policy-Making.* Ann Arbor: University of Michigan Press, 2000.

Rosen, Harvey. *Public Finance,* 2d ed. Homewood, Ill.: Irwin Press, 1988.

Mathew Manweller

Morrison v. Olson 487 U.S. 654 (1988)

Morrison v. Olson was a Supreme Court case that upheld the law providing for a special prosecutor to be appointed to investigate the presidency and the executive branch.

In 1978 Congress included specific procedures for a special prosecutor (independent counsel) as part of its reform act, the ETHICS IN GOVERNMENT ACT OF 1978. This act was written and enacted by Congress, in part, as a response to the corrupt practices exposed during the WATERGATE scandal of the Nixon administration. Those provisions were included in this legislation to allow for the appointment of a special prosecutor when congressional investigations indicated the need to prosecute high-ranking government officials. Specifically, the Ethics in Government Act explained the powers of the office, provided for the selection process of the special prosecutor, the length of the special prosecutor's term of office, and the division (the "special division") under which the special prosecutor would serve.

It is the selection process of the special prosecutor that comes under legal attack in *Morrison v. Olson,* 487 U.S. 654 (1988). In Article II, section 2 of the U.S. Constitution we find the appointments clause that provides for the appointment powers of the president for major administrative and judicial offices. This provision of the Constitution also allows Congress to appoint persons to minor or inferior administrative offices. At question in this U.S. Supreme Court case is whether or not the office of the special prosecutor is a major or minor administrative office. This is important because if it is a major administrative office, then the president has the authority to appoint and fill vacancies (as well as removal authority). However, if it is a minor administrative office, then Congress may have either retained this authority to appoint or remove persons from the office or delegated the authority to another branch or government entity.

The facts behind this controversy are as follows. A special prosecutor, James McKay, was initially appointed according to the provisions of the Ethics in Government Act of 1978 to investigate the role of the Justice Department in some activities regarding the Environmental Protection Agency and the Land and Natural Resources division of the Department of Justice. McKay resigned before the investigation concluded. Therefore, a new special prosecutor was appointed by three federal judges to replace him, as stipulated in the 1978 Act. As the investigation continued, however, Theodore Olson and others who were being targeted by the special prosecutor's office were not cooperating with the newly appointed special prosecutor. Olson in particular refused to cooperate, claiming that the special prosecutor was a major administrative office and therefore under the authority of the president. Since the new special prosecutor had not been appointed by the pres-

ident, Olson argued that he did not need to recognize the office and did not need to cooperate. According to Olson, the special prosecutor was not an inferior office.

In addition to challenging the validity of the selection process for the special prosecutor, Olson also argued in his case that the "special division" created by the Ethics in Government Act of 1978 violated provisions of the U.S. Constitution (Article III). Finally, Olson contended that the act itself was a violation of the separation-of-powers principle upon which our government's distribution of powers is founded.

Writing for the majority in a 7-1 decision, William Rehnquist, chief justice of the United States, concluded that the office of the special prosecutor and its division, the "special division," are not in violation of the appointments clause in Article II, section 2. Simply put, the special prosecutor's office is a minor or inferior administrative office and not a major administrative office, as Olson claimed in his case. Therefore, Congress and not the president has the authority to determine how the special prosecutor shall be appointed as well as to establish the powers of the independent counsel's office and the length of his or her term. Finally, the chief justice stated that the "special division" did not violate Article III of the Constitution and that the Ethics in Government Act of 1978 did not violate our principle of separation of powers.

For more information

Epstein, Lee, and Thomas G. Walker. *Constitutional Law for a Changing America: Institutional Powers and Constraints,* 3d ed. Washington, D.C.: Congressional Quarterly Press, 1998.

Jolly Ann Emrey

Myers v. United States 272 U.S. 52 (1926)

Myers v. United States was an important Supreme Court case that sought to answer questions regarding the accountability of the administrative bureaucracy to the executive branch and ultimately to the president of the United States.

Under the terms of a law passed by Congress in 1876, first-, second-, and third-class postmasters could only be removed from office with the approval of the Senate. The idea was that since the Constitution required Senate consultation in the appointment of these officials, removal also should require the advice and consent of that body. The requirement was political in nature and grew out of the Jacksonian era SPOILS SYSTEM that had made almost all executive branch offices and officials highly politicized and subject to highly partisan presidential whims.

This particular case began in 1920 when Myers—a postmaster first class in Portland, Oregon, since 1917—was removed from office by the postmaster general of the United States. The postmaster general, acting on direct instructions from President Wilson and clearly in violation of the 1876 act, removed Myers without any consultation with the Senate. The order from President Wilson came in the midst of a heated battle over a proposed law that would place the same senatorial consultation requirements on the president when he wished to remove the comptroller general of the United States. The Myers firing was, in essence, a protest over what the executive branch viewed as meddling on the part of the Congress in the hiring and firing of executive branch officials.

Myers protested his firing and eventually sued in the U.S. Court of Claims to recover the salary lost by his allegedly illegal firing. After losing in the court of claims, the administrator of the Myers estate, Lois Myers, appealed to the U.S. Supreme Court. The basis of the Supreme Court case was a claim against the unfettered removal power of the president as being in violation of the constitutional requirement of advice and consent by the senate in appointment of administrative officers.

The decision of the Court was 6-3, with the opinion in the case being announced by Chief Justice (and former president) Taft striking down the 1876 law as it pertained to the removal of postmasters. The decision in the case relied on an originalist interpretation of the Constitution. Citing the notes from the 1787 convention, Taft and the Court argued for the necessity of a strong executive branch that possessed the power necessary to carry out the constitutional requirement that "the laws be faithfully executed." That power, according to the majority opinion in this case, extends to the power to remove officials that are subordinates of the president who are performing clearly executive functions and who may not be fulfilling the responsibilities of their office. The power to remove, they argued, meant the power to control.

As a second argument, the Court noted that the framers of the Constitution had included specific language regarding senatorial consultation in the appointment process but had omitted that language in regard to the removal of those officers. Taft argued that had the framers intended the Senate to be involved, the Constitution would contain that language in the enumerated power of the Congress or in the limitation on executive power in Article 2. Because it did not, the Congress did not have the authority to insert itself into that process by statute.

Myers v. United States created a strict interpretation of the doctrine of separated powers by suggesting that the only permissible overlapping of power between the three branches is the overlapping specifically mandated by the Constitution. The issues in *Myers* have been revisited many times as the Supreme Court has attempted to strike a reasonable and workable balance between the constitutional branches of government as mandated by the SEPARATION OF POWERS doctrine. As the executive bureaucracy has continued to expand in size and in function, the strict interpretation of *Myers* quickly became unworkable in practice and was revised considerably only nine years later in *HUMPHREY'S EXECUTOR V. UNITED STATES* 295 U.S. 602 (1935).

For more information

Foster, James, and Susan Leeson. *Constitutional Law: Cases in Context.* Englewood Cliffs, N.J.: Prentice Hall, 1998.

O'Brien, David M. *Constitutional Law and Politics: Struggles for Power and Governmental Responsibility.* New York: W. W. Norton, 1991.

David A. May

N

Nader, Ralph (1934–) *consumer advocate, presidential candidate* Ralph Nader is a consumer advocate, a former presidential candidate of the Green Party, and a hero to many on the American Left.

Born in Connecticut in 1934 to Lebanese immigrants, Nader attended Princeton University and Harvard University Law School. He came to prominence in 1965 with the publishing of *Unsafe at Any Speed: The Designed-in Dangers of the American Automobile*. The book's thesis was that the main cause of car injuries was not driver error, as the auto industry often claimed, but the inherent engineering and design deficiencies of the vehicles themselves. The book led to the establishment of the National Highway Traffic Safety Administration and a host of new automobile safety regulations, and it also established Nader as the foremost consumer advocate of his era.

Building on his initial success, Nader began to use the host of college-age idealists who gravitated toward him to launch investigations into a variety of industries, including meat, energy, and communications. These groups of students soon became known as "Nader's Raiders," so named for their willingness to confront key political actors to obtain information. Nader's Raiders published a host of reports in the late sixties and early seventies, all of which have reflected Nader's philosophical commitment to providing customers with information on the health, safety, and environmental impact of the products they buy and eliminating government subsidy of large corporations. He believes that the United States is a country ruled by huge, nondemocratic corporations and wants to make these corporations more accountable for their actions so as to return control of the country's most important decisions to the country's citizens.

Nader continued his consumer advocacy throughout the seventies and eighties, forming countless groups dedicated to applying the Nader philosophy to countless policy areas. He resurfaced on most people's radar in 1996, when the Green Party chose him as its presidential candidate. He frustrated many party members by refusing to actively campaign. Party regulars must have forgiven him by 2000, when they again nominated Nader, who this time embraced the nomination and campaigned heavily. His

Ralph Nader   (ALEX WONG/GETTY IMAGES)

campaign message reflected the same ideals and attacked the same targets against which he had fought for the previous 35 years, with special emphasis placed on his opposition to free trade agreements like NAFTA for their alleged negative effects on the American worker. Many in the Democratic Party worried that Nader's candidacy would siphon votes from Democratic nominee Al Gore and cost him the election, and many blamed Nader when Gore lost the election in Florida (and consequently the presidency) to George W. Bush by fewer than 1,000 votes. Nader's total vote share in Florida did exceed Bush's margin of victory, but so too did the votes of several other third-party candidates.

For more information
Bollier, David. *Citizen Action and Other Big Ideas: A History of Ralph Nader.* Center for Responsive Law, 1991. Available online. URL: http://www.nader.org/history_bollier.html.

Brien Shelley

National Aeronautics and Space Administration (NASA)

NASA is an acronym for the National Aeronautics and Space Administration, the primary federal agency responsible for space exploration.

On 4 October 1957, Americans listening to the evening news were alarmed to learn that the Soviet Union had successfully launched an artificial satellite, Sputnik 1. To meet the Soviet challenge, President Eisenhower signed the National Aeronautics and Space Act (Public Law 85–568) on 29 July 1958.

The new agency was made civilian to avoid intermilitary service rivalry and to promote peaceful space research. The act creating NASA also abolished the National Advisory Committee for Aeronautics (NACA) organized on 13 March 1915 during the Wilson administration to do research in the field of aerodynamics.

NASA is now one of the largest of the federal government's independent executive agencies. NASA's mission is to conduct basic space research, develop human space enterprises (e.g., communications satellites), and transfer useful technology to the public.

NASA's administrator, appointed by the president and serving at his pleasure, heads the agency. The Office of the Administrator conducts planning and operations to perform NASA's mission. It houses advisory, staff, and program offices. Advisory offices include the NASA Advisory Council. Staff offices include the Office of Headquarters Operations.

The different program offices—directing NASA's five "enterprises"—report to the Office of the Director. The program offices include the

Office of Aerospace Technology, the Office of Biological and Physical Research, Office of Earth Science, Office of Space Science, the Office of Space Flight, and the Office of Space Communications.

NASA centers across the country conduct many programs. Each center reports to its respective program office. For example, the Kennedy Space Center on Merritt Island, Florida, is managed by the Office of Space Flight (space shuttle program). Major centers include the Goddard Space Flight Center, Johnson Space Center, Marshall Space Flight Center, Jet Propulsion Laboratory, Langley Research Center, Stennis Space Center, Glenn Research Center, and the Ames Research Center.

NASA supporters have included scientists, engineers, technological companies, as well as its congressional supporters. Opponents have criticized the high cost of space research, arguing that money "wasted in space" would be better spent on the poor on Earth. NASA's budget is less than 1 percent of the total federal budget.

Lavish spending on a crash program led to NASA's most dramatic success—the landing of men on the Moon (20 July 1969). However, NASA failures have included the tragic losses of the *Apollo 1, Challenger,* and *Columbia* and their crews.

The space station programs have involved well over a dozen countries. International cooperation has its own brand of politics that will expand as more countries become involved in space exploration. Plans for future missions are guided by NASA Strategic Plan 2000, which seeks to answer basic research questions about the universe.

For more information
Launius, Roger D. *NASA: A History of the U.S. Civil Space Program.* Malabar, Fla.: Krieger Publishing Company, 1994.
McCurdy, Howard E. *Inside NASA: High Technology and Organizational Change in the U.S. Space Program.* Baltimore: Johns Hopkins University Press, 1993.

A. J. L. Waskey

national debt Government debt is composed of the accumulated federal deficits of the U.S. government, net of surpluses, from the founding of the republic to the present. Legally, it comprises the debt of the U.S. Treasury. The main components of the national debt are marketable securities (U.S. government bonds) in the hands of U.S. citizens and foreigners (including foreign governments) and nonmarketable debt held by U.S. government agencies (principally, the social security trust fund).

The gross national debt totaled some $5,629 billion at the end of fiscal year 2001, including $2,219 billion in nonmarketable debt held by U.S. government agencies. Of the remaining $3,410 billion, $511 billion of federal securities was held by the Federal Reserve Banks, to be used mainly for management of the money supply through open-market operations (i.e., buying and selling U.S. Treasury securities in order to expand and contract the money supply).

The use of nonmarketable securities has been a source of federal "borrowing" from other federal programs, principally social security, which ran cash surpluses throughout the 1990s. In recent years, social security has received more in taxes and other receipts than it paid out in benefits. The Treasury has used these surpluses to fund other spending. In exchange, Treasury securities have been given to social security, to be exchanged for cash at some future date. In effect, the U.S. government owes this money to itself. Nonmarketable debt is not sold to the public or issued to outside agencies, and it is not traded by investors on the secondary debt markets. Most of it—over $2 trillion—is a bookkeeping entry on U.S. government accounts. Ultimately, this "internal debt" will have to be satisfied through additional taxes in order to pay social security and other benefits that have been promised to U.S. citizens.

The growth of the national debt has been a source of controversy for over three decades. A related concern is the growing amount of interest that must be paid on the federal debt, which exceeded 10 percent of federal outlays in fiscal year 2001. The problem worsens when the federal government runs budget deficits. In any given year in which there is a deficit, the federal debt will grow by at least the amount of the deficit, but it can grow faster than the deficit when the government "borrows" trust fund balances. The projected budget surpluses through 2010 will help shrink the amount of debt held by the public. Federal debt as a percentage of gross domestic product also is expected to fall. This will have the positive effect of reducing interest payments as a proportion of federal outlays.

The gross debt will continue to grow, however, due to increasing amounts of Treasury securities held by U.S. government agencies (i.e., nonmarketable debt). Consequently, while the projected gross federal debt in 2007 will reach $5,953 billion, the nonmarketable component will nearly double, to $4,352 billion. At some point, nearly all of this debt will have to be repaid.

For more information

General Accounting Office. *Federal Debt: Answers to Frequently Asked Questions—An Update.* Document No. GAO/OCG-99-27. Washington, D.C.: General Accounting Office, May 1999.

Mikesell, John L. *Fiscal Administration,* 5th ed. Fort Worth, Tex.: Harcourt Brace, 1999.

Peterson, Peter. *Facing Up.* New York: Simon & Schuster, 1993.

Robert S. Kravchuk

National Labor Relations Board The National Labor Relations Board (NLRB) is the independent federal government agency responsible for resolving private-sector labor-management disputes—with the exceptions of agriculture, airlines, and railroads—that arise under the National Labor Relations Act (NLRA) of 1935 and its amendments.

Established by the NLRA, the NLRB has quasi-judicial powers to administer certification and decertification elections by secret ballot to determine whether or not employees in a recognized bargaining unit want to be represented by a union. It also rules on charges of unfair labor practices filed by either labor or management. NLRB decisions can be appealed to the federal courts.

Based in Washington, D.C., the NLRB consists of a five-person board whose members are appointed by the president with the consent of the Senate. According to longstanding custom, the president appointed three members from his party, including the chair, and two members from the opposition party who were generally supportive of the board's mission. But in the 1990s the Republican-controlled Congress demanded and got the power to select the two minority party members, who, many critics contend, have been antagonistic to labor. There is also a general counsel, also appointed by the president with the consent of the Senate, who serves a four-year term. The general counsel is in charge of investigating and prosecuting unfair labor complaints and also oversees the NLRB's field offices.

Many unionists have become disenchanted with the NLRB's time-consuming and cumbersome handling of the election process. Workers must file a petition with the NLRB signed by 50 percent of the bargaining unit's employees in order to request an election. But first, the NLRB must hold a hearing to determine whether or not the workers constitute a bargaining unit covered by the NLRA. Employers are entitled to take part in the hearing and can use it to sway the date and terms of the election to their advantage. NLRB rules require that the election be held at the workplace, rather than a neutral site. In theory, employers are not supposed to use this advantage to persuade their workers to vote against unionization, but in practice this provision is difficult to enforce. Union organizers are not allowed on the employer's premises, which makes it more difficult for them to communicate their message to workers. In Canada, by contrast, getting 50 percent of the workers to sign cards is enough to recognize the union as the bargaining agent.

The NLRB also rules on charges of unfair labor practices, but cases can take years to be adjudicated, and employers have more options at their disposal. For example, employers can file secondary boycott charges before both the NLRB and, since the TAFT-HARTLEY ACT, in federal court, but unions can only seek redress before the NLRB. While it is illegal for employers to fire workers for organizing activities, the NLRB's backlog means that they may not hear the case for years. Presidents Reagan and George H. W. Bush made a series of antilabor appointments to the NLRB, which weakened labor rights and lengthened the appeals process. It is not uncommon for employers to take advantage of these developments to delay recognition of the union. Consequently, many unions have grown disillusioned with the NLRB and have effectively been discouraged from organizing new workers.

For more information

Gould, William B. *Labored Relations: Law, Politics, and the NLRB—A Memoir.* Cambridge, Mass.: MIT Press, 2000.

Hardin, Patrick et al. *The Developing Labor Law: The Board, the Courts, and the National Labor Relations Act,* 4th ed. Washington, D.C.: Bureau of National Affairs, 2001.

Human Rights Watch. *Unfair Advantage: Workers' Freedom of Association in the United States under International Human Rights Standards.* New York: Human Rights Watch, 2000.

Vernon Mogensen

National Performance Review   National Performance Review also known as the National Partnership for Reinventing Government (NPR), was established and existed during the Clinton-Gore administration as an interagency task force to improve government by creating a government that, in the words of former vice president Al Gore, "works better, costs less, and gets results Americans care about." The NPR was officially closed and became part of history when Al Gore lost the 2000 presidential election. However, the general premise of NPR—a government that is performance oriented and customer focused—will most likely live on but may be given a different management reform name.

NPR's main purpose, or main mission and goals, consisted of establishing trust in government through pursuing outcomes focused on: providing the best customer service; increasing electronic access to government, or E-GOVERNMENT; achieving outcomes no one agency can achieve alone; and embedding reinvention in government's culture. The first report issued by NPR in 1993 had over 1,200 recommendations. Gore approached these goals by creating various intergovernmental teams consisting of members from across the federal government. Some of the councils created by NPR to develop and implement innovative ideas were the Chief Financial Officers Council, President's Management Council, the Government Information Technology Services Working Group, and the National Partnership Council.

Some classify NPR's history into two distinct parts, Clinton-Gore's first administration and Clinton-Gore's second administration. Others discuss NPR's efforts by dividing its history into three phases. The first focused on government process reforms; the second phase asked the question of what government should do; and the third phase focused on the development of special activities designed to work on problem agencies and programs.

The first interagency task force approached implementing the interagency recommendations at three levels of government: government-wide, agency specific, and employee focused. Several of the first interagency recommendations included reducing the workforce by 252,000 positions, decreasing internal agency regulations by half, and requiring agencies to set customer service standards.

In 1994 NPR established the Hammer Award to recognize teams of federal employees who improved services by using innovative ideas and solutions. The hammer was chosen for this award as a symbol to reflect a change in how government does business. The New York regional office of the Department of Veterans Affairs was the first recipient of the Hammer Award for its improved customer service in administering benefits to veterans in the region. Many felt the Hammer Award was the first time federal employees were publicly recognized for their contributions to improving government. The award also served as a way to spread the word of reinvention through the federal government and, when publicized by the local media, to the general public.

To signal a change in the way government does business, the phrase "reinventing government" became closely associated with the NPR. Various government agencies and programs became designated "reinvention laboratories." Examples include the Customs Service, Bureau of Reclamation, and the Occupational Safety and Health Administration. All three reinvention laboratories implemented successful changes that resulted in better service.

The second round of interagency recommendations gave increased attention to the basic question of what government should be doing. The last few years of NPR primarily focused on improving coordination of government programs and reducing management problems in what were classified as high-impact agencies. NPR defined high-impact agencies as those dealing directly with taxpayers and where management problems would have a great service impact and high political risk. There was also increased focus on the regulatory system and identifying which enforcement processes could be altered to reflect a partnership approach rather than an enforcement-type approach to doing business.

During NPR's tenure from 1993 to 2000 it claimed overall successes that included: reducing the era of big government, changing government to be more performance- and results-oriented, improving service to the public, changing the way government works with business and communities, transforming access to government through technology, making the government a better place to work, and cost savings associated with improved services.

Overall, NPR made a tremendous effort to further reform the way government does business. The effort will no doubt live on through a different management reform name, but it will possess the same intentions.

For more information

Ingraham, Patricia W., et al. *Transforming Government Lessons from the Reinvention Laboratories*. San Francisco: Jossey-Bass, 1998.

U.S. General Accounting Office. *Management Reform: GAO's Comments on National Performance Review's Recommendations*. Publication GAO/OCG-94-01. Washington, D.C.: U.S. Government Printing Office, 1993.

Jamie F. Green

National Science Foundation The National Science Foundation (NSF) is an independent agency created to stimulate scientific research and the application of science in daily life. It was established by the U.S. government in 1950 (under the National Science Foundation Act) "to promote the progress of science; to advance the national health, prosperity, and welfare; and to secure the national defense." It was formed in part to turn the large research machine developed during World War II toward peacetime applications of science and engineering.

The NSF carries out its mission by providing funding and other support for a wide variety of activities involving both traditional disciplines and interdisciplinary studies, as well as both pure and applied science. These activities are divided into 11 main areas:

1. Initiate and support scientific and engineering research, as well as education programs at all levels (including K–12), and assess the impact of research on industrial development and the general welfare of U.S. citizens.

2. Provide graduate fellowships in the sciences and in engineering, with the goal of increasing the number of students in these disciplines and providing them opportunities for advanced research.

3. Foster the exchange of scientific information between scientists and engineers in the United States and foreign countries through meetings, joint projects, etc.

4. Support the development and use of computers and other scientific technologies, primarily for research and education in the sciences.

5. Evaluate the status and needs of the various science and engineering disciplines, and use these studies to determine how the NSF can work with other federal and nonfederal programs to ensure needs are being met.

6. Provide a clearinghouse for data on scientific and technical resources in the United States, including a register of scientific and technical personnel in the United States, and provide this information to other federal agencies so they can use it in forming policy. This is related to the NSF's mission to ensure that science plays an important role in policy decisions.

7. Determine the total amount of federal money received by universities and other organizations for scientific and engineering research, including both basic and applied; determine where additional resources are needed to build necessary facilities for research; and report this information annually to the president and the Congress.

8. Initiate and support scientific and engineering activities related to international cooperation, national security, and the effects of science and technology on society.

9. Initiate and support special applied scientific and engineering research as requested by the president (usually in support of specific challenges to the nation).

10. Promote national policies focused on basic research and education in the sciences and engineering. Strengthen research and innovations in education in the sciences and engineering, including independent research by individuals, throughout the United States.

11. Support activities designed to increase the participation of women and minorities, and other underrepresented groups, in science and technology.

To carry out this mission, the NSF is guided by the National Science Board of 24 part-time members and a director, each appointed by the president with the advice and consent of the U.S. Senate. Other senior officials include a deputy director appointed by the president and eight assistant directors.

For more information

England, J. M. *A Patron for Pure Science: The National Science Foundation's Formative Years.* Washington, D.C.: National Science Foundation, 1982.

Douglas Crawford-Brown

The National Security Act of 1947   The National Security Act of 1947 was a law that reorganized the defense and intelligence institutions of the United States to fight the cold war. The act created the NATIONAL SECURITY COUNCIL, the CENTRAL INTELLIGENCE AGENCY, the U.S. Air Force, the JOINT CHIEFS OF STAFF, the National Security Resources Board, and a national military establishment headed by a secretary of defense.

World War II had demonstrated the need for greater coordination of effort and pooling of resources to create more efficiency and eliminate waste and duplication. The issue was especially problematic within the military, where the army was constantly fighting with an only technically subordinate air corps and with the navy. The National Security Act of 1947 attempted to solve this problem. It created a national military establishment headed by a secretary of defense who was a member of the cabinet but not the head of his own department. An independent Department of the Air Force was also created by removing the air corps from the army. Each of the now three services was headed by a civilian secretary who also enjoyed cabinet status, with the inherent ability to go over the head of the secretary of defense. The act also made permanent the wartime Joint Chiefs of Staff, formalizing the interaction between the senior officer in each of the military services.

A 1949 amendment to the act created the DEPARTMENT OF DEFENSE as a cabinet agency and made the army, navy, and air force subordinate agencies without cabinet rank. Additional amendments in 1953 and 1958 and the GOLDWATER-NICHOLS DEPARTMENT OF DEFENSE REORGANIZATION ACT OF 1986 further unified the armed forces.

In addition to streamlining the military, the act aimed at improving coordination among all executive agencies involved in the security arena. The National Security Council (NSC) was created to streamline the flow of information from the several bureaucracies responsible for the many issues related to security. The NSC created a vehicle to bring together existing agencies in a formal setting. Its statutory members are the president, vice president, secretary of state, and secretary of defense, with the director of central intelligence and chairman of the Joint Chiefs of Staff as statutory advisors.

Other members vary based on the desires of the president and the existing security environment, but the national security adviser and White House chief of staff are always included. Below the NSC itself are the Deputies Committee and Policy Coordinating Committee, both of which consist of more-junior policy experts who do most of the detailed staff work. The usage and prestige of the NSC varies based on the prefer-ence of the president, with some presidents relying quite heavily on the NSC and others preferring to rely primarily on their secretary of state.

The Central Intelligence Agency (CIA) was created by the act as the first peacetime civilian intelligence-gathering agency in U.S. history. It is independent of the cabinet and headed by the director of central intelligence, who is both head of the CIA as well as the coordinator for all the intelligence agencies in the U.S. government. In this latter capacity, the DCI has authority over all the intelligence assets of the Defense Department, State Department, and several independent intelligence-gathering agencies. Many analysts have noted that this power is often observed only in the breach, as intelligence agencies are even more loath to share information than other bureaucracies.

For more information

Caraley, Demetrious. *The Politics of Military Unification: A Study of Conflict and the Policy Process.* New York: Columbia University Press, 1966.

National Security Act of 1947 (PL 235-61 Stat. 496). July 26, 1947.

Snow, Donald M., and Eugene Brown. *United States Foreign Policy: Politics beyond the Water's Edge,* 2d ed. New York: Bedford/St. Martin's, 2000.

James H. Joyner, Jr.

National Security Council The National Security Council is an entity of the federal government that was first established by the National Security Act of 1947 for the purpose of determining "at the highest level of government the relationships between national objectives and military policy, in peacetime and in war."

The National Security Council is made up of only four statutory members: the president of the United States, the vice president, the secretary of defense, and the secretary of state. Additionally, the National Security Council has statutory advisors. These statutory advisers are the director of the Central Intelligence Agency and the chairman of the Joint Chiefs of Staff. The chief of staff to the president, the counsel to the president, and the assistant to the president for economic policy are invited participants at National Security Council meetings. Other executive agency and department heads are also invited to attend as the nature of policy discussion warrants.

The original configuration of the National Security Council included the Office of Civil and Defense Mobilization. This office was absorbed by the Office of Emergency Preparedness and has now been replaced by the Federal Emergency Management Agency. The National Security Council reflects operationally the decision-making style of the president. Ideally, information would flow up to the council in a way that each of the departments below would be a source of information for decision making. The shift in global politics has led to the inclusion of economic concerns in the national security discussion. Coupled with the cooperative posture nations have adopted, it is increasingly important to monitor the foreign-policy impact on domestic issues and vice versa. The National Security Council directs intelligence collection activity by offering guidance and establishing priorities. Sensitive intelligence activity and the cognizance of counterintelligence is reviewed by the National Security Council with recommendations made to the president.

The National Security Council is responsible for evaluating the quality of the intelligence received and has three major functions. According to Jordan et al., the three functions performed by the National Security Council are: "resource allocation, policy planning, and coordination and monitoring of operations." The goal is to shape future events and to plan for contingencies. The coordination and monitoring functions are to ensure that the policies get implemented in accordance with the plan. The size and complexity of this task requires revenue that is secured by the National Security Council with the assistance of the Office of Management and Budget. In addition, the National Security Council conducts analysis of military capability, taking into consideration not only estimates of force but situational factors influencing the power relationships around the world.

The degree and the nature of the influence wielded by the National Security Council is determined by the president and in accordance with his perceived configuration of the world. Although its purpose has remained the same, the extent of reliance on the National Security Council, its areas of focus, and the use of specially assigned executive committees or interagency task forces have varied with each presidential administration.

For more information

Dougherty, James E., and Robert L. Pfaltzgraff, Jr. *Contending Theories of International Relations*, 4th ed. New York: Longman, 1997.

Huntington, Samuel P. *The Common Defense*. New York: Columbia University, 1961.

Jordan, Amos A., William J. Taylor, and Michael J. Mazarr. *American National Security*. Baltimore: Johns Hopkins University Press, 1999.

Olivia M. McDonald

National Transportation Safety Board

The National Transportation Safety Board (NTSB) is an independent federal agency that began operations in the DEPARTMENT OF TRANSPORTATION (DOT) under the Independent Safety Board Act with two major tenets within its mission: to safeguard modes of transportation and to investigate major accidents.

The NTSB began operations on 1 April 1967 as an independent federal agency, and it remains that way today despite markedly different funding arrangements. The NTSB initially relied on the DOT for its funding and administrative support at the outset. In 1975, the Independent Safety Board Act was passed, and this allowed the NTSB to break its ties to the DOT. Congress commissioned the NTSB to act as an independent and unbiased agency with the responsibility of investigating major accidents in the foremost modes of transportation, as well as the duty to issue recommendations directed to safeguard transportation modes. The agency also was to provide guidelines to prevent future accidents but without enforcement powers.

The jurisdiction of the agency includes the railway systems, the airlines, the highways of the United States, the nation's pipeline system, and the marine travel ways. The agency operates every day of the year and has investigated over 100,000 accidents and has issued over 11,000 recommendations regarding safety improvements. It has been estimated that over 80 percent of the recommendations offered by the NTSB have been adopted by those persons charged with the duty to effect change in their transportation systems.

The agency also assists overseas when directed to do so, and it has been called upon to act when there has been an accident involving U.S.-made products or with U.S.-registered vessels. The impartiality of the agency sets it apart as one of the most effective tools for safeguarding the public in their use of transportation systems. The agency points out that the cost of the agency to the public is nominal (approximately 25 cents per U.S. citizen) when compared with the impact it has on the public at large.

The recommendations that the NTSB makes are mostly retroactive because some problems or issues are not realized until after an accident has happened. Yet, these recommendations still impact the industries in an effective manner. The DOT sets guidelines and—with the help of state and local authorities—enforces them. Transportation companies have the onus to comply and ensure the safety of the public. The safe transportation of materials, the maintenance of the companies' products, and safe operation are all examples of regulated activities. The public also has a duty to maintain and develop the knowledge necessary to operate or participate in the use of any transportation device. In this way,

despite its often retroactive approach, the agency can improve the safety of future operations, and each player in the equation can be a part of the changes.

The NTSB does not perform criminal investigations, but it often works with criminal investigators such as the FEDERAL BUREAU OF INVESTIGATION. Some critics argue that the NTSB lobbies and pressures industries, with the result being an inundation of burdensome regulation. Since the NTSB does not enforce regulations, it appears that this criticism is unwarranted. The NTSB rather appears to have significant power to effect change in the industry by offering its recommendations, which are then co-opted by the regulatory agencies. The agency continues to be true to its ideals and maintains a high-profile image in the nation's transportation industries. The agency head often appears before Congress to report agency findings. The NTSB publishes quarterly reports that can be found on its website.

For more information
Lebow, Cynthia C., ed. *Safety in the Skies: Personnel and Parties in the NTSB Aviation Accident Investigations.* New York: Rand, 1999.
National Transportation Safety Board. *National Transportation Safety Board.* Washington, D.C.: National Transportation Safety Board, 1995.
National Transportation Safety Board. www.ntsb.gov.

Ernest Alexander Gomez

natural resource damage assessments
Natural resource damage assessments (NRDAs) involve a federal process to (1) receive compensation for spills of oil and/or hazardous substances that subsequently damage natural resources and (2) address resource recovery or restoration efforts. This effort started in the 1980s and involves two federal agencies that have developed separate, federally approved rules and procedures, the U.S. Department of Interior (US DOI) and the U.S. Department of

Commerce, National Oceanographic and Atmospheric Administration (U.S. DOC, NOAA). The approved rules apply to assessments of economic losses (economic damages in the adopted language) that result from such spills in waterways under U.S. jurisdiction.

The US DOI was given legal responsibility and authority to (1) develop procedures to use in the case of hazardous-substance spills and oil spills in all navigable waters of the United States under the Comprehensive Environmental Response, Compensation, and Liability Act of 1980 (CERCLA), amended by the Superfund Act of 1986 (SARA), and (2) seek legal means to recover assessed economic damages that can result from spills of hazardous substances. The legal liabilities and responsibilities are stipulated in CERCLA of 1980 and SARA of 1986, commonly referred to as CERCLA by practitioners. Oil was not included within CERCLA because it was previously covered under the Clean Water Act (CWA, enacted in 1970 as the Water Quality Improvement Act—partially in response to the famous Santa Barbara oil spill—amended by the Federal Water Pollution Control Act of 1972, and further amended in 1977).

However, the rules and procedures developed by the US DOI also refer to oil spills. For both the CWA and CERCLA, these laws provide that natural-resource damages are to be compensatory and not punitive, following common-law principles relating to damages (compensatory damages are favored over punitive damages). The first versions of these procedures were published in 1986 and in 1987, referred to as "type B" rules and as "type A" rules, respectively. These were subsequently revised in 1994 and in 1996 as required by federal court order.

In 1990, the Oil Pollution Act was passed, which gave the US DOC, NOAA, legal responsibility and liability over oil spills in the nations' waterways. For all oil spills that occurred after 1 August 1990, OPA 1990 supersedes the regulations, responsibilities, and liabilities stipulated in the Clean Water Act. However, OPA does not regulate crude oil and petroleum products, which are either treated as hazardous substances under CERCLA or under the CWA. NOAA's procedures were published in 1996 after undergoing an extensive period of development and formulation beginning in 1990.

NRDA rules and procedures are referred to as liability rules by economists. The procedure involves both fines and penalties or damage awards to return the injured environment back to predamaged levels. Parties become legally responsible for any and all damages from such spills. Damage awards include the sum of response costs, social damages, and restoration costs (sometimes these include the cost of purchasing equivalent natural resources). Difficulties consist of measuring social damages and the costs of restorations. It remains unknown whether such tools (1) affect behavior so as to limit random pollution events or (2) allow society to collect adequate social damages to return injured resources back to predamaged levels.

For more information

Ofiara, D. D., and J. J. Seneca. *Economic Losses from Marine Pollution: A Handbook for Assessment.* Washington, D.C.: Island Press, 2001.

Douglas D. Ofiara

neutral competency   Neutral competency is a concept that proposes that public administrators should be nonpartisan and be able to effectively and efficiently perform the duties of their positions in an objective manner. This school of thought encompasses the politics-administration dichotomy, and the idea can be understood briefly in the now-famous slogan, "Take the administration out of politics." The desire for objectivity, i.e., being able to do a job without political interference, exists today just as it did when the concept was born.

The concept of neutral competency has its roots in MAX WEBER's and Woodrow Wilson's ideas, as well as countless others. The demand for executives and administrators to be above the political fray came on the heels of public criticisms of the government bureaucracy. The spoils system was supposed to allow administrators to appoint skilled employees, but the result was that administrators filled positions with family and friends who did not have the skills necessary to do the job. This created government inefficiency and made many administrators ineffective.

The proponents of neutral competency (separating the politicos from the administrators) believed that this style of management embodied the idea of representation of the public. By separating the work of the administrator from the work of the politician, the administrator could tend to the tasks of his job without preference. It is believed that the freedom to complete administrative tasks free from political influence would ensure that decisions and actions taken by administrators were done efficiently and effectively, thereby providing for the public in an unbiased manner.

The concept of neutral competency grew after the Civil War, and bipartisan representation and commission-style administration became commonplace. The movement for neutral competency led to the creation of the Interstate Commerce Commission and other like agencies. Although these agencies had very different administrative operations, conceptually they were the same. Most agencies included overlapping leadership and terms for commission members, and they were granted discretion or secure tenure in order to remove the volatility associated with a political crisis. A merit-based promotional system grew from this idea, and many called for the removal of political appointing power, cessation of arbitrary promotions or dismissals, positional and responsibility classification created by clearly established job duties, and the banning of political activities by civil servants. The Civil Service Commission and other agencies acted in the role of administrative watchdog and demanded competence of public servants.

Today, most public servants work under a merit-based promotional system and are given great leeway in keeping their jobs despite errors (as long as those errors were made in the best interests of the agency mission). The training of public-sector employees has also improved, and the selection process weeds out individuals that do not meet the minimal requirements for each position. Many in the public administration field believe that the city-manager concept is one of the great accomplishments of neutral competency. The idea of neutral competency has spread into others realms of administration, such as in the running of nonprofit organizations, beyond the field of public administration.

For more information

Kaufman, Herbert. "Emerging Conflicts in the Doctrines of Public Administration." *American Political Science Review* 50, no. 4 (December 1956): 1057–1073.

Stillman, Richard J., II. *Preface to Public Administration.* New York: St. Martin's Press, 1991.

Ernest Alexander Gomez

new public administration   The new public administration movement refers to a refocus of public management toward responsive and socially equitable implementation of public programs.

In 1968, a gathering of young academics in public administration met at the MINNOWBROOK CONFERENCE site at Syracuse University in New York. The purpose of the conference was to identify how public administration as a discipline was to meet the demands of the 1960s and 1970s for more social services and public programs. In the past, the discipline focused on running government like a business, with concerns focused on efficiency and economy while maintaining accountability to the citizens. The focus of the conference was to expand the emphasis on these traditional concepts to include responsiveness.

This "new public administration" was to have at its center social equity in the implementation of programs by public service employees. According to H. George Frederickson, one of the contributors to the conference and a continued supporter of the new-public-administration approach, this meant that bureaucrats needed to be more responsive to the public, who were considered customers or clients under the new public administration approach. The new public administrators would include normative and prescriptive ideals of democracy such as fair and equal treatment. Most of all, public administrators were to focus on the needs of the citizen as a client of the public program rather than on the efficiency of the process.

The new public administration approach was to replace several of the past goals for bureaucrats working in the public sector. First, administrators were to be recognized not as neutral or value-free decision makers as they had been in the past. Instead, they were expected to seek good management practices while implementing the values of social equity in their programs. Second, public administrators were to be change agents in the workplace by eliminating policies and structures that systematically inhibited social equity. Finally, the new public administrator was to function as a second-generation behavioralist, acting as a seeker of social justice while maintaining a scientific approach toward implementation. The analytical skills applied in previous decades to efficient management were now also to be used to achieve the goal of social equity. Ultimately, the new public administrator had to balance efficiency, economy, and equity.

Today, the new public administration is generally taught as one approach that can guide bureaucrats. While the concepts are accepted by most students studying public administration, it has been difficult to implement many of the tenets in the workplace. Nonetheless, the new public administration approach continues to serve as an ethic or as a guidepost for public administrators. A collection of the papers presented at the Minnowbrook Conference was edited and published by Frank Marini, then editor of the *Public Administration Review* journal.

For more information

Frederickson, H. George. *The Spirit of Public Administration.* San Francisco: Jossey-Bass, 1997.

Marini, Frank, ed. *Toward a New Public Administration: The Minnowbrook Perspective.* Scranton, Pa.: Chandler Publishing, 1971.

Kelly Tzoumis

Nixon, Richard (1913–1994) *37th president of the United States*

Richard Milhous Nixon, the 37th American president, was born and grew up in poverty in Whittier, California, the son of a Quaker grocer and gas station operator.

After graduating from Whittier College in 1934 and Duke University Law School in 1937, Nixon practiced law in California, worked in the Office of Price Administration in Washington, and served in the Pacific theater during World War II. Following the war, Nixon defeated the Democratic incumbent to win election to the U.S. Congress as a Republican from California's 12th Congressional District, a seat he held from 1947 to 1951. In 1950 Nixon defeated Helen Gahagan Douglas in a bitterly fought campaign to win a U.S. Senate seat. Nixon drew national attention in the House and Senate for his anticommunist positions and for his prominent role in the Alger Hiss case. In 1952, Nixon won the Republican Party's vice-presidential nomination, and he went on to serve as President Dwight D. Eisenhower's vice president from 1953 to 1961. In 1960, Nixon won the Republican Party's presidential nomination, but he lost to Democrat John F. Kennedy in a close election. Two years later, after a stinging defeat in California's gubernatorial race, Nixon announced his retirement from politics.

Nixon returned to political life in 1968, winning the Republican Party's presidential nomination yet again and defeating Democrat Hubert

Humphrey and American Independent George C. Wallace to win the presidency with 43 percent of the popular vote and 301 electoral votes. As president, Nixon demonstrated an inordinate predilection for secrecy and isolation, often keeping important diplomatic and domestic initiatives from cabinet members and members of Congress. He exhibited deep suspicion and distrust toward the federal bureaucracy, especially the State Department, and over the course of his presidency he limited his exposure to his cabinet secretaries and increasingly centralized policy making in the White House. During his second term, he reshuffled his cabinet, replaced suspect political appointees with loyalists throughout the bureaucracy, and presented a proposal to reorganize the federal bureaucracy into four large policy areas (natural resources, community development, human resources, economic affairs) under the control of four "supersecretaries" answering to the president. However, Nixon's reorganization efforts were eventually overwhelmed by the WATERGATE scandal and left largely unimplemented.

The Nixon administration oversaw a flurry of activity in foreign affairs, negotiating the Seabed Treaty (1970), the Chemical Weapons Treaty (1971), a Strategic Arms Limitation Treaty (1972), and the Antiballistic Missile Treaty (1972) with the Soviet Union. Nixon also was the first American president to visit the Soviet Union and the People's Republic of China. Although he had claimed during the election campaign that he had a "secret plan" to end the war in Vietnam, as president he expanded the fighting into neighboring Cambodia and Laos while reducing American troop levels in the region. However, secret negotiations with the North Vietnamese in Paris, spearheaded by Nixon's national security advisor, Henry Kissinger, led to a peace agreement in January 1973 that would result in a U.S. withdrawal from the Vietnamese conflict. Overriding Nixon's veto, Congress passed the WAR POWERS ACT later that year to limit the president's ability to wage war without congressional sanction.

Nixon expressed little interest in domestic policy, but rising inflation, a lackluster economy, and domestic unrest periodically forced him to divert his attention from foreign affairs. To combat inflation, Nixon imposed wage and price controls in 1971, and in 1972 the administration adopted a program of revenue sharing, returning billions of dollars in federal revenues to state and local governments with few restrictions as to how they should be spent. Other important domestic initiatives during the Nixon administration included a series of major crime bills, the Environmental Quality Policy Act of 1969, the Water Quality Improvement Act of 1970, the National Air Quality Standards Act of 1970, the Resource Recovery Act of 1970, the Consumer Product Safety Act of 1972, and the Water Pollution Act (passed over Nixon's veto in 1972).

Nixon easily defeated his Democratic opponent, South Dakota senator George McGovern, to win reelection in 1972 with 61 percent of the popular vote and 520 electoral votes, one of the most lopsided presidential victories in American political history. However, the Watergate scandal, which began as a botched break-in of the Democratic Party's Washington offices in 1972, would come to dominate Nixon's second term, as continuing investigations revealed systemic abuses of power and that a cover-up of the White House's involvement in the affair was orchestrated from within the Oval Office. On 9 August 1974, Nixon resigned after the House Judiciary Committee voted to recommend three articles of impeachment against the president to the full House. He was succeeded by his vice president, Gerald R. Ford of Michigan.

For more information

Aitken, Jonathan. *Nixon, A Life*. Washington, D.C.: Regnery Publishing Co., 1994.

Hoff, Joan. *Nixon Reconsidered*. New York: Basic Books, 1995.

Reeves, Richard. *President Nixon: Alone in the White House*. New York: Touchstone, 2001.

William D. Baker

nongovernmental organizations (NGOs)
See NONPROFIT SECTOR.

nonprofit corporation   A nonprofit corporation is an organization created for the purposes of delivering social-welfare and other services and programs to different groups in society. The importance of nonprofit corporations arises from the fact that many of them perform functions in the United States that often are performed by the public sector.

Legally, nonprofit or not-for-profit organizations are corporations created under state and federal law. Unlike business corporations, which are created to make profits or dividends that are distributed to shareholders or investors, state and federal law prevents nonprofits from doing this. Instead, any profits or dividends that are produced must go back into the organization. State laws determine the structure of nonprofits. Generally, these laws require that all nonprofits have a governing board that oversees the organization, with an executive director, who reports to the board, serving as the main person who runs the corporation and oversees its staff.

Nonprofits are often described as "mission-driven." While for-profit businesses may have a mission they serve in order to make money, nonprofit organizations are created to fulfill specific purposes, such as finding cures for cancer or other diseases, helping the poor, housing the homeless, or serving other educational or social-welfare functions. Under federal law, certain nonprofits can obtain a tax-exempt status. To this end, the Internal Revenue Service (IRS) code describes many nonprofits as what has come to be called §501(c)(3) entities. This U.S. Code 26 §501(c)(3) reference refers to a specific section of the IRS code, which indicates that a nonprofit can be tax exempt if it is: "operated exclusively for religious, charitable, [or other specified] purposes, . . . and which does not participate in, or intervene in (including the publishing or distributing of statements), any political campaign on behalf of (or opposition to) any candidate for public office."

If a nonprofit is recognized as a §501(c)(3) entity, it does not have to pay income taxes, and contributions to it can be considered as charitable contributions that can be deducted to reduce the donor's income tax obligations. Yet in return for these privileges, §501(c)(3) entities may not engage in partisan politics and they must disclose many of their financial records to the public.

The point of discussing §501(c)(3) entities is that while federal law recognizes some nonprofits as tax exempt, not all of these organizations are. Instead, federal and state law recognizes a huge range of nonprofit organizations in the United States, all organized for a wide variety of purposes. These organizations include the American Red Cross, the American Cancer Society, the Salvation Army, and the Catholic Church, as well as museums, colleges, hospitals, foundations, and a host of other entities. They range in size from perhaps one-person operations to multibillion-dollar operations, all serving specific populations as defined by their mission statements. In the United States there are well over 1 million nonprofit agencies and organizations.

Nonprofit corporations fulfill many functions, but an increasingly important role for them in recent years has been to perform functions that either supplement what the government does, or to perform quasi-governmental services through contracts they have received from federal, state, or local governments. For example, some nonprofits are under contract with city governments to provide housing or homeless shelters to qualifying individuals or families. As a result, the NONPROFIT SECTOR has become very important in public administration, often serving as government surrogates or alternative service providers for programs and services often considered to be exclusively the province of the public sector and public administration.

For more information

Carver, John. *Boards That Make a Difference: A New Design for Leadership in Nonprofit and Public Organizations.* San Francisco: Jossey-Bass, 1997.

Ott, J. Steven. *Understanding Nonprofit Organizations.* Boulder, Colo.: Westview Press, 2001.

David Schultz

nonprofit sector   The nonprofit sector refers to a host of organizations in American society that provide a wide range of goods and services to broad segments of the population. Oftentimes the nonprofit sector is seen as an alternative to the government when it comes to servicing specific social needs.

The nonprofit sector is also often called the "independent sector," and it consists of many voluntary private organizations often referred to as nonprofits or nonprofit organizations. Outside the United States, these entities are often referred to as nongovernmental organizations (NGOs). Among the defining characteristics of the nonprofit sector is that organizations do not exist for the purposes of making private profits or dividends that are distributed to shareholders. Instead, these organizations are voluntarily created to fulfill specific educational, religious, cultural, and social-welfare functions ranging from helping the disadvantaged, providing medical care and housing, and operating museums to serving specific populations such as members of different ethnic, racial, or religious groups.

Internationally, NGOs such as the World Bank and the International Monetary Fund are also important in providing financial assistance and loans to national governments. Thus, nonprofits often perform duties that are similar to what are traditionally associated with the public sector. This means that NONPROFIT CORPORATIONS are similar to private-sector corporations in that they are privately run for a specific purpose, but they may share many public-sector characteristics in that they also mirror what governments may do.

Within the United States, nonprofits can perhaps trace their origins to the voluntary public associations or societies that formed early in American history. Alexis de Tocqueville wrote in his 1840 *Democracy in America* that voluntary associations easily rise and flourish in the United States, with people eager to form groups to address a variety of social causes and problems. It is from these voluntary associations, perhaps, that the nonprofit arose, with poorhouses, orphanages, and volunteer fire and police departments leading the way. Out of them many famous organizations arose, including JANE ADDAMS'S HULL-HOUSE in Chicago, Illinois, in 1889, which provided numerous services to the poor, and Clara Barton's American Red Cross, which was founded in 1881. Since that time, millions of other nonprofits and NGOs have arisen, and the total value of the goods and services they deliver is in the billions of dollars, and the number of people that they serve is in the millions.

Besides performing many governmentlike services without regard for profit, the nonprofit sector possesses several other defining traits. For example, they are mission driven and organized for clearly defined purposes. Second, much of the work performed by nonprofits or NGOs is delivered by volunteers. Third, much of the money used to fund nonprofits has traditionally come from private and voluntary contributions from donors. As a result, some describe the nonprofit sector as the world of charities and charitable giving, where compassion, sympathy, and empathy are the primary values that define the behavior of individuals and organizations who are involved. This contrasts with the private sector, where the desire for personal financial gain is what is supposed to motivate behavior.

Over the years the nonprofit sector has undergone significant changes. Starting in the 1960s, the number of nonprofit organizations began to grow dramatically, partly in response to collaborations with government agencies that increasingly turned to them either to be alternative service providers or to supplement government activity. A characteristic of nonprofits during this time was that most were small operations, often employing only a few people. Yet by the 1990s there were pushes to consolidate, transforming the independent sector from a world of small "mom and pop" agencies to large organizations such as the United Way, the American Red Cross, and Catholic Charities, employing thousands of people, serving millions of people, and handling billions of dollars. This push toward consolidation also meant a drive toward professionalizing nonprofits.

The growth of the nonprofit sector, while good in many respects, also has led to many concerns. First, the drive to professionalize may be crowding out volunteers from many organizations, thereby raising the costs associated with the delivery of goods and services. These increased costs have also led to the need to raise more money, and this has forced many nonprofits either to become more dependent upon government contracts for money, or to spend more time fund-raising, or to become more involved in partnerships in the private sector. All of these activities raise critical concerns regarding how independent the nonprofit sector still is.

Moreover, with the demand to expand services has come calls for the nonprofit sector to be more responsible in how it spends its money, forcing many entities to adopt practices generally more characteristic of the private sector. As nonprofit groups continue to evolve in that direction, critics complain that nonprofits are losing their distinct identity and their capacity to promote many of their traditional ethical values of compassion and empathy.

Finally, a last set of concerns regarding the evolution of nonprofits and NGOs is their increased political power and lack of accountability. With so many of the groups undertaking traditional governmental functions, the complaint is that these groups are exercising political power without being subject to the same checks for the public as are governmental bodies. For example, the public does not have a right to elect members of the nonprofit boards or attend meetings. NGOs such as the International Monetary Fund or the World Bank have the capacity to force sovereign governments to adopt certain policies, and the people in those countries do not have much say over them. Thus, many NGOs and nonprofits are accused of acting in an antidemocratic fashion. Given these criticisms, the nonprofit sector is facing more media and public scrutiny than in the past, placing pressures upon many organizations to change their practices.

For more information

Carver, John. *Boards That Make a Difference: A New Design for Leadership in Nonprofit and Public Organizations.* San Francisco: Jossey-Bass, 1997.

Fischer, Marilyn. *Ethical Decision Making in Fund Raising.* New York: John Wiley & Sons, 2000.

Ott, J. Steven. *Understanding Nonprofit Organizations.* Boulder Colo.: Westview Press, 2001.

———. *The Nature of the Nonprofit Sector.* Boulder, Colo.: Westview Press, 2001.

David Schultz

North American Free Trade Agreement

In December of 1992, the heads of state of Canada, Mexico, and the United States signed the North American Free Trade Agreement, or NAFTA. NAFTA was approved by the U.S. Congress in 1994, and the agreement went into effect 1 January 1994. NAFTA creates a framework for each country to eliminate its barriers to the others' exports. In addition to eliminating trade barriers among the three countries, the agreement also provides greater openness in the trade of services and in foreign investment. The agreement also allows for the three countries to cooperate and coordinate on environmental and labor issues.

During the years of its negotiation, there was a great deal of opposition to NAFTA. Workers' and environmental groups argued that NAFTA would compromise Canadian and U.S. labor and environmental standards by allowing imports from Mexico, whose standards are less rigid.

These groups also argued that by eliminating restrictions on foreign investment, NAFTA would provide an inducement for Canadian and U.S. firms to relocate to Mexico.

Proponents of NAFTA, on the other hand, argued that NAFTA would create a win-win scenario for all three countries by expanding trade and investment opportunities, in turn contributing to economic growth for all three. Proponents also argued that rather than lowering labor and environmental standards in Canada and the United States, NAFTA would serve to improve Mexico's standards. In addition, supporters of NAFTA argued that by expanding economic openness in Mexico, political openness would occur as well. Finally, proponents argued that NAFTA, by fostering economic cooperation among the three countries, would also foster cooperation in other areas, particularly immigration and drug trafficking.

The results of NAFTA have been mixed. Trade and investment among the three countries have increased, but the increase in trade and investment was a trend that was occurring before NAFTA was negotiated. Canadian and U.S. labor and environmental standards have not been weakened as a result of NAFTA, but neither have Mexico's standards significantly improved. Immigration and drugs still remain contentious issues among the three countries. On the other hand, although Canadian and U.S. firms did take advantage of new investment opportunities in Mexico, the exodus of jobs to Mexico that had been feared by its opponents did not occur. Indeed, during the first five years of NAFTA, unemployment rates in the United States were among the lowest in the nation's history.

Another positive consequence of the agreement is that NAFTA may have had some small role in bringing about the first truly free election in Mexico's history. With the election of the current president Vicente Fox and the erosion of single-party rule, the Mexico of today is a more democratic country than the Mexico with which Canada and the United States negotiated NAFTA.

For more information

Mayer, Frederick W. *Interpreting NAFTA: The Science and Art of Political Analysis.* New York: Columbia University Press, 1998.

Nader, Ralph, ed. *The Case against Free Trade: GATT, NAFTA, and the Globalization of Corporate Power.* San Francisco: Earth Island Press, 1993.

Orme, William A. *Understanding NAFTA: Mexico, Free Trade, and the New North America,* 2d ed. Austin: University of Texas Press, 1996.

United States Trade Representative. http://www.ustr.gov/regions/whemisphere/ nafta.shtml.

Steven G. Jones

notice and comment   Notice and comment in administrative law refers to a particularized set of procedures through which an administrative agency solicits public participation in the rulemaking process. The precise nature of the procedures followed differs, depending upon both the agency and the type of rule making under consideration. When agencies engage in legislative rule making, they must satisfy certain minimum requirements provided under the ADMINISTRATIVE PROCEDURE ACT (APA).

Historically, one aspect of the expansion of the executive branch during the New Deal era was the creation of administrative agencies, which were granted considerable power to give force to complex legislation by creating rules. Criticism soon arose, and the agencies were sometimes described as a fourth branch of government: unelected, unaccountable to the people, and mysterious in its operations. The Administrative Procedure Act of 1946 was a response to these concerns and mandated that agencies follow requirements designed to increase openness and transparency in their activities. Included in these requirements are the notice and comment procedures, which must be followed when an agency engages in legislative rule making. The notice requirements relate to how an agency must inform the public that it intends to promulgate certain rules, and the comment requirements relate to how an agency must accept input from interested members of the public.

The purpose of the notice requirement is to provide the public with information about rules that an agency is considering adopting, in order to allow interested persons to participate and to formulate responses to proposed actions by agencies. Another purpose underlying the notice requirement is to increase the accountability of decision makers within administrative agencies. The purpose of the requirement that agencies receive public comment is to provide agencies with information, to expose the agencies to suggestions and criticisms, and to facilitate positive relationships between governmental agencies and the public that they serve.

When an agency is required to provide notice under the APA, the notice must contain the following three types of information. First, the notice must contain a statement of the time, place, and nature of any public rule-making proceedings. Second, the notice must state the legal authority under which the agency proposes the rule. Third, the language of the proposed rule or a description of the issues involved in the proposal must be included.

The notice must either be published in the FEDERAL REGISTER or provided individually to all persons subject to the proposed rule. Additional requirements may apply to some agencies and to some types of rule making. For example some types of legislative rule making may require a hearing or more specific types of notice. Thus, the APA is a starting point rather than the only source of notice-and-comment requirements for agency rule making. Also, some agencies have chosen to follow notice-and-comment procedures in instances such as interpretative rule-making activities, where they are not required, or to provide more extensive notice-and-comment procedures, such as a formal hearing, than

required by law. Where legislation such as the APA does not require certain notice-and-comment procedures to be followed in a particular instance, and the agency chooses not to follow them, courts are generally powerless to invalidate the rule on the basis that greater public participation should have been allowed, except where required to preserve constitutional rights.

Requirements regarding public comments are fairly simple. Agencies are required to consider any comments that are received in writing or at an oral hearing. After consideration of relevant comments, agencies are required to incorporate a concise statement of the basis and purpose of the rule. Generally, agencies will note important or helpful comments in the preamble to the final rule when it is officially promulgated. It is not necessary for an agency to create rules that agree with public comments or for the agency to refute comments in disagreement with the final rule. However, by carefully responding to public comments, an agency may demonstrate its rule to be the product of an informed, thorough, and reasoned decision-making process worthy of respect and judicial deference. Similarly, if an agency neglects to respond to significant public comments or to explain its position in light of concerns reflected in public comments, a court may be more likely to invalidate the rule if it is challenged.

For more information

Fox, William, Jr. *Understanding Administrative Law,* 2d ed. New York: Matthew Bender, 1992.

U.S. Code. Title 5, sec. 553.

U.S. Senate. *Administrative Procedure Act, Legislative History.* 79th Cong., 2d sess., 1946. S. Doc. 248.

Demetra M. Pappas

Nuclear Regulatory Commission   The Nuclear Regulatory Commission (NRC) began as the Atomic Energy Commission (AEC), which was established by Congress under the Atomic Energy Act of 1946. The subsequent Atomic

Energy Act of 1954 moved the country forward in developing commercial applications of nuclear power and gave the AEC responsibility for both developing nuclear power and regulating its safety (specifically with respect to radiation protection, plant siting, and environmental quality). An important feature of the AEC at this time is that its mission was to improve safety without jeopardizing the commercial growth of the nuclear industry. As a result, critics charged that the mission had an inherent conflict.

This conflict led Congress to pass the Energy Reorganization Act in 1974, creating the Nuclear Regulatory Commission (NRC) and the DEPARTMENT OF ENERGY (DOE). The DOE was given the task of developing nuclear power, and the NRC was given the task of overseeing issues of reactor safety, protection of public health, and development of regulations. These regulations focus on the use of nuclear materials for power production as well as in a variety of applications in medicine, industry, and research. The NRC regularly publishes standards for radiation protection and the use of these nuclear materials, establishes requirements on reactor design and operation (intended to reduce the probability and severity of accidents), considers siting and design of new reactors, and reviews performance of existing power plants.

In addition, the NRC is charged with regulating nuclear materials, including theft or diversion of these materials. This task stems from the fact that some nuclear materials can be hazardous if used inappropriately, and they can also be used in construction of weapons. A particularly important issue related to this task is the development of storage facilities for spent nuclear fuel, particularly the fuel rods of reactors after they have been used. The NRC has regulatory control over these materials, and any waste management policies (including development of a national repository for high-level radioactive waste) must meet NRC safety requirements.

For more information

George T. Mazuzan. *Controlling the Atom: The Beginnings of Nuclear Regulation 1946–1962.* Berkeley: University of California Press, 1984.

Samuel J. Walker. *Containing the Atom: Nuclear Regulation in a Changing Environment, 1963–1971.* Berkeley: University of California Press, 1992.

———. *Permissible Dose: A History of Radiation Protection in the Twentieth Century.* Berkeley: University of California Press, 2000.

Occupational Safety and Health Administration

Occupational Safety and Health Administration The Occupational Safety and Health Administration (OSHA) is the federal government agency charged with the regulatory responsibility for ensuring that U.S. workers have safe and healthful workplaces.

Established by the Occupational Safety and Health Act of 1970, OSHA began its institutional existence in 1971. A part of the DEPARTMENT OF LABOR, it is based in Washington, D.C., with 10 regional offices around the nation. OSHA is headed by an assistant secretary of labor, who is appointed by the president to an open-ended term with the consent of the Senate. It is responsible for setting workplace safety and health standards and enforcing employer compliance through workplace inspections and fines for serious violations. OSHA also provides safety and health information and training to workers and employers, and it works with the National Institute of Occupational Safety and Health, which conducts medical research on workplace hazards and makes recommendations to OSHA for standards.

OSHA was the result of a political compromise reached between congressional Democrats and the Nixon administration. By the late 1960s, it became increasingly clear to organized labor and liberal Democrats that the uneven, patch-work quilt of state regulations was inadequate to control the widespread proliferation of workplace hazards in a highly industrialized economy. Seeking to increase his electoral support among the blue-collar "silent majority," President Nixon agreed to sign OSHA legislation, but he insisted that it maintain a strong state presence. Consequently, 23 states have their own enforcement plans, which can be based on their own or OSHA's standards but must meet OSHA's minimum standards. In addition, three states have their own plans just for their public-sector employees. Workplaces with fewer than 11 people and agricultural workers are exempt from OSHA's jurisdiction.

Since its inception, OSHA has been constantly under attack by corporate interests that chaff at its oversight and by Republicans who try to cut its budget, if not dismantle the agency outright. As measured by its mission—to ensure that Americans have safe workplaces—OSHA has been chronically underfunded and understaffed for its entire history. Its 1,170 inspectors are hard-pressed to cover the numerous workplaces under its jurisdiction, and the fines levied by the agency are routinely reduced, if not overturned on appeal to the Occupational Safety and Health Review Commission. During the Reagan administration, corporate interests mounted a major effort to "reform" OSHA, i.e., to weaken its regulatory authority through increased reliance on voluntary compliance programs. This trend continues today.

OSHA's biggest success has been in preventing imminent hazards. Indeed, the occupational mortality rate has fallen 50 percent and the workplace injury rate has declined 40 percent since the agency's inception. However, it has promulgated few new chemical and environmental standards to prevent occupational illnesses and health problems, despite major changes in the work process during the past three decades. The recent demise of its ergonomics standard, designed to prevent the proliferation of repetitive-strain illnesses in the workplace, illustrates OSHA's status as a besieged government agency. The ergonomics standard was 10 years in preparation and survived budget shortfalls and attacks from corporate and congressional opponents before it was finally promulgated by President Clinton shortly before leaving office. However, in an unprecedented move, the Republican-controlled Congress and President George W. Bush took less than two months to repeal the standard in 2001 on the grounds that it would be too expensive.

For more information

McGarity, Thomas O., and Sidney A. Shapiro. *Workers at Risk: The Failed Promise of the Occupational Safety and Health Administration.* Westport, Conn.: Praeger, 1993.

Mogensen, Vernon L. *Office Politics: Computers, Labor, and the Fight for Safety and Health.* New Brunswick, N.J.: Rutgers University Press, 1996.

Noble, Charles. *Liberalism at Work: The Rise and Fall of OSHA.* New Brunswick, N.J.: Rutgers University Press, 1986.

Vernon Mogensen

Office of Government Ethics The Office of Government Ethics (OGE) is an executive branch agency responsible for providing leadership in the establishment of conflicts-of-interest policies and standards-of-conduct regulations for executive departments and agencies; for overseeing the programs implemented by the agencies to ensure high ethical standards among their officers and employees, including the administration of the public and confidential financial-disclosure systems; and for ordering corrective actions for regulations violations by individuals or agencies (5 C.F.R. part. 2600).

Created by the ETHICS IN GOVERNMENT ACT of 1978 (EGA) (PL 95-521; as amended, 5 U.S.C. App.), OGE was originally placed in the Office of Personnel Management. To fulfill a campaign pledge "to guarantee integrity in the executive branch of government" after the government scandals of the 1970s, President Jimmy Carter had proposed such an office in the ethics legislation promoted by his administration in May 1977. Though the final version of the law extended to legislative, judicial, and executive employees, upon signing the act on 26 October 1978, the president recalled his pledge and noted OGE's executive branch role in making government "open, honest and free from conflicts of interests" (Weekly Compilation of Presidential Documents. Vol. 14, No. 43 [1978]).

The OGE became an independent agency on 1 October 1989, as part of the Office of Government Ethics Reorganization Act of 1988 (PL 100-598) and received added supervisory responsibilities under the Ethics Reform Act of 1989 (PL 101-194) when Congress established post-employment, outside earned income, and outside employment restrictions on certain federal employees. President Bush's Executive Order 12674, "Fourteen Principles of Ethical Conduct for Congressional Officers and Employees" (3 C.F.R. 1989 Compilation, pp. 215–216), the standards of conduct regulations (5 C.F.R. Parts 2634–2641), and the conflicts-of-interest criminal statutes (primarily 18 U.S.C. §§ 201–209;

216; 218–219) make up a substantial part of OGE guidance responsibilities.

The director of OGE is appointed by the president with the advice and consent of the Senate for a five-year term. To fulfill OGE's mission, he/she is assisted by a deputy director and four offices. The offices and some of their major duties include the following: the Office of Government Relations and Special Projects performs OGE's liaison function to the Office of Management and Budget and to Congress; advises foreign governments on anticorruption programs; and assists the director when advising either the President's Council on Integrity and Efficiency or the Executive Council on Integrity and Efficiency. The Office of General Counsel and Legal Policy provides branch-wide ethics program policies and regulations development, agency-level legal and policy implementation assistance, and statutory and regulatory advisory opinions; initiates executive branch administrative ethics corrective actions; makes referrals to the Department of Justice for criminal conflict of interest violations; and answers media requests for information.

The Office of Agency Programs provides each executive branch department and agency ethics office with various materials, opportunities, updates, and advice for ethics training; conducts scheduled yearly on-site ethics program reviews to ensure that each agency's program, counseling, and training are tailored to its needs and goals and is being implemented properly; collects, tracks, reviews, and certifies the annual and termination public financial-disclosure reports of Senate-confirmed presidential appointees and each executive agency's "designated agency ethics official," and processes Freedom of Information requests for the reports; and monitors proper certification of any ethics agreements (including recusal, waivers, divestiture, and blind trusts) by newly confirmed appointees. The Office of Administration and Information Management provides and coordinates essential administrative support services to all OGE programs.

The very concept of a government ethics program has prompted diverse reactions. It appears to some that insurance of public-employee integrity under EGA is equated with paperwork. The appearance of conflicts of interest is primarily eliminated through financial disclosure, since OGE has no mandate to address the "other dimensions of performance and character" needed to prevent government corruption. OGE directors have recognized, however, that it is the day-to-day maintenance of each agency's ethics program—supplemented by the values of each executive and employee, coupled with the public's ability to access disclosure information and make its own judgment on the integrity of public official—that are the keys to meeting the loftier goals of ethics legislation.

For more information

Comstock, Amy. Interview by Paul Lawrence. *Business in Government Hour.* Radio interview transcript. 22 August 2001. Available online. URL: http://www.endowment.pwcglobal.com/radio/comstock_frt.asp.

Maletz, Donald J., and Jerry Herbel. "Beyond Idealism: Democracy and Ethics Reform." *American Review of Public Administration* 30, no. 19 (March 2000): 19–46.

U.S. Office of Government Ethics. *Guidelines for Conducting Reviews of Ethics Programs at Executive Branch Agencies.* Washington, D.C.: U.S. Office of Government Ethics, May 2001.

U.S. Office of Government Ethics. *An Ethics Handbook for Executive Branch Employees.* Washington, D.C.: U.S. Office of Government Ethics, January 1995.

Kathleen M. Simon

Office of Management and Budget

The Office of Management and Budget (OMB) is often referred to as the president's budget office.

The OMB has a broad mandate for public-policy development and coordination across a number of functions of government. The director of OMB, who is a presidential nominee and confirmed by the Senate, carries out these functions as a member of the president's cabinet. OMB, a staff office within the EXECUTIVE OFFICE OF THE PRESIDENT, employs about 550 people, most of whom are career civil servants. While there are staff members who certainly have expertise in budgeting, many of its employees have training and experience in such areas as economics, public and business administration, statistics, and public policy areas as diverse as the activities of the federal government.

Some of the confusion about OMB's true role may stem from its beginning as the Bureau of the Budget (BOB) in the DEPARTMENT OF THE TREASURY after the passage of the Budget and Accounting Act of 1921. This law still provides much of OMB's legal authority to coordinate the development and implementation of the president's budget each fiscal year. This requires OMB to request budget plans from each executive branch agency, conduct its own independent analysis of the agency's budget request, and then make recommendations on what should be included for each agency in the president's budget request to the Congress. Once the Congress has appropriated funds to the agencies, OMB then works to ensure that the funds are spent consistent with the spending laws and policies of the presidential administration.

Unlike many federal agencies, OMB does not provide a good or service to the public. It does produce the president's budget document each year, but mostly it oversees the work of other federal agencies. One way it does this is by setting government-wide policy on a wide array of matters, ranging from how agencies procure goods and services to how they ensure the privacy of the public's sensitive information held in agency data stores. In addition to budget oversight and government-wide policy making, OMB staff also review other kinds of documents and plans produced by federal agencies.

While some of these responsibilities result from public laws enacted since the creation of

the BOB in 1921, others arise from the desire to have presidential administrations "speak with one voice" on important issues. As an example, before an executive branch official can testify before Congress, OMB staff review the draft testimony for consistency with the policies of the president. OMB staff also review such federal agency documents as reports to Congress, their strategic plans, regulations, surveys of the public, and their plans to invest in information technology.

Despite the relatively small size of OMB compared with the rest of the federal government, its proximity to the president and the White House along with its oversight and coordinating roles across a number of areas of government give it enormous power and responsibility.

For more information

Greider, William. "The Education of David Stockman." *Atlantic Monthly* 248, no. 6 (December 1981): 27–40.

Tomkin, Shelly Lynne, and Stephen J. Wayne. *Inside OMB: Politics and Process in the President's Budget Office (American Political Institutions and Public Policy)*. New York: M. E. Sharpe, 1998.

Steve H. Holden

Office of Personnel Management   The Office of Personnel Management (OPM) is the federal governmental agency responsible for all federal personnel activities except presidential appointees.

OPM is classified as an independent federal agency, like the National Aeronautics and Space Administration (NASA) and the Central Intelligence Agency (CIA), which means that it is not under the direct supervision of the EXECUTIVE OFFICE OF THE PRESIDENT as many of the bureaucratic agencies are. This is significant because the Office of Personnel Management (OPM) must be independent of any political influence in order to ensure that it is run without political bias favoring one party over another party. Just as with other independent federal agencies, the OPM accepts its mission and guidelines from the legislative branch of the government. Congress passes laws that provide direction and regulation on the administration of the OPM; however Congress cannot micromanage the operations of the office.

The government is run by people who coordinate with other people to keep every federal department, bureau, agency, and office doing the jobs that need to be done in the common interest of the American people. In 1996, the federal government employed over 2,847,000 people, and it is the responsibility of the OPM to ensure that the right people are hired for the right jobs, are adequately trained and retrained when necessary, receive proper promotions, receive proper pay for the work they are doing, and get fired only when necessary because of poor job performance. The OPM also has the daunting responsibility for resolving conflicts between and among people who work for the government, as well as dealing with any discrimination or harassment problems. It must also ensure the fair treatment of every federal employee and every job applicant.

The management of human resources has not always been based on fair and nonpartisan practices. The history of personnel management reveals that government employees were usually chosen according to the spoils system. This system was based much more on who knew whom in high places in the government. President Andrew Jackson was well noted for firing most of the people in government positions of responsibility when he first got into office and replacing them with people who would support his agenda and politics.

Obviously this did not go over very well with the opposing political party or with the fired government employees. Congress finally passed the PENDLETON ACT of 1883, which established the American civil service system. This act professionalized human-resource management in the government and set up specific requirements for equitable recruitment, examination, and classification of public employees based upon the merit system. In other words, government jobs were now going only to people who were qualified to perform the jobs adequately, regardless of political affiliation.

With the professionalization of public personnel management came both benefits and challenges. The most commonly heard problem with the current system is that of inflexibility and rigidity. The OPM is seen by many as a system that is so entrenched in bureaucracy and rules that it inhibits productivity, frustrates good employees, works against good management, and fails to respond to the needs of America's citizens.

The benefits of professionalizing public-personnel management have been felt by a much more diverse group of citizens than was possible before the Civil Rights Act of 1964 was passed by Congress. Government personnel offices on every level of government were then instructed to examine their own hiring practices for discrimination. This evaluative practice was further advanced by the Equal Employment Opportunity Act of 1972, the Civil Service Reform Act of 1978, and the Americans with Disabilities Act in 1990. The congressional acts were all designed to create a representative bureaucracy of personnel management that would be better able to respond to the needs of America's citizens.

For more information
Office of Personnel Management. http://www.opm.gov.

Lesele H. Rose

O'Hare Truck Service, Inc. v. City of Northlake 518 U.S. 712 (1996)

O'Hare Truck Service, Inc. v. City of Northlake is a U.S. Supreme Court decision that held that a state may not terminate the services of an independent contractor based on his or her political affiliation or exercise of political expression. This decision, along with its companion case, *Board*

of Commissioners, Wabaunsee County v. Umbehr,
518 U.S. 668 (1996), extended the First Amendment protections awarded to public employees in
the previous landmark cases of ELROD V. BURNS
(427 U.S. 347) and BRANTI V. FINKEL (445 U.S. 507)
to independent contractors in certain instances.

In *O'Hare,* a tow truck operator was removed
from a rotation list of businesses that provided
towing services to the city when the owner
refused to make a contribution to the mayor's
reelection campaign and supported the mayor's
opponent in the election. The Supreme Court
held that, while at-will employees may generally
be terminated without cause, adverse decisions
regarding their employment can not be made in
retaliation for the exercise of their First Amendment rights of political affiliation and expression.

In effect, under *O'Hare* the government can no
longer discharge, refuse to hire, or refuse to promote an independent contractor on the basis of
his or her political affiliation unless party affiliation is an appropriate requirement for effective
performance of the job in question. Alleged violations must be considered on a case-by-case basis
using the tests established in *Elrod* and *Branti*
(political affiliation) and the balancing test of
Pickering v. Board of Education (391 U.S. 563) for
restrictions of freedom of speech. The dissenting
justices, led by Justice Antonin Scalia, expressed
doubts about the effect of the *O'Hare* decision on
the system of political patronage long established
in the United States and predicted that the vague-
ness of the majority decision, which did not spell
out a clear rule for determining when independent contractors must be treated the same as public
employees, would create confusion, conflicting
decisions, and increased litigation.

However, in a time when formerly publicly
supplied services such as garbage collection,
sewage treatment, and towing are routinely contracted out to nongovernmental operators, it no
longer seems reasonable to draw a distinction
between public employees and independent contractors where the protection of First Amendment rights is concerned. Indeed, making such a

distinction might lead governments to contract
out even more services in order to avoid First
Amendment restrictions and preserve the patronage system. The flood of litigation feared by the
dissenting justices in *O'Hare* has not come to
pass, at least in part because plaintiffs suing
under *O'Hare* have a heavy burden of proving
that they were treated adversely based on their
political affiliation and that the job in question
did not reasonably require a particular political
affiliation to be performed effectively. Moreover,
governments can still terminate independent
contractors for poor performance or budgetary
reasons. Although there have indeed been conflicting decisions in cases decided in the lower
federal courts, the only adverse effect has been
on the political patronage system, which many
consider to be outdated and not worthy of judicial protection.

For more information
Chemerinsky, Erwin. "Speech Rights of Government
    Contractors. Supreme Court Review." *Trial* 33
    (January 1997): 64–66.
Koenig, Heidi. "Free Speech: Government Employees
    and Government Contractors." *Public Administra-
    tion Review* 57 (January/February 1997): 1–3.

Celia A. Sgroi

ombudsman   An ombudsman is an independent official given the authority and responsibility
of addressing complaints about governmental or
other organizational actions.

One definition of "ombudsman" proposed by
the U.S. Ombudsman Association, while specifically setting standards for the governmental
ombudsman, is that of "an independent, impartial public official with authority and responsibility to receive, investigate or informally address
complaints about government actions, and,
when appropriate, make findings and recommendations and publish reports."

The concept of the ombudsman originated in
Sweden. *Ombudsman* is a Swedish word that has

been used for centuries to describe a person who represents or protects the interests of another. Most ombudsman offices have been established within the public sector, but there are significant examples of such private offices. The key concepts of the ombudsman, whether private or public, ordinarily include accessibility by the public to the authorized ombudsman, a recognized procedure for processing grievances, and impartiality and independence of the ombudsman.

Interest in the ombudsman arose most notably, in the United States, during the 1970s. Ombudsman offices were established at many levels of government. Examples at the federal level include the U.S. Department of Education, the Environmental Protection Agency, the National Institutes of Health, and the Small Business Administration at the federal level. Other examples include the states of Alaska, Arizona, Hawaii, Iowa, and Nebraska and specific governmental functions, such as the National Long Term Care Resource Center funded by the U.S. Administration on Aging and operated by the National Citizens' Coalition for Nursing Home Reform. In addition, an ombudsman can be found in a variety of nonprofit organizations (National Public Radio) and many commercial organizations (Kodak and GE Capital). Newspapers have frequently established the ombudsman as an avenue for newspaper readers to respond to local and national news coverage. For example, the *St. Louis Post-Dispatch* and the *Washington Post* have been leaders in offering their readers the ombudsman as a method for addressing citizen complaints.

For more information

American Bar Association. http://www.abanet.org/adminlaw/ombuds/home.html.

Ombudsman Association. http://ombudstoa.org.

U.S. General Accounting Office. *The Role of Ombudsmen in Dispute Resolution.* GAO-01-466. Washington, D.C.: General Accounting Office, 2001. http://www.gao.gov.

U.S. Ombudsman Association. http://www.usombudsman.org.

Jerry Stephens

outsourcing Outsourcing is said to occur when an organization arranges for a function, good, or service to be performed outside the organization. The rationale for this is an increased capacity for the organization to maintain focus on its core business instead of being distracted by activities that can be provided externally. Outsourcing cushions the organization from uncertainty in aspects of its environment. It has become particularly common in large corporations and the public sector.

Typically, a public-sector funding body arranges for a nongovernment organization or individual to provide a service or perform a function defined by the public sector for a fee. This may occur in any portfolio area, but it is particularly common in the provision of utilities such as water and refuse collection, human resource activities, IT services, and human services such as support for people with disabilities, health services, and welfare provision to unemployed people. Organizations include private for-profit businesses and nonprofit public bodies.

There are a number of ways of making these arrangements. The government body can use a range of competitive tendering methods to identify the most suitable provider. A suitable provider can be chosen on the basis of prior knowledge to provide goods or services at a stipulated price. Alternatively, the government body may invite a selection of providers to tender, or the tender process may be an open one, in which providers are sought through advertisements in the press and other promotions. It may be a fixed tender process, in which the exact amount of available funding is disclosed, a process in which a funding range is suggested, or an uncapped budget that the aspiring provider must decide upon. Typically, the potential providers are assessed using indicators of efficiency and effectiveness as well as capacity to meet the requirements of the contract. This is established by such measures as prior experience and comments by referees.

The activity of outsourcing has gained favor since the financial strictures of the 1980s, which saw government and public-sector service providers face economic constraints. Neoliberal thought also gained momentum at this time and was highly influential in the search for solutions to these difficulties. Neoliberalism is based in the doctrine of the free market ultimately providing the most appropriate solutions to economic problems. This view has recently been extended to include community and social problems. Outsourcing is the application of "the invisible hand" of the market, including competition, to social problems previously believed unsuited to this treatment. This is also consistent with the doctrine of small government prevalent in much of the Western world during the 1990s and 2000s.

Outsourcing is likely to continue as an approach to service provision. Outsourcing is also an effective means of reducing risk and budget overruns, as the primary organization is protected from economic vagaries by the fixed contract.

Outsourcing by government is believed to be beneficial because of reduced infrastructure and salary costs. Its weaknesses are precisely the same: the loss of government assets and the lack of control over the provision of these often-essential goods and services are frequently lamented as a diminution of the quality of service over which government has little real control.

For more information

Claremont, James. *Privatisation and Outsourcing: An Annotated Bibliography.* Canberra: Lionel Murphy Library, Attorney-General's Dept., 1997.

Dinerman, Gloria. "The Angst of Outsourcing." *Information Outlook* 1, no. 4 (April 1997): 21–25.

Domberger, Simon. *The Contracting Organization: A Strategic Guide to Outsourcing.* Oxford and New York: Oxford University Press, 1998.

Reilly, Peter. *Outsourcing: A Flexible Option for the Future?* Brighton, England: Institute for Employment Studies, 1996.

Worthington, John, ed. *Reinventing the Workplace.* Boston: Architectural Press, 1997.

Megan Alessandrini

P

Patent and Trademark Office The U.S. Patent and Trademark Office is managed by the undersecretary of commerce for intellectual property, who has an additional, official title, director of the U.S. Patent and Trademark Office (USPTO). The commissioner of trademarks assists the director with trademark matters, and the commissioner of patents assists the director with processing approximately 300,000 patent applications annually, maintaining patent records, publishing official documents, and advising and informing the president on governmental affairs concerning patents.

Congress created the U.S. Patent Office as a bureau of the State Department in 1802 to handle the unanticipated volume of patent applications filed annually, following the enactment of the first patent laws in 1790. The Constitution mandated that Congress enact these laws to improve the competitiveness of U.S. industry by encouraging technological and scientific advancement. In 1845, the office was transferred to the Department of the Interior, and in 1925, the office was placed under the auspices of the Department of Commerce, where it remains today. The words *and Trademark* were added to the title of the office in 1975 to more accurately reflect the USPTO's current functions.

It is common for nonattorneys to confuse copyrights, trademarks, and patents with one another. These legal classifications serve the common purpose of protecting the product of an individual's creativity, but they apply to different manifestations of that originality.

A copyright's owner has the exclusive right to reproduce the copyrighted work and also to: prepare derivative works, distribute copies or sound recordings of the copyrighted work, and perform or display the copyrighted work publicly. The copyright protects the *form* of expression rather than the subject matter of the writing. For instance, the author of a copyrighted book about dogs has the exclusive privilege of using words in the sequence in which they appear in the book. However, the author cannot prevent others from writing books about dogs.

A trademark is a word (Kleenex), symbol (Apple Computers' profile of an apple), or device (Energizer bunny) that is used in connection with specific goods or services and identifies the source of the goods or services in a manner that distinguishes them from similar goods or services produced or provided by other individuals or businesses. The individual who owns a trademark can prevent others in the same business from using the same or a very similar mark, but that individual cannot prevent others from producing or selling similar goods or services under a different mark. A U.S. business that builds items or provides services that are sold in other states or countries may, but is not required to, register its trademark with USPTO. The advantage of registration is that it creates a public record of the trademark to notify others that they cannot use the same or a similar trademark to market similar goods or services.

A patent grants the inventor a monopoly—or right to exclude others from making, using, advertising as "for sale," selling, or importing the invention—for a period of 20 years after the date on which the application for the patent was filed at USPTO. Although monopolies are generally prohibited under U.S. law, this specific, time-limited right is allowed because society benefits when USPTO publishes the inventor's description of the previously unknown device or process. It is important to note that patents issued by USPTO are effective only within the United States, U.S. territories, and U.S. possessions.

After the USPTO receives a patent application, a patent examiner must search USPTO's files to determine: (1) whether the current application describes a device or process that is sufficiently different from previous items and processes that it would not be obvious to a person with ordinary knowledge of the invention's type of technology; and (2) that the device or process was not previously patented in the United States, described in a printed publication anywhere in the world, or in public use or for sale in the United States before the current patent application was filed. When an application fulfills these requirements and the inventor has paid the issuance fee, USPTO sends a copy of the patent to the inventor and publishes the patent in USPTO's public records.

Each patent issued by USPTO falls into one of the three types of patents. A *utility* patent may be granted to an individual who invents or discovers a new and useful process, machine, manufactured item, or composition of materials, or a new and useful improvement of an existing device or process. A utility patent remains in effect only if the inventor makes timely payment of periodic maintenance fees required by USPTO. A *design* patent may be granted to an individual who invents a new, original, and ornamental design for a manufactured item; and a *plant* patent may be granted to an individual who invents or discovers, and then asexually reproduces, a new, distinct variety of plant.

If a patent application does not fulfill USPTO requirements, the examiner rejects the application. The inventor may then amend the application, and again submit it to USPTO. If the application is rejected a second time, resubmission is allowed only if the inventor appeals the matter to the Board of Patent Appeals and Interferences. If this appeal also results in rejection of the application, the inventor may challenge this decision in a court of law.

If a patent examiner discovers that two individuals have filed patent applications describing nearly identical devices, the examiner must initiate an "interference," which is an administrative proceeding that determines which invention was completed earlier.

An inventor may sell some or all of the privileges granted by a patent, provided a copy of this transfer of rights is filed with USPTO. It is common for an inventor to sell to another business the right to manufacture the invention. This type of agreement, or license, requires that the manufacturer pay the inventor fees, or royalties, based on sales of the invention.

Although the patent concept is recognized throughout the world, each nation has its own distinct set of laws. Fortunately, a treaty signed by the United States, Canada, and nearly 100 other nations, facilitates filing patent applications in many nations. The nations that signed the treaty agree that when a citizen of one signatory nation applies for a patent in another signatory nation, the country that receives that application must treat it as if the inventor were its own citizen. Additionally, if an inventor files an application for a foreign patent within a year of applying for a patent in his/her own country, the foreign application is treated as if it were filed on the same date as the application in the inventor's home country. The 1978 Patent Cooperation Treaty, signed by the United States and 30 other countries, further facilitates filing patent applications for the same device or process in several countries. Participants in this treaty have agreed on a standard patent application form that is accepted in all of those countries and have further agreed to utilize the same method of searching for existing patents.

The *Patents Official Gazette* and *Trademarks Official Gazette,* both of which the USPTO publishes weekly, describe patents issued and trademarks registered by USPTO. Records of already-issued patents, patent applications filed since 29 November 2000, and records of assignment of patent rights are maintained by USPTO and are accessible to the public.

For more information

N.Y.S. Library. Patent information files. Available online. URL: http://www.nysl.nysed.gov/patents.htm#e.

U.S. Patent and Trademark Office. http://www. uspto. gov/web/offices/pac/doc/general/whatis.htm.

Beth Simon Swartz

Peace Corps   The Peace Corps is a U.S. government agency that sends civilian volunteers to foreign countries to teach various skills.

The Peace Corps was founded in 1961 by President John F. Kennedy, who observed, "Think of the wonders skilled American personnel could work, building goodwill, building the peace." The Peace Corps's mission is to transfer skills in fields such as education, public health, law, environmental protection, and business development in promotion of democracy, open society, and free-market economy. To this end, it recruits and trains individual Americans to live and work with host-country counterparts on a grass-roots level.

The Peace Corps stresses that it is not a funding agency or a provider of products or supplies; rather, it is a nonmilitary, non-intelligence-gathering organization, nonsectarian and nonpolitical (although clearly a government agency financed by the U.S. government). Its headquarters is in Washington, D.C., with recruiting offices in major U.S. cities.

Currently, about 7,000 Peace Corps volunteers serve in 91 countries (about half of the world's independent nations). The Peace Corps is present in a country by invitation only, i.e., the host country must request Peace Corps presence. There is wide variation in host-country conditions. Many are new nations seeking to develop modern infrastructure, while some have a history of industrialization and (e.g., in the countries of the former Soviet Union) seek to upgrade technical skills as well as develop managerial and financial practices in order to foster a Western-style, free-market economy.

Volunteers are recruited from universities and other venues through media advertising and personal contacts from paid, full-time recruiters, all of whom have successfully completed Peace Corps service. The application process is arduous, and only a fraction of all applicants is accepted. To be accepted as a volunteer, one must be an American citizen, a college graduate or have significant experience in a desired field, in reasonably good health, and unhampered by legal impediments. Most important, an applicant must demonstrate a desirable skill that can be transferred to a host country.

An applicant who is accepted into the Peace Corps becomes a volunteer and is assigned to a host country and a specific job in that country. A volunteer is expected to commit to two years of service, plus several months of training in the local language and culture. Service is strictly voluntary, so a volunteer is free to leave the Peace Corps at any time. However, volunteers are strongly encouraged to complete their service as planned.

Volunteers are not paid a salary but are provided with a monthly stipend that allows them to live in reasonable comfort and safety at approximately the level of their average host-country counterparts. The Peace Corps staff provides medical care, some transportation, and other support, but the volunteer is expected to function independently at the assigned job and become involved in local community outreach activities and participate in local cultural events. A volunteer is considered to be on duty around the clock, every day, as a positive example of America.

Volunteers include many new college graduates, although, increasingly, more older people with significant career expertise are volunteering. There is no upper age limit. Most volunteers are single, but married couples are also accepted.

For more information
Bannerjee, Dillon. *So You Want to Join the Peace Corps. What to Know Before You Go.* Berkeley, Calif.: Ten Speed Press, 2000.
Peace Corps. http://www.peacecorps.gov.

Elsa M. Shartsis

Pendleton Act   The Pendleton Act institutionalized merit appointments in the U.S. federal public service.

Prior to the Civil War, the individuals employed in the U.S. federal civil service were often placed in their positions as a form of patronage. Awarding jobs in the civil service was seen as a mechanism for "paying back" or rewarding political support. Even those who earned their appointments were increasingly expected to contribute time and money to partisan activities in order to keep their appointments. Elections resulted in a major staff turnover as individuals more loyal or committed to newly elected public officeholders replaced staff who were let go because they supported the losing candidate or who had refused to actively support the newly elected public officeholder.

From the public's point of view, this was tolerable, as the federal civil service was seen to be relatively ineffective and inconsequential. However, as the civil service became more complex and more important to the ongoing operation of the country, employees often required more specialized skills, and continuity between elections became more essential. Sensing this, public support for changes in the civil service appointment process grew in the 1870s.

A pivotal event occurred when President Garfield was assassinated by Charles Guiteau. Guiteau's grievance related to his disappointment in not being appointed to his desired office. This event galvanized public opinion that pressured Congress to change the civil service appointment system.

In 1883 Senator George Pendleton sponsored, and Congress passed, the Pendleton Act, an act to "regulate and improve the civil service of the United States." The act authorized the president to appoint three commissioners to serve as the "United States Civil Service Commission." The commission was charged with establishing examinations for testing the "fitness" of applicants for the public service and with ensuring that positions were classified in a system that would ensure that the highest-scoring individuals on particular exams were placed in the appropriate positions.

The Pendleton Act also required a probationary period for all positions and clearly stated that position holders were not required to contribute to any political fund or participate in partisan political activity and that they could not face discipline or removal for refusing to respond to such requests. The Pendleton Act further required that the commission ensure that the federal jobs were distributed among the states on a proportional basis, relative to population.

The passage of this act initiated the development of a merit-based civil service in the United States. For the first time, a law guaranteed federal civil service hiring based on merit. As technical and management skills have become increasingly vital to the functioning of a modern-day civil service, the principles outlined in the Pendleton Act have become even more important. The Pendleton Act created the framework that led to the development of a professional federal civil service that provides stability across political administrations.

For more information

U.S. Info. http://usinfo.state.gov.

U.S. Office of Personnel Management. http://www.opm.gov/index.htm.

Michael Henry

Pentagon   The Pentagon is the world's largest office building, whose name has come to symbolize the DEPARTMENT OF DEFENSE, which inhabits the building. Located in Arlington County, Virginia, directly across the Potomac River from the District of Columbia, on 34 acres (13.8 hectares), it is 71 feet high, five stories tall, and has five concentric rings named A, B, C, D, E. It has 6.5 million square feet of floor area, of which 3.7 million square feet are offices. There are 17.5 miles of corridors. The entire complex, including parking lots, covers 583 acres.

Groundbreaking occurred on 11 September, 1941. As the U.S. Army prepared for the impending conflict of World War II, the Department of War found itself housed in 17 buildings as its staffs dramatically expanded. This proved chaotic and interfered with efficiency. Although the Department of War had opened a new building that year, it too proved to be too small. Brigadier General Brehon B. Somervell, chief of the construction division of the army, took less than four days to develop plans for a facility that could handle a staff of 40,000. Its shape came from the five roads that surrounded the original agricultural-station farm location.

Because the project was estimated to cost over $35 million, the War Department had to convince Congress to appropriate the money. They argued that the navy could take over some of the offices that they were going to abandon, saving $22 million in a proposed new building for the Department of the Navy. The government also would save $3 million a year in rental fees on War Department offices. The remaining vacated offices would lessen the office-space shortage in Washington D.C. Finally, the new building would save money in travel time, and efficiency would increase from 20 to 40 percent.

Several congressmen felt the new office building was going to be a white elephant after the war ended and objected to taking land that was meant for Arlington National Cemetery. Nevertheless, on August 25, Congress agreed to the plan. The next day, under pressure from certain congressmen, President Franklin Roosevelt decided to move the location of the building about three-fourths of a mile southwest of Arlington to the "Northwest Triangle."

The architects were George E. Bergstrom and the John T. McShain Company of Philadelphia. After Pearl Harbor, a fourth and fifth floors were added to the plans. At peak times, 13,000 workers were involved in the project, and a total of 6 million cubic yards of dirt were moved and 435,000 cubic yards of concrete was poured. On 15 January 1943, the Pentagon was completed at what the War Department claimed was a cost of $63 million but more than likely exceeded $80 million.

The Pentagon is three times the size of the Empire State Building. To put its size in perspective, the Capitol building would fit in any of the five sections of the Pentagon. It currently houses 23,000 employees of the Defense Department. With its banks, shopping establishments, subway station, and cafeterias, it resembles a minor city. There are over 200,000 telephone calls daily, and over 1.2 million pieces of mail pass through the building monthly. Yet, given this immense size, it is designed so that an individual can move from one location in the building to any other in 10 to 15 minutes. The design and size of the building allow for the most efficient administration of the military.

In this large complex the Defense Department performs a myriad of tasks. Not only is it home to the Joint Chiefs of Staff, but it also headquarters the administration of each of the armed services and houses the public-relations and industry-coordination aspects of the modern American military. Special events and conferences are held on a regular basis inside the complex. The Pentagon also has become a model for other public-sector buildings. This large building was attacked by terrorists on 11 September 2001. Yet, it still remains the nation's largest office building and continues to function at peak efficiency.

For more information

Goldberg, Alfred. *The Pentagon: The First Fifty Years.* Washington, D.C.: History Office of Secretary of Defense, 1992.

Rogner, E. A. *Pentagon, "A National Institution": Its History, Its Functions, Its People.* Alexandria, Va.: D'Or Press, Dearengor, 1986.

Smith, Perry McCoy. *Assignment: Pentagon: The Insider's Guide to the Potomac Puzzle Palace.* Washington, D.C.: Pergamon-Brassey's, 1989.

T. Jason Soderstrum

performance auditing   Performance auditing is an integral part of the process in democratic governments by which citizens and their representatives hold government agencies accountable for efficient, effective, and equitable conduct. A performance audit is an objective, systematic examination of evidence to independently assess the performance of a government program against objective criteria. This definition is based on *Government Auditing Standards,* published by the U.S. GENERAL ACCOUNTING OFFICE (GAO). The GAO establishes the rules by which all types of govern-

ment audits in the United States must be conducted.

Performance auditing, like financial auditing, is based on the principles of independence, verification, and third-party reporting. This means that auditors are independent of management (usually the executive branch of government), base their findings and conclusions on evidence, and report their conclusions to others outside of management (usually a legislative body and the public). However, where financial auditing is primarily concerned with the proper reporting of financial data, performance auditing is primarily concerned with reporting on and improving critical aspects of program performance.

Unlike financial audits, which almost always are conducted on a government-wide basis, performance audits vary widely in scope and topic. Some audits may focus on narrow issues of management control and compliance in particular programs or activities, while others may address broad government-wide policy issues.

Performance audits can influence programs and policies in several ways. First, the auditors' independence allows them to base their conclusions on an objective analysis of evidence, which in turn adds to the credibility of the auditors' reports. Second, performance audits can influence the policy development process by independently identifying and reporting on problems, which are then added to the policy agenda. Finally, the auditors' conclusions about program results can significantly influence decisions about the allocation of resources.

In the United States, performance auditing is practiced at the federal level, in most state governments, and in many local governments. Examples of performance audits from various levels of government are available online. At the federal level, performance audits are conducted both by Offices of the Inspector General, which exist in every major agency, as well as by the GAO. GAO audits are available on the Internet at gao.gov. State audits are available through the National State Auditors Association at nasact.org. Local government audits are available online through the website of the National Association of Local Government Auditors at www.nalga.org.

Performance audits are also conducted in other countries throughout the world. Central government agencies, equivalent to the GAO in the United States, are referred to generically as "supreme audit institutions." Australia, the United Kingdom, and Sweden are among the countries having supreme audit institutions that conduct performance audits. Examples of the work of these and other countries' supreme audit institutions can be found online through the "membership directory" section of the website of the International Organization of Supreme Audit Institutions at intosai.org.

For more information

Funkhouser, Mark. "The Spread of Performance Auditing among American Cities." dissertation, University of Missouri—Kansas City, Kansas City, Mo., 2000.

Raaum, Ronell B., and Stephen L. Morgan. *Performance Auditing: A Measurement Approach.* Altamonte Springs, Fla.: Institute of Internal Auditors, 2001.

Wheat, Edward M. "The Activist Auditor: A New Player in State and Local Politics." *Public Administration Review* 51, no. 5 (1991): 385–392.

Mark Funkhouser

performance budgeting   Performance budgeting is a type of public-sector budgeting that uses information on the performance of an agency or program to help determine the level of resources allocated to it. The aim is to provide governments with information that allows them to determine how efficient and effective current activities are and whether better value-for-money can be achieved by changing the level or mix of resources allocated.

Over the last 40 years, there has been a succession of performance-budgeting initiatives within the public sector. Program budgeting was introduced by the Johnson administration as a goal-oriented approach to resource allocation and was later widely adopted elsewhere. It was complemented by the Nixon administration's introduction of MANAGEMENT BY OBJECTIVES. Each of these initiatives aligned well with management reforms that introduced structured strategic and operational planning into the business sector. However, program budgeting suffered from difficulties in defining and reliably measuring performance in public-sector situations where there is no competitive market for services. As well, attempts to hold managers accountable for performance did not differentiate between the factors they control and those they do not. Refinements aimed at overcoming these impediments are continuing on various fronts.

In the United States, the Government Accounting Standards Board established the Service Efforts and Accomplishments project in the late 1980s to develop comparable performance measures for common types of government services (see www.gasb.org). Similarly, in Australia, the Productivity Commission publishes each year a report on government services, which provides a time-series of performance information that lists benchmarks for comparisons between the various states (see www.pc.gov.au/gsp/index.html). However, this level of performance information is generally not comprehensive enough or detailed enough to be used for budgeting.

Following the lead of the New Zealand government, a number of governments—notably state and federal governments in Australia—have introduced performance budgeting systems known as "accrual output budgeting." These systems look at performance by recognizing the tension between a government's short-term interest as the "purchaser" of services from an agency and its longer-term interest as the "owner" responsible for maintaining the productive capacity of the agency. As purchasers, governments want to acquire the level and mix of services that best meets the outcomes they want, at least cost. As owners, governments have an interest in maintaining and expanding the assets they control (physical infrastructure and intellectual capital) to meet current and future service delivery needs.

These recent trends in performance budgeting have been criticized for not holding managers accountable for outcomes (that is, the actual impacts that government agencies have on society), on the basis that politicians would not be willing to accept this responsibility. At the same time, though, there are increasing signs of governments publishing "report cards" that attempt to quantify their performance (see, for example, www.treasury.alberta.ca). As these evolve and improve, governments are using them to ensure that agency planning processes are more closely aligned with government priorities and, potentially, as a more targeted basis for performance budgeting.

For more information
Organization for Economic Cooperation and Development. Journal on budgeting. Available online. URL: http://www.oecd.org.

Bob Shead

performance management Performance management describes a process that either an organization or an individual within an organization goes through in order to provide the best program, product, or service possible at the lowest cost. It is also used to assist in decision making and program improvement. The process of performance management consists of four major phases: planning, measuring, monitoring, and reporting. It has been used in the federal, state, and local governments with varying degrees of success. Legislation known as the GOVERNMENT PERFORMANCE AND RESULTS ACT OF 1993 spearheaded the federal government's use of performance management.

In phase one, other organizations and individuals set goals and create performance plans. The goals describe, in a broad and general way, the long-term results that an organization or individual hopes to achieve. For example, a goal might be "to provide cleaner roads." Goals reflect the vision and mission of an organization. An organization's vision is usually a future-oriented statement about what it seeks to achieve or to be, and it often includes values or beliefs that are important to the organization, its employees, and its customers. A mission is a concise statement that answers the questions of why an organization exists, what an organization does, and for whom and how the organization does what it does.

Objectives are similar to goals but are more specific and often tied to the immediate future. Objectives follow the SMART criteria of being: specific, measurable, attainable, results-oriented, and time-limited. One of the related objectives might be "to increase by 20 percent the number of roads swept last year."

A strategy is the specific action an organization intends to take to achieve its goals and objectives. Using the goal of clean roads, a strategy might be to purchase a new machine to sweep roads. Both the internal and external environments are examined as the organization creates goals, objectives, and strategies.

Phase two involves measuring performance in an attempt to capture what the organization does and assess how well it does it. Measures are categorized as input, output, outcome, or efficiency. Input measures are the resources—people or money—it takes to produce a service or product. Outputs are the services delivered or the amount of work completed, such as "the number of miles of road swept." Outcomes are the benefits or impacts of a program on customers or the public. Outcomes measure the results, such as "the cleanliness of streets." Often customers or the public are asked for their opinions of a service through a survey. Their opinions are considered an outcome, such as "the percentage of citizens that rate the city's streets as clean." An efficiency measure shows the relationship between inputs and outputs or outcomes. "The number of miles swept per employee" is an example. Standards are also set to determine acceptable levels of performance based on the measures. For example, does an organization want to sweep 2,000 or 20,000 miles of road?

Phases three and four involve monitoring and reporting. Once measures and standards are created, the organization must then collect and analyze the data. The results are compared with the objectives and standards established for that year. If the data show that the organization did not meet its standards or achieve its results, the organization must address the problem. Sometimes, measures will illustrate that an organization accomplished one objective but not the other. For example, what if the organization swept all the roads it intended to, but the public still thought the roads were dirty? The organization must analyze the causes, and make changes accordingly. Or the data may reveal that the organization is doing a good job. The organization should continue efforts to improve and attempt to provide even cleaner roads at less expense. Over time, priorities may shift, e.g., the organization decides that clean roads are less important than other issues or programs. In this case, the organization needs to undergo the cycle of performance management again, using the performance measures and evaluation to help plan for the future.

People also go through the phases of performance management. A person sets goals and objectives that answer the questions of "what you do at your job" and "why you do it." Together, an employee and his/her employer create standards to measure the employee's performance. At the end of the year, the employee is evaluated on whether he/she completed the objectives. This process is often referred to as a performance review or performance appraisal. When the employer rates the employee, the employer is qualifying how well the person did their job. The process starts again with new goals being set for the upcoming year. The goals and objectives are created to encourage the person to perform better in the upcoming year.

For more information

Gaebler, Ted, and David Osborne. *Reinventing Government: How the Entrepreneurial Spirit Is Transforming the Public Sector.* New York: Plume, 1993.

Government Accounting Standards Board. http://accounting.rutgers.edu/raw/gasb/.html.

Sharon Friedrichsen

performance measures Performance measures are indicators that quantify the outcomes or results and the efficiency of government programs. Performance measures are used for both internal monitoring and management and for increased public accountability.

To provide a fair and useful picture of agency performance, individual performance measures should be reported as part of a balanced set that includes at least the following types of measures:

- Inputs. These are measures of resources used or costs. Usually the numbers reported are dollars or numbers of staff.
- Outputs. These are measures of the amount of work completed. The numbers reported are usually counts of work accomplished. Examples might be "lane miles paved" or "classes held."
- Outcomes. These are measures of the result of the work conducted. Usually outcomes are broken down into intermediate and end outcomes. For example, an intermediate outcome of a parent involvement program at a local school might be that the children of participating parents have better school attendance. An end outcome might be that these children have better grades.
- Efficiency. Efficiency measures are ratios of inputs to outputs or inputs to outcomes. In the previous example, the efficiency measures might be cost per participating parent and cost per student with improved grades.
- Explanatory. Explanatory measures provide context for understanding reported performance measures. Continuing the example

above, an explanatory measure might be the percent of children participating in the program whose families meet certain income guidelines. The validity of a set of performance measures depends on the correct initial selection of measures and then accurate data collection procedures.

Many governments have established overall systems of performance measurement in the context of "managing for results." In *Making Results-Based State Government Work,* a 2001 publication of the Urban Institute, the authors refer to managing for results as the system a government uses "to focus its decisions and activities on the results, as well as costs and physical outputs, of government activities and actions." Managing for results in the federal government is largely driven by the GOVERNMENT PERFORMANCE AND RESULTS ACT OF 1993 (GPRA). GPRA requires federal agencies to develop and report performance measures. The U.S. GENERAL ACCOUNTING OFFICE's reports on performance measures prepared by individual federal agencies can be accessed through their website (www.gao.gov).

The Governmental Accounting Standards Board (GASB) establishes standards for government accounting and financial reporting. Since 1987, the GASB has been encouraging governments to report performance information. GASB's work can be accessed through its website (www.seagov.org). An example of the type of report contemplated by the GASB is *City of Portland Service Efforts and Accomplishments 2001: Eleventh Annual Report on City Government Performance,* prepared by the Portland city auditor. The report is available online (www.ci.portland.or.us/auditor).

The International City/County Management Association (ICMA) assists cities and counties in collecting performance data. Currently, approximately 130 communities participate in the ICMA program, all following a consistent set of definitions to allow for accurate comparisons of inputs, outputs, and outcomes. Performance data are collected in 15 services areas, including police, fire, parks, and libraries.

For more information

Governmental Accounting Standards Board. *Concept Statement No. 2 of the Governmental Accounting Standards Board, Service Efforts and Accomplishment Reporting.* Norwalk, Conn.: Governmental Accounting Standards Board, 1994.

Hatry, Harry P. *Performance Measurement: Getting Results.* Washington, D.C.: Urban Institute Press, 1999.

Mark Funkhouser

performance review   Performance review is an ongoing process of monitoring and evaluating performance. The concept was devised as a way of holding organizations and individuals accountable for achieving results. It is also used as a method to stimulate and improve performance. The concept grew from a belief that organizations do not always produce products and services in an effective and efficient manner and sometimes lose sight of why they were created in the first place.

This school of thought led President Clinton and Vice President Gore to create an interagency task force called the National Partnership for Reinventing Government, which was later renamed the National Performance Review. The purpose of the National Performance Review was to reform or "reinvent" government to put the customer first, to lower costs, and to improve performance. Benchmarking was also part of the National Performance Review. Benchmarking involves comparing an organization's performance with that of another organization or evaluating an organization's own performance over time.

For individuals, performance review entails a series of meetings between the individual and his/her supervisor. This process is often referred to as a performance appraisal. The purposes of performance review at the individual level are to help the employee focus on the essential components of his/her job; promote communication between the employee and the supervisor; assist the employee in knowing how he/she fits within the organization; and promote personal accountability for one's performance.

A performance appraisal or review process usually takes place over a period of several meetings. During the first meeting, the employee and his/her supervisor set goals and objectives related to the employee's essential job functions. Goals are statements that generally describe what a person intends to accomplish. Objectives are more specific statements that attempt to quantify the goal. For example, an individual's goal may be "to provide excellent customer service" and the objective may be "to answer 95 percent of all incoming calls by the second ring." A person may have more than one objective related to a goal. Usually, the goals and objectives are aligned with the larger goals of the organization.

During this first meeting, rating criteria are usually established that will be used to determine if goals and objectives were met. Since goals and objectives are based on job functions, the person is really being measured on how well he/she performed throughout the year. The rating criteria are typically based on a scale from one (corresponding to a person needing improvement) to five (a person performing in an outstanding manner).

The second meeting is a midyear assessment of the employee's performance. During this time, goals and objectives may be revised, depending on the external environment. This meeting also provides an employee with feedback on his/her performance so that the person can improve his/her performance before the final review.

The third meeting occurs at the end of the year. The supervisor rates the employee on the extent of his/her completion of the objectives established at the beginning of the year. Goals and objectives for the upcoming year are also created. The performance review enables an employee to know how well he/she has performed during the year and how to perform better in the upcoming year.

Some performance review systems have included incentives based on an individual's performance. Often, people are paid a monetary bonus for achieving their objectives, commonly known as "pay for performance." Another incentive is to link the performance of an organization to its budget. In this scenario, if an organization performs well and makes improvements to save money, the savings are put back into the organization's budget, and the manager is given more leeway in deciding the use of these funds. A third incentive is to allow managers flexibility in managing and adapting their division or program in exchange for their increased accountability for what happens to the programs and services they provide.

Holding people accountable for achieving predetermined standards of performance does have some inherent problems. First, factors in the external environment often impede one's ability to accomplish the stated objectives, despite his/her best efforts. Second, people sometimes set goals and objectives that are easily obtainable and do not try to improve their performance over time. Third, people may attempt to manipulate the measurement data to guarantee that the data illustrate that they met the stated objectives. Fourth, the performance appraisal process may become a contentious situation if conducted by untrained personnel and without consistent and objective rating criteria in place.

For more information

Gore, Albert. *From Red Tape to Results: Creating a Government That Works Better and Costs Less.* Washington, D.C.: National Performance Review, 1993.

Hatry, Harry. *Performance Measurement: Getting Results.* Washington, D.C.: Urban Institute Press, 1999.

Sharon Friedrichsen

Personnel Administrator of Massachusetts v. Feeney 442 U.S. 256 (1979)

Personnel Administrator of Massachusetts v. Feeney held that a classification disadvantaging women was not unconstitutional sex discrimination if there was no intent to discriminate on the basis of sex. The case dealt with a challenge to a Massachusetts program that granted an absolute lifetime preference to veterans over nonveterans in state civil service employment. The program provided that veterans who passed the civil service exam and who applied for state positions would automatically be ranked higher on the hiring list than nonveterans no matter their respective scores on the exam.

As a result of congressional statutes such as a male-only draft and since-repealed quotas on the number of women who could serve in the military, at the time of this litigation 98.2 percent of veterans in Massachusetts were men and only 1.8 percent were women. Consequently, the veteran preference adopted by the state had the effect of severely disadvantaging women in gaining state employment, including Helen Feeney who had consistently scored highly on the civil service exam but was passed over by veterans scoring lower on the exam but given the preference.

The legal issue in *Feeney* was whether this was sex discrimination against women in violation of the U.S. Constitution's Fourteenth Amendment equal protection clause. By a 7-2 decision the U.S. Supreme Court, in an opinion by Justice Potter Stewart, held that it was not.

Applying a rule that it had previously adopted in race discrimination cases in *Washington v. Davis*, 426 U.S. 229 (1976), the Court held that a discriminatory *effect* was insufficient to show an equal-protection violation. For the equal protection clause to be violated, one must show a discriminatory *purpose* for passage of the law.

The classification in this case was problematic because it was not one obviously based on sex; it was between veterans and nonveterans, not men and women. In such cases, where there is no obvious sex classification, the Court set a very high burden of proof challengers must meet in order to show a discriminatory purpose: the plaintiff must successfully show that the state established this program because of "its discriminatory effect and not merely in spite of" it.

Justices Thurgood Marshall and William Brennan dissented, arguing that the severe discriminatory impact upon women resulting from this preference program was so clearly foreseeable that the state should bear the burden of proof to show that sex-based considerations played no part in the decision to enact it.

The *Feeney* case is significant for providing guidelines to public policy makers and administrators, who regularly make classifications in the law. Previously, the U.S. Supreme Court had held that government classifications based on sex would have to meet a more stringent constitutional test than other types of classifications. Whereas most government classifications between different types of people (e.g., tax rates based on amount of income) are required only to be "reasonable," government classifications based on sex must be substantially related "to an important" governmental objective (*Craig v. Boren*, 429 U.S. 190 [1976]). *Feeney* clarified for policy makers and administrators when the courts would deem a classification to be one based on sex, thus requiring the more-stringent constitutional test, and when it would not, thus utilizing only the mere reasonableness test.

For more information

Goldstein, Leslie Friedman. *The Constitutional Rights of Women: Cases in Law and Social Change,* rev. ed. Madison: University of Wisconsin Press, 1988.

Mezey, Susan Gluck. *In Pursuit of Equality: Women, Public Policy, and the Federal Courts.* New York: St. Martin's Press, 1992.

Michael W. Bowers

planned programming budgeting system (PPBS)

PPBS (planned programming budgeting system) is the decision-making process that the executive branch of the U.S. government adopted in 1965 to help make its annual expenditure budgets. The main feature of PPBS was that budget decisions were to be based on analyses of the effectiveness of agencies' programs. PPBS was formally abandoned government-wide in 1971, primarily because (1) budget makers were unable to adequately analyze the great number of complex funding options that PPBS presented; (2) politicians were wary of how PPBS could reduce the range of objectives they could pursue in their policies; and (3) civil service executives were wary of how PPBS could reduce their discretion over administration.

PPBS was a very rational way of deciding how much money to spend on which activities in government. Rational budget makers determine their policy objectives, identify possible policies and programs, assess the extent to which each policy and program meets their objectives, compare their policy and program options, select the policies and programs that best meet their objectives, and adopt them through the budget.

Previous budgeting systems, such as line-item budgeting, allocated resources to agencies and activities based on how economically agencies would spend their budgets on inputs, or on how efficiently agencies' activities would turn inputs into outputs. PPBS proposed to allocate resources based on how effectively agencies' outputs would achieve the desired outcomes of policies and programs—in other words, how effectively the policy and program options under consideration would meet the government's objectives. Budget makers would use their knowledge of the causes of social phenomena and the consequences of government activity to predict both the costs and the effects of programs, compare these costs and effects both between programs with similar objectives and between programs with dissimilar objectives, and use the budget to allocate resources to the programs that they thought would provide the most "value for money."

The major advantage of PPBS was that it helped focus budget makers' attention on how well policies and programs actually worked. Using policy analysis and program-evaluation techniques to assess the cost effectiveness of policies and programs may have helped budget makers decide which proposed policies and programs would receive new funding in the budget, as well as identify the existing policies and programs that were good candidates for either increased or decreased funding. It would seem, for example, that PPBS helped Robert McNamara prepare budgets in the Department of Defense, where it was first introduced in 1961. By helping focus attention on how well policies and programs worked, PPBS may have helped budget makers ensure that agencies' activities contributed to the administration's overall objectives.

PPBS had two major disadvantages. The first was that it was impossible for budget makers to fully understand the causes of social phenomena and the consequences of government activities, and so it was impossible to accurately predict the costs or the effects of programs. Too little was known about these complex causal relationships to identify exactly how, for example, spending a billion more dollars on school lunches would affect the health of children, their ability to learn, or their future competitiveness in global labor markets.

The second disadvantage was that politicians and civil service executives saw that increased transparency of the objectives and results of their policies and programs could highlight cases where the objectives of policies were overtly political and where the results of programs were disappointingly low. They were often unwilling to identify the true objectives or the true results of policies and programs, for fear that criticism of those objectives or results would reduce their ability to respond to multiple political and administrative pressures, or even lead to cuts in their budgets. For these and other reasons, analyses were often not used to inform budgetary decisions. In general, PPBS had little effect on actual patterns of resource allocation.

It is important to appreciate how PPBS was supposed to work and why it failed, because the idea of budgeting more rationally has enduring appeal and continues to influence the design of budgeting systems. Indeed, the performance budgeting system envisioned by the GOVERNMENT PERFORMANCE AND RESULTS ACT OF 1993 (GPRA) is based on the same rational budgeting principles on which PPBS was based. Rational budgeting does have the potential to improve resource allocation decisions, but its elements should perhaps be applied only where causal relationships are well understood and where political sensitivities are low.

For more information

Schick, Allen. "The Road to PPB: The Stages of Budget Reform." *Public Administration Review* 26, no. 4 (December 1966): 243–258.

———. "A Death in the Bureaucracy: The Demise of Federal PPB." *Public Administration Review* 33 (March/April 1973): 146–156.

Wildavsky, Aaron. "The Political Economy of Efficiency: Cost-Benefit Analysis, Systems Analysis, and Program Budgeting." *Public Administration Review* 26, no. 4 (December 1966): 292–310.

David I. Dewar

planning   Planning is the formal decision-making process that can be used by governments to determine what policies and programs they will adopt in order to influence or prepare for future situations. There are many different types of planning that governments can carry out. Types of planning can range from very broad and strategic, where senior politicians and civil servants attempt to chart a path for their organizations to a desirable future position within their political and policy environments, to very narrow and operational, where managers attempt to forecast future tasks and identify the organizational structures and resources necessary to carry

them out. Planning can also be characterized by the general policy area in which a government acts. For example, urban planning refers to the planning of how cities are built and how they function and grow. The word *planning* has even come to be associated with the attempts of communist regimes and some wartime governments to centrally control and direct the production and consumption of a wide variety of goods and services in their economies, often many years into the future. Here we will focus on generic policy planning, which operates at a level of detail (and provides a crucial link) between strategic and operational planning for any given policy area.

Policy planning is deciding on a course of policy action that will be carried out to do some good in the future. In government, planning processes—at least on paper—tend to be very rational and analytical. Planning may involve the following steps: (1) set long-term goals or derive them from statements of the organization's vision, values, mission, or strategy; (2) forecast future situations; (3) identify policy options, i.e., ways the government can meet its goals by either influencing those future situations or preparing for them; (4) evaluate the options against the goals, compare them, and select the best one(s); (5) specify the required program activities. Rather than simply hoping things turn out well or reacting to situations as they arise, governments can benefit from being proactive, i.e., acting in advance of those situations. Planning is particularly useful when there are many policy actors and policy actions involved, because plans—as common, detailed, and relatively stable statements of purpose and activity—can help executives coordinate and control their organizations.

There are four basic reasons why governments plan. First, governments may plan to prevent something negative from happening. For example, governments may detect a threat of terrorist attacks occurring within their borders and plan ways of identifying and stopping the attacks, such as infiltrating terrorist organizations and searching bags at airports. Second, governments may plan to ensure that something positive does in fact happen. For example, governments may identify the benefits of knowing more about outer space and plan ways of increasing such knowledge, such as taking pictures with the Hubble space telescope and conducting experiments on the international space station. In these two scenarios, governments decide on a course of action to prevent a particular situation or event that otherwise would occur, or to bring about a particular situation or state of affairs that otherwise would not occur. A plan is a blueprint of how a government will prevent or bring about an event or state of affairs. It is a road map that specifies not only the destination but also the steps it will take between the present and the future point in time when the situation either will or will not arise.

Third, governments may plan to mitigate the negative consequences associated with a situation that cannot be prevented. For example, governments may forecast that a natural disaster might occur within their borders and plan ways of responding should it actually occur, such as evacuating the injured and airlifting food to survivors. Evacuations and airlifts are part of a contingency plan in case of disaster. Fourth, governments may plan to take advantage of the potentially positive consequences associated with a situation that could occur in the future. For example, governments may forecast that foreign countries might wish to become democracies and ask for help in doing so, and then plan ways of responding to such requests should they actually occur, such as scrutinizing elections and providing education on good business practices. In these two scenarios, governments decide on a course of action to prepare themselves to mitigate or take advantage of a situation that they think may, on its own, arise in the future. Again, a plan is a blueprint of how a government will prepare itself for an eventuality; in other words, it is a road map that specifies not only the destination but also the steps it will take between the present and the future point in time when the situation arises.

Three things are clear from the above examples. First, planning is important. Effectively influencing or preparing for future situations often requires governments to act through public policy far in advance and to coordinate the work of many people. Without a clear plan that everyone who needs to be involved can follow, available in time for all the necessary actions to be carried out (especially in sequence), governments will find themselves simply reacting to events rather than proactively influencing or preparing for them. However, due to globalization and other forces, the range of situations that may be influenced or prepared for by governments may be shrinking, as might be the amount of lead time that governments could possibly have to influence or prepare for them. If so, the importance of planning may be declining.

Second, planning is difficult. For a number of reasons, planning processes—especially the more formalized and logical ones—cannot always help governments influence or prepare for the future. First, the policy goals and criteria of a good plan are often vague and highly contested. Second, forecasts of future economic, social, and other conditions and of the situations that may arise are almost always inaccurate. Third, planners rarely fully understand and can measure the causes and consequences of those situations, as well as what policy actions could be taken to prevent, bring about, mitigate, or take advantage of them. Fourth, planners and policy makers often do not know how to translate the general idea of policy action into the specific activities of actual programs. Fifth, policy makers may be too busy responding to short-term problems to be proactive in influencing or preparing for long-term situations. Sixth, smaller organizations do not always have the resources or capacity to properly plan. Seventh, the planning process can be so slow, and the environments can change so quickly, that plans become out of date by the time they are implemented, and the more detailed and inflexible the plans are, the less discretion politicians and managers have to alter their behavior in response to shifting priorities, emerging knowledge, or changing conditions. Finally, if changes to the plan are desired but the plan tightly coordinates the activities of many different parts of the organization, changes to one part of the plan will affect all the other parts and can cause the entire plan to unravel.

Third, planning alone is insufficient. Planning to do something is of little value if the plan itself is never accepted or followed. While planning can help governments identify what actions should be taken to achieve their goals, planning is not action itself, and so must be followed by the sound execution of the plan as well as by an evaluation of how well the plan worked in the end. Planning is only one in a series of steps in the broader policy process and only one in a wide range of management functions in any organization.

Evidently, formal policy planning cannot always help governments to fully influence and prepare for future events. Nevertheless, policy planning can—particularly when it adds intuition and creativity to analytical skills—help governments achieve some successes, avoid some failures, and be ready to respond to some events. Indeed, the importance of planning is reflected in the many repeated attempts to link it to the budgetary process, as is done in the federal government under the Government Performance and Results Act of 1993. Given the limitations of planning, though, policy makers should not rely on it too heavily.

For more information
Bryon, John M., ed. *Strategic Management in Public and Voluntary Services: A Reader.* New York: Pergamon Press, 1999.

Mintzberg, Henry. *The Rise and Fall of Strategic Planning: Reconceiving Roles for Planning, Plans, Planners.* New York: Macmillan, 1994.

Wildavsky, Aaron. "If Planning Is Everything, Maybe It's Nothing." *Policy Sciences* 4 (1973): 127–153.

David I. Dewar

planning, history of   Planning is a professional field that focuses on the rational preparation for future growth and revitalization of rural, suburban, and urban communities. Planning emphasizes responsible and fair decision making for regions regarding social, economic, and environmental problems. The field of planning requires that practitioners promote the best use of a community's land and resources for recreational, institutional, residential, and commercial purposes. In short, planning is collective action for the public good that focuses on building the infrastructure for present needs as well as future growth.

Historically, the goal of planning has been to create urban infrastructure and to connect urban environments to rural environments. City and urban planning rose in response to late-19th-century industrialization. Practitioners applied concepts from design, engineering, law, and the social sciences to create the art and science of planning. Yet, in recent years, practitioners of planning have become involved in many types of socioeconomic and environmental activities within communities, such as traffic congestion, air pollution, the effects of economic growth and development on community values, and others.

In his influential book *Planning in the Public Domain,* John Friedman explains that the intellectual traditions of planning are rooted in a broad range of fields, including systems engineering, neoclassical economics, public administration, scientific management, sociology, the German historical school, pragmatism, historical materialism, and utopianism. Each of these fields has influenced the evolution of planning theory in some way. Specifically, public administration can be linked with planning because it is concerned with the function of public-oriented central planning, the conditions for its success, and the relation of planning to politics.

The formal history of the practice of American planning goes back to the Ordinance of 1785, which provided for the rectangular land survey of the old Northwest. Some scholars have called this survey the largest single act of national planning in U.S. history. Additionally, the World's Columbian Exposition in Chicago in 1893 commemorated the 400th anniversary of the discovery of the New World. This exposition inaugurated the American City Beautiful movement and the start of the urban-planning profession.

The development of the field of planning as a profession began in 1909 at the First National Conference on City Planning held in Washington, D.C. That same year, the first course in city planning in the United States was inaugurated in Harvard College's Landscape Architecture Department. In 1914, five years later, Flavel Shurtleff wrote the first major textbook on city planning, titled *Carrying Out the City Plan*. Frederick Law Olmsted, Jr., became the first president of the newly founded American City Planning Institute in 1917. This organization would eventually become the American Institute of Certified Planners.

In 1978, the American Institute of Planners (AIP) and the American Society of Planning Officials (ASPO) merged to create the American Planning Association (APA). The American Planning Association (APA) is a nonprofit public-interest and research organization for urban, suburban, regional, and rural planners. The association has an affiliated professional institute, the American Institute of Certified Planners (AICP). Professional planners who have completed the educational and experience requirements of the AICP, and have successfully passed a written exam, qualify as certified planners.

For more information

Campbell, Scott, and Susan S. Fainstein, eds. *Readings in Planning Theory*. Cambridge: Blackwell Publishers, 2002.

Friedman, John. *Planning in the Public Domain: From Knowledge to Action*. Princeton, N.J.: Princeton University Press, 1987.

Hall, Peter. *Cities of Tomorrow*. Cambridge: Blackwell Publishers, 1996.

Elizabeth Corley

Plunkitt, George Washington (1842–1924)

New York politician George Washington Plunkitt was a leader of the New York City Democratic Party's political machine (Tammany Hall).

Born in 1842 in an Irish-American shantytown on Manhattan Island called Nanny Goat Hill, Plunkitt quit school at age 11 to go to work in a butcher shop. Eventually he owned his own store and later engaged in contracting for harbor construction.

Plunkitt's career in politics had begun early in his life. By 1876, he had worked his way up the Tammany Hall ladder from election district captain to assembly district leader. Eventually he held many offices. He was Tammany leader (ward boss) of the 15th Assembly District, sachem of the Tammany Society, and chairman of the Elections Committee of Tammany Hall. He also held the public offices of state senator, assemblyman, police magistrate, county supervisor, and alderman. At one time he held four public offices simultaneously and drew salaries from three of them.

Plunkitt told his story to William L. Riordon of the *New York Evening Post* in a series of interviews at "Plunkitt's Office"—Graziano's bootblack stand in the New York County Court House. The interviews were published in newspapers as *A Series of Very Plain Talks on Very Practical Politics*. Plunkitt's *Talks* were a frank description of how to succeed in the Tammany machine.

Plunkitt's political life was one of constant contact with the people of his district, usually the poor and recent immigrants. Personal attention gained political appreciation from people and eventually their vote at the polls. It was Plunkitt's philosophy that the individual should be involved in politics to get something directly from political participation. The gain from voting for people like Plunkitt would be favors, help with the government, jobs, contracts, and—for the poorest—coal or food. On election day it was whiskey for the vote of the down-and-out. To Plunkitt this was just practical politics and not corruption. As a result, Plunkitt was in favor of the spoils system and adamantly opposed to the "curse" of civil service reforms.

Plunkitt believed in "honest graft." To Plunkitt, directly stealing out of public funds was just plain crookedness. However, to use inside information to cheaply buy up land wanted by the government and then to sell it at a large profit was "honest graft." Plunkitt also liked to say about insider information on government contracts that he "seen his opportunities and he took 'em." He was born poor but, from success in his political career, died a millionaire.

The politics of Plunkitt and other politically "practical men" have been criticized by Daniel P. Moynihan, Lincoln Steffens, and others. They might have been politically successful, but they lacked the vision to change society for the better.

For more information

Riordon, William L. *Plunkitt of Tammany Hall: A Series of Very Plain Talks on Very Practical Politics, Delivered by Ex-Senator George Washington Plunkitt, the Tammany Philosopher, from His Rostrum—The New York County Court House Bootblack Stand.* New York: E. P. Dutton, 1963.

A. J. L. Waskey

pocket veto   A pocket VETO occurs when, under certain circumstances, the president keeps a bill "in his pocket" (i.e., ignores it) rather than signs it into law or vetos it outright. After 10 days, the ignored bill, de facto, is considered vetoed.

The framers of the Constitution set up the law-making process so that presidents cannot hold a bill indefinitely, and therefore a pocket veto can only occur during the last 10 days of a congressional session in very limited circum-stances. The Constitution gives the president 10 days to consider a bill once it has passed both houses of Congress. If the president ignores a bill that has been sent to his desk by the Congress, the bill automatically becomes law after a period of 10 days.

However, the exception is in the last 10 days of a congressional session. Sometimes the Congress sends a bill to the president and then adjourns. If this occurs, the president can simply "pocket" the bill, neither signing nor vetoing the bill. After 10 days, the bill is a victim of a pocket veto. For example, Congress may send a bill on school safety to the president. Seven days later, Congress adjourns. If the president has not signed or vetoed the bill by that time, the bill becomes pocket vetoed after three more days.

The pocket veto is especially effective because Congress does not have the opportunity to override a pocket veto. The only way Congress can avoid a pocket veto is to extend the session so that Congress is still in session after the required 10 days have expired. This is very rare, because most members of Congress need to return home to campaign. Since Congress cannot override a pocket veto with a two-thirds vote, the bill must be reintroduced at the beginning of the next session if Congress wants the bill to become law.

There was some debate as to when a president can use a pocket veto. Nixon tried to use the pocket veto when Congress simply went into recess, not adjournment. Senator Edward Kennedy challenged this action, and in *Kennedy v. Sampson* (511 F.[2d 430 D.C. Cir 1974]) the Supreme Court agreed with Senator Kennedy.

There are political reasons a president might want to use the pocket veto. Sometimes Congress sends the president a popular bill that he does not like. If the bill is vetoed, it might attract unfavorable press attention, or members of Congress might criticize the president. However, with a pocket veto, the president can claim that the bill was not overtly vetoed. The pocket veto can be a way to kill a bill without facing the resulting political consequences.

Since 1789, presidents have vetoed 2,532 bills. Of those, 1,067 were pocket vetoes. Presidents Grover Cleveland and Franklin Roosevelt used the pocket veto more than any other presidents.

For more information

Congressional Record. 13 November 2000. House. H11852–H11865.

Spitzer, Robert J. *The Presidential Veto: Touchstone of the American Presidency.* Albany: State University of New York Press, 1988.

Mathew Manweller

police power Police power describes governments' general authority to protect public health, safety, morals, and welfare. Police power is exercised mainly through legislation or administrative-agency rule making.

In the United States, police power has distinctive meaning when referring to state and local governments on one hand and the national government on the other. In the former, police power describes regulation under state or local authority and connected to states' reserved powers under the Tenth Amendment to the U.S. Constitution. Local governments are administrative units of the state. In contrast, the national government's regulatory authority depends upon specific legislation or agency rules. Analogous national authority to state police power must find appropriate validation in the Constitution or legislation. The most extensive use of federal regulatory authority, similar to state police power, has occurred through the U.S. Constitution's Commerce Clause (art. I, sec. 8) and subsequent federal legislation, such as environmental protection and food safety.

State and national government police power is central to questions about the scope of governmental authority in economic, political, and social issues. Government use of police power may limit individuals, groups, or corporations from engaging in activities that government deems to have negative social or economic consequences, e.g., government can bar discriminatory denial to individuals of public accommodations because of a persons' race, or government can prevent children from working in hazardous occupations. In federal systems, central questions occur whether the state/locality or national government has exceeded its police power under the national or state constitution or legislation.

Local and state governments possess police power to limit individuals' property rights. Zoning, a largely 20th-century phenomenon, is part of governmental police power to regulate use of land to enhance the public welfare. Court and societal customs can limit states' exercise of police powers that violate state or national constitutions, legislation, or due process of law. New situations may introduce new avenues for the use of governmental police power. In 2001 the newly created U.S. Office of Homeland Security may expand the police powers of the federal government to regulate individual activities, thus creating additional tensions between societal definitions of security and individual liberties.

For more information

Gilman, Howard. *The Constitution Besieged: The Rise and Demise of Lochner Era Police Powers Jurisprudence.* Durham, N.C.: Duke University Press, 1993.

Steven Puro

policy advice Policy advice is a process to inform decision making in organizations and government, where the action that results is based on choosing one of a series of options that arise from analysis of the issue, taking into consideration all of the influential factors relating to the spending of money on programs or to the establishment of a new way of doing something in society.

The provision of policy advice within organizations or government helps people make better decisions in relation to spending money or arranging services in society by providing them with as much information on the issue as possible. Policy advisers analyze complex issues that are interlinked with society's needs and choices based on value systems. This is why policy advice is sometimes called an art, since it involves looking carefully at behavior in society as well as intentions and action. However, there is a logical approach to arriving at the range of options available to any decision maker. All the ideas and values, including why the issue warrants attention, are placed inside a meaningful framework so that the issue in question can be properly discussed. It also enables the adviser to separate fact from fiction and discuss the research in the context of value choices. The options that are developed come from this process of analysis, which is known as the policy development phase.

The options are then presented for discussion. It is necessary to discuss the issues and take information from people who have an interest in the decision. This is called consultation and occurs with internal and external stakeholders.

The discussion process also includes a close examination of the cost of any policy, as this is fundamental to whether the final decision and policy itself will work. For example, an organization or government considers building a new hospital because the population is growing in a particular area. The decision to look at the issue could come from a variety of sources, from an election commitment to build a new hospital in the area or a recommendation from the planning department to consider this issue. A policy adviser will look at the relevant issues, ranging from population data to research on what types of hospitals are appropriate to how much money it is going to cost.

There are generally multiple decisions involved in any policy advice, and a good policy is one that incorporates a great deal of flexibility, so that as people's opinions change it is not necessary to go back to the development phase. Policies that do not function effectively in practical application are common, and policy makers

must recognize that policy is a flexible instrument to guide change. Thus the policy advice concerning the building of a new hospital in the growing suburb will also have some alternatives to building, such as ways in which people can receive health care without building a new hospital. Policy advice is therefore very similar to planning for the future, since it is based on a thorough examination of people's attitudes, including what government wants to happen and input from those who may be affected by any long-term decisions.

Modern policy making equates to the old saying, "Who needs to know?" There have to be choices on whether to act on issues, the scope of acting, and the choice about the interrelating issues. The affiliation of policy advice with art is further evidenced by the sense of expression in policy and the sense of purpose in the nature of the process. In other words, policy advice is an art because it needs to reflect dynamism in life, society, and action.

For more information

Colebatch, H., and P. Lamour. Chap. 3 in *Market, Bureaucracy and Community.* London: Pluto Press, 1994.

Hogwood, B. W., and L. H. Gunn. "Analysing Public Policy." Chap. 2 in *Policy Analysis for the Real World.* Oxford: Oxford University Press, 1984.

Angela Magarry

policy design   Policy design is one step in the policy-making process that encompasses agenda setting, policy formulation and design, implementation, and evaluation.

Policy design is determining what the policy problem is and the solutions to remedy the problem. Essentially, a policy design identifies the purpose of the policy, the agencies that will implement the policy and the actions they will take to solve the policy problem, the intended recipients of the policy, the rules governing the implementation and administration of the policy, and the rationale supporting the policy. Numerous actors may participate in the process of determining a policy design. These actors may be from either the private or public sector and include elected officials, legislators, nonelected government officials, interest groups, research organizations, and the mass media.

Within the United States, federal, state, and local governments formally establish public policies through the adoption of legislation. However, the policy design that the legislature adopts may represent the intentions not only of the elected officials who enact the policy, but also a wide range of policy actors who lobby the legislature to adopt their policy preferences. Public-policy scholars broadly define these policy actors as comprising policy communities that possess professional or scientific expertise in specific policy areas. Policy communities may supply government officials, both elected and bureaucratic, with policy designs that support their understanding of the policy problem and solution. The actors that make up the policy community, also known as the policy subsystem, vary over time and across policy areas and governmental units. Because these actors represent various institutions, it is argued that institutions shape the actor's values and actions in the policy design process.

Intrinsic to the process of policy design is determining the policy problem. Often members of policy communities, government bureaucracies, and other interested parties identify policy problems through stories that convey economic or social decline or portray serious problems that threaten the general public's welfare. The definition of the policy problem has consequences for establishing the solution to the problem. Policy makers may construct a policy problem because they have a ready-made policy solution they seek to institute.

Policy making is complex and can be a nonlinear process. While previously established public policies may shape how policy makers and interested parties perceive a policy problem and its solutions, in periods of economic, political, or social change, entire policy designs may be scrapped and new ones adopted. Policies are subject to design and redesign. In determining a policy design, policy makers may not follow a straightforward process where they define the policy problem and then consider the appropriate solution to it. Policy solutions may exist prior to the identification of a policy problem, or they may occur during the policy implementation or evaluation stages.

In its adoption of the legislation, the U.S. Congress and state or local legislatures may adopt a distributive, redistributive, allocational, or regulative policy design. A distributive policy design is one where public resources are used to stimulate or support economic growth. In cities, policies that provide property tax abatements to real estate developers who build residential or commercial space in blighted neighborhoods are distributive policies.

Redistributive policy designs direct public resources to benefit those organizations or individuals who generally are economically or socially disadvantaged. The federal Section 8 housing-choice policy, which provides rent subsidies that allow low-income families to rent housing from the private housing market, is an example of a redistributive policy.

Allocational policy designs are neither distributive nor redistributive. Instead, they direct public resources to pay for governmental services such as the operation of the government's executive, legislative, and judicial branches of government. Regulative policy establishes government regulations such as legally established air quality standards.

A policy design also specifies policy tools, i.e., the implementing agencies and the actions they will take to implement the policy. Examples of policy tools include proclamations, public service announcements, speeches by public officials, voluntary incentives, legal sanctions, grant funding for programs that support policy goals, and technical assistance to aid public or private groups that are involved in the policy implementation.

For more information

Heclo, Hugh. "Issue Networks and the Executive Establishment." In *The New American Political System,* edited by Anthony King. Washington, D.C.: American Enterprise Institute for Public Policy, 1978.

Howlett, Michael, and M. Ramesh. *Studying Public Policy: Policy Cycles and Policy Subsystems.* Oxford, U.K.: Oxford University Press, 1995.

Ingram, Helen, and Anne Larason Schneider. *Policy Design for Democracy.* Lawrence: University of Kansas Press, 1997.

Kingdon, John. *Agendas, Alternatives, and Public Policies.* Boston: Little Brown, 1984.

Lindblom, Charles. "The Science of Muddling Through." *Public Administration Review* 19 (spring 1959): 79–88.

Lowi, Theodore. "Four Systems of Policy, Politics and Choice." *Public Administration Review* 32, no. 4 (1972): 298–310.

Peterson, Paul E. *City Limits.* Chicago: University of Chicago Press, 1981.

Sabatier, Paul. "The Need for Better Theories." In *Theories of the Policy Process,* edited by Paul Sabatier. Boulder, Colo.: Westview Press, 1999.

Stone, Deborah. *Policy Paradox.* New York: W. W. Norton & Company, 1997.

Melissa Pavone

policy evaluation   During the policy evaluation process, the programs related to the designed policy are analyzed in order to assess and improve the ways in which policies and programs are conducted. The process extends from the earliest stages of defining and designing programs through their development and implementation. Another similar definition that completes the previous one states that evaluation is the systematic assessment of the operation and the outcomes of a program or policy, compared with a set of explicit standards, as a means of improving the program or policy. Evaluation is the fourth phase of the public policy analysis cycle (the previous ones being problem definition, decision making, and policy implementation).

At one time evaluators believed that a study that responded to the questions of the study sponsor would almost automatically be used. But in the past decades we have learned that this is not always true. Evaluation can pursue both overt and covert purposes. Among the former, we find responsibility (a search for information to make better decisions or to reconsider previous ones), program improvement, and basic knowledge (in order to have a comprehensive view of reality). But evaluation can also be used as a subterfuge to delay a decision (postponement) or to provide legitimacy (window dressing) or self-glorification because of the success of a program (public relations).

There are two main approaches to conducting an evaluation. The first one is called the goals-based evaluation, which measures goal attainment and therefore requires that a program have clearly specified goals. But many times, as we have just stated, policy and program objectives are general and ambiguous. That is why a second approach is needed: the pluralistic evaluation. This second methodology considers that the values and the opinions of the different groups of actors involved in a program (such as stakeholders, policy designers and implementers, evaluators, and citizens) are important. Also, this type of evaluation is carried out in order to influence the political decision-making process. Finally, the pluralistic evaluation is a political decision in itself, and therefore it has political power.

Designing an evaluation means making decisions about what to measure. Several kinds of evaluations can be performed depending on the guidelines chosen. Therefore, depending on time and intention, there are three different types of evaluation: ex ante evaluation (which is carried out before the decision of implementing a policy is taken), implementation evaluation (which takes place while action is carried out), and ex post evaluation (which is performed once the policy is completely implemented; in other words, this evaluation intends to measure results, effects, outputs, and outcomes).

Two types of research techniques can be used when carrying an evaluation out: quantitative (including questionnaires) and qualitative methodologies (including literature review, in-depth interviews, and focus groups). In fact, the critical feature about data collection is that the methods match the central focus of the inquiry. Nevertheless, many times, both kinds of approaches will be needed because of the complexity of the policy goals and the number of actors involved.

Finally, there is the issue of location. There is a long tradition of controversy about whether in-house or outside evaluation is preferable. Neither of them has a monopoly of advantages. In any case, it is recommended that the following factors be considered: administrative confidence, objectivity, understanding of the program, potential for utilization, and autonomy.

For more information

Weiss, C. K. *Evaluation,* 2d ed. Upper Saddle River, N.J.: Prentice Hall, 1998.

Mila Gascó

policy formulation   Policy formulation occurs when policy makers try to develop alternative proposals or strategies for addressing public problems. When confronted with several competing alternatives, individual policy makers may devise their own proposal. This stage of the policy making process is often not simple or straightforward. As a result, many public administrators and policy makers are stymied because they cannot agree on what to do.

For example, in the 1980s, President Ronald Reagan's administration could not agree on how to revise the order that required set-asides for hiring of minority government contractors. As a result, the order remained intact and continues to define federal affirmative action policy.

Two questions usually arise over policy formulation: (1) how is public policy formulated, and (2) who formulates public policy? Different types of policy formulation occur depending on government's ability to understand the nature of the problems it confronts. For example, government may lack a basic factual understanding of a problem, such as the military capabilities of another country. In addition, government may not understand the causes of the problem. What created the problem in the first place? If government does not know the underlying causes of a problem, such as poverty, how can they devise proposals to address it?

Different kinds of policy formulation arise from the lack of factual understanding and the lack of knowledge about the causes of a problem. Routine policy formulation occurs when policy makers have a factual understanding of the problem and know its causes. They are able to simply adjust routine policies, already in place, to redress the problem. Craftsman policy formulation occurs when policy makers have a theory of what causes the problem but lack a factual understanding of it. For example, the United States understands what the causes of terrorism are, but it often lacks factual information on the destructive capabilities of individual terrorist organizations. Conditional policy formulation occurs when policy makers have sufficient facts about the problem but lack a theory of its causes. Economic policy making often produces conditional policy formulation. Creative policy formulation—the most difficult of all—exists when policy makers have neither an adequate factual information base or a theory of causation. Creative policy formulation requires policy makers to enter into uncharted territories, putting forward policy solutions that have no precedent. Dealing with complex problems such as finding a cure for a new disease often forces creative policy formulation.

Numerous actors are involved in the process of policy formulation, such as the public bureaucracy, legislators, interest groups, think tanks, and presidential commissions and task forces. Often alternative policy proposals are generated by governmental agencies. Staffed by experts in a particular field of public policy, such as agricultural policy or energy policy, public agencies are well positioned to devise policy proposals. Due to the creation of congressional information providers such as the Congressional Research Service and the General Accounting Office, members of Congress are more able to get involved in policy formulation. At the state level, state legislative information agencies also give assistance to state legislators, making it easier for them to formulate policy alternatives. Interest groups are frequently at the helm of policy formulation, going to legislators with policy proposals in hand or with specific legislation already drafted.

At the state level, interest groups are even more influential in policy formulation because state legislators often do not have the time, the staff, or the expertise to address highly technical issues. Think tanks, which sometimes resemble interest groups, are research organizations in the private sector that work under contract for government agencies, providing them technical assistance and analysis. Think tanks, such as the Brookings Institution, the American Enterprise Institute, the Heritage Foundation, and those based in universities, are expected to provide more creative and innovative solutions to problems. Presidential commissions and task forces are often employed by presidents as a means of developing bipartisan policy alternatives and solutions to problems. They may be used to take pressure off the president, to help the president garner support for certain policy proposals, or to create an image of government concern about a problem or issue.

Policy formulation is one of the most important processes in policy making. It asks the question: what should be done about a problem? It may produce enduring solutions to problems or it may delay choosing among policy alternatives due to lack of political support or resources.

For more information

Anderson, James E. *Public Policymaking,* 4th ed. Boston: Houghton Mifflin, 2000.

Peters, B. Guy. *American Public Policy: Promise and Performance,* 5th ed. Chappaqua, N.Y.: Seven Bridges Press, 1999.

Ruth Ann Strickland

policy impact   A policy impact is the effect a public policy has on society (i.e., people and organizations). These effects can be either intended or unintended and either positive or negative.

For example, a natural resources agency might increase the minimum fine it levies against firms that expel waste into public waterways. This policy (i.e., the higher minimum fine) has the intended impact of improving the quality of rivers and lakes. However, some firms might find alternative ways of disposing of their waste on land or in the air. If this were the case, then ground or air pollution would increase as a result of the policy, and these increases would be an unintended impact of the policy. To use another example, suppose the speed limit were raised on a highway system. A positive impact is that travelers arrive at their destinations sooner, while a negative impact would be an increased accident rate.

The people and organizations affected by a policy can be sorted between the policy targets (those for whom the policy was intended) and others. Defining a policy target depends on the particular policy. Food stamps, for example, are provided to people with low incomes, while the Women, Infants, and Children program is intended to assist women with low incomes and their children. Federal student loans are available to most college students, while Pell

Grants are designed for lower-income students. Small-business loans are available to firms that meet certain size restrictions and are not intended for large corporations. Knowing for whom a policy is intended is important. It might be the case that a policy has positive but unintended impacts on nontargets but has no impact on the policy targets. Such information is very useful when policy makers reformulate the policy.

Determining what impacts a policy has is referred to as policy impact analysis. The tools and techniques used for this analysis usually fall under the domain of program evaluation.

For more information

Mohr, Lawrence. *Impact Analysis for Program Evaluation.* Newbury Park, Calif.: Sage, 1995.

Peters, B. Guy. *American Public Policy: Promise and Performance,* 5th ed. New York: Chatham House, 1999.

Jason Palmer

policy implementation   In the policy implementation stage of the policy process, the programs related to the designed policy are activated to produce results and effects that will solve a given public problem. In this sense, to implement a policy means to take action, to perform, to carry out programs.

Policy implementation is the third phase of the public policy analysis cycle (the previous ones being problem definition and decision making and the fourth phase being policy evaluation). At this stage, policy makers and implementers have to plan what must be done. Since implementation of public policy is not an exact science, sometimes there is no clear-cut answer of how to proceed. However, the basic components of implementation are usually provided. A listing is made of who will participate, the manner and amount of funding allocation, and reporting requirements for those charged with carrying out the implementation of the policy.

Two different analytical approaches can be used when implementing a public policy. The first one is the top-down model (also called administrative model or rational-Weberian model). It takes a policy decision by central government and then poses a number of questions about the implementation. These include: (1) To what extent are the actions of the implementing officials and target groups consistent with the objectives and procedures outlined in the policy decision? (2) To what extent are the objectives attained over time (that is, to what extent are the impacts consistent with the objectives? (3) What are the principal factors affecting policy outputs and impacts, both those relevant to the official policy as well as other politically significant ones? and (4) How is the policy reformulated over time on the basis of experience? As one can deduce, this perspective is based on the fact that it is possible to keep the public-policy design process (which always goes first) completely separated from the public-policy implementation phase. Therefore the public-policy designers are different from the public-policy implementers, the designers being on the top of the organization and the implementers underneath them. Their roles are also different. The first ones make decisions (they are the political actors), while the second ones take action (they are the technical actors).

The alternative approach to the top-down model is led by Aaron B. Wildavsky, who states that (1) programs are not totally perfect, (2) a program may pursue several goals at the same time, (3) public administrations are not always transparent and rational, and (4) society is often hostile and contradictory. That is why he proposes a new methodology based on the hypothesis that there is no difference between the role played by public-policy designers and the role played by the policy implementers during the public-policy analysis cycle. Both contribute to the process in a different way. Therefore, the content of a public policy depends both on its implementation and on the decision taken. In other words, from this perspective, the implementation process involves several institutional, political, and social groups of actors (such as public administration levels, administrative organizations, or affected citizens) and, therefore, it leads to the building of a policy network or policy community that deals with the action programs the policy involves.

For more information
Pressman, J. L., and A. Wildavsky. *Implementation,* 3d ed. Berkeley: University of California Press, 1984.

Mila Gascó

policy output   An output of a policy is a product that follows the passing of a law or executive or judicial decision. Examples of a policy output include the creation of a public program, a public information notice about a polluted river, or the racial integration of public schools through busing. These outputs result from the activities of government, done either by the program's employees themselves or by third parties hired by the government.

A policy output is part of the policy process, the transformation of inputs into outputs and impacts. It is a middle stage in this process and closely related to policy implementation. However, it is a narrower term than implementation in that outputs are tangible, while implementation incorporates both outputs and the processes that generate those outputs. For example, a policy output might be defined as the increase in the proportion of minority students at a city's suburban high schools. Policy implementation would be defined to include not only this output, but also the roles of principals and other administrators; union officials; bus drivers; the additional financial resources needed to expand school bus services and routes; and the response of citizens, parents, and students to the integration.

For more information
Peters, B. Guy. *American Public Policy: Promise and Performance,* 5th ed. New York: Chatham House, 1999.

Jason Palmer

policy window   *Policy window* is a concept used to describe a moment in time when opportunities exist for policy advocates to forward a particular public policy onto the government agenda or to draw attention to a particular public problem.

The most vivid example of this metaphorical "window" is associated with the space program. Here, a launch window will open that suggests the weather is right; Earth, Moon, and planets are in alignment; and other variables are in their proper places to allow for a successful mission launch. As in a policy window, the opportunity to launch exists for only a short period of time. If managers (NASA or otherwise) fail to take advantage of this open window, they may not get another chance for quite some time, if ever.

Policy windows can be predictable or unpredictable. That is, policy advocates may know that a particular window will open each year as a program's annual funding is renewed. On the other hand, policy windows may open as the result of a crisis, which could not have been known in advance. For example, the high-school shootings at Littleton, Colorado, offered a window of opportunity for gun-control advocates to promote their cause. This was an unpredictable event (a crisis) that offered proponents of gun control a unique chance to press their agenda and highlight a problem.

Policy advocates must be prepared for the opening of a policy window, because major changes in public policy may result. For example, the terrorist acts of 11 September 2001, in which aircraft were flown into the World Trade Center and the Pentagon opened a policy window for advocates of airline safety to press their case for increased security. Further, the annual federal budget process offers education policy advocates a chance to pursue renewed education efforts as the budget goes before Congress each year.

The concept of a policy window is one way of understanding why some policies emerge on the government agenda and others do not. If a policy window is closed, policy advocates may not be able to promote a policy or program. If the window is open, which is the result of a variety of factors, chances for success and promotion greatly increase.

For more information

Kingdon, John W. *Agendas, Alternatives, and Public Policies.* New York: HarperCollins, 1995.

Robert A. Schuhmann

politics-administration dichotomy The politics-administration dichotomy refers to the separation of partisan political activity from civil administration, particularly in the procedures for appointing civil servants.

Countries differ in the extent of partisan influence in the operation of their civil services. Traditionally, the British "Westminster" system of appointing permanent officers on seniority or merit has been contrasted with the modern U.S. system of patronage or "spoils," by which an incoming government installs its favorites to replace those of the previous administration, especially at the senior levels. In a Westminster system, civil servants have little contact with elected members other than their own minister, and engagement in direct partisan activity is regarded as unethical.

In the Westminster system that is followed in the Commonwealth countries, the roles of legislative and executive branches are combined in the person of the elected minister, who is accountable to Parliament for the administration of the department. Powers are separated by maintaining the independence and tenure of the civil servant head of the department, who offers "frank and fearless" advice to the minister.

Advocates of the U.S. system argue that an incoming government needs to place people it can trust in the senior positions if it is to implement its agenda for reform. Advocates of Westminster systems argue that trust, stability, and efficiency are increased if a government knows that its officers have no partisan axes to grind. International observers of the 2000 U.S. presidential ballot in Florida could identify no institution that was able to ensure that the result was fair and free of partisan bias.

Confusing policy with politics

Confusion of the terms *politics* and *policy* clouds understanding of the proper separation of politics from public administration. When university lecturer Woodrow Wilson (later U.S. president) in 1886 wrote that "administration lies outside the proper sphere of politics," he can hardly have imagined that his paper would be quoted a century later as authority for the view that elected members make policy and public officials simply carry it out. Policy is a statement by a high level of authority on how to handle commonly recurring sets of circumstances. Policies establish a framework in which a public-sector agency can make decisions where a discretion is to be exercised. An objective of policy is to make the response of the agency predictable and fair to all affected citizens.

It is a fundamental of ethical government in a democracy that departments have a duty to implement the policies of the government of the day. However, this does not mean that departments are empty vessels into which partisan policy is poured. Good policy does not arise from a vacuum. It has its roots in detailed and thoughtful research, intellectual inquiry, and analysis. The maxim "Ministers make policy, public servants carry it out," is just a simplistic old cliché.

Also, *politics* is an ambiguous word. Although the formulation of policy can be nonpartisan, it inevitably is political in the sense that policy decisions affect the distribution of benefits and burdens by the modern state and necessarily are value-laden.

A careful reading of Wilson's paper makes clear that his concern was that public administration should be free from partisan obligations, be recognized as a skilled profession, and be generally seen as aloof from the "hurry and strife" of political life. He was advocating an independent, nonpartisan civil service dedicated to the public interest, not a passive and subservient one concerned only with administrative minutiae.

For more information

Bridgman, Peter, and Glyn Davis. *Australian Policy Handbook*. New South Wales: Allen & Unwin, 1998.

Wilson, Woodrow. "The Study of Administration." *Political Science Quarterly* 56 (1941): 481–506.

Geoff Edwards

POSDCORB   POSDCORB is an acronym that represents the seven main functions of an executive in an organization: planning, organizing, staffing, directing, coordinating, reporting, and budgeting.

In the early to mid-1990s, management experts, who became known as classical organizational theorists, like LUTHER GULICK, Lyndall Urwick, and Henri Fayol, established a core set of principles that was to assist in achieving optimal performance of an organization. These principles were considered the scientific approach to management.

The goal of scientific management was to have relationships among employees, management, and the organization clearly defined so that efficiency of production could be achieved. Some of the principles include division of work, span of control, unity of command, and the work of the executive. The division-of-work principle is based on specialization of skills and the coordination of work by organization or the dominance of a particular idea.

The span-of-control principle asserts that an organizational unit should have a small number of employees reporting to a supervisor so that control is maintained. The unity-of-command principle is where there is one supervisor issuing guidance for each staff person to avoid confusion or conflict from multiple directions. Taken together, these three principles provide guidance on how an organization could be arranged so that it can efficiently function. The organization was to be rigidly hierarchical to achieve optimal performance.

As part of these management principles, one of the major focuses of the classical organizational theorists was on the role of the chief executive. The six job functions of the executive could be separated into subdivisions of the organization. HERBERT SIMON pointed out that these principles were really more like proverbs, since they contained inherent contradictions and were reflective of a rigid organizational structure. While many of the principles of the classical organizational theorists are no longer useful today in modern organizations, POSDCORB remains a concept that continues to have some limited usefulness in describing the functions of the executive. It lacks the more current notions of organizational behavior, which include motivation, employee needs, morale, and working in teams.

For more information

Fayol, Henri. *Industrial and General Administration*. London: Sir I. Pitman and Sons, 1949.

Gulick, Luther, and Lyndall Urwick, eds. *Papers on the Science of Administration*. New York: Institute of Public Administration, Columbia University, 1937.

Simon, Herbert. "The Proverbs of Administration." *Public Administration Review* 6 (1946): 53–67.

Kelly Tzoumis

postmodern public policy   Postmodern public policy is a form of analysis that differs from modernist accounts of public administration.

Postmodern analysis has three elements. First, it assumes that the field of public policy is simply part of a grand narrative of the unquestioned superiority of liberal democratic capitalism. The argument is that this form of political organization should be regarded as but one story in the advancement of humanity. The second strand of postmodern thought borrows from linguistic theory, which regards language as a cultural construct where meaning is not inherent in things but is tangential. As such, words carry different meanings depending on the context and period; for instance, the word "gay" has multiple meanings, which have changed over time. In this linguistic construction, there is a slippage between symbols and what they purport to represent as reality. As such, multiple meanings emerge and are contested in the public arena. For instance, the O.J. Simpson trial is read in many ways (e.g., as a case of domestic violence, as discriminatory police processes, as trial by media, etc.) without any discourse being agreed upon or establishing a stable truth.

Third, postmodern theory is profoundly concerned with aesthetic styles—notably in the fields of architecture, the arts, literature, media, cinema, and television—where repetition, deconstruction, recycling, remakes, citation, and irony have come to be a dominant form of representation. Many postmodern theorists see the emergence of this stylistic trope as proof of a new historic era where modernism has either been replaced by or coexists with postmodern sensibilities. Given this perspective, politics and public administration cannot be analyzed in terms only of their supposed essence; one must also consider how they are represented and how they represent themselves to the public. That is, in the postmodern approach to government, politics takes on the form of simulations rather than genuine efforts to address problems or construct good government.

Moreover, citizens come to know about government from these repeated images, symbols, and signs, and this in turn reproduces the same forms over and over again. It is as if political reality does not occur unless you see it as a produced image on television, sometimes in endless repeats (as in the 9/11 terrorist implosion of the World Trade Center).

The difference between the postmodern form of analysis and that of modernist interpretations of public policy can be illustrated by referring to the example of "the war on drugs" used by Charles Fox and Hugh Millar. These two authors argue that there are four ways to address this government program. The first approach is in a modernist framework, which depicts the "war on drugs" as a genuine strategy by governments to address a real problem. A second modernist interpretation, Fox and Miller offer, is to regard the "war" as irrational because its terminology and methods (police, custodial, and military) are counterproductive, promoting rather than eliminating illegal drug activity. Their third interpretation regards the use of the notion of a "war on drugs" as an ideological ploy, pursued by governments to demonize certain sections of the population and to appeal to other sections of the electorate, principally middle-class (white) voters.

Their final and postmodern interpretation considers the "war on drugs" as but a set of stylistic images and simulated models divorced from both the meaning of the words used and the material reality itself. Moreover, this form of representation and simulation comes to be depicted as reality itself and becomes the only reality that the public knows regarding the drug problem. In the postmodern world, particular language forms and symbols come to take the place of reality, so that codes—such as arrest statistics, rising prison numbers, drug confiscations—become the reference point in themselves, read off in terms of "winning the war" if, indeed, there is a "war" at all. These codes are repeatedly cross-referenced in diverse forms, such as political advertisements, media releases, party political platforms, news footage, talk-show discussions, film plots, television dramas, etc., so that "image" comes to dominate the perception of the drug issue in America.

For the public administrator, the postmodern condition has two basic dilemmas. First, truth is uncertain, and the conditions of proof will vary across discourses. Truth involves trusting in some community, e.g., the medical profession and the truth of their discourse, while denying another community and their discourse, say faith healers. The dilemma for public administrators is not merely what interpretation of the truth about the "real" they accept, but how to defend that decision in a world where the game of uncertainty has an inverse effect. That is, the more there is disputation over truth, the more people tend to believe in fiction. This leads to a second problem for public administrators in that they have to be aware of the role that representation plays in contemporary society where, after 70 years of mass communication, the public is saturated by narratives that are characterized by irony, quotation, self-conscious allusion, and nostalgic recycling of concepts and codes. As such, when a public issue appears, it is likely to be subject to this aesthetic, where it will sit cheek-by-jowl with other concerns, all open to the pervasive ironic stance that looks with boredom at politics.

Some claim that the postmodern condition has depoliticizing effects. Consider the case that there is a medical report on the positive benefits of the public distribution of heroin, based on a successful European model, which has gained the backing of a public health body. Now the report might appear as a news item on *Good Morning America;* then by noon it has been reworked as a current-affairs item, with recycled sensationalized footage of drug addicts in, say, Amsterdam; by the time of the evening programming it is satirized on panel shows, with cross-referencing to the opening scene from the film *Pulp Fiction* (with its debate on the little differences between Europe and America); by midnight it is the butt of jokes on the David Letterman show. In short, a serious issue has been coded and recoded, evoking a "so what" response from the audience.

Notwithstanding the nihilism that this might imply, public administrators should remain positive, as audiences and participants alike are aware of postmodern codes and styles. One only has to remember the 1992 presidential election campaign in which George H. W. Bush sought to attack Bill Clinton via a series of codes that questioned his personal life and liberal values. In response, Clinton recoded this criticism as Bush merely recycling his 1988 campaign against Michael Dukakis, thereby successfully transcoding the message into one that showed Bush being a passé president. In sum, public policy can be effective if it recognizes both the contingency of truth and the power of the postmodern aesthetic.

For more information

Fox, Charles, and Hugh T. Miller. "The Deprecating Public Policy Discourses." *American Behavioral Scientist* 41, no. 1 (September 1997): 64–89.

McCarthy, Greg. "Two and Two Make One: The Collapse of the State Bank of South Australia." *Policy Organisation and Society* 11 (summer 1996): 85–111.

Gregory McCarthy

privacy   Privacy is a legal, political, and social term that means different things in different contexts.

At its simplest level, it means a state in which others do not know things about you, a state of seclusion. It may be seen as a right to personal privacy, to be free from surveillance and observation. In another context privacy connotes the state in which an individual is able to keep information about him or herself from others, or to control its use, i.e., information privacy.

There has been an increase in government surveillance in the wake of the World Trade Center disaster, particularly in the United States. The subsequently enacted legislation gives the government expanded abilities to conduct online searches and seizures and regulate financial institutions. This increased surveillance makes the individual's right to information privacy more important.

The legal protection given to privacy also differs among legal jurisdictions. In some jurisdictions, principally the United States, privacy receives constitutional protection in addition to protection through a myriad number of laws governing specific contexts, e.g., credit, door-to-door sales, health information, bank records, etc.

In addition to the concerns of individuals about privacy in an online environment, most countries are also subject to international obligations, which necessitate some form of privacy protection. The Universal Declaration of Human Rights (UDHR), adopted in 1948, includes Article 12:

> "No one shall be subjected to arbitrary interference with his privacy, family, home or correspondence, nor to attacks upon his honour and reputation. Everyone has the right to the protection of the law against such interference or attacks."

Article 17 of the International Convention on Civil and Political Rights is almost identical to Article 12 of the UDHR. This convention imposes binding obligations on its member states.

In an Internet environment, a major concern of consumers and regulators is the need for sellers to respect customer privacy. In doing so they should adhere to the National Principles for the Fair Handling of Personal Information. Based on the Guidelines Governing the Protection of Privacy and Transborder Flows of Personal Data (1980) of the Organization for Economic Cooperation and Development (OECD), these principles establish a benchmark for the handling of personal information and provide guidelines about the collection, use, disclosure, quality, security, access, and correction of personal information.

The OECD National Privacy Principles (NPP) are reflected in the European Privacy Directive and in the legislation of countries like Australia. The National Privacy Principles relate to:

- **Collection of personal information.** Collection must be necessary for an organization's activities. It must be collected lawfully and fairly, and as a general principle, with the individual's consent.
- **Use and disclosure of personal information.** Information can only be used or disclosed for its original purpose unless the person has consented to its use or disclosure for another purpose. Exemptions may apply to initial contact for direct marketing if consent wasn't practicable originally. Other common exceptions include law enforcement needs; public safety; need for medical research; need to manage, fund, and monitor a health service; and to prevent or lessen a threat to a person's life.
- **Accuracy of personal information.** Organizations must take reasonable care to ensure that they keep personal information accurate, complete, and up-to-date.
- **Security of personal information.** Organizations must take reasonable steps to protect the personal information that they hold from misuse, loss, and unauthorized access, modifications, or disclosure.
- **Openness of the organization's practices.** Organizations that collect personal information must be able to document their practices

A surveillance camera disguised as a street lamp watches from a street corner in New York City. (SPENCER PLATT/ GETTY IMAGES)

and make the information available upon request.

- Access and collection rights. Organizations must give individuals access to their personal information and allow them to correct it or explain something with which they disagree, unless that explanation would invade someone else's privacy. Another exception is where this would compromise a fraud investigation.
- Use of government identifiers. Restrictions are placed on the use of government agency identifiers so that people are not misled or confused.
- Anonymity. Organizations must give people the option of entering into transactions anonymously where it is lawful and practicable. An example of where it would be unlawful would be the opening of a bank account.
- Restrictions on transborder data flows. Organizations can transfer the personal information about an individual to a foreign country only if they believe that the information will be protected by a law or a contract that upholds privacy principles similar to the NPP's.
- Special provisions for sensitive information. A higher level of privacy protection applies to sensitive personal information. This includes health information, political beliefs, religious affiliation, sexual preferences, membership in political parties, etc.

There are those who argue that the OECD privacy guidelines, formulated in 1980 before the existence of the Internet, need modification in the light of this new technology. The guidelines were, however, brought about by the introduction of computers into economic and social life and the recognition that the proliferation of computer systems would mean a reduction in the power of individuals to control the personal information collected and stored about them. The guidelines are also technology neutral so as to be flexible enough to apply to new technology. The OECD has also published a number of documents elaborating on the application of the privacy guidelines in the context of the Internet.

It may happen that the major protection of an individual's privacy may come less from the law than from technology itself. The World Wide Web Consortium (W3C) has developed its new Platform for Privacy Preferences (P3P). With this technology, organizations can express their privacy policy in XML. The user can enter into a P3P-compliant browser the information they are willing to share and direct how it can be used. This saves consumers the chore of hunting privacy documents and wondering whether they provide the same protection as other privacy policies. Using this technology, the software compares the user's preferences with the privacy policy to see whether consumer expectations match what the policy proclaims to deliver. However, one problem with this technology is that there is no body to enforce the privacy protection that firms say they provide. The greater use and availability of encryption software should also help to ensure a greater level of privacy protection.

Education, especially of vulnerable groups such as children (Children's Online Privacy Protection Act of 1998, 15 USC sec. 6501), will also play an important role in privacy protection. Recent U.S. legislation restricts the personal information that net providers can collect from children under 13 without the permission of their parents.

These developments make it clear that, for a long time to come, privacy issues will remain high on the agenda of governments, consumers, and business.

For more information

Bernstein, Debra, and Jonathan Winer. "Business Implications of the US Anti-Terorrism Law." Available online. URL: http://gigalaw.com/articles/2001/bernstein-2001-11.html. Downloaded July 2003.

OECD; Directorate for Science, Technology and Industry; Committee for Information, Computer and Communications Policy; Group of Experts on Information Security and Privacy. *Privacy Protection in a Global Networked Society.* DSTI/ICCP/REG(98)6/FINAL. Washington, D.C.: OECD Publishing, 1998.

Sholtz, Paul. "The Changing Definition of Privacy." Available online. URL: http://www.zdnet.com/filters/printerfriendly/0,6061,2815772-2,00.html.

Turrow, Josephy. *Privacy Policies on Children's Websites: Do They Play by the Rules?* Annenberg Public Policy Center, University of Pennsylvania. Available online. URL: http://www.appcpenn.org. Downloaded March 2001.

Eugene Clark

privatization Privatization describes a process of transferring government assets and services to the private sector.

Privatization most commonly denotes the sale of state-owned assets to private owners. Broadly defined, privatization also includes the formation of other relationships between government and the private sector, including agreements for services formerly performed by government to be performed by privately owned businesses, and transactions that utilize private investors to finance infrastructure projects. Today, privatization is most commonly associated with the process of reducing government control of the economy in former communist and emerging economies as part of structural transitions to market economies. Privatization has been a global trend since the early 1980s, when the government of Margaret Thatcher began a pathbreaking program of privatization in the United Kingdom, followed later by other countries in western Europe and elsewhere. In the United States, attention has focused on efforts to privatize electricity generation and distribution, and on proposals to privatize the management of retirement funds collected through the Social Security system.

Privatization is a political process as well as an economic process, and specific political and economic considerations determine the goals and methods of privatization. The main goal of privatization is to reduce the role of government in the economy and free government of financial commitments connected with that role. Reducing public-sector ownership is especially attractive for emerging economies in which assistance to unprofitable state-owned enterprises consumes a significant amount of resources and results in considerable external debt. Other goals of privatization include freeing private businesses from subsidized competition; obtaining sales proceeds to finance government objectives; broadening the ownership of important assets; and improving the performance of specific enterprises by increasing accountability, improving incentives for performance, cutting costs, and accelerating innovation.

There are a variety of techniques that can be used for privatizing a state-owned enterprise, depending on specific political and economic circumstances and results sought. Some of these methods are described as follows. Small-business auctions are public auctions to the highest bidder and are generally not used for larger enterprises. An advantage is that this method is highly transparent and publicly promotes privatization by allowing for broad participation. Offerings to strategic investors are offers to a select group of potential investors. This technique allows parties to work out detailed investment plans and address various economic and political factors. However, this technique is time-consuming and has the aura of "backroom deals" due to the lack of transparency.

Initial public offerings (IPOs) involve the sale of shares directly to the public. An advantage of this method is broad participation. A drawback is that it is expensive, does not bring new capital to the firm, may not result in a change in management, and requires the existence of a formal stock market. Joint-venture investments by government and the private sector are cooperative arrangements in which the government retains some control. For this reason, it is often utilized by countries not fully supportive of privatization. Mass privatization programs involve a distribution of vouchers to the general public, which can later be exchanged for stock. An advantage is that this method does not rely on an established stock market and may facilitate enforcement of transfer restrictions. Build-own-operate/build-own-transfer programs are methods to finance large infrastructure projects by obtaining private-sector financing and operation in exchange for fees paid to government. Finally, as a last resort, asset liquidation is appropriate where there is no going-concern value to preserve.

For more information
Scott, Hal S., and Philip A. Wellons. *International Finance,* 5th ed. New York: Foundation Press, 1998.

Olga Sekulic

procedural due process Procedural due process is one of the most important criteria by which legislative and executive enactments and judicial proceedings are judged. This concept is critical to public administration in that it serves as a limit on how decisions are made and implemented.

Derived in part from the phrase in the English Magna Carta (1215) referring to "the law of the land," the concept of due process has come to embody both general ideas of fairness and specific guarantees designed to ensure such fairness in the first 10 amendments, or Bill of Rights, and other constitutional provisions.

On occasion, American courts invalidate laws on the basis that the objects they are trying to accomplish are invalid (so-called substantive due process), but, except in cases involving fundamental rights—privacy, for example, or those involving limitations of freedom of speech, press, or religion specifically forbidden by the Constitution—courts generally allow state officials to decide on the proper content of laws and devote most of their attention to matters of procedure.

Although a provision in the Fifth Amendment (1791) prohibited the national government from depriving any individual of "life, liberty, or property, without due process of law," the phrase was rarely used to invalidate legislation in the 18th or 19th centuries. It has received much more prominence since the Fourteenth Amendment (1868) adopted a similar restriction on actions by state governments. Indeed, this provision has been the primary vehicle by which the guarantees in the Bill of Rights, previously interpreted only to limit the national government, have now largely been used to limit the states as well. Most Supreme Court justices took the view that due process required "fundamental fairness," or they selectively incorporated individual provisions of the Bill of Rights and applied them to the states. However, over time, and especially during the years of the Warren Court, Court majorities applied almost all the provisions that once limited actions by the national government to the states as well.

Procedural due process can apply to a variety of situations involving those accused of, or on trial for, crimes as well as a variety of administrative situations, where inadequate processes can often prove to be as controversial as unjust outcomes. Thus, the idea of procedural due process is often used to ascertain the reasonableness of governmental searches and seizures under the Fourth Amendment, the rights of individuals on trial as guaranteed in the Fifth Amendment, and the right to counsel in the Sixth Amendment.

Similarly, in *Goldberg v. Kelly,* 397 U.S. 254 (1970), the Court invalidated the suspension of welfare benefits without a hearing, even though it failed to apply a similar standard to disability benefits in *Mathews v. Eldridge,* 424 U.S. 319 (1976). (In *Goss v. Lopez,* 419 U.S. 565 [1975], the Court further insisted that, although students were not necessarily entitled to a formal hearing, they were entitled to know and be able to respond to evidence against them before being expelled from school.) In *Memphis Light, Gas & Water Division v. Craft,* 436 U.S. 1 (1978), the

Court refused to allow a utility to disconnect services before providing an administrative hearing. Generally interpreting procedural due process requirements less strictly than the Warren Court, the Burger and Rehnquist Courts continue to recognize the truth of Justice Felix Frankfurter's observation in *McNabb v. United States*, 318 U.S. 332 (1943) at 347, that "the history of liberty has largely been the history of observance of procedural safeguards."

For more information

Abraham, Henry J., and Barbara A. Perry. *Freedom & the Court*, 7th ed. New York: Oxford University Press, 1998.

John R. Vile

program evaluation   By "program evaluation," most public-policy and -administration scholars are referring to the systematic inquiry of a public program's purposes, operations, and impacts. Public programs (organizations created by a government agency for the purpose of providing goods or services to clients and/or citizens, e.g., the Head Start preschool program) are evaluated because a group of people, called stakeholders, would like to know something about the program.

For example, stakeholders might want to know if the program's operations are being implemented efficiently, if all of the program's clients are being treated fairly, or whether the program is achieving its goals. The stakeholders usually do not conduct the evaluation themselves but instead hire a researcher or a research team to address these questions.

Program-evaluation researchers use techniques that are similar to those used by other researchers:

- Identify the research question(s) (what the stakeholders want to know)
- Locate previous research on evaluations of similar programs or evaluation questions
- Detail the methods to be used to answer the question
- Identify the types and sources of data needed
- Implement the evaluation (i.e., investigate the program using the methods listed above)
- Write a report explaining the purpose of the evaluation, what the questions are, how they were answered, what the findings are, and what implications that has for the stakeholders

Depending on the evaluation question and the data needed to answer the question, researchers use many different methods to evaluate the program. These methods are typically classified along a continuum from qualitative to quantitative. When researchers use qualitative methods, they focus on data that can be obtained by written documents and oral interviews. They might attempt to discover, for example, the program's history, stakeholders' perceptions of the program's strengths and weaknesses, and clients' perceptions on service delivery. Here, a researcher might interview parents of Head Start students to see how responsive they believe program staff are to their needs.

When using quantitative methods, researchers use numerical data on service delivery. Questions that are appropriate for quantitative methods include: (1) How many service units were delivered last year? (2) How much does one unit cost? and (3) Is a racial or socioeconomic group receiving a disproportionate share of the program's benefits? These methods include, among others, regression analysis, time-series analysis, and cost-benefit analysis. Many times, stakeholders will want to know much about a program. Thus, evaluation researchers will use both qualitative and quantitative methods in their effort to address all of the stakeholders' questions.

Evaluation researchers face many challenges in conducting evaluations. These include disagreement among stakeholders, the political context of the program and its evaluation, and ethical dilemmas. If a Head Start parent reported that the staff were unresponsive to a student's educational needs, the researcher should not disclose the parent's identity to program staff. Professional associations, such as the American Evaluation Association, have developed standards and guidelines for the proper conduct of a program evaluation. These include identifying and including evaluation stakeholders; providing valid, reliable, and timely information; and protecting the rights of individuals (especially the program's clients) involved in the evaluation.

For more information

American Evaluation Association. http://www.eval.org/.

Manski, Charles F., and Irwin Garfinkel, eds. *Evaluating Welfare and Training Programs.* Cambridge, Mass.: Harvard University Press, 1992.

Rossi, Peter H., Howard E. Freeman, and Mark W. Lipsey. *Evaluation: A Systematic Approach,* 6th ed. Newbury Park, Calif.: Sage, 1999.

Jason Palmer

Program Evaluation and Review Technique (PERT)

PERT was developed to meet the challenge of highly complex, first-ever, one-of-a-kind programs.

Planners schedule work for projects in conditions of certainty and uncertainty. As projects in the 20th century became ever more complex and unusual—dams, tunnels, space programs—involving vast resources with large numbers of people working for months or years, new methods of management for working under conditions of uncertainty were needed.

The navy's Special Projects Office invented PERT in order to achieve fully integrated planning in managing the Polaris weapons system. In 1958 Admiral W. F. Raborn established a research team composed of D. G. Malcolm, J. H. Roseboom, C. E. Clark, and W. Fazar, who developed PERT.

To use PERT, a project is analyzed. Complex projects may have hundreds or many thousands of events. Every task in the project is arranged in a network of activities over a time scale as an interrelated series of events. Each event is numbered and graphically connected with arrows to show activity relationships. PERT can effectively use computers to display graphically the network of predecessor and successor events as well as parallel events. The graphic display gives managers day-to-day control of the whole program. After all the events are listed in a network, their times for accomplishment are calculated. PERT managers often face situations where the tasks have never been performed before, so they calculate three possible times for each event: a pessimistic time, a likely time, and an optimistic time.

After the times are assigned, a computer can run simulations to show the critical path in the network. The critical path is the longest path of events. Any delay along the critical path will delay the whole project's completion. Other paths will have slack time, that is, tasks that can be completed without pressure. As work on the project is completed, computer updates can show any delays. Late completion of slack-time events may change the critical path, or events may be shifted to other paths in order to complete the project on time.

The basic PERT plan just described is called PERT/time because it focuses on the time restraints. In addition PERT/cost has been developed to manage the costs of a program.

PERT was developed at the same time as the critical path method (CPM). They are similar network-scheduling techniques, but they differ in terminology, time values assigned, and in other ways. Features from each are sometimes used together.

PERT has been used by the Federal Aviation Agency, the Atomic Energy Commission, the Office of Management and Budget, and others. Typical uses include installing new administrative procedures, planning a presidential inaugural ball, or reducing processing time for grants-in-aid.

For more information

Miller, R. W. *Schedule, Cost and Profit Control with PERT.* New York: McGraw-Hill, 1963.

Moder, Joseph J. *Project Management with CPM, PERT, and Precedence Diagramming,* 3d ed. New York: Van Nostrand Reinhold Company, 1983.

A. J. L. Waskey

progressive property tax A progressive property-tax system places a greater burden of responsibility for the tax on the more wealthy citizens of a jurisdiction relative to those citizens of lower wealth.

Most states mandate tax assessment of real estate on some basis of fair market value or use value, which is fair market value of the property restricted to a specific use. Tax assessment is the procedure performed by appointed or hired personnel of the local government that determines what the value of the house or commercial building is for purposes of taxing the owner. One expectation contained in this mandate is the legal requirement of equity. If inequities are present in a tax system, the result is that some subset of the population is required to pay a higher proportion of their wealth to the tax collector while another subset of the population pays less of their wealth. Two forms of potential inequities exist in the property tax, horizontal and vertical. State legislators require local assessing authorities to attain vertical and near horizontal equity in assessment practices.

Horizontal inequities occur when the tax level varies significantly across households with near equal capacity to pay or, in the case of the property tax, with similar house values. Horizontal inequity will be present, in isolated instances, in nearly every property tax system induced by variations in local real estate markets and their information asymmetries. Excessive horizontal inequities signal inconsistent valuation procedures by the assessor and/or a mandated variation in the time between assessments of similar properties.

Vertical inequality arises from the systematic over or under assessment of properties of different value. It can be expressed as significant differences in the assessed-value to market-value ratios of low-, medium-, and high- priced properties. Inequities of this nature are referred to as vertical inequities because the inequity varies as the home value moves up or down the value range. Vertical inequities occur when the effective tax rates are lower for citizens with a higher ability to pay (regressive), or when the tax structure results in higher effective tax rates for citizens with higher ability to pay (progressive). When vertical inequity exists, such inequities should be addressed through reappraisal or other corrective actions.

The principal focus in the evaluation of assessment procedures has been to test whether inequities are a function of poor assessment practices or the result of wide variations in localized real estate market events. A number of factors have been identified as contributing to the possibility of property tax inequities.

- The infrequency of assessment coupled with the rate of change in the value of real estate
- The subjectivity of the appraiser and the often limited information relative to characteristics internal to the structure
- The political environment, which can influence the assessment process by creating an artificial ceiling on the assessed value of high-valued housing, often owned by citizens with political clout
- A tendency, on the part of assessors, to center the value estimates to the mean, a behavior that will increase the estimate for low-valued houses and decrease the estimate for high-valued housing
- The limitations inherent in statistical methods employed by assessors to conduct mass appraisals
- The limited comparability of marginal properties, i.e., those at the extreme bottom and top in terms of value

Though the property tax has been maligned throughout much of its history, it has been, and remains, the major source of tax revenue for local governments in the United States. Recently, local property taxation has been under attack for reasons associated with assessment inequity, as well as for the use of funds for public services, such as public schools. The result of this heightened interest has been the creation of property tax restructuring legislation in California, Michigan, Massachusetts, Florida, and Indiana.

While the property tax has been referred to as the worst tax, there remains a strong case for local governments to rely on the property tax to generate revenue for service provision. Considering the characteristics (reliability, stability, and balance) that continue to make the property tax a prominent source of state and local public revenue, property taxes are not likely to be eliminated. The property tax appears destined to remain a major factor for financing education, infrastructure, and other local governance, and it will very likely become increasingly important that the property tax systems of the future operate both efficiently and fairly.

For more information

Fisher, Ronald. *State and Local Public Finance,* 2d ed. Chicago: Irwin, 1996.

Mikesell, John. *Fiscal Administration: Analysis and Applications for the Public Sector,* 5th ed. Fort Worth, Tex.: Harcourt Brace College Publishers, 1999.

Brent C. Smith

project management   Project management is an undertaking that has a beginning, middle, and end that is carried out to achieve a goal.

A project is a problem scheduled for solution. Project management seeks to solve the problem by bringing together money, manpower, and materials in order to do or build something. Projects themselves may be small (writing a book), medium (making a movie), or enormous (the Manhattan Project during World War II). Managers often face unique problems because they are undertaking a project never previously attempted.

Project management as a discipline arose in the 1960s in response to the need to manage the American space program. Thereafter it moved quickly into the military, civilian government, and business. Project management can also be called product management, matrix management, or construction management.

Project management differs from ordinary operations found in organizations that endure indefinitely. Ordinary operations, such as supplying an agency, deal with repetitive routines. Projects are unique and temporary. In addition, projects often need resources only part-time, while permanent organizations use their resources permanently.

Projects move through a predictable life cycle of conception, planning, execution, and completion. The goal of a project is to complete it on time, under budget, and as specified in the project plan. This means that during the project, managers will work with details to ensure the quality of the work, that costs are controlled, and that schedules are kept.

Once the decision to do a project is made, it must be planned. Every task in a project will be organized into the work breakdown structure (WBS). The WBS is like a hierarchical organization chart of personnel in an organization, but with the tasks in their logically subordinate rankings. When every task is assigned a place in the WBS, it is scheduled, people are assigned, resources are allocated, and the costs are estimated. Supervising the execution of the project plan is the job of the manager, who works with teams of people to accomplish the project's component tasks.

Projects are usually planned and managed with project-management computer programs. The software allows managers to view the scheduled tasks in GANTT CHART views, or PERT (PROGRAM EVALUATION AND REVIEW TECHNIQUE) views, or in many other views, depending upon the sophistication of the program.

Project management is often difficult because project managers must recruit manpower and material from other managers. This frequently requires the exercise of excellent political skills of leadership, persuasion, and negotiation.

Modern governments authorize many projects annually. These may be highway projects, infrastructure projects, research projects, military projects, or grants-in-aid to any number of clients for development of local or state governments or even for civilian groups. Many managers belong to the Project Management Institute.

For more information

Forsberg, Kevin, Hal Mooz, and Howard Cotterman. *Visualizing Project Management: A Model for Business and Technical Success.* New York: Wiley, 2000.

Lewis, James P. *Project Planning, Scheduling & Control: A Hands-On Guide to Bringing Projects in on Time and on Budget.* Chicago: Irwin Professional Publishing, 1995.

A. J. L. Waskey

public-choice theory Public-choice theory is the branch of political science that attempts to explain voter outcomes and political processes by economic theory and game theory, i.e., by analyzing the strategies that rational actors (bureaucrats, voters, legislators, and politicians) use in trying to achieve their goals.

In 1986, James Buchanan received the Nobel Prize in economics for his groundbreaking work in public-choice theory, a new perspective directed toward the study of politics based on economic principles and therefore aimed to make the interrelationships between politics and the economy more understandable.

Generally speaking, public-choice theory is a social science that studies the decision-making behaviors of government officials from the perspective of economic theory. This perspective is interested in answering the following question: how are decisions made outside of a private market context? Therefore, it is a theory that can be seen as the intersection of two disciplines: political science and economic theory. In Buchanan's own words, "It takes the methods and approaches that economists have traditionally applied to the private sector and extend those to the political sectors, to politics."

Indeed, the public-choice theory takes the same principles that economists use to analyze people's actions in the marketplace and applies them to people's actions in collective decision making. Particularly, it analyses the roles of bureaucrats, voters, legislators, and politicians. In this context, "choice" is the act of selecting from among alternatives. "Public" refers to people. But people do not choose. Choices are made by individuals, and these choices may be "private" or "public." A person makes private choices as he goes about the ordinary business of living. He makes "public choices' when he selects among alternatives for others as well as for himself. Such choices become the objects of inquiry in the public choice theory.

The public-choice theory seems to have taken hold in five different areas:

1. Budget. The explanation of the budget deficit regime is the best example of the public-choice thinking. Buchanan explains that "the key to public choice is common sense. And common sense tells you that a politician is very much like the rest of us. A politician who's seeking office or seeking to remain in office is responsible, as he should be, to constituents. He wants to go back to a constituency and tell them that he's either lowered their taxes, or he's brought them program benefits. You plug that into politics and you have a natural proclivity of a politician to create deficits."

2. Monetary policy. The public-choice theory looks at the behavior of Federal Reserve Boards as well as other monetary institutions

from an incentive/constraint-structures point of view.

3. Operation of democracies. Much attention has been given in the public-choice field to the problem of voting. In fact, one of the chief underpinnings of public-choice theory is the lack of incentives for voters to monitor government effectively. Also, public-choice scholars have looked at the ways politicians interact with each other, the voters, and their supporters to achieve their own goals. Finally, public choice has much to say about the use of rent-seeking, which is the act of obtaining special treatment by the government at the expense of the rest of the people.

4. Growth of special interests. Public-choice scientists examine the options involved with solving the many social dilemmas resulting from living in groups or collectives. Public-choice scholars address the challenge of determining what is the best "of the imperfect solutions" given that the private market is not "the" solution and neither is the public one (i.e., the government).

5. Constitutional framework. Public-choice theorists attempt to examine the system of government in which the people governed define their government by means of a constitution. The emphasis is on rules. In this sense, Buchanan says that "we were the first to start analyzing the Constitution from an economic point of view. There were other people who analyzed particular voting rules, like majority voting, but we put that in a constitutional structure and provided an argument for choices among voting rules."

Definitively, public choice is an application of neoclassical economic tools (self-interest and utility maximization) to explain political behavior. This behavior gives rise to the design of specific public policies, which is why this theory is important to public administration science. For example, the design of representative government is often flawed in that, even if most legis-lators wanted to balance the budget, individual legislators desiring reelection cannot risk voting for specific expenditure cuts and/or tax increases.

For more information
Buchanan, James, and T. Gordon. *The Calculus of Consent.* Ann Arbor: University of Michigan Press, Ann Arbor Paperbacks, 1962. Available online. URL: http://www.econlib.org/library/Buchanan/buchCv3Contents. html.

Mila Gascó and Fran Equiza

Public Employment Relations Board The Public Employment Relations Board (PERB) is a state-level, independent, quasi-judicial agency created to ensure the rights of employees of a state, county, city, town, or village government, or of a school district, public authority, or other special service district, to decide to or decline to join a union. PERBs also exist to protect the right of unions composed of public employees to engage in collective bargaining with public employers.

Since the 1935 enactment of the National Labor Relations Act, individuals working in the private sector have had the right to unionize and to bargain collectively with employers. However, employees of federal, state, and local government and public agencies had no parallel rights until 1967, when the Taylor Law granted employees of New York's state and local governments and agencies the right to unionize; granted public employee unions the right to bargain collectively with public employers; and created the Public Employment Relations Board to protect these rights of public employees and their unions. Since 1967, 35 additional states have created PERBs or agencies with similar or identical functions. Congress passed the CIVIL SERVICE REFORM ACT of 1978, which created the MERIT SYSTEMS PROTECTION BOARD (MSPB), an agency similar to a PERB, and also granted federal government and agency employees unionization and collective bargaining rights parallel to those taken for granted by state and local public employees for 11 years and by private-sector employees for 43 years.

Currently, employees of all federal government branches and agencies—and of all state and local governments and agencies in the 36 states with laws similar to New York's—benefit from statutes that guarantee these employees the right to organize and to bargain collectively with their employers. Public-sector employers must consult with the employees' union prior to effecting any changes in the employees' terms or conditions of employment.

A PERB is responsible for monitoring and gathering information about state and federal agencies' decisions that might impact public employees, and for using these data to ensure public employers' compliance with civil service laws or other statutes or rules relevant to non-federal public employees. Each PERB must define the actions that it considers to be "improper labor practice." Improper union actions typically include mismanagement of the labor force, abuse of authority, unjust treatment of "whistleblowers," and denial of opportunity for employees to form collective-bargaining units. Improper employee actions include striking in violation of statutory prohibitions against this activity, "whistleblowing" based on false allegations, and violations of a reasonable code of behavior promulgated by a particular public employer. When improper practice allegations are made by an employee against an employer, or by an employer against an individual employee or a union, PERB is empowered to act an an umpire to attempt to achieve resolution of the dispute at hand.

Most of a PERB's work involves mediation to solve a dispute in a manner that is acceptable to and equitable for both parties. A PERB relies on this useful procedure to solve disputes arising from contract negotiations between a public employer and its employees' union, or when it becomes necessary to resolve an impasse that arises from collective-bargaining negotiations, or when public employees threaten to strike if the employer fails to meet a certain demand.

If mediation efforts fail during negotiations by public employees who are not involved in public-safety-related work, a PERB may decide to conduct a legislative hearing. Most commonly, these hearings result in the legislature's demand that both parties resume negotiations. Occasionally, however, state legislatures unilaterally impose terms and conditions of employment for a period of less than one year.

In other cases in which mediation fails to resolve a disagreement, the PERB appoints a fact finder who then conducts hearings, takes testimony, accepts briefs containing the arguments of both the public employer and employee, and proposes nonbinding settlement suggestions. In the event that one party refuses to accept the fact finder's report, a PERB can require that the parties meet again and submit to conciliation proceedings.

Stalled negotiations between a public employer and a union of law enforcement officers, fire fighters, or other public-safety employees are expected from the usual conciliation and mediation procedures noted above. Instead of a legislative hearing or appointment of a fact finder, when public safety may be at risk, the PERB appoints an arbitrator. Both parties to the dispute are bound by the results of the arbitration.

The Office of Personnel Management, which manages the U.S. CIVIL SERVICE SYSTEM, is responsible for ensuring that federal agencies make employment decisions in accordance with the merit (or civil service) system's laws and rules, and that these agencies do not engage in prohibited personnel practices. The MSPB's Office of Special Counsel is responsible for investigating allegations of both employees' and employers' prohibited personnel practices and for prosecuting violators of merit system rules and regulations.

When a public employee initiates an MSPB "improper practice" proceeding and specifically alleges that the employer discriminated against him or her, the MSPB may request that the Equal Employment Opportunity Commission review the case. However, if the public employer prevails in an employee-initiated "improper practice" proceeding that does not involve an allegation of discrimination, the employee-complainant may appear before MSPB to appeal the administrative decision.

All MSPB final decisions are subject to review by the U.S. Court of Appeals for the Federal Circuit that includes the public employer's place of business.

The FEDERAL LABOR RELATIONS AUTHORITY (FLRA) is the appropriate forum for certain complaints that involve a federal agency employer but are unrelated to practices prohibited by the federal merit system. For instance, the FLRA has authority to determine whether a federal employees' bargaining unit is appropriate in terms of the specific employers and the number and skill level (clerical, skilled, or professional) of employees involved. The FLRA also oversees elections in which employees can choose to be represented by a union and resolves disputes regarding the negotiability of employment issues, unfair labor practice complaints, and arbitration awards.

The FLRA's Office of General Counsel investigates unfair labor practice complaints and prosecutes them before the agency. Within the FLRA, the Federal Service Impasse Panel resolves negotiation impasses between federal employers and the unions representing their employees.

It is valid to summarize the foregoing detailed information on federal and state public employee rights, and the procedures to enforce those rights, with this statement: state-level PERBs and the federal MSPB protect the rights of the employees of all federal, state, and local governments, government agencies, and other public entities to be represented by unions, and they further protect the right of these unions to engage in collective bargaining with public employers in matters involving terms and conditions of employment.

For more information
New York State Public Employment Relations Board. www.perb.state.ny.us.
Merit Systems Protection Board. www.mspb.gov.

Beth Simon Swartz

public goods   Public goods, in the language of economics, are goods and services that are nonrivalrous in consumption (the supply is not depleted by consumption) and nonexcludable (all people can take advantage). Commonly, this means that they are not provided efficiently by private markets.

Examples are national defense and street lighting. Public goods include not only tangible things like public roads, but also services like town planning that reserves space for future roads. Markets undersupply public goods because nonpayers cannot be excluded from enjoying the benefits (called the "free-rider" problem). Private markets rely upon a direct connection between what people pay and the goods and services they receive.

Goods and services that display some of the above characteristics can be classified as "impure" public goods. Goods may be impure because of partial rivalry and congestion (supply is limited, such as a busy urban street) or partial excludability (users may form a "club," such as for an electric grid or toll road). In practice, most goods lie between the fully "pure" category and the fully "impure" or private category.

The free gifts of nature such as fresh air and fisheries are sometimes referred to as public goods (though they are depletable, they are nonexcludable), but they are really "common pool resources." Other relevant terms include "merit goods" such as creative arts, which are not provided in sufficient quantity or equitability by markets without government subsidy; "network goods" such as vaccination, the value of which actually increases as more people use them; "nonrejectable goods," which applies to public goods such as defense that individuals cannot avoid consuming; "marginal cost of supply," which for nonrivalrous goods is zero; and the "public benefit," which may or may not be served by supplying some specific "public good," commercial broadcast signals being an example.

Many books use the term *public goods* loosely. It is best regarded as a concept. There are many difficult-to-classify variants. For example, personal health services may be supplied privately and exclusively, but if the health of individuals improves, then the whole community benefits.

Confusion also arises because individuals *can* be excluded from many goods from which they should not be excluded. Scientific knowledge and the Internet are examples. In principle they should be freely available for the benefit of world citizens, and they grow only as they are shared. In practice, it is possible to partly commodify or privatize them by making them accessible only to those prepared to pay, such as through license fees or sponsorship or by purchasing scientific journals or specialized equipment. In this way there is a distinction between the economic and ethical meanings of the term public good.

In the Western democracies after the early 1970s, neoliberal economics became the dominant economic ideology. Its simple coherence and appeal to the politically powerful led to widespread downsizing of government agencies, intensifying the undersupply of public goods. This particularly disadvantages the poor, who lack enough purchasing power to obtain substitutes from private markets. But not only the poor depend upon public goods: as the definition makes clear, all citizens can benefit. Anyway, private markets cannot function effectively unless certain public goods such as prudential regulation, contract law, and physical infrastructure are adequately supplied.

The tendency of low-taxing, small-government societies to produce conditions of "private affluence and public squalor," i.e., an undersupply of public goods, was publicized by J. K. Galbraith in *The Affluent Society* in 1957. A chronic undersupply deepens inequality and poverty.

However, not all products supplied by governments are public goods; and public goods are supplied not only by governments but also by individuals, not-for-profit organizations, and commercial firms. Mostly, firms exist to produce finite stocks of goods and services that are exchanged for profit only with those who pay, so they are not public goods. However, firms can produce public goods by philanthropy, through prepayment by advertisers, as a by-product of their commercial operations, or under contract or instruction from governments. A firm that cleans up pollution or places useful information in the Internet's public domain is generating a public good.

Public goods can be intra- or intergenerational, depending on who benefits. If their supply is beyond the power of individual nation-states or their effects transcend national borders, such as a reduction in greenhouse gases, they are termed "global public goods."

A study of public goods is worthwhile because it highlights how many goods and services, often taken for granted, depend upon governmental, collective, or unpaid activity and how crucially important they are for the effective operation of a modern society. It also highlights the threat that privatization or granting private rights such as patents over common property can pose to public goods and hence to public well-being.

For more information

Kaul, Inge, Isabelle Grunberg, and Marc Stern, eds. *Global Public Goods: International Cooperation in the 21st Century*. New York: Oxford University Press, 1999.

Stretton, Hugh, and Lionel Orchard. *Public Goods, Public Enterprise, Public Choice*. Basingstoke, U.K.: Macmillan, 1994.

Geoff Edwards

public interest   Public interest refers to the stake that the community at large has in an issue under consideration, i.e., the interests that people have in common with members of the public generally.

There are many variants—the common good, the commonweal, the will of the people—and each may be defined distinctively. The term *national interest* is normally adopted in foreign affairs and *public interest* in domestic ones, but the two terms may be defined differently.

The notion that there is a public sphere of activity to be contrasted with a private one is strongest in the individualistic West. People separate their behavior in private transactions from their civic responsibilities; evidence is clear that they expect their governments to act in the public interest and vote accordingly. References to "national interest" first appeared in 16th-century Europe, though the concept dates back to Aristotle and the ancient Greeks. The concept does not translate easily into tribal societies, where one's prime loyalty is to one's clan or village and the world beyond the mountain scarcely exists; or in some modern (e.g., Asian) societies, where service to one's community takes precedence over satisfaction of individual wants.

"Public interest" overlaps with "ethics," but the concepts are not the same. It is possible to erect a reciprocal definition: "acting in the public interest" may be one item in a code of ethics, and ethical conduct is just one aspect of serving the public interest. Approaches to the public interest can be classified according to the method used to define what it means. For example:

Rationalist approaches: individuals are rational beings who can well judge what is in their best interests. The public interest constitutes a summation of these private interests, moderated by pluralist-style debate among competing interest groups.

Elitist or representative approaches: the public interest is what political leaders or parliaments in positions of authority determine it is, provided that they are well advised in a democratic manner and that discourse is unfettered.

Idealist or natural law approaches: the public interest follows from what people of character and goodwill acting according to their consciences determine it to be. Acceptance of some objective standard of human well-being, such as the United Nations' Millennium Declaration, as the object of public policy is consistent with this approach.

Institutionalist approaches: civil society (non-government civic organizations) or the civil service are the custodian of the public interest.

All approaches are problematic. Aligning public interest with the views of popular opinion places it at the mercy of demagogues, commentators, advertisers, and offices of propaganda. Aligning it with the deliberative opinions of the representative legislature confuses it with democracy, a different concept altogether, and places upon the legislature the burden of being always honest, noble, and well-informed. The pluralist approach of relying on interest groups to bargain a way forward is also unsatisfying, as it disregards the inequality of power relations in any society: the views of the strongest negotiator may prevail and can be entirely self-interested. The same defect plagues any approach relying on procedures or codes: rules can reflect the interest of those who set them.

Approaches based upon the deliberations of "reasonable men" consulting their consciences don't explain how differences in race, temperament, upbringing, religious faith, or political orientation can be reconciled. Nor can the courts, overall, act as guardians of the public interest, because historically their role has been to protect private rights from overbearing kings, cheats, or bullies.

PUBLIC-CHOICE THEORY, which assumes that the public interest will arise spontaneously by aggregating the preferences of individuals, such as through market mechanisms, is an invention of neoliberal economics and derives no support from religion, philosophy, history, or geopolitics. This theory leads to undersupply of public goods such as environmental quality and social justice.

Some analysts argue that public interest is defined in terms of the well-being only of the citizens of the country under discussion; others argue that everyone is a global citizen, a member of a common humanity, so has a personal interest in ensuring the well-being of nationals of other countries, particularly the poor. Modern environmentalism has revealed the dependence of all people on the earth's basic ecosystem services, hence a common interest in ensuring their protection.

For practicing civil servants, the imprecision in the term is softened where modern legislation includes a definition of the public interest to guide civil servants when exercising administrative discretion. In the United States, any model for describing the public interest must allow that reformers with vision can carry a people forward to where they would go if they had sufficient understanding about the issues. The public interest is not static but is being redefined continually as knowledge and insight evolve.

Although imprecise, the term *public interest* is analytically very useful. It sets a standard and by contrast allows mean, selfish, and corrupt actions to be revealed as such.

For more information
Lewin, Leif. *Self-interest and Public Interest in Western Politics.* Oxford, U.K.: Oxford University Press, 1991.

Geoff Edwards

public personnel system   A public personnel system is a complex arrangement of rules, laws, practices, and technology for recruitment, selection, training, motivation, evaluation, and compensation of employees working for governments. Often, especially in a large jurisdiction, such as a state or the federal government, there is more than one personnel system or there are variations on a single system. These variants may be based on which type of employees are covered by the system, what organizational entity or individuals administer the system, and the particular values that are emphasized.

There are several basic values that infuse public personnel systems. Most common are: merit, individual rights, social equity, and responsiveness. In day-to-day operations these values sometimes are in conflict. Value emphasis varies with the type of employees covered and who administers the system. The most fundamental distinction in personnel systems is between the political appointment system, the CIVIL SERVICE SYSTEM, the collective bargaining system, and special systems such as for scientific, technical, and protective services.

Merit
An example of merit, for example, is competition among a pool of candidates for employment, where only the better qualified will be employed. This value also governs other personnel decisions such as promotions and pay increases. Merit also means that values that do not have relevance to performance, such as loyalty to political officials, are not to be considered in personnel decision making. Merit is most characteristic of the civil service system, although it is not uncommon to find political appointments of scientific and technical personnel who are first qualified by merit but politically appointed.

Individual rights
Civil servants are citizens and therefore are afforded individual rights under the U.S. and state constitutions, as well as other laws. Thus, the constitutional rights of freedoms of speech, association, beliefs, protection from illegal search and seizure, and others generally prevail. There may be exceptions, however, in certain circumstances. For example, freedom of speech does not mean that a public employee can compromise a procedure by providing information that would favor one group over another. Other laws are concerned with various other freedoms and

rights, such as protection from employment discrimination because of race, ethnicity, or gender, or protection from sexual harassment.

In addition to these substantive rights, various procedural ones under the U.S. and state constitutions and other laws are afforded public employees of the civil service system. For example, civil service system employees may not be deprived of property without due process of law. Once a civil service system employee is regularly appointed (after a probationary period), the employee is considered to have a property right in employment. Removal of this right from an employee is subject to at least employee notification of reasons, and an opportunity must be provided for a hearing to present the employee's side of the story where disciplinary or performance issues are involved.

The collective-bargaining system stems from employee rights of association and various enabling laws of public jurisdictions. Collective bargaining usually has been superimposed on the civil service system. It is an arrangement whereby employees as members of union bargaining units negotiate with management on various conditions of employment through their bargaining agent. The outcome is a contract for a fixed period of time, at the end of which bargaining can be reinitiated, perhaps involving some of the same or different issues. Unions also represent member employees in grievance procedures and before civil service commissions and hearing officers in disciplinary hearings.

Social equity

Social equity means that individuals should be accorded preference in selection and promotion in public positions based on previous sacrifices (e.g., veterans) or discrimination (e.g., minorities, women, the disabled) that have prevented them from competing fairly for jobs. Preference as reverse discrimination is illegal. However, extra efforts in recruitment and ensuring equality of opportunity and growth experiences that help to develop and qualify them for career growth are not illegal.

For more information

Thompson, Frank. *Classics of Public Personnel Policy,* 2d ed. Pacific Grove, Calif.: Brooks/Cole Publishing, 1990.

Gilbert B. Siegel

public policy Public policy refers to the process whereby the members of a geographic area or political unit make choices that address their areas and issues of concern.

"Public" reflects the preferences and actions of a group of people, most commonly through their joint voice as reflected in their governing institutions and especially their governments. "Policy" refers to rules, management strategies, processes, and plans allowed by the public to address their areas of concern. These strategies, processes, and plans can be both intentional and accidental. Often, jurisdictions develop an approach to address a given issue or concern, such as crime. Other times, the absence of a strategy or plan to address a given issue establishes a de facto plan, namely the intent to not take action in a given area. The presence or absence of such a plan would also be a public policy.

Control over policy choices can be exerted by the public directly (for example through voter initiatives) and indirectly (where near-total control is ceded to a third party, most often the government, to act as the public's agent). Historically, and in nondemocratic political structures, public policy was established through edicts from the ruler and his or her authorized agents. Such choices were binding on communities through the powers and authority that they granted their monarch. The derivation of that power and authority can be military, political, economic, religious, or traditional.

In modern democracies, public policies are typically generated by the governing (legislative) and administrative (executive) branches of the government. Often, general approaches to addressing a given concern are specified by the legislative body and used by the executive body to prescribe rules and procedures to implement the approach.

The term *public policy* is used not only to describe that process and its consequences, but also the general set of tools and mechanisms through which these choices are made. Whether it be by fiat, legislative voting, administrative rule making, public assent, or default, the ways that choices are made in the interest of the people is an important aspect of the public policy process.

Public policy also refers to a field of academic research and training that has developed around the tools and processes associated with public decision making and priority setting described above. The field as an academic discipline emerged in the 1960s as the academic and political communities sought ways to maximize the effectiveness of the United States's ever-expanding investment in public programs. Since then it has emerged as one of the fastest growing areas of professional training and education. Students in the field of public policy typically focus on the tools and processes whereby the body politic addresses areas of mutual concern.

Public policy differs from public administration in that it focuses on the "public" problems requiring action, while public administration focuses on the process through which they are solved. Public policy retains the public administrative processes as one of the sets of resources available to address problems.

For more information

McCool, Daniel C., ed. *Public Policy Theories, Models, and Concepts.* Englewood Cliffs, N.J.: Prentice Hall, 1995.

Theodoulou, Stella Z., and Matthew A. Cahn, eds. *Public Policy: The Essential Readings.* Englewood Cliffs, N.J.: Prentice Hall, 1994.

Michael Shires

public-private partnerships *Public-private partnerships* is a broad term that refers to a con-

tractual arrangement between public- and private-sector partners. Typical arrangements usually involve a government agency contracting with a private-sector partner to operate, maintain, or manage a facility or a project that provides a public service.

The General Accounting Office lists several forms of public-private partnerships. Some types of partnerships include: build/operate/transfer (BOT) or build/transfer/operate (BTO), where the private partner builds a facility, operates the facility for a certain time, and then transfers the facility to the agency at the end of a specified time. The BTO model is similar to the BOT model except that the transfer to the public owner takes place at the time that construction is completed.

Build/own/operate (BOO): A contractor constructs and operates a facility without transferring ownership to the public sector, and there is no obligation for the public sector to purchase the facility.

Contract services: A public partner (federal, state, or local government agency or authority) contracts with a private partner to provide or maintain a specific service.

Lease/purchase: The private sector finances and builds a new facility, which it then leases to a public agency.

Tax-exempt lease: A public partner finances capital assets or facilities by borrowing funds from a private investor or financial institution.

Other forms of public-private partnerships may include: design/build (DB), design/build/operate (DBO), sale/leaseback, and turnkey.

The debate concerning ways in which our government could streamline costs, promote efficiency, and enhance overall management is very much a part of the public-private partnership discussion. Many advocates claim that partnerships change the relationship between government and the private sector for the better, promoting collaboration rather than conflict.

Moreover, these agreements maximize the skills and assets of each sector (public and private) as they deliver a service for the use of the general public. Through this collaboration, each party will also share in the risks and rewards potential in the delivery of that service.

Public-private partnership supporters also believe that there are certain elements that are necessary for them to succeed. One of these elements includes a commitment from a political leader who can assure the general public that the partnership has support and is beneficial to the community. The public sector should also be an active partner with appropriate monitoring. Additionally, a good business plan is an essential component of a successful partnership and should clearly define the roles of the public and private entities. Finally, all affected parties, including potential employees and any other interested parties, should be well informed as the partnership develops.

Opponents of these agreements argue that the public sector becomes the net loser in some partnerships because private benefits, such as community goodwill, and public costs are not measured the same way. Others fear that public agencies will shift controversial or difficult tasks to the private sector, for example, shifting revenue-generating duties to the private entities while leaving tasks that require subsidies to the public sector, which could further reinforce stereotypes of private efficiency and public waste.

There are also practical concerns with public-private partnerships. Attempts to ensure accountability make the public sector inflexible and slow moving. However, the private sector moves at a fluid pace because its decisions are not subject to public comment and other legislative procedures. In order to function, both partners must adjust to each other's pace. For example, private partners must submit their business plans, while their public partners may experience concerns from the community if they are too beholden to the private sector.

The history of public-private partnerships has revealed that they should be evaluated according to short-term objectives, rather than locking either side into a permanent arrangement.

For more information

Government Accounting Office. *Public-Private Partnerships: Terms Related to Building and Facility Partnerships.* Washington, D.C.: Government Accounting Office, April 1999.

National Council for Public-Private Partnerships. *How Partnerships Work.* Washington, D.C.: National Council for Public-Private Partnerships, 2002.

National Council for Public-Private Partnership. http://www.ncppp.org.

Cherylyn A. Harley

public works infrastructure   Public works infrastructure is generally considered to include all of the improvements to real property owned by a government, whether it be federal, state, county, or municipal. This term gained popularity during the past couple of decades, ever since the public began hearing and reading about the deteriorating condition of our nation's public improvements on television screens and in newspapers across the country.

The government's capital facilities are wearing out due to their age and lack of proper maintenance. Infrastructure is also deteriorating because of increasingly tight budgets, created by the public's unwillingness to pay more taxes. With fewer state and federal grant programs, needed capital projects have been deferred, if not postponed indefinitely. "Public works infrastructure" is synonymous with public facilities, capital improvements, capital assets, capital plant, and related terms. Because of the magnitude of this problem, both in size and in dollars, this issue is likely to be the focus of national attention for many years to come.

With declining tax dollars, politicians at all levels of government found it easier to fund more-visible public services, such as police, fire, and recreation programs. When a shortage of public funds exists, the limited funds available are typically used to finance a government's operations or public services. Capital projects, normally included in multiyear capital improvement plans, are put on a back burner until better financial times. But, during the late 1990s, the condition of our nations's infrastructure fell into a state of decline in cities, counties, and states throughout the country. This had led to the topic of our public works infrastructure being the subject of an increasing number of studies. Scholars, researchers, public officials, and practitioners have examined the condition of our nation's capital assets. Many articles and studies have served to focus public attention on various issues surrounding the proper funding for the maintenance and replacement of our government's public works infrastructure.

While the political debate is still underway regarding our country's public works infrastructure, no solutions appear to be looming on the horizon. Since restoring America's infrastructure is truly a national problem, the required leadership must come from the highest levels of government. An informed and educated electorate is necessary to help solidify public opinion on an acceptable long-term solution to restoring our government's infrastructure, at all levels. A national infrastructure policy is needed to provide the necessary direction to the many state, county, and municipal units of government that must grapple with the task of improving the condition of America's deteriorating capital assets. As our country enters the 21st century, this issue will be high on the national agenda in the years ahead.

For more information

Kemp, Roger. *America's Infrastructure: Problems and Prospects.* Danville, Ill.: Interstate, 1986.

Office of Technology Assessment. *Rebuilding the Foundations: A Special Report on State and Local Public Works Financing and Management.* Washington, D.C.: U.S. Government Printing Office, 1991.

Rosen, Howard, and Ann Durlein Keating, eds. *Water and the City: The Next Century.* Chicago: Public Works Historical Society, 1991.

Roger L. Kemp

R

racial profiling   Racial profiling is the stopping of individuals or suspected criminals based upon their race or skin color.

Racial profiling involves the claim that police and law enforcement officials are detaining individuals in traffic enforcement simply because of their race or skin color. Oftentimes the pretext for the stopping is the claim that the individual fits some profile of a person wanted for a crime. Or individuals are stopped in their cars on the basis that they have committed a minor traffic infraction. Evidence that racial profiling exists began to appear in the media in the middle to late 1990s when newspapers revealed that the New Jersey State Police were using racial profiles to stop and detain motorists. Since then, statistics gathered in other areas, such as New York City, Denver, Minneapolis, and St. Paul, Minnesota, as well as in other cities and states, demonstrate that people of color are disproportionately more likely to be stopped than are whites.

Another aspect of racial profiling surfaced after the terrorist attacks in the United States on 11 September 2001. There were calls to stop, detain, or single out individuals who looked Islamic or Arabic, especially when boarding airplanes, because they were suspected of having ties to terrorist groups or activities. Several news stories surfaced about individuals who were also harassed because they fit this profile, even though they had no terrorist affiliations. Moreover, the U.S. government also investigated many groups that had ties to Islam or the Arabic world, and critics claimed that these investigations were a form of racial profiling.

Those who denounce profiling say that the issue raises important legal questions regarding racial, religious, or ethnic discrimination. These issues may arise out of either the equal protection or due process clauses of the Fourteenth Amendment. In fact, racial profiling is sometimes referred to as "driving while black." The singling out of individuals solely based upon their race or skin color is unconstitutional. The statistics on who is stopped by the police is pointed to as evidence of either de jure or de facto discrimination.

Others deny that the statistics reveal discrimination, saying these stops are not motivated by race but are simply a sign of aggressive policing and efforts to apprehend criminals. Police are

Mohammad Aslam
Pervez
Pakistani
DISAPPEARED
in the USA

Asian and Arab immigrants participate in a rally in front of the Immigration and Naturalization Services building in New York City. The protesters were demanding an end to the racial profiling, detentions, and deportations that many immigrants have been subjected to since the attacks of 11 September 2001. (SPENCER PLATT/GETTY IMAGES)

thus stopping individuals on the basis of reasonable suspicion that a crime has been committed or that the person stopped is a criminal. In fact, in *Brown v. City of Oneonta*, 195 F. 3d 111 (2d Cir. 1999), a federal court ruled that in some cases race could be used as a reason to justify an investigatory stop.

While racial profiling has focused mostly on police stops, other statistics reveal that whites and people of color are treated very differently in the entire criminal justice system. This means that the initial stopping of people of color makes it more likely that they will face additional interaction with the criminal justice process. All of these instances could be considered examples of racial profiling.

For example, whites are more likely to be offered bail than people of color. Whites are much less likely to receive prison sentences than people of color, and whites are much less likely to be prosecuted—or are prosecuted less aggressively—for drug offenses than are people of color.

In the area of the death penalty, several studies have confirmed that whites are less likely to be placed on death row than people of color and that whites are much less likely to receive a prison sentence if they murder a person of color than is an African American who murders a white person. For example, in 2000, 37 states, the military, and the U.S. government imposed the death penalty for a variety of crimes, with over 40 percent of those on death row being African-American. African Americans are 12 percent of the population.

From 1930 until 1993, 3,859 persons in the United States were executed. Of those, 2,066 were black. During this same time period, of 455 people executed for rape, 405 were black. From 1976 until 1993, 176 people in the United States have been executed. Of those, 40 percent were black. Even though whites and blacks are victims of homicide in about equal numbers, 80 percent of those sentenced to death and executed have been individuals who killed whites.

A 1990 Government Accounting Office (GAO) study entitled *Death Penalty Sentencing* concluded that "[t]hose who murdered whites were found to be more likely to be sentenced to death than those who murdered blacks." GAO and other studies by the American Bar Association, Congress, and the Death Penalty Information Center have found that those who murder whites are far more likely to be sentenced to death that those who murder blacks. Similarly, a 1994 House Judiciary Subcommittee on Civil and Constitutional Rights report indicated that prosecution of the 1988 federal Anti-Drug

Abuse Act appears racially tainted. Of those prosecuted under the act, 75 percent have been white and 24 percent black. But in death penalty prosecutions, 78 percent have been black and 11 percent white.

Racial profiling or racial disparities exist on several levels in the criminal justice system, raising questions regarding the explanation and possible remedy for this different treatment.

For more information

"Civil Rights Commission Cites Improper Use of Racial Profiling by New York City Police." *Jet* 98, no. 4. (July 3, 2000): 4.

Derbyshire, John. "In Defense of Racial Profiling: Where Is Our Common Sense?" *National Review* 53 (February 19, 2001): 20.

Walker, Samuel, et al. *The Color of Justice: Race, Ethnicity, and Crime in America.* Belmont, Calif.: Wadsworth, 2000.

David Schultz

RAND   RAND is America's largest nonprofit, nonpartisan think tank. Headquartered in Santa Monica, California, it is a leading producer of rigorous analysis that influences public policy in the United States and throughout the world. Its motto reflects the purpose to which it has committed itself since its inception: to be "a nonprofit institution that helps improve policy and decision making through research and analysis." RAND has a well-trained staff of more than 1,600, some 65 percent of whom have Ph.D.s or M.D.s. RAND is a leading producer of research on public policy issues in many diverse fields.

RAND was formed in December 1945. Originally called "Project RAND," it was designed to bring an interdisciplinary team together to perform scientific planning that would allow the U.S. Army, the Army Air Forces, and the U.S. Navy to make effective use of research and technology. Its name came from "R and D," an abbreviation for research and development. In 1946 it issued its first publication, "Preliminary Design of an Experimental World-Circling Spaceship," looking at potential use of manufactured satellites. In 1948, it was incorporated as a nonprofit corporation dedicated to "the public welfare and security of the United States." The RAND Corporation took leave of its old quarters within the Douglas Aircraft Company and set about on its independent course. In the decades that followed, RAND has been credited with reshaping the landscape of quantitative policy analysis. It is widely known for its major contributions to the field of system science and the techniques of systems analysis. It built one of the world's first computers, JOHNNIAC, and built one of the first terminal-based computer networks. In 1962, a RAND scholar looking to design computing systems capable of surviving nuclear attack originated the concept that is today the foundational principle of the Internet.

Two RAND researchers in the area of computing, Herb Simon and Harry Markowitz, went on to become Nobel laureates. RAND was also responsible for advancing the fields of quantitative analysis, developing many modern linear programming techniques and mathematical optimization techniques concurrently with their colleagues in Europe and the Soviet Union. Their 1955 book *A Million Random Digits with 100,000 Normal Deviates* is still widely used today. While its origins are military and RAND is still home today to three military-focused federally funded research and development centers (FFRDCs), it is also one of the premier research institutions in the world studying social policy concerns such as education, public health, transportation, social welfare, and the environment. RAND scientists continue to analyze public health problems, evaluate school reform, develop cost models for the public medical system, evaluate alternative tort systems for civil justice, and explore the economic impacts of global warming.

RAND is also home to the largest doctoral program in policy analysis in the world—the RAND Graduate School of Policy Studies. This unique program immerses its students in the practicalities of real-world policy analysis while providing a rigorous program of course work and research to train leading scholars. It was founded in 1970 as one of the eight original schools of public policy and accesses RAND's professional staff of more than 600 scholars to engage students in the art and science of public policy analysis.

For more information
RAND Corporation. http://www.rand.org.

Michael Shires

Reagan, Ronald (1911–   ) *40th president of the United States*   Ronald Reagan was the 40th president of the United States, serving in office from 1981 to 1989. Reagan's presidency was marked by efforts to reduce the size of the federal government, balance the budget, reduce numerous social programs, and increase the military budget for the country. His lasting legacy as president may be less in what he achieved in terms of specific programs, but more in terms of a major attitudinal change among the American public toward the role of the government in society.

Ronald Reagan was born in Tampico, Illinois, in 1911 and attended Eureka College. After graduation he became a sports announcer. Eventually he became a movie actor, starring in 53 films over a period of two decades. While an actor in the 1950s, he was elected president of the Screen Actors Guild and became involved in heated disputes involving the search for communists in Hollywood. While initially a Democrat, Ronald Reagan turned increasingly conservative and became a political spokesman for the conservative movement. He became a Republican, supported Barry Goldwater for president in 1964, and eventually successfully ran for governor in California in 1966, serving a total of two terms from 1967 to 1980.

In 1980 he ran for president of the United States with George Bush as his vice-presidential running mate, winning a decisive victory over Jimmy Carter. In 1984 Reagan was reelected president with one of the largest margins of victory ever.

Ronald Reagan became president at a time when many of the assumptions that had governed the federal service since the Progressive and New Deal eras were being challenged. He also came to office at a time when antigovernment feelings were mounting and the nation was facing severe economic problems, including rising budget deficits, high inflation, and growing unemployment. In his first inaugural speech he stated that "government was part of the problem, not the solution," thereby setting a tone that declared that the solution to the many problems at hand resided in reducing the size of the federal government by returning more power to the states or to the free market. The lynchpin of what would be called the "Reagan Revolution" resided in several policies.

First, Ronald Reagan ushered in an economic theory called supply-side economics. Invented by Arthur Laffler, the theory stated that tax cuts would free up money for private investment in the economy. The goal was that significant tax cuts would produce enough economic growth that, even with a lower tax rate, there would be more tax revenue from a larger economy to pay for government services. The Kemp-Roth tax bill, passed in 1981, enacted this philosophy. However, instead of the economy growing, the budget deficit grew significantly and the economy went into a severe recession, with unemployment breaking 10 percent in 1982.

A second prong of the Reagan Revolution was to continue the deregulation of the economy that had begun under President Carter. The belief was that over-regulation of businesses had produced too much paperwork and red tape, making it difficult for companies to comply with government rules.

A third aspect of the Reagan Revolution was a reorganization of the federal government in order to give the president greater control over the bureaucracy. Reagan successfully appointed conservatives to many cabinet positions who shared his political views. Especially critical were his appointments to the Office of Management and Budget, who oversaw many of Reagan's key goals, including efforts to reduce paperwork, federal regulations, and government spending. For example, under David Stockman, his first OMB director, the agency was empowered to review the regulations of other agencies and limit unnecessary paperwork or ensure that proposed regulations were cost-effective. The president also successfully employed the recently passed Civil Service Reform Act of 1978 to move around members of the Senior Executive Service to achieve greater control over various agencies and programs.

Finally, in 1981, members of the federal air controllers union, PATCO, representing about 15,000 employees, were fired by the president after they had gone out on strike. This strike clearly violated the Taft-Hartley provisions that made strikes by federal employees illegal. Approximately 5,000 never went on strike or returned, thus leaving 11,301 controllers out of work. Subsequently, the Federal Aviation Administration moved to have the government decertify or withdraw union recognition from PATCO, which it did, and the decision was eventually upheld in federal court. The firing of PATCO employees not only demonstrated a clear resolve by the president to take control of the bureaucracy, but it also sent a clear message to the private sector that unions no longer needed to be feared.

The Reagan presidency launched several programs that sought to improve the performance of the public sector. In 1981, Reagan created the President's Private Sector Survey on Cost Control (PPSSCC), otherwise known as the Grace Commission, to review the personnel and organizational practices of the federal government and to make recommendations for ways to eliminate duplication, unnecessary procedures, waste, etc. The commission was funded privately, and it produced 47 reports that included 12,000 pages, 38 volumes, and almost 2,500 recommendations for reform and potential savings.

In Reagan's first term, partisan and nonpartisan use of REDUCTIONS IN FORCE (RIFs) were used to somewhat decrease the size of the federal government. However, from 1984 on, the size of the federal civilian employment increased steadily, surpassing the Carter administration levels and topping out at 3,090,699 in 1988 at the end of the Reagan administration. This was the largest civilian employment level since the end of World War II. Increases in employment did not occur uniformly but were concentrated in the Defense, State, and Justice Departments as well as the Veterans Administration, with cuts still occurring in many domestic and regulatory agencies.

In Reagan's second term, independent counsel Lawrence Walsh was appointed to investigate claims that the Reagan administration had illegally diverted military arms to the government of Iran in exchange for the release of American hostages held by that country, with some of the profits from the arms sales being used to support a marginally covert war against the Sandinista regime that came to power in Nicaragua in the summer of 1979. The scandal, eventually known as IRAN-CONTRA, involved several members of the Reagan administration, including members of the National Security Council and the Department of Defense. Several members of the Reagan administration were convicted of illegal activity, with many of those convictions overturned on appeal. While the president himself was never indicted, the special prosecutor concluded that Reagan was aware of the arms-for-hostages diversion.

By the end of the Reagan era, it was unclear either how much he had changed the organization of the federal service or how much power the president had taken back from Congress, the courts, or the bureaucracy. The size of the federal government was larger than it had been since the end of the World War II, and the budget deficit was also at record levels. Yet the real lasting legacy of the Reagan presidency was not in his policies so much as in a rhetoric and a set of values that ushered in a more conservative era that questioned the value and role of the federal government in addressing and solving social and economic problems.

For more information

Ingraham, Patricia. *Legislating Bureaucratic Change: The Civil Service Reform Act of 1978.* Ithaca, N.Y.: SUNY Press, 1984.

Schultz, David, and Robert Maranto. *The Politics of Civil Service Reform.* New York: Peter Lang Publishing, 1998.

Walsh, Lawrence. *Firewall: The Iran-Contra Conspiracy and Cover-Up.* New York: W. W. Norton & Company, 1998.

David Schultz

redistributive policy   Redistributive policy is policy that provides benefits to certain groups but does so while taking away from others.

Redistributive policy reallocates resources. Government tries to ensure that those in dire need receive the basic necessities such as food, shelter, and clothing. For instance, the redistributive policy relates to the school lunch program because the wealth of society is redistributed to this program for the benefit of those less fortunate. Other examples of this type of policy include social security, welfare, and tax policies. Taxation, for instance, redistributes income based on the assumption that it brings about a better society in terms of income equality.

On the other hand, it is not clear how far a society is willing to go in accepting a strong redistributive policy, since some people may strongly disagree with the redistribution of their income. In their view, "to justify income redistribution, it is necessary to show that individuals somehow do not have a just title to the income they earned." The role of such justification is set upon bureaucracies that are responsible for creating the redistributive policies, which they must then implement. However, many consider distribution policy self-contradictory, because what government gives with one hand it takes away with the other. Some opponents of distributive policies consider that although redistribution raises the income of the poor, it provides an incentive for able-bodied individuals to choose welfare benefits over work.

In 1965 President Lyndon Johnson launched the most ambitious effort in American history to eliminate poverty. Known as the Great Society, this effort consisted of a variety of social programs designed to alleviate the problems of the poor. Declaring that "the days of the dole in this country are numbered," Johnson sought to provide short-term assistance to the able-bodied poor in the belief that it would enable recipients to lift themselves out of poverty; the smaller population of individuals who could not work would receive long-term support.

An enormous number of people entered the welfare rolls as a result of Great Society programs. However, the hope that they would use the programs as "a hand, not a handout" was unrealized. Thus, by providing income to those individuals who do not work, welfare discourages recipients from entering the labor force and encourages workers to join the welfare rolls, aggravating the unemployment problem and lowering the rate at which the economy can grow.

Some people oppose redistribution because they do not wish to give up their income to the poor. On the other hand, some people support redistribution because they do not object to spending other people's income on the poor.

For more information

Stigler, George J. "Director's Law of Public Income Redistribution." *Journal of Law and Economics* 13 (April 1970): 1–10.

Thurow, Lester C. "The Income Distribution as a Pure Public Good." *Quarterly Journal of Economics* 85 (May 1971): 327–328.

Wildasin, David E. "Income Redistribution in a Common Labor Market." *American Economic Review* 81 (September 1991) 757–779.

Raissa Muhutdinova-Foroughi

red tape   Red tape refers to bureaucratic procedures that are seen as unnecessary, duplicative, or wasteful, thus contributing to delays and creating a sense of frustration. This frustration may flow from a perceived lack of responsiveness by government officials or agencies, or it may involve the perception of excessive paperwork or unnecessary procedures as impediments to productive activities. Barry Bozeman, one of the leading scholars on red tape, defines red tape as "rules, regulations and procedures that remain in force and entail a compliance burden but do not advance the legitimate purposes the rules were intended to serve."

Historically, red tape refers to the narrow ribbons used at one time in England and America to tie up packets of legal and government documents. The term was popularized in the 19th century by Sidney Smith, Thomas Carlyle, and Herbert Spencer. The image projected is one of endless lengths of ribbons, which parallels the idea of excesses of government.

One of the earliest scholars to conduct research on red tape was a sociologist by the name of Alvin Gouldner. Gouldner suggested that red tape is determined not only by the situation itself but also by the frame of reference through which red tape is viewed. In other words, he was suggesting that the existence of red tape was related both to objective, external conditions (such as the presence of rules and procedures) and subjective conditions (e.g., the way the individual viewed those rules). In his research, Gouldner found that individuals who exhibited high levels of alienation tended to perceive red tape to a greater degree than those exhibiting lower levels. More-recent studies have helped to confirm these earlier findings. Those who experience high levels of alienation in their work environments are more likely to rationalize their frustrations by pointing to the presence of high levels of red tape.

One of the most often quoted works on the topic is Herbert Kaufman's *Red Tape: Its Origins, Uses and Abuses.* Kaufman argues that we, as citizens, are largely to blame for red tape because most rules and regulations result from the multiplicity of demands we have generated on government. According to Kaufman, red tape is not the product of incompetent government officials, but rather, it is an inevitable by-product of our political system that attempts to be accountable to diverse and oftentimes competing interests. In addition, these accountability requirements (i.e., red tape) may provide citizens protection against the arbitrary and capricious exercise of bureaucratic power while ensuring fairness and consistency in the treatment of clients.

For example, once a new government program is created, new rules are put into place to make sure that funds are expended appropriately. This, in turn, may require the creation of new forms and documentation to justify how that money is being spent. These kinds of requirements are designed to ensure accountability to the public and to minimize waste, fraud, or abuse. Yet, some might see these requirements, rooted in a legitimate purpose, as red tape. Where does one draw the line between a legitimate accountability requirement and a dysfunctional rule, and according to whom? The citizen may see this as red tape, while the public manager may see this as a legitimate accountability requirement. It soon becomes clear that oftentimes it is hard to distinguish between the two. As Kaufman states, one person's red tape may be another's treasured procedural safeguard. Kaufman also notes that efforts to eliminate red tape in government will ultimately fail because we would be appalled by the resurgence of abuse that various rules and procedures currently prevents.

For more information

Bozeman, Barry. *Bureaucracy and Red Tape.* Upper Saddle River, N.J.: Prentice Hall, 2000.

Kaufman, Herbert. *Red Tape: Its Origins, Uses, and Abuses.* Washington, D.C.: Brookings Institution, 1977.

Patrick G. Scott

reductions in force In the federal government, layoffs of government employees are called reductions in force, or RIFs.

The term *RIF* refers to both the layoff of federal government employees as well as the system that determines which employees can stay in their agencies or departments when employment reductions are necessary. A significant aspect of the RIF process focuses on the rights of employees to remain when positions are being eliminated from their organization. The RIF process is the responsibility of the OFFICE OF PERSONNEL AND MANAGEMENT (OPM), which is responsible for the administration of the federal civil service system. RIF's regulations are part of the Veteran's Preference Act of 1944 and are codified in Sections 3501-3503 of Title 5 of the U.S. Code.

RIF's regulations require that the Office of Personnel and Management take into consideration four factors when there is a plan to terminate employees in the federal government. These four factors include (1) the type of position, (2) veteran's preference, (3) length of service, and (4) performance ratings. Federal government agencies are required to use RIF procedures when one or more employees will be separated or demoted for a reason such as lack of work, reorganization within a department or agency, a lack of funds, or certain cases where individuals are being reemployed or reinstated into a position. However, RIF procedures may not be used to take disciplinary or job-performance-related actions against an employee.

Before an agency implements a reduction in force, it must first define both a competitive area and a competitive level. A competitive area is the boundary within which employees compete for retention in their jobs. The competitive area is both geographical and organizational. In other words, the RIF may occur in Dallas or Chicago and not occur in Washington, D.C. The organizational boundary refers to the part of the organization that will experience the RIF. This may be all or part of an agency, such as a department or regional office. The organization then must develop a competitive level based on grouping positions that have similar characteristics such as qualifications, duties, working conditions, and pay and work schedules (full-time, part-time). The four retention factors are applied, and a listing of all employees in the order of their retention standing is developed. Under a RIF, employees with the highest retention standing have "bumping" or "retreating" rights to an available position in the same competitive area. Bumping means displacing another employee who is in a lower group based on his or her retention standing.

Federal agencies initiating a RIF must give employees at least 60 days notice before they are reached for a RIF personnel action. In addition, any employee who is part of a RIF process for more than 30 days has the right to appeal to the MERIT SYSTEMS PROTECTION BOARD and the right to file a grievance if the employee is a member of a bargaining unit covered by a labor union. Since 1995 all executive departments and agencies provide career-transition assistance, and all federal employees who receive a notice of separation by a RIF are eligible for placement assistance in other federal government positions.

For more information

Bulger, Brian W., and Carolyn Curtis Gessner. "Sign of the Times: Implementing Reductions in Force." *Employee Relations Law Journal* 17 (winter 1991/1992): 431–438.

U.S. House Committee on Government Reform and Oversight. Subcommittee on Civil Service. *Federal Downsizing: The Costs and Savings of Buyouts versus Reductions-in-force.* 1996.

Dahlia Bradshaw Lynn

regulation When applied to organizations or individuals, the word *regulation* refers to the maintenance of a standard of behavior. It can also be used to describe a rule prescribed for the management of some matter.

Regulation can occur in relation to the performance of machinery, biological structures, and animals. Before any regulation can be undertaken or even discussed, the objective sought must be known. In the science of governance (CYBERNETICS), regulation is the process of removing variety. Controlling or eliminating variables reduces variety in a dynamic system. This requires selecting controllers to eliminate each variable. Regulation then depends upon there being a requisite variety of controllers. This is referred to as the Law of Requisite Variety, or Ashby's Law.

The word *control* can also be used in the same sense as regulation. However, it is useful to reserve the term *control* for static systems and *regulation* for dynamic systems. For example, a throttle on the engine of a land vehicle is not a dynamic system. It will remain in any position selected by the driver. However, the speed of a land vehicle depends not only on the position of the throttle but also the slope of the terrain. The process of selecting throttle settings from feedback information on the speed of the vehicle is used to regulate its speed.

For more information

Ashby, W. R. *An Introduction to Cybernetics.* London: Methuen, 1968.

Shann Turnbull

regulatory capture Regulatory capture refers to the controversial view that administrative agencies, ostensibly created to police activities of private economic entities in the public interest, actually promote those private interests. If accurate, regulatory capture raises doubts about government accountability and political control of administrative agencies.

Debates over regulatory capture take place within the context of disputes about the fundamental nature of American national government and politics.

At base, these disputes swirl around the role that groups play in American politics and government. For James Madison, groups—he called them "factions" in *Federalist* No. 10—were an unavoidable fact of political life. The "mischiefs" of factions posed the greatest danger to republican government. Consequently, "[t]he regulation of these various and interfering interests forms the principle [sic] task of modern legislation. . . ."

In the early 20th century, what Madison perceived as the bane of "popular government" became the basis of good government by a school of thought know as "pluralism." Pluralist theorists such as Arthur Bentley and David Truman reasoned that, first, politics merely reflects group competition; second, because Americans belong to various groups, all interests will be represented and no single group will dominate (termed "crosscutting cleavages"); and third, if a group was not formally organized, it existed as a "latent group" that would organize when its interests were threatened.

Although pluralist analyses remain influential, their shared assumptions have been criticized by theorists like E. E. Schattschneider and C. Wright Mills. Schattschneider countered that what he called "the pressure system" has an inherent "business or upper class bias," famously observing: "The flaw in the pluralist heaven is that the heavenly chorus sings with an upper class accent. Probably about 90 percent of the people cannot get into the pressure system."

Regulatory-capture arguments complement Schattschneider's. The strongest version holds that government promotes monopoly by creating boards and commissions that are "captured" by—and "regulate" on behalf of—producers that utilize regulation to prevent competition. Another version of the regulatory-capture thesis holds that regulatory agencies (euphemistically called "independent"), operating under the influence of business groups, shape policy primarily to benefit these favored "client groups." A third version involves "IRON TRIANGLES," "sub-governments," and "policy regimes." Common to these three terms is the privatization of public policy making. The argument goes: in specific substantive policy areas—for example, agriculture, banking, transportation, public works—regulatory agencies + congressional committees + special interests form a mutually beneficial triangle to govern narrowly. Such "incest groups" (Ripley and Franklin) allegedly dominate policy making, share personnel ("revolving door"), and are largely impervious to external political constraints.

All three versions of the regulatory-capture thesis have been criticized severely. Critics come in three varieties. "Neo-Madisonians," such as Theodore Lowi, argue that the problem is not regulatory capture but "hyperpluralism"—the fact that the pluralist system is out of control, with government trying to appease too many groups. Others contend that a combination of congressional reform, media scrutiny, divided government, fragmentation of interests, and spending restraints has weakened iron triangles. Still others maintain that contemporary policy making is a game played out within "policy domains" (Browne).

For more information

Browne, William P. *Cultivating Congress: Constituents, Issues, and Interests in Agricultural Policymaking.* Lawrence: University of Kansas Press, 1995.

Lowi, Theodore. "The Public Philosophy: Interest-Group Liberalism." *American Political Science Review* 61 (1967): 5.

Ripley, Randal B., and Grace A. Franklin. *Congress, the Bureaucracy, and Public Policy,* 4th ed. Chicago: Dorsey, 1987.

Schattschneider, E. E. *The Semi-Sovereign People: A Realist's View of Democracy in America.* New York: Holt, Reinhart and Winston, 1960.

James C. Foster

regulatory policy Regulatory policy is defined as administrative control of individuals, institutions, businesses, and agencies through administrative action or inaction to regulate behavior that is in violation of law.

The Interstate Commerce Commission (ICC) was the first state regulatory agency. It was established in 1887 in response to 19th-century laissez-faire capitalism that matured into oligopoly, trusts, and monopoly, with monopolistic practices taking the form of exorbitant prices for goods, reduced quality of goods sold, and rate discrimination. The ICC asserted control by establishing standards and procedures, by imposing auditing and reporting requirements, and by enforcing sanctions. The process of regulation typically focuses on one of three areas: regulation directed toward prices and the products of natural monopolies such as public utilities; regulation directed toward health and safety issues, such as that associated with the drug industry; and regulation directed toward oligopolistic industries, i.e., industries that have a limited number of producers and sellers and hence limited competition. An example of an oligopolistic industry would be transportation, and more specifically the airline industry.

The goal of regulating natural monopolies and oligopolistic industries, along with the myriad associated activities that are classified as social regulation—such as monitoring the quality of drugs sold legally in this country or the quality of air and water—is in place primarily to protect the public. The bottom line in government is stated as the preservation of the inalienable rights of life, liberty, and the pursuit of happiness. Regulatory activity is part of the structure for preserving those rights. Mechanisms to preserve the security of rights are designed to protect them from threat of depletion, erosion, or obsolescence. Regulatory activity seeks to prop up that which is weak but deemed worthy of preservation.

Some regulatory mechanisms are designed to forestall the collapse of that which would otherwise become weakened, as in the case of regulatory review of pension funds. There are preventive review mechanisms designed to secure that which would otherwise be lost to the public. These mechanisms are designed to prevent adverse factors from reaching a level at which they might jeopardize the quality of life, such as environmental and health-related issues. Mechanisms designed to interrelate the derivative goals to maximize the coverage, quality, and stability. Regulatory mechanisms are designed to regulate the actions, actors, and outcomes that have competing interpretations in the exercise of societal rights. According to Mitnik, "Regulatory policies impose government limits on individual choice in order to restrict 'unacceptable' behavior."

Regulation policy seeks to protect people from harm. People are prohibited from selling unsafe drugs, from competing unfairly in the marketplace, or from polluting the air and water. Familiar regulatory agencies include the Food and Drug Administration and the Securities and Exchange Commission. The Federal Reserve and the Federal Deposit Insurance Corporation protect the business from the "hazards of market competition," primarily at the federal level. At the state level, agencies regulate the insurance industry, public utilities industries, and banks that do not use federal deposit insurance. The state regulates occupations and professions such as law, medicine, and barbering. Local government regulates local business, land use (zoning), public health-related matters, and morality concerns. There is also regulation that goes on across levels of government, such as issues related to law enforcement. Commerce receives heavy regulation in areas concerning regulation of prices, fraud, unfair practices, and monopolistic action. In addition, securities, stockyards, commodity futures trading, and national labor relations are under regulatory scrutiny. The goal is to maximize the public good even at the cost of limiting individual activity.

For more information

Jones, Charles O. *An Introduction to the Study of Public Policy.* New York: Thompson Publishing, 1997.

Olivia M. McDonald

regulatory tax A regulatory tax is a tax imposed to regulate some product or practice rather than simply to raise revenue.

The revenue from a regulatory tax may be useful to a government, but the main purpose of the tax is to penalize, or even to prevent, the sale of a product or engagement in an antisocial activity. For example, alcohol and tobacco are heavily taxed as "sin taxes" to reduce consumption. Companies producing alcohol have to pay a regulatory tax in the form of a license fee.

Control of narcotics began with regulation of the opium trade and eventually resulted in a series of taxes to regulate a range of narcotics and other drugs such as marijuana. These regulatory taxes were later expanded to control organized crime. The taxing of the manufacture and distribution of firearms and other weapons, such as machine guns, was enacted in part to control organized crime.

Gambling is regulated with taxes on gambling devices. In addition, those engaged in gambling professionally pay a gambler's tax. The courts have limited the scope of the gambler's tax as violating the Fifth Amendment protection against self-incrimination, because some states have laws making the purchase of a national gambling stamp prima facie evidence of violation of state gambling laws.

Regulatory taxes can also be used to protect producers. The use of protective tariffs is a common form of regulatory tax on imported goods. At one time, oleomargarine was taxed in order to protect the dairy industry. Congress also taxed futures in grain commodities and cotton at the behest of agricultural groups.

Sometimes a regulatory tax is designed to protect public health. Congress has sought to protect children with a prohibitive tax on child labor (later declared unconstitutional). It also imposed a regulatory tax on white-tipped matches. The tax was imposed in the early 1900s to protect industrial workers making phosphorus-tipped matches from "phossy jaw," a degenerative disease caused by prolonged exposure to phosphorus. Heavy taxes on smokestacks (effluent tax) seek to regulate air-quality conditions.

States and localities engage in regulatory taxation as a part of their reserved police powers to regulate the health, safety, welfare, and morals of the community. The federal government levies regulatory taxes through the commerce clause of the U.S. Constitution. The courts rarely review regulatory taxes because it is their policy not to enquire into the motivation of Congress in adopting federal legislation.

Sometimes the laws of the two levels work together. The federal tax on gambling devices, for example, helps states enforce antigambling laws.

Regulatory taxes are often preferred by advocacy groups. They believe the regulatory results are better and require less political effort than having a bureaucracy create regulatory rules.

Some regulatory taxes are hidden. For example, hidden in the income tax code are provisions that give unfavorable treatment for certain kinds of activities or products.

For more information
Lee, R. Alton. *A History of Regulatory Taxation*. Lexington: University Press of Kentucky, 1973.

A. J. L. Waskey

Rehabilitation Act of 1973   The Rehabilitation Act of 1973 was passed by Congress to establish programs promoting employment opportunities and independent living for individuals with disabilities. This act also prescribes that individuals with disabilities will have equal access to facilities, programs, and activities run by the federal government, the U.S. Postal Service, and any other organization that receives federal funds. The full text of the act can be found at 29 U.S.C. secs.791 et seq.

The call for equal rights and opportunities for individuals with disabilities is generally known as the Independent Living movement. The idea underlying this movement is that individuals with disabilities not only have the same rights as any other individual, but should also have the same opportunities as far as possible depending upon the limiting nature of their disability. Accordingly, the Rehabilitation Act not only prohibits discrimination against individuals with disabilities, but also mandates affirmative steps designed to put individuals with disabilities on a level playing field from which to seek those opportunities.

In order to ensure that individuals with disabilities are able to utilize available opportunities, the act requires that any employer who receives federal funding must make reasonable accommodations so that a qualified individual with a disability can perform his or her job. Thus, an employee who develops a mental illness that slows down his or her ability to complete paperwork but who still retains the same degree of accuracy should likely be given longer to complete tasks, particularly if the position is a salaried rather than an hourly one. Similarly, the act requires that a subsidized housing complex is required to install ramps, grab bars, and other assistive devices for tenants with disabilities. Employers, housing providers, schools, and other recipients of federal funds are required to make such reasonable accommodations unless doing so would create an undue financial or administrative burden or fundamentally alter the nature of the program.

One of the most controversial requirements of the Rehabilitation Act is the requirement that government employers and independent contractors who contract with the federal government take affirmative action to hire individuals with disabilities. Contrary to common belief, however, this affirmative action requirement does not equal a quota system but simply requires such employers to take affirmative steps, such as targeted advertising, to ensure that individuals with disabilities are aware of the employment opportunities available and given an equal chance to apply for such opportunities.

The Rehabilitation Act was the first significant civil rights legislation passed for individuals with disabilities. Its passage paved the way for even broader legislation such as the INDIVIDUALS WITH DISABILITIES EDUCATION ACT OF 1974 and the AMERICANS WITH DISABILITIES ACT (ADA) of 1990. The ADA extends many provisions of the Rehabilitation Act to private employers, housing providers, schools, and similar organizations not just government ones.

For more information

Consumer's Guide to Disability Rights Laws. Washington, D.C.: U.S. Department of Justice, Civil Rights Division, Disability Rights Section, 1999.

Middleton, Renee A., Carolyn W. Rollins, and Debra A. Harley. "The Historical and Political Context of the Civil Rights of Persons With Disabilities: A Multicultural Perspective for Counselors." *Journal of Multicultural Counseling & Development* 27, no. 2 (April 1999): 105.

Martha M. Lafferty

representation   Representation refers to the multiple ways that interests or people may have their views heard or expressed in a popular government or democracy such as the United States. There are three separate but related perspectives on what representation means:

First, there is demographic representation, which is the transformation of public bureaucracies into representative political institutions through the partisan, social, and attitudinal composition of their workforces.

Second, there is descriptive representation, wherein public bureaucracies illustratively represent large-scale interests in the society through various symbolic and functional measures, including, but not limited to, institutional title, organizational structure, and administrative mission. This is sometimes evident in the names of government departments and agencies that represent well-organized interests within society, such as departments of agriculture, labor, and commerce.

Third, there is interest representation, wherein interest groups or individuals represent a narrow range of issues relative to representation by more traditional and broadly conceived agencies. Citizen participation in administration can assume various forms, such as citizen advisory groups.

Identifying these various meanings of representation is worthwhile because it allows us to better understand and appreciate the range and scope of influences within society that attempt to determine the behavior of public agencies in a political context. A fundamental question concerning public agencies and administrators is whether they are representatives despite their bureaucratic commitments and features. Specifically, is it consistent with democratic theory to propose that government administrative agencies perform some representative function along with their delegated administrative duties pertaining to policy formation, development, implementation, and evaluation? Is it proper to ask government bureaucrats to act as public trustees, particularly in the absence of free and open elections to provide for their accountability?

Although there are some who would argue that it is possible for bureaucrats to fulfill this representative role, others would contend that it is not only difficult, but also dangerous to democratic government. Because public bureaucrats are nonelected officials, their representative activity might be inconsistent with the tenets of democratic theory that link representation to elections. Thus, the concept of representation in the context of public administration remains complex and controversial within the framework of a representative democracy.

For more information

Krislov, Samuel, and David H. Rosenbloom. *Representative Bureaucracy and the American Political System*. Westport, Conn.: Praeger Publishers, 1981.

Ryden, David. *Representation in Crisis*. Albany: State University of New York Press, 1996.

Maurice C. Sheppard

representative bureaucracy The concept of representative bureaucracy theorizes that government bureaucracies can better develop and implement effective and efficient public policies if they foster the creation of a public workforce that is representative of the diverse communities and individuals these organizations serve.

There are two primary approaches to representation in this context. One approach is demographic representation. This approach contends that because individuals with equivalent backgrounds undergo similar socialization experiences, these comparable individuals can better understand how the formation of attitudes and values lead to certain behaviors and conditions than those with dissimilar backgrounds. For example, women administrators might be more supportive of Equal Employment Opportunity Commission (EEOC) policies than their male counterparts.

Another approach is interest representation. This approach contends that government administrative agencies tend to serve a narrow range of specialized interests within the broader society. For example, Department of Defense (DOD) contract representatives with ties to private-sector interests can provide more efficient and effective contract services to business and market entities than DOD contract representatives lacking such personal and professional relationships.

Common to both approaches is the notion that a public administration that is representative of segments of a broader society can better access, interpret, and act to represent these segments in the public policy process. While tension may exist between the two approaches, they are not mutually exclusive.

This matter is significant for two primary reasons. First, it proposes that by having the public sector more closely resemble particular segments of the broader society, the policy process improves as these individuals—with unique expertise, information, and ideas—enhance policy analysis, formation, development, implementation, and evaluation. Second, because a representative bureaucracy can reflect the needs of a diverse set of social groups, it shows a commitment by government toward supporting, in practice, the idea that all members of society have equal access to government offices. In essence, by having public-sector bureaucracies more closely resemble target populations, government enhances the legitimacy of public policy, government officials, and bureaucratic offices. Representative bureaucracy, therefore, proposes to enhance the quality of service in the public sector and the legitimacy of government by contending that merit-based public administration is most effective and efficient when government agencies are compatible with their social environment.

Criticism of representative bureaucracy usually takes three forms. First, because the process of socialization is continuous, individuals upon entering the public sector will replace existing similarly demographic or other interest alliances with a new alliance to the public organization and its culture and values. Second, some of the goals of representative bureaucracy may tend to be incompatible with the missions and cultures of many public-sector organizations. Third is the charge that representative bureaucracy, according to either of the approaches discussed above, skews the public-policy process in such a manner that broader societal issues do not receive adequate attention and resources. J. Donald Kingsley's *Representative Bureaucracy* was the first book to examine public workforce representation with later studies analyzing bureaucratic representation in terms of broader socioeconomic factors such as race, gender, and ethnicity.

For more information

Kingsley, J. Donald. *Representative Bureaucracy, an Interpretation of the British Civil Service.* Yellow Springs, Ohio.: Antioch Press, 1944.

Krislov, Samuel, and David H. Rosenbloom. *Representative Bureaucracy and the American Political System.* Westport, Conn.: Praeger Publishers, 1981.

Selden, Sally Coleman. *The Promise of Representative Bureaucracy.* Armonk, N.Y.: M. E. Sharpe, 1997.

Maurice C. Sheppard

reproductive freedom   Reproductive freedom refers to the removal of social and legal impediments to access to the most effective contraception. This includes practical sex education on effective contraception, avoiding sexually transmitted diseases, and access to medically competent abortions. Reproductive freedom has been challenged by many religious and social conservatives.

Reproductive freedom in its various dimensions is a high-priority concern of the women's movement, which is committed to expanding women's choices in directing their lives. Nothing so constrains such choices as the all-consuming commitment of parenthood. This is especially true for women who still take on the predominant role in child rearing.

Restrictions on the means of controlling the rate of human reproduction have been part of American criminal law since the latter part of the 19th century. The restrictions on such control came as the technology for reproduction control became more effective. Not only were abortions under most circumstances criminalized throughout the land, but a number of states also criminalized contraception using chemical or barrier methods. It was not until *Griswold v. Connecticut,* 381 U.S. 479 (1965), that the Supreme Court, basing its decision on an inferred right of privacy, ruled that the decision to practice contraception was none of the state's business.

Although numerous states were beginning to liberalize their restrictions on abortion through state legislation, the Supreme Court struck down all laws criminalizing abortion by judicial fiat in *Roe v. Wade,* 410 U.S. 113 (1973). Relying on the aforementioned right of privacy inferred from the Fourth, Fifth, and Ninth Amendments, *Roe* specifically laid down the following rules: if the pregnant woman, the abortion providers, and the hospital or clinic are willing, the state may not ban abortions in the first trimester (three months) of pregnancy; states may regulate abortion in the interest of the health of the pregnant woman in the second trimester; and the state may ban abortions in the last trimester unless the health (broadly defined) of the pregnant woman is threatened. The Court's decision was based more upon medical and sociological fact than legal precedent. In the first trimester, abortions performed by competent medical personnel are safer than childbirth. However, abortion becomes progressively more dangerous in the second trimester, giving the state a compelling interest in protecting the pregnant woman. In the third trimester, the fetus becomes viable outside the womb, and the now independent new life is another compelling state interest. This viability criterion is becoming increasingly vulnerable because developing technology has rendered the unborn viable at progressively earlier points in the pregnancy.

Opposition to the legality of abortion and opposition to the legality of contraception are related. One might logically suppose that people who find abortion abhorrent would encourage contraception in order to prevent the unplanned and unwanted pregnancies that generate the demand for abortion. However, the reality is that the same individuals in the forefront of the fight against legal abortion, the "pro-life movement," are the ones leading the fight against public encouragement of contraception and sex education. The

A woman holds prescription contraceptives.
(Tim Matsui/Getty Images)

religious right, the Vatican, and groups like Joseph Schiedler's Pro-Life Action Committee vigorously oppose all three methods of controlling one's reproduction. Schiedler, a leading antiabortion activist, epitomized this perspective when he characterized contraception as "mutual masturbation."

The common thread in these struggles is the question of whether people should be able to engage in sexual activity without the fear of pregnancy or sexually transmitted diseases. In other words, should people be able to engage in sexual activity purely for pleasure without the intent to procreate. These three issue areas—abortion rights, contraception, and sex education—are dimensions of the broader concept of reproductive freedom. The assumption of those who wish to suppress abortion, sex education, and contraception appears to be that the ability to engage in sexual activity without the risk of pregnancy or disease encourages promiscuity. Western religious tradition has tended to regard sexual activity outside of marriage for mere pleasure as immoral, and social conservatives further argue that traditional sexual morality and family stability are inseparable.

Pro-life advocates—the label given to opponents of abortion rights—have succeeded in placing a number of hurdles for people seeking abortions under the guise of second-trimester regulations to protect the pregnant woman: a 24-hour waiting period, a lecture on alternatives to abortion, parental notification in the case of pregnant minors, etc. A set of such barriers was upheld in *Planned Parenthood of Pennsylvania v. Casey,* 505 U.S. 833 (1992). The special attention to discouraging sexuality in minors, exemplified in the parental-notification provision, was further advanced by a "gag rule" imposed by presidential decree in the Reagan years that withheld federal funds from clinics that gave contraceptive advice to minors. This was removed by President Clinton.

However, frustrated by their inability to reverse *Roe,* pro-life forces have taken to direct action to reduce the incidence of abortion. Congress reacted to attempts to physically block clinic access and harass clients with legislation restricting the activities and proximity of protesters. A growing pattern of violence against and harassment of abortion providers and their families, including the murder of two physicians and three other clinic employees, has resulted in a sharp decrease in the number of professionals willing to provide abortion services. This violence continued through 2000 as Father John Earl drove his car through a Rockford, Illinois, women's center and then attacked the center with an ax. In March of that year, a bomb exploded in an Asheville, North Carolina, abortion clinic. Thus, while such services may be legal, in many parts of the country they are effectively unavailable because it is increasingly difficult to find medical personnel willing to perform them.

Much controversy has been generated on this issue by a form of late-term abortion sometimes called "partial birth abortion" but medically termed "dilatation and extraction." While this is the safest means of late-term abortion, the procedure strikes others as close to infanticide, as a viable fetus is partially removed from the womb and its brains sucked from its skull. The Supreme Court in *Stenberg v. Cahart,* June 2000, struck down a Nebraska ban on this procedure as "too broadly worded" and posing "an undue burden on women." This undue-burden principle is the vague principle used by the Court in judging the regulation of abortion. In July of that year, the Sixth Circuit Court struck down a Kentucky law banning late-term abortions citing *Stenberg.* Also in 2000, a New Jersey court struck down a parental notification requirement.

The controversy over abortion rights is based on conflicting views as to when a fertilized egg becomes a human being. The issues surrounding reproductive freedom are based on conflicting views on the morality of sex for pleasure, not reproduction. Since these conflicts cannot be resolved by further information, they will remain bitter for the foreseeable future.

For more information

Djerassi, Carl. *The Politics of Contraception: Birth Control in the Year 2001*. San Francisco: W. H. Freeman & Co., 1981.

Frohock, Fred. *Abortion: A Case Study in Law and Morals*. Westport, Conn.: Greenwood Press, 1983.

Tribe, Lawrence. *Abortion: The Clash of Issues*. New York: W. W. Norton & Co., 1990.

Lawrence Mayer

revenue sharing Revenue sharing is a practice by which the federal government transfers funds it collects from income tax revenues to state and local governments to use as they desire, with few strings attached.

Revenue sharing originated in the United States in the mid-19th century, but its most recent and ambitious incarnation came with the State and Local Fiscal Assistance Act of 1972. This program, signed into law by President Richard M. Nixon, permitted the almost unconditional transfer of federal funds to state and local governments. Its supporters believed that the infusion of federal funds would allow state and local governments to better satisfy their fiscal priorities, and that revenue sharing would allow subnational political officials more flexibility in determining how to allocate funds to best meet the needs of their jurisdictions.

Prior to the enactment of revenue sharing in 1972, federal assistance to the states was generally confined to narrowly defined categorical grant programs. Categorical grants were funds appropriated by Congress for specific purposes, allocated by a precise formula, and subject to detailed conditions imposed by the national government. From the 1960s until the presidency of Lyndon B. Johnson, the federal government used these grants to provide funds to, or withhold them from, state and local governments in order to urge these governments to further national needs.

Beginning in the 1960s, criticism of the federal grant system began to mount. Categorical grants came to be viewed as inflexible and administratively inefficient, and state and local political leaders sought more discretion in deciding how to use federal funds. When Walter Heller, the chairman of Johnson's Council of Economic Advisers, formulated the outlines of a revenue-sharing plan, his idea attracted the attention of local, state, and national political leaders. What became known as the Heller-Pechman plan (Joseph Pechman chaired a task force appointed by Johnson to refine the Heller proposal) called for the regular distribution of a portion of the federal personal income tax to the states. In addition, the states would have greater freedom in deciding how to use federal funds than they did in the case of categorical grants. While Johnson eventually abandoned the idea, Nixon embraced it as part of his "new federalism" campaign to reinvigorate state and local governments and bring political decision making closer to the people. Pressure by state and local officials and support from powerful House of Representatives committee chairman Wilbur Mills led to the passage and enactment of the State and Local Fiscal Assistance Act in 1972.

The 1972 revenue-sharing program authorized the return of $30.2 billion to state and local governments over a five-year period, and it was reauthorized in 1976 and again—but only for local governments—in 1980 and 1983. The allocation of funds was determined by a formula whereby a state's government would received one-third of the total funds authorized, and local governments would receive the remaining two-thirds. Local governments could use shared revenues for a variety of purposes, including public safety, public transportation, health, recreation, libraries, and social services.

The 1980 and 1983 reauthorizations of revenue sharing were more limited in scope than earlier versions of the program, and in 1986, revenue sharing became a victim of federal deficit reduction, which was then the most pressing domestic policy issue. In addition, economic recession, inflation, projected shortfalls in the

Social Security system, and the declining relative power of the state and local lobby in Congress also contributed to the demise of revenue sharing. Despite the fact that the revenue sharing program distributed over $83 billion in 14 years to 39,000 localities, it died in undramatic fashion in Congress, with no debate on its merit or success. However, the influence of revenue sharing is perhaps still being felt: many believe revenue sharing set the stage for the devolution movement in the 1990s, when state and local governments played a more important role in formulating, financing, and administering domestic policy.

For more information

Department of the Treasury. Office of Revenue Sharing. *Revenue Sharing, 1972–1986: A Plain-Language Explanation of the Revenue Sharing Program.* Washington, D.C.: Government Printing Office, 1985.

Wallin, Bruce A. *From Revenue Sharing to Deficit Sharing: General Revenue Sharing and Cities.* Washington, D.C.: Georgetown University Press, 1998.

Kathleen Grammatico

risk management Risk management is a systematic process for the development and implementation of policies, practices, or specific actions to identify, assess, manage, and monitor risks relevant to any activity.

Common public-sector examples of risk management include workplace safety audits, development of fire management plans for forests, and assessment of investment proposals for financial exposures. The purpose is to help reduce the occurrence of unexpected or unwanted events that could adversely affect the activity, prevent or reduce loss before the event occurs, or minimize the consequences after the event. Risk management tends to focus on what can go wrong, but it should also consider opportunities for improvement. The general principles of risk management apply to any

activity, but the level of detail and attention can vary considerably. Greater attention will naturally be given to the risk management of events that may endanger life, have significant property or financial impacts, or that can frequently disrupt a beneficial activity. Statutes such as workplace safety legislation, duty of care provisions, and government financial management and audit policies all require that risks be properly managed.

In public administration, risk management can occur at both the program and project level. Programs are generally ongoing activities that are administered by public-sector agencies to achieve general public policy objectives, for example education and public health. Program risks are usually defined broadly at the agency level, for example the likelihood of the government approving a particular policy position or the potential for overrun of budgeted expenditure. Specific risks within a program area of the agency can then be developed in more detail. In contrast, projects are tasks with specific objectives and time frames undertaken by agencies consistent with the broader program goals. Projects may be physical activities such as construction of a building, or they may be ideas, for example the development of a policy proposal or an organizational change. Project risks are specific to a particular project, and their management is essential to ensure the project is successfully delivered on time and within budget. Project risks need to be considered in relation to the project and also in the context of the broader program risks.

Public-sector agencies incorporate risk management activities into their corporate governance and their general business planning and management processes at a number of organizational levels. Managers within an agency are accountable for risk management activities relevant to their areas of responsibility within the agency. Ultimately, however, responsibility for risk management for programs and specific projects lies with the board or chief executive, who must ensure that internal management processes and controls are in place to manage risks relevant to the agency's activities.

The implementation of risk management may vary in different public agencies, but the general process is the same. The first step is to establish the context for the risks. An environmental scan is often done. It is also important to establish clear responsibilities and the scope and structure of the risk management process from the beginning so that the risk of a poor process is also properly managed. The second step is to identify the risks, establish what could happen, and how and why they may occur. The third step is to assess the risks in terms of likelihood and consequences of occurrence. Analyses of historical data or modeling techniques are often used at this stage. The fourth step is to evaluate the risks against relevant criteria and set risk priorities. The fifth step is to treat the risks, which can be done in a number of ways.

Risk can be avoided by ceasing the activity, transferring the risk through insurance or by contracting out the activity, or reducing the risks by changing the way the activity is done. An important role of governments and the public sector in treating risks for the community is to regulate and control certain types of activities. Appropriate monitoring and review processes are also required. However, not all risks are within a manager's control. Some risks remain, and provision must be made for their potential impacts. Risk management must be an ongoing process because risks are constantly changing.

The principles and processes for risk management are now codified by many organizations worldwide, e.g., Australia Risk Management Standard, AS/NZS 4360: 1999; and Guidelines for Managing Risk in the Australian and New Zealand Public Sector, SAA/NZS HB143: 1999.

For more information
Bernstein, Peter L. *Against the Gods: The Remarkable Story of Risk*. New York: Wiley, 1996.

Richard Muncey

rules committees A rules committee is a group of legislators who work to set guidelines for the legislative process.

Article I, Section 5 of the U.S. Constitution states that each house of Congress "may determine the Rules of its Proceedings." To that end, both houses of Congress and many state bodies have permanent rules committees that regulate the legislative process. Broadly, these rules committees may have jurisdiction over parliamentary procedure, the management of the legislative institution, ethical standards, lobbying and elections, and the rules for consideration of specific bills on the floor.

The Rules Committee of the U.S. House of Representatives became a standing committee in 1880, although the membership and jurisdiction of the committee have changed over time. One primary responsibility of the House Rules Committee as it relates to the legislative process, is the sponsorship of special rules that set procedures for the consideration of a bill. These rules are generally directed at the ability of legislators to offer amendments on the legislative floor. Within the U.S. House, there are four common types of rules that can be applied to a piece of legislation. An open rule allows amendments to be offered on the floor, while a modified open rule allows amendments within a certain time limit. In contrast, a closed rule prohibits amendments, and a modified closed rule only allows certain types of amendments to be offered.

The Rules Committee also proposes rules that set a specific date and time for the consideration of a bill. Without this power, legislators would have to deliberate legislation in the order of its placement on the legislative calendar, which occurs once it is advanced from committee. Therefore, since the chairperson of the Rules Committee is usually a member of the majority party, the use of these rules allows the majority in the House to set their own schedule for consideration of bills on the floor. By setting rules for floor debate beforehand, the Rules Committee—and therefore the majority party—has the ability to maintain control of the legislative process, something very important when 435 members have their own policy goals.

The roles of the rules committees in the U.S. House and U.S. Senate are quite different. While the House committee, as noted, has jurisdiction over the scheduling of bills and application of open and closed rules, the Senate Committee on Rules and Administration oversees a variety of issues, including those related to federal elections, chamber rules, the administration of federal buildings, and presidential succession. In order to regulate floor debate, members of the Senate adopt unanimous-consent agreements, in which leaders from both parties work out an arrangement to set the rules for debate on a piece of legislation. The scheduling of bills on the floor is the result either of a unanimous-consent agreement or of the preferences of the majority leader.

The jurisdictions of rules committees at the state level may include some or all of the areas overseen by the committees at the federal level. Typically, rules committees at the state level have less of an impact on the daily legislative calendar than does the House Rules Committee. Rules committees at the state level tend to deal more with the rules of the legislative chamber and the administration of the legislative institution, which can include overseeing office space and even staff parking.

For more information

Davidson, Roger H., and Walter J. Oleszek. *Congress and Its Members,* 8th ed. Washington, D.C.: Congressional Quarterly Press, 2002.

Robinson, James A. "The Role of the Rules Committee in Regulating Debate in the U.S. House of Representatives." *Midwest Journal of Political Science* 5, no. 1 (1961): 59–69.

Thomas: Legislative Information. http://thomas.loc.gov.

Tracy McKay Mason

Rutan v. Republican Party of Illinois 492 U.S. 62 (1990)

Political patronage has mani-

fested itself in public administration in myriad ways, including exerting influence on decision making by and about personnel in the public sector. Most recently, however, the trend has been to curtail patronage. This trend can clearly be seen in a trio of cases handed down by the U.S. Supreme Court, culminating in the Court's opinion in *Rutan v. Republican Party of Illinois,* 492 U.S. 62 (1990).

In 1939, in response to the perceived excesses of existing patronage systems, Congress passed the Hatch Act, which, among other things, limited political activity by public employees. As merit appointment of public employees took hold in the 1960s, court challenges to patronage increased, reaching the U.S. Supreme Court in the 1970s. Beginning with ELROD V. BURNS 427 U.S. 347 (1976), which declared the practice of patronage dismissal unconstitutional, and continuing with BRANTI V. FINKEL 445 U.S. 507 (1980), which held that employees' political speech is protected by the First Amendment, the Supreme Court declared patronage an endangered practice. The Court was not unanimous, however, as the justices acknowledged the value of patronage in furthering a strong two-party system.

Where *Elrod* and *Branti* dealt with dismissal, *Rutan* raised the question of patronage in personnel decisions such as hiring, promotion, transfer, and recall of employees following layoffs. As Justice Brennan succinctly noted in the opening of the opinion he wrote for a divided court, "[t]o the victor belong only those spoils that may be constitutionally obtained" (*Rutan,* at 65). At issue was a practice implemented by the governor's office in Illinois instituting a hiring freeze, exceptions to which had to be processed exclusively through that office. In reality, personnel decisions were conditioned on support by the Republican Party. Cynthia B. Rutan claimed she had repeatedly been denied promotion based on lack of support by the Republican Party. Similarly, three other petitioners were denied promotion, transfer, or recall based on party affiliation.

A fifth petitioner claimed he was not hired based on lack of political support.

Grounded in constitutional law, the court held that such decisions "based on political affiliation or support are an impermissible infringement on the First Amendment rights of public employees." Taking care to detail the ways these decisions may negatively impact employees, the court noted that there are other means to assure an effective workforce, such as performance-based discipline. The rule in *Elrod* and *Branti* that permits party affiliation to be taken into consideration for top policy-making positions was left intact. The dissent authored by Justice Scalia opines that "that categorical pronouncement reflects a naive vision of politics and an inadequate appreciation of the systemic effects of patronage in promoting political stability and facilitating the social and political integration of previously powerless groups."

Rutan symbolizes the demise of patronage as a major force in public employment practice. It is also symbolic of the role that the courts play in defining acceptable personnel practices. Both trends are significant ones in public personnel administration.

For more information

Shafritz, Jay M., et al. *Personnel Management in Government,* 5th ed. New York: Marcel Dekker, 2001.

Holly Taylor Sellers

S

sales tax   Sales taxes represent the largest single source of revenue for state and local governments, providing approximately 20 percent to total annual general revenue. Sales taxes in the United States are confined to the state and local level, as there is no U.S. national sales tax. Both state and local governments collect sales taxes. Combined state and local collections range from 4 percent in Hawaii to 9.78 percent in Oklahoma. Some purchases are exempt from sales tax; the exact product type varies by state. For example, some states tax prepared and unprepared foods, while others tax only prepared food. Nearly every state charges a general sales tax on residential telephone use; fewer than 10 states charge sales tax on medical services.

There has not been much talk of a national sales tax since the beginning of the Second World War. During this period, as the United States was increasing its involvement in the war and faced with increasing costs, policy makers considered the sales tax as a possible source of new revenue. The sales tax emerged as a leading contender, at least in some policy circles. During that period income tax revenue was depressed, and the sales tax was viewed as a supplement to the income tax. Today, any discussion of a national sales tax is surrounded with notions of replacing the income tax on the basis of equitable tax burden. Proponents argue a national sales tax on nonessential items forces those with the greatest ability to pay the tax to bear the burden.

The state and local governments where a business is physically located collect most sales taxes. For sales conducted between parties in different states, the consumer is responsible for reporting the purchase and paying the tax. For decades, potential sales tax collections from catalog sales have been forgone by states. The business conducted on the Internet represents another potential source of revenue that is lost to state governments. There are a number of arguments against taxing Internet commerce, most centering on concerns that levying sales tax would slow the growth of e-commerce. This fear triggered action by the legislature and the enactment of the Internet Tax Freedom Act, which, among other things, provides a moratorium on Internet tax collections. As part of the act, the Advisory Commission on Electronic Commerce was created to study Internet tax issues and make recommendations.

In 1999, U.S. state and local governments collected $203 billion in general sales tax revenues. According to a report by the General Accounting Office of the U.S. Congress, as much as $12 billion in sales tax revenue goes uncollected on consumer-to-business and business-to-business Internet e-commerce. Proponents of expanded state taxing authority usually offer three arguments in support of their position: fairness to businesses that provide products and services "nonelectronically" or traditionally; the threat that lost revenue will inhibit states and localities from providing essential services and infrastructure; and neutrality, or the idea that taxes for goods should be uniform regardless of how they are purchased. This debate is expected to continue into the foreseeable future and will involve both state and national lawmakers. There is also the possibility that this war between state governments and business interests on the taxation of electronic commerce will be conducted not on the floor of the legislature, but in the courtroom, restricting public involvement in the process.

For more information

Fisher, Ronald. *State and Local Public Finance,* 2d ed. Chicago: Irwin, 1996.

Lukas, Aaron. *Should Internet Sales Be Taxed?* Washington, D.C.: Cato Institute's Center for Trade Policy Studies, April 1999.

Mikesell, John. *Fiscal Administration: Analysis and Applications for the Public Sector,* 5th ed. Fort Worth, Tex.: Harcourt Brace College Publishers, 1999.

Brent C. Smith

sales taxes on remote commerce Sales taxes on remote commerce refers to the ability and wisdom of governments levying a sales tax on goods bought by their citizens from companies located outside the borders of their city, state, or country. Remote commerce includes catalog sales as well as e-commerce sales, but the main point of contention is on merchandise sold through the Internet, and it has risen to become a major public policy issue today.

The public policy issues in taxing remote sales are complicated, however, especially given the national scope of the problem. In *Quill v. North Dakota* 504 U.S. 298 (1992) (viewable at http://supct.law.cornell.edu/supct/html/91-0194.ZO.html), the U.S. Supreme Court ruled that states lack the authority to require businesses outside their borders to collect sales tax owed by citizens on purchases made using the Internet, mail, or telephone unless the seller has a physical presence in the citizen's state. In that case, the court stated that Congress has the authority to resolve this, which they did temporarily by enacting the 1998 Internet Tax Freedom Act [Public Law 107-75], placing a moratorium on any new taxes on e-commerce sales. Originally for a three-year period from October 1998, the act was extended in October 2001 for another three-year period [PL 105-277].

This federal preemption has created a hiatus during which a national solution might be found. However, in order to impose a uniform national system of sales tax collections on remote sales, a uniform system of tax policy needs to be in place so that retailers can reasonably rely upon their ability to comply with all the state and local tax laws. Given the current variety of sales tax rates and bases, especially at the local level, a simple solution is not likely in the near future.

Taxing of remote sales can be viewed from the perspective of consumers, retailers, and government:

Consumers

Consumers, well-known for adopting tax avoidance behavior, enjoy the avoidance of paying state and local sales taxes on remote sales, although shipping costs usually more than offset any tax savings. For example, an item purchased at a main-street retailer for $100 might have sales tax of 5 percent, or $5. The same item, if bought for $100 on the Internet, might not have the 5 percent sales tax, but instead might have a $7.50 shipping charge. Usually, however, there is a price advantage in purchasing through the Internet, so the $100 item might only cost $90, with $7.50 shipping, for a total of $97.50, a savings over the $105 total price at the main-street merchant.

Consumers also argue that state and local sales and use tax revenue is used to pay for state and local services, which are not demanded in remote sales transactions. The primary advantages of remote sales to the consumer, it appears, are convenience and selection: one can compare the prices, features, and availability of a variety of products without leaving one's home.

Consumers have argued in defense of the tax exemption that e-commerce enjoys, noting that Article 1, section 9 of the U.S. Constitution precludes taxes or duties on articles exported from any state. However, this same constitutional provision states that "[n]o preference shall be given by any regulation of commerce or revenue to the ports of one state over those of another: nor shall vessels bound to, or from, one state, be obliged to enter, clear or pay duties in another." It could be argued that a remote, tax-exempt purchase is given a preference over a local purchase for which a sales tax is paid, and thus it should be constitutionally disallowed.

Retailers

Main-street merchants insist that consumer savings of sales taxes offers e-commerce and other remote merchants an unfair competitive advantage. The fabric of the local community is threatened, they say, by their price disadvantage in having to collect sales taxes on purchases. If consumers appreciate the ease with which purchasing decisions can be made on remote sales, then they should be expected to pay more for that service in higher shipping charges, not less in sales taxes. Those consumers use the local services (i.e., streets, law enforcement, fire protection, etc.) that sales tax revenue pays for, so they should be expected to help pay for those services. Indeed, the delivery companies need sound roads, bridges, and streets to ship the goods to the consumer, yet these remote transactions do not contribute to pay for them.

Competition from remote merchants has exacerbated a problem that main-street merchants have already been experiencing with the growth of "big box" retailers, such as Wal-Mart and Home Depot. Were remote commerce taxed on the same basis as local businesses, main-street retailers feel that more business would "stay home," and their competitive position would be enhanced.

Government

It may appear that consumers' tax-avoidance behavior is actually tax evasion, since a state use tax, and usually a local use tax, is owed on goods purchased elsewhere and used or stored within the state. National research shows that the total lost state and local tax revenue from remote sales in 2001 would be $16.4 billion, increasing to $66.2 billion in 2011. Of this amount, $13.3 billion in 2001 is due to e-commerce alone, growing to $54.8 billion in 2011. Nationally, this amounts to an average of over 2.5 percent of state total tax revenue in 2001, rising to over 6.5 percent in 2011. In Florida, where sales tax is a high percentage of state tax collections, these percentages are 4.6 percent and 11.5 percent, respectively. (Data are from "State and Local Sales Tax Revenue Losses from E-Commerce: Updated Estimates," Knoxville, Tennessee, September 2001.)

For more information

California Taxpayer's Association. *Cal-Tax Digest.* March 2000. Available online. URL: http://www.caltax.org/MEMBER/digest/mar2000/mar00-3.htm.

Golden-Mumane, Laura. "E-Commerce and Internet Taxation." *Information Today* (June 2000). Available online. URL: http://www.findarticles.com/ cf_dls/m0DPC/6_8/62767117/pl/article.jhtml? term=.

Geoff Withers

Sarbanes-Oxley Act of 2002 The Sarbanes-Oxley Act of 2002 is a federal law that regulates the financial practices and reporting of corporations. The act was passed in reaction to news that several companies in the United States had falsified their financial reports.

In the fall of 2001 and into 2002, several companies in the United States admitted that they had misreported their financial data. These stories came to public attention when Enron Corporation, a large energy company, went bankrupt and it was revealed that they had submitted incorrect or false reports regarding their finances. These reports claimed that the corporation was in good financial health when, in fact, they failed to disclose that Enron actually had numerous debts totaling tens of millions of dollars, if not more. In addition, there were allegations that executives and officers at the company loaned themselves corporate money and lied to the employees and stockholders regarding the company's finances, resulting in both losing billions of dollars in the value of their pension funds and stock investments. This occurred after the executives and officers—who knew about Enron's real financial situation—had sold their stock before it collapsed.

Under federal law, corporations are required to report their finances to the SECURITIES AND EXCHANGE COMMISSION (SEC), the U.S. govern-

Enron employees leave the company's headquarters after being laid off in December 2001 in Houston, Texas. (JAMES NIELSEN/GETTY IMAGES)

ment agency that regulates corporations. Among the financial reports required to be submitted was an audit of the company's books. In the case of Enron, Arthur Andersen was the firm hired to do its auditing. Congressional hearings and testimony revealed that Arthur Andersen helped Enron hide information about its finances. When these reports were made public, and while both companies were under congressional investigation, Arthur Andersen began shredding documents that were being subpoenaed by Congress. As a result of this activity, Arthur Andersen was convicted of obstruction of justice.

In addition to Enron and Arthur Andersen, several other companies during 2001–2002 also reported that they had misreported their finances, including Xerox, WorldCom, Merck, Adelphia, and Tyco International. These revelations resulted in a significant drop in the value of many stocks and in a public demand for Congress to subject corporations and auditors to increased regulation. One of the concerns growing out of these investigations was that many auditing agencies had a conflict of interest in the performance of their financial reviews. They were supposed to provide independent reviews of a company's finances, but because companies such as Arthur Andersen also sold other services to the businesses they were auditing, the auditing firm was unable to perform a fair and impartial review.

The Sarbanes-Oxley Act of 2002 is the legislation that Congress passed to regulate the financial practices of business corporations and auditors. Among the many provisions of the act, one of them now requires the chief operating officer (COO) and the chief financial officer (CFO) of corporations to certify under oath that the reports they are filing with the SEC are true and accurate and that they comply with all SEC requirements. The act prohibits corporations from making personal loans to officers and members of the board of directors, and it gives new legal protections to whistle-blowers or individuals who report illegal corporate activity to the government. These rules make it harder to fire or retaliate against employees who file these complaints.

Finally, to address the problems surrounding the auditing of corporations, companies that perform audits would also be prevented from selling other services. To enforce this rule and others, a new Public Company Accounting Oversight Board was created to oversee the accounting profession. This board was given the power to make rules regulating auditing firms and to initiate criminal investigations.

For more information

American Institute of Public Accountants. http://www.aicpa.org/info/sarbanes_oxley_summary.htm.

David Schultz

satisficing   *Satisficing* is a term coined in 1955 by HERBERT SIMON to describe his belief that people make decisions that, while not necessarily the best, are good enough or satisfactory.

Herbert Simon (1917–2001)—a Nobel Prize winner (economic sciences), prolific author, and well-respected scholar of political science, organizational theory, and public administration—believed that no human decision can be completely rational; that is, it is impossible, he argued, for a person to have full knowledge about the possible variables within the problem at hand, its possible outcomes, or the multiplicity of choices. Human decisions are subject to an array of constraints and uncertainties, and the information on which decisions are based is, at best, incomplete. Thus, while human decision making may be purposeful, it cannot be completely rational; rather, it is "bounded rationality." Instead, people make decisions that are satisfactory. This, in Simon's words, is satisficing.

For more information

March, James G. "Bounded Rationality, Ambiguity and the Engineering of Choice." *Bell Journal of Economics* 9 (1978): 587–608.

Simon, Herbert A. "A Behavioral Model of Rational Choice." *Quarterly Journal of Economics* 69 (1955): 99–118.

Linda K. Shafer

school vouchers School vouchers involve giving public money to parents of students in failing schools in order to offset the costs of private school education.

School-choice initiatives are programs that allow parents to choose which school their children will attend. For example, school-choice programs might allow parents to send their children to a magnet school, a charter school, or an alternative school. Advocates of school choice believe that it encourages schools to experiment, compete, and specialize.

One type of school-choice program is a school voucher system. School vouchers can be publicly or privately funded. A privately funded school voucher is similar to a scholarship. A student receives a voucher and can use it to pay for tuition at any private school. However, publicly funded school vouchers allow students to attend private schools at public expense. Specifically, a publicly funded voucher is a specific amount of public money given to a student who has withdrawn from a public school. The student can then use that voucher to help pay for private-school tuition.

Currently, there are very few publicly funded school voucher programs in the United States. At the state level, Vermont and Maine have public voucher systems. At the city level, Cleveland and Milwaukee have public voucher systems.

School vouchers that use public monies for private schools are controversial. Those who support school vouchers believe that vouchers help promote competition, accountability and access to quality schools. School-vouchers advocates argue that school competition, like market competition, promotes quality. This competition will come in the form of higher pay for teachers, better working and learning environments, and better academic offerings. These advocates believe that if schools are forced to compete for students and quality teachers, schools will have to improve in order to attract such people.

In addition, school-voucher advocates believe that school choice leads to school accountability. It can be argued that public schools are a monopoly and therefore act like an unresponsive bureaucracy. However, when parents have the ability to leave the school and "take their business elsewhere," schools will be forced to respond. The argument is, schools that meet parental demands will survive, and those that do not will fold. School voucher supporters also believe that vouchers give lower-income students access to private schools that have otherwise been limited to wealthier patrons. The public funding of school vouchers allows poorer students to pay for private-school tuition.

In response to these arguments, opponents of school vouchers argue that publicly funded school vouchers drain money from public schools, do not work, segregate schools based on class and race, and are unconstitutional. Besides the argument that vouchers do not improve student performance, opponents of vouchers fear that if public education money is spent to send students to private schools, public schools will become worse, not better. For each student that accepts a voucher, public schools would lose a certain amount of funding from the state. Opponents of vouchers also feel that private schools will "skim" the best students from the public schools. Private schools have the right to accept or reject applicants. Opponents fear this could lead to a situation where private schools reject students based on race and socioeconomic status. The end result, they suggest, could be private schools with all the high-achieving students and motivated parents, and public schools without these elements.

In addition, opponents of vouchers argue that they are unconstitutional. The First Amendment of the U.S. Constitution prevents the government from supporting religious activities. Voucher

A young girl holds up a sign in support of school vouchers in front of the U.S. Supreme Court, Washington, D.C. (Mark Wilson/Getty Images)

opponents believe that public monies being spent on private religious schools violates the concept of "separation of church and state." The Supreme Court recently rejected this argument. In *Zelman v. Simmons-Harris* the Court concluded that vouchers are given to private individuals who have a choice to spend the money on secular or parochial schools. To the Court, this distinction meant that the state is not giving public funds directly to religious schools, and therefore does not violate the establishment clause.

There has been considerable research into the effectiveness of school vouchers. Unfortunately, the results have been inconclusive, and arguments about methodology have been common. Some studies have shown that vouchers help African-American students and elevate mathematics scores. Other researchers have claimed that vouchers make little to no difference with respect to student test scores.

For more information
Peterson, Paul, and David Campbell. *Charters, Vouchers, and Public Education.* Washington, D.C.: Brookings Press, 2001.
Witte, John. *The Market Approach to Education.* Princeton, N.J.: Princeton University Press, 2000.

Mathew Manweller

scientific management Scientific management is a term for the management philosophy of FREDERICK WINSLOW TAYLOR.

The late 1800s was a period of rapid industrialization in the United States. It was also an age of inefficiency, corruption, political immorality, and wasting of the nation's natural resources. Reformers argued that new, efficient methods of management and public administration were needed for conservation of resources, full productivity, and increased benefits to all.

Taylor was a production engineer who believed that a mental revolution in the minds of both workers and management was needed to meet the problems of the day. Taylor developed a management philosophy using scientific methods in order to make work rational and efficient, with increased production. Taylor's engineering experiences convinced him that the problems of industrial production were due to two major failings: poor management and inefficient labor.

To solve the first problem, Taylor argued that well-educated managers should take charge of planning and controlling work. They were no longer to be authoritarian whips nor to operate by a rule-of-thumb method. Instead they were to engage in a cooperative effort to recruit, train, supervise, and reward labor for increased production.

To deal with the inefficiency of labor, three changes were needed. First, efficiency would be improved through work design. By studying the labors of individual laborers in shops and factories, standard methods, or "the one best way" to do each job, would be determined. In this way Taylor sought to eliminate waste in the time and effort to do a job. Second, tools were to be designed for doing each job most efficiently and provided by the organization. Finally, motivation to work was to be stimulated by a piece-rate bonus plan.

These three solutions would eliminate "soldiering," which Taylor saw as the great problem with labor. For Taylor workers were naturally lazy, and their ideological "soldiering" created a practical slowdown of work in the belief that there was a limited supply of work and that it was unwise to work one's self out of a job.

Taylor's philosophy of management was most clearly spelled out in "Shop Management" (1903), *Scientific Management* (1911), and his testimony to the Select Committee of the House of Representatives (1912). The term "scientific management" to describe Taylor's ideas was first used by Louis Brandeis in the 1911 Eastern Rate Case before the Interstate Commerce Commission.

Scientific management's impact upon business and public administration has been great. The value of scientific management in rationalizing production, on the development of mass-production techniques, and on public administration has been immense. As a movement, it has declined, but this is mainly due to its absorption into American cultural values. Reengineering in the 1990s was another form of scientific management in action.

For more information
Nelson, Daniel. *Frederick W. Taylor and the Rise of Scientific Management*. Madison, Wis.: University of Wisconsin Press, 1985.
Schracter, Hindy L. *Frederick Taylor and the Public Administration Community*. Buffalo: State University of New York Press, 1989.

A. J. L. Waskey

secretary of defense The secretary of defense is the chief adviser to the president of the United States on defense policy and the chief administrator of the DEPARTMENT OF DEFENSE.

A member of the cabinet, the secretary of defense is appointed by the president and must be confirmed by the U.S. Senate. The secretary of defense exercises direct control over the JOINT CHIEFS OF STAFF, Office of Secretary of Defense, the uniformed services (the army, navy, and air force; the Marine Corps is a subordinate branch of the navy), and a number of civilian defense agencies. The secretary is also a statutory member of the National Security Council. While many secretaries of defense have previous uniformed military experience, some even as generals and admirals, the position has always been held by a civilian.

The secretary of defense is arguably the most powerful member of the cabinet. The Department of Defense is by far the largest federal bureaucracy, in terms of both budget and personnel. The defense budget routinely comprises nearly half of all discretionary spending ($336 billion in FY 2002 versus $382 billion for all other categories) and employs 1.37 million active-duty uniformed personnel, 669,000 civilians, and another 1.28 million uniformed military reservists.

The office was created with the National Security Act of 1947. Originally, the secretary of defense was head of the National Military Establishment, a small agency that coordinated the cabinet-ranked Departments of Army, Navy, and Air Force. A 1949 amendment to the National Security Act consolidated these departments under the secretary of defense in a single Department of Defense, removing cabinet status from the individual services. Despite this move, early secretaries of defense found that they had little power, because the individual services still controlled most aspects of budgeting, planning, and coordination within the military. A 1958 amendment to the National Security Act helped change this, by removing the service chiefs from the operational chain of command and having the four-star unified commanders in chief, or CINCs (pronounced "sinks"), report directly to the secretary of defense.

Because most long-term planning and budgeting takes place outside of the operational commands, the services continue to wield enormous power. This has been exacerbated by the designation of the chairman of the Joint Chiefs of Staff, a subordinate of the secretary, as the principal military adviser to the president by the GOLDWATER-NICHOLS DEPARTMENT OF DEFENSE REORGANIZATION ACT OF 1986. The independent power of the chairman, the continued influence of the individual services, and congressional wrangling over the distribution of the largest pool of discretionary money have all hindered secretaries of defense in their efforts to centralize the control of military planning and spending.

For more information

Sarkesian, Sam C. *U.S. National Security: Policymakers, Processes, and Politics,* 3d ed. Boulder, Colo.: Lynne Reiner, 2002.

Snow, Donald M., and Eugene Brown. *United States Foreign Policy: Politics beyond the Water's Edge,* 2d ed. Boston: Bedford/St. Martin's, 2000.

James H. Joyner, Jr.

Section 8 housing   Section 8 housing is a federal program that provides government-funded housing assistance to low-income individuals.

Section 8 housing was initiated by Congress as part of the Housing and Community Development Act of 1974. While the U.S. DEPARTMENT OF HOUSING AND URBAN DEVELOPMENT is the federal agency that administers Section 8 funding, the funding is generally disbursed to recipients by state and local public housing authorities. Under the program, low-income individuals and families who qualify for Section 8 assistance only have to pay 30 percent of their gross adjusted income toward rent, and the remaining portion of their rent is paid by the government.

The social policy underlying the Section 8 program is that all individuals have the right to live in decent housing. However, in our capitalist society, many balk at the idea of providing anything beyond the most basic shelter to individuals who are not able to afford rental prices or buy a home. So there is continued debate about the appropriate standard of quality for such housing and at what income level to cease offering such assistance.

When this program was first initiated there were two types of Section 8 assistance available, project based and tenant based. As a result of efforts to reform the Section 8 program, no new project-based communities are being built, and federal aid to such existing communities will be cut off over the next several years. This move toward only tenant-based assistance is due to the sentiments that recipients of housing assistance should have more choices about where to live and, similarly, that recipients of such aid should not be clustered together and segregated from individuals who do not receive such aid. Today a majority of Section 8 funding recipients are given vouchers that can be applied to a portion of their rent. Because Section 8 housing vouchers are portable, eligible recipients are able to obtain housing from any provider who will agree to participate in the program and offers rent affordable with the voucher.

While housing providers who receive federal money, such as public housing authorities and private landlords who participate in tax credit programs, are required to accept Section 8 vouchers, most private housing providers are free to choose whether or not to accept these vouchers. Many private housing providers opt not to accept individuals who receive Section 8 assistance, ostensibly because of the paperwork required to be a housing provider in the program, and because of the stringent inspection standards local housing authorities require all Section 8 properties to undergo annually. It also seems likely that some housing providers refuse to accept Section 8 recipients in order to indirectly discriminate against minorities and families with children, since those groups are the most frequent recipients of Section 8 assistance. Accordingly, some cities have extended their fair-housing provisions to prohibit housing discrimination based on source of income and require all covered housing providers to accept tenants with Section 8 vouchers.

For more information

Johnson-Spratt, Kim. "Housing Discrimination and Source of Income: A Tenant's Losing Battle." *Indiana Law Review* 32 (1999): 457.

U.S. Department of Housing and Urban Development. http://www.hud.gov.

Martha M. Lafferty

Securities and Exchange Commission   The Securities and Exchange Commission (SEC) is a federal agency created after the stock market crash of 1929.

The collapse of the stock markets made it clear that the securities business was not sufficiently regulated and that investors and the U.S. economy had suffered devastating losses as a result. In the aftermath of the stock market crash, Congress held hearings and passed legislation to regulate the securities industry. Their purpose was to restore confidence in the financial markets and protect investors. The Securities Act of 1933 required companies to provide financial information to investors and prohibited fraud in the sale of securities. The Securities Exchange Act of 1934 created the Securities and Exchange Commission (SEC), whose purpose was to protect investors and maintain the integrity of the securities markets.

The SEC consists of five commissioners appointed by the president, one of whom is designated by the president to be the chairman. In 1934, President Franklin Roosevelt appointed Joseph P. Kennedy to be the first chairman of the SEC. The commissioners meet periodically to interpret securities laws, amend existing rules or propose new ones, and enforce the securities laws and regulations. In addition to the commissioners, the SEC is divided into four divisions (corporation finance, market regulation, investment management, and enforcement) and 18 offices. It is a relatively small agency (2,900 employees) with a great deal of responsibility.

A major concern of the SEC is ensuring that investors obtain sufficient information about companies to make informed decisions to buy or sell securities. All publicly traded companies are required by law and regulations to file financial information with the SEC, which also regulates the stock markets, brokers, and investment advisers. The SEC also oversees the Securities Investor Protection Corporation (SIPC), which insures securities and cash in customer accounts in member brokerage firms against the failure of those firms. Fraud, deceptive practices, and insider trading are primary targets of securities law that are investigated and prosecuted by the SEC. Another major responsibility is to prevent conflicts of interest among companies and individuals participating in the sale and transfer of securities.

The Enforcement Division of the SEC investigates possible violations of the securities laws and brings civil litigation or administrative proceedings against violators. Civil actions may result in injunctions to prohibit activities in violation of the law, as well as substantial monetary fines. Administrative proceedings may result in censure, being barred from practice in the securities business, or fines. The SEC Enforcement Division brings about 500 civil actions each year.

As the securities industry has become ever more complex, the weaknesses in the SEC's current regulatory scheme have been made increasingly evident. One problem is that regulation of financial advisers differs, depending on what type of product they sell Regulation of financial advisers and brokers dealing in stocks, mutual funds, hedge funds, and other products needs to be harmonized. Other reform proposals involve strengthening rules for disclosure of financial information, oversight of financial markets, disclosure of possible conflicts of interests by financial analysts, and tightening up on regulation of standards for the accounting industry. With the collapse of the multibillion-dollar Enron Corporation at the end of 2001 and the resulting criminal investigation launched by the U.S. Department of Justice, investors, employees, securities industry professionals, and Congress are demanding changes in how the SEC regulates the securities industry and the stock markets.

Particular areas of concern are the partnership arrangements that permitted Enron and other companies to conceal billions of dollars of debt from their investors, deceptive practices, insider trading that allowed Enron management to cash out millions of dollars of stock while leaving uninformed investors to face enormous losses, and substantial conflicts of interest in the accounting industry that prevented disclosure of Enron's true financial condition. It is likely that a financial collapse of such magnitude will result in substantial reform of the SEC and its regulatory practices.

For more information
"SEC Pushes for Fuller Disclosure; Securities: Officials Feel Pressure to Restore Investor Confidence after Enron's Fall." *Los Angeles Times,* 14 Feb 2002, p. A1.
U.S. Securities and Exchange Commission. http://www.sec.gov/.

Celia A. Sgroi

Selective Service System   The Selective Service System is a federal government agency and a governmental process for bringing civilians into military service.

The system developed out of a national tradition opposing large standing armies and favoring the use of a militia and volunteers to fight the nation's wars. Conscription of citizens for the military had previously been used during the Civil War (by both the Union and the Confederacy) and during World War I. The draft was revived with the signing by President Franklin D. Roosevelt of the Selective Training and Service Act of 1940. This legislation was replaced by the Selective Service Act of 1948, a measure that regulated the draft from 1948 until its abolition in 1973, when the United States shifted to an all-volunteer military service.

Along with the introduction of an all-volunteer military service, mandatory registration with the Selective Service System was suspended in

1975. However, following the invasion of Afghanistan by the Soviet Union in 1980, a requirement that all men between the ages of 18 and 26 be registered for a potential military draft was reinstated. Through a proclamation signed that year by President Jimmy Carter, all eligible men must register with the Selective Service System within 30 days of their 18th birthday. Registration is done at U.S. post offices and at U.S. embassies overseas.

There have been occasional proposals to abolish the Selective Service System. One recent effort is that of the Cato Institute, which in 1997 urged Congress to abolish the system as "a relic of a different time and a different world."

For more information

Flynn, George Q. *The Draft, 1940–1973.* Lawrence: University Press of Kansas, 1993.

Selective Service System. http://www.sss.gov.

United States Government Manual. Washington, D.C.: U.S. Government Printing Office.

U.S. Code, Title 50 Appendix, secs. 451–473.

Jerry E. Stephens

Seminole Tribe of Florida v. Florida 517 U.S. 44 (1996)

Seminole Tribe of Florida v. Florida, was a Supreme Court decision that restricted severely the ability of Native Americans to sue states that would not enter into negotiations with tribes that wanted to offer gambling on their land. Specifically, the Supreme Court ruled that the Native American tribes that were being stonewalled by some state governments in their effort to get the rights to offer commercial casinos on reservations could not sue states under the auspices of the 1988 INDIAN GAMING REGULATORY ACT (IGRA) when states were not negotiating "in good faith."

For example, officials in the governor's office of the state of Florida continually held discussions with the Seminole tribe but found multiple ways of stalling and preventing negotiations for tribal gambling in that state to proceed at a reasonable pace. Thus, the state was intentionally preventing the tribe from being able to offer full-scale casino games. After the *Seminole v. Florida* decision, the tribe cannot sue the state for this intentional stonewalling. The case marks a significant change in public policy that is in favor of states and against the interest of Native American tribes.

The 5-4 decision by the Court was along ideological lines, with the more conservative justices (Scalia, Rehnquist, Thomas, O'Connor, and Kennedy) voting in the majority in favor of states and the more liberal justices (Breyer, Ginsburg, Souter, Stevens) voting in the minority in favor of the tribes. The case pivoted on the majority's conclusion that the U.S. Constitution's Eleventh Amendment guarantee to the states of sovereign immunity protects them against lawsuits by Native American tribes. States should negotiate for a compact in good faith, as specified by the IGRA, but if they do not, then the tribes have no standing in court.

Though the *Seminole v. Florida* decision has prevented since 1996 lawsuits filed by tribes against states that do not negotiate in good faith, most tribes in the United States that wanted to offer casinos were able to begin doing so (and still do so) under the specifications of the IGRA between 1988, when that legislation was signed into law, and 1996.

The most famous Native American casino is operated by the Mashantucket Pequot Indians and is located in Foxwoods, Connecticut. In terms of square footage, it is the largest casino in existence. It is also immensely profitable, given its location between Boston, Massachusetts, and New York, New York. The Pequots won from Connecticut the right to offer full-scale casinos only after a federal court in 1991 agreed with them that the state of Connecticut had not negotiated in good faith. Such a decision, without the Supreme Court overturning *Seminole v. Florida,* could not happen today.

For more information

Mason, John Lyman, and Michael Nelson. *Governing Gambling*. Washington, D.C.: Brookings Institution Press, 2001.

Mason, W. Dale. *Indian Gaming: Tribal Sovereignty and American Politics*. Norman: University of Oklahoma Press, 2000.

John Lyman Mason

Senior Executive Service The Senior Executive Service (SES) was established by Title IV as part of the CIVIL SERVICE REFORM ACT OF 1978. The creation of the SES was designed to help address a number of problems. Among them were (1) the lack of a uniform system for managing executive government positions, (2) a low level of attention paid to certifying managerial skill and expertise, (3) limited authority and flexibility to appoint or reassign individuals to meet program/agency needs, and (4) a growing need to increase the pay and status of top-level career administrators.

Consisting of senior-management-level federal employees, the purpose of the service is to "ensure that the executive management of the Government of the United States is responsive to the needs, policies and goals of the nation and otherwise is of the highest quality." The goals of the Senior Executive Service include improving the executive management of government, selecting and developing senior executives with leadership expertise, holding executives accountable for performance and linking pay with performance, and ensuring an executive system guided by public interest and free from improper political influence.

The SES's 7,000 members include high-level managerial, supervisory, and other executive-level positions throughout the executive branch of the federal government. Certain positions are excluded from the Senior Executive Service, such as those within the judicial branches of government as well as intelligence-gathering agencies (such as the Central Intelligence Agency) and the Foreign Service. By providing one distinct personnel system for all members, the Senior Executive Service was envisioned as an opportunity to improve executive management in government by selecting and developing outstanding senior executives and to provide a system that held individuals accountable for and rewarded both individual and organizational performance.

The Office of Personnel Management distributes executive openings to each federal agency on a two-year basis upon an agency request. Senior-level administrators and managers who are eligible for the SES can voluntarily choose to leave their federal civil service positions in return for multiyear performance contracts that have the potential for providing greater salaries, career growth, and job flexibility.

For more information

Huddleston, M. W., and W. W. Boyer. *The Higher Civil Service in the U.S.: Quest for Reform*. Pittsburgh, Pa.: University of Pittsburgh Press, 1996.

U.S. Office of Personnel Management. "Executive Core Qualifications." Available online. URL: http://www.opm.gov/ses/ html.

Dahlia Bradshaw Lynn

separation of powers Separation of powers is a distinctive feature and integral part of the American constitutional polity and the administration of public affairs. The principle of the separation of powers is embedded in the U.S. Constitution, especially in the first section of each of the first three articles of the Constitution, in which the tripartite arrangement of legislative, executive, and judicial powers is adumbrated.

The principle of separating powers, strongly advocated by the likes of James Madison, in part due to his reading of like analysts of Locke and Montesquieu especially, fears the exercise of arbitrary power more than any disadvantages caused by shared power. As a result, shared governance and its concomitant, political friction, is a necessary and proper characteristic of our political architecture.

The animating purpose of the principle of separation of powers is clearly seen in the words of Associate Justice Louis D. Brandeis: "The doctrine of the separation of powers was adopted by the convention of 1787, not to promote efficiency but to preclude the exercise of arbitrary power. The purpose was, not to avoid friction, but, by means of the inevitable friction incident to the distribution of the governmental powers among three departments, to save the people from autocracy." As a result, we have, in the design and fabric of our system of public policy making, autonomous institutions but not completely independent institutions.

The principle of separation of powers entails what James Madison referred to as "the necessary partition of power among the several departments as laid down in the Constitution." One of Madison's principal concerns was not simply how to craft such a "necessary partition" in a governing document, but more important, how to maintain such a separation of power in practice. For Madison—and what we see of separation of powers in the text of the Constitution is largely a Madisonian vision—separating governmental powers was based on logic and experience. "But what is government itself," Madison asked, "but the greatest of all reflections on human nature? If men were angels, no government would be necessary. If angels were to govern men, neither external nor internal controls on government would be necessary." Thus, the attempt by the framers of the Constitution to establish and maintain a political system that would provide for power and protect liberty concurrently was, in the words of Justice Brandeis, "a classic expression of the eighteenth-century hope that freedom could be secured by calculated inefficiency in government."

In such a system, whereby authority is allocated among distinct actors at different levels of government, the actors are separated but they are not hermetically sealed from one another. The policy makers are interdependent but not isolated, distinct but not distant. Power and responsibility are intermingled among the three branches as these dispersed powers function to produce a workable government. We find here an explicit, intentional effort to cabin power without making impossible its necessary and proper exercise. Of course, since the inception of the republic, the crucial issues and critical debates in the American polity invariably flow from the subtleties and puzzles that inevitably arise due to the application of the doctrine of separation of powers in internal and external affairs.

For more information

Fisher, Louis. *Constitutional Conflicts between Congress and the President.* Lawrence: University of Kansas Press, 1997.

Neustadt, Richard E. *Presidential Power: The Politics of Leadership.* Boston: Wiley, 1960.

Stephen K. Shaw

September 11, 2001, events of   See EVENTS OF 11 SEPTEMBER 2001.

sexual harassment policy   Sexual harassment consists of illegal behaviors in the workplace, such as requesting sexual favors as a condition of continued employment and creating a work environment that makes it hard, if not impossible, for individuals to perform their duties.

Since the EQUAL EMPLOYMENT OPPORTUNITIES COMMISSION (EEOC) first issued rules defining sexual harassment in 1980 and declared it a form of sex discrimination prohibited under the Civil Rights Act of 1964, the awareness of the implications of sexual harassment in the workplace has risen among policy makers, public administrators, business owners, and corporations in the United States. A precise definition of sexual harassment is not easy to obtain. Generally, however, the EEOC has defined it:

Unwelcome sexual advances, requests for sexual favors, and other verbal or physical conduct of a sexual nature constitute sexual harassment when (1) submission to such conduct is made either explicitly or implicitly a term or condition of an individual's employment, (2) submission to or rejection of such conduct by an individual is used as the basis for employment decisions affecting such individual, or (3) such conduct has the purpose or effect of unreasonably interfering with an individual's work performance or creating an intimidating, hostile, or offensive working environment.

Two basic types of sexual harassment exist: quid pro quo and hostile work environment claims. *Quid pro quo* is a legal phrase which generally means "something for something." In sexual harassment policy, a quid pro quo plaintiff claims that a supervisor or someone in a position of authority offered workplace benefits in exchange for sexual favors or threatened to take away benefits if sexual favors were not exchanged. In a quid pro quo sexual harassment claim, workers assert that because of their gender they are forced to meet demands or comply with conditions that other workers do not face.

One of the first and most influential quid pro quo cases was *Barnes v. Costle,* 561 F. 2d 983 (1977), in which a three-judge U.S. Court of Appeals claimed that a woman forced to have sex to keep her job would not have been a victim "except for her womanhood." Under this precedent, quid pro quo sexual harassment had a legal basis for redress by holding that employees who spurned the sexual advances of their supervisors should not lose their jobs. More recently, employers can also be held responsible for a supervisor's behavior even when they have no knowledge of the harassing behavior. According to *Faragher v. City of Boca Raton, Florida,* 118 S. Ct. 2275 (1998), employers should distribute their policies on sexual harassment and establish preventive and complaint procedures to protect themselves against sexual harassment charges.

The U.S. Supreme Court held in *Meritor Savings Bank v. Vinson,* 477 U.S. 57 (1986), that sexual harassment included the creation of a hostile work environment as a direct harm. Further, the Court ruled that it did not matter whether the victim voluntarily submitted to advances or submitted under duress as long as sexual advances were shown to be unwelcome. If a hostile work environment severely impairs an employee's ability to function and creates an abusive work environment, the employer is usually liable for the discriminatory acts of supervisors. Furthermore, another Supreme Court ruling in *Harris v. Forklift Systems, Inc.,* 510 U.S. 17 (1993), held that the hostile or abusive work environment does not have to be psychologically injurious as long as the environment interferes with the employee's work performance. All employers should know that sexual harassment is not limited to males harassing females. Under existing case law, female superiors can also be held liable for harassing male employees. Similarly, the courts have ruled in favor of plaintiffs in same-sex harassment cases, holding that same-sex harassment cases are actionable under Title VII of the Civil Rights Act of 1964.

Compared with the 1980s, with 5,849 sexual harassment claims filed with the EEOC, the 1990s have witnessed an explosion of EEOC sexual harassment filings, with a total of 37,725 from 1990 until 1999. This may be partly attributed to changing social attitudes toward reporting sexual harassment in the workplace. Largely, however, the legal environment has been altered by court interpretations of sexual harassment. These court decisions have expanded the definition of sexual harassment and have made it easier for plaintiffs to come forward. In addition, states have adopted fair-employment practices that prohibit sexual harassment, and many of their laws are more stringent than federal law.

Judgments in sexual harassment cases routinely exceed $1 million. Not including the legal fees for defending against sexual harassment civil suits, which average around $250,000 per civil suit, the U.S. Department of Labor estimates that workplaces in the United States lose $1 billion annually from absenteeism, low morale, new employee training, and employee replacement costs related to sexual harassment. "EEOC Settles Bias Suit For $2.8 Million against TWA," "Harassment Costs Ford: $8-Million Payout Joins $10 Million to Educate Workers," and "Mitsubishi Settles Sexual Harassment Suit for $34 Million" are just a few of the headlines that alert us to the costs of not formulating successful sexual harassment prevention and grievance policies. Given the costs associated with sexual harassment, employers in the private and public sectors should take the development of sexual harassment preventive policies and grievance procedures seriously.

For more information

Levy, Anne C., and Michele A. Paludi. *Workplace Sexual Harassment*, 2d ed. Upper Saddle River, N.J.: Prentice Hall, 2002.

Strickland, Ruth Ann. "Sexual Harassment: A Legal Perspective for Public Administrators." *Public Personnel Management* 24 (winter 1995): 493–513.

Ruth Ann Strickland

Simon, Herbert (1916–2001) *economist, management specialist* Herbert Simon was a cross-disciplinary intellectual who made numerous contributions to public administration. He was responsible for challenging the mid-20th-century model of the rational economic man by offering up the concept of the SATISFICING man, which was based on the assumption of bounded rationality.

Born in Milwaukee, Wisconsin, on 16 June 1916, Simon was educated in political science at the University of Chicago, where he received a B.A. in 1936 and a Ph.D. in 1943. In addition to 52 years of teaching, researching, and publishing in the fields of artificial intelligence, psychology, administration, and economics, Simon was awarded some of the disciplines' highest honors, most notably the Alfred Nobel Memorial Prize in Economic Sciences in 1978 and the National Medal of Science in 1986.

In his book *Administrative Behavior* (1947), Simon advocates the use of the scientific method in studying administrative phenomena and states that decision making is the center of administration. Simon argues that it was unrealistic, in fact impossible, for decision makers to use the optimizing model, cost-benefit analysis, or the Progressives' ideal of system-wide planning because of bounded rationality—the limits of human ability to process information. According to Simon, these economic-based models of decision making require individuals to recognize all of their possible choices and be able to calculate the consequences of each one.

Simon described three kinds of boundaries associated with human rationality: (1) individuals are limited by unconscious skills, habits, and reflexes; (2) individuals are limited by values that may influence decision making; and (3) individuals are limited by the extent of their knowledge about things relevant to performing tasks. Accordingly, when decision makers are faced with complex problems, they forgo optimizing—which involves determining precisely the best solution and is beyond human capabilities—and instead "satisfice" or make choices that are good enough, rather than the best. Simon referred to this decision maker as the administrative man—one who deals with the daily uncertainties of decision making in the public sector and must cope with his or her own human limitations and lack of knowledge about the particular problem to be solved.

Take, for instance, the shift supervisor at a nuclear power plant. On an ordinary day she is concerned with scheduling workers, making sure that those employees who are working are doing their assigned tasks, and monitoring the overall operation of the power plant. However, when a warning light comes on signaling a potential problem in the nuclear reactor, the shift supervisor, who is by no means an expert in the operation of the plant's multiple safety systems, must immediately take action by making a decision that is "good enough." She cannot optimize because there is not enough time, the system is too complicated, and she lacks the capacity to understand the technical specifications of each of the literally thousands of components that make up the operating system. Thus, she "satisfices," or makes a decision that will both satisfy and suffice given the circumstances.

Simon also examined the willingness of workers to obey commands from superiors. According to Simon, workers will obey only those commands that are perceived to be within a "zone of acceptance," or reasonable. Chester Barnard referred to this concept as the "zone of indifference." If a supervisor tells a subordinate to perform a given task in a specified manner, the subordinate will not object as long as the request appears reasonable; however, if the suggestion lies outside of the "zone of acceptance," then the worker will offer resistance or even disobey the order altogether.

Besides challenging the assumptions of mid-20th-century economic theory, Simon is most noted for the extent of his cross-disciplinary contributions. In addition to receiving top honors in economics, computer science, and psychology, Simon was awarded honors in public administration and artificial intelligence. Simon drew upon both the natural and social sciences in developing theories, and it was the language of computers that enabled Simon to develop models for both human and organizational problem solving that remains valuable for public administrators today.

For more information

Simon, Herbert. *Administrative Behavior.* New York: Free Press, 1947.

Simon, Herbert A. "The Proverbs of Administration," *Public Administration Review* 6 (1946): 53–67.

Jonathan Greenblatt

Small Business Administration   The Small Business Administration (SBA) is a federal agency created in 1953 for the purpose of assisting, advising, educating, and protecting the interests of small businesses and their owners.

While the phrase *small business* usually evokes the image of a small, family-owned and -operated retail store, the SBA is dedicated to working with a broad range of commercial ventures, including but not limited to: growing and harvesting agricultural crops; fishing; mining; hydroelectric and fossil fuel electric power generation; manufacture of pet foods, pesticides, chocolate products, explosives, computers, and electronic products; and provision of postal, courier, warehousing, and information services. For each type of business, the SBA establishes the upper limit of "small," expressed in terms of the number of individuals employed by a business, or by the annual receipts of a business.

The U.S. economy is directly linked to the success of small businesses. These enterprises, responsible for 47 percent of all sales in the United States, employ 53 percent of the private-sector workforce. Federal government statistics indicate that the number of small businesses started through self-employment grew 40 percent between 1976 and 1996, and statistics show continuation of this trend toward increasing prevalence, popularity, and importance of small businesses. Additionally, current data showing that 52 percent of small businesses are home-based also indicate that this percentage is likely to increase as technological advances allow more entrepreneurs to operate profitable commercial endeavors without leasing or purchasing space intended solely for business purposes.

By assisting small businesses, SBA helps the United States maintain its competitive position in the increasingly diverse world marketplace. Agency statistics demonstrate that small businesses are not afflicted with the inertia that prevents larger enterprises from adopting new, more efficient methods of accomplishing tasks, or from quickly adapting to new technology or software. For instance, a disproportionately high percentage of innovative ideas and devices are introduced by small businesses, and a similarly large percentage of high-technology jobs are found in small businesses.

In most situations, the SBA does not loan money directly to small businesses. Instead, SBA guarantees banks' loans to small businesses that do not meet the usual criteria required to borrow money but need working capital for business startups; financing construction or expansion of a business's physical plant; or acquiring equipment, facilities, machinery, supplies, or materials that are necessary to maintain the competitive position of a small business.

When a community has been ravaged by a natural disaster, such as a flood, tornado, or fire, SBA makes an exception to its general "no direct loans" policy. SBA's reason for making its own funds available in this situation is that the agency's own, prior experience has demonstrated that a devastated community can recover its vitality only if the local economy is quickly stabilized with sufficient capital to expedite rebuilding the businesses that provide jobs and essential goods and services for the community.

In collaboration with federal purchasing agencies and private contractors, SBA has developed policies and procedures ensuring the award of a "fair proportion" of government and large private contracts to small businesses, particularly those owned by disadvantaged groups or women.

SBA seeks to reach out to as many entrepreneurs as possible and to provide services to not only maintain viability of business ventures, but to also encourage success of a broad range of endeavors that are involved with many different sectors of the U.S. economy. As part of this effort to communicate with and assist every type of small business, SBA has created a network of "resource partners," including lenders, development companies, and business resource centers. In accordance with SBA's policy of using the most current technology available to provide assistance and support to small businesses, SBA information and services are available at both SBA offices throughout the United States and SBA websites on the Internet.

For more information

American Bar Association. *ABA Legal Guide for Small Businesses*. Washington, D.C.: American Bar Association, 2000.

Small Business Administration. http://www.sba.gov.

Small Business Administration publications. http://www.sbaonline.sba.gov/aboutsba/indexprofile.html.

Beth Simon Swartz

social capital   Social capital refers to the interactions and networks formed by society in general and its subsequent collective value.

Sociologist Pierre Bourdieu was the first to use the term *social capital* in the late 1970s to describe the advantages and opportunities accruing to people through membership in certain communities. Another sociologist, James S. Coleman, used the term to describe a resource that emerges among people as a result of their interpersonal ties. He defined social capital according to its function within the social structure, stating that the changing relationships among individuals create a form of capital that is as important as monetary, physical, or human capital for achieving success.

Coleman's theories of social capital refer to the aspects of a social structure that facilitate action and include both vertical and horizontal associations, the vertical associations characterized by hierarchical relationships and an unequal distribution of power, and the horizontal associations formed among peers. According to Coleman, individuals possess social capital and use it as a resource for action embedded in the relationships between and among them. In a similar sense, the World Bank defines social capital as the "norms and social relations embedded in social structures that enable people to coordinate action and to achieve desired goals." It refers to the collective value of all social networks and the trust, reciprocity, information, and cooperation generated by those social networks. Whereas physical capital refers to material objects and human capital refers to traits and abilities possessed by individuals, social capital "refers to connections among individuals—social networks and the norms of reciprocity and trustworthiness that arise from them."

Any occurrence that makes individuals less dependent upon one another destroys social capital. Drawing from economic models, Coleman viewed social capital like other forms of capital in that it depreciates over time if the social relationships are not maintained or renewed. Social capital, which exists to varying degrees in all organizations, is useful because it facilitates the achievement of organizational goals that would not be achieved in its absence.

There are two types of social capital: (1) bonding social capital that strengthens relationships within a network, and (2) bridging social capital that links one network with another, thus expanding opportunities for disseminating information and developing reciprocity. Robert Putnam, in his article "Bowling Alone: America's Declining Social Capital" (*Journal of Democracy* [1995]: 65–78), identified three elements that are necessary for the development of social capital—trust, reciprocity, and dense social networks. Trust is of prime importance as it forms the foundation for building social capital. Reciprocity refers to the give and take that occurs between individuals and groups. Even if the return is not immediate, social capital relies upon the assumption that all actions are reciprocal in nature. Dense, well-connected networks rich in reciprocity confer the greatest benefits, as a key feature of social capital is the benefit derived from coordination and cooperation among the members of an association.

Social capital tends to be cumulative, so that the components of trust, communication, rich networks, and shared norms increase with each successful interaction. A positive experience in one endeavor builds trust, social connections, and information that facilitates future interactions and collaborations among individuals and groups.

The decline of civic engagement in American society has been documented over the past 40 years. For example, membership in organizations such as religious congregations, civic and fraternal orders, labor unions, the Boy Scouts, the Red Cross, and parent-teacher associations has steadily declined.

For more information

Coleman, James S. *Foundations of Social Theory.* Cambridge, Mass.: Harvard University Press, 1990.

Putnam, Robert D. *Bowling Alone.* New York: Simon and Schuster, 2000.

Sharon Timberlake and Douglas D. Ofiara

social entrepreneurship Social entrepreneurship refers to the adaptation of market-based for-profit entrepreneurial techniques and approaches to the nonprofit sector.

Social entrepreneurship has gained momentum in the face of an identified and apparently growing gap between the provision of services for which government has traditionally had a responsibility and the demand for services arising in the community at large. Recognition of these unmet needs by nonprofit and charitable organizations has presented a dilemma. While private-sector organizations are obviously unable to provide services for those unable to pay for them, many nonprofit organizations have goals and missions to do just this. Social entrepreneurship has emerged as a means to generate the resources needed to address these problems. It is also regarded by many as a major change in the approach to welfare.

This is a new and emerging term, the definition for which is not fixed. There are four definitions that are currently in use, with different levels of emphasis on means and outcomes:

- Social entrepreneurship as the adoption of business expertise and market-based skills to the community sector

- Social entrepreneurship as cross-sectoral collaboration, for example between governance and community, or business and community
- Social entrepreneurship as the introduction of initiatives intended to produce far-reaching outcomes in the form of dramatic measurable change
- Social entrepreneurship that involves an innovative and original process, with a dramatic and positive outcome. This should be as the result of surplus-generating activities utilized to create social benefits.

At a practical level, social entrepreneurship operates as a type of rallying cry for nonprofit organizations in the new century, as they deal with globalization, shrinking welfare expenditure, and arguably reduced power and capacity of the nation-states to address welfare issues. Social entrepreneurs have led by example, adopting innovative solutions for long-term social problems for which resources are scarce. The triple bottom line of profit, community, and environment—often espoused by market corporations in plans and annual reports—is used to persuade corporate decision makers that it is in their interest to collaborate with the nonprofit sector.

Typically, this can take a number of forms, including direct donation of funds, in-kind support through the provision of the corporation's goods at reduced or no cost, and the facilitation of employee volunteering of time and expertise. Suffice it to say, activities vary enormously in scale and field of endeavor while sharing characteristics of flexibility, innovation, and capacity to result in social change.

Networks of like-minded organizations have sprung up all over the Western and non-Western world. Ideas and expertise are thus shared in a way that exemplifies the market contrast between market entrepreneurs and social entrepreneurs.

For more information

Canadian Centre for Social Entrepreneurship. http://www.bus.ualberta.ca/CCSE.

Community Wealth Ventures, Inc. http://www.communitywealth.org.

Megan Alessandrini

Social Security Administration   The Social Security Administration (SSA) is the government organization charged with administering the Social Security system of the United States.

Since 1995, the SSA once again exists as an entirely independent government agency, as it did in the 1940s and early 1950s. However, it has gone through a number of organizational incarnations since first being founded as the Social Security Board (SSB) during Franklin Delano Roosevelt's presidential administration in 1935.

This shifting organizational history was inaugurated on 29 June 1934, when Roosevelt appointed the Committee on Economic Security to make recommendations to the Congress on policy responses to the Great Depression. The Social Security Act of 1935 was the major piece of resulting legislation, under whose terms the SSB was first created. Consisting of three presidentially appointed commissioners, directing such personnel as could be donated by other agencies, the SSB at first had no budget, facilities, or staff of its own. By the time it was absorbed in the new subcabinet level Federal Security Agency in 1939, however, the SSB had overseen the creation of field offices and records, the distribution of applications (through the Post Office) for Social Security numbers, and (in March 1937) the paying out of the first low, old-age-assistance benefits to pensioners. In 1939, legal amendments also brought dependents' and survivors' benefits into the ambit of programs to be administered by the SSB.

It was not until after the Second World War, by order of President Harry Truman in 1946, that the SSB was abolished and the Social Security Administration was first established under that name. In 1953, when President Dwight

Eisenhower abolished also the Federal Security Agency itself, the SSA became part of the newly created Department of Health, Education and Welfare (HEW). The responsibilities of the HEW expanded upon the passage of legislation expanding the definition of disability in 1956, the Medicare program in 1965, as well as the Supplemental Security Income (SSI) program enacted under President Richard Nixon in 1972. Though legal changes in 1977 meant that Medicare and Medicaid were to be administered by the Health Care Financing Administration, the SSA had control of the SSI program.

The SSA remained a major part of the renamed DEPARTMENT OF HEALTH AND HUMAN SERV-ICES (HHS), which HEW became in 1980. In some respects, the SSA's responsibility contracted when the Omnibus Budget Reconciliation Act of 1981, under President Ronald Reagan, phased out students' benefits and young parents' benefits for children older than age 16. However, the 1980s also marked the reascendance of arguments that the SSA should become an independent agency again, with the 1981 National Commission on Social Security Reform (or the Greenspan Commission) recommending the matter be studied. After options were outlined in 1984 and legislative proposals followed, a law passed both houses of Congress unanimously in 1994, with President Bill Clinton signing it on August 15 of that year.

The SSA is today arguably an "agency under stress," according to Derthick. President Bill Clinton's term has made for new challenges and mixed messages, in that the welfare reform bill of 1996 has led to major restructuring of welfare programs at the same time as presidential promises were issued to "save Social Security First" in 1998. Expanding concepts of policy-relevant social risks have made for difficulties of assessment, with evidence existing to question, for example, the reliability of SSA disability determinations for mental disorders. Finally, as in all bureaucracies public and private, discretion in policy implementation raises vital problems of accountability to decision makers within the SSA. Such discretion may need to be limited by legislative curbs.

For more information

Derthick, Martha. *Agency under Stress: The Social Security Administration in American Government.* Washington, D.C.: Brookings Institution, 1990.

Kubitschek, C. A. "Social Security Administration Nonacquiescence: The Need for Legislative Curbs on Agency Discretion." *University of Pittsburgh Law Review* 50, no. 2 (1989): 399–456.

Okpaku, S. O., A. E. Sibulkin, and C. Schenzler. "Disability Determinations for Adults with Mental Disorders: Social Security Administration vs.

A 1934 poster for Social Security. (LIBRARY OF CONGRESS)

Independent Judgements." *American Journal of Public Health* 84, no. 11 (1994): 1791–1795.

Social Security Administration. http://www.ssa.gov/history/.

Eero Carroll

South Dakota v. Dole, Secretary of Transportation 483 U.S. 203 (1987)

In *South Dakota v. Dole, Secretary of Transportation,* the U.S. Supreme Court examined a federal mandate that states raise their legal drinking age to 21 as a condition for receiving federal highway funds.

In 1982 Congress passed the National Minimum Drinking Age Act (23 U.S.C. 158), which instructed the U.S. secretary of transportation to withhold from a state a portion of federal highway funds if the state allowed persons under 21 to purchase, possess, or consume any alcoholic beverage. South Dakota, which permitted persons 19 years old or older to purchase beer containing up to 3.2 percent alcohol, challenged the constitutionality of the law in U.S. District Court for the District of South Dakota, arguing that Article I of the Constitution bars the conditional grant of federal funds to states and that the Twenty-first Amendment to the Constitution allows states to make their own laws concerning alcohol. The district court dismissed the case and South Dakota appealed the ruling to the federal Court of Appeals for the Eighth District, but its claim was rejected there as well. The state then moved to appeal the case to the U.S. Supreme Court.

The U.S. Supreme Court upheld the appeals court decision in a 7-2 decision under Chief Justice Rehnquist, who also wrote the opinion. Justices Brennan and O'Connor dissented. In the Court's written opinion, Chief Justice Rehnquist argued that although Congress cannot regulate the drinking age directly, "the Constitution empowers Congress to 'lay and collect Taxes, Duties, Imposts, and Excises, to pay the Debts and provide for the common Defense and general Welfare of the United States.' Incident to this power, Congress may attach conditions on the receipt of federal funds."

Chief Justice Rehnquist went on to argue that the spending power of Congress was not unlimited. Based on the Constitution, he argued that (1) Congress's exercise of the spending power must be in pursuit of the general welfare, which Congress is allowed to determine; (2) if Congress tries to set conditions on funds received by states, it must make those conditions clear and unambiguous, so that states can make a knowledgeable choice; and (3) conditions on federal grants might be illegitimate if they are unrelated "to the federal interest in particular national projects or programs."

The Court's answer in this case was to argue that because the funds were for highway construction, and the federal government could argue that drunk driving was a problem on highways affecting the general welfare, indirect encouragement of specific state policies to obtain uniformity in state drinking-age laws is a valid use of the spending power. The net effect of the case was to expand the power of Congress to enact spending legislation by allowing it to use this power to encourage states to adopt policies consistent with the preferences of the national government. Thus, this case expanded the power of the national government at the expense of the states.

For more information

Gray, Virginia, Russell L. Hanson, and Herbert Jacob. *Politics in the American States: A Comparative Analysis,* 7th ed. Washington, D.C.: CQ Press, 1999.

Donald P. Haider-Markel

sovereign immunity   Sovereign immunity is a legal doctrine that protects government from lawsuits seeking money damages.

Two related theories support this legal doctrine. In the early Middle Ages, the English king was sovereign; his power might be checked by a group of barons (as in Magna Carta of 1215) or, later, by the Parliament. Since the king appointed judges, the courts couldn't be used to limit the king's power. In the modern period, some claim the sovereign (the president, the prime minister) acts on behalf of all the people. For that reason, no single individual should have the right to go to court to challenge a decision of the sovereign.

To a lawyer in the 21st century, "sovereign immunity" is the power of a government to define the forum, procedure, and limits on suits against itself. In some situations, legislation and court decisions have supported or upheld claims by the sovereign, perhaps a state governor, of immunity from suit. In other situations, legislation and court decisions effectively waived immunity, thereby allowing citizens to sue the sovereign.

This doctrine applies differently to four types of governments.

Sovereign immunity of the American federal government. The Supreme Court ruled in *United States v. Nordic Village* (1992) that statutes waiving the sovereign immunity of the United States "must be construed strictly in favor of the sovereign." That is, if a citizen or government employee seeks to sue the federal government and the federal government has not waived its immunity, our courts will not further consider the suit. Since the Constitution clearly states (Art. I, sec. 9) that no federal monies shall be paid out except "in consequence of appropriation made by law," federal sovereign immunity is more a defense against money judgments against the United States than a limit on citizens' suits against the federal government. Alternatively, the citizen can seek remedial legislation or take his complaint directly to the sovereign.

Sovereign immunity of American state and local governments. The Eleventh Amendment says that federal judicial power "shall not . . . extend to any suit against one of the . . . states by citizens of another state" or foreigners. In other words, outsiders can't sue a state in federal court. In the last years of the 20th century, the Rehnquist Supreme Court generally upheld claims of state sovereign immunity from suits filed in federal courts. For example, the Supreme Court held that a state could not be sued in federal court for patent infringement (*Florida Prepaid v. College Savings Bank*, 1999) or for employment discrimination in violation of the Americans with Disabilities Act (*University of Alabama v. Garrett*, 2001). These decisions create situations in which state and local governments can ignore otherwise valid federal laws.

Regarding suits potentially filed in state courts, the state legislature determines when sovereign immunity is waived for itself and for other governments (cities, school boards, etc.) within the state. Most state legislatures have given up some portion of their sovereign immunity. For example, most states permit citizens involved in a crash with a state-owned vehicle to sue the state for money damages. Also, when a state operates a business (as in the operation of college dormitories), the state is subject to the same rules as a business operating a similar facility.

Sovereign immunity of American Indian tribes. How can an Indian tribe in North Carolina or Massachusetts operate a large bingo hall when state law prohibits gambling and casinos? The Constitution (Art. 1, sec. 8) gives the Congress the power "to regulate commerce . . . with Indian Tribes." As interpreted by the Supreme Court, this means an Indian tribe is subject to suit only when Congress has authorized the suit or the tribe has specifically waived its "sovereign immunity" (*Three Affiliated Tribes v. World Engineering*, 1986). On Indian land, a tribe can assert its sovereign immunity from the enforcement of state gambling laws. Instances exist where individuals have joined together claiming to be a distinct Indian tribe and then seek federal recognition of their tribe, thereby allowing a lucrative bingo hall to be built on tribal lands.

Sovereign immunity in international relations. Until the past century, immunity of one foreign nation from suits in the courts of another nation was an undisputed principle of international law. Each nation was sovereign and could not be forced into the courts of a foreign land. In the first half of the 20th century, nations—particularly the Soviet Union and states in Eastern Europe—set up commercial trading and banking entities. International traders in other countries claimed that "immunity" of states engaged in these activities was not required by international law because "sovereign immunity" gave these state trading firms and banks an unfair advantage in competition with private firms in other lands. There is now a consensus in international and American law that a foreign state is immune from the jurisdiction of another nation's courts, except with respect to claims arising out of activities that can be carried on by businesses or private persons.

For more information

Florida Prepaid v. College Savings Bank, 119 Sup.Ct. 2199 (1999).

Gifis, Steven. *Barron's Dictionary of Legal Terms.* New York: Barron's Educational Series, 1983.

Jacobs, Clyde Edward. *The Eleventh Amendment and Sovereign Immunity.* Westport, Conn.: Greenwood Press, 1972.

Three Affiliated Tribes v. World Engineering, 457 U.S. 138 (1986).

United States v. Nordic Village, 503 U.S. 30 (1992).

University of Alabama v. Garrett, 99 Sup.Ct. 1240 (2001).

Volokh, Eugene. "Sovereign Immunity and Intellectual Property." *Southern California Law Review* 73 (2000): 1161.

Gayle Avant

spoils system   The spoils system is a practice whereby government benefits and jobs are given only to faithful followers of the political party in power. Closely aligned with the concept of "machine politics" of the 19th century, friends of those in power were rewarded with public positions, while enemies were often punished and removed from public employment.

During the 1800s a public office was viewed more as a prize to be won by those victorious at the ballot box than as a position to be earned through the virtues of skill, knowledge, and a commitment to serving the public. Rather than a competitive merit-based system such as the one in place today, government positions were awarded based on someone's connection to the party in power. "To the victor belong the spoils of the enemy," declared Senator Marcy in 1832. Since then, his name has been linked to the spoils system.

The spoils system was embedded in the spirit of the times, which suggested that the "common man" was capable of performing any and all positions in public service. As a result, after each election, communities would see sweeping changes in those employed by government. Gone were employees faithful to the previous party, and in their place would arrive employees who were faithful to the new party. This process would prove more and more damaging to public service provision as the skills required of public servants became more complex. As changes emerged on the public service landscape, no longer could the "common man" manage municipal water treatment plants, traffic and highway improvements, and sophisticated financial matters. Waste, corruption, incompetence, and graft became ever present in government employment, in part a direct result of the spoils system.

The difficulties associated with the spoils system reached their symbolic nadir with the assassination of President James A. Garfield on 2 July 1881, by "disgruntled office seeker" Charles J. Guiteau. Guiteau believed the president owed him a diplomatic position (ambassador to France) because of his support for Garfield in the election of 1880. As a result of this and other events, the Civil Service Reform Act of 1883 was enacted at the federal level in an effort to limit the fallout from an overly zealous spoils system.

In the end, civil service reform and the need for merit-based civil service would minimize the influence of the spoils system. Remnants of spoils remain in public service; however, at most levels of public employment, merit rather than party affiliation is the norm.

For more information

MacDonald, Austin. *American City Government and Administration*. New York: Thomas Crowell, 1938.

Ross, Bernard H., and Myron A. Levine. *Urban Politics*, 5th ed. Itasca, Ill.: F. E. Peacock, 1996.

Robert A. Schuhmann

state-level administrative procedure acts

State-level administrative procedures acts are state replications of the spirit of corresponding federal administrative procedures acts. There are two areas where states utilize administrative procedures in the conduct of their business.

The first of these areas is the establishment of administrative rules or regulations that govern the operations of various state agencies. Common use of these administrative rules is found in fish and game rules, prison conduct rules, social welfare eligibility rules, and university and school conduct rules. These rules are crafted by the relevant state agency under the following general guidelines:

- Rules are legislatively authorized in the statutes.
- Draft rules are circulated to interested parties.
- Notice of a hearing is provided in a newspaper of general circulation.
- Interested parties have an opportunity to present written and oral testimony on the draft rules.
- After hearings, the final rules are drawn up and notice is given of intent to file.
- The final rules are filed with the appropriate state officer. When the rules are filed, they

have the "force and effect" of law and are enforced as appropriate. In the case of fish and game rules, the enforcement may be via the criminal justice system. In the case of university rules and regulations, the enforcement may be via an administrative hearing committee.

State administrative procedures acts also often provide for the rules and conduct of "contested case" hearings held under the authority of the administrative rule. For example, a student at the state university is accused of disrupting the operations of the animal laboratory in the medical school, where experiments are conducted to measure the effects of a drug or medicine on laboratory animals. While the disruption may well be a criminal act (breaking and entering, disruption of government operations, etc.), the act by one member of the university (the student) could be seen to endanger the entire university. If the university had an administrative rule that prohibited its members (students, faculty, and employees) from disrupting university operations, charges might be filed against the student, not for a criminal charge, but rather for an administrative charge—disrupting the operations of the university.

Under this scenario, the accused student would be given a contested-case administrative hearing. At such a hearing:

- A statement of charges would be provided to the accused student
- A statement of the possible sanctions or punishments that could be awarded would be provided to the student
- A statement of the rules of the hearing, including the membership of the committee that would hear the charges, would be provided.
- The student would be able to receive copies of evidence to be used against him.
- The student would be able to seek assistance from other parties. (Some states permit attorneys to represent parties in contested case hearings.)

- The student would be able to confront and question witnesses who testified against him.
- The student could testify in his own behalf but could not be required to testify.
- The student would receive a copy of the findings of the committee and be given notice of his appeals within the university if he was not satisfied with either the findings or the sanction that might be imposed by the committee. After all administrative remedies had been exhausted, the student could appeal his case to the state or federal courts. These administrative hearings provide quasi-judicial means to deal with grievances, problems, and disciplinary cases within the state agencies and their operations.

The advantage to the state in these administrative procedures provisions is the ability to move more quickly to refine rules and regulations such as fish and game bag limits, or to recognize that agencies have special expertise and needs that are generally best protected in an in-house manner, such as in the example of the university disruption above.

In both the creation of rules and administrative hearings, protection of the rights of the public and the individual is provided by an open hearing process in the rule drafting and adjudication. Rules are checked by the appropriate state officer in the case of rule making; in the case of adjudication, the result can be appealed to the formal court system.

For more information
Administrative Codes for American States: Hawaii. *Revised Statutes,* chap. 91.

Bruce L. Bikle

strategic management Strategic management is a doctrine that provides tools for managers in their effort to analyze the organization's internal attributes and its external conditions, and on that basis to decide about basic action lines in order to achieve the overall goals of the organization. Thus, the basic idea of strategic management is to ensure that the organization is capable of high performance and of long-term profitability when interacting with a competitive environment.

The word *strategy* derives from the Greek *strategos,* referring to military leadership. It entered the English vocabulary in the 1680s. It originally encompassed the overall view of what must be done to win a war.

Strategic management in its modern form emerged and became widely practiced in the business sector after World War II, but spread rapidly to voluntary and public organizations as well. It gained ground in the 1960s when corporate planning was transformed into fashionable strategic planning. This was a time of a rapidly changing business environment and increased competition. The writers behind this new doctrine were Alfred Chandler, H. Igor Ansoff, and Kenneth Andrews. Ansoff's *Corporate Strategy* (1965) was possibly the single most influential work in this field. At that time, the focal point was determining the proper combination of products and markets for a firm.

Strategic planning lost some of its popularity in the 1970s and in the following decade, when it was largely replaced by a concept of strategic management. Strategic thinking had broadened to include issues of organizational capability and management of change. Later, the implementation of strategy also gained increasing attention among those who applied and developed this management concept further.

There are two broad families in the field of strategic thinking. The older one is analytically oriented, hard-line strategic thinking, including such approaches as the planning school, design school, and positioning school. The other family of approaches can be called soft-line strategic thinking, emphasizing the role of people, social relations, and the actual strategy process. Its early forms include the excellence factors of Peters and Waterman. In the course of time, it became a diffuse field of approaches, including the learning school, the cultural school, logical incrementalism, and many others.

Early developments of strategic management occurred in hard-line strategic thinking. This is visible in such models of portfolio management as the BCG Matrix and McKinsey's model. Another approach that spread worldwide in the 1980s and 1990s was based on conceptions developed by Michael Porter, whose 1980 seminal book *Competitive Strategy* opened up an analytical view to the question of how an organization can achieve long-term competitive advantage.

Strategic management is about building a "big picture" for an organization and bringing coherence to a perceivably fragmented world. It is about the organization's ability to understand what is happening in the environment, identifying need for change, mapping out options, and designing strategies and implementing them. This is, in fact, how it has contributed to the management practices of various organizations. Some organizations have been very successful in applying these techniques and methods, yet there are cases that have failed because of "paralysis of analysis" or other reasons.

The strategy process contains the following formal basic elements: defining the point of departure of an organization's strategy process, identifying strategic issues, formulating mission statements or broad goals, undertaking external and internal analyses (e.g., SWOT—strength, weakness, opportunities, threats—analysis), designing strategies and action plans, implementing a strategy, and monitoring and assessing performance. The key outcome of this process is a strategic plan that helps managers to steer an organization for long-term success.

For more information

Hitt, M., R. E. Freeman, and J. S. Harrison. *The Blackwell Handbook of Strategic Management.* Oxford, U.K.: Blackwell, 2001.

                              Ari-Veikko Anttiroiko

strategic planning   Strategic planning is a tool or mechanism for an organization to plan and communicate what the organization does, where it wants to go in the future, and how it will get there.

Beginning a strategic planning process requires assessing the organization's purpose by consulting both internal and external customers. Strategic plans generally include goals, objectives, performance measures, and strategies or activities. There is variation among the requirements for strategic planning across federal, state, and local governments. To maximize strategic planning potential, it should be used to direct setting goals and allocating resources to achieve results over time.

For most practitioners of strategic planning, one of the more complex issues is distinguishing between output goals and outcome goals. An outcome goal should be a description of the intended results, effects, or consequences that will occur from carrying out a program or activity. Output goals are descriptions of the level of activity or effort that will be produced over a period of time or by a specified date, including a description of the characteristics and attributes (e.g., time lines) established as standards in the course of conducting the activity or effort.

Also referred to as "managing for results" or "results-based management," strategic planning should begin with the development of a short mission statement that clearly states what the organization does and why it exists. At the federal level, strategic planning is mandated by the Government Performance and Results Act of 1993 and should contain the following strategic planning elements.

The first element a strategic plan should contain is a comprehensive mission statement covering the major functions and operations of the agency. General goals and objectives, including outcome-related goals and objectives, for the major functions and operations of the agency are required in the strategic plan. A description of how the goals and objectives are to be achieved, including a description of the resources required to meet those goals and objectives—operational processes, skills and technology, human capital, information—should also be included. A description of how the performance goals included in annual performance plans are related to the general goals and objectives of the strategic plan is needed, along with the identification of key factors external to the agency and beyond its control that could significantly affect achievement of the general goals and objectives. Finally, the strategic plan should include a description of the program evaluations used in establishing or revising general goals and objectives, along with a schedule for future program evaluations.

Each federal government agency should have a copy of its strategic plan accessible to the public and available on its website. The Treasury Department's website lists 11 goals in its strategic plan for 2000–2005. Each of Treasury's goals has corresponding objective and performance goals. One of the Treasury Department's goals—to manage the federal government's accounts—has the corresponding objective to ensure all federal payments are accurate and timely.

At the federal level, strategic plans are to cover at least five years and should be revised at least every three years. Strategic planning is by no means an easy process to improve an organization's planning efforts or performance. Among the various complexities is the need to include an effective assessment and explanation of linkages between goals, measures, and strategies. Many have referred to strategic planning as a major change in the way government has historically been conducted. As with most significant organizational changes, the visible successes of strategic planning have been slow. However, because the Government Performance and Results Act is a law requiring strategic planning, organizations should continue to improve strategic planning efforts.

For more information

Broom, C., et al. *Performance Measurement Concepts and Techniques,* 3d ed. Washington, D.C.: American Society of Public Administration's Center for Accountability and Performance, n.d.

U.S. General Accounting Office. *Managing for Results: Critical Issues for Improving Federal Agencies' Strategic Plans.* Publication no. GAO/GGD-97-180. Washington, D.C.: U.S. Government Printing Office, 1997.

U.S. Office of Management and Budget. *Circular A-11, part 2. Preparation and Submission of Strategic Plan, Annual Performance Plans, and Annual Program Performance Reports.* Washington, D.C.: U.S. Government Printing Office, July 2000.

Jamie Green

street-level bureaucrat *Street-level bureaucrat* is a term coined by Michael Lipsky to describe those government and service workers who provide direct services to clients. Examples of street-level bureaucrats include police officers, welfare caseworkers, and legal-aid office workers and attorneys.

In Lipsky's model of street-level bureaucrats, the clients often are those who have little power and are poor, minority-group members, or lacking the skills to negotiate the bureaucratic channels of government. Many of the clients of street-level bureaucrats are not voluntary. Criminal defendants, offenders dealing with police, and those who have immediate needs for welfare or social services are there under order or lack of other means to solve their problems.

Street-level bureaucrats utilize a great deal of discretion in their work. While the street-level bureaucrat is supposed to follow rather extensive and detailed administrative rules, policies, and procedures in the conduct of her/his work, these bureaucrats often find ways of exercising discretion to meet the needs of the clients for immediate care or services. Reasons for these incidents of discretion often include the perception that the system and the rules take too long, that adequate funding is not available to meet the needs of the client, or that the rules do not apply in the case at hand.

Another factor that contributes to the wide use of discretion is the ambiguous nature of much of the work of street-level bureaucrats. Policing is a good example. Many people believe that police are on duty to "do" law enforcement activity. But the actual conduct of law enforcement activity is a small part of a police officer's day. What police do in many cases is maintain order and provide service. Faced with the need to maintain order or to find the best way to provide services, many police officers innovate or judge the situation somewhat differently than the "official" job description might indicate. For example, it is common for a police officer not to arrest a suspect in a minor crime because of the burden of the paperwork in an arrest, the officer's belief that it won't do any good to arrest the person, or the officer's belief that it will actually undermine the task of maintaining an orderly community.

These situations can lead agency administrators and managers to view street-level bureaucrats as free agents who operate outside of the established rules, regulations, and job descriptions. This situation of broad discretion and "on the street" problem solving to get the job done can lead to the feeling by the street-level bureaucrats that the managers in headquarters "do not know what is happening on the street."

Street-level bureaucrats are thus distinguished by their ability to use discretion to get their work done and provide services to the public, but they are also subject to burnout and prone to cynicism concerning the established bureaucracy and the administrators who supervise these programs.

For more information

Lipsky, Michael. *Street Level Bureaucracy: Dilemmas of the Individual in Public Services.* New York: Russell Sage Foundation, 1980.

Bruce L. Bikle

strict scrutiny   Strict scrutiny is one of the standards applied by the U.S. Supreme Court in determining the constitutionality of laws or regulations created by the elected branches of government. While strict scrutiny is a relatively recent development in constitutional adjudication, it has become one of the most important standards for the protection of rights under the Constitution.

In the mid 1930s, the Supreme Court began reexamining the long-held belief that all rights are equal under the law. Despite the fact that the Constitution itself makes no hierarchical division among rights, justices such as William O. Douglas and Frank Murphy have argued that some were clearly more important than others. These and other liberally minded judges began to assert that some freedoms, such as those found in the First Amendment, were fundamental to any truly democratic process, and that those rights are clearly more important than others. Their argument was basically that democracy could continue without vigorous protection of property or other rights, but that it could not long exist without freedom of speech or of the press precisely because those rights are fundamental to the democratic enterprise.

This was not simply an academic debate, however. The logical conclusion for this type of argument was that legislation or executive action that impinged on these "preferred" or "fundamental" rights deserved far less judicial deference than legislation limiting the exercise of other, less important rights. This conclusion led to a two-tiered system for testing the constitutionality of laws passed by Congress or actions taken by the executive.

Laws that limit the exercise of nonpreferred or nonfundamental rights are judged on the basis of their reasonableness, subjected to only minimal scrutiny. If the law or regulation is reasonably related to a legitimate government purpose, then the law or regulation is normally presumed by the Supreme Court to be a constitutional exercise of power. Reasonableness represents a relatively low standard for the government to meet and makes regulation of nonfundamental rights relatively easy.

Laws that limit the exercise of fundamental or "preferred" freedoms are subject to a much higher standard of strict scrutiny. In cases involving preferred freedoms, the Supreme Court reverses its usual assumption of constitutionality of laws passed by Congress. Any law that limits the exercise of fundamental rights or freedoms is assumed by the Supreme Court to be unconstitutional until the government can show otherwise by meeting the strict-scrutiny standard.

Under strict scrutiny, the government must show that the law in question is tailored as narrowly and specifically as possible to accomplish its ends. It must demonstrate that the law in question is the least restrictive alternative capable of achieving those ends. A much higher bar to reach than reasonableness, strict scrutiny requires that the government show that the case before the Court represents a "clear and present danger" or that the legal limitation of the right constitutes a "compelling state interest" with no other, better alternative available to accomplish the same ends.

Strict scrutiny demands that any governmental limitations on our most important freedoms be scrutinized with the utmost care. It requires that any limitation of those rights be not just a reasonable exercise of governmental power but, rather, a limitation in furtherance of a "compelling interest" on the part of the state. Strict scrutiny requires not only that government pass good laws but also that it pass the best law.

For more information

O'Brien, David M. *Constitutional Law and Politics: Struggles for Power and Governmental Responsibility.* New York: W. W. Norton & Co., 1991.

Stephens, Otis H., Jr., and John M. Scheb II. *American Civil Liberties.* New York: West Publishing, 1999.

David A. May

subgovernments   Subgovernments operate as triads of power comprising a small circle of people with a vested interest in controlling a particular aspect of policy development and doing so with limited outside influence.

A subgovernment has three legs and comprises people from government, a related government agency, and a relevant interest group. The subgovernment acts independently from government branches but succeeds in controlling a fairly narrow range of programs because the parties only influence each other in the process of shaping policy. The subgovernment becomes dominant in the policy development process because it has a lock on controlling the decisions and outcomes in shaping such policies. But how does a subgovernment emerge, and why is it so effective in the policy development process?

A subgovernment seems to be impenetrable to external influence. People within it seem to dominate the outcomes of policy making because they create the terms and conditions within which the inner circle of interest operates. The subgovernment exists only because it meets the mutual interests of the interacting participants in controlling the agenda and shaping policy.

A subgovernment is therefore defined as an interlocking set of reciprocally supportive relationships that exists among a bureaucratic agency, the government, and a clientele group. This interlocking set of supportive relationships is why subgovernments have been called "cozy triangles." The players all know each other, they never stray beyond their particular field of interest, and they control the process because they have the information and power to do so.

All three legs of power find mutual support from the others, and policy is produced by this tripartite interaction. The notion of a subgovernment as an iron triangle is best explained by way of an example.

A typical government has jurisdiction over core societal issues such as health, and there is a department of health as well as a range of interest groups oriented toward health issues. The government has an elected member responsible for health, and this person engages with the head of the agency (the department of health) in order to learn about the department and its operations and to lend support to the agency's aims and objectives. The agency head needs the government to approve the agency's budget or to pass legislation that enables the agency to act on a specific health-related issue. It might be a sub-departmental agency devoted to a particular special interest of government in health, e.g., disease control. Both parties—government and agency—have a need to interact in a practical and effective manner, and a close relationship is established.

At the same time, government must be aware of what the client interest group(s) think of aspects of health, so in turn, it engages the relevant lobby groups. The common interest is a need to learn about the activities of each and to gain support for the public policy that is in focus. A close relationship is established, and a triangle of interests is formed whereby the government interacts with the agency, which interacts with the interest group, which in turn interacts with the government. All of the interactions have a purpose and a desired outcome. The key to the interaction is simply that it is with the same set of players and, therefore, is cozy.

The triangle is hard to break into by outside participants. Instead, participants often just switch locations. For example a participant of, say, the agency moves on, and he/she generally moves on to the associated interest group, thereby keeping the triangle of interest intact.

Subgovernments rarely exist today because of the high degree of transparency required of government, agencies, and interest groups. Each is subject to greater scrutiny than was the case when subgovernments dominated in the early 1950s. Most policy development now occurs with greater emphasis on mixing the relationships to gain input from a wider range of interested parties capable of participating in the policy development processes of government or its agencies. This has reduced the capa-bility for subgovernments to form and dominate the outcome.

Some observers have suggested that despite the continual injection of new issues and interests to the process, all that has happened is that the triangle has become floppy, resembling more of a hexagonal framework of interest. The power relationships have remained the same, but there are more players attempting to control the agenda. Consequently, there is less homogeneity and reciprocity in support than if it were a triangular affair, as more negotiation and compromise among the vested groups is required. Regardless of the shape of the framework of policy, the intent is still the same: each party wants to cooperate to achieve a certain outcome.

See also IRON TRIANGLES.

For more information

Heclo, H. "Issue Networks and the Executive Establishment." In *The New American Political System*, edited by Anthony King. Washington, D.C.: American Enterprise Institute, 1978.

Lowi, T. *The End of Liberalism*. New York: Norton, 1969.

Angela Magarry and Graham Magarry

substantial evidence Court review of actions by administrative agencies raises a question common to all cases on appeal: what standard does the reviewing court use to evaluate the decision? For judicial review of agency fact finding, courts have adopted "substantial evidence" as the appropriate standard.

A precise definition of substantial evidence has thus far eluded the courts. However, the history of cases describing the standard reveals a standard similar to that employed by courts when reviewing findings of facts made by juries. That is, if the record as a whole supports the finding by the agency, the court will not disturb the finding. Implicit in this definition is the prerequisite that the court is reviewing proceedings "on the record."

Early in the 20th century, as the scope of federal government activity increased—most notably in the realm of regulating interstate commence—appeals challenging agency actions also increased. In the interest of judicial efficiency, and out of deference to agency expertise in its realm of activity, the U.S. Supreme Court stated that factual findings of regulatory agencies would not be disturbed if they were supported by substantial evidence (*ICC v. Union R. Co.*, 222 U.S. 541, 547-548 [1912]).

Adoption of the ADMINISTRATIVE PROCEDURES ACT (APA) in 1946 signaled a move toward regularizing the work of government. Consistent with the larger constitutional scheme, judicial review of agency actions serves as part of the system of checks and balances incorporated into the APA. Section 706 of the act incorporates the substantial-evidence standard by stating that a reviewing court shall set aside agency actions, findings, and conclusions found to be unsupported by substantial evidence (5 U.S.C. sec. 706 [2][E]). Cases appealed to the Supreme Court following adoption of the APA raised the question of what this standard means. In *Universal Camera Corp. v. NLRB*, 340 U.S. 474 (1951), the Court likened the standard to that used for court review of jury findings.

More recently, the Supreme Court has analogized the substantial-evidence standard to that which could satisfy a "reasonable jury" (*Allentown Mack Sales and Service, Inc. v. NLRB*, 522 U.S. 359, 367 [1998]), a standard that is consistent with the definition set forth in the *Universal Camera* case decided 47 years earlier. Discussing application of the substantial-evidence standard to patent cases, the Supreme Court reiterated that "[t]his Court has described the APA court/agency 'substantial evidence' standard as requiring a court to ask whether a 'reasonable mind might accept' a particular evidentiary record as 'adequate to support a conclusion.' *Consolidated Edison* [*Co. v. NLRB*, 305 U.S. 197 (1938)] at 229" (*Dickinson v. Zurko*, 527 U.S. 150, 162 [1999]).

Regarding the actual application of this standard, it has been noted that the standard does vary based on the type of case. However, the common theme of court deference to agency action exists across case types, and courts are generally not inclined to reverse agency findings.

For more information
Strauss, Peter L., et al. *Administrative Law,* 9th ed. New York: Foundation Press, 1995.

Holly Taylor Sellers

sunset clauses   Insertion of sunset clauses in legislation has the effect of automatically terminating the regulation or functions of government (or government agency or board) on a certain date, as prescribed by the legislature. If legislators wish to continue the regulation or practice, they must act by passing a bill to that effect or the regulation/function will disappear from sight, like the sunset at the end of a day.

Sunset legislation takes on a number of time frames and forms, for example, from a short period of time (six months) in regard to experimental legislation to a longer time span (10 to 12 years) for legislation that automatically reviews all laws, agencies, boards, and functions of government. At first glance, sunset clauses appear to be a mere mechanistic means of reviewing legislative initiatives, but at their essence, sunset clauses go to deep philosophical questions over the role of government. Proponents of sunset clauses come from polar opposite positions. Libertarians tend to support sunset clauses as a weapon to wind back the state; at the other pole, communitarians are known to support sunset clauses as a means of making government laws and functions fulfill the role of creating public good.

In the early 1970s, sunset clauses became an issue of considerable dispute in the American Congress, where views were divided on their uses and their cost effectiveness. The concept of sunset clause then moved to the state legislatures and gradually gained support in a number of American states. By the turn of the century, 20 states had, to differing degrees, sunset clauses in their legislative systems.

The most prominent state to adopt sunset legislation was Texas, which did so in 1976. As a result, all government agencies and boards are reviewed in a 12-year cycle by the Texas Sunset Advisory Commission, which ascertains whether they should continue in existence, and, if so, how they could be improved. In Texas, as in other states, this process of review has become a site for political debate and lobbying. A clear example of this was over the September 2000 review of the Texas Natural Resources Conservation Commission, where environmental groups made submissions to the review and organized public rallies and petitions in an effort to improve and expand the agency's ability to protect the environment. In contrast, industrial opponents of the agency sought to weaken its powers.

At the national level, sunset clauses are now advocated as a means of protecting citizen rights. For example, in response to the antiterrorist laws that were promulgated after the 2001 terrorist attack on America, civil libertarians in America and Canada have argued for sunset clauses in these acts to protect the long-term civil rights of citizens in the two countries. In sum, sunset clauses are promoted as both a way of responding to exceptional circumstances and as a regular means for reviewing legislation and public agencies.

For more information
Sunset Advisory Commission. http://www.sunset.state.tx.us.

Gregory McCarthy

super-majority voting   Super-majority voting provisions require a greater than majority vote for decisions within a given legislative body.

Super-majority voting provisions are often part of a broader set of statutory and constitutional provisions, including: a balanced budget, limits on taxes and spending, and requirements for voter approval for new taxes.

New tax and spending limits have been introduced in a number of states requiring voter approval to raise taxes, super-majority vote requirements for the legislature to exceed tax and spending limits, and sanctions on government officials who violate these limits. This approach to fiscal discipline has been especially important in states that provide for citizen initiative and referendum to incorporate fiscal rules in their constitutions. Partly in response to this taxpayer revolt, state legislators have also introduced constitutional and statutory limits on the growth of taxes and spending, including super-majority vote requirements to increase taxes. As of 2003, 14 states now require a super-majority vote to raise taxes, and 13 states have introduced this legislation.

When these fiscal discipline mechanisms are incorporated in the constitution, they are more likely to constrain the growth of government. Statutory provisions are often perceived as less stringent constraints that can be ignored or evaded by legislators. In Colorado, for example, the constitutional tax and spending limits imposed through citizen initiative now constrain the growth of state and local government. Voter approval is required for any increase in taxes at all levels of government. The legislature can increase taxes in a temporary emergency, but this requires a two-thirds vote of both houses.

At the federal level, a constitutional amendment to require a super-majority vote to raise taxes has been introduced in Congress. Further, 29 states have passed a resolution calling for a constitutional convention to balance the federal budget. It is likely that such a balanced-budget provision would be accompanied by other fiscal discipline mechanisms now contained in state constitutions, including tax and spending limits, voter approval to raise taxes, super-majority vote

Table 1
The following 14 states require a super-majority to raise taxes

Arizona $\frac{2}{3}$*	Constitutional requirement adopted in 1992
Arkansas $\frac{3}{4}$*	Applies to taxes levied since 1934 Primarily pertains to sales and alcohol beverage taxes
California $\frac{2}{3}$*	Constitutional requirement adopted in 1980
Colorado $\frac{2}{3}$*	Temporary emergency taxes only, otherwise voter approval required
Delaware $\frac{3}{4}$*	Constitutional requirement adopted in 1980
Florida $\frac{3}{5}$*	Applies only to corporate income tax, was adopted in 1971 Florida also requires a $\frac{2}{3}$ majority of voters for any taxes proposed by constitutional amendment, which was adopted in 1996 by initiative
Louisiana $\frac{2}{3}$*	Adopted in 1996
Mississippi $\frac{3}{5}$*	Adopted in 1970
Missouri $\frac{2}{3}$*	Requires voter approval for any taxes that exceed $50 million or 1% of state revenues, whichever is less Adopted a constitutional amendment in 4/96
Nevada $\frac{2}{3}$*	Requires $\frac{2}{3}$ of elected legislature or voter approval Constitutional amendment adopted in 1996
Oklahoma $\frac{3}{4}$*	Requires $\frac{3}{4}$ of elected or voter approval Constitutional requirement adopted in 1992
Oregon $\frac{3}{5}$*	Constitutional requirement adopted 5/21/96
South Dakota $\frac{2}{3}$*	Required to enact new tax or increase existing tax rate or base Adopted in 1978, amended to apply to new taxes in 1996
Washington $\frac{2}{3}$	Tax increases raising revenue under the tax limitation require a $\frac{2}{3}$ vote of the legislature Any increase above the tax limitation requires voter approval Adopted in 1993

The following states have introduced legislation for a super-majority vote to increase taxes

Georgia	Provides that any new tax or an increase in any tax or license fee be approved by $\frac{3}{5}$ of the legislature
Hawaii	Amends the state constitution; provides that the levy of a new tax, an increase in tax rates, or repeal of a tax exemption or credit shall require the enactment of a law by $\frac{2}{3}$ of the elected members of each house of the legislature
Illinois	Proposes an amendment requiring a $\frac{3}{4}$ vote of each house on any bill increasing state revenue by increasing a tax on income or on the selling price of any personal property
Indiana	Requires a referendum to impose or increase any state tax without a $\frac{2}{3}$ majority vote in each house

Maine	Proposes an amendment to the Constitution of Maine to require a vote of $\frac{3}{5}$ of each house to enact or increase a tax or license fee
Michigan	Requires a $\frac{3}{5}$ vote of the legislature to raise certain taxes
Minnesota	Amends constitution to require a $\frac{3}{5}$ vote in each house for any bill that increases income or sales taxes
New Hampshire	Requires any change in state taxes after 1 July 1997 to be passed by a 60% majority in each house
New York	Proposes an amendment requiring a $\frac{2}{3}$ super-majority vote by each house on any bill increasing or decreasing taxes
Rhode Island	Proposes an amendment that would require a super-majority vote by each house on any bill that would increase the rate or amount of existing taxes or license fees
South Carolina	Requires a $\frac{2}{3}$ majority vote on the second reading of any bill imposing a new tax affecting more than 50% of the state's population
Tennessee	Requires a $\frac{2}{3}$ vote before all tax increases by any governmental body are to be approved
Utah	Requires a super-majority vote before the legislature can raise any taxes

* Indicates majority required by elected officials in each house of the legislature

to exceed these limits, and sanctions that would assure enforcement of the limits. A constitutional convention accompanied by a thorough national debate and referendum may be the best way to achieve a consensus and to formally incorporate such provisions in the U.S. Constitution. But amending the U.S. Constitution through a constitutional convention has proven to be a lengthy and difficult process.

For more information
Poulson, Barry W. "Designing a State Fiscal Constitution." In *Saving the States*. Washington, D.C.: American Legislative Exchange Council, 1993.

Supplemental Security Income Supplemental Security Income (SSI) is a nationwide federal income supplement program, established by Congress in 1972, designed to help the low-income elderly, blind, or disabled.

The SSI program was created to establish uniform eligibility criteria and benefit amounts for people receiving assistance under various former federal-state assistance programs. The origins of SSI are in the 1935 Social Security Act. In the original act, programs were introduced for low-income elderly (age 65) and blind individuals. In 1950, programs for needy disabled individuals were added. The Social Security Act was the first national welfare program in the United States. The establishment of public support for millions of citizens was a departure in a country priding itself on rugged individualism. It represented a significant policy shift from radical self-reliance to the recognition of the responsibility of government for the social and economic well-being of its people.

Despite substantial federal financing, income-assistance programs evolving from the Social Security Act—including the Old Age Assistance (OAA), Aid to the Blind (AB), and Aid to the Permanently and Totally Disabled (APTD)—were essentially state programs. Federal law did not specify maximum or minimum standards but provided matching funds to support whatever payment levels the states established. Over the years, state programs became complex and inconsistent, with as many as 1,350 administrative agencies involved and payments varying more than 300 percent from state to state. In the early 1960s, the "crazy quilt" of 50 state-operated, federally assisted welfare programs drew criticism. Responding to these concerns, Congress passed and the president approved the SSI program (Public Law 92-603, enacted 30 October 1972). The new program was historic in that it shifted from the states to the federal government the responsibility for determining who would receive assistance and how much assistance they would receive. The first SSI payments were disbursed in 1974.

In FY 2002, the SSI program was expected to pay monthly benefits to more than 6.6 million Americans. In contrast, the Social Security program will provide financial protection to over 152 million workers and their families, and monthly retirement, disability, and survivor benefits will be dispensed to approximately 45 million Americans. SSI recipients are usually eligible for benefits under other social welfare programs, including Medicaid and federal food stamps, because of stringent SSI income and asset guidelines. In 2002, for example, SSI eligibility guidelines limited the amount of personal income and resources an individual could possess to $2,000 ($3,000 for a married couple), including cash, bank accounts, land, personal property, and life insurance. In 2002, the maximum monthly SSI payment amount to individuals was $545, $817 for eligible

couples. Payments are usually lower, however. SSI recipients are encouraged to work, and although benefit amounts are not reduced dollar-for-dollar, earned income is counted against income and asset limits. Thus, in some cases, there may be disincentives for SSI recipients to obtain employment. States are permitted to provide additional supplementary income at their discretion.

The Social Security Administration is the federal agency that oversees both the SSI and Social Security programs. There are differences in how the programs are funded, however. SSI revenues are derived from general funds of the U.S. Treasury, while the Social Security program is funded through revenues generated through payroll withholding taxes under the Federal Insurance Contributions Act (FICA). States that provide supplementary payments draw from state funds. The Social Security Administration retains responsibility for administering the Social Security program, but applications to the program are administered locally.

For more information

Social Security Administration. *Understanding Supplemental Security Income.* 2002. Available online. URL: http://www.ssa.gov/notices/supplemental-security-income/.
———. *Social Security Online: History Page.* 2002. Available online. URL: http://www.ssa.gov/history/law.html.

Lisa Dicke

supply-side economics   *Supply-side economics* is a term that comes from a policy practice that was first followed during President Ronald Reagan's administration. It involves a policy whereby taxes were reduced to stimulate the economy. As such, it uses a tool under the domain of FISCAL POLICY.

Fiscal policy works to help stimulate the economy by increasing government spending or by reducing taxes. Both work in different directions. Here we are concerned with the effect of taxes. The idea is that if households or private firms receive a tax cut, they will have more income/wealth to spend or invest. Considering first consumers, if they receive a tax cut (this also could be a tax rebate), they could respond by either increasing spending or by saving more, thereby, increasing the amount of money available for investment. The spending side will increase the demand for goods and services in the economy, hence this effect is not a supply-side effect. But increases in savings can cause more capital to be available to firms to use to expand production, and this will cause the aggregate supply curve to bulge, ultimately increasing output and reducing unemployment. Here the same effect occurs for a tax policy that lowers taxes to firms and corporations.

There are other policies that can affect the overall supply curve in the economy. These include deregulation of industries, and changes in trade policies. Deregulation works on the principle that regulation results in added costs to firms, and without those costs firms would produce more goods, causing the overall supply curve to increase. Trade policies can benefit domestic firms when cheaper imported goods are kept out of a country. If these trade policies were not present, domestic firms would cut back production, reduce employment, and the overall supply curve could change.

For more information

Ekelund, R. B., Jr., and R. D. Tollison. *Macroeconomics: Private Markets and Public Choice.* Reading, Mass.: Addison-Wesley Longman, 1997.

Douglas D. Ofiara

suspect classification

suspect classification   Suspect classification arises when an intentional governmental action is directed against a person because of the person's race, ethnicity, religion, or alien status.

The U.S. Supreme Court first declared the doctrine in *Korematsu v. United States,* 323 U.S.

214, 216 (1944), where it held that "all legal restrictions which curtail the civil rights of a single racial group are immediately suspect," and that "courts must subject them to the most rigid scrutiny." *Korematsu* dealt with the federal government and the due process clause of the Constitution's Fifth Amendment. The Court later applied its suspect-classification doctrine to the states through the Fourteenth Amendment's equal protection clause.

The U.S. Constitution outlaws only invidious distinctions. Invidiousness connotes hostility or contempt, stigmatizing the individual as morally inferior because of his or her group identity. It can be shown by (1) a history of purposeful unequal treatment against individuals because of their involuntary membership in a disfavored group or (2) where a group is so politically disadvantaged that it has no opportunity for a fair hearing in the ordinary political process.

The traditional test in cases not involving suspect classes or fundamental rights is a tolerant one. So long as the state demonstrates that the means it has selected are reasonably related to accomplishing a legitimate (constitutional) end, the court will defer to the legislature. However, when a government practice adversely affects the exercise of a constitutional right, such as the freedom of speech, or threatens to injure the status of a suspect class, as the Jim Crow laws of the South did, the courts are not so relaxed. State action adversely affecting a suspect class must pass muster under the far sterner STRICT SCRUTINY test. The state must demonstrate that the means it has selected to accomplish its compelling interest are least intrusive on individual rights.

The Supreme Court has refused to include gender, age, poverty, sexual orientation, mental retardation, or illegitimacy as suspect classes. The Court's unwillingness to expand the suspect classification principle may reflect its concern with containing its own powers. Mindful of the political and popular reaction to judicial invalidation of New Deal legislation in the 1930s, the federal courts are sensitive to the propriety of intruding unnecessarily into legislative judgments. These doubts are also traceable to the tension between the practice of judicial review by unelected judges appointed for life and the ideal of democratically accountable government.

As the federal courts refused to expand suspect classes under the U.S. Constitution, litigation shifted to state courts and constitutions. State supreme courts such as California's used their state constitution to hold that poverty was a suspect class when public education is provided (*Serrano v. Priest,* 18 Cal. 3d, 728, 557 P.2d 929 [1976]). State constitutions have also been the basis of new liberties, such as the right to die.

Diligent public administrators often find the doctrine of suspect classification a burden on their attempts to ensure affirmative action (affecting race and ethnicity), to maintain order and discipline in public schools and prisons (affecting religious practices), and to implement successful school finance programs (affecting the poor). On the other hand, the doctrine also holds the hostile or prejudiced administrator to a high standard of accountability. The doctrine is one aspect of the government's continuing struggle to balance the demands of fair and effective administration.

For more information
Reed, Douglas S. *On Equal Terms.* Princeton, N.J.: Princeton University Press, 2001.

Timothy J. O'Neill

systems analysis   Systems analysis is both a diagnostic tool that can be used to identify and explain the past effects or results of programs, and a prognostic tool that can be used to predict the future effects or results of programs. It treats policy areas as systems and attempts to model the cause-and-effect relationships found within them.

When a policy area is complex, systems analysis can help policy makers identify the component parts and study how each interacts with the others, thus facilitating both a better understanding of the policy area and the development of programs in that area. It was popularized in the 1950s and 1960s as providing the theoretical basis for more rational decision making in government, and it is currently making a comeback under the cover of approaches such as PERFORMANCE MANAGEMENT and PERFORMANCE BUDGETING. However, to the extent that policy areas are too complex to analyze properly and decision makers in government must respond to a wide range of purely political pressures, systems analysis has limited usefulness.

In public policy studies, systems analysis (not to be confused with systems theory) views society as being made up of systems within which underlying policy issues and governmental policy actions (i.e., programs) interact to produce social phenomena or outcomes. According to Wildavsky, systems analysis "builds models that abstract from reality but represent the crucial relationships" between components of those systems, i.e., between underlying policy issues and programs. A key feature of systems analysis is that it does not simply identify the characteristics of existing social phenomena, but also seeks to identify the reasons why those particular phenomena came to be. Underlying this feature of systems analysis is causal theory, which examines components of policy systems and attempts to discover causal relationships between them. Systems analysis uses causal theory to explain the underlying policy issues that cause social phenomena, as well as to identify what the effect of particular programs on social phenomena are or would be.

There are two basic applications of systems analysis. The first application is modeling how a single social phenomenon is the product of multiple underlying issues and the effects of multiple government programs. The second application is modeling how a single government program itself combines with multiple underlying issues and the effects of other government programs to produce a variety of social phenomena. Both applications of systems analysis can produce models that help decision makers better understand not only the causes of policy problems and policy opportunities, but also how specific programs would interact with underlying policy issues and perhaps with other programs to solve those problems or exploit those opportunities.

Decision makers can use this knowledge of the effects of programs to make better decisions and plans about programs. Systems analysis can help decision makers in government to identify the factors that must be addressed in order to achieve policy objectives, translate those factors into program terms, evaluate and compare existing and potentially new programs against the achievement of policy objectives, and ensure implementation of the most cost-effective programs by influencing departments' and agencies' policies, budgets, and specific management practices.

For example, systems analysis can be used to help formulate and implement labor market policies. Let us say that some of the key objectives of labor market policies are to increase employment and increase productivity. Initial systems analytical studies could identify the underlying policy issues (i.e., reasons why employment and productivity may be low), such as individual workers not having the knowledge or skills that are demanded by employers. Further systems analytical studies could then identify policy options and programs that could address those issues, such as increasing the participation of employers in the development of school curricula or subsidizing particular forms of training. Decision makers could then use this information to help determine which programs achieve the labor market policy objectives in the most cost-effective way, and act accordingly.

Systems analysis does, however, have many limitations. One set of limitations concerns upper limits to our understanding of the causal theory behind programs, which imposes upper limits to the methodology that can be used to model policy systems. The cause-and-effect relationships at work in a policy system that collectively produce a social phenomenon are so numerous, and often so poorly understood, that systems analysts typically fail to measure and analyze critical underlying policy issues or aspects of programs. Also, it can be difficult to find ways of measuring these issues and aspects that are both accurate and precise.

Another set of limitations concerns operational limitations to analysis. Not only can some kinds of data be very costly to gather (or simply not be available), but the volume and complexity of data can overwhelm analysts, especially if the analysts themselves have not been specially trained for the task. And even if the effects of programs can be evaluated or predicted, this would be of little value if the objective of programs are vague or unstated, since program objectives could not then be used as a yardstick against which to assess the desirability of those effects. A final set of limitations concerns political disincentives. Systems analysis ideally involves the clear identification of program objectives and past program performance. Senior civil servants and politicians alike are often reluctant to produce information on their programs that could highlight the "real" but unpopular objectives behind a program, or to reveal the extent to which the program has failed to achieve its more laudable objectives, for fear that their programs will be cancelled or modified or that their reputations will be tarnished. As the old saying goes, "a dog will not fetch the stick with which it will be beaten."

The use of systems analysis in public policy studies peaked in the 1950s and 1960s, when it was first developed by the RAND Corporation and applied to policy making and budgeting in the Department of Defense and later across the federal government. With some exceptions, these early attempts to use systems analysis to inform decision making achieved only limited success, and systems analysis in general was judged to consume more resources and time than it was worth. Like other forms of "scientific" and "rational" decision making, systems analysis may be elegant in theory but futile or worse in practice when it is applied to complicated or contentious situations in the real world. Nevertheless, the idea of systems analysis and rational decision making in general has considerable intuitive appeal and is making a comeback in many governments, both in the United States and around the world. Practitioners should, however, ensure that its use is limited to areas of public policy where results are easily measured and where political sensitivities are low. Even when applied in those areas, it should be used only in combination with other techniques of policy analysis and development.

For more information

Hitch, Charles, and Roland McKean. *The Economics of Defense in the Nuclear Age.* Cambridge, Mass.: Harvard University Press, 1960.

Quade, E. S., and W. I. Boucher. *Systems Analysis and Policy Planning: Applications in Defense.* New York: American Elsevier, 1968.

Wildavsky, Aaron. "The Political Economy of Efficiency: Cost-Benefit Analysis, Systems Analysis, and Program Budgeting." *Public Administration Review* 26, no. 4 (December 1966): 292–310.

David I. Dewar

T

Taft-Hartley Act The Taft-Hartley Act, formally known as the Labor-Management Relations Act, was the most significant effort by Congress to weaken the National Labor Relations (Wagner) Act of 1935, which gave workers the right to organize into unions.

Taft-Hartley was a reaction against the growth of labor power and cold-war fears of communism. Under the Wagner Act, unions organized millions of new members and gained a presence on the American political landscape. When World War II ended, so did wage controls and labor's no-strike pledge, and many unions struck in order to recoup deferred pay increases. Sponsored by Senator Robert Taft and Representative Fred Hartley, it was passed by a Republican-controlled Congress over President Truman's veto in 1947 with support from conservative and moderate Democrats.

Taft-Hartley forbade the closed shop, which prohibited the hiring of nonunion workers; provided for decertification elections if 50 percent of union members in a bargaining unit decided they wanted to vote on whether or not to retain the union as their bargaining agent; created the Federal Mediation and Conciliation Service to settle disputes before they reached the strike stage; required employers to submit requests to it for a 60-day "cooling off" period before termination of contract; authorized the U.S. government to seek injunctions imposing an 80-day "cooling off" period on any strike the president declared to be a threat to the national interest; required unions to publicly disclose their financial statements; forbade direct union contributions to political campaigns; ended the "check-off" system whereby employers collected union dues; and prohibited management employees from joining unions. It also gave employers the right to sue unions for strike-related contract infringements. This provision had the unintended consequence of centralizing and strengthening the international unions at the expense of the locals, since the latter were now required to submit their collective-bargaining agreements to the former for legal approval.

Taft-Hartley was also influenced by the cold-war backlash, which sought to root out communists from the labor movement by requiring that union leaders take an oath that they were not members of the Communist Party in order to retain federal collective-bargaining rights under the NLR Act. With few exceptions most unions complied with the non-Communist affidavits requirement. The unions that did not comply were expelled by the CIO (Congress of Industrial Organizations). The states were given the option to become so-called right-to-work states by banning union and agency shop agreements. This provision has had a particularly devastating effect on labor's ability to organize new members in the West and the South, where it all but put a halt to the large-scale organizing drive known as Operation Dixie.

Labor leaders decried Taft-Hartley as a "slave labor law" and helped Truman win in 1948, but their campaign success never translated into repeal or modification of Taft-Hartley's rough edges. The Carter administration made a modest attempt to roll back some of its harshest features but was rebuffed by an increasingly pro-business Congress. Taft-Hartley remains as an effective restraint on organized labor's ability to organize and strike.

For more information

Forbath, William. *Law and the Shaping of the American Labor Movement.* Cambridge, Mass.: Harvard University Press, 1991.

Gold, Michael. *An Introduction to Labor Law.* Ithaca, N.Y.: ILR Press, 1989.

Snyder, Francis, and Douglas Hay, eds. *Labour, Law and Crime: An Historical Perspective.* London, New York: Tavistock, 1987.

Taylor, B. *Labor Relations Law.* Englewood Cliffs, N.J.: Prentice Hall, 1987.

Tomlins, C. *The State and the Unions: Labor Relations, Law and the Organized Labor Movement, 1880–1960.* New York: Cambridge University Press, 1985.

Vernon Mogensen

Tammany Hall   Tammany Hall was an often corrupt, sometimes benevolent political "machine" that dominated politics in New York City (up to 1898 mainly in Manhattan) from the 1850s until the mid-1930s. It sprang from a workingman's and artisans' club, the Society of St. Tammany, founded in 1786 and named for an Indian chief. Its members were known as "braves," its leaders "sachems," and its headquarters the "Wigwam."

Many of those who joined it worked actively under the leadership of Aaron Burr to secure the election of the Jefferson-Burr ticket in 1800. In 1805 its heads had the Tammany Society chartered by the state legislature as a charitable association. Shortly afterward, they formed a political organization that, because it met in the Wigwam, was known as Tammany Hall. Though the Tammany Society continued to be legally separate from Tammany Hall, the leaders of the society exerted considerable influence over the hall and the hall's powerful executive committee until World War II. Moreover, Tammany Hall became (not without opposition) the official New York County Democratic Party.

Although Tammany Hall was justifiably known as the ladder on which immigrant groups (especially the Irish) ascended to political power, the Tammany Society began as an anti-immigrant, "nativist" club. However, by the time Andrew Jackson was elected president in 1828, it had started recruiting newcomers to the country, mainly Irish and German.

By the 1850s many Hall-backed public officials were corrupt. The city council at this time already contained many Tammanyites and was so venal that it was collectively known as the "forty thieves." A ring headed by William M. Tweed, who in the early 1860s founded and ran the executive committee and thus became the hall's boss, stole millions in public funds through, e.g., kickbacks from inflated bills submitted by builders and other individuals doing business with the city.

In 1871 the Tweed Ring was exposed. Boss Tweed was convicted and died in jail in 1878. His successor as hall boss and thus Democratic leader of New York County was "Honest John" Kelly, its first Roman Catholic chief. Though Kelly himself was not on the take, graft and ballot-box stuffing were not uncommon during his

A political cartoon portraying William M. Tweed as a bullying schoolteacher giving New York City comptroller Richard B. Connolly a lesson in arithmetic. The exaggerated bills for the building of a county courthouse are posted on the wall. (LIBRARY OF CONGRESS)

reign. However, it was the jobs at the hall's disposal, plus the aid given to individuals in need by Tammany (assembly) district leaders and committeemen (for example, finding temporary quarters for people rendered homeless by a fire), that made it politically successful. A populace grateful for these boons voted for the hall's candidates so regularly that it ruled the city for seven of the eight decades between 1854 and 1934.

Kelly was succeeded in 1886 by Richard Croker. During Croker's tenure, district leaders such as George Washington Plunkitt gained fortunes by what Plunkitt openly called "honest graft," including using his position as an insider to dis-

cover where the city wanted to locate a park, buying the parcel cheaply, and then selling it to the municipality for a high price. Croker himself was adept at the "honest graft" game and tolerated a lot of "dishonest graft" paid by saloon-keepers, brothel madams, prostitutes, and gamblers to policemen and Tammany politicians. In 1902, when Croker departed for England and Ireland to raise and run his horses, the taciturn Charles F. Murphy became the hall's boss. Under Murphy, corruption declined, and two of his protégés, Alfred E. Smith and Robert F. Wagner, were to have glorious careers as New York State governor and U.S. senator, respectively. However, in

1913 he secured the impeachment and conviction of Governor William Sulzer, whose sole crime was his refusal to bow to Tammany's wishes on patronage and other matters.

Murphy's death in 1924 started the hall's executive committee and its following on a decline from which they never recovered. His immediate successors were much less competent, and large-scale municipal corruption reared its ugly head again during the mayoralty of Tammanyite Jimmy Walker from 1926 through much of 1932. Reform mayor Fiorello H. La Guardia (1934–45) and Franklin Roosevelt's New Deal programs, such as unemployment compensation, stripped the hall of its two major pillars of political support: patronage and aiding the needy. In 1943 the Tammany Society was so financially strapped that it had to surrender its imposing headquarters on 17th Street. It disappeared from sight in the 1950s.

During that decade, Carmine DeSapio from Greenwich Village headed Tammany Hall's Executive Committee (previously infiltrated by organized crime) and tried to restore its control over New York City's government. He did get Robert F. Wagner, Jr., elected mayor in 1953. However, DeSapio's efforts ended in failure when Wagner successfully ran for reelection in 1961 on an anti-Tammany platform and DeSapio himself was defeated by a reform Democrat in a district leadership contest. This loss forced him to resign as leader of the New York County Democratic Party. Since then, neither that county party nor any other political organization can be justly referred to as "Tammany Hall." No one misses the venality of many of Tammany Hall's leaders, but quite a few regret the passing of an organization that gave help to those in trouble without subjecting them to miles of red tape.

For more information

Allen, Oliver E. *The Tiger: The Rise and Fall of Tammany Hall.* Reading, Mass.: Addison-Wesley, 1993.

Myers, Gustavus. *The History of Tammany Hall,* 2d ed. New York: Boni and Liveright, 1917.

Daniel C. Kramer

tax increment financing Tax increment financing (TIF) was first authorized in 1952 for use by redevelopment agencies in California and has been adopted in several states for urban renewal and similar purposes.

TIF provides a vehicle whereby certain types of public improvements that promote urban redevelopment can be financed through the issuance of bonds, known as tax allocation bonds (TABs). These infrastructure improvements, in turn, facilitate development or redevelopment of real estate within the area by private developers. The bonds are then redeemed by revenues from either an ad valorem property tax or a municipal sales tax, or both. The tax revenue is derived from the "increment" that is realized from increased economic activity in the area that is redeveloped, i.e., the amount above the base tax revenue that existed prior to the redevelopment. TIF districts, such as urban renewal authorities and downtown development authorities, are established to use this financing mechanism.

In practice, any increased tax base in the redevelopment area does not accrue to the benefit of the governments that were there prior to the establishment of the TIF district. Instead, any increased revenue from the expanded tax base goes directly to the TIF, usually only for the repayment of bonds but sometimes to pay for the operational expenses of the TIF district. For example, increased taxable value in a TIF district may not be included in the total valuation for assessment of the county. The county's normal millage levy is applied to the TIF district, however, and the revenue that it generates is then distributed directly to the TIF district. In a sales tax TIF, the revenue from increased sales may be distributed directly to the TIF district or, if state-collected, may be distributed by the state to the city, which then transmits the TIF share to the TIF district.

Public officials who support the use of TIF to finance public improvements are numerous, as are detractors. Generally, it is popular because it is seen as a way to generate new revenue without raising taxes. The downside of TIF financing is twofold: First, the speculative nature of the improvements rely on growth to generate the revenue necessary to repay the debt. Therefore, if the economy turns down, or if the redevelopment area is not successful due to poor planning or competition for growth in other geographical areas, the revenue may not follow, which could cause default on the bonds. Critics point out that this use of a government mechanism to support essentially private development is putting the government at risk for private profit.

Second, other governments that overlap the TIF district often object to the use of this financing mechanism, since their revenues do not benefit from the increased growth that results from the redevelopment. This is particularly onerous when the growth creates increased demand on services but not the funds to pay for those services. For example, a school district might see increased enrollment from the families that move into a redeveloped residential area, but the property tax that derives from that increased development will be used for many years to pay for the public improvements that were necessary to support the development.

The problems related to TIF financing have led to a number of lawsuits between local governments as well as legislation requiring concurrent approval of such redevelopment plans by the affected governments. Not all such legislation has been successful. Some municipalities have been known to share a percentage of their revenues with overlapping jurisdictions. Some states require a percentage of the incremental revenues for specified purposes. For example, in California, 20 percent of the incremental revenue must be used to support low- and moderate-income housing.

For more information

"Tough Times for TIF's." *Congressional Quarterly* (February 1994).

Geoff Withers

Taylor, Frederick Winslow (1856–1915)

inventor, management specialist Frederick Winslow Taylor was the inventor of time-motion study and the father of SCIENTIFIC MANAGEMENT.

Frederick Winslow Taylor, praised as a great seminal thinker and denounced by others, was born 20 March 1856 in Philadelphia, Pennsylvania, the son of a wealthy lawyer. His mother was an ardent feminist and abolitionist. His family was Quaker with a strict lifestyle.

Taylor attended Phillips Exeter Academy in New Hampshire in 1872. An ardent sportsman and an excellent student, he passed the entrance examination for Harvard with honors but did not enter because of developing eye trouble. In 1875, after successful eye treatments, he became an apprentice pattern maker and machinist at the Enterprise Hydraulic Works in Philadelphia.

In 1878 he went to work for Midvale Steel Company as a machine-shop laborer. He advanced rapidly to shop clerk, machinist, gang boss, foreman, maintenance foreman, head of the drawing office, and chief engineer. While at Midvale Taylor introduced time-study experiments (1881), thereby creating a new profession. He also experimented with a piece-rate bonus system. His subsequent theories of management science grew from these experiences. Studying at night, he earned a degree in mechanical engineering from Stevens Institute of Technology in 1883 through a correspondence course. In 1884 Taylor became chief engineer at Midvale. He soon organized a new type of machine shop. While at Midvale and elsewhere, he received over 40 patents for various inventions.

Over the years Taylor was a consulting engineer in management to many prominent firms, ending with the Bethlehem Steel Corporation.

While at Bethlehem he performed time-study experiments in shoveling and pig-iron handling. Taylor retired at age 45 in order to promote the principles of scientific management by lecturing at universities and professional societies. Living at home in Philadelphia, he sought to care for his adopted children and wife, Louise, who was experiencing episodes of depression.

The American Society of Mechanical Engineers elected him president in 1906. The University of Pennsylvania awarded him an honorary doctor of science degree, also in 1906. Among his influential publications are "Notes on Belting" (first appearing in the *Transactions of the Society of Mechanical Engineers,* 1894), "A Piece-rate System" (1895), "Shop Management" (1903), and "On the Art of Cutting Metal" (1906). *The Principles of Scientific Management* was published commercially in 1911.

Taylor testified in 1912 before a special committee of the House of Representatives investigating systems of shop management, especially Taylor's system at the Watertown Arsenal. Thereafter Congress outlawed the use of stopwatches by civil servants, not lifting the ban until 1949. Still, Taylor continued to promote scientific management with many associates, including Frank and Lillian Gilbreth, Henry Gantt, and Charles Bedaux.

Taylor died unexpectedly on 21 March 1915 in Philadelphia. In 1993 his adopted son Robert, a successful investment banker, gave $10 million to the Stevens Institute of Technology, Hoboken, New Jersey, to help preserve his father's papers.

For more information

Kanigal, Robert. *The One Best Way: Frederick Winslow Taylor and the Enigma of Efficiency.* New York: Viking, 1997.

A. J. L. Waskey

Taylorism   Taylorism is a name for the teachings of FREDERICK WINSLOW TAYLOR.

Taylor and his followers called his ideas SCIENTIFIC MANAGEMENT. Taylor's ideas were advocated by the Taylor Society, formed about 1910 and expanded by many prominent individuals active in advancing scientific management, including Henri Fayol, Edward D. Jones, the Gilbreths, Henry Gantt, Harrington Emerson, Carl G. Barth, Sanford E. Thompson, H. King Hathaway, and many others.

Taylor's ideas have often been opposed. The managers where Taylor worked opposed him because they believed he was attacking their authority. Taylor was denounced by workers who felt their special craft knowledge was threatened and by unions seeking negotiated wages. "Taylorism" is a synonym for "scientific management," but the first term is most frequently used by critics or opponents. Critics have claimed that Taylorism developed into a philosophy of human control that took away the workers' creative involvement and substituted central administrative control. For others Taylorism is a mechanistic philosophy that reduces workers to cogs in a machine.

Some critics have claimed Taylor was merely a "time-study analyst" promoting a management tool for reducing wages. Others say that he was not original, or that he was so technology oriented that he ignored the human and social aspect of work. Other criticisms are that his studies were inaccurate, meaningless measurements. Others have alleged that his management philosophy was really an ideology of control. Many of these criticism are unwarranted. However, after Taylor's death in 1915, there were many whose attempts to put his ideas into action did seek to reduce workers to cogs in a machine in an inhuman fashion. Today *Taylorism* is used by many critics to mean a backward style of management that seeks to eliminate all worker initiative and depends upon labor discipline for its effectiveness.

Taylor started introducing his ideas into public administration after 1905 in government arsenals and later in navy yards. The attempt at the

Watertown Arsenal near Boston aroused a strike even before he arrived. Despite a ban on the use of stopwatches in government agencies, Taylor's ideas were adopted by the federal and state governments. Position-classification systems are an example of Taylor's influence.

Taylor's ideas have had no geographical or ideological boundaries. His thought has spread to Japan, India, and Europe and beyond. In Russia, V. I. Lenin had originally opposed Taylorism, but at the end of World War I he advocated it for developing Soviet industry. Aspects of his ideas were used by the Fascists in Italy. There are also cases of Nazis using stopwatch efficiency to advance their totalitarian cause. In fairness to Taylor, these applications were a perversion of his thought.

Taylor's ideas have deeply influenced corporate management, classical public administration theory, and the federal government's operation.

For more information

Haber, Samuel. *Efficiency and Uplift: Scientific Management in the Progressive Era, 1890–1920.* Chicago: University of Chicago Press, 1964.

Waring, Stephen P. *Taylorism Transformed: Scientific Management Theory since 1945.* Chapel Hill: University of North Carolina Press, 1994.

A. J. L. Waskey

teledemocracy Teledemocracy refers to deliberative and participatory forms of democracy in which the use of Interactive Computer Terminals (ICTs) has an important role. It reflects a political dimension of the coming of the information age.

Early ideas of teledemocracy were presented by R. Buckminster Fuller and Erich Fromm, among others. In the late 1960s and early 1970s, new projections emerged mainly as a critique of the existing system of elitist representative democracy and, on the other hand, in support of rising hopes that electronic media and communication tools could mark a radical turn in democratic practice. The academics and futurists who developed these ideas further include Amitai Etzioni, Alvin Toffler, Ted Becker, Christa Slaton, and Benjamin Barber. Theodore (Ted) Becker is the founding father of the post-Newtonian conception of teledemocracy and among the first—if not the very first—to coin the term *teledemocracy* in print in the early 1980s.

Ideal types of democracy—representative, associative, direct, and participatory democracy—are based on the mechanisms that characterize each of them: representation based on elections; aggregating interests on the basis of membership in associations; direct participation and involvement in the act of decision making; and participation in deliberative processes in the preparation, planning, and implementation of public policies. In contrast to these basic models, the concept of teledemocracy is historically rooted in technological development. The prefix *tele* is of Greek origin, meaning "at a distance." Thus, the only thing this concept defines is that the system in question is democratic or relies on the "rule by the people," and that technology is used in conducting related democratic practices. In practice, however, most of the advocates of teledemocracy tend to search for citizen-centered alternatives to traditional representative democracy.

In discussions of teledemocracy, the technology is important, yet it is not the main point. Rather, teledemocracy is, above all, about new forms of democracy. This is also why it matters: teledemocracy is needed to overcome the limitations of representative democracy. It is a way to give ordinary people a voice and a stake in the collective decision-making processes. This is also how it is intended to change public administration and policy. It favors citizen-centered and participatory solutions to administrative, and democratic processes.

In the early phase, the conceptions of teledemocracy were rather narrow, but in the course of time they broadened and became more contextual. The earliest conception of teledemocracy was based on romantic ideas that echo the democracy of ancient Greece. From this point of view, it was seen normatively as an electronically mediated form of direct democracy. Another, rather limited view may be called the "communicational" approach, for it emphasizes computer-mediated processes of communication and dialog among political leaders, administrators, and citizens.

Broader views of teledemocracy opened horizons to a new democratic paradigm. They originated in the 1970s, culminating in the writings of Ted Becker and Christa Slaton. This approach relies on direct and participatory forms of democracy utilizing such tools as scientific deliberative polling, electronic town meetings, and new democratic uses of the Internet. The broadest conceptions go even further, as they build a kind of postmodern hybrid model of democracy and governance. These ideas aim at radical renewal of the foundations of the entire democratic system to meet the challenges of information-society development, globalization, and postmodern condition.

Teledemocracy can, in principle, be used synonymously with such terms as electronic democracy, digital democracy, cyberdemocracy, or online democracy, but their roots and emphases differ. Even though the concept of teledemocracy was originally based on the idea of direct democracy, i.e., of unmediated political communication and decision making, in the early 21st century it is usually understood in a broader sense to indicate the overall transformation of democratic systems.

For more information
Becker, Ted, and Christa Slaton. *The Future of Teledemocracy.* Westport, Conn.: Praeger, 2000.

Ari-Veikko Anttiroiko

Temporary Assistance for Needy Families
Temporary Assistance for Needy Families (TANF) is a federal program designed to reform the nation's welfare system.

The Personal Responsibility and Work Opportunity Reconciliation Act of 1996 created the TANF block grant, which replaced the AID TO FAMILIES WITH DEPENDENT CHILDREN (AFDC) program. The explicit goals of the TANF program, as specified in the law, are to: provide assistance to needy families so that children can be cared for in their own homes or in the homes of relatives; end the dependence of needy parents on government benefits by promoting job preparation, work, and marriage; prevent and reduce the incidence of out-of-wedlock pregnancies and establish annual numerical goals for preventing and reducing the incidence of these pregnancies; and encourage the formation and maintenance of two-parent families. This new program is the culmination of years of public debate about national welfare policy.

The TANF program made significant changes in the relationships between the federal government and the states with regard to welfare policy, giving states flexibility to create new cash-assistance programs for families with children. The most obvious of these changes is the end of the open-ended entitlement to funding under the AFDC program, in which state expenditures were matched by federal funds. Under TANF, states receive a block grant based on their expenditure level under the AFDC program. In addition to using funds from the block grant, they are required to maintain a historical level of spending that includes state funds, known as maintenance of effort.

The total federal block grant is $16.8 billion each year through federal fiscal year (FY) 2002, the end of the initial period for which the program was funded. The number of families receiving TANF benefits has decreased dramatically. In January 1993, 14.1 million people received benefits under the AFDC program. By December of 1999, the number of TANF recipients was 6.3 million.

In addition to providing cash benefits to families, TANF funds can be used for a wide variety of services to help families become self-sufficient. For example, a family might receive cash assistance as well as vouchers for child care and transportation. The state could also provide employment-related services, such as job-readiness preparation and funds for uniforms. The types of benefits and services vary a great deal from state to state.

Though the legislation includes minimum requirements in certain areas, it provides states with considerable flexibility to establish policies that exceed the minimum requirements; in other areas, the legislation provides complete state discretion. Following are examples of some of the major changes in federal policy.

Under AFDC, there were no restrictions on the number of months families were eligible to receive assistance; if a family met eligibility requirements, it was entitled to benefits. Under TANF, payments to families that include an adult are limited to 60 months, with certain exceptions, and states may establish shorter time limits. In fact, there is no requirement that states make cash payments to families. Assistance can be provided in other forms, such as vouchers or payment for supportive services.

The new welfare law encourages states to move recipients into work and gives states the ability to develop their work requirements within broad federal parameters. Under AFDC, nonexempt recipients were required to participate in work activities once the state determined they were ready or as state resources permitted. Under TANF, nonexempt recipients are required to participate in work activities within 24 months, although states can impose work requirements sooner.

Under AFDC, families receiving assistance could not have more than $1,000 in countable resources. This limit excluded the value of certain assets, including the value of a vehicle worth up to $1,500. Under TANF, there is no limit regarding assets, including vehicle exclusions, giving states the flexibility to set their own asset rules.

Under AFDC, payments to families were based on needs standards established by each state. Rules for counting income, in particular earned income, were explicitly defined by federal rules. Under TANF, states have complete flexibility to establish payment levels and rules for counting income.

In return for the flexibility that states have under the program, the legislation includes performance goals, such as work participation rates, and incentives and penalties related to performance. An example is a bonus for reduction of out-of-wedlock births.

The TANF program is generally considered to be successful, as evidenced by substantial reductions in caseloads during the late 90s. However, it is also true that the strong economy during this time was a major factor contributing to caseload reductions. One criticism of the program is that states have focused on reducing the number of families that receive benefits rather than reducing poverty.

For more information

Administration for Children and Families. http://www.acf.dhhs.gov/programs/ofa.

American Public Human Services Association. http://www.aphsa.org/.

Welfare Information Network. http://www.welfareinfo.org.

Mark Ragan

Tenure of Office Act of 1867   The Tenure of Office Act of 1867 provided that all federal officials whose appointment required Senate confirmation, once approved, could not be removed without the consent of the Senate. It was passed on March 2 over the veto of President Andrew Johnson (who had become president upon the assassination of Abraham Lincoln). The act held that when the Senate was not in session, the president was permitted to suspend an official, but if the Senate refused to concur in the removal, the official must be reinstated in his position. It was unclear whether the act applied to cabinet officials appointed by a previous president, such as Secretary of War Edwin Stanton, a Lincoln appointee.

In the summer of 1867, with Congress not in session, Andrew Johnson decided the time had finally come to replace Edwin Stanton with a new secretary of war. Stanton had become increasingly at odds with Johnson and the rest of his cabinet and had been conspiring with hard-line Radical Republicans in Congress to thwart Johnson's policies on Reconstruction, which were considered too soft and "Lincol-nesque" by the radicals who wished to punish the South.

On 5 August 1867, Johnson sent Stanton the following message: "Public considerations of high character constrain me to say that your resignation as Secretary of War will be accepted." Stanton refused to resign, forcing Johnson to send Stanton a second letter suspending him from office, ordering that he cease all exercise of authority, and transferring power to a new secretary of war, Ulysses S. Grant.

On 3 January 1868, the new Congress met and refused to concur in the removal of Stanton by a vote of 35 to 16. The president, however, refused to accept the Senate's decision, believing the Tenure of Office Act to be an unconstitutional infringement on the power of the executive. Wishing to bring about a court test of the constitutionality of the act, Johnson dismissed Stanton, but the Supreme Court, intimidated by the radicals, refused to take on the case. General Ulysses S. Grant, whom Johnson appointed secretary ad interim, turned the office back to Stanton when the Senate refused to approve his dismissal.

Hoping to obtain a lower-courts review of the act's constitutionality, Johnson on 21 February 1868, appointed General Lorenzo Thomas, adjutant general of the army, to the post of secretary of war. Stanton balked at leaving the office he had reoccupied since January. Charles Sumner, one of the Senate's leading Radical Republicans, sent Stanton a one-word telegram: "Stick."

Impeachment proceedings began within days. Johnson's alleged violation of the Tenure of Office Act was the principal charge in the impeachment proceedings against him. When this move to impeach President Johnson failed by one vote in May of 1868, Stanton finally gave up.

Later Presidents Ulysses Grant and James Garfield complained vigorously about the Tenure of Office Act. It was modified in Grant's administration and was in large part repealed in 1887, at the urging of President Grover Cleveland. Finally, in 1926 the Supreme Court declared its principles unconstitutional, thus permitting presidents to fire their cabinet members at will. This has provided the president with great power in enforcing his will upon his cabinet officers, but it comes at the expense of stifling public expression of any concerns a cabinet member may have with the president or his policies.

For more information
Benedict, Michael Les. *The Impeachment and Trial of Andrew Johnson*. New York: W. W. Norton & Company, 1999.

Craig Donovan

Theory X   Theory X attempts to explain a specific human management style or approach.

Douglas McGregor was researching different management styles, and in 1960 he developed two very different theories of management style that he called Theory X and THEORY Y. These theories provide us with two opposing ideas about how people, particularly in management, tend to view human behavior both at work and in organizational life.

McGregor's theories had a profound effect upon the human-resource management field because he built upon the work of a well-respected motivational theorist by the name of ABRAHAM MASLOW. Maslow had developed a five-part, hierarchical theory, which explained that people have essential needs that must be met on five levels of their lives and that each lower level must be satisfied before the person becomes motivated to reach the next higher level. McGregor developed this further by explaining that Maslow's *Hierarchy of Needs* worked from both the manager's perspective and from the worker's point of view. The hierarchy of needs, from the lowest to the highest, follows these steps: physiological needs (food, shelter, etc.), safety and security needs, social and affection needs, esteem or status needs, and finally the need for self-actualization.

One of McGregor's greatest contributions to the understanding of personnel management was the fact that managers did indeed deal with people according to their unique, personal perspectives. This idea was important because the most commonly held belief about management was the *productivity model* of management, which was built upon the scientific approach to management. Instead, McGregor was showing how people, both workers and managers, are not like machines but are motivated by their own assumptions and beliefs. He explained that you could tell what those assumptions and beliefs were by the way people talked to each other and behaved within their organizations.

McGregor found that the dominant style of management under the productivity model of management was based upon the assumption that the manager's role is to control employees primarily by coercion. According to Theory X, this controlling, coercive style is required because:

All people inherently dislike work and will avoid putting much effort into it whenever possible.
People have to be controlled, directed, coerced, or threatened with punishment in order to get them to adequately perform their job duties.
People do not want responsibility, even to the point where they expect the manager to have complete control over their duties, and that people have little or no ambition.

Above all, people want security in their jobs and lives.

Theory X has both a hard and a soft version. The hard approach can be characterized by "the stick" with which to figuratively beat workers over the head. The hard approach is meant to motivate the worker by threatening the loss of something of value to the worker based upon Maslow's hierarchy of needs, like firing or demoting the worker.

The soft approach in Theory X can be characterized by "the carrot" in front of the worker's nose to motivate hard work. This is done by dangling rewards in front of the worker, again in terms of the values that the worker currently holds according to Maslow's hierarchy. These rewards can be as concrete as more pay or additional vacation time, or they may be as abstract as tempting someone with personal recognition for a job well done. This is commonly done with employee-of-the-month recognition or some such reward.

For more information

Heil, G. *Douglas McGregor Revisited: Managing the Human Side of the Enterprise.* New York: Wiley Publishers, 2000.
McGregor, D. *The Human Side of the Enterprise.* New York: McGraw-Hill, 1960.

Lesele H. Rose

Theory Y   Theory Y is a contemporary management theory regarding human motivation and behavior in the workplace. This theory is part of a body of management research about the importance of social and psychological factors in the workplace and of human relations in organizations (referred to as the human relations school).

Theory Y, outlined in the book *The Human Side of the Enterprise* by social psychologist Douglas McGregor in 1960, is based on his examination of management practices in business and industry and the assumptions about human behavior that are part of supervisory and management decisions regarding employees. McGregor argued there are two alternative views of employees in the workplace (THEORY X and Theory Y), and both provide a set of assumptions regarding human nature and what motivates people in the workplace.

Under the traditional view of workers (which McGregor called Theory X), managers and supervisors recognized the need to assume significant direction and control of the organization and employees. Assumptions within Theory X about human motivation included the view that employees basically disliked work, were irresponsible, and unable to work without direct supervision. Workers were seen as having little ambition and could only be motivated by punishment to become productive workers and ultimately support the goals of their employer. The alternative view, put forward by McGregor (Theory Y), was based on the belief that direction and control must be replaced by supportive relationships to ensure worker productivity and effort.

Assumptions about human motivation within Theory Y include the beliefs that work can be a source of satisfaction as workers have the potential to enjoy their jobs, be highly motivated, handle responsibility, and be able to direct their own work without constant supervision. Under Theory Y, managers would be more effective because their employees are able to control their own work behavior rather than having to depend on external supervision and control.

Modern-day managers and supervisors who adapt the Theory Y view of employees see workers as capable of a high degree of motivation, as active contributors, both committed and involved in their organization. Theory Y includes a number of strategies to help achieve high levels of productivity and quality among workers. These include decentralized decision making by involving employees in decisions, participatory management by involving employees in the management of work efforts, and expanding individual job duties to make work more personally interesting. These techniques challenge employees and provide them with a sense of involvement and responsibility. As the basis for running organizations, the Theory Y concept, in an ideal world, encourages all employees to feel that the goals of the organization are important to them and that their jobs are meaningful and contribute to organizational objectives. Equally important within Theory Y is the relationship between employees and their supervisors. In order to perform their jobs effectively, employees need the support of their supervisors. By giving this support, managers help make their workers effective.

For more information

Heil, G. *Douglas McGregor Revisited: Managing the Human Side of the Enterprise.* New York: Wiley Publishers, 2000.

McGregor, D. *The Human Side of the Enterprise.* New York: McGraw-Hill, 1960.

Dahlia Bradshaw Lynn

Theory Z   Theory Z is a Japanese style of management that is characterized by lifelong employment, slow promotion, and evaluation with a collective decision-making process.

William Ouchi introduced Theory Z to the United States in 1981. Theory Z is based on a Japanese managerial system of industry that was in place by World War II. In this system, major firms are clustered around a bank with hosts of satellite companies. The satellite companies produce products for one of the major firms. The best and the brightest Japanese males are selected for employment in major firms, whereas women and the less talented males are employed in the satellite companies. Those employed in major firms enjoy benefits, such as lifelong employment, not granted to those in satellite companies. Lifelong employment is defined as a permanent job placement until the age of 55. Upon retirement at age 55, retirees are given a bonus that is typically six years' worth of their annual salary and a part-time job in a satellite company. This rotation makes room for new graduates. Those working in satellite companies receive a bonus but cannot continue employment with the company, so they either start a small business or move in with relatives after retirement.

Also inherent in this system is slow promotion and evaluation. After new graduates are hired, it is generally 10 years before they will be evaluated and promoted based on merit. Until that time, all employees are promoted at the same time and given the same pay raise. Employees are also expected to work in several different departments during this time. Japanese workers are not specialized in a certain field of expertise. They have a nonspecialized career path. As a result of working in different departments, they have the opportunity to see how the entire organization works.

Theory Z is a set of beliefs, values, and principles that are very much engrained in the cultural and social identity of the country. The basic tenets of Theory Z are productivity, trust, and subtlety. Trust and subtlety lead to increased productivity, and they develop over time because of lifelong employment. Because workers will have to work with each other for quite some time, it is mutually beneficial to resolve conflicts and create an open atmosphere that leads to trust. Once trust is established, an intimate working relationship develops that fosters subtlety. In this case, subtlety leads to a unique problem-solving approach where workers can make decisions and implement changes that are not questioned by superiors because trust and loyalty is implicit in their relationship. Loyalty is such a big part of this relationship that when workers decide to go on strike, they give an advanced notice of the strike. After the strike, they return to work and make up the production lost on the previous day(s) without overtime.

Another unique feature of the Theory Z is the decision-making process. Everyone impacted by a decision will have a chance to give input instead of being dictated to by a superior. A team of three will be assembled to speak with everyone involved, in some instances more than 60 people. Discussions continue until a general consensus is reached. This process is time-consuming, but everyone affected by a decision gives their input, which further increases trust between managers and subordinates.

Theory Z is contrasted with Douglas McGregor's Theory X and Y, which refer to a manager's assumptions about workers. THEORY X managers assume workers are lazy and irresponsible; whereas, THEORY Y managers assume workers are hardworking and responsible and should be treated accordingly. Traditional American organizations that adhere to this philosophy are called type A organizations. Not all organizations in the United States adhere to this philosophy. Ouchi refers to organizations that have applied Theory Z as type Z organizations. Some companies and organizations in the United States have adopted Theory Z with great success, such as New York City's Bureau of Motor Equipment, Hewlett-Packard, Samsung, and Procter & Gamble.

Because the United States is so culturally and ethnically diverse, Theory Z has to be modified to work within American organizations. To get workers to conform to the same principles and beliefs, companies and agencies subscribe to an organizational philosophy, mission statement, or strategic plan. Lifelong employment is not guaranteed, but long-term employment may occur unofficially. Once employees buy into the philosophy and mission of the organization, they are more inclined to work at various jobs in different departments to become generalized rather than specialized. Promotions and evaluations are slow, but not as slow as in companies in Japan. Quality circles and work teams are used to get everyone involved in the decision-making process.

For more information

Lewis, James. *Excellent Organizations: How to Develop & Manage Them Using Theory Z*. New York: J. L. Wilkerson Pub., 1985.

Ouchi, William G. *Theory Z: How American Business Can Meet the Japanese Challenge.* Reading, Mass.: Addison-Wesley, 1981.

La Loria Konata

total quality management and continuous quality improvement (TQM/CQI)

Total quality management and continuous quality improvement (TQM/CQI) refer to a group of concepts and techniques that involve employees in continuously improving the quality of organizational performance, with quality being determined by persons who receive the organization's products or services.

Though TQM/CQI was originally aimed at improving business operations, such as manufacturing and sales, it is now widely applied by governments as well (for example, federal government defense contracts administration and municipal government public-works activities). The key measure of organizational performance in TQM/CQI is quality as defined by customers. More than the final consumers of products, services, decisions, etc., customers are also persons inside and outside the organization who participate in the production of these final outputs. Thus, suppliers of various elements to the production process, such as those of a material, electronic, or intellectual nature, consider those functional units that "consume" their "products" as customers.

Asking customers their opinions about their needs helps in the development of performance measures of quality. For example, a public transit agency might ask its customers, "What is most important to you as a public transit rider?" Customers might define quality as meeting of schedules, feeling safe while using public transit, cleanliness of buses or trains, etc.

There can be several performance measures. Organizations that are serious about applying TQM/CQI must introduce major changes in work management. Many so-called bureaucratic problems in organizations result from compartmentalization of functional units. Compartmentalization is done because complex functions need to be subdivided into manageable groups. There is also need to utilize resources of all types well. Thus, a county public-works department separates road construction from engineering by placing these functions in separate organizational units. In so doing they are using their human and material resources well. Engineers carry out the design and land-acquisition activities, and equipment operators and surveyors physically construct the roads. While this is an oversimplification, it points out one basis for bureaucratic problems. Sometimes separateness leads to conflicts, such as misunderstandings about requirements, miscommunication of schedules, and lack of coordination in general. Providing the road to the public is the purpose, and the tasks of these units are different aspects of the same process, which will result in the road as a public benefit. TQM/CQI emphasizes the whole process, which is supposed to yield final outputs, not only a process within a separate unit.

Organizing for improvement may involve several levels of committees and action groups, or it may maintain a relatively flat structure. Committees at a higher level may focus on overall concerns such as mission, values, expected organizational structure, reward systems, and personnel policies. At lower levels are improvement teams. Here, the labor force involved in production must be trained in teamwork and problem-solving methods and must actively participate in improvement activities as ongoing commitments. Supervisors facilitate these activities rather than acting as controllers.

The implicit assumption about worker motivation is that involvement in efforts to improve work is an important motivator of both performance and satisfaction in the workplace. These assumptions are based on the now-classical observations by writers such as William Ouchi. (*Theory Z: How American Business Can Meet the*

Japanese Challenge, Reading, Mass.: Addison-Wesley, 1981).

There are realities in public-sector organizations that make quality initiatives difficult to achieve. First are statutory and other legal requirements that dictate who does what, where, when, and how. The bureaucratic insularity discussed above often is dictated by legislation that ties function to organization. Though other departments may in fact be part of a process, their statutory independence may lead them to resist cooperation. For cooperation to occur, it may be necessary to change legislation, sometimes difficult to achieve for a variety of reasons. Examples of difficulties are: political resistance by powerful interest groups, insufficient higher management authority, and what are thought to be good practices or fair and ethically correct behavior in particular legislation.

Not uncommonly in government, seemingly opposed functions are provided through the same service-delivery channels. This also makes a quality emphasis difficult. For example, through patrol of highways, state troopers render various services to motorists. They also regulate motorists through the same patrol channel. The public as customers will no doubt view the output of motorists assisted as quality, but will they assign the same value to citations written?

Cooperation with suppliers is also difficult. Often, there are government requirements for competitive bidding. These may inhibit candor in the supply process. Usually, the government buyer is motivated by the criterion of highest quality for lowest cost, while the supplier might inflate costs or obscure quality differences in order to make a profit.

Despite these types of problems there is a remarkable record of quality improvement achievements by all levels of American governments. A 1989 survey by a consulting firm revealed that 66 percent of responding federal organizations had introduced the quality philosophy, and 12 percent had carried out major initiatives. The Federal Quality Institute, in cooperation with the National Technical Information Service, provides training, technical assistance, and a large database on experiences with federal quality programs. The States of Wisconsin and Minnesota have conducted significant statewide programs, while departmental initiatives were carried out in California, Michigan, Florida, Arizona, Arkansas, and Pennsylvania. Local governments too have initiated TQM/CQI programs. Though many more cities and counties have proceeded with quality efforts since the early 1990s, early leaders were Ft. Collins, Colorado; Madison, Wisconsin; Phoenix, Arizona; Rocky Mount, North Carolina; Volusia County, Florida; and Austin, Texas.

For more information

Carr, David K. *Excellence in Government, Total Quality Management in the 1990s.* Arlington, Va.: Coopers and Lybrand, 1990.

Gilbert B. Siegel

transactional costs   Transactional costs are the costs of information gathering, decision making, contracting, and controlling that are involved in any human interaction.

Generally speaking, an economic definition of transactional costs states that those are the costs of measuring what is being exchanged and enforcing agreements. In the larger context of societal evolution, they are all the costs involved in human interaction over time. Nevertheless, when we refer to transactional costs, from the new institutional economic point of view, the understanding of this term becomes more complex.

In 1937, Ronald Coase published his article "The Nature of the Firm," where he first explained the term "transactional cost." In order to understand what he meant by that, it is important to know the significance of the transaction concept. Many scientists, among whom Williamson is one of the most outstanding, believe a transaction occurs when a good or service is transferred across a technologically separable interface, i.e., is physically delivered. Given this, a transaction can take place within firms (resulting in an internal or intrafirm transaction) or across markets (giving rise to external or market transactions). These are called economic transactions. But transactions can also be political. That means "deliveries" can occur between politicians, bureaucrats, and interest groups. Indeed, both economic and political transactions are special kinds of social transactions; they are social actions that are necessary for the information and maintenance of the institutional framework in which economic and political activity take place.

In this context, transactional costs are the costs associated with the efforts that go into choosing, organizing, negotiating, and entering into even the most mundane contracts that either economic or politic human interaction impose. These costs are generally independent of the price of the contracted product or service itself.

There are three typical types of transactional costs: market transaction costs, managerial transaction costs, and political transaction costs. The first type arises from using the market. Coase states that "in order to carry out a market transaction it is necessary to discover who it is that one wishes to deal with, to inform people that one wishes to deal with and to what terms, to conduct negotiations leading up to a bargain, to draw up the contract, to undertake the inspection needed to make sure that the terms of the contract are being observed, and so on." Therefore, market transaction costs include search and information costs, bargaining and decision costs, and supervision and enforcement costs.

Managerial transaction costs are the result of exercising the right to give orders within a firm. Basically, the main concern here has to do with implementing the labor contracts that exist between a firm and its employees. That is why they include the costs of setting up, maintaining, or changing an organizational design as well as the costs of running the organization.

Finally, the political transaction costs are the ones associated with the running and adjusting of the institutional framework of a polity. Some scholars refer to them as the costs of supplying public goods by collective action, and therefore they state that such costs can be understood as analogous to the managerial ones. In this sense, political transactional costs comprise the costs of setting up, maintaining, and changing a system's formal and informal political organization (for example, the costs associated with the establishment of the legal framework, the administrative structure, the military, or the educational system) and the costs of running a polity (for instance, current outlays for legislation, defense, the administration of justice, or transport but also the costs of monitoring, making decisions, or giving official orders).

As seen, this last category of costs is the one that really matters to public administration because it includes the costs involved in the political process and the political organization (e.g., the costs of setting up a political party or pressure group), the result of which are public policies.

Although the transaction-costs model dates back to the 1930s, this perspective is still largely used not only to explain economic and market phenomena such as vertical integration, outsourcing, corporate governance, and the boundaries of the firm, but also to illustrate the political behavior related to issues such as the benefits of the prohibition of tobacco smoking and alcohol consumption or the investment in public education.

For more information

Furubotn, E., and R. Richter. *Institutions and Economic Theory. The Contribution of the New Institutional Economics*. Ann Arbor: University of Michigan Press, Ann Arbor Paperbacks, 2000.

Mila Gascó and Fran Equiza

tribal nation sovereignty Tribal nation sovereignty refers to the right of tribes located within the United States to have self-government as sovereigns.

Nearly 600 tribal nations have a government-to-government relationship with the United States. Tribal nations are recognized as governments in the commerce clause, which acknowledges congressional power "To regulate Commerce with foreign nations, among the several States, and with the Indian Tribes." Tribes were originally dealt with by the United States through the treaty process. In 1871 Congress declared that no new treaties would be made between the United States and tribes, but many treaties created before that time remain in effect. The limited sovereignty of tribes has been recognized by the executive branch, Congress, the Supreme Court, and the states.

Two of the seminal cases defining the governmental status of tribal nations are *Cherokee Nation v. Georgia,* 30 U.S. 1 (1831), and *Worcester v. Georgia,* 31 U.S. 515 (1832). In *Cherokee Nation* the Supreme Court defined tribes as "dependent domestic nations" reliant upon the federal government for protection. In *Worcester,* the Court acknowledged that tribal nations possessed "territorial boundaries, within which their authority is exclusive," and that they are "distinct, independent political communities, retaining their original natural rights." The states were prohibited in *Worcester* from interfering with tribal authority on tribal land protected by the federal government, although President Andrew Jackson refused to enforce the decision. Tribal sovereign authority has been diminished in more recent cases, yet it remains a judicially recognized principle.

One example of congressional recognition of tribal nation sovereignty is the Indian Child Welfare Act (1978). This law recognizes the sovereign right of tribal governments to determine the placement of tribal children in adoption and foster-care decisions. States are required to give notice to the tribe if a case involves an Indian child. If the tribe requests jurisdiction, the matter must be handed over to the tribe for resolution, with some exceptions. Other examples of the recognition of tribal nation sovereignty include the issue of gaming and Environmental Protection Agency recognition of tribal clean water standards.

Throughout the 1800s and early 1900s, Congress randomly bestowed U.S. citizenship upon individual tribal members, and at times whole tribes, with an expectation that tribal allegiance would end. In 1868, when the Fourteenth Amendment declared, "All persons born or naturalized in the United States and subject to the jurisdiction thereof, are citizens of the United States and of the State wherein they reside," tribal members were not considered to be included. Congress and the Supreme Court instead considered tribal citizenship and U.S. citizenship mutually exclusive.

Congress in 1924 declared that all Indians were U.S. citizens and in 1940 declared that citizenship took effect at birth. No longer were tribal citizenship and U.S. citizenship considered to be mutually exclusive. Tribal members have a tricitizenship. As citizens of the tribe, the United States, and the state, tribal members vote in tribal, federal, and state elections. Tribal nation sovereignty and U.S. citizenship for tribal members are recognized as compatible.

For more information

Getches and Wilkinson. *Federal Indian Law: Cases and Materials,* 4th ed. St. Paul, Minn.: West Publishing, 1998.

Tebben, Carol. "An American Trifederalism Based upon the Constitutional Status of Tribal Nations." *U. Penn J. of Constitutional Law* (symposium issue, Winter 2002–2003): 318–356.

Carol Tebben

triple bottom line Triple bottom line refers to a concept in modern commercial administration that is designed to highlight that consideration of only one measurement of success—the financial bottom line—is inadequate in a number of respects. Triple-bottom-line thinking insists that there are at least two other aspects of doing business that require equal consideration and active managerial attention—the social impacts (e.g., health, welfare, and safety) and the environmental impacts that a company's activities may be having.

Advocates of triple-bottom-line reporting are quick to remind skeptics that having three reporting considerations instead of one is also necessary for, indeed irretrievably linked to, the financial bottom line. Financial success itself is reliant upon not only economic sustainability but also social and environmental sustainability. A company that can meet the needs of the present in terms of social and environmental impact, without compromising the needs of the future, is, so the thinking goes, more likely to appeal to investors and customers alike, and thus be financially successful. Advocates promote the triple bottom line by using it as a selling point in the marketplace and appealing to customers concerned about the environment and about reducing risk to workers, consumers, and the public in general.

The term *triple bottom line* was the brainchild of John Elkington, a British environmentalist and chairman of the London-based consultancy, SustainAbility Ltd. He developed the idea that companies need to be able to measure and display "sustainability" using a range of measurable performance indicators.

Moves have been made since the early 1990s to list, measure, and compare the performance of companies that meet "sustainability" criteria. There has been tracking (audited by Price Waterhouse Coopers) of those companies that were identified by self-reported responses as having met agreed performance indicators. In September 1999, the Dow Jones Sustainability Group Index (DJSGI) was published for the first time, introducing to analysts and investors alike the notion of sustainability as a performance indicator. "Sustainable" is defined according to a range of criteria designed to measure a firm's performance in economic, environmental, and social terms. The final ratings are based upon the ability of a company to encourage stakeholder relationships, respect human rights, ensure appropriate employment conditions, and foster an environment of anticorruption, among other things. The index is currently composed of 229 firms (market value $4.3 trillion) across 22 countries. These firms (including Fujitsu, Unilever, Skandia, and Honeywell) are, according to the index, the top 10 percent of companies (in each of 68 worldwide industries) operating from sustainability-related management practices.

It is still too early to tell whether the current enthusiasm for triple-bottom-line thinking will lead to major changes in the operation of the business community and the public sector.

For more information

SustainAbility. http://www.sustainability.co.uk.

Rick Sarre

U

unfunded mandates Unfunded mandates are rules and constraints imposed by legislative, executive, or judicial actions of one level of government on other sectors in the economy.

Although mandates can refer to regulations imposed on private profit and nonprofit entities, the term was coined to describe regulations imposed by one level of government on other governments, whether it be federal mandates applied to state and local governments or state mandates applied to their local jurisdictions. Mandates can consist of either affirmative obligations to take action on a policy problem, such as the treatment of municipal sewage, or a constraint or prohibition against certain policy actions, such as the recent federal preemption of state taxation of Internet access fees.

Mandates is a broad term that actually covers several distinct tools used to regulate activities of other levels of government. Mandates are most often viewed as direct orders, where one level of government orders another to comply with policy standards, such as federal clean water standards, with the penalty of civil or criminal sanctions. However, when governments regulate one another, other strategies have been deployed.

Grants in aid have become a widely used vehicle for project mandates; recipients of funding are bound to follow a wide range of rules as a condition for obtaining the grant. Federal courts have ruled that mandates attached to grants are less coercive and therefore more permissible than direct orders because, technically, states or localities can choose not to apply for funding, although for major grant programs this is not a practical option.

Preemption is another strategy where federal or state governments assert a regulatory policy that prevents other levels of government from pursuing their own regulatory schemes in that area. In some cases, the preemption is complete and prohibitive of any related action by other governments, while in other cases the preemption is partial, where other governments may continue to play a role as long as their standards and policies are consistent with minimum standards.

The federal government has relied more on the use of various forms of mandates since the 1970s. As the federal role in domestic policy expanded, the grant was often the initial instrument used to assert a national presence, but this has been followed by various forms of mandates as national officials and groups became stronger and more insistent on projecting national goals. Mandate advocates argue that state or local governments would not on their own provide sufficient resources or protections for national priorities or vulnerable clientele, whether it be environmental protection or handicapped education. Some suggest that states and localities are engaged in a competition with other jurisdictions for new businesses and higher-income residents, which serves to undermine their support for redistributive policies involving commitments to vulnerable groups. More recently, national business interests have joined the chorus supporting certain mandates and preemptions to guarantee uniform regulatory policies across all 50 states.

The growing use of mandates has prompted a debate on their implications for governance. Absent any restraint, unfunded mandates undermine accountability by permitting one government to experience the joy of enacting benefits without also having to realize the pain of paying for those benefits. Costs imposed by mandates can indeed be significant—nearly $28 billion in new costs were estimated to be imposed on states and localities by federal mandates enacted between 1983 and 1990. Such costs can be paid for by higher taxes, but more often than not they force lower levels of government to distort their priorities by limiting resources for other unique local needs. Mandates carry nonfiscal implications as well. Even when funded or partially by federal or state governments, mandates often impose a "one size fits all" set of rules and approaches that undermine our systems' capacity to respond to diverse needs in flexible ways.

The debate over unfunded mandates has ushered in a wave of reforms. Many states have adopted statutory or constitutional restrictions attempting to rein in the ability of their legislatures to impose unfunded mandates on local governments. Most states attempt to make mandated costs more visible by reporting estimates to the legislature during debates. Some have gone further to require state government to reimburse local jurisdictions for costs associated with state mandates, although legislatures have often continued to pass unfunded mandates when compelling interests are at stake.

At the federal level, growing pressures from state and local governments culminated in passage of the 1995 Unfunded Mandates Reform Act. This act permits mandate opponents to raise a point of order against proposed unfunded mandates in pending legislation under consideration by the Congress. The point of order does not prevent mandates from being enacted, since it can be overridden by a majority of each chamber, but it does promote accountability by prompting a separate vote on the issue of mandating itself. This new act did achieve modest success in deterring certain mandates from reaching the floor of the Congress and prompting mandate sponsors to modify others to reduce their projected state and local costs.

However, important mandates continued to be passed, particularly those exempt from coverage of the reform, such as conditions of federal grants, reflecting the continued appeal of mandates as a tool of government to both parties at the national level. The Supreme Court has joined the mandate debate at the federal level by ruling in the 1990s against direct federal commandeering of state and local governments to enforce federal regulatory policies. Although these rulings have inserted the Court as a source of restraint, nonetheless Congress retains considerable authority because the Court's rulings do not yet extend to the mandate tools most commonly deployed at the federal level—conditions of grants and federal preemptions of state and local regulatory authority.

For more information

Advisory Commission on Intergovernmental Relations. *Federally Induced Costs Affecting State and Local Government*. Washington, D.C.: ACIR, 1995.

Fix, Michael, and Daphne A. Kenyon, eds. *Coping with Mandates*. Washington, D.C.: Urban Institute Press, 1990.

Posner, Paul L. *The Politics of Unfunded Mandates: Whither Federalism?* Washington, D.C.: Georgetown University Press, 1998.

Paul L. Posner

United States Constitution

The U.S. Constitution is the nation's most important legal document, serving as the fundamental law paramount to all other written laws. It also establishes the basic structure of government under which administrative decisions are implemented.

Whereas the British forebears had an unwritten constitution, the delegates who met at the Constitutional Convention in Philadelphia in the summer of 1787 thought that governmental responsibilities would be clearer and liberties would be more secure if the United States had a document unchangeable by ordinary legislative means, enforceable in courts, and granting and limiting governmental powers. The convention included a total of 55 delegates from all of the 13 states (except Rhode Island) that were bound by the Articles of Confederation. George Washington presided at the convention, although fellow Virginian James Madison is often thought to have been the most influential delegate.

The confederal system, under which a weak unicameral Congress constituted the only branch with substantive authority, had allowed states to dominate and had given Congress too little authority over matters of common concern, like interstate commerce. Rather than revising this system, authors of the Virginia Plan, whose blueprint dominated discussion during the first two weeks of the convention, proposed an alternative federal system. It advocated a government where powers were divided among three branches, each of which was expected to provide checks and balances against excesses by the others. The Constitution reflected numerous compromises between large and small states and between those from the North and South. Compromises between large and small states centered chiefly on representation in Congress, and those between North and South largely involved issues of slavery and commerce.

The Constitution reflects the framers' philosophies of government and their compromises. The document consists of a preamble and seven articles (most with multiple sections), and it now has 27 amendments. The preamble is best known for lofty language laying the foundation of the new Constitution in the authority of "We the people" and in articulating the goals of the new document, which included creating "a more perfect Union."

Consistent with the framers' view that the legislative branch would be the most important, Article I describes this branch and is the Constitution's longest. It creates a bicameral legislature. Membership in the lower house (currently set at 435 voting members), the House of Representatives, is based on population. (Slaves were originally counted as three-fifths of a person.) States are equally represented, each with two Senators (thus giving that body a current membership of 100) in the upper house, or Senate. Originally chosen by state legislatures until the ratification of the Seventeeth Amendment (1913) during the Progressive Era, Senators are now chosen, like members of the House, by direct popular election. Elections reflected the framers' commitment to representative democracy over an extended land area, which, they hoped, in accord with James Madison's arguments in *Federalist* No. 10, would promote justice by moderating the passion and influence of factions or interest groups. Members of the House of Representatives are elected for renewable two-year terms and those of the Senate for six years. Laws require majorities of both Houses and either presidential concurrence or passage by a two-thirds majority of both Houses over a presidential veto. The Supreme Court invalidated an alternative "legislative veto" mechanism in *Immigration and Naturalization Service v. Chadha* (1983).

Article I, section 8 lists a variety of congressional powers including some, like control over interstate commerce, that Congress did not have under the Articles of Confederation. In addition to enumerated powers, the necessary and proper clause (the last clause of Art. I, sec. 8) has also provided the basis for judicial recognition of implied powers, such as the power, recognized in *McCulloch v. Maryland* (1819), of establishing a national bank. Congressional powers are limited both by provisions in Article I, section 9—Congress cannot, for example, adopt retroactive criminal laws (known as ex post facto laws) or legislative punishments (known as bills of attainder)—and by subsequent amendments like the first 10 amendments, known as the Bill of Rights. The Senate has special responsibility for confirming presidential nominations to the judicial branch and to diplomatic posts and for approving treaties by a two-thirds vote. Congress has the power to declare war and is vested with the "power of the purse" in appropriating and spending money.

Article II creates and describes the presidency. Partly influenced by the founders' belief that George Washington would be the first to hold this office, the presidency is occupied by a single individual who is elected through a system of indirect election known as the electoral college. It allows states to choose electors who cast ballots for president based on their combined representation in the House and Senate and almost always reflects the popular vote. Presidents serve for four-year terms. The president is designated as "commander in chief" of the armed forces, thus assuring civilian control of the military. Although the specific terminology is not used, the president is recognized as both head of government, with many domestic responsibilities, and head of state, representing the nation's interests in foreign affairs.

The president also has responsibility to make top-level appointments, subject to Senate confirmation. The Constitution does not explicitly say who can remove such officers, but Court decisions, most notably *Myers v. U.S.* (1926), have generally upheld the president's power over all executive appointments whose members do not perform quasi-judicial or quasi-legislative functions. In addition to the "power of the sword," the president is expected to enforce the laws, which he does in part through a variety of cabinet offices that the president heads. Presidents have significant power over legislation through use of their veto power. Presidential powers have expanded with the proliferation of media outlets that allow presidents to appeal directly to the people for the support of programs and policies that they favor.

Article III outlines the judicial branch of government, whose members are appointed by the president, confirmed by the senate, and serve for life terms. The only constitutionally designated court is the Supreme Court, which currently consists of eight associates and one chief justice, who exercise what has been called the "power of judgment." This Court currently sits atop a hierarchy of lower federal trial courts known as district courts and lower appellate courts, or courts of appeal. Cases involving the federal Constitution may also reach the U.S. Supreme Court from the highest court within each state. At least since the Supreme Court's decision in *Marbury v. Madison* (1803), American courts have exercised the power known as judicial review, which allows them to decide whether or not laws which arise in the course of cases coming before them are constitutional or not. This power is often enhanced by the ambiguity of some constitutional language and by theories of unenumerated rights. Courts also exercise statutory interpretation by deciding on the meaning of ambiguous laws.

Article IV outlines the relation between the national government and the states. Some powers are exercised exclusively by the national government; some powers are denied to one or both governments; many powers are exercised concurrently by both state and national governments; and others (as the Tenth Amendment affirms) are reserved to the states. States are charged with responsibilities related to protecting the rights of citizens of other states, extraditing criminals, and the like. The national government is committed to preserving a republican form of government within the states and coming to their aid when needed. Because the Constitution created a federal system, the national government has the right to act directly on its citizens rather than having to go through the states, as under the Articles of Confederation. Since the Civil War, there has been general agreement that states do not have the rights of nullifying federal laws or seceding from the Union.

Article V seeks to forestall violent means of change by outlining a process for amending the Constitution. Such amendments are proposed by two-thirds majorities in both houses of Congress and ratified by three-fourths majorities of the states. Although they have not yet done so, two-thirds of the state legislatures may also call an Article V convention to propose amendments. Article V specifies that states cannot be deprived of their equal suffrage in the Senate without their consent.

Article VI contains a number of miscellaneous provisions, the most important of which is the supremacy clause found in the second paragraph. This clause, which recognizes the supremacy of the national constitution and requires state judges to uphold this document, is one of the supports for judicial review. Article VII provided for sidestepping the requirement for unanimous consent to constitutional changes under the Articles of Confederation by providing that the new constitution would go into effect when ratified by special conventions in nine or more states. This mechanism helped bypass state legislatures wary of giving up some of their powers and arguably gave the new Constitution a more popular base than it would otherwise have had.

Over time, the Constitution has been increasingly democratized both by changing mores and by formal amendments. The first 10 amendments, or Bill of Rights, adopted shortly after ratification of the Constitution (1791), forestalled a second convention by affirming the framers' commitment to such rights as freedom of religion, speech, and press; their distaste for general warrants; and their belief in the necessity of rights for individuals accused of, on trial for, or being punished for crimes. A number of amendments, most notably the Fifteenth (1870), Seventeenth (1913), Nineteenth (1920), Twenty-third (1961), Twenty-fourth (1964), and Twenty-sixth (1971), have expanded voting rights to new groups or struck down obstacles to such voting. Most important were the Fifteenth Amendment, designed to prohibit race from being used as an obstacle to voting (the amendment proved initially ineffective), and the Nineteenth Amendment, which extended voting rights to women. Other amendments have clarified states' rights, modified the electoral college, provided for a national income tax, limited a president to two full terms, provided for cases of presidential disability, and the like.

Amendments Thirteen through Fifteen, all adopted shortly after the U.S. Civil War, were designed to eliminate slavery, extend to all U.S. citizens fundamental rights, and prohibit voting discrimination on the basis of race. In so doing, these amendments aligned the Constitution more closely with the goals of freedom and equality that had been enunciated in the Declaration of Independence (1776). Over time, judicial interpretations of the Fourteenth Amendment (1868) have served as the vehicle through which most provisions in the Bill of Rights have been applied not only to the national government but also to the states.

For more information

Peltason, J. W., et al. *Understanding the Constitution,* 15th ed. Fort Worth, Tex.: Harcourt, 2000.

Vile, John R. *A Companion to the United States Constitution and Its Amendments,* 3d ed. Westport, Conn.: Praeger, 2001.

John R. Vile

United States foreign policy   United States foreign policy consists of those strategic mechanisms that are employed to protect U.S. national interest in the international arena, primarily by means of diplomacy but also through the use of military intervention.

The structure, institutions, and decision making processes that make up American foreign policy have multiple origins.

Constitutional and legal basis of foreign policy

The constitutional and legal basis of American foreign policy can be traced to Articles I and II on the United States Constitution, which describes the respective roles of the president and Congress. Under Article II, the president of the United States has the power to make treaties, appoint and receive ambassadors to and from foreign countries for purposes of diplomacy, and to serve as commander in chief of the armed forces. Under Article I, Congress has the power to approve treaties, to declare war, to create, maintain, and regulate the armed forces, and to regulate international trade.

Both the president and Congress share responsibilities in foreign policy and national defense. The pattern has been for Congress to submit to the leadership of the president in issues of national defense. As commander in chief, the president has initiated military force around the world on over 160 occasions compared to Congress's official declaration of war five times. The relationship between the president and Congress has been best described as a "system of overlapping competing powers" where the executive and legislative branches of government are constitutionally required to cooperate in the protection of the national interest from any and all international threat.

Origins of U.S. foreign policy values

The first attempt to undertake an American foreign policy originated during the Revolutionary War and then under the Articles of Confederation. The Articles of Confederation had produced a loose organization of states, and one of the failures of this first constitution for the United States was that each of the states seemed to create its own foreign policy in competition against the others. The result was that it was difficult to form a truly national foreign policy with the national government speaking with one voice.

In revising the Constitution in 1787, the founders tried to strike a balance between giving the new office of the presidency too much power in foreign policy versus making it an institution that was too feeble or weak to react to national threats. The basis for constitutional provisions eventually adopted is described in detail in the *Federalist Papers*. In general, there is evidence that the framers intended Congress to be the primary institution responsible for foreign policy, but over time a significant amount of power has gravitated to the president.

Characteristics of U.S. foreign policy decision making

American foreign policy decision making has several characteristics. First, the foreign policy process involves various stages of development and implementation. However, it differs from domestic policy development on two key points. First, because much of foreign policy has to do with negotiation and securing the most beneficial posture ranging from issues of trade to issues of war, secrecy is a dominant factor. Hence, in the case of foreign policy, public interest is represented by Congress. Moreover, within Congress there are elected officials who undertake the oversight of the foreign-policy challenges and help provide the information needed to make strategic decisions. Therefore, the information element that would drive public opinion domestically on internal policies is more restricted in the foreign-policy domain.

A second characteristic of foreign policy that makes it unique is that it has been best depicted as a pendulum that repeatedly swings

Protesters jab a caricature of the Statue of Liberty during a protest in front of the U.S. embassy in Manila, Philippines. (CALDERON/GETTY IMAGES)

to and fro from a posture of isolationism to a posture of interventionism. By *isolationism* scholars mean periods in which the United States directs its attention and resources toward internal issues of the country and its populace. On the other hand, by *interventionism* it is meant that the country is actively seeking to protect or secure that which is threatened either politically or, if need be, militarily, for the interest of the country. Throughout various times in American history, U.S. foreign policy has displayed both interventionist and isolationist characteristics.

A third theme driving American foreign policy decision making has been a policy debate between realism and idealism. Realism is depicted as "Old World diplomacy." The goal of realism is to sus-

tain the nation by any means necessary, including the use of force. The tools of power politics that have been used include military force, secret diplomacy, the balancing of power among different nations, and the containment of other superpowers by allying with other countries. Examples of realism include the diplomacy and military buildup used to confine communism and the Soviet Union during the cold war, or the use of military power to disarm Iraq in 2003.

Idealists see the survival of a nation depending upon compromise and cooperation. Idealism in foreign policy tends to stress human rights, international organization, open diplomacy, economic development through free trade, international law, and collective security. Examples of idealism in foreign policy include the pursuit and protection of human rights during the presidency of Jimmy Carter and the move to create the League of Nations under President Woodrow Wilson.

Realism and idealism form a continuum. The foreign policy stance that is considered Neorealist focuses upon power distribution in the international arena. The neo-idealist or neo-liberal stance is international interdependence in law, economics, and policy interest.

A fourth and increasingly important theme in American foreign policy making revolves around the use of economic and not military power to secure desired objectives. Trade expansion has as its goal the securing of new markets so that Americans can sell goods to other countries. The idea behind use of trade as a tool of foreign policy is that the United States could use its economic leverage to influence other countries.

However, expansion of trade has also been associated with what other parts of the international community refer to as "cultural imperialism." Cultural imperialism describes products that are generated in the United States as being tied to values that support a way of thinking that differs significantly from other portions of the world. Because of technological advances especially, it is thought that these products bolster a kind of "Americanization" of thought and value throughout the world. In addition, some accuse the United States of using certain international organizations, such as the World Trade Organization, the World Bank, and the International Monetary Fund, as fronts simply to support American interests.

A final theme that emerges in discussions of American foreign policy is over the issue of unilateralism versus multilateralism. Unilateralism refers to the United States's undertaking foreign policy initiatives on its own without consulting its allies, whereas multilateralism is undertaking a foreign policy in consultation with allies and in cooperation with international institutions such as the United Nations.

Critics of American foreign policy assert that the United States often views itself as the leader of the world or the "world's policeman" and therefore believes it can do what it wants because of its military and economic power, regardless of what international law or international opinion holds. An example of this position is criticism of the decision of the United States to invade Iraq in 2003 without express language from the United Nations' Security Council authorizing the use of force.

On the other hand, defenders of unilateralism argue that the country needs to take unilateral action because, in fact, America is the most powerful nation in the world and, therefore, it has a special obligation to act when other nations do not or cannot. President George W. Bush defended his decision to invade Iraq as necessary to disarm that nation and to eliminate the roots of world terrorism.

For more information

Boyer, Paul S., ed. *The Oxford Companion to United States History.* New York: Oxford University Press, 2001.

Goldwin, Robert A., and Robert A. Licht, eds. *Foreign Policy and the Constitution.* Washington, D.C.: American Enterprise Institute Press, 1990.

Johnson, Paul. *A History of the American People.* New York: Harper Perennial, 1997.

Pfiffner, James P. *The Strategic Presidency: Hitting the Ground Running.* Lawrence: University of Kansas Press, 1996.

Sunstein, Cass R. *Designing Democracy: What Constitutions Do.* New York: Oxford University Press, 2001.

Tindall, George Brown, and David E. Shi. *America: A Narrative History,* 4th ed. Vol. II. New York: W. W. Norton, 1996.

Urdang, Laurence, ed. *The Timetables of American History.* New York: Simon and Schuster, 1996.

Weismann, Max, ed. *Mortimer J. Adler's the Great Ideas: From the Great Books of Western Civilization.* Chicago: Open Court, 2001.

Olivia M. McDonald

United States Postal Service The United States Postal Service (USPS) is the second oldest department or agency in the U.S. federal government.

In 1775, the Continental Congress named Benjamin Franklin the first postmaster general. After the ratification of the U.S. Constitution, the new U.S. Congress passed the Act of September 22, 1789 (1 Stat. 70), which temporarily established a post office and created the Office of the Postmaster General. At that time there were 75 post offices and about 2,000 miles of post roads. Although detailed provisions were made for the postal services in 1792, it took 80 years for the Post Office Department (POD) to be established as an executive department by Congress in 1872.

Almost 100 years later, the 1970 Postal Reorganization Act transformed the POD into the USPS, a quasi-private federal agency in the executive branch of the U.S. government. The new USPS officially began operations on 1 July 1971. Despite the changes produced by the reorganization, the mission of the USPS remained the same:

> The Postal Service shall have as its basic function the obligation to provide postal services to bind the Nation together through the personal, educational, literary, and business correspondence of the people. It shall provide prompt, reliable, and efficient services to patrons in all areas and shall render postal services to all communities (Title 39 of the U.S. Code). While the USPS receives no federal monies, it is subject to congressional oversight by the Subcommittee on the Postal Service of the House Committee on Government Reform and Oversight. The purpose, structure, and most of the internal functions (i.e., hiring under the Merit System Protection Board) of the USPS are governed by legislation. Although the USPS is not a government corporation, it is frequently identified as such and has been included in major government corporation studies.

With nearly 800,000 employees, it is now the largest federal civilian employer in the United States and the second largest civilian employer in the world. It collects, processes, and delivers 182 billion pieces of mail per year. As mandated by the Reorganization Act, it is also a financially self-sustaining organization. The USPS operates solely on the revenues of postal products and services (totaling more than $63 billion in fiscal year 1999), and does not receive any federal tax dollars. The USPS is a vital component of the nation's economy, delivering hundreds of millions of messages and conducting billions of dollars in financial transactions with 8 million businesses and 250 million Americans each day.

For more information

U.S. Postal Service. http://www.usps.com/history/his1.htm.

Tina Nabatchi

United States v. National Treasury Employees Union 513 U.S. 454 (1995)

United States v. National Treasury Employees Union (1995) confirmed that the First Amendment right to free speech protects federal government employees' ability to speak and write about topics unrelated to their jobs.

In 1989, Congress enacted the Ethics Reform Act. One provision of the act prohibited federal government employees from receiving honoraria, which are payments for making appearances at meetings, giving speeches, or writing articles. Congress created the prohibition after a report by a national commission evaluating government salaries raised concerns about officials in the legislative, executive, and judicial branches supplementing their incomes by accepting payments for giving speeches and meeting with interest groups. The commission expressed concern that government officials' decisions on policy issues might be influenced by their desire to obtain honoraria.

The prohibition on honoraria was challenged in court by several government employees and by two unions representing government workers. The government employees had received honoraria for speaking and writing during off-duty hours about subjects that were unrelated to their work for the government. For example, a government microbiologist wrote articles about dance performances in his spare time. An aerospace engineer lectured about African-American history, and a postal-service employee gave talks to groups about religion. They claimed that the prohibition on honoraria improperly violated their First Amendment right to freedom of speech.

The U.S. Supreme Court had previously said that Congress can impose job-related limitations on the job-related speech of public employees in *Snepp v. United States,* 444 U.S. 507 (1980). That case concerned a former Central Intelligence Agency (CIA) officer whom the government sought to prevent from writing a book about the CIA's activities in the Vietnam War. In order to limit the speech of its employees, the government must show that its interests in promoting efficient public service outweigh the employee's right to speak. When the Supreme Court examined the government's claimed interests to justify the prohibition on honoraria, the justices rejected the government's claim that its interests outweighed the employees' rights.

The government claimed that the ban on honoraria was needed to ensure that federal officers do not misuse or appear to misuse their power by accepting compensation for their unofficial writing and speaking activities. The Court noted, however, that the government provided no evidence that any misconduct related to such honoraria had occurred among lower-level federal employees. The Supreme Court supported the lower-court decisions that prevented enforcement of the law against federal employees involved in the lawsuit. The Court also invited Congress to consider additional legislation that would more carefully define and justify the circumstances in which it was necessary to prohibit honoraria because of a close connection between the compensated activity and the employee's governmental duties.

The Supreme Court's decision reinforced the principle that people do not surrender their constitutional right to freedom of speech merely by virtue of becoming a government employee. Government employees do not have unlimited free speech rights, because the Supreme Court permits limitations when the government's interests in prohibiting certain expressions outweigh the employees' rights. However, the nature of and justifications for limiting free speech must be carefully specified. Courts will not automatically accept all claims by government concerning the purported need to limit public employees' right to express themselves.

For more information

Rohr, John A. *Public Service, Ethics, and Constitutional Practice.* Lawrence: University Press of Kansas, 1999.

Salkin, Patricia E. *Ethical Standards in the Public Sector: A Guide for Governmental Lawyers, Clients, and Public Officials.* Chicago: ABA Publishing, 1999.

Christopher Smith

United States v. Wurzbach **280 U.S. 397 (1929)** In *United States v. Wurzbach* the Supreme Court upheld a law regulating federal campaign contributions.

The 1925 federal Corrupt Practices Act prohibited members of Congress from collecting campaign contributions from officers or employees of the U.S. government. The 1925 act was one of the first attempts by Congress to limit campaign contributions in national elections. The law was prompted by the belief that large sums of money created corruption in the political process. Congress also feared that the federal workforce might be coerced into donating money to a candidate for fear of losing their jobs.

In the Supreme court case of *United States v. Wurzbach,* the constitutionality of that law was tested. Wurzbach followed the Court decision in *United States v. Newberry,* 256 U.S. 232 (1921), in which the Supreme Court had limited Congress's ability to regulate primary elections. Those elections, used to choose candidates to run in the general election in November, were controlled and regulated by state governments. The *Wurzbach* case saw the federal government claim jurisdiction over primary elections.

Wurzbach was running for Congress in the Republican primary in the state of Texas. While the 1925 act prohibited such donations in federal elections, the law did not specifically mention primary elections. After Wurzbach collected money from federal employees to fund his campaign, he was charged with violating the law as it was applied to the Republican primary election. A federal district court dismissed the charge, stating that the law was not intended to be used against primary elections because such elections were the constitutional field of the states.

The federal government appealed to the U.S. Supreme Court, which heard the case in 1930. Speaking for a unanimous court, Justice Oliver Wendell Holmes wrote that the 1925 act was to be interpreted broadly to include primary elections. According to Holmes, Article I, section 4 of the Constitution granted Congress the power over the time, place, and manner of holding federal elections. This power included primary elections where candidates were chosen to represent a political party in the general election. The Court also ruled that Congress intended to prevent coercion of federal employees to donate money to federal candidates for fear of losing their jobs, a goal that government could advance without violating the constitution.

The *Wurzbach* decision was one of the first Court opinions granting the federal government power to limit campaign contributions for primary elections. It contradicted the Mulberry decision in which the Court had limited federal control over primaries. It also allowed for further congressional legislation, including the 1940 Hatch Act which placed monetary limits on donations to congressional candidates. Wurzbach was followed a decade later by the better known decision in *U.S. v. Classic* (313 U.S. 229) (1941) in which Congress' power over primary elections was extended by the Court.

For more information

Luna, Christopher. *Campaign Finance Reform.* New York: H. W. Wilson, 2001.

Mutch, Robert. *Campaigns, Congress and the Courts: The Making of Federal Campaign Finance Law.* New York: Praeger Publishing, 1988.

Douglas Clouatre

U.S. Department of State

U.S. Department of State   The United States Department of State, better known as the State Department, is a cabinet-level agency of the U.S. government primarily responsible for managing the FOREIGN POLICY of the United States and assisting American citizens abroad.

The State Department was created by an act of Congress in 1789 along with the War and Treasury Departments. President George Washington appointed Thomas Jefferson to serve as the first head, or secretary, of this department commencing in 1790. The list of individuals who have served as secretary of state has included James Madison, James Monroe, John Quincy Adams, Martin Van Buren, and James Buchanan, all of whom would subsequently be elected president of the Untied States. Two former secretaries of state, John Marshall and Charles Evans Hughes, would become chief justices of the United States Supreme Court. Other secretaries have included distinguished politicians such as Senators Daniel Webster and John Calhoun. Madeleine Albright, named by President Bill Clinton in 1997, was the first female secretary of state, and in 2001 President George W. Bush named Colin L. Powell, the first African-American to hold this position. Generally the secretary of state serves as the chief diplomat for the United States government, often traveling the world to meet or work with other countries on matters regarding peace, war, and the promotion of U.S. interests.

The secretary of state leads the primary agency in the United States entrusted with developing, coordinating, and implementing American foreign policy. This task includes serving the United States abroad as the official representative of the government. This means that when the government wishes to undertake treaty negotiations with other countries, or international agencies such as the United Nations, the State Department is generally given primary responsibility to act on its behalf. In addition, the State Department also manages the foreign-affairs budget, as well as other foreign-affairs resources, and it provides support and guidance to the U.S. diplomatic corp, including American ambassadors, who serve in embassies and consulates around the world. These embassies and consulates also serve as contact points for foreign individuals or individuals who wish to travel or immigrate to the United States.

Besides managing the country's foreign affairs, the State Department performs many critical functions for U.S. citizens. It is this department that issues passports to American citizens so that they may travel abroad. The State Department provides assistance and protection to U.S. citizens who are abroad. It provides warnings about security or safety threats to Americans in different countries, and foreign service workers may provide assistance to American citizens abroad who have been accused of or been a victim of a crime. Finally, the State Department also works with American compa-nies to help them in their efforts to do business in foreign countries.

The State Department is organized into several bureaus or agencies, each with its own undersecretaries. There are undersecretaries for political affairs, arms control, and international security. The Department of State also has programs that address cultural and educational affairs and human rights, and there are bureaus that specialize in certain regions of the world, such as Asia or Latin America, or which handle specific issues, such as refugees.

Overall, the Department of State is one of the most important cabinet agencies in the United States. Without it, U.S. citizens would be severely limited in their ability to travel, and it would be impossible for the government to make and implement foreign policy decisions.

For more information

Allison, Graham T., *Essence of Decision: Explaining the Cuban Missile Crisis*. New York: Pearson, 1999.

Mead, Walter Russell. *Special Providence: American Foreign Policy and How It Changed the World*. New York: Routledge, 2002.

Sweeney, Jerry K. *America and the World, 1776–1998: A Handbook of United States Diplomatic History*. Prospect Heights, Ill.: Waveland Press, 2000

U.S. Department of State. http://www.state.gov.

David Schultz

V

value-added tax (VAT) VAT refers to the value-added tax, which is generally assessed on the value of goods and services. It is also frequently referred to as a "general tax," in that it applies to all commercial activity, or as a "consumption tax," which means that the tax is visible at all stages through the production and distribution chain.

The VAT is usually assessed as a percentage of the price of the product or service and is therefore not a charge to the company or producer's profit or income but, rather, a levy on the price charged. In most applications of the VAT, there is a system of deductions where the producer of the product or service can deduct the amount of tax it pays related to input costs from the amount of VAT it collects when selling its product or service, hence making the tax "neutral."

There has been a wide-ranging debate about the fairness and effectiveness of the VAT, although the European Union, Canada, and other countries have adopted it. The benefits of the VAT include the revenue-neutral characteristic of the tax that avoids taxation at multiple levels of production, which otherwise would be compounded before being passed on to the consumer. In the context of the shift from manufacturing-based economies to increased service-based economies, VAT can serve to spread the tax burden over a wide range of economic activity. VAT applies to services and goods, while more traditional sales taxes are usually applied to goods only.

Criticism of the VAT focuses on the amount of increased revenue it generally brings governments, money that would otherwise be fueling the economy. In addition, the cost to business of administering the VAT (i.e., recording tax paid and received on every item or service sold) is often cited as a weakness of the VAT.

Finally, opponents of the VAT point to the fact that unlike progressive sales taxes, individuals of all incomes contribute to paying the tax, although there is usually a low-income cutoff below which those with low incomes pay minimal or no income tax. Proponents of the VAT suggest that direct income-transfer payments to low-income individuals can offset this "unfairness."

While the debate over the VAT continues in most countries, most economic observers agree that the VAT is a tax that will continue to be adopted by more countries.

For more information

Bradford, David F. *Fundamental Issues in Consumption Taxation*. Washington, D.C.: AEI Press, 1996.

Delegation of the European Union to the United States. http://www.eurunion.org/legislat/VATweb.htm.

Ebrill, Liam, et al. *The Modern VAT*. Washington, D.C.: International Monetary Fund, 2001.

Michael Henry

Vermont Yankee Nuclear Power Corp. v. Natural Resources Defense Council 435 U.S. 519 (1978)

Vermont Yankee represents the concept that administrative agencies that have met the requirements for rule making should be granted deference to their procedures by reviewing judicial courts.

In this unanimous U.S. Supreme Court decision written by then Justice Rehnquist, the Court held that when an administrative agency has followed rule-making procedures mandated by law or by the ADMINISTRATIVE PROCEDURE ACT (APA), the courts may not impose their "own notion of which procedures are 'best' or most likely to further some vague, undefined public good." Only in "extremely rare" circumstances may courts impose additional procedural requirements on administrative agencies.

At issue was the granting of a construction permit by the Atomic Energy Commission (AEC, now the Nuclear Regulatory Commission) to the Vermont Yankee Nuclear Power Corporation. Concerns were raised regarding Vermont Yankee's disposal and storage of highly toxic nuclear waste from the proposed plant. As part of the process, the AEC proposed and adopted a rule that included the environmental impact of the waste disposal, but ultimately the practical effect was to diminish the waste-disposal problem. During the rule-making process, the only evidence supporting the waste-disposal segment was a 20-page report, and the AEC did not allow a cross-examination of the report's author. During the process, all other APA rule-making requirements were followed by the AEC.

The Natural Resources Defense Council (NRDC) filed suit, and the D.C. Circuit Court of Appeals held that by not allowing a cross-examination, the AEC's rule-making procedures were inadequate, thus overturning the agency's rule. The U.S. Supreme Court overturned the court of appeals's decision, concluding that absent "constitutional constraints or extremely compelling circumstances," administrative agencies should be free to determine their own rule-making procedures. It is the discretion of administrative agencies, and not judicial courts, to determine when extra procedures are needed in rule making. Justice Rehnquist held that there were compelling reasons to avoid this sort of "Monday morning quarterbacking" by the courts over agency decision making. Most notably, judicial review would be "totally unpredictable," while agencies would be compelled to use procedures normally reserved only for adjudicatory hearings, and thus turn rule making into judicial, courtlike proceedings.

The *Vermont Yankee* opinion was controversial. Some scholars contend that the Court ignored APA's section 559, which imposes minimum, but not maximum, requirements on agency rule-making procedures. Others argue that the Court was correct in respecting the procedures sanctioned by the Congress, and that agencies, and not courts, are the experts in fact-finding procedures. However, the U.S. Supreme Court has not been consistent in its deference to agency rule-making procedures and has occasionally mandated court-imposed additional requirements.

For more information

Byse, Clark. "*Vermont Yankee* and the Evolution of Administrative Procedure: A Somewhat Different View." *Harvard Law Review* 91 (1978): 1,823–1,845.

Davis, Kenneth C. "Administrative Common Law and the *Vermont Yankee* Opinion." *Utah Law Review* (1980): 3–17.

J. Michael Bitzer

veterans preference The veterans preference is applied to persons who meet requirements associated with service in the armed forces. Eligible veterans receive preference in obtaining employment with the federal government and an improved retention standing in the event of a reduction in force.

The Veterans Preference Act was passed in 1944. The intent of this legislation was to provide a competitive advantage for veterans returning to the civilian workforce following their service in World War II. The public-policy consideration was the relative competitiveness of veterans who had been removed from the civilian work force. Preference recognizes the economic loss suffered by citizens who have served their country in uniform and acknowledges a larger obligation owed to disabled veterans. Consistent with the concept of loss, veterans preference may also apply to the mother of a deceased veteran and the widow/widower of a veteran.

Preference is applied when federal agencies hire from civil service registers. Candidates for jobs are evaluated and ranked on a register according to a civil service examination score. The examination score is a summation of points assigned to the job-related knowledge, skills, and abilities that a candidate demonstrates on the job application. A preference-eligible veteran will have five points added to the examination score. Disabled veterans have 10 points added to the score.

To receive preference, a veteran must have been separated from the army, navy, air force, Marine Corps, or Coast Guard with an honorable or general discharge. Historically, Congress has defined eligibility for preference for those who were either disabled or served in declared wars. An ongoing series of legislation has expanded the eligibility definition of preference to include military service in conflicts that are not declared wars. Grenada, Somalia, and Panama are examples of designated military conflicts that qualify veterans for preference.

Under the Civil Service Reform Act of 1978, a disabled veteran with a service-connected disability of 30 percent or more may be noncompetitively selected for a job. The disability must be documented by the Department of Defense and the Department of Veterans Affairs. This hiring authority is optional for agencies. Agencies that do not want to select a 30 percent disabled veteran must notify the veteran and the U.S. Office of Personnel Management and allow a 15-day appeal period.

Not all veterans qualify for preference points. According to Public Law 95-454, nondisabled veterans who retire at or above the rank of major are not eligible for preference. After the initial selection for a federal job, veterans compete equally with all other candidates for subsequent job openings. In 1999, 25 percent of the federal civilian workforce had exercised veterans preference to obtain employment.

The Department of Labor Veterans Employment and Training Service investigates complaints associated with veterans preference. The Veterans Employment Opportunities Act of 1998 allows preference-eligible veterans to complain when a violation of rights relating to preference occurs.

For more information
United States Code, Titles 5 and 38.
United States Office of Personnel Management. www.opm.gov/veterans.

Richard J. Van Orden

veto Veto refers to the power of a chief executive (a president, governor, or mayor) to keep a proposal passed by a legislative body (the congress, state legislature, or city council) from becoming law, in whole or part.

Typically in the United States, a bill must pass the legislature and be approved by the chief executive to become law. If the chief executive refuses to approve the bill, that is, if he or she vetoes it, it cannot become law except under extraordinary circumstances. The legislature can override a veto by reapproving the measure with some super-majority vote, often a two-thirds vote. However, overriding a veto is difficult, so the veto is a powerful tool for the chief executive.

The veto is an important part of the checks and balances of the U.S. system of government, since it limits the power of the legislature. In most parliamentary systems, the legislative branch has virtually unfettered lawmaking power. More than simply a negative power to stop legislation, the veto also forces the legislature to consider the wishes of the chief executive in lawmaking. Passing a bill is hard and time-consuming work. Once they have passed a bill, legislators generally want to see it become law. The ever-present threat of a veto forces legislators to work with the chief executive throughout the process so that he or she will sign it into law.

There are several types of vetoes with which different U.S. chief executives have been empowered by their constitutions:

- Package veto: The package veto (or just "the veto") allows the chief executive to stop an entire bill from becoming law. The chief executive formally states that he or she is vetoing the bill and sends a message to the legislature explaining why. The president, all governors, and many mayors have this power.

- POCKET VETO: This is a form of the package veto by which the president and 15 governors can stop a bill passed at the end of a legislative session from becoming law simply by not signing it, that is, by "putting it in his or her pocket." With the legislature adjourned, no further action can be taken on the bill and it dies.

- Line-item veto: Forty-two governors have the power to veto individual "line items" (specific expenditures) from a spending bill, allowing the rest of the bill to pass into law. Variants of the line-item veto exist in a few states, such as the reduction veto, which allows the governor to reduce a spending line without eliminating it entirely, and the so-

called wheel-of-fortune veto that Wisconsin governors enjoy, which allows them to eliminate individual words and letters from spending bills.

- Amendatory veto: Fifteen governors have the power to send a bill back to the legislature with a request for specific changes. If the legislature votes to accept these changes, the governor promises to sign it.

Presidents have long envied the power of the governors' line item veto and advocated it for the presidency. Some argue that such a change would allow the president to reduce government spending. However, research in the states has shown that the line-item veto does not necessarily do this. Congress has been reluctant to grant this power to the president, both because it would reduce its own power and because there is a question as to whether such a change could be accomplished through legislation or if it would require a constitutional amendment. In 1996, Congress finally passed a law granting the president a very limited line-item veto. But in *Clinton v. City of New York* (1998), the U.S. Supreme Court declared this law to be an unconstitutional violation of the separation of powers between the executive and legislative branches.

For more information
Watson, Richard A. *Presidential Vetoes and Public Policy.* Lawrence: University Press of Kansas, 1993.

Christopher Z. Mooney

Violence Against Women Act   The Violence Against Women Act of 1994 (VAWA), was passed by Congress as part of the Violent Crime Control and Law Enforcement Act of 1994 and signed by President Bill Clinton.

By passing VAWA, Congress agreed that gender-based violence against women is a form of sex discrimination. By adding a gender-specific civil-rights provision (i.e., if a crime against a woman is motivated by gender animus, that crime violates the woman's civil rights under federal law), VAWA complemented existing federal civil rights legislation. In *United States v. Morrison, et al.* and *Brzonkala v. Morrison* (2000), however, the Supreme Court ruled that Congress exceeded its constitutional exercise of federal authority and invalidated the key portion of the act that gave women the right to file federal civil rights suits and sue their alleged attackers in federal court.

Gender-motivated violence against women was a serious problem long before 1994, but it was not a subject of congressional hearings and testimony until 1990, when Congress began to study the extent of violence against women in the United States. After listening to four years of exhaustive hearings about the degree and impact of gender-motivated violence, Congress concluded that it affected women not only as citizens but as consumers and producers—full and free participants—in the market and thus was within the scope of its authority under the U.S. Constitution, specifically the commerce clause (Article I, clause 3) and the Fourteenth Amendment (equal protection). Congress passed VAWA as part of the Violent Crime Control and Law Enforcement Law of 1994, which was then signed by President Bill Clinton.

VAWA had several core goals: bolster women's safety on the streets and in their homes; ensure protection of their civil rights and equal justice in the court system; protect battered immigrant women and children; and reduce stalking and domestic violence. Soon after President Clinton signed the omnibus crime bill, the U.S. Department of Justice—as mandated by the act—created the Violence against Women Office. VAWA also required that the National Academy of Sciences develop a research agenda to study violence against women, which resulted in the National Institute of Justice and the Centers for Disease Control and Prevention working together. In addition, VAWA established a national domestic violence hotline.

Congress committed federal funds for the years 1995 to 2000 toward combating violence against women, including, for instance, millions of dollars to states and local communities: for training of police officers and building programs for law enforcement on how to respond to and deal with violent crimes against women; for prosecutors, police, and prevention services; and for victim-witness counselors.

On the eve of its expiration in 2000, Congress reauthorized VAWA as one of the sections of the Victims of Trafficking and Violence Protection Act of 2000, which was then signed by President George Bush.

For more information

Violence Against Women Office, Office of Justice Programs, U.S. Department of Justice. http://www.ojp.usdoj.gov/vawo/.

Linda K. Shafer

W

Waldo, Dwight (1913–2000) *public administrator, writer* Dwight Waldo was one of the 20th century's leading public administration theorists. He is the author of numerous works, many of which focused on the intellectual roots of the field of public administration and the oftentimes uneasy relationship between public administration and political science.

After receiving his Ph.D. from Yale University in 1942, Waldo worked in Washington, D.C., at the Office of Price Administration and later at the Bureau of the Budget. In 1946 he joined the faculty at the University of California, Berkeley, and later taught at the Maxwell School at Syracuse University until his retirement in 1979. Waldo also served as editor in chief of the *Public Administration Review* from 1966 to 1977.

Waldo is perhaps best known for his book, *The Administrative State: A Study of the Political Theory of American Public Administration* (1948). In this work Waldo provides a fundamental challenge to some of the existing premises that were embraced by such orthodox scholars as LUTHER GULICK and Lyndall Urwick. As an example, Waldo asserts that the orthodox movement's exaltation of the values of economy and efficiency was misguided.

Rather, the pursuit of such values must be accomplished within the context of other ends rooted in our constitutional framework. After all, Waldo reasoned, the German concentration camps during World War II were ruthlessly "efficient" but obviously inimical to our constitutional and democratic values. Thus, it is not efficiency per se, but efficiency toward some ends. Redirecting our focus toward more substantive ends is where our efforts should lie.

Waldo also challenged the prevailing belief that a "science" of public administration could be achieved. Because the practice of administration is culturally and contextually bound, it can never attain the status of a science in the truest sense of the word. In other writings Waldo challenged the orthodox belief in the separation of politics and administration. From his own wartime administrative experience, Waldo understood that a public administration based on the progressive drive to root out corruption by removing politics from administration was not in accord with administrative realities. Administrators can and do play a political role in the formation and implementation of public policy on a daily basis.

In the late 1960s and early 1970s Waldo helped spawn a new intellectual movement in the field, known as the NEW PUBLIC ADMINISTRATION. This movement originated out of an academic conference in upstate New York comprising rising "young turks" who sought to address and redefine the major questions facing the field during these turbulent times. The new public administration called for scholars to elevate the value of equity alongside the values of economy, efficiency, and effectiveness. The proceedings of this conference were published as a book in 1971, entitled, *Toward a New Public Administration: The Minnowbrook Perspective.*

In 1979 the American Society for Public Administration named its highest honor for lifetime academic contributions the Dwight Waldo Award.

For more information

Waldo, Dwight. *The Administrative State: A Study of the Political Theory of American Public Administration.* New York: Ronald Press, 1948.

Patrick G. Scott

War Powers Act

War Powers Act   The War Powers Act refers to the law that prohibits the president of the United States from waging war beyond 60 days without congressional approval.

The War Powers Act mandates that the executive branch, if possible, is to notify Congress before committing troops. Once committed, only Congress can extend their mission beyond said period of time. The legislative branch can authorize presidential action through several means, including a temporary waiver or a formal declaration of war. Under certain circumstances such as troop safety, this deadline can be extended by another 30 days. The stated purpose of the law was to "insure that the collective judgments of both the Congress and the President will apply to the introduction of United States Armed Forces into hostilities, or into situations where imminent involvement in hostilities is clearly indicated by the circumstances, and to the continued use of such forces in hostilities or in such situations."

The War Powers Act was a means of preventing the nation from becoming embroiled in prolonged unpopular acts and a check on presidential foreign policy. The act was created on 7 November 1973 in the aftermath of the Vietnam War. Congress felt that President Lyndon Johnson had been given too much power as a result of the Gulf of Tonkin Resolution. Many felt Presidents Johnson and Nixon had waged a war with far more sweeping powers than the Constitution permitted. Not only were there concerns over escalation of the war, but some members felt that both administrations had lied about U.S. participation in Vietnam.

The first major test of the law was the Persian Gulf War in 1991. While the Congress approved President Bush's actions, there were several members of the administration who felt the law was unconstitutional and that the president had a right to proceed with the military operation no matter what the Congress decided.

In 1974, Congress passed the Hughes Ryan Act to strengthen the War Powers Act. It required the president to report any nonintelligence, non-CIA actions to the relevant legislative committee in a timely fashion. Its purpose was to guarantee that proper oversight committees received all relevant information regarding covert activities. This law was believed to help Congress in making proper decisions. There has been a great amount of criticism of this act because of congressional leaks to the press.

Congress added another amendment to the War Powers Act when it passed the Boland Amendment on 8 December 1982. This law stated that governmental intelligence agencies were not allowed to provide military support, training, and equipment "for the purpose of overthrowing the Government of Nicaragua." This legislation was designed to prevent the RONALD REAGAN administration from supporting the Contra rebels in their battle against the communist government. The Reagan administration tried to subvert the law by having members of the National Security Council (NSC), which they considered to be a nonintelligence agency, provide funds to the Contras, thus leading to the infamous IRAN-CONTRA public hearings in which Oliver North, John Poindexter, and others were brought before Congress. To this date, no president has challenged the constitutionality of this law regulating his use of military force.

For more information

Burgess, Susan R. *Contest for Constitutional Authority: The Abortion and War Powers Debates.* Lawrence: University Press of Kansas, 1992.

Hall, David Locke. *The Reagan Wars: A Constitutional Perspective on War Powers and the Presidency.* Boulder, Colo.: Westview Press, 1991.

Turner, Robert F. *Repealing the War Powers Resolution: Restoring the Rule of Law in U.S. Foreign Policy.* Washington, D.C.: Brassey's, 1991.

T. Jason Soderstrum

Watergate   *Watergate* is a term that refers to the series of scandals surrounding the campaign to reelect President Richard Nixon in 1972, scandals that ultimately led to Nixon's historic resignation from the presidency in 1974.

The name *Watergate* derives from the apartment complex of that name in Washington, D.C., that housed the headquarters of the Democratic Party. That headquarters was broken into by a set of operatives headed by G. Gordon Liddy working for Nixon's Committee to Reelect the President (CREEP). The incident was dismissed by the Nixon administration as a "third rate burglary." However, Judge John Sirica learned that one of the putative burglars had been pressured from higher up to plead guilty. This led to a grand jury investigation, to the appointment of a special prosecutor, and to televised congressional investigations, most notably the one under Senator Sam Ervin.

Meanwhile, two investigative reporters from the *Washington Post,* Bob Woodward and Carl Bernstein, undertook an investigation of their own aided by leaks from a still-unidentified person or persons within the administration whom they called "Deep Throat." Their investigation uncovered the link between the burglary and CREEP. Their work attests to the potentially powerful role the media can play in mobilizing support for, or opposition to, public officials.

The alleged misdeeds took the form of using powerful and putatively neutral administrative tools of the presidency to harass and punish mere active political opposition and support of the 1972 Democratic candidate for president. These activities included using defense intelligence to intercept overseas mail of prominent Democrats to gather material to be used against them, using the Internal Revenue Service to audit tax returns of prominent Democrats, and having the FBI gather damaging dossiers on political opponents and information using illegal wiretaps. These and similar activities were especially offensive because they served to make democratic elections less competitive. As such, these actions to win at all costs constituted a frontal assault on the democratic political process itself. That is why the Watergate scandals were deemed by many to be more serious than scandals that enriched their perpetrators (such as the Teapot Dome affair under President Harding) or scandals involving inappropriate sexual activities (such as those surrounding President Clinton).

Eventually, former White House Counsel John Dean testified before the Ervin Committee about extensive efforts to cover up the unraveling scandal. The coup de grâce for the administration was probably when one official revealed to the Ervin Committee that Nixon had set up a taping system to record all White House conversations. Against determined resistance from the Nixon administration, the tapes were subpoenaed by the committee and the special prosecutor. The tapes revealed that Nixon and his close aides were heavily involved in a series of attempts to cover up the unraveling scandal.

They also showed Nixon in an unflattering light, obsessed with revenge against perceived social and political enemies. A number of Nixon's closest aides, including Dean, John Erlichman, Bob Haldeman, and Attorney General John Mitchell, resigned and some were sent to prison.

The issues in the Watergate affair involved more than a question of the president engaging in illegal behavior. Thus, what one senator regarded as the defining question of the affair, "What did the president know and when did he know it?" does not get to the heart of matter. Other presidents have engaged in illegal behavior and even in attempts to cover up such behavior. Nixon's behavior in 1972 (and at other times in his career as in the race for governor of California in 1960) was sui generis because it involved an assault on the democratic political process itself.

For more information

Dean, James. *Blind Ambition.* New York: Simon and Schuster, 1976.

Pynne, Ronald, ed. *Watergate and the American Political Process.* New York: Praeger Publishers, 1975.

Woodward, Bob, and Carl Bernstein. *All the President's Men.* New York: Simon and Schuster, 1987.

Lawrence Mayer

water rights   Fresh water is one of the most precious commodities in the world. Who owns fresh water in the United States? Interestingly, states determine many of the specific criteria of water ownership.

Native American people have traditionally viewed water rights as belonging to them. This is still reflected in such agreements as the water rights compact among the Seminole tribe of Florida, the State of Florida, and the South Florida Water Management District. For the most part, however, water rights did not become a major administrative and political issue in the United States until large-scale settlement of territories.

Utah is a very dry state, and therefore water use has always been a very political and important issue. According to the Utah Division of Water Rights:

> The Utah pioneers in the late 1840's [sic] were the first Anglo-Saxons to practice irrigation on an extensive scale in the United States. Being a desert, Utah contained much more cultivable land than could be watered from the incoming mountain streams. The principle was established that those who first made beneficial use of water should be entitled to continued use in preference to those who came later. This fundamental principal was later sanctioned and is known as the Doctrine of Prior Appropriation. This means those with earliest priority dates who have continuously used the water since that time have the right to water from a certain source before others with later priority dates.

All waters in Utah are public property. A water right is "a right to the use of water based upon 1) quantity, 2) source, 3) priority date, 4) nature of use, 5) point of diversion and 6) physically putting water to beneficial use."

Another state where water is a precious and high-demand commodity is California. Prior to 1872, water rights could be acquired by simply taking and "beneficially using water." Subsequently, California has enacted a series of increasingly complex rules for water rights and water use. These are the result of great pressure on a finite supply of fresh water for farming, ranching, and recreational, industrial, and residential use.

The complexity of water rights is best illustrated by the extensive effort to define and spell out the regulation for riparian water rights in California.

> No California statute defines riparian rights, but a modification of the common law doctrine of riparian rights has been established in this State by decisions of the courts and confirmed by the provisions of section 3, Article XIV of the California Constitution (see California Water Code sections 100, 101). Lands within the watershed of a

natural watercourse, which are traversed thereby or border thereon, with the exceptions and limitations hereinafter indicated, may be riparian. Each owner thereof may have a right, which is correlative with the right of each other riparian owner to share in the reasonable beneficial use of the natural flow of water, which passes his land. No permit is required for such use. The State Water Resources Control Board's (SWRCB) policy is to consider natural flow as not including return flows derived from use of ground water, water seasonally stored and later released, or water diverted from another watershed.

Another example is South Dakota's law [codified Law (SDCL) 46-1-3], which states that "all water within the state is the property of the people of the state but the right to the use of water may be acquired by appropriation as provided by law." In South Dakota a water appropriation is an authorization granted by the state Water Management Board to "make a private, beneficial use of the state's water resources."

One fascinating aspect of scarce water is the buying and selling of water rights, which have in some cases become a commodity like oil, land, or mineral rights. The following description of a water-rights firm provides a good perspective on this aspect of water rights.

The Water Rights Market brings together buyers and sellers of water, water rights, and water-related properties throughout the western United States. Whether you wish to buy or sell groundwater, surface water, or shares in conservancy districts or ditch companies, WaterRightsMarket.com covers them all. If you need to increase your water supply for farm, ranch, and agricultural irrigation, municipal water supply, in-stream flow quantities, or other water resources requirements, search the "for sale" listings and place a "wanted" listing. If you wish to sell water rights, place a "for sale" listing and search the "wanted" listings. Water leases and trades are also accommodated."

In Washington State waters collectively belong "to the public and cannot be owned by any one individual or group. Instead, individuals or groups may be granted rights to use them. A water right is a legal authorization to use a predefined quantity of public water for a designated purpose. This purpose must qualify as a *beneficial use*. Beneficial use involves the application of a reasonable quantity of water to a non-wasteful use, such as irrigation, domestic water supply, or power generation, to name a few. An average household uses about 300 gallons of water per day."

As in most states, Washington State has an elaborate administrative structure for granting water rights uses as well as for terminating water rights for violations of the regulatory provisions.

Recent important issues related to water rights in the United States include water facility security. As the *National Water Rights Digest* reported (http://www.ridenbaugh.com/nwrd/), "the aftereffects of the September 11 terrorist attacks in New York, Washington and Pennsylvania reached even the unlikely field of water rights. After those attacks, a number of water storage facilities were reviewed for additional security to guard against attack. Lake Mead facilities near Las Vegas were one example of a facility receiving additional security." In fact, protection of water sources was a major component of the long-range plans of the Office of Homeland Security.

Another major water-rights issue is the relationship between water supply, energy needs, and the Endangered Species Act. In particular, the problem revolves around the damming up of water during drought periods (the West had a water shortage in the late 1990s and early 2000s), and the release of water for fish and other wildlife has become a contentious issue with environmentalists, farmers, electric power generators and power users, and municipal (residential) water users. For example, 1,400 farmers were cut off in April 2001 from water they have received for decades, affecting 90 percent of the 200,000 acres watered by the Klamath Project in Oregon. This federal Bureau of Reclamation decision was based on the requirements of the Endangered Species

Act. In one incident, angry farmers cut the chains that had been put in place to lock the water diversion system and opened the flow of water to their farms in violation of federal mandates and law.

With increasing population pressure on scarce water resources, the issue of water rights promises to be one of the most contentious and politically charged environmental public-policy problems, especially in the Plains States, the West, and the Southwest of the United States.

Steffen W. Schmidt

Weber, Max (1864–1920) *sociologist* Max Weber is generally credited with being the founder of modern sociology and one of the most influential modern thinkers on the nature of authority. His views on bureaucratic organization have been tremendously influential upon the public sector and government personnel policies.

Max Weber was born 21 April 1864 in Erfurt, now a part of modern-day Germany. While a child, he moved to Berlin and subsequently attended the Universities of Gottingen and Berlin. In 1894 he was appointed professor of political economy at the University of Freiburg and subsequently held positions at a number of German universities. He died in June 1920, a victim of the postwar influenza epidemic in Europe.

Weber left behind a large quantity of notes, lectures, essays, and other writings. He did not publish a great number of books. *The Protestant Ethic and the Spirit of Capitalism* (1905), *Economy and Society* (1914), and *General Economic History* (1923) are the best-known. His impact on modern ideas has, however, been enormous. Contemporary concepts of rationalism, bureaucracy, charisma, authority, power, legitimacy, and understanding (*verstehen*) have been decisively influenced by Weber's work.

In *The Protestant Ethic and the Spirit of Capitalism,* Weber proposed an alternative to Karl Marx's explanation for the rise of capitalism. While not completely disagreeing with Marx's materialistic interpretation of history, he rejected it as too narrow. Weber observed that capitalism had originated and subsequently developed much more quickly in Protestant societies than those dominated by Roman Catholicism. Weber argued that the ideas defining Protestantism, particularly Calvinism and Puritanism, led to an otherworldly asceticism and work ethic that fit well with the economic motives of capitalism. The rise of capitalism is therefore a product of the ideas that dominate human life and not simply the evolution of the economic system.

Weber's account of how human history evolves focused on the development of scientific rationalism as well as capitalism. Power is exercised in all societies. The question we ask is always whether the exercise of power in any particular case is legitimate. So what establishes the grounds of legitimacy? In other words, what makes us believe that someone or some government has authority over us and is not merely coercing us? Why do we feel we ought to obey their commands?

Weber argued that there are three types of authority: charismatic, traditional, and rational-legal. The first is where authority rests on a belief in the divine ground of the person speaking. It is thus important to note that charisma means much more than mere popularity. Traditional authority is based on the idea that because we have always done things a certain way, that way is therefore good.

In general, the path of world history has meant that societies have moved away from these two types of authority and toward rational-legal authority. The world is thus "disenchanted" as the old views of religion and tradition are often debunked by science and a rationalistic approach to law and government. The world thus seems to move inevitably toward enlightenment, toward a scientific world view in which all aspects of human life are rationalized through technology and bureaucratic organization.

Weber provided a profound account of the nature of bureaucracy and the forms of bureaucratic organization and thinking. Weber described a bureaucracy as one of the most rational and efficient means to organize authority. He described a public bureaucracy consisting of hierarchal authority where civil servants are employed on the basis of merit, serving under civil service protections that guaranteed them a lifelong vocation. The purpose of these protections was to ensure that public servants would make the best technical decisions, freed from worries that politics or political pressure would influence their decisions.

While Weber's views on bureaucracy were influential in creating modern views of how government agencies should be organized, he also argued that the bureaucratization of life is the depersonalization of life. It means the rise of the emotionally detached, professional expert. His fear was that we are living through the development of a society dominated by "specialists without spirit or vision." Modern societies are thus at a crossroads; they must consider carefully the nature of scientific and bureaucratic rationalism in order to assess its effects on the human condition.

For more information

Bendix, Reinhard. *Max Weber: An Intellectual Portrait.* Garden City, N.Y.: Anchor Books, 1962.

Mommsen, Wolfgang J. *The Political and Social Theory of Max Weber.* Translated by Michael Steinberg. Chicago: University of Chicago Press, 1989.

Weber, Max. *From Max Weber: Essays in Sociology.* Edited and translated by H. Gerth and C. Wright Mills. New York: Oxford University Press, 1947.

Patrick N. Malcolmson

welfare economics   Welfare economics is the branch of microeconomic theory that is concerned with measuring economic performance. It is normative theory in that its fundamental theorems describe the basic conditions for achieving optimum economic efficiency.

Welfare economics involves the study of conditions under which markets perform well and those under which markets can fail to deliver optimal amounts of goods and services, e.g., where environmental pollution results from a manufacturing process. When this occurs, the prices paid for the product may not include compensation for the costs imposed by the pollution. Under such circumstances, welfare economics calls for government intervention to correct for a "market failure." Thus, in applied settings, welfare economics provides useful criteria for designing effective public-policy instruments.

The central concept for evaluating policy proposals is the Pareto efficiency criterion, named for its originator, Italian economist Vilfredo Pareto. This criterion holds that any allocation of resources is efficient if the only way to make some person better off is to make at least one other person worse off. For example, a tax policy is Pareto efficient if no one can get a tax cut without also requiring someone else to pay more taxes. It turns out that the Pareto criterion is not an adequate basis for public policy making, however, since most of the tasks of governments will necessarily involve redistributing resources from some citizens for expenditure on the needs of others. (A common example would be paying for primary education by taxing property owners, including those without school-age children.) Consequently, welfare economists since Nicolas Kaldor and John R. Hicks in the 1930s adopted the "Pareto potential improvement criterion," which holds that any outcome is optimal provided that the net benefits to all of society outweigh the costs imposed on those who pay for them.

The lessons of welfare economics teach, among other things, that wherever possible, it is best to allocate goods and services throughout a society using the vehicle of free, competitive markets. Pareto-efficient outcomes will result where competitive markets can operate without impediment. However, markets can fail in cases where goods are produced by a single firm (a monopoly) or a few firms (an oligopoly). Also, markets simply do not exist for certain so-called public goods, such as national defense, that society may demand but that are not feasible to supply via markets. Further, as mentioned above, certain costs to society—such as pollution—may not be captured in market prices (i.e., an external cost or "externality" may be present). The theory of market failure therefore implies that, in the absence of governmental intervention, markets can sometimes provide too much or too little of certain goods and services. When that occurs, welfare economics describes the means that can be used by governments to correct for such problems, e.g., a corrective tax to capture the external costs of production in the selling price of the affected goods.

Important economics topics that are either a part of the subject matter of welfare economics or are related to it—and some of the principal authorities on those subjects—include: externalities and market failure (Arthur Pigou); general equilibrium analysis (Leon Walras); the theory of the "second best" (Kelvin Lancaster, Richard Lipsey); theories of collective choice and collective action (Mancur Olson, Ronald Coase); the economic theory of democracy (Anthony Downs, Kenneth Arrow); cost-benefit analysis of government expenditures (John Krutilla); the theory of optimal taxation (Nicholas Stern); economics of the public sector (Joseph Stiglitz); and public choice and governmental failure (James M. Buchanan, Gordon Tullock).

For more information

Johansson, Per-Olov. *An Introduction to Modern Welfare Economics.* New York: Cambridge University Press, 1991.

Stiglitz, Joseph A. *Economics of the Public Sector,* 3d ed. New York: W. W. Norton & Co., 2000.

Varian, Hal. *Intermediate Microeconomics: A Modern Approach,* 6th ed. New York: W. W. Norton & Co., 2003.

Robert S. Kravchuk

welfare reform   Welfare reform refers to efforts to modify the rules and requirements of the programs that support poor families.

Most recently, welfare reform efforts culminated in the creation in 1996 of the TEMPORARY ASSISTANCE FOR NEEDY FAMILIES (TANF) program, now the nation's primary program for assisting needy families with benefits and services designed to encourage work and self-sufficiency. But efforts to reform welfare programs started well before the creation of the TANF program.

Until 1996, the nation's basic welfare program was the AID TO FAMILIES WITH DEPENDENT CHILDREN (AFDC) program. Enacted in the 1930s as Title IV-A of the Social Security Act, AFDC was administered by the states with federal and state funding. The federal government matched state expenditures at rates ranging from 50 to 80 percent, depending on state per capita income. The program provided income support for families with a child under 18 (or under 21, if in school) in which at least one parent was absent, disabled, or unemployed. States set income limits and benefit levels; the federal government established broad eligibility requirements. The program was available in all states and was considered an individual entitlement; if a family qualified, benefits had to be provided. For many years, there were no requirements that adults included in the grant had to seek employment.

Most of the early efforts to reform the AFDC program occurred at the federal level. Beginning in the 1960s, Congress enacted and funded a series of work programs, such as the Work Incentive (WIN) program, designed to move recipients from the welfare rolls to work. However, even with these programs, the number of families on welfare continued to increase.

A significant change in the AFDC program occurred in 1988, with passage of the Family Support Act. This legislation created the Job Opportunity and Basic Skills (JOBS) training program as well as the first federal child care programs. For the first time, states were required to have increasing percentages of able-bodied adult recipients engage in work or educational activities.

But this effort to reform the nation's welfare program was generally acknowledged to have failed to reduce the level of dependency. Beginning in the early 1990s, the federal government gave the states greater flexibility to implement program changes to reduce dependency and increase participation in work activities through "waivers," which allowed states to ignore federal requirements in certain areas. By 1996, 32 states were granted waivers.

But even with this relaxation of federal control, many state governors and program administrators pressed for greater autonomy. An increasing number of policy experts agreed that there were fundamental flaws in the AFDC program and that the solution had to come at the state and local level rather than from the federal government. From 1993 to 1996, legislative proposals from the Clinton administration and from members of Congress were debated. There was a great deal of acrimony between the Republican Congress and the Democratic administration, and in early 1996, President Clinton vetoed a Republican-sponsored bill.

However, by August of 1996, a historic consensus of federal and state officials from both political parties came together. Congress enacted and the president signed the Personal Responsibility and Work Opportunity Act of 1996. The new law replaced the AFDC program with the Temporary Assistance for Needy Families program. No longer would state expenditures be matched with federal funds. Instead, TANF is a block grant totaling $16.8 billion per year, under which states receive a capped amount of funding. In return for limits on

A protester participates in a demonstration against welfare reform in New York City. (MARIO TAMA/GETTY IMAGES)

funding, states have great flexibility in using TANF funds to implement programs that emphasize work and family self-sufficiency, and to provide a variety of benefits and services to assist families. No longer is there an individual entitlement to cash benefits, and there is a five-year limit on benefits.

These and other changes are generally referred to as "welfare reform." However, it is a bit of an oversimplification to consider only the changes related to creation of the TANF program as welfare reform. Many of the other programs that come into play in assisting needy families have also been modified over the last two decades. The Child Support Enforcement program has been strengthened; the Medicaid program has been expanded; child-care programs have been enacted and expanded; the Food Stamp program has been amended; and work programs have been consolidated, all with the goal of providing the supports that children and families need to move from welfare dependency to self-sufficiency.

These programs continue to evolve, just as the characteristics and needs of the poor change. Welfare reform in 1996 is the latest, and one of the most significant, changes since the federal government became the primary source of funding and programs for the poor. Ironically, one of the fundamental characteristics of the legislation is a new federalism, moving authority from the federal government to the states, where programs like AFDC began.

Welfare reform is generally considered to have been successful. In January 1993, 14.1 million people received benefits under the AFDC program. By December of 1999, the number of TANF recipients was 6.3 million. But it is also true that economic factors played a significant role in this decrease in the number of families receiving assistance and an increase in employment of the poor. As economic conditions change, TANF and related programs will be tested. Only then will we know the true effects of welfare reform.

For more information

American Public Human Services Association. http://www.aphsa.org/reform/timeline.htm.

Department of Health and Human Services. http://aspe.hhs.gov/hsp/index.htm.

Mark Ragan

Whyte, William H. (1917–1999) *organizational theorist* William H. Whyte was a social observer, urbanologist, and lifelong student of organizational behavior who heavily influenced late-20th-century urban planning, especially the design of human-sized and human-friendly city spaces.

Whyte won fame in 1956 when *The Organization Man,* a highly readable study of the role of major corporations in American life, appeared. The book's thesis is that large corporations so completely co-opt the lives of their employees and their families that any individuality is smothered, and corporate advances are made at the expense of the individual and not because of individual inspiration. Whyte, then an editor at *Fortune* magazine and admittedly not a psychologist, convincingly argued that the embrace of the organization substituted for family and regional loyalty, religion, and personal interests of all kinds and turned entire communities into virtual company towns, their residents marching in lockstep. This chilling description of the conformity of suburban postwar America remains a classic of sociological literature. *The Organization Man* has sold over 2 million copies and is still in print.

Whyte went on to extensive involvement in urban planning and policy. He championed the city. He enjoyed high-density life and lived in New York City for most of his life. He perfected the technique of closely and painstakingly documenting what people actually did in public spaces, the better to plan for those spaces. His advice—often followed—to municipal planners was to make public spaces inviting and usable in ways that people actually wanted. He shared Jane Jacobs's idea that many people, together in a public space, are a deterrent to crime because many eyes are witnesses and people consciously or unconsciously look out for each other. This notion directly translates to a robust street life.

Whyte was for many years Distinguished Professor at Hunter College of the City University of New York, a consultant on many building and planning projects for New York, and editor of the master plan for New York. His people-centered philosophy contrasts sharply with that of Robert Moses, who, as New York's master builder for many decades, preferred superhighways and superscaled buildings over established street-life-centered neighborhoods and pedestrian-accessible public spaces.

Whyte addressed sprawl and urban revitalization and advocated sane development, but his heart was always in the city. He authored many articles and short studies (and one novel) as well as several books that remain essential to municipal planners, graduate schools, and urban designers. All of Whyte's works share the same clear, readable (and often dryly humorous) style and appeal to professionals and laypersons alike.

For more information

Whyte, William H. *The Organization Man*. Philadelphia: University of Pennsylvania Press, 2002.

Elsa M. Shartsis

Wickard v. Filburn 317 U.S. 111 (1942)

The *Wickard v. Filburn* decision by the Supreme Court played an important part in upholding the constitutionality of New Deal legislation and extended the commerce power of Congress. In 1937–38 the Congress passed a series of laws commonly called the "Second New Deal" seeking to get the United States out of the Great Depression. To eliminate overproduction in agriculture and increase prices paid to farmers, the Agricultural Adjustment Act of 1938 set acreage allotments for production of several agricultural products, including wheat.

An Ohio farmer, Roscoe Filburn, was allotted 11.1 acres, actually planted 23 acres of wheat, and refused to pay the $117 fine imposed by the federal government for producing 239 "excess" bushels of wheat. Filburn's lawyer claimed his client fed most of his wheat to livestock on the farm. Therefore, Filburn's wheat was not in "interstate commerce." Since the Constitution gives the Congress power only to regulate commerce between the states (Art. I, sec. 8), the Agricultural Adjustment Act of 1938 and the fine imposed were unenforceable.

Justice Jackson led the Court in deciding that Filburn's wheat production, though small, did contribute to total wheat production, which was in interstate commerce. The Supreme Court upheld the Agricultural Adjustment Act of 1938, including its allotment and penalty provisions. Flowing from the *Wickard* decision, it was clear Congress could, under its power over commerce, regulate intrastate activities closely related to interstate commerce and set the terms for interstate transportation of products and services.

For more information

Mason, A. T. *American Constitutional Law*, 13th ed. New York: Prentice Hall, 2002.

Nowack, John E., et al. *Constitutional Law*. St. Paul, Minnesota: West Publishing, 1978.

Gayle R. Avant

Wilson, Woodrow (1856–1924) *38th president of the United States*   Woodrow Wilson, the 38th president of the United States, is considered to be the father of modern American public administration. Wilson was born in Staunton, Virginia, in 1856 but spent his formative years in Augusta, Georgia, and Columbia, South Carolina. As an undergraduate Wilson attended Davidson College and the College of New Jersey (now Princeton University). He studied law at the University of Virginia and received a Ph.D. in history in 1886 from the Johns Hopkins University.

Wilson taught at Bryn Mawr College and Wesleyan University, and in 1890 he accepted a professorship at Princeton University. In 1902 he was selected as president of Princeton and served until 1910, when he was elected governor of New Jersey. As governor, Wilson successfully pushed for a number of reforms, including the use of direct primaries, regulation of public utilities, and antitrust legislation. In 1912 Wilson secured the Democratic Party's nomination and was elected president of the United States. With the help of a Democratic majority in Congress, Wilson was able to achieve several important initiatives, including the imposition of lower tariffs, the creation of the Federal Trade Commission, and the passing of new laws restricting child labor. Wilson was reelected in 1916 on the platform, "He kept us out of War."

Although Wilson initially opposed U.S. intervention in World War I, Germany's increasing aggression against the United States compelled him in April 1917 to urge Congress to issue a declaration of war in order to make the world "safe for democracy." Following the Allied victory, Wilson penned his famous "fourteen points" peace plan that would fundamentally restructure the conduct of international affairs. His plan called for the United States and other nations to solve their differences through the creation of a League of Nations, the forerunner of today's United Nations. Wilson's plan, however, was never ratified by the U.S. Senate because of the opposition of isolationist Republicans, led by Senator Henry Cabot Lodge.

As a member of the Progressive movement, Wilson became an outspoken advocate for governmental reform. In his famous 1887 essay, "The Study of Administration," Wilson called for a separation of politics from administration; in other words, he sought to remove what he saw as the corrupting influence and intrusion of political officials in the day-to-day business of government. His views echoed those of other Progressives who were concerned about the corrupting influence of patronage politics at the time. Wilson wrote,

"Administration lies outside the proper sphere of politics. Administrative questions are not political questions." Wilson believed that such a separation was necessary in order to make government more efficient and more businesslike. He also noted that "it is the object of administrative study to discover, first, what government can properly and successfully do, and, secondly, how it can do these proper things with the utmost possible efficiency and at the least possible cost either of money or of energy." This "politics/administration dichotomy" would become the foundation for the classical, orthodox public administration movement.

Wilson is the author of several other works, including *Congressional Government* (1885), *The State* (1890), and *A History of the American People* (1902). Wilson died in Washington, D.C., on 3 February 1924.

For more information

Wilson, Woodrow. "The Study of Administration." *Political Science Quarterly* 2 (June 1887): 197–222; reprinted 50 (December 1941): 481–506.

Patrick G. Scott

World Trade Organization   The World Trade Organization (WTO) is an international organization that enforces free trade among countries.

Following World War II, the democratic, capitalist allies met in Bretton Woods, Vermont, to establish a postwar economic system. That system, known as the Bretton Woods system, was based on three fundamental goals: a stable world financial system that would ensure international liquidity; an open system of international trade; and a mechanism for assisting in the reconstruction of war-torn economies. The GENERAL AGREEMENT ON TARIFFS AND TRADE (GATT) was the mechanism for pursuing the second of those goals, an open system of international trade. Rather than establishing a permanent international organization to monitor and regulate international trade, GATT created a treaty framework under which nations would gradually reduce tariff barriers to trade in manufactured goods. By the late 1980s, the size of membership in GATT and the scope of trade issues had increased to the point that many GATT members felt that a permanent organization with substantive monitoring and dispute-settlement powers was needed. Consequently, the GATT members created the World Trade Organization (WTO) in 1994.

The WTO expands the scope of the GATT in several ways. First, it creates a permanent organizational structure to monitor compliance with GATT obligations. Second, it expands the scope of trade issues not originally covered by GATT, most notably trade in agricultural products, trade in services, and trade issues related to intellectual property rights. Third, it establishes regular meetings for further reductions in trade barriers among WTO's member states. Fourth, and to many observers, most important, it establishes a permanent dispute-settlement body with the authority to rule on member states' compliance with their obligations under GATT and other international trade agreements.

Of course, not everyone is satisfied with the GATT/WTO requirements. In spite of specific provisions that provide exceptions for "least-developed country Members," many developing countries believe that the rules of the regime favor the advanced, industrialized countries at the expense of the developing countries. They argue that the GATT should allow them more "catch-up" time and grant them additional

A South Korean farmer burns grain during the World Trade Organization protest rally on 2 December 2001 in downtown Seoul. Some 20,000 farmers, students, and supporters protested against the WTO's new movement that is expected to force open South Korea's rice market. (CHUNG SUNG-JUN/GETTY IMAGES)

exceptions to GATT and WTO rules. In addition, many labor, environmental, and human rights groups in the industrialized economies argue that GATT and the WTO promote trade and investment at the expense of workers rights and environmental protection.

The anti-WTO adherents and their arguments were brought to the forefront of the debate on international trade at the opening of the most recent round of GATT negotiations, the so-called Millennium Round, which took place in November 1999 in Seattle, Washington. Protesters were able to disrupt the negotiations to the point that they were postponed a full day. In addition, the negotiators were unable to accomplish any substantive work; they were not even able to agree to an agenda for future negotiations. In spite of the setbacks at Seattle, trade ministers at the last WTO meeting in Genoa, Italy, were able to agree on a modest agenda for deepening the provisions established by the original WTO agreement. This agenda includes reviews of issues of concern to developing countries and a recommitment to international labor and environmental standards as established by international treaties.

For more information

Jackson, John H. *The World Trade Organization: Constitution and Jurisprudence.* London: Royal Institute of International Affairs, 1998.

Krueger, Anne O., ed. *The WTO as an International Organization.* Chicago: University of Chicago Press, 2000.

Schott, Jeffrey J., ed. *The WTO after Seattle.* Washington, D.C.: Institute for International Economics, 2000.

Steven G. Jones

Z

zero-based budgeting Zero-based budgeting is a system of allocating resources in which the budget is developed from a "clean sheet," usually each year.

A zero-based budget process generally requires the proposed expenditure across the whole organization or government to be assessed and justified. Zero-based budgets tend to be used where there is a concern about the size or growth in expenditure or where there is a need to allocate a larger amount of funding to a new priority than is available from revenue growth or from expenditure cuts at the margin.

In 1977, the U.S. federal government introduced a form of zero-based budgeting that required agencies to specify what levels of performance could be achieved at differing spending levels, one of which was to be below the current spending level. Some jurisdictions still mandate the use of zero-based budgeting in legislation, although the cost of reviewing the entire budget each year can make this impractical.

The zero-based approach is contrasted with INCREMENTAL BUDGETING, in which attention is focused only on changes from the previous budget. Incremental budgeting is much less time consuming, as it accepts that the bulk of expenditure does not need to be justified each year, whereas zero-based budgeting requires all expenditure to be reviewed. On the other hand, it is also less effective in facilitating a change in priorities. One way of reducing the costs of zero-based budgeting is to schedule a rolling review of parts of the budget over a period of several years.

Zero-based budgeting can be used in conjunction with other budget processes, including input budgeting and PERFORMANCE BUDGETING. Where it is used with input budgeting, an agency's expenditure needs to be justified on a line-by-line basis, whether it is classified according to its type (for example, employee costs) or function (for example, registry operations). Where zero-based budgeting is used with a performance budgeting system, it should be less resource-intensive because the review can focus on judgments about the quantity and quality of services, or other performance measures, rather than on individual expenditure lines.

A hybrid approach—part incremental and part zero-based—can also be used. This is the case where some costs are seen to be locked in or are best forecast using historical trends (thus being budgeted for incrementally), while others will vary according to an external factor, such as the level of demand, and would be justified accordingly.

For more information
Government Accounting Office. http://www.gao.gov.

Bob Shead

APPENDICES

DECLARATION OF INDEPENDENCE

Action of Second Continental Congress, July 4, 1776.

The unanimous Declaration of the thirteen United States of America.

We hold these truths to be self-evident, that all men are created equal, that they are endowed by their Creator with certain unalienable Rights, that among these are Life, Liberty, and the pursuit of Happiness. That to secure these rights, Governments are instituted among Men, deriving their just powers from the consent of the governed. That whenever any Form of Government becomes destructive of these ends, it is the Right of the People to alter or to abolish it, and to institute new Government, laying its foundation on such principles and organizing its powers in such form, as to them shall seem most likely to effect their Safety and Happiness. Prudence, indeed, will dictate that Governments long established should not be changed for light and transient causes; and accordingly all experience hath shown, that mankind are more disposed to suffer, while evils are sufferable, than to right themselves by abolishing the forms to which they are accustomed. But when a long train of abuses and usurpations, pursuing invariably the same Object, evinces a design to reduce them under absolute Despotism, it is their right, it is their duty, to throw off such Government, and to provide new Guards for their future security. Such has been the patient sufferance of these Colonies; and such is now the necessity which constrains them to alter their former Systems of Government. The history of the present King of Great Britain is a history of repeated injuries and usurpations, all having in direct object the establishment of an absolute Tyranny over these States. To prove this, let Facts be submitted to a candid world.

HE has refused his Assent to Laws, the most wholesome and necessary for the public good.

HE has forbidden his Governors to pass Laws of immediate and pressing importance, unless suspended in their operation till his Assent should be obtained; and when so suspended, he has utterly neglected to attend to them.

HE has refused to pass other Laws for the accommodation of large districts of people, unless those people would relinquish the right of Representation in the Legislature, a right inestimable to them and formidable to tyrants only.

HE has called together legislative bodies at places unusual, uncomfortable, and distant from the depository of their public Records, for the sole purpose of fatiguing them into compliance with his measures.

HE has dissolved Representative Houses repeatedly, for opposing with manly firmness his invasions on the rights of the people.

HE has refused for a long time, after such dissolutions, to cause others to be elected; whereby the Legislative powers, incapable of Annihilation, have returned to the People at large for their exercise; the State remaining in the mean time exposed to all the dangers of invasion from without, and convulsion within.

HE has endeavoured to prevent the population of these States; for that purpose obstructing the Laws of Naturalization of Foreigners; refusing to pass others to encourage their migrations hither, and raising the conditions of new Appropriations of Lands.

HE has obstructed the Administration of Justice, by refusing his Assent to Laws for establishing Judiciary powers.

HE has made Judges dependent on his Will alone, for the tenure of their offices, and the amount and payment of their salaries.

HE has erected a multitude of New Offices, and sent hither swarms of Officers to harass our People, and eat out their substance.

HE has kept among us, in times of peace, Standing Armies without the Consent of our legislatures.

HE has affected to render the Military independent of and superior to the Civil power.

HE has combined with others to subject us to a jurisdiction foreign to our constitution, and unacknowledged by our laws; giving his Assent to their Acts of pretended Legislation:

FOR quartering large bodies of armed troops among us:

FOR protecting them, by a mock Trial, from Punishment for any Murders which they should commit on the Inhabitants of these States:

FOR cutting off our Trade with all parts of the world:

FOR imposing Taxes on us without our Consent:

FOR depriving us in many cases, of the benefits of Trial by Jury:

FOR transporting us beyond Seas to be tried for pretended offences:

FOR abolishing the free System of English Laws in a neighbouring Province, establishing therein an Arbitrary government, and enlarging its Boundaries so as to render it at once an example and fit instrument for introducing the same absolute rule into these Colonies:

FOR taking away our Charters, abolishing our most valuable Laws, and altering fundamentally the Forms of our Governments:

FOR suspending our own Legislatures, and declaring themselves invested with power to legislate for us in all cases whatsoever.

HE has abdicated Government here, by declaring us out of his Protection and waging War against us.

HE has plundered our seas, ravaged our Coasts, burnt our towns, and destroyed the Lives of our people.

HE is at this time transporting large armies of foreign mercenaries to compleat the works of death, desolation and tyranny, already begun with circumstances of Cruelty & perfidy scarcely paralleled in the most barbarous ages, and totally unworthy the Head of a civilized nation.

HE has constrained our fellow Citizens taken Captive on the high Seas to bear Arms against their Country, to become the executioners of their friends and Brethren, or to fall themselves by their Hands.

HE has excited domestic insurrections amongst us, and has endeavoured to bring on the inhabitants of our frontiers, the merciless Indian Savages, whose known rule of warfare, is an undistinguished destruction of all ages, sexes and conditions.

IN every stage of these Oppressions We have Petitioned for Redress in the most humble terms: Our repeated Petitions have been answered only by repeated injury. A Prince, whose character is thus marked by every act which may define a Tyrant, is unfit to be the ruler of a free people.

NOR have We been wanting in attention to our British brethren. We have warned them from time to time of attempts by their legislature to extend an unwarrantable jurisdiction over us. We have reminded them of the circumstances of our emigration and settlement here. We have appealed to their native justice and magnanimity, and we have conjured them by the ties of our common kindred to disavow these usurpations, which would inevitably interrupt our connections and correspondence. They too have been deaf to the voice of justice and of consanguinity. We must, therefore, acquiesce in the necessity, which denounces our Separation, and hold them, as we hold the rest of mankind, Enemies in War, in Peace Friends.

WE, therefore, the Representatives of the UNITED STATES OF AMERICA, in GENERAL CONGRESS, Assembled, appealing to the Supreme Judge of the world for the rectitude of our intentions, do, in the Name, and by Authority of the good People of these Colonies, solemnly publish and declare, That these United Colonies are, and of Right ought to be FREE AND INDEPENDENT STATES; that they are Absolved from all Allegiance to the British Crown, and that all political connection between them and the State of Great Britain, is and ought to be totally dissolved; and that as FREE AND INDEPENDENT STATES, they have full Power to levy War, conclude Peace, contract Alliances, establish Commerce, and to do all other Acts and Things which INDEPENDENT STATES may of right do. And for the support of this Declaration,

with a firm reliance on the Protection of Divine Providence, we mutually pledge to each other our Lives, our Fortunes and our sacred Honor.

JOHN HANCOCK.

Georgia
  BUTTON GWINNETT
  LYMAN HALL
  GEO. WALTON
North Carolina
  WILLIAM HOOPER
  JOSEPH HEWES
  JOHN PENN
South Carolina
  EDWARD RUTLEDGE
  THOMAS HEYWARD, JR.
  THOMAS LYNCH, JR.
  ARTHUR MIDDLETON
Maryland
  SAMUEL CHASE
  WILLIAM PACA
  THOMAS STONE
  CHARLES CARROLL
  OF CARROLLTON
Virginia
  GEORGE WYTHE
  RICHARD HENRY LEE
  THOMAS JEFFERSON
  BENJAMIN HARRISON
  THOMAS NELSON, JR.
  FRANCIS LIGHTFOOT LEE
  CARTER BRAXTON
Pennsylvania
  ROBERT MORRIS
  BENJAMIN RUSH
  BENJAMIN FRANKLIN
  JOHN MORTON
  GEORGE CLYMER
  JAMES SMITH
  GEORGE TAYLOR
  JAMES WILSON
  GEORGE ROSS
Delaware
  CAESAR RODNEY
  GEORGE READ
  THOMAS M'KEAN
New York
  WILLIAM FLOYD

PHILIP LIVINGSTON
FRANCIS LEWIS
LEWIS MORRIS
New Jersey
RICHARD STOCKTON
JOHN WITHERSPOON
FRANCIS HOPKINS
JOHN HART
ABRAHAM CLARK
New Hampshire
JOSIAH BARTLETT
WILLIAM WHIPPLE
MATTHEW THORNTON
Massachusetts-Bay
SAMUEL ADAMS
JOHN ADAMS

ROBERT TREAT PAINE
ELBRIDGE GERRY
Rhode Island
STEPHEN HOPKINS
WILLIAM ELLERY
Connecticut
ROGER SHERMAN
SAMUEL HUNTINGTON
WILLIAM WILLIAMS
OLIVER WOLCOTT

IN CONGRESS, JANUARY 18, 1777.

ARTICLES OF CONFEDERATION

Agreed to by Congress November 15, 1777 then ratified and in force, March 1, 1781.

Preamble

To all to whom these Presents shall come, we the undersigned Delegates of the States affixed to our Names send greeting.

Articles of Confederation and perpetual Union between the states of New Hampshire, Massachusetts-bay Rhode Island and Providence Plantations, Connecticut, New York, New Jersey, Pennsylvania, Delaware, Maryland, Virginia, North Carolina, South Carolina and Georgia.

ARTICLE I

The Stile of this Confederacy shall be "The United States of America".

ARTICLE II

Each state retains its sovereignty, freedom, and independence, and every power, jurisdiction, and right, which is not by this Confederation expressly delegated to the United States, in Congress assembled.

ARTICLE III

The said States hereby severally enter into a firm league of friendship with each other, for their common defense, the security of their liberties, and their mutual and general welfare, binding themselves to assist each other, against all force offered to, or attacks made upon them, or any of them, on account of religion, sovereignty, trade, or any other pretense whatever.

ARTICLE IV

The better to secure and perpetuate mutual friendship and intercourse among the people of the different States in this Union, the free inhabitants of each of these States, paupers, vagabonds, and fugitives from justice excepted, shall be entitled to all privileges and immunities of free citizens in the several States; and the people of each State shall free ingress and regress to and from any other State, and shall enjoy therein all the privileges of trade and commerce, subject to the same duties, impositions, and restrictions as the inhabitants thereof respectively, provided that such restrictions shall not extend so far as to prevent the removal of property imported into any State, to any other State, of which the owner is an inhabitant; provided also that no imposition, duties or restriction shall be laid by any State, on the property of the United States, or either of them.

If any person guilty of, or charged with, treason, felony, or other high misdemeanor in any State, shall flee from justice, and be found in any of the United States, he shall, upon demand of the Governor or executive power of the State from which he fled, be delivered up and removed to the State having jurisdiction of his offense.

Full faith and credit shall be given in each of these States to the records, acts, and judicial proceedings of the courts and magistrates of every other State.

ARTICLE V

For the most convenient management of the general interests of the United States, delegates shall be annually appointed in such manner as the legislatures of each State shall direct, to meet in Congress on the first Monday in November, in every year, with a power reserved to each State to recall its delegates, or any of them, at any time within the year, and to send others in their stead for the remainder of the year.

No State shall be represented in Congress by less than two, nor more than seven members; and no person shall be capable of being a delegate for more than three years in any term of six years; nor shall any person, being a delegate, be capable of holding any office under the United States, for which he, or another for his benefit, receives any salary, fees or emolument of any kind.

Each State shall maintain its own delegates in a meeting of the States, and while they act as members of the committee of the States.

In determining questions in the United States in Congress assembled, each State shall have one vote.

Freedom of speech and debate in Congress shall not be impeached or questioned in any court or place out of Congress, and the members of Congress shall be protected in their persons from arrests or imprisonments, during the time of their going to and from, and attendence on Congress, except for treason, felony, or breach of the peace.

ARTICLE VI

No State, without the consent of the United States in Congress assembled, shall send any embassy to, or receive any embassy from, or enter into any conference, agreement, alliance or treaty with any King, Prince or State; nor shall any person holding any office of profit or trust under the United States, or any of them, accept any present, emolument, office or title of any kind whatever from any King, Prince or foreign State; nor shall the United States in Congress assembled, or any of them, grant any title of nobility.

No two or more States shall enter into any treaty, confederation or alliance whatever between them, without the consent of the United States in Congress assembled, specifying accurately the purposes for which the same is to be entered into, and how long it shall continue.

No State shall lay any imposts or duties, which may interfere with any stipulations in treaties, entered into by the United States in Congress assembled, with any King, Prince or State, in pursuance of any treaties already proposed by Congress, to the courts of France and Spain.

No vessel of war shall be kept up in time of peace by any State, except such number only, as shall be deemed necessary by the United States in Congress assembled, for the defense of such State, or its trade; nor shall any body of forces be kept up by any State in time of peace, except such number only, as in the judgement of the United States in Congress assembled, shall be deemed requisite to garrison the forts necessary for the defense of such State; but every State shall always keep up a well-regulated and disciplined militia, sufficiently armed and accoutered, and shall provide and constantly have ready for use, in public stores, a due number of filed pieces and tents, and a proper quantity of arms, ammunition and camp equipage.

No State shall engage in any war without the consent of the United States in Congress assembled, unless such State be actually invaded by enemies, or shall have received certain advice of a resolution being formed by some nation of Indians to invade such State, and the danger is so imminent as not to admit of a delay till the United States in Congress assembled can be consulted; nor shall any State grant commissions to any ships or vessels of war, nor letters of marque or reprisal, except it be after a declaration of war by the United States in Congress assembled, and then only against the Kingdom or State and the subjects thereof, against which war has been so declared, and under such regulations as shall be established by the United States in Congress assembled, unless such State be infested by pirates, in which case vessels of war may be fitted out for that occasion, and kept so long as the danger shall continue, or until the United States in Congress assembled shall determine otherwise.

ARTICLE VII

When land forces are raised by any State for the common defense, all officers of or under the rank of colonel, shall be appointed by the legislature of each State respectively, by whom such forces shall be raised, or in such manner as such State shall direct, and all vacancies shall be filled up by the State which first made the appointment.

ARTICLE VIII

All charges of war, and all other expenses that shall be incurred for the common defense or general welfare, and allowed by the United States in Congress assembled, shall be defrayed out of a common treasury, which shall be supplied by the several States in proportion to the value of all land within each State, granted or surveyed for any person, as such land and the buildings and improvements thereon shall be estimated according to such mode as the United States in Congress assembled, shall from time to time direct and appoint.

The taxes for paying that proportion shall be laid and levied by the authority and direction of the legislatures of the several States within the time agreed upon by the United States in Congress assembled.

ARTICLE IX

The United States in Congress assembled, shall have the sole and exclusive right and power of determining on peace and war, except in the cases mentioned in the sixth article — of sending and receiving ambassadors — entering into treaties and alliances, provided that no treaty of commerce shall be made whereby the legislative power of the respective States shall be restrained from imposing such imposts and duties on foreigners, as their own people are subjected to, or from prohibiting the exportation or importation of any species of goods or commodities whatsoever — of establishing rules for deciding in all cases, what captures on land or water shall be legal, and in what manner prizes taken by land or naval forces in the service of the United States shall be divided or appropriated — of granting letters of marque and reprisal in times of peace — appointing courts for the trial of piracies and felonies commited on the high seas and establishing courts for receiving and determining finally appeals in all cases of captures, provided that no member of Congress shall be appointed a judge of any of the said courts.

The United States in Congress assembled shall also be the last resort on appeal in all disputes and differences now subsisting or that hereafter may arise between two or more States concerning boundary, jurisdiction or any other causes whatever; which authority shall always be exercised in the manner following.

Whenever the legislative or executive authority or lawful agent of any State in controversy with another shall present a petition to Congress stating the matter in question and praying for a hearing, notice thereof shall be given by order of Congress to the legislative or executive authority of the other State in controversy, and a day assigned for the appearance of the parties by their lawful agents, who shall then be directed to appoint by joint consent, commissioners or judges to constitute a court for hearing and determining the matter in question: but if they cannot agree, Congress shall name three persons out of each of the United States, and from the list of such persons each party shall alternately strike out one, the petitioners beginning, until the number shall be reduced to thirteen; and from that number not less than seven, nor more than nine names as Congress shall direct, shall in the presence of Congress be drawn out by lot, and the persons whose names shall be so drawn or any five of them, shall be commissioners or judges, to hear and finally determine the controversy, so always as a major part of the judges who shall hear the cause shall agree in the determination: and if either party shall neglect to attend at the day appointed, without showing reasons, which Congress shall judge sufficient, or being present shall refuse to strike, the Congress shall proceed to nominate three persons out of each State, and the secretary of Congress shall strike in behalf of such party absent or refusing; and the judgement and sentence of the court to be appointed, in the manner before prescribed, shall be final and conclusive; and if any of the parties shall refuse to submit to the authority of such court, or to appear or defend their claim or cause, the court shall nevertheless proceed to pronounce sentence, or judgement, which shall in like manner be final and decisive, the judgement or sentence and other proceedings being in either case transmit-

ted to Congress, and lodged among the acts of Congress for the security of the parties concerned: provided that every commissioner, before he sits in judgement, shall take an oath to be administered by one of the judges of the supreme or superior court of the State, where the cause shall be tried, 'well and truly to hear and determine the matter in question, according to the best of his judgement, without favor, affection or hope of reward': provided also, that no State shall be deprived of territory for the benefit of the United States.

All controversies concerning the private right of soil claimed under different grants of two or more States, whose jurisdictions as they may respect such lands, and the States which passed such grants are adjusted, the said grants or either of them being at the same time claimed to have originated antecedent to such settlement of jurisdiction, shall on the petition of either party to the Congress of the United States, be finally determined as near as may be in the same manner as is before prescribed for deciding disputes respecting territorial jurisdiction between different States.

The United States in Congress assembled shall also have the sole and exclusive right and power of regulating the alloy and value of coin struck by their own authority, or by that of the respective States — fixing the standards of weights and measures throughout the United States — regulating the trade and managing all affairs with the Indians, not members of any of the States, provided that the legislative right of any State within its own limits be not infringed or violated — establishing or regulating post offices from one State to another, throughout all the United States, and exacting such postage on the papers passing through the same as may be requisite to defray the expenses of the said office — appointing all officers of the land forces, in the service of the United States, excepting regimental officers — appointing all the officers of the naval forces, and commissioning all officers whatever in the service of the United States — making rules for the government and regulation of the said land and naval forces, and directing their operations.

The United States in Congress assembled shall have authority to appoint a committee, to sit in the recess of Congress, to be denominated 'A Committee of the States', and to consist of one delegate from each State; and to appoint such other committees and civil officers as may be necessary for managing the general affairs of the United States under their direction — to appoint one of their members to preside, provided that no person be allowed to serve in the office of president more than one year in any term of three years; to ascertain the necessary sums of money to be raised for the service of the United States, and to appropriate and apply the same for defraying the public expenses — to borrow money, or emit bills on the credit of the United States, transmitting every half-year to the respective States an account of the sums of money so borrowed or emitted — to build and equip a navy — to agree upon the number of land forces, and to make requisitions from each State for its quota, in proportion to the number of white inhabitants in such State; which requisition shall be binding, and thereupon the legislature of each State shall appoint the regimental officers, raise the men and cloath, arm and equip them in a solid-like manner, at the expense of the United States; and the officers and men so cloathed, armed and equipped shall march to the place appointed, and within the time agreed on by the United States in Congress assembled. But if the United States in Congress assembled shall, on consideration of circumstances judge proper that any State should not raise men, or should raise a smaller number of men than the quota thereof, such extra number shall be raised, officered, cloathed, armed and equipped in the same manner as the quota of each State, unless the legislature of such State shall judge that such extra number cannot be safely spread out in the same, in which case they shall raise, officer,

cloath, arm and equip as many of such extra number as they judge can be safely spared. And the officers and men so cloathed, armed, and equipped, shall march to the place appointed, and within the time agreed on by the United States in Congress assembled.

The United States in Congress assembled shall never engage in a war, nor grant letters of marque or reprisal in time of peace, nor enter into any treaties or alliances, nor coin money, nor regulate the value thereof, nor ascertain the sums and expenses necessary for the defense and welfare of the United States, or any of them, nor emit bills, nor borrow money on the credit of the United States, nor appropriate money, nor agree upon the number of vessels of war, to be built or purchased, or the number of land or sea forces to be raised, nor appoint a commander in chief of the army or navy, unless nine States assent to the same: nor shall a question on any other point, except for adjourning from day to day be determined, unless by the votes of the majority of the United States in Congress assembled.

The Congress of the United States shall have power to adjourn to any time within the year, and to any place within the United States, so that no period of adjournment be for a longer duration than the space of six months, and shall publish the journal of their proceedings monthly, except such parts thereof relating to treaties, alliances or military operations, as in their judgement require secrecy; and the yeas and nays of the delegates of each State on any question shall be entered on the Journal, when it is desired by any delegates of a State, or any of them, at his or their request shall be furnished with a transcript of the said journal, except such parts as are above excepted, to lay before the legislatures of the several States.

ARTICLE X

The Committee of the States, or any nine of them, shall be authorized to execute, in the recess of Congress, such of the powers of

Congress as the United States in Congress assembled, by the consent of the nine States, shall from time to time think expedient to vest them with; provided that no power be delegated to the said Committee, for the exercise of which, by the Articles of Confederation, the voice of nine States in the Congress of the United States assembled be requisite.

ARTICLE XI

Canada acceding to this confederation, and adjoining in the measures of the United States, shall be admitted into, and entitled to all the advantages of this Union; but no other colony shall be admitted into the same, unless such admission be agreed to by nine States.

ARTICLE XII

All bills of credit emitted, monies borrowed, and debts contracted by, or under the authority of Congress, before the assembling of the United States, in pursuance of the present confederation, shall be deemed and considered as a charge against the United States, for payment and satisfaction whereof the said United States, and the public faith are hereby solemnly pleged.

ARTICLE XIII

Every State shall abide by the determination of the United States in Congress assembled, on all questions which by this confederation are submitted to them. And the Articles of this Confederation shall be inviolably observed by every State, and the Union shall be perpetual; nor shall any alteration at any time hereafter be made in any of them; unless such alteration be agreed to in a Congress of the United States, and be afterwards confirmed by the legislatures of every State.

CONCLUSION

And Whereas it hath pleased the Great Governor of the World to incline the hearts of the legislatures we respectively represent in Congress, to approve of, and to authorize us to ratify the said Articles of Confederation and perpetual Union. Know Ye that we the undersigned delegates, by virtue of the power and authority to us given for that purpose, do by these presents, in the name and in behalf of our respective constituents, fully and entirely ratify and confirm each and every of the said Articles of Confederation and perpetual Union, and all and singular the matters and things therein contained: And we do further solemnly plight and engage the faith of our respective constituents, that they shall abide by the determinations of the United States in Congress assembled, on all questions, which by the said Confederation are submitted to them. And that the Articles thereof shall be inviolably observed by the States we respectively represent, and that the Union shall be perpetual.

SIGNATORIES

In Witness whereof we have hereunto set our hands in Congress. Done at Philadelphia in the State of Pennsylvania the ninth day of July in the Year of our Lord One Thousand Seven Hundred and Seventy-Eight, and in the Third Year of the independence of America.

On the part and behalf of the State of New Hampshire:

Josiah Bartlett
John Wentworth Junior

On the part and behalf of the State of Massachusetts Bay:

John Hancock
Francis Dana
Samuel Adams
James Lovell

Elbridge Gerry
Samuel Holten

On the part and behalf of the State of Rhode Island and Providence Plantations:

William Ellery
John Collins
Henry Marchant

On the part and behalf of the State of Connecticut:

Roger Sherman
Titus Hosmer
Samuel Huntington
Andrew Adams
Oliver Wolcott

On the Part and Behalf of the State of New York:

James Duane
William Duer
Francis Lewis
Gouverneur Morris

On the Part and in Behalf of the State of New Jersey:

Jonathan Witherspoon
Nathaniel Scudder

On the part and behalf of the State of Pennsylvania:

Robert Morris
William Clingan
Daniel Roberdeau
Joseph Reed
John Bayard Smith

On the part and behalf of the State of Delaware:

Thomas Mckean
John Dickinson
Nicholas Van Dyke

On the part and behalf of the State of Maryland:

John Hanson
Daniel Carroll

On the Part and Behalf of the State of Virginia:

Richard Henry Lee
Jonathan Harvie
John Banister
Francis Lightfoot Lee
Thomas Adams

On the part and Behalf of the State of No Carolina:

John Penn
Corns Harnett
Jonathan Williams

On the part and behalf of the State of South Carolina:

Henry Laurens
Richard Hutson
William Henry Drayton
Thomas Heyward Junior
Jonathan Matthews

On the part and behalf of the State of Georgia:

Jonathan Walton
Edward Telfair
Edward Langworthy

THE CONSTITUTION OF THE UNITED STATES OF AMERICA

We the people of the United States, in order to form a more perfect union, establish justice, insure domestic tranquility, provide for the common defense, promote the general welfare, and secure the blessings of liberty to ourselves and our posterity, do ordain and establish this Constitution for the United States of America.

ARTICLE I

Section 1. All legislative powers herein granted shall be vested in a Congress of the United States, which shall consist of a Senate and House of Representatives.

Section 2. The House of Representatives shall be composed of members chosen every second year by the people of the several states, and the electors in each state shall have the qualifications requisite for electors of the most numerous branch of the state legislature.

No person shall be a Representative who shall not have attained to the age of twenty five years, and been seven years a citizen of the United States, and who shall not, when elected, be an inhabitant of that state in which he shall be chosen.

Representatives and direct taxes shall be apportioned among the several states which may be included within this union, according to their respective numbers, which shall be determined by adding to the whole number of free persons, including those bound to service for a term of years, and excluding Indians not taxed, three fifths of all other Persons. The actual Enumeration shall be made within three years after the first meeting of the Congress of the United States, and within every subsequent term of ten years, in such manner as they shall by law direct. The number of Representatives shall not exceed one for every thirty thousand, but each state shall have at least one Representative; and until such enumeration shall be made, the state of New Hampshire shall be entitled to choose three, Massachusetts eight, Rhode Island and Providence Plantations one, Connecticut five, New York six, New Jersey four, Pennsylvania eight, Delaware one, Maryland six, Virginia ten,

North Carolina five, South Carolina five, and Georgia three.

When vacancies happen in the Representation from any state, the executive authority thereof shall issue writs of election to fill such vacancies.

The House of Representatives shall choose their speaker and other officers; and shall have the sole power of impeachment.

Section 3. The Senate of the United States shall be composed of two Senators from each state, chosen by the legislature thereof, for six years; and each Senator shall have one vote. Immediately after they shall be assembled in consequence of the first election, they shall be divided as equally as may be into three classes. The seats of the Senators of the first class shall be vacated at the expiration of the second year, of the second class at the expiration of the fourth year, and the third class at the expiration of the sixth year, so that one third may be chosen every second year; and if vacancies happen by resignation, or otherwise, during the recess of the legislature of any state, the executive thereof may make temporary appointments until the next meeting of the legislature, which shall then fill such vacancies.

No person shall be a Senator who shall not have attained to the age of thirty years, and been nine years a citizen of the United States and who shall not, when elected, be an inhabitant of that state for which he shall be chosen.

The Vice President of the United States shall be President of the Senate, but shall have no vote, unless they be equally divided.

The Senate shall choose their other officers, and also a President pro tempore, in the absence of the Vice President, or when he shall exercise the office of President of the United States.

The Senate shall have the sole power to try all impeachments. When sitting for that purpose, they shall be on oath or affirmation. When the President of the United States is tried, the Chief Justice shall preside: And no person shall be convicted without the concurrence of two thirds of the members present.

Judgment in cases of impeachment shall not extend further than to removal from office, and disqualification to hold and enjoy any office of honor, trust or profit under the United States: but the party convicted shall nevertheless be liable and subject to indictment, trial, judgment and punishment, according to law.

Section 4. The times, places and manner of holding elections for Senators and Representatives, shall be prescribed in each state by the legislature thereof; but the Congress may at any time by law make or alter such regulations, except as to the places of choosing Senators.

The Congress shall assemble at least once in every year, and such meeting shall be on the first Monday in December, unless they shall by law appoint a different day.

Section 5. Each House shall be the judge of the elections, returns and qualifications of its own members, and a majority of each shall constitute a quorum to do business; but a smaller number may adjourn from day to day, and may be authorized to compel the attendance of absent members, in such manner, and under such penalties as each House may provide.

Each House may determine the rules of its proceedings, punish its members for disorderly behavior, and, with the concurrence of two thirds, expel a member.

Each House shall keep a journal of its proceedings, and from time to time publish the same, excepting such parts as may in their judgment require secrecy; and the yeas and nays of the members of either House on any question shall, at the desire of one fifth of those present, be entered on the journal.

Neither House, during the session of Congress, shall, without the consent of the other, adjourn for more than three days, nor to any other place than that in which the two Houses shall be sitting.

Section 6. The Senators and Representatives shall receive a compensation for their services, to be ascertained by law, and paid out of the treasury of the United States. They shall in all cases, except treason, felony and breach of the peace, be privileged from arrest during their attendance at the session of their respective Houses, and in going to and returning from the same; and for any speech or debate in either House, they shall not be questioned in any other place. No Senator or Representative shall, during the time for which he was elected, be appointed to any civil office under the authority of the United States, which shall have been created, or the emoluments whereof shall have been increased during such time: and no person holding any office under the United States, shall be a member of either House during his continuance in office.

Section 7. All bills for raising revenue shall originate in the House of Representatives; but the Senate may propose or concur with amendments as on other Bills.

Every bill which shall have passed the House of Representatives and the Senate, shall, before it become a law, be presented to the President of the United States; if he approve he shall sign it, but if not he shall return it, with his objections to that House in which it shall have originated, who shall enter the objections at large on their journal, and proceed to reconsider it. If after such reconsideration two thirds of that House shall agree to pass the bill, it shall be sent, together with the objections, to the other House, by which it shall likewise be reconsidered, and if approved by two thirds of that House, it shall become a law. But in all such cases the votes of both Houses shall be determined by yeas and nays, and the names of the persons voting for and against the bill shall be entered on the journal of each House respectively. If any bill shall not be returned by the President within ten days (Sundays excepted) after it shall have been presented to him, the same shall be a law, in like manner as if he had signed it, unless the Congress by their adjournment prevent its return, in which case it shall not be a law.

Every order, resolution, or vote to which the concurrence of the Senate and House of Representatives may be necessary (except on a question of adjournment) shall be presented to the President of the United States; and before the same shall take effect, shall be approved by him, or being disapproved by him, shall be repassed by two thirds of the Senate and House of Representatives, according to the rules and limitations prescribed in the case of a bill.

Section 8. The Congress shall have power to lay and collect taxes, duties, imposts and excises, to pay the debts and provide for the common defense and general welfare of the United States; but all duties, imposts and excises shall be uniform throughout the United States;

To borrow money on the credit of the United States;

To regulate commerce with foreign nations, and among the several states, and with the Indian tribes;

To establish a uniform rule of naturalization, and uniform laws on the subject of bankruptcies throughout the United States;

To coin money, regulate the value thereof, and of foreign coin, and fix the standard of weights and measures;

To provide for the punishment of counterfeiting the securities and current coin of the United States;

To establish post offices and post roads;

To promote the progress of science and useful arts, by securing for limited times to authors and inventors the exclusive right to their respective writings and discoveries;

To constitute tribunals inferior to the Supreme Court;

To define and punish piracies and felonies committed on the high seas, and offenses against the law of nations;

To declare war, grant letters of marque and reprisal, and make rules concerning captures on land and water;

To raise and support armies, but no appropriation of money to that use shall be for a longer term than two years;

To provide and maintain a navy;

To make rules for the government and regulation of the land and naval forces;

To provide for calling forth the militia to execute the laws of the union, suppress insurrections and repel invasions;

To provide for organizing, arming, and disciplining, the militia, and for governing such part of them as may be employed in the service of the United States, reserving to the states respectively, the appointment of the officers, and the authority of training the militia according to the discipline prescribed by Congress;

To exercise exclusive legislation in all cases whatsoever, over such District (not exceeding ten miles square) as may, by cession of particular states, and the acceptance of Congress, become the seat of the government of the United States, and to exercise like authority over all places purchased by the consent of the legislature of the state in which the same shall be, for the erection of forts, magazines, arsenals, dockyards, and other needful buildings;—And

To make all laws which shall be necessary and proper for carrying into execution the foregoing powers, and all other powers vested by this Constitution in the government of the United States, or in any department or officer thereof.

Section 9. The migration or importation of such persons as any of the states now existing shall think proper to admit, shall not be prohibited by the Congress prior to the year one thousand eight hundred and eight, but a tax or duty may be imposed on such importation, not exceeding ten dollars for each person.

The privilege of the writ of habeas corpus shall not be suspended, unless when in cases of rebellion or invasion the public safety may require it.

No bill of attainder or ex post facto Law shall be passed.

No capitation, or other direct, tax shall be laid, unless in proportion to the census or enumeration herein before directed to be taken.

No tax or duty shall be laid on articles exported from any state.

No preference shall be given by any regulation of commerce or revenue to the ports of one state over those of another: nor shall vessels bound to, or from, one state, be obliged to enter, clear or pay duties in another.

No money shall be drawn from the treasury, but in consequence of appropriations made by law; and a regular statement and account of receipts and expenditures of all public money shall be published from time to time.

No title of nobility shall be granted by the United States: and no person holding any office of profit or trust under them, shall, without the consent of the Congress, accept of any present, emolument, office, or title, of any kind whatever, from any king, prince, or foreign state.

Section 10. No state shall enter into any treaty, alliance, or confederation; grant letters of marque and reprisal; coin money; emit bills of credit; make anything but gold and silver coin a tender in payment of debts; pass any bill of attainder, ex post facto law, or law impairing the obligation of contracts, or grant any title of nobility.

No state shall, without the consent of the Congress, lay any imposts or duties on imports or exports, except what may be absolutely necessary for executing its inspection laws: and the net produce of all duties and imposts, laid by any state on imports or exports, shall be for the use of the treasury of the United States; and all such laws shall be subject to the revision and control of the Congress.

No state shall, without the consent of Congress, lay any duty of tonnage, keep troops, or ships of war in time of peace, enter into any agreement or compact with another state, or with a foreign power, or engage in war, unless actually invaded, or in such imminent danger as will not admit of delay.

ARTICLE II

Section 1. The executive power shall be vested in a President of the United States of America. He shall hold his office during the term of four years, and, together with the Vice President, chosen for the same term, be elected, as follows:

Each state shall appoint, in such manner as the Legislature thereof may direct, a number of electors, equal to the whole number of Senators and Representatives to which the State may be entitled in the Congress: but no Senator or Representative, or person holding an office of trust or profit under the United States, shall be appointed an elector.

The electors shall meet in their respective states, and vote by ballot for two persons, of whom one at least shall not be an inhabitant of the same state with themselves. And they shall make a list of all the persons voted for, and of the number of votes for each; which list they shall sign and certify, and transmit sealed to the seat of the government of the United States, directed to the President of the Senate. The President of the Senate shall, in the presence of the Senate and House of Representatives, open all the certificates, and the votes shall then be counted. The person having the greatest number of votes shall be the President, if such number be a majority of the whole number of electors appointed; and if there be more than one who have such majority, and have an equal number of votes, then the House of Representatives shall immediately choose by ballot one of them for President; and if no person have a majority, then from the five highest on the list the said House shall in like manner choose the President. But in choosing the President, the votes shall be taken by States, the representation from each state having one vote; A quorum for this purpose shall consist of a member or members from two thirds of the states, and a majority of all the states shall be necessary to a choice. In every case, after the choice of the President, the person having the greatest number of votes of the electors shall be the Vice President.

But if there should remain two or more who have equal votes, the Senate shall choose from them by ballot the Vice President.

The Congress may determine the time of choosing the electors, and the day on which they shall give their votes; which day shall be the same throughout the United States.

No person except a natural born citizen, or a citizen of the United States, at the time of the adoption of this Constitution, shall be eligible to the office of President; neither shall any person be eligible to that office who shall not have attained to the age of thirty five years, and been fourteen Years a resident within the United States.

In case of the removal of the President from office, or of his death, resignation, or inability to discharge the powers and duties of the said office, the same shall devolve on the Vice President, and the Congress may by law provide for the case of removal, death, resignation or inability, both of the President and Vice President, declaring what officer shall then act as President, and such officer shall act accordingly, until the disability be removed, or a President shall be elected.

The President shall, at stated times, receive for his services, a compensation, which shall neither be increased nor diminished during the period for which he shall have been elected, and he shall not receive within that period any other emolument from the United States, or any of them.

Before he enter on the execution of his office, he shall take the following oath or affirmation:— "I do solemnly swear (or affirm) that I will faithfully execute the office of President of the United States, and will to the best of my ability, preserve, protect and defend the Constitution of the United States."

Section 2. The President shall be commander in chief of the Army and Navy of the United States, and of the militia of the several states, when called into the actual service of the United States;

he may require the opinion, in writing, of the principal officer in each of the executive departments, on any subject relating to the duties of their respective offices, and he shall have power to grant reprieves and pardons for offenses against the United States, except in cases of impeachment.

He shall have power, by and with the advice and consent of the Senate, to make treaties, provided two thirds of the Senators present concur; and he shall nominate, and by and with the advice and consent of the Senate, shall appoint ambassadors, other public ministers and consuls, judges of the Supreme Court, and all other officers of the United States, whose appointments are not herein otherwise provided for, and which shall be established by law: but the Congress may by law vest the appointment of such inferior officers, as they think proper, in the President alone, in the courts of law, or in the heads of departments.

The President shall have power to fill up all vacancies that may happen during the recess of the Senate, by granting commissions which shall expire at the end of their next session.

Section 3. He shall from time to time give to the Congress information of the state of the union, and recommend to their consideration such measures as he shall judge necessary and expedient; he may, on extraordinary occasions, convene both Houses, or either of them, and in case of disagreement between them, with respect to the time of adjournment, he may adjourn them to such time as he shall think proper; he shall receive ambassadors and other public ministers; he shall take care that the laws be faithfully executed, and shall commission all the officers of the United States.

Section 4. The President, Vice President and all civil officers of the United States, shall be removed from office on impeachment for, and conviction of, treason, bribery, or other high crimes and misdemeanors.

ARTICLE III

Section 1. The judicial power of the United States, shall be vested in one Supreme Court, and in such inferior courts as the Congress may from time to time ordain and establish. The judges, both of the supreme and inferior courts, shall hold their offices during good behavior, and shall, at stated times, receive for their services, a compensation, which shall not be diminished during their continuance in office.

Section 2. The judicial power shall extend to all cases, in law and equity, arising under this Constitution, the laws of the United States, and treaties made, or which shall be made, under their authority;—to all cases affecting ambassadors, other public ministers and consuls;—to all cases of admiralty and maritime jurisdiction;—to controversies to which the United States shall be a party;—to controversies between two or more states;—between a state and citizens of another state;—between citizens of different states;—between citizens of the same state claiming lands under grants of different states, and between a state, or the citizens thereof, and foreign states, citizens or subjects.

In all cases affecting ambassadors, other public ministers and consuls, and those in which a state shall be party, the Supreme Court shall have original jurisdiction. In all the other cases before mentioned, the Supreme Court shall have appellate jurisdiction, both as to law and fact, with such exceptions, and under such regulations as the Congress shall make.

The trial of all crimes, except in cases of impeachment, shall be by jury; and such trial shall be held in the state where the said crimes shall have been committed; but when not committed within any state, the trial shall be at such place or places as the Congress may by law have directed.

Section 3. Treason against the United States, shall consist only in levying war against them, or in adhering to their enemies, giving them aid and comfort. No person shall be convicted of treason unless on the testimony of two witnesses to the same overt act, or on confession in open court.

The Congress shall have power to declare the punishment of treason, but no attainder of treason shall work corruption of blood, or forfeiture except during the life of the person attainted.

ARTICLE IV

Section 1. Full faith and credit shall be given in each state to the public acts, records, and judicial proceedings of every other state. And the Congress may by general laws prescribe the manner in which such acts, records, and proceedings shall be proved, and the effect thereof.

Section 2. The citizens of each state shall be entitled to all privileges and immunities of citizens in the several states.

A person charged in any state with treason, felony, or other crime, who shall flee from justice, and be found in another state, shall on demand of the executive authority of the state from which he fled, be delivered up, to be removed to the state having jurisdiction of the crime.

No person held to service or labor in one state, under the laws thereof, escaping into another, shall, in consequence of any law or regulation therein, be discharged from such service or labor, but shall be delivered up on claim of the party to whom such service or labor may be due.

Section 3. New states may be admitted by the Congress into this union; but no new states shall be formed or erected within the jurisdiction of any other state; nor any state be formed by the junction of two or more states, or parts of states, without the consent of the legislatures of the states concerned as well as of the Congress.

The Congress shall have power to dispose of and make all needful rules and regulations respecting the territory or other property belonging to the United States; and nothing in this Constitution shall be so construed as to prejudice any claims of the United States, or of any particular state.

Section 4. The United States shall guarantee to every state in this union a republican form of government, and shall protect each of them against invasion; and on application of the legislature, or of the executive (when the legislature cannot be convened) against domestic violence.

ARTICLE V

The Congress, whenever two thirds of both houses shall deem it necessary, shall propose amendments to this Constitution, or, on the application of the legislatures of two thirds of the several states, shall call a convention for proposing amendments, which, in either case, shall be valid to all intents and purposes, as part of this Constitution, when ratified by the legislatures of three fourths of the several states, or by conventions in three fourths thereof, as the one or the other mode of ratification may be proposed by the Congress; provided that no amendment which may be made prior to the year one thousand eight hundred and eight shall in any manner affect the first and fourth clauses in the ninth section of the first article; and that no state, without its consent, shall be deprived of its equal suffrage in the Senate.

ARTICLE VI

All debts contracted and engagements entered into, before the adoption of this Constitution, shall be as valid against the United States under this Constitution, as under the Confederation.

This Constitution, and the laws of the United States which shall be made in pursuance thereof; and all treaties made, or which shall be made, under the authority of the United States, shall be the supreme law of the land; and the judges in every state shall be bound thereby, anything in the Constitution or laws of any State to the contrary notwithstanding.

The Senators and Representatives before mentioned, and the members of the several state legislatures, and all executive and judicial officers, both of the United States and of the several states, shall be bound by oath or affirmation, to support this Constitution; but no religious test shall ever be required as a qualification to any office or public trust under the United States.

ARTICLE VII

The ratification of the conventions of nine states, shall be sufficient for the establishment of this Constitution between the states so ratifying the same.

Done in convention by the unanimous consent of the states present the seventeenth day of September in the year of our Lord one thousand seven hundred and eighty seven and of the independence of the United States of America the twelfth. In witness whereof We have hereunto subscribed our Names,

G. WASHINGTON: Presidt. and deputy from Virginia

New Hampshire: JOHN LANGDON, NICHOLAS GILMAN

Massachusetts: NATHANIEL GORHAM, RUFUS KING

Connecticut: Wm: SAML. JOHNSON, ROGER SHERMAN

New York: ALEXANDER HAMILTON

New Jersey: WIL LIVINGSTON, DAVID BREARLY, WM. PATERSON, JONA: DAYTON

Pennsylvania: B. FRANKLIN, THOMAS MIFFLIN, ROBT. MORRIS, GEO. CLYMER, THOS. FITZSIMONS, JARED INGERSOLL, JAMES WILSON, GOUV MORRIS

Delaware: GEO: READ, GUNNING BEDFORD JUN, JOHN DICKINSON, RICHARD BASSETT, JACO: BROOM

Maryland: JAMES MCHENRY, DAN OF ST THOS. JENIFER, DANL CARROLL

Virginia: JOHN BLAIR—, JAMES MADISON JR.

North Carolina: WM. BLOUNT, RICHD. DOBBS SPAIGHT, HU WILLIAMSON

South Carolina: J. RUTLEDGE, CHARLES COTESWORTH PINCKNEY, CHARLES PINCKNEY, PIERCE BUTLER

Georgia: WILLIAM FEW, ABR BALDWIN

BILL OF RIGHTS

The Conventions of a number of the States having, at the time of adopting the Constitution, expressed a desire, in order to prevent misconstruction or abuse of its powers, that further declaratory and restrictive clauses should be added, and as extending the ground of public confidence in the Government will best insure the beneficent ends of its institution;

Resolved, by the Senate and House of Representatives of the United States of America, in Congress assembled, two-thirds of both Houses concurring, that the following articles be proposed to the Legislatures of the several States, as amendments to the Constitution of the United States; all or any of which articles, when ratified by three-fourths of the said Legislatures, to be valid to all intents and purposes as part of the said Constitution, namely:

AMENDMENT I

Congress shall make no law respecting an establishment of religion, or prohibiting the free exercise thereof; or abridging the freedom of speech, or of the press; or the right of the people peaceably to assemble, and to petition the government for a redress of grievances.

AMENDMENT II

A well regulated militia, being necessary to the security of a free state, the right of the people to keep and bear arms, shall not be infringed.

AMENDMENT III

No soldier shall, in time of peace be quartered in any house, without the consent of the owner, nor in time of war, but in a manner to be prescribed by law.

AMENDMENT IV

The right of the people to be secure in their persons, houses, papers, and effects, against unreasonable searches and seizures, shall not be violated, and no warrants shall issue, but upon probable cause, supported by oath or affirmation, and particularly describing the place to be searched, and the persons or things to be seized.

AMENDMENT V

No person shall be held to answer for a capital, or otherwise infamous crime, unless on a presentment or indictment of a grand jury, except in cases arising in the land or naval forces, or in the militia, when in actual service in time of war or public danger; nor shall any person be subject for the same offense to be twice put in jeopardy of life or limb; nor shall be compelled in any criminal case to be a witness against himself, nor be deprived of life, liberty, or property, without due process of law; nor shall private property be taken for public use, without just compensation.

AMENDMENT VI

In all criminal prosecutions, the accused shall enjoy the right to a speedy and public trial, by an impartial jury of the state and district wherein the crime shall have been committed, which district shall have been previously ascertained by law, and to be informed of the nature and cause of the accusation; to be confronted with the witnesses against him; to have compulsory process for obtaining witnesses in his favor, and to have the assistance of counsel for his defense.

AMENDMENT VII

In suits at common law, where the value in controversy shall exceed twenty dollars, the right of trial by jury shall be preserved, and no fact tried by a jury, shall be otherwise reexamined in any court of the United States, than according to the rules of the common law.

AMENDMENT VIII

Excessive bail shall not be required, nor excessive fines imposed, nor cruel and unusual punishments inflicted.

AMENDMENT IX

The enumeration in the Constitution, of certain rights, shall not be construed to deny or disparage others retained by the people.

AMENDMENT X

The powers not delegated to the United States by the Constitution, nor prohibited by it to the states, are reserved to the states respectively, or to the people.

OTHER AMENDMENTS
TO THE CONSTITUTION

AMENDMENT XI

(1798)

The judicial power of the United States shall not be construed to extend to any suit in law or equity, commenced or prosecuted against one of the United States by citizens of another state, or by citizens or subjects of any foreign state.

AMENDMENT XII

(1804)

The electors shall meet in their respective states and vote by ballot for President and Vice-President, one of whom, at least, shall not be an inhabitant of the same state with themselves; they shall name in their ballots the person voted for as President, and in distinct ballots the person voted for as Vice-President, and they shall make distinct lists of all persons voted for as President, and of all persons voted for as Vice-President, and of the number of votes for each, which lists they shall sign and certify, and transmit sealed to the seat of the government of the United States, directed to the President of the Senate;—The President of the Senate shall, in the presence of the Senate and House of Representatives, open all the certificates and the votes shall then be counted;—the person having the greatest number of votes for President, shall be the President, if such number be a majority of the whole number of electors appointed; and if no person have such majority, then from the persons having the highest numbers not exceeding three on the list of those voted for as President, the House of Representatives shall choose immediately, by ballot, the President. But in choosing the President, the votes shall be taken by states, the representation from each state having one vote; a quorum for this purpose shall consist of a member or members from two-thirds of the states, and a majority of all the states shall be necessary to a choice. And if the House of Representatives shall not choose a President whenever the right of choice shall devolve upon them, before the fourth day of March next following, then the Vice-President shall act as President, as in the case of the death or other constitutional disability of the President. The person having the greatest number of votes as Vice-President, shall be the Vice-President, if such number be a majority of the whole number of electors appointed, and if no person have a majority, then from the two highest numbers on the list, the Senate shall choose the Vice-President; a quorum for the purpose shall consist of two-thirds of the whole number of Senators, and a majority of the whole number shall be necessary to a choice. But no person constitutionally ineligible to the office of President shall be eligible to that of Vice-President of the United States.

AMENDMENT XIII

(1865)

Section 1. Neither slavery nor involuntary servitude, except as a punishment for crime whereof the party shall have been duly convicted, shall exist within the United States, or any place subject to their jurisdiction.

Section 2. Congress shall have power to enforce this article by appropriate legislation.

AMENDMENT XIV

(1868)

Section 1. All persons born or naturalized in the United States, and subject to the jurisdiction thereof, are citizens of the United States and of the state wherein they reside. No state shall make or enforce any law which shall abridge the privileges or immunities of citizens of the United States; nor shall any state deprive any person of life, liberty, or property, without due process of law; nor deny to any person within its jurisdiction the equal protection of the laws.

Section 2. Representatives shall be apportioned among the several states according to their respective numbers, counting the whole number of persons in each state, excluding Indians not taxed. But when the right to vote at any election for the choice of electors for President and Vice President of the United States, Representatives in Congress, the executive and judicial officers of a state, or the members of the legislature thereof, is denied to any of the male inhabitants of such state, being twenty-one years of age, and citizens of the United States, or in any way abridged, except for participation in rebellion, or other crime, the basis of representation therein shall be reduced in the proportion which the number of such male citizens shall bear to the whole number of male citizens twenty-one years of age in such state.

Section 3. No person shall be a Senator or Representative in Congress, or elector of President and Vice President, or hold any office, civil or military, under the United States, or under any state, who, having previously taken an oath, as a member of Congress, or as an officer of the United States, or as a member of any state legislature, or as an executive or judicial officer of any state, to support the Constitution of the United States, shall have engaged in insurrection or rebellion against the same, or given aid or comfort to the enemies thereof. But Congress may by a vote of two-thirds of each House, remove such disability.

Section 4. The validity of the public debt of the United States, authorized by law, including debts incurred for payment of pensions and bounties for services in suppressing insurrection or rebellion, shall not be questioned. But neither the United States nor any state shall assume or pay any debt or obligation incurred in aid of insurrection or rebellion against the United States, or any claim for the loss or emancipation of any slave; but all such debts, obligations and claims shall be held illegal and void.

Section 5. The Congress shall have power to enforce, by appropriate legislation, the provisions of this article.

AMENDMENT XV

(1870)

Section 1. The right of citizens of the United States to vote shall not be denied or abridged by the United States or by any state on account of race, color, or previous condition of servitude.

Section 2. The Congress shall have power to enforce this article by appropriate legislation.

AMENDMENT XVI

(1913)

The Congress shall have power to lay and collect taxes on incomes, from whatever source derived, without apportionment among the several states, and without regard to any census of enumeration.

AMENDMENT XVII

(1913)

The Senate of the United States shall be composed of two Senators from each state, elected by the people thereof, for six years; and each Senator shall have one vote. The electors in each state shall have the qualifications requisite for electors of the most numerous branch of the state legislatures.

When vacancies happen in the representation of any state in the Senate, the executive authority of such state shall issue writs of election to fill such vacancies: Provided, that the legislature of any state may empower the executive thereof to make temporary appointments until the people fill the vacancies by election as the legislature may direct.

This amendment shall not be so construed as to affect the election or term of any Senator chosen before it becomes valid as part of the Constitution.

AMENDMENT XVIII

(1919)

Section 1. After one year from the ratification of this article the manufacture, sale, or transportation of intoxicating liquors within, the importation thereof into, or the exportation thereof from the United States and all territory subject to the jurisdiction thereof for beverage purposes is hereby prohibited.

Section 2. The Congress and the several states shall have concurrent power to enforce this article by appropriate legislation.

Section 3. This article shall be inoperative unless it shall have been ratified as an amendment to the Constitution by the legislatures of the several states, as provided in the Constitution, within seven years from the date of the submission hereof to the states by the Congress.

AMENDMENT XIX

(1920)

The right of citizens of the United States to vote shall not be denied or abridged by the United States or by any state on account of sex.

Congress shall have power to enforce this article by appropriate legislation.

AMENDMENT XX

(1933)

Section 1. The terms of the President and Vice President shall end at noon on the 20th day of

January, and the terms of Senators and Representatives at noon on the 3d day of January, of the years in which such terms would have ended if this article had not been ratified; and the terms of their successors shall then begin.

Section 2. The Congress shall assemble at least once in every year, and such meeting shall begin at noon on the 3d day of January, unless they shall by law appoint a different day.

Section 3. If, at the time fixed for the beginning of the term of the President, the President elect shall have died, the Vice President elect shall become President. If a President shall not have been chosen before the time fixed for the beginning of his term, or if the President elect shall have failed to qualify, then the Vice President elect shall act as President until a President shall have qualified; and the Congress may by law provide for the case wherein neither a President elect nor a Vice President elect shall have qualified, declaring who shall then act as President, or the manner in which one who is to act shall be selected, and such person shall act accordingly until a President or Vice President shall have qualified.

Section 4. The Congress may by law provide for the case of the death of any of the persons from whom the House of Representatives may choose a President whenever the right of choice shall have devolved upon them, and for the case of the death of any of the persons from whom the Senate may choose a Vice President whenever the right of choice shall have devolved upon them.

Section 5. Sections 1 and 2 shall take effect on the 15th day of October following the ratification of this article.

Section 6. This article shall be inoperative unless it shall have been ratified as an amendment to the Constitution by the legislatures of three-fourths of the several states within seven years from the date of its submission.

AMENDMENT XXI

(1933)

Section 1. The eighteenth article of amendment to the Constitution of the United States is hereby repealed.

Section 2. The transportation or importation into any state, territory, or possession of the United States for delivery or use therein of intoxicating liquors, in violation of the laws thereof, is hereby prohibited.

Section 3. This article shall be inoperative unless it shall have been ratified as an amendment to the Constitution by conventions in the several states, as provided in the Constitution, within seven years from the date of the submission hereof to the states by the Congress.

AMENDMENT XXII

(1951)

Section 1. No person shall be elected to the office of the President more than twice, and no person who has held the office of President, or acted as President, for more than two years of a term to which some other person was elected President shall be elected to the office of the President more than once. But this article shall not apply to any person holding the office of President when this article was proposed by the Congress, and shall not prevent any person who may be holding the office of President, or acting as President, during the term within which this article becomes operative from holding the office of President or acting as President during the remainder of such term.

Section 2. This article shall be inoperative unless it shall have been ratified as an amendment to the Constitution by the legislatures of three-fourths of the several states within seven years from the date of its submission to the states by the Congress.

AMENDMENT XXIII

(1961)

Section 1. The District constituting the seat of government of the United States shall appoint in such manner as the Congress may direct: A number of electors of President and Vice President equal to the whole number of Senators and Representatives in Congress to which the District would be entitled if it were a state, but in no event more than the least populous state; they shall be in addition to those appointed by the states, but they shall be considered, for the purposes of the election of President and Vice President, to be electors appointed by a state; and they shall meet in the District and perform such duties as provided by the twelfth article of amendment.

Section 2. The Congress shall have power to enforce this article by appropriate legislation.

AMENDMENT XXIV

(1964)

Section 1. The right of citizens of the United States to vote in any primary or other election for President or Vice President, for electors for President or Vice President, or for Senator or Representative in Congress, shall not be denied or abridged by the United States or any state by reason of failure to pay any poll tax or other tax.

Section 2. The Congress shall have power to enforce this article by appropriate legislation.

AMENDMENT XXV

(1967)

Section 1. In case of the removal of the President from office or of his death or resignation, the Vice President shall become President.

Section 2. Whenever there is a vacancy in the office of the Vice President, the President shall nominate a Vice President who shall take office upon confirmation by a majority vote of both Houses of Congress.

Section 3. Whenever the President transmits to the President pro tempore of the Senate and the Speaker of the House of Representatives his written declaration that he is unable to discharge the powers and duties of his office, and until he transmits to them a written declaration to the contrary, such powers and duties shall be discharged by the Vice President as Acting President.

Section 4. Whenever the Vice President and a majority of either the principal officers of the executive departments or of such other body as Congress may by law provide, transmit to the President pro tempore of the Senate and the Speaker of the House of Representatives their written declaration that the President is unable to discharge the powers and duties of his office, the Vice President shall immediately assume the powers and duties of the office as Acting President.

Thereafter, when the President transmits to the President pro tempore of the Senate and the Speaker of the House of Representatives his written declaration that no inability exists, he shall resume the powers and duties of his office unless the Vice President and a majority of either the principal officers of the executive department or of such other body as Congress may by law provide, transmit within four days to the President pro tempore of the Senate and the Speaker of the House of Representatives their written declaration that the President is unable to discharge the powers and duties of his office.

Thereupon Congress shall decide the issue, assembling within forty-eight hours for that purpose if not in session. If the Congress, within twenty-one days after receipt of the latter written declaration, or, if Congress is not in session, within twenty-one days after Congress is required to assemble, determines by two-thirds vote of both Houses that the President is unable to discharge the powers and duties of his office, the Vice President shall continue to discharge the same as Acting President; otherwise, the President shall resume the powers and duties of his office.

AMENDMENT XXVI

(1971)

Section 1. The right of citizens of the United States, who are 18 years of age or older, to vote, shall not be denied or abridged by the United States or any state on account of age.

Section 2. The Congress shall have the power to enforce this article by appropriate legislation.

AMENDMENT XXVII

(1992)

No law varying the compensation for the services of the Senators and Representatives shall take effect until an election of Representatives shall have intervened.

HOW A BILL BECOMES A LAW

How a bill becomes a law in a state legislature or the U.S. Congress is one of the most arcane and complicated decision-making processes that any institution undertakes. This is no accident. The legislative process is designed to be complicated and difficult. Americans are suspicious of government as a threat to their personal liberty, so our political institutions are designed to limit governmental power as much as possible. In addition, the passage of a law is a significant event that can have major impacts on people and business, and so it is important that considerable thought be given to it. And given the variety of interests and values of U.S. citizens, there must be many opportunities for people to have input into lawmaking.

The legislative process is a complex path along which a bill travels, generally clearing one obstacle after another in a specific order as it moves toward becoming law. Failure to pass any one of these obstacles successfully will keep the bill from becoming law. Thus, it is much easier to stop a bill than to see it successfully through to final passage. Each of the obstacles is, in fact, a test of the quality of the bill. Most bills do not survive one of these tests and therefore do not become law.

To become law, a bill must be considered in and approved by both legislative chambers (in the Congress and most state legislatures, this is the House of Representatives and the Senate) in exactly the same form, and then be approved by the chief executive (i.e., the governor or president).

The process begins when a legislator introduces a bill in his or her chamber. The bill is then giving a first reading in that chamber and is referred to a committee of that chamber for consideration. Legislative chambers organize committees by policy area to divide up the labor of evaluating bills. The committee evaluates the bill and gets input on it by holding public hearings. The committee then reports its recommendation on the bill to the full chamber. The bill is then given a second reading, at which time the full chamber considers the bill and ways it might be changed (amended) to make it more acceptable to various legislators and the groups of people they represent. After all attempts to amend the bill at second reading are completed, the bill moves to third reading, at which time each member of the chamber votes aye or nay on the full bill, and no more amendments can be made to it.

If the bill receives a majority of the chamber's vote at third reading, it passes that chamber and is reported to the other chamber, where the entire process of readings, committee consideration, and amendment is repeated. If the bill passes the second chamber unamended, it moves on to the chief executive's desk for consideration. If the bill does not pass the second chamber in any form, it is dead and will not become law in that legislative session. If the bill passes the second chamber, but is amended in any way in that chamber, it goes back to the first chamber for reconsideration. (Remember, the bill must pass both chambers in exactly the same form to move on to the chief executive.) The first chamber might vote to accept the second chamber's amendments, or if not, the second chamber might vote to take back its own amendments. If neither chamber is willing to give in completely, the chamber leaders may appoint a conference committee consisting of members of both chambers whose job it is to arrive at a compromise that will be acceptable to both chambers. If the conference committee is able to report out a compromise bill, each chamber votes on it, with no amendments allowed.

If both chambers pass the conference committee's bill, or if the bill passes both chambers in identical form without a conference committee, it is sent to the chief executive for his or her consideration. The chief executive has the option of approving the bill by signing it or of killing the bill be vetoing it. If he or she signs the bill, it becomes law on the effective date specified in the bill or by other rule of the legislature.

If the bill fails to move successfully past any stage of the legislative process, it will not become law. Thus, the process by which a bill becomes a law is long, complex, and difficult, but it helps assure that laws will not be passed without a good deal of thought and consideration of the interests of all citizens.

See also POCKET VETO; VETO.

For more information

Oleszek, Walter J. *Congressional Procedures and the Policy Process,* 5th ed. Washington, D.C.: Congressional Quarterly Press, 2000.

Christopher Z. Mooney

LOOKING FOR GOVERNMENT INFORMATION

Information on the workings of our government is more accessible than ever thanks to the World Wide Web. Much of that information has always been—and still is—available through government depository library programs, but it is no longer necessary to travel to these collections, especially for selected key publications. From congressional committee reports to the *U.S. Code* itself and from city council meeting minutes to state legislation, you can literally watch government happen from your computer.

STARTING POINTS

Of course, not everything is in one place, even on the World Wide Web. There are a number of good starting points that will help lead you to the information you need. It is useful to have more than one good starting point: the right one will vary depending on your question.

There are two very good resources for **state and local government information.** If you need information on a specific state, try State and Local Government on the Net (http://www.statelocalgov.net/), which provides a clear, standardized menu for navigating to state home

pages and their legislative, executive, and judicial branches; boards and commissions; and cities and counties. If, instead, you have a topic and would like to know how states compare, the main menu of StateSearch (http://www.nascio.org/stateSearch) provides a list of categories from which you can choose. These categories link you to the state pages relating to your topic. For example, if you would like to compare the constitutions of several states, choosing "constitutions" from the main menu will take you directly to a list of links to the constitutions of all 50 states.

One caveat on state and local government web pages: there is no standardization. For example, many, but not al, cities post their city council minutes. It often is a matter of resources and/or priorities at the local level.

There are a number of good starting points for **federal government information.** Again, the site you choose will depend on your needs. If the federal government and its processes are new to you, a good first stop is *The Guide to Law Online* from the Library of Congress (http://www.loc.gov/law/guide/index.html). It is an annotated guide to key documents of governments around the world. Following the links to U.S. information will bring you to overviews of each of the branches of government and the Constitution, with links to informational pages, such as *How Our Laws are Made,* and to the documents created by the legislative process, such as *The U.S. Code* and *The Congressional Record.*

Once you are familiar with the context of federal documents, you may want to try *GPO Access* (http://www.access.gpo.gov/su_docs/index.html). The U.S. Government Printing Office, the official disseminator of federal information, is responsible for this site. The official versions of the most important documents of the legislative process are available here and can be searched by keyword. Because this is such an important source, I will be referring to it throughout this essay.

If you are looking for "how-to" information as a citizen (e.g., information on federal benefits, getting a passport), the best starting point is FirstGov (http://www.firstgov.gov/).

For a comprehensive starting point with links to local, state, federal, foreign, and international government information, visit the University of Michigan Documents Center (http://www.lib.umich.edu/govdocs/).

SPECIALIZED INFORMATION

Federal Laws

There are a number of reliable sites that provide access to the *U.S. Code.* Once again, the site you choose depends on your needs. While a keyword search of an entire document can be a useful tool, sometimes browsing is more effective; it is easier to see the context of the information. The Legal Information Institute at Cornell University hosts a site that provides access to the *Code* by table of contents ("title"). Within each title, you can either do a keyword search or follow the hierarchy through the chapters to a specific section (http://www4.law.cornell.edu/uscode). The *GPO Access* site also provides keyword searching. For

example, to see whether there is anything in the *U.S. Code* on wind energy, I entered "wind energy" as a keyword phrase and got a list of results that included Title 42, Chapter 100, Section 9206, *Wind Resource Assessment,* which includes an order to "establish standard wind data collection and siting techniques." This law came into effect in the year 2000.

Federal Legislation

The legislative process is well documented at *Thomas,* a website from the Library of Congress that is named after Thomas Jefferson (http://thomas.loc.gov). The site includes: bill summaries, complete text, and status; the *Congressional Record;* committee information; and roll call votes. It is very up-to-date and provides multiple search options. When I entered "wind energy systems" (using the same terminology as the *U.S. Code* for this topic), I discovered that a number of bills have been introduced, including one "to enhance energy conservation, research and development and to provide for security and diversity in the energy supply for the American people." It was interesting to see that this bill saw a flurry of activity in the months following the terrorist attacks in New York and Washington, D.C.

Congressional Hearings

The real work on a bill happens in the House and Senate committees. The meeting and hearing schedules for each of these committees is posted on their web page, which can be reached through *Thomas.* Many of the committees make transcripts of their hearings available on their pages; some now include audio files. However, the information provided varies from committee to committee. *GPO Access* maintains its own pages of House and Senate documents, which generally have more comprehensive coverage of hearings transcripts than the committee pages (http:// www.access.gpo.gov/congress/house/index.html; http://www.access.gpo.gov/congress/senate/index.html). These are handy for browsing. If you would like to do a keyword search for hearings on a specific topic, go instead to the *GPO Access Congressional Hearings* page (http://www.access.gpo.gov/congress/cong017.html), which provides a search engine. Following through on my search for congressional information on "wind energy," I found links to more than two dozen related hearing transcripts, including *Alternative Energy Sources on Public Lands,* the testimony of the legislative director of the American Wind Energy Association.

While most hearings are available to the public, the committee may ultimately choose not to release a transcript. Testimony submitted by witnesses in writing is more widely available than question-and-answer testimony. Also, transcripts of sessions prior to the mid-1990s are not as likely to be available online. The next step, then, would be to visit your local federal depository library. Many of these libraries subscribe to commercial publications—online, print, and in microform—that make these documents more accessible. One example of a tool you may find there is the *CIS Index to Unpublished U.S. Senate Committee Hearings,* which will help you identify hard-to-find hearings from the mid-1800s to the 1960s. The transcripts themselves are available on microfiche. For example, using this tool (online or in print), I searched to see whether anything concerning wind energy was discussed within this time frame. I discovered that a hearing was held in 1951 discussing the potential authorization of research and development in this area. If I wanted to read the testimony, I would note the CIS number needed to locate the full text on microfiche and visit my local depository library. Not every depository library subscribes to these publications and databases, however, so call ahead to inquire.

Finally, thanks to the World Wide Web, you can actually watch Congress in action from your computer; the C-SPAN website provides access to live web broadcasts of testimony and other discussions at the Capitol (http://www.c-span.org).

Federal Rules

The *Code of Federal Regulations* (CFR) contains rules enforced by the various agencies of the federal government, arranged by subject ("title"). For example, the Employment and Training Administration of the Department of Labor has rules on the protection of informants in investigations and hearings. Like the legislative process that keeps the *U.S. Code* relevant, there is a process associated with the development of rules in the federal government. Proposed rules are published daily in the *Federal Register.* The *Register* also includes a variety of notices from federal agencies and organizations, and executive orders and other presidential documents. The *GPO Access* website provides both keyword search and browse capabilities of the full text of these publications. Using this search engine, I learned that wind energy does meet the definition of "energy property" for purposes of the energy investment credit.

Government Reports

Good lawmaking requires good information. Congress relies on several federal agencies for nonpartisan information. Much of this information is also available to the public. These are all excellent sources of policy information.

When a committee recommends a bill to the full body, it does so with an accompanying "report" that summarizes the scope and intent of the proposed bill and estimates the associated costs or revenues. Sometimes a report will be a more general, policy-related document, rather than information about a specific bill. They are available through *Thomas,* starting with the 104th Congress.

The Government Accounting Office (GAO) assists Congress by producing analysis and recommendations concerning existing federal programs and agencies; it is an oversight agency. Reports are published daily and can be viewed in full in the GAO website (http://www.gao.gov/). Both the GAO site and *GPO Access* have keyword search capabilities. GAO has done a number of reports on alternative energy, including *Renewable Energy: DOE's Funding and Markets for Wind Energy and Solar Cell Technologies.*

The Congressional Budget Office (CBO) provides Congress with nonpartisan analysis of the budgetary and economic impact of pending legislation. These reports are available on the CBO website (http://www.cbo.gov/).

The Library of Congress does research for members of Congress through its Congressional Research Service (CRS). CRS reports are often considered confidential and are not readily available to the public. However, individual members of Congress, federal agencies, and nongovernmental organizations make selected reports available on their websites. The Law Library Resource Xchange (LLRX) maintains a website (http://www.llrx.com/features/crsreports.htm) with links to these sites.

More Information

The depth of government information available on the Web is impressive. However, it is not always easy to find, the emphasis is on current information, and not everything is published there. In addition, democracy is messy and there is not any one agency or person to make sure that everything that should be published—on the Web or in print—actually is. Your state or local depository library can be a valuable source of additional and/or archival information. One of the most valuable things you will find there is the knowledgeable staff. To locate a nearby federal depository library, go to http://www.access.gpo.gov/su_docs/locators/findlibs/. These same libraries also usually collect state and local documents or, at the very least, help you locate a library that does.

For more information

Robinson, Judith Schiek. *Tapping the Government Grapevine: The User-Friendly Guide to U.S. Government Information Sources,* 3d ed. Phoenix, Ariz.: Oryx Press, 1998.

Kate Borowske

INDEX

Boldface page numbers refer to main entries in the encyclopedia; *italic* page numbers indicate illustrations.